INDIA IN
A NEW KEY

In this evocative exploration of modern India, Narain D. Batra masterfully weaves the narrative of India's rise from 'Nehru's socialistic pattern of society to Modi's entrepreneurial digital India,' thereby challenging some of the shibboleths which are so prevalent in India and the wider world when it comes to thinking about the twenty-first century aspirational India. As the world is forced to engage with India of today on New Delhi's terms, this book carries an important message about the vitality of Indian democracy that, for all its flaws, manages to open up new possibilities every day for Indians of all stripes and how India's economic energy today strengthens the nation's democratic fabric. A remarkably fresh and buoyant take on India's evolution over the last more than seven decades, devoid of the usual pessimism that has become so fashionable in writings on the subject.

—Harsh V. Pant
Professor of International Relations, King's College London, and Director, Studies and Head of the Strategic Studies Programme at Observer Research Foundation

INDIA IN A NEW KEY

NEHRU TO MODI: 75 YEARS OF FREEDOM AND DEMOCRACY

NARAIN D. BATRA

RUPA

First published by
Rupa Publications India Pvt. Ltd 2022
7/16, Ansari Road, Daryaganj
New Delhi 110002

Sales Centres:

Allahabad Bengaluru Chennai
Hyderabad Jaipur Kathmandu
Kolkata Mumbai

ISBN: 978-93-5520-328-1

Second impression 2022

10 9 8 7 6 5 4 3 2

The moral right of the author has been asserted.

Printed at Parksons Graphics Pvt. Ltd, Mumbai

For

Dr Nikhil N. Batra
Ishu Sudarshan Khurana
Poonam Ashwani Kumar
Noris Ashok Kumar
Nikki and Varsha

In Remembrance
Shyam Sunder

Aano bhadra krtavo yantu vishwatah.
Let noble thoughts come to me from all directions.

—Rig Veda 1.89.1

My Lord! Open up for me my heart
And ease for me my task
And untie the knot of my tongue
That they may understand my speech.

—Qur'an, Surah 20:25–28 (Prayer of Moses)

Hinduism…is essentially inclusive and ever-growing,
ever-responsive…gives the freest scope to imagination,
speculation and reason.

—Mahatma Gandhi

Fear of serious injury alone cannot justify oppression of free
speech and assembly. Men feared witches and burnt women.
It is the function of speech to free men from the bondage of
irrational fears.

—Justice Louis D. Brandeis

The very concept of objective truth is fading out of the world.
Lies will pass into history.

—George Orwell

CONTENTS

Introduction

BORN AGAIN INDIA

Do I dare
Disturb the universe?
In a minute there is time
For decisions and revisions which a minute will reverse.

—T.S. Eliot

After more than seven decades since India achieved freedom from Britain, with 'calm of mind, all passion spent'—as John Milton wrote—and the furies of vengeance back to their subterranean abode, it seemed to me, as a historical explorer, that the creation of Pakistan was perhaps one of the greatest unintended contributions, an asset more than a loss, to the newly independent India.

The contrarian idea was initially startling; and almost sacrilegious. Some of the recent and most significant historical scholarship, such as the monumental work of the historian's historian Ramachandra Guha, *India After Gandhi*, a voluminous 'what of' and 'what if' of historical events, meandering scene after scene, episode after episode, layer upon layer; and the fascinating anecdotal, historical account of Patrick French's *India: A Portrait*, in the tradition of oral history, for example, explicitly or implicitly dwell upon the horrendous events of 1947 as the primordial historic force foreshadowing the future, allocating the blame for the breakup of the Indian subcontinent on political players; or on the confluence of historical events beyond anyone's control.

Of particular interest is Sunil Khilnani's thought-provoking exploration of *The Idea of India* as 'the wager of India's modern, educated, urban élite…(who) had no single, clear definition of this idea…(though) it had the capacity to entertain diverse, often contending visions of India'.[1] The argument that 'contemporary India is unequivocally a creation of the modern world', challenges historical facts because the idea of India had begun much before Mohandas Karamchand Gandhi arrived from South Africa on the Indian political scene and turned the idea of India into a mass movement.

The idea of India began when Queen Victoria proclaimed that she was the Empress of India. Since then, especially spurred and nurtured by the prolonged flowering of the Bengal Renaissance, the quest of Indian leaders, looking inward and outward, had been not only to break away from the British Empire but also to build a strong but flexible constitutional framework, a dynamic political system that could contain the paradoxical aspirations of the people for separateness and togetherness.[2]

In 1947, the British Crown handed over to the Indian National Congress (INC), not an idea of India to wager upon or play with, but a country with 330 million people, hundreds of princely states and hosts of other intractable problems, which challenged its leaders and called forth the best in them. India was a historical and geopolitical actuality, not an idea invented by a group of aspirational elites. The Indians, after a prolonged freedom struggle, got India back from the British Empire. Pakistan was certainly built on an idea; a politically ingenious idea that the Muslims of the subcontinent were so distinctively separate from the Hindus that they must have their own homeland. For this, the glory must go to Mohammed Ali Jinnah, most deservedly called by its people the Quaid-e-Azam, the great leader. Jinnah founded a nation based on an idea.

In the course of time, the proposition began to grow in my mind that by creating a new nation for the Muslims of the subcontinent, Jinnah inadvertently freed the INC from the burden of the two-nation theory and strengthened the Indian leaders' aspirations and determination to experiment with freedom so that they could play the game of democracy on their own terms.

The idea that a segregated hierarchical society, which spoke in a thousand tongues, dared to create a level playing field through federal-parliamentary democratic practices for everyone, from the untouchable to the twice-born, was challenging and seemed worth pursuing, especially after I had published *The First Freedoms and America's Culture of Innovation: The Constitutional Foundations of the Aspirational Society.*

I wondered what made the United States one of the most dynamic, desirable and liveable societies, thereby decisively rejecting the decline-and-fall paradigm, vide Paul M. Kennedy, Niall Ferguson and Fareed Zakaria. In *The First Freedoms*, I argued how individual liberties stimulated innovative behaviour in America. The system of dynamic freedoms, the First Amendment, has created through turbulence and harmony, a perpetually self-renewing vibrant society that has so far negated the decline-and-fall patterns of history. I wondered if this system of dynamic freedoms could have been a model for the Indian leaders, many of whom had been well versed in Western jurisprudence and constitutionalism.

Four decades of being away from India and living in the United States created in me what Bertolt Brecht called *Verfremdungseffekt, distanciation*, a kind of yogic detachment that holds me back from losing myself into the narrative of the India into which I was born, giving me the ability to be a critical observer and eschew any tendency towards false sympathy or misplaced empathy. John Keats called it 'Negative Capability', when one is 'capable of being in uncertainties, Mysteries, doubts, without any irritable reaching after fact and reason', giving the observer the ability to overcome egocentricity and self-consciousness, and live in a state of openness and acceptance to all contradictory experiences in order to identify events and objects under scrutiny, a necessary condition to be a historian.[3]

The idea of India, in the Westphalian sense of sovereignty, which began to take shape in 1858 after Queen Victoria's proclamation to 'the Princes, Chiefs and Peoples of India,' and more so especially when, in 1877, Queen Victoria appropriated the title of the Empress of India (aggregating and subsuming the broken-up Mughal

Hindustan), was based on the brute might of the British Empire, unlike the 13 states that voluntarily formed the United States of America in 1789; or the evolution of European nations into the European Union beginning with the Maastricht Treaty in 1993. In the course of time, nonetheless, the brute force of the British Empire in India was tempered with the seductive soft power of its parliamentary democracy, the deep founts of its Oxbridge universities and the Inns of Court, the beauty of its English language, literature and Shakespeare, its hierarchical class system with its retinues and rituals, sportsmanship epitomized in cricket, and by and large its cultural accessibility of which Gandhi, Jawaharlal Nehru, Bhimrao Ramji Ambedkar, Subhas Chandra Bose and Jinnah were some of the most enlightened progeny.

The British Indian Empire, in the course of time, became more or less an empire of the willing. To create a free India modelled on the British parliamentary democracy, India had to cast off—as an ocean liner would do in distress—the unnecessary burden of what would become Pakistan. Nay, perhaps, it was the other way around. By separating Pakistan from the subcontinent, Jinnah left India free to explore its own democratic future unencumbered by the two-nation theory.

Freedom is a hydra-headed, brute creative force. Not every nation can handle freedom. A free society as an open social system tends to move towards chaos; therefore, the inevitable destiny of a free society as an open system is authoritarianism *unless* it is founded on a dynamic self-renewing system in equilibrium based on checks and balances. For me, as a historical voyager, it was worth exploring what freedom was doing to India; and more importantly, why freedom was not breaking up India and pushing it towards authoritarianism, a country as crazily and brazenly diverse, from Tamil Dravidian linguistic tribalism in the deep south to Kashmir touch-me-not isolationism in the extreme north; the Naga head-hunting (metaphorically and perhaps literally speaking) separatism in the Himalayan fastness of the Northeast to the Khalistan bloody zest for a homeland for the Sikhs of Punjab; the West Bengal and Kerala socialism-and-communism model of a just society to the

Gujarat-Mumbai rugged entrepreneurialism for creating wealth; and the vast Hindi-speaking Middle India with its extended belly of cow-worshipping. And then there were the Muslims, who had been left behind 'butt-naked' by Partition, as a wayside shopkeeper of Delhi's Ballimaran Bazaar, remarked—in colourful language—about the early years of Independence, when I happened to wander through the labyrinthine streets of the bazaar.[4]

On 12 April 2002, after the firebombing of a train in Godhra in Gujarat that had triggered Hindu–Muslim riots, one of the worst inter-religious riots since India's independence, Prime Minister Atal Bihari Vajpayee gave a much-criticized, politically incorrect speech in Goa, in which he talked about Muslims' unwillingness or inability for peaceful coexistence with other communities.[5] He was reported to have said:

> Wherever Muslims live, they don't like to live in co-existence with others, they don't like to mingle with others; and instead of propagating their ideas in a peaceful manner, they want to spread their faith by resorting to terror and threats. The world has become alert to this danger.[6]

Vajpayee, arguably the most beloved politician after Nehru, was unselfconsciously paraphrasing and repeating what Jinnah had said during his most historic speech on 3 March 1940, in Lahore. Heir to Sir Syed Ahmed Khan's two-nation theory, in his speech Jinnah postulated and rationalized why Muslims and Hindus could not live together. Because they belong to 'different and distinct social orders,' and can never 'evolve a common nationality' since they

> ...belong to two different religious philosophies, social customs, and literature[s]. They neither intermarry nor interdine together, and indeed they belong to two different civilisations which are based mainly on conflicting ideas and conceptions...[they] derive their inspiration from different sources of history...have different epics, their heroes are different, and different episodes...To yoke together two such nations under a single state, one as a numerical minority and

the other as a majority, must lead to growing discontent, and final destruction of any fabric that may be so built up for the government of such a state.[7]

After more than three decades of Jinnah's momentous path-breaking Lahore Resolution speech for the creation of Pakistan, ironically, Sheikh Mujibur Rahman of East Pakistan said in his address to his Bengali speaking people on 7 March 1971, that Bengalis could no longer coexist with West Pakistanis and must do or die: 'The struggle this time is a struggle for emancipation, the struggle this time is a struggle for independence [Bengali: *Ebarer sangram amader muktir sangram, ebarer sangram swadhinatar sangram*].'[8] Bangabandhu Sheikh Mujibur Rahman wanted liberation from Jinnah's Muslim Pakistan in the same manner as Jinnah had wanted liberation from the Hindu-majority India.

On the Friday morning of 15 August 1947, when Jawaharlal Nehru, heir to Mahatma Gandhi and the Buddha and the European Enlightenment, raised the Indian Tricolour on the ramparts of the Red Fort—the palace of the seventeenth-century Mughal Emperor, Shah Jahan—in Delhi, India gained its freedom twice. India was free from the 90-year shining glory of the British 'Inglorious' Empire. And India was free from the burden of the 'Land of the Pure' dreams of Jinnah's Indian Muslim League that had rolled up its flag and retreated into the newly created Muslim nation of Pakistan. India was free to do experiments with freedom. India was free to confront its most hideous demon, its ancient ethos of divinely ordained segregation. India was free to build the structures of freedom, the federal-parliamentary political system to achieve unity through multiplicity. India was free to experiment with secular democratic socialism to create a just society.

Nehru's democratic socialism, along with the Soviet-style central planning, did not fulfil the economic aspirations of rapid growth but it did bind the nation by bringing all national and regional parties under the federal-parliamentary umbrella. By building for the nation a platform of secular socialist ideology reinforced by the centrally planned economy, the rhythms of Five-Year Plans and the general elections, Nehru and the Congress party immunized Indian masses to the temptations of the Soviet and Chinese-style bloody revolutions. Even the Bharatiya Jana Sangh, the Hindu nationalist party that would eventually become the Bharatiya Janata Party (BJP), did not reject the authoritarian central control over the economy.

In the early years of Independence, the Indian people would not have accepted the marketplace entrepreneurial economy of the capitalist West, the United States. Nevertheless, under its democratic socialism programme, the Congress party did allow the private sector to have a limited role. And thanks to the space left for private businesses in the mixed socialist economy model—including myriad mom-and-pop stores and small-and-medium entrepreneurs whose energy, adaptability, survivability, shrewdness, and buoyancy in the narrow bazaars of India since time immemorial had empowered and enriched millions—the animal spirit of the marketplace entrepreneurial economy roared when Prime Minister P.V. Narasimha Rao and Finance Minister Manmohan Singh, under compelling economic circumstances in the 1990s, opened up India's economy. Once the economic horizons opened up and Indians began to have the taste for growing wealth through the dynamics of a free marketplace, there was no going back.

Transitioning from democratic socialism under the Narasimha Rao-Manmohan Singh era to the rule of the right-wing BJP, which had assimilated the Jana Sangh's Hindu nationalism and the Swatantra Party's free enterprise ideology, had been comparatively smooth. Indians wanted to be rich and they knew it was possible to be rich. To paraphrase William Butler Yeats—Indians had fed their hearts on fantasies of growing rich and their hearts had grown hungry from the fare and they wanted more and more. India was ravenous. Nehru's democratic-socialism commitment to social justice did not disappear, however. In its new garb of social welfare-ism, it's as much a part of the BJP as it had been for the Congress party from Nehru through Manmohan Singh, the thirteenth prime minister of India. Most importantly, the competition of the global marketplace would challenge India and create the need for competencies, aptitudes and skills that lead to a merit-and-talent based society. The marketplace would churn up India as the electoral democracy had been doing since the times of Nehru.

Nehru was a master of creative illusions. The democratic socialism and non-alignment that Nehru had created, kept India together in spite of the nation's age-long fissiparous tendencies. Socialism did not create wealth but Nehru was such a powerful and influential intellectual force that everyone went along with his ideological views long after he had become part of history—a history that he had helped create. Most of the intellectual and political class members, regardless of their convictions, went along with the flow, the Great Nehru Flow, the leftist flow of their political bases on which they depended, in order to continue to be politically something, to remain politically relevant, to remain in power. That was the psychological make-up of thousands and thousands of politicians, journalists and academics, the hordes who willy-nilly went along with the tidal wave, the mainstream flow, like flotsam and jetsam. The BJP, a Hindu nationalist and populist political party, did not have to struggle with such internal contradictions or cognitive dissonance. Its evolutionary growth has been steady and consistent and without any disruptive changes.

How the BJP evolved from its genesis in the Rashtriya Swayamsevak Sangh-Jana Sangh's inward-looking religious ideology to a broad-based mainstream free-market, entrepreneurial all-India political party by playing the game of democracy, has been the most remarkable political development in India. Narendra Modi, a hardscrabble son of entrepreneurial Gujarat, transformed Nehru's democratic socialist India into a democratic entrepreneurial digital India. And this is the story that the book tells: how Indians have been playing the game of democracy from Jawaharlal Nehru to Narendra Modi to uphold 'the India Constant'.

The book explores three major historical themes. Part One, 'The Freedom House That Nehru Built', deals with India's post-Independence formative years, as to how during the Nehru era, Indian leaders doused the Partition-generated communal inferno; rehabilitated millions of refugees from Pakistan; controlled and domesticated revolutionary communist forces; managed to feed the hungry and designed the Constitution of India as a fluid dynamic system, a strong and flexible federal-parliamentary system to assimilate and integrate 565 princely states, including Portuguese Goa and French Pondicherry as well as satisfy regional, cultural and linguistic aspirations through federalism. In many ways, this was a most remarkable time for India because Nehru, through his policy of non-alignment and economic development based on democratic socialism, placed India on the world stage, giving Indians the illusion of a great power without the necessary accoutrement of economic and military foundation—an illusion that was shattered by China's predatory aggression on India's northeastern and northwestern Himalayan regions in 1962.

Part Two, 'Creator and Destroyer', deals with how, during her long tenure as India's prime minister, Indira Gandhi incorporated Sikkim into the Indian Union, created six new states, broke up Pakistan and helped the birthing of a new nation, Bangladesh, carried on the Green Revolution that freed India from the food dependency on the US, experimented with authoritarianism by imposing the Emergency and brutally fought the Sikh-Khalistan militancy, for which she paid with her life. India burned with anger and hatred, nonetheless, remained one and unbroken. Her son Rajiv Gandhi, who led the Congress party to win the Lok Sabha election of 1984, was seen entering the Indian political scene as Mr Clean, but in the course of the next few years his image became sullied with political expediencies, damaging compromises, corruption scandals and general incompetence for managing crises, including the handling of the Sri Lankan civil war, for which he paid with his life when a Sri Lankan Tamil suicide bomber blew him up at an election rally.

His (though not immediate) successor, Narasimha Rao, facing an acute economic crisis, took bold measures to change India's course and in the process put India on the threshold of marketplace economy, which was the beginning of the end of Nehru's socialistic pattern of society. The rise of regional leaders strengthened federalism and made the game of democracy complicated, as was demonstrated by the most unfortunate tragic event, the destruction of the Babri

Masjid in 1992 by Hindu zealots claiming the site for their own Hindu God, Ram. Going into the 1996 general election, the Indian people had forgotten Rao's achievements and remembered only the pain and the suffering, ensuing riots, bombings, hijacking, kidnapping and the rising prices; and they shoved him into the dustbin of history. Politicians would learn that in democratic India there are no heroes and that voters seek their own interests in elections and could turn their back on them any time.

Part Three, 'As the Millennium Turned', recounts and explores a new phase of Indian democracy, the working of coalition governments under Atal Bihari Vajpayee and Manmohan Singh, of which India had already some limited experience in the 1970s. Under the short-lived coalition governments from 15 May 1996, through 17 April 1999, India saw the United Front-led coalition government headed by H.D. Deve Gowda followed by another brief one headed by Inder Kumar Gujral. However, Vajpayee's BJP-led National Democratic Alliance (NDA) 13-month coalition government was the most momentous in the history of coalitions: India became a nuclear weapons state; Vajpayee took a bus journey to meet with Pakistan's prime minister, Nawaz Sharif, which resulted in the Lahore Declaration for peaceful resolution of disputes.

The 1999 general election was pivotal because India was entering an era of stable coalition governments. After the thirteenth general election, the BJP-led NDA gave India a stable government for a full five-year term. Vajpayee, nevertheless, had to face, in quick succession, one bloody crisis after another: the Kargil War, the hijacking of the Kathmandu–Delhi–Kabul Air India flight by terrorists and the Pakistan-based terrorist attack on the Indian Parliament, followed by a massive buildup of troops that brought India and Pakistan to the brink of a nuclear war. And then came the burning of the train at Godhra in Gujarat, from where the flames of hell leapt up and bounced from town to town in a most horrific, uncontrollable wave after wave of unspeakable barbarism. In 2004, when Indians were called to elect the fourteenth Lok Sabha, they threw the centre-right Vajpayee government out and brought in the centre-left, Congress-led United Progressive Alliance (UPA) coalition government under Manmohan Singh, under whose administration India joined the trillion-dollar GDP (gross domestic product) club.

Singh tried to move India away from socialism to a limited free market economy. In reaching the landmark India–US Nuclear Energy Agreement, he carried out a most herculean task of bringing India out of the nuclear backstreet to the status of an acknowledged nuclear power. As Singh was trying to make peace with President Pervez Musharraf, Pakistani terrorists launched a seaborne attack on Mumbai in November 2008, reminiscent of the 9/11 attacks in New York in 2001. During Singh's tenure, India had an extraordinary economic growth, lifting millions out of poverty. Nonetheless, voters did not forgive the UPA coalition government for corruption scandals, rising inflation and failure to fight back terrorists. In the 2014 general election, Indian voters gave the pro-business BJP an overwhelming parliamentary majority and offered Prime Minister Narendra Modi a chance to liberate India from the shackles of deadened socialism and hasten the country on the path of a digital age and marketplace economy, making India aspirational as an emerging global power. The 2019 general election raised Modi to greater heights of mass idolization than ever before, ranking him at par with Nehru and Indira Gandhi: the two most esteemed leaders since India began experimenting with freedom.

In more than seven decades since Independence, India gradually changed from Nehru's socialistic pattern of society to Modi's entrepreneurial digital India, dealing with its internal contradictions by playing the game of democracy, and in the process becoming the sixth-largest economy in the world. And with *Chandrayaan* exploring the moon, she became a space nation, ranking with the United States, Russia and China.

I wrote *India in a New Key* for a global audience that needs to have a fresh perspective on a democratic India as a model of possibilities for political, economic and social developments and conflict resolution; and for those people who would be engaging with India as seriously as they are doing with China now. Modi is the most influential and highly regarded, albeit controversial, political figure in India today. As a statesman, he ranks with Xi Jinping of China and other powerful leaders in the world. Modi's phenomenal political rise has opened the doors for millions of aspirants at the bottom of India's pyramid. The world must know how India plays the game of democracy that has facilitated the rise of this wayside man to the top of the political pyramid; and the tryst he would make with India's destiny. The ultimate question is: can Narendra Modi, as he spurs India to a five-trillion-dollar economy, create a unified Indian consciousness as Jawaharlal Nehru had done?

PART ONE

The Freedom House That Nehru Built

1

IN THE BEGINNING,
THERE WAS JAWAHARLAL

This amazing man, his noble bearing, keen eyes and warm and disarming smile, made a very deep impression on me.

—Mikhail Gorbachev

I always admired your ardent wish for peace and the absence of bitterness in your consideration of the antagonisms that had in the past divided us. Yours is indeed a heavy burden and responsibility, shaping the destiny of your many millions of countrymen, and playing your outstanding part in world affairs. I wish you well in your task. Remember 'The Light of Asia!'

—Winston Churchill

At the beginning of the time when India became free from British rule, there was a beloved and trusted leader, Jawaharlal Nehru, who, on the midnight of 15 August 1947, spoke to his people and the world on the floor of the Constituent Assembly of India, in some of the most inspiring and poetic words uttered in the English language:

Long years ago we made a tryst with destiny, and now the time comes when we shall redeem our pledge… At the stroke of the midnight hour, when the world sleeps, India will awake to life and freedom. A moment comes, which comes but rarely in history, when we step out from the old to the new, when an age ends, and when the soul of a nation, long suppressed, finds utterance. It is fitting that at this solemn moment we take the pledge of dedication to the service of India and her people and to the still larger cause of humanity with some pride...We end today a period of ill fortune and India discovers herself again.[1]

It must have taken the first prime minister of free India, the undisputed leader of the nation, immense psychological and moral courage to transcend the bloody spectacle of the killing fields of the vast Indo-Gangetic plains and the exodus of millions of wretched and helpless brutalized people that accompanied the partition of the subcontinent, and audaciously assure the people that it was the beginning of a new India and that they would have a bright future. But that's the stuff great leaders are made of. Partition was collateral damage and the price paid for freedom, not only from the British colonial rule but also—and more importantly—from the burdens and the encumbrances of the Muslim League under the leadership of Mohammed Ali Jinnah and the party's two-nation theory of Hindu–Muslim socio-cultural incompatibility, which an overwhelming majority of Muslims of the subcontinent had accepted as reality. 'The achievement we celebrate today,' Nehru said optimistically, 'is but a step, an opening of opportunity, to the greater triumphs and achievements... That future is not one of ease and resting but of incessant striving so that we may fulfil the pledges we have so often taken.'[2]

The most important job was to create a sense of peace and security by bringing religious communal riots unleashed by Partition under control; the rehabilitation of 6–7 million drained, deprived, hostile Hindu-Sikh refugees who were forced to leave their rich, fertile lands, businesses and homes; the security of the Muslims who opted to stay behind in India or of those who wanted to go to Pakistan; the division of financial assets as well as military and administrative personnel between India and Pakistan; and the integration of the princely states with Indian Union. Equally challenging and urgent was the problem of governance based on the principles of representative democracy of a vast and disparate country and the establishment of a parliamentary constitutional system of governance responsive to the people. Throughout the long-drawn-out political struggle for independence, people's democratic aspirations, including fighting poverty, inequality, social oppression and injustices through rapid but planned socio-economic development, had been built up. Most importantly, how would India play the game of democracy? Would free, democratic India give up Mahatma Gandhi's non-violent, passive-active resistance, Satyagraha, hartals (strikes), bandhs (shutouts), fasts-unto-death, and individual and mass movement mode of bringing about sociopolitical changes? Or, would this grassroots political mode that gave the people a sense of instant empowerment become an essential part of the parliamentary democracy? Then there was the question of India's place in the world, keeping in mind the country's long struggle against imperialism and the imperative need to avoid recolonization by becoming an appendage of the Cold War blocs.

Nehru created hope from the wreckage of Partition that the British Empire had left behind and pushed Indians to dream big. Indians began to share his zest for life, his sense of drama, his 'no life without risk' attitude, believing, as William Wordsworth had once said, that it was 'a great privilege for people of this generation to live during this period of India's long history… I have believed that there is nothing more exciting in the wide world today than to work in India'.[3] Through the hustle and bustle of democracy, regularly scheduled free and fair elections, the tempo and progression of Five-Year plans, the constant beat of socialism and secularism, and the commitment to nonalignment-based friendships, Nehru would give Indians a sense of self-respect that they had never felt before. And transcending the sufferings of Partition, he would make India take great leaps forward.

Even before Nehru, there were many national and regional leaders of great ability, integrity and political acumen who had waged a tough struggle for independence under the charismatic tutelage of Mohandas Karamchand Gandhi. A saint-like politician, who is reverently addressed as Mahatma (in Sanskrit: great soul), he was one of the greatest political geniuses of modern times. He mesmerized Indians and lifted them up. And at first, they listened to him, they followed him, they imitated him, but finally, they found him too difficult to understand and thus, they killed him. His followers included some of the brightest and the toughest who, like him, had assimilated the best from the West and the East, including Sardar Vallabhbhai Patel, who helped integrate the princely India with the Republic; Islamic scholar Maulana Abul Kalam Azad, who wistfully wrote *India Wins Freedom*; the tall massively built Pathan, Abdul Ghaffar Khan aka Frontier Gandhi; Rajendra Prasad, who would become the first president of the Republic of India; C. Rajagopalachari, Governor General, state chief minister, writer and interpreter of the classics such as the Mahabharata, and later the co-founder of the Swatantra Party; Bhimrao Ramji Ambedkar, the great constitutionalist and Dalit leader; Jayaprakash Narayan, socialist and Sarvodaya leader; Syama Prasad Mookerjee, the fiery leader and founder of the Bharatiya Jana Sangh; Sarvepalli Radhakrishnan, philosopher, diplomat and the second president of India; and communist leaders like Puran Chand Joshi and Ajoy Ghosh, who would demonstrate that communism and democracy were not incompatible. There were many capable state leaders, including Govind Ballabh Pant of Uttar Pradesh, Bidhan Chandra Roy of West Bengal and Morarji Desai, a stoic Gandhian from Bombay Presidency (present-day Valsad district in Gujarat)—leaders who played stabilizing roles in spite of their sharp ideological differences. Above all, there was the INC, whose widespread organizational networks, horizontal and vertical, reached out from village grassroots through district and state levels to the national echelon that left no one untouched.

CONTROLLING THE COMMUNAL INFERNO

In the aftermath of Independence, the greatest threat to India came from within. This threat came as furious out-of-control communal fire, hatred and violence that had its genesis in the Muslim League's call for Direct Action Day of 16 August 1946. Although it hastened the call for Partition and the creation of Pakistan, this day fuelled the inter-religious communal fire that had started travelling from village to village, city to city, and from one refugee caravan to another. But the gods of freedom were still smiling on India because the inter-religious communal infernos were limited to the Indo-Gangetic killing fields. Most of India, especially the South, was almost free from the Hindu–Muslim communal violence. Fortunately, the South sometimes thinks differently from the rest of India. And it was the South, with its immense intellectual powers and capacity for resistance, which would go on to shape the destiny of India.

After Partition, when Nehru, Patel and other Indian leaders found that the Hindu–Muslim communal situation was beyond control, beyond the ordinary law and order situation, that the capital of free India, Delhi, might collapse like a house of cards, whom did they call? They controlled their mighty egos and approached Lord Mountbatten to help contain such a precarious situation. Mahatma Gandhi told Indians to despise British imperialism but not the British people, whom he, like most other Indian leaders, respected and admired. In the first few years of India's independence, Lord Mountbatten, the last viceroy of India, played an important role in stabilizing the political situation.

Surprisingly, more than the political leaders, it was a most savvy and astute southern 'non-politician' politician from Kerala, V.P. Menon, who understood the gravity of the situation and demanded some tough measures to be enforced. As an eyewitness to the unfolding chaos and as a top official in the home ministry working with Sardar Patel, he observed that the most urgent task was to restore law and order, quell the communal madness, create a sense of security for the Muslims staying in India and the safe departure for those who wanted to go to Pakistan. No less crucial was the safety and settlement of Hindu and Sikh refugees escaping from Pakistan. 'It was particularly essential,' he said, 'that Delhi should be saved from the impending chaos at whatever cost. Danger to the Capital meant a threat to the very existence of the nascent Dominion.'[4]

India chose Lord Mountbatten, who was highly regarded by Indian politicians, especially Nehru and Patel, as the first governor-general of the Union of India. Menon thought that Mountbatten could help save the calamitous situation, and he should be asked to return to Delhi from his Simla (now Shimla) vacation. Both Nehru and Sardar Patel readily agreed with the suggestion, and so did Lord Mountbatten, who promptly returned to Delhi in early September 1947. A high-powered Emergency Committee, under the chairmanship of Lord Mountbatten, and consisting of cabinet ministers including Nehru, Patel and others, as well as top military, police and civilian officers, was formed. The daily scene of action was the Map Room; 'the purpose of which was to provide factual and up-to-date information to all concerned with regard to the place and number of disturbances and the location and movement of refugees.'[5] Since the disturbed region consisting of New Delhi and Old Delhi, as well as the surrounding villages, was too large to be managed by a single committee, the responsibility was devolved to zonal administrators and their committees, who were vested with the power and resources to stop large scale rioting, and whose work was coordinated at the Central Control Room.

But once the political, military, and law-and-order machinery was set in motion, it restored people's confidence, resulting in the restoration of peace due to:

> the steadfastness and loyalty of majority of its citizens, who were more than ready to give their help and co-operation... Nothing was more inspiring and nothing cheered one so much as the spontaneous way in which men and women of all ages, classes and shades of opinion came forward to work at all hours—if need be, round the clock—in a disciplined manner at a task which they realized was one of great humanity.[6]

Restoring peace had been a humongous task, but by December 1947, the sense and sensibility of common humanity had returned, for which credit must be given—where it's due—to Lord Mountbatten who 'agreed to take over the helm of responsibility at that critical stage, and it redounds to the statesmanship of Nehru and Patel that they unhesitatingly and confidently offered it to him'.[7]

But it was too premature to celebrate the victory gained over the deeply ingrained communal forces in India. On 30 January 1948, a grief-stricken Nehru told the people of India, 'Our beloved leader, Bapu as we called him, the Father of the Nation, is no more.' Speaking on All India Radio, he said:

> The light has gone out of our lives and there is darkness everywhere... The light has gone out, I said, and yet I was wrong. For the light that shone in this country was no ordinary light... that light represented something more than the immediate present; it represented the living, the eternal truths, reminding us of the right path, drawing us from error, taking this ancient country to freedom.

Referring to Nathuram Godse as a madman, Nehru said, 'For I can only call him mad who did it, and yet there has been enough of poison spread in this country during the past years and months, and this poison has had an effect on people's minds.' The Mahatma's death was not the end of the story because, as he continued, 'We must face this poison, we must root out this poison, and we must face all the perils that encompass us, and face them not madly or badly, but rather in the way that our beloved teacher taught us to face them.'

Nehru attempted to transform the national tragedy into a lesson for nation-building, reminding the people that, instead of being angry over the action of the madman,

> We have to behave like strong and determined people, determined to face all the perils that surround us, determined to carry out the mandate that our great teacher and our great leader has given us, remembering always that if, as I believe, his spirit looks upon us and sees us, nothing would displease his soul so much as to see that we have indulged in any small behavior or any violence.

Although he was agnostic and secular in outlook, Nehru seemed deeply spiritual in invoking the guiding spirit of the Mahatma, reminding the people that he (the Mahatma) would have wanted above all nothing but the unity of the people, therefore, '...we should, in strength and in unity, face all the troubles that are in front of us... hold together, and all our petty troubles and difficulties and conflicts must be ended in the face of this great disaster'.

Instead of considering it merely the act of a madman, he reminded the people of the deeper symbolic meaning of the tragic event, 'A great disaster is a symbol to us to remember all the big things of life and forget the small things of which we have thought too much.' The Mahatma's death was not in vain because, '[i]n his death he has reminded us of the big things of life, the living truth, and if we remember that, then it will be well with India'.[8]

What to do when free speech and political protests, constitutionally guaranteed democratic rights, disrupt the game of democracy? In a December 1947 letter to state chief ministers, one of the most innovative modes of communications he had developed to keep regional leaders informed and under his political umbrella, Nehru wrote:

> We have a great deal of evidence to show that the RSS is an organisation which is in the nature of a private army and which is definitely proceeding on the strictest Nazi lines, even following the technique of organisation. *It is not our desire to interfere with civil liberties* [emphasis added]. But training in arms of large numbers of persons with the obvious intention of using them is not something that can be encouraged... *Unfortunately, a number of Congressmen, without thinking, are attracted to this development of fascist and Nazi modes of thought and practice* [emphasis added]. I have ventured, therefore, to draw your attention to this for we will ignore it at our peril.[9]

He saw no difference between the Muslim League and the Rashtriya Swayamsevak Sangh (RSS), saying:

> The wave of fascism which is gripping India now is the direct outcome of hatred for the non-Muslims (Hindus) which the Muslim League preached among its followers for years...

accepted the ideology of fascism from the Nazis of Germany…
The ideas and methods of fascist organization are now gaining
popularity among the Hindus also and the demand for the
establishment of a Hindu State is its clear manifestation.[10]

At every public platform, through public speeches, radio broadcasts,
parliament speeches, private correspondence and letters to state
chief ministers, Nehru continued his relentless campaign against
religious communalism.

On the point of secularism and protecting and safeguarding
minorities, he had the full support of his Congress colleagues,
especially the next in leadership and command Sardar Vallabhbhai
Patel, the deputy prime minister and home minister, whose secular
credentials remain unimpeachable. Patel repeatedly said on many
occasions, 'Ours is a secular state…Here every Muslim should feel
that he is an Indian citizen and has equal rights as an Indian citizen.
If we cannot make him feel like this, we shall not be worthy of our
heritage and of our country.'[11] On another occasion Patel said, 'We
have just heard people shouting that Muslims should be removed
from India. Those who do so have gone mad with anger. I am a
frank man. I say bitter things to Hindus and Muslims alike. At the
same time I maintain that I am a friend of Muslims.'[12]

Writing to industrialist M.B. Birla, he said:

> I do not think it will be possible to consider India as a Hindu
> state with Hinduism as the state religion. We must not forget
> that there are other minorities whose protection is our primary
> responsibility. The state must exist for all irrespective of caste
> and creed.[13]

Patel, nonetheless, expected full loyalty to India from the Muslims
who decided not to go to Pakistan in spite of the fact that the
majority of them had supported the Muslim League's demand for a
separate homeland. But Patel's immediate concern was the RSS, the
right-wing Hindu nationalist organization whose Hindutva ideology
might have inspired Nathuram Godse, Gandhi's assassin.

The RSS was founded in 1925 by a physician from Nagpur,

central India, Dr Keshav Baliram Hedgewar, for rejuvenating Hindu society.[14] He was deeply inspired by the works of revolutionary Bengali groups such as Anushilan Samiti, the great Hindu ascetic and philosopher Aurobindo Ghosh, and later Vinayak Damodar Savarkar, the author of *Hindutva*. In the aftermath of the assassination of Gandhi, the Government of India banned the RSS on 4 February 1948 and arrested several of its leaders, including its chief, M.S. Golwalkar. But since there was no direct link between the RSS leadership and Gandhi's assassination, Golwalkar and other leaders were acquitted of the conspiracy charges. The ban on the RSS nevertheless continued until the organization accepted Home Minister Sardar Patel's demands, including its renunciation of violence, loyalty to the Constitution of India, acceptance of and respect for the National Flag and a written democratic constitution for the organization.[15]

Soon after accepting the government-imposed conditions, the RSS, while maintaining its original character and ideology, developed its political organization, the Bharatiya Jana Sangh, under the leadership of Syama Prasad Mookerjee and several prominent RSS volunteers, including Deendayal Upadhyay, Balraj Madhok and Atal Bihari Vajpayee. In the 1980s, the Bharatiya Jana Sangh would evolve into a free-market-oriented, right-wing nationalist party, the BJP that would eventually rule the country under the leadership of Atal Bihari Vajpayee; and later under Narendra Modi, who, in his own way would unite India the way Nehru had done in his day. Had the RSS been totally banned, the organization with its massive network of branches (shakhas) would have gone underground and sabotaged the game of democracy.

COMMUNISTS MORE DANGEROUS THAN COMMUNALISTS

Indian communists' challenge to a democratic India, the ruling INC, and Nehru's leadership and his vision of India was no less serious than that from religious communalism. And it's one of his greatest achievements that Nehru eventually brought Indian communists and other leftist revolutionaries into the democratic mainstream. But it wasn't that easy. In February 1948, the CPI, at its second party congress held in Calcutta (now Kolkata), called for a democratic revolution in India, condemning the Nehru government as 'reactionary'. The newly elected CPI General Secretary B.T. Ranadive asked the party to contend with 'a so-called Independence,' and continue the struggle against British toadies, using all kinds of means. He added, 'Strikes, mass rallies, demonstrations, and armed struggles must be used to challenge this false sense of freedom.'[16]

The hereditary rulers in Tripura in the Northeast as well as in Kerala and Andhra Pradesh region in the south became easy targets of the CPI's new revolutionary programme. It was in Telangana, then part of the Hyderabad State, however, that the communists had the most popular support, and raised a people's militia to fight against the Nizam and big landlords. But the insurgency was brutally put down, and the CPI gave up its revolutionary platform. Ranadive was condemned for his left adventurism and fired from his position as the party's general secretary. The party's national leadership, including S.A. Dange, Chandra Rajeswara Rao and P.K. Vasudevan Nair, began building up public support by championing the cause of the poor and by unionizing textile workers, bank employees and unorganized sector workers.

In the first general election of 1952, the CPI contested 49 seats and won 16, thereby becoming the leading opposition party in the Lok Sabha.[17] In the 1957 general election, the party won the Kerala state election and formed the first democratically elected communist government. E.M.S. Namboodiripad became the state's first chief minister, whose progressive agenda, including land reforms and education policies, would transform Kerala into a standard-bearer of peaceful socialist revolution, under the so-called 'Kerala Model', an alternative to Nehru's democratic socialism. The Kerala communist-democratic experiment paved the way for Jyoti Basu, a Middle Temple (London) barrister and a leader of the Communist Party of India (Marxist)—the CPI(M)—who would rule as West Bengal chief minister from 1977 through 2001, the longest-serving head of an Indian state. Eventually, the communists, like other Indian political parties, would split into factions, some nationalists and others internationalists, some pro-Chinese (including the underground Maoists and the Naxalites) and others pro-Soviet, and play the Indian game of democracy by forming coalitions and sharing power with like-minded parties at the state level and the Centre.

Nehru felt less uncomfortable with the Indian communists, whose ideological goals of socialism he broadly shared, because in his view '...the communists, with all their faults, function in terms of serious economic solutions [sic]'; it's the dogma and violence of their approach that is to be repudiated and if 'they can divest themselves of this obsession and accept the discipline of our parliamentary democracy in good faith, there is not much difference between their goal of socialism and ours'. But on the other hand, he said, 'parties...like the Jana Sangh and Swatantra, seem to be organized around plainly fascist and feudal concepts without any social or economic basis...they are dangerous to the country and our values of democracy and socialism'.[18]

Ironically, the communists and their ideology would dissipate in the coming decades, and rightist parties like the BJP (the political offspring of the Jana Sangh) and the Swatantra Party, after going through the processes of political mergers and recombinant transformations, would give India new social and economic dynamism. By giving his opponents—and even those whom he might have despised—plenty of space to grow, Nehru, with his remarkable capacity for democratic tolerance, let Indians develop and play the game of democracy in the legal framework of parliamentary federalism that the founders had created.

REHABILITATION AND RESETTLEMENT

Thirty-five million Muslims who could not or did not want to go to Pakistan, regardless of their past affiliations with the Muslim League, were protected and stayed in India. They had to be emotionally, psychologically and politically rehabilitated and strengthened to accept the new realities of free India, where their loyalty would be constantly questioned. They, too, had to pay the price of the broken Indian freedom. But on the bright side, their large presence would strengthen India's secularism and give the country a legal and moral rationale for bonding and integrating a majorly Muslim populated Jammu and Kashmir with the Indian Union. On the other hand, there was almost a complete ethnic cleansing of the Hindus and Sikhs in West Pakistan, where some were forcibly converted to Islam, more than a million were massacred, and hundreds of thousands of women were kidnapped and raped.[19] The massacre of Muslims and the kidnapping and rape of Muslim women were equally horrific. These kidnapped women were later repatriated to their respective countries—Hindu and Sikh women to India and Muslim women to Pakistan.[20] About eight million Hindu and Sikh refugees came to India column by moving column, caravan by straggling caravan, and train by burning train. Millions of East and West Pakistan refugees had to be sheltered, housed, fed and resettled, which, apart from necessitating the judicious allotment of limited available cultivable lands, also required providing them with government jobs as well as space and resources for working on their own.

GIFT OF THE REFUGEES

Hindu and Sikh refugees, destitute and brutalized, were nonetheless bringing to India something precious: professional skills and entrepreneurial spirit; and they were hungry and willing to work and daring to break new ground. They would upturn barren lands into green fields. They would transform the British imperial Delhi beyond recognition.[21] They—the Kapoors, the Anands, the Chopras and thousands of other refugees—would harness the so-called Bollywood creative and artistic energies for telling melodramatic and epic stories infused with a hurly-burly, song-and-dance culture aimed at the masses cutting across caste and creed, turning Bombay into India's melting pot. Bombay would become 'Meri Jaan' (My Love) for the best and the brightest in India. And these displaced millions listened to Nehru, and they loved him, and they believed in him, and they shared his new vision of India.

Research done regarding the impact of the transfer of skills on the agricultural practices that the refugees brought to India indicated that the 'places with more activity by displaced persons as a result of the Partition were more likely to experience higher agricultural yields, although such increases are only observed after the advent of the Green Revolution in India (in the late 1960s), which could have occurred due to 'the relative education of the refugees, which made them more likely to take up technologies and new methods of cultivation that were part of the Green Revolution.'[22]

These highly productive refugee farmers from the fertile lands of Lyallpur (now Faisalabad) and other parts of West Pakistan would turn Indian Punjab into the food bank of the nation. A similar impact of the skills of refugees was seen in West Bengal when its jute mills were cut off from their jute growing areas in East Pakistan and which instigated and motivated India to grow its own jute. The new jute cultivation areas in India 'correlate strongly with areas that received migrants from East Pakistan,' for which a 'likely reason is that refugees from East Pakistan came with knowledge specific to cultivating and growing the crop'. And consequently, 'while the Partition lines and a trade embargo disrupted a flourishing industry in the short run, refugee specific knowledge may have mitigated long-term damage to this industry.'[23]

More than the agricultural transformation in Punjab and the revival and rehabilitation of jute and other industries attributed to East Pakistan's Bengali Hindu refugees, Partition opened to India, the floodgates of brainpower. Intellectuals, professionals, artists and creative people who would rejuvenate India in diverse fields, including luminaries such as the theoretical physicist Amal Kumar Raychaudhuri; economist-philosopher and Nobel laureate Amartya Kumar Sen; film personalities Asit Sen, Bimal Roy, Mithun Chakraborty, Mrinal Sen and Haradhan Bandopadhyay; singer Geeta Dutt; historians Hem Chandra Raychaudhuri and Jadunath Sarkar; General J.N. Chaudhuri of Hyderabad fame; the most durable communist leader and the longest-serving state chief minister, Jyoti Basu; astrophysicist Meghnad Saha; writer Nirad Chaudhuri; cricketer Pankaj Roy; statistician and five-year plan economic planner and advisor Prasanta Chandra Mahalanobis; and Higgs-Boson physicist Satyendra Nath Bose, to name a few. But these luminaries did not need much help from the government because Calcutta, Delhi, Bombay and other cities where they spread their luminous wings had always been their homes away from home.

A dispassionate observer might say, however, that while East Pakistan refugees gifted India with creativity and brainpower, West Pakistan refugees brought with them entrepreneurial and organizational energies, not belittling however the great contribution made by économist-prime minister, Dr Manmohan Singh, writer Khushwant Singh, poet, lyricist and film director Gulzar (Sampooran Singh Kalra), Nobel Laureate biochemist Har Gobind Khorana; and not the least, freedom fighter Acharya J.B. Kripalani, among many others.

Altogether the Bengali, Punjabi and Sindhi refugees, in the course of time, transformed India into a dynamic nation. But before they could do so, the refugees had to be rehabilitated and resettled. The challenge of the resettlement of about eight million refugees brought forth the best in the government in terms of organization, logistics, land allotment, housing, food distribution, health and sanitation, and schooling. How did they do it? A month after Independence, the Government of India established the Ministry of Relief and Rehabilitation, tasking it with the resettlement and rehabilitation of 7.95 million refugees—4.7 million from West Pakistan and 3.25 million from East Pakistan.[24] The problem was not just about saving the newly independent country from a massive human disaster that came in the form of displacement of people. The first and foremost challenge was making arrangements for the sheer survival of the millions who had flooded the country for which the government established more than 200 refugee camps, some big enough to accommodate 300,000 people. The displaced people from West Pakistan were dispersed in Punjab, Delhi, Uttar Pradesh, Gujarat, Bombay, Madhya Pradesh and Rajasthan. While the migration from West Pakistan was completed by the end of 1947, the refugee flow from East Pakistan was still in a continuous flux. Unlike the West Pakistan refugees, who came in one big flood, the Bengali Hindu refugees came in wave after wave, crossing into Tripura and into West Bengal where most of them moved into Calcutta and the neighbouring districts, Nadia and 24 Parganas, thereby putting extreme pressure on the state. Later, some Bengali refugees were settled in Assam, Odisha, Madhya Pradesh and Bihar. In Delhi, refugees from East Pakistan were rehabilitated in what was earlier known as the East Pakistan Displaced Persons Colony; today, we know that place as Chittaranjan Park.

According to official accounts, by the end of 1951–52, the government had settled a vast majority of displaced agriculturalists from West Pakistan. Besides, the government distributed ₹80 million as 'loans for the purchase of bullocks, fodder, seeds and other agricultural equipment, repair and construction of houses and wells, etc., and for the maintenance of families for the initial period of six months following the allotment of land'. Regarding East Pakistan's rural refugees, it was estimated that 3,30,000 out of 4,70,000 Bengali rural families had been settled in the eastern states by 1951–52, but since the influx of refugees continued, the situation remained fluid.[25] Depending upon the Hindu–Muslim communal situation, East Pakistan's Hindu refugees kept coming to India in varied numbers, ranging from a trickle to wave after wave.

In 1958, the government of India launched an ambitious resettlement scheme, the Dandakaranya Project, for their settlement; 'a grand project that deserves to succeed, if only because of the hope of a new life that it seemed to offer to the many homeless refugees from East Pakistan, who are still leading a demoralised existence on doles in camps,' according to a report in *The Hindu*. Of the 20,000 East Bengal refugees expected in the Project, only 1,464 had arrived by March 1959. The Dandakaranya Development Authority blamed the refugees for their tardiness.[26]

The government's purpose was not only to resettle the Bengali Hindu refugees but also help develop the tribal population of the area where the project was located. But the project faced resistance, because 'political elements in West Bengal have continuously sought to exploit the unhappy condition of the refugees in camps and to teach them to resist resettlement in areas outside Bengal,' *The*

Hindu stated.[27]

The urban refugees' resettlement presented a different set of challenges. The urban Hindus and Sikhs who migrated from West Pakistan were mostly professionals, industrialists, traders, merchants and small shopkeepers. In order to absorb them, the economy had to expand and create a space for them. Of the 2.5 million urban refugees from West Pakistan, 1.5 million refugees were settled in evacuee houses and for the remaining, the government embarked upon a massive home-building programme at an estimated expenditure of nearly ₹600 million.[28] Many new cooperative settlement colonies and towns were established, including Faridabad and Nilokheri (in Haryana), Rajpura and Tripuri in Punjab, Sardarnagar and Ulhasnagar in the Bombay region, Gandhidham in Kutch, Gujarat, and Govindpuri and Hastinapur in Uttar Pradesh. A most well-planned, modern and beautiful city, Chandigarh, was established as the capital of Punjab (and now Haryana as well). It was designed by the Swiss-French architect Le Corbusier and includes the Capitol Complex with the high court, legislative assembly, the Panjab University, the Rock Garden, and the Open Hand symbolic monument. With the building of Chandigarh, Hindu and Sikh refugees had transcended beyond the trauma of Partition. In the east, new townships at Fulia, Habra and Baigachi were established for East Pakistan Hindu refugees. But most of the urban settlements of refugees in West Bengal, Assam, Bihar and Orissa were left to private individuals who were provided with developed plots and loans.

Employment opportunities for displaced people were created through employment exchanges and by making job reservations for refugees in Indian Railways and other public sector establishments. The government also provided technical and vocational training to willing and capable refugees and helped them in the allotment and construction of business premises and industrial undertakings. Moreover, the government granted loans for small as well as large-scale businesses. New schools and colleges were opened, and deserving students were given free tuition, stipends and cash grants for books. One of them was a Sikh boy from the village of Gah in

Punjab—Manmohan Singh, who would go on to become a most successful and transformative finance minister and later the prime minister of India, who opened India up to the global competition. Another refugee boy born in Jhelum (now in Pakistan), Inder Kumar Gujral, would go on to become a successful diplomat and politician and also have a brief stint as prime minister.

The government also established the Rehabilitation Finance Administration to help displaced businesspersons set up large-scale businesses. Moreover, the government helped finance refugee entrepreneurs to revive and redevelop the evacuee abandoned stores and industrial establishments, apart from financing the development of new markets for enterprising refugees in various townships. By the end of the 1952 fiscal year, the government had spent about ₹900 million on rehabilitation schemes, which included rural resettlement and technical training and education schemes, apart from the urban housing loans and the Rehabilitation Finance Administration loans.[29] It was a massive undertaking that, besides boosting the national economy, also called forth the best in the government, private enterprises as well as voluntary organizations that worked with the authorities. In crisis mode, India works the best.

GIVE US OUR DAILY BREAD OR ELSE...

By the time India became independent, the Great Bengal Famine of 1943 that had—thanks to the callousness and inhumanity of the policy of Winston Churchill's War Cabinet and the colonial administration—killed about three to four million people, four times more than Partition killed, had become a distant memory.[30] For the British, India growing food and its distributive management policy had become part of the wartime food economy, without any concern for the welfare of the Indian people. The British Indian government introduced food procurement levies, price controls and rationing as well as subsidized prices for the poorer sections, which, although had alleviated shortages, covered only 20 per cent of the population. For the rest of the population, 'there was the open market or the black market,' because, since the government procured food grains at below the market prices, the black market flourished during the war.[31] Partition aggravated the post-World War II calamitous food situation and the Government of India, burdened with refugee rehabilitation and resettlement crises, had no choice but to continue the colonial-time food management policy including price controls, procurement policies and rationing.

The Nehru Government launched the Grow More Food campaign which, in spite of setting targets for extra food production for each state, was not able to produce enough to meet the growing demand. The government had to depend on imports that cost ₹200–250 million per year, pressuring its already limited foreign exchange reserves.[32] In addition to the refugee resettlement, the defence of Jammu and Kashmir put increasing budgetary pressures. Nehru vowed for food production self-sufficiency, equating it with freedom and exhorted the nation to produce more. But due to primitive agricultural infrastructure, dilapidated rural economy, hidebound peasantry and exploitative landlordism, mere populist appeals to grow more food to achieve economic independence weren't good enough. Most of the cultivators who 'were scraping a living on small plots with little access to irrigation, let alone fertilizers or tractors, were paradoxically both a hindrance and one of the only tools at hand to solve India's "food problem".'[33] But to mobilize scattered masses of subsistent peasantry into a disciplined food production force, was beyond any democratic government to resolve, in spite of the fact that the INC had a widespread grassroots political machine.

One of the most seemingly bizarre schemes introduced was the Van Mahotsav, a forestation and reforestation programme for planting tens of millions of trees. It was a brainchild of the erudite food minister, Dr Kanaiyalal Maneklal (K.M.) Munshi, and was based on the idea that forests not only produced food (on which some tribals depended) but also attracted more rains, apart from preventing land erosion, which though true, did not solve the immediate problem of food production or equitable distribution of scarce food resources. When Munshi, also known by his pen name of Ghanshyam Vyas, suggested that forest products might be used as food, he was laughed at: 'Maybe bark...boiled...and seasoned with newspaper cuttings containing the Food Minister's speeches will be a better proposition... For dessert we must have wood—slabs of it—and a plateful of sawdust in honour of the master brain that conceived such a brilliant idea.'[34] The Van Mahotsav programme was accompanied by a campaign for making compost, which farmers could use as fertilizer, but it did not enthuse the farmers and few cared for the outlandish schemes. Of course, the Grow More Food Programme was much more than just growing trees and making compost, because 'hundreds of wells were drilled, fertilizers and improved varieties of seed were made available for purchase, and hundreds of thousands of rupees were loaned to farmers to help them buy these items.'[35] But this was not good enough. It would take years of education and persuasion and demonstrable benefits before the Indian farmer would adopt scientific farming methods. Until then, the average Indian farmer would depend upon the kindness or the vagaries of the monsoon.

To allocate food from surplus states to deficit ones, the Union Food Ministry depended upon the food production and procurement data from the states. The food redistribution between surplus and deficit states not only depended upon the availability of surpluses but also on how accurate the estimates were. Besides, farmers and middlemen had greater incentives to sell their food in the black market rather than sell it to the government at procurement levy prices. For a long time, India would depend upon the dual food distribution system, the unauthorized free market (black market) food for those who could afford it and the procurement levy-based rationing for the rest. In the early years of independence, the food problem showed the emerging tensions in the functioning of the federal system. How scarce resources between the Centre and the states should be allocated 'turned into a cacophonous row, with many provinces constantly pressing the Centre for a greater allocation of grains,' because 'the gap between food production and consumption encouraged hoarding, which in turn caused prices to rise...a sense of crisis grew because the production of food ultimately depended on the one thing the government could neither command nor cajole, but which everyone could monitor: the weather.'[36] But unfortunately, the monsoon gods were not seen to be kind to India for the first five years after Independence.

The monsoons have always been unreliable as well as indispensable in spite of the fact that India has the largest acreage of arable and cultivable land in the world, comparable only to the United States. India's food problem has been more than its dependency on the vagaries of the monsoons. In the course of time, the country would realize that feeding India's millions was essentially the problem of science, technology and political management. Until then, the monsoons, sometimes its excesses and sometimes its scarcities, would create rolling disasters from region to region, as they did, for example, during 1947–1952: droughts, cyclones and river floods that damaged or destroyed crops in Bihar, West Bengal, Uttar Pradesh, Kashmir, and in many parts of the south. The monsoons never blessed or cursed all parts of India even-handedly and consequently, although the 1943 Bengal Famine conditions did not exist anywhere, the marginalized population, especially in the rural areas, suffered disproportionately. For the less fortunate of the population, landless labourers and small farmers, the food crisis was aggravated due to poverty and perhaps inaccessibility to ration shops. Deaths due to starvation were reported in Bihar and eastern Uttar Pradesh. In some areas the cattle perished while in other areas people migrated in search of food and work.

But the fatalistic attitude had changed in India and for the post-Independence food crisis, Indians did not blame their fate, the monsoons or the gods. The people confronted the government for its failure to manage the food crisis in which the free and vociferous print news media and the political opposition parties joined them. In 1951, thousands of people participated in protests and hunger marches in Punjab, West Bengal and Delhi, in which they were supported by Socialist Party leaders including Ram Manohar Lohia and Jayaprakash Narayan, who demanded,

If the Government of India are unable to feed the people,

> which is their primary duty...they must then say so and resign.
> Let the people choose a new government...Hungry and Naked
> India Demands Bread Clothing and Houses...A Government
> that cannot end blackmarketing [sic] and corruption has no
> right to exist.[37]

Populous street democracy was becoming an important part of the game of democracy that India would play in the future. The government learnt that asking semi-starving people to miss a meal, as Nehru did on 1 May 1951, in a radio broadcast, had limitations. What forced the government to adopt practical measures to manage the food crisis was India's forthcoming first general election on which the Congress party and Nehru had staked their democratic reputations. Nehru and the INC won the 1952 general election and grounded Indian democracy on a solid foundation, thanks to its pragmatic attitude rather than phony slogans like Grow More Foods Grow More Trees and Miss a Meal. Instead of depending upon food nationalism and letting people starve, India turned to global food markets for food security. It entered into food aid agreements with Australia and Canada and barter deals with Russia, China and Argentina. The US Congress and President Harry S. Truman were unresponsive to India's request for food aid due to its non-alignment policy, but eventually, the US agreed to give India a US$190 million wheat purchase loan.[38]

NEHRU UNBOUND

Jawaharlal Nehru was born on 14 November 1889 in Allahabad (now Prayagraj). As a leader, he was passionate about children's education as he was extremely fond of them. The children, in turn, always affectionately addressed him as 'Chacha (Uncle) Nehru'. His birthday later came to be celebrated as Children's Day every year. He would celebrate this day by releasing a dove into the skies, symbolizing peace. Nehru made Indians feel good about themselves and about their nation.

Allahabad (now Prayagraj) is an ancient city at the confluence of the mighty Himalayan rivers—the Triveni Sangam—of the

Ganga, the Yamuna and the mythic Saraswati, where the Kumbh Mela is held and vedic hymns are chanted. The consecrated rivers drain the sprawling Indo-Gangetic plains, the birthplace of India's great epics, the Ramayana and the Mahabharata, the birthplace of Buddhism, and the playground of marauders, conquerors and empire builders, from the Maurya Empire of Asoka through the Mughal Empire of Akbar to the British Empire of Queen Victoria. Jawaharlal Nehru was deeply imbued with a sense of history as well as with ancient Indian philosophical and humanist heritage, about which he wrote beautifully in *The Discovery of India*, during his 1942–46 imprisonment for his participation in the Quit India Movement under the leadership of Mahatma Gandhi.

As a child, Nehru was fed with a silver spoon and home-taught by private tutors and governesses, as was the custom with most Indian elite families. His father, Motilal Nehru, a prosperous barrister in Allahabad, was a political person and had served as president of the INC in 1919 and again in 1928. Born in a Kashmiri Brahmin family, his ancestors had migrated to the plains during the sunset of the Mughal Empire. The atmosphere at Anand Bhavan, the palatial home Motilal Nehru had built in the then Allahabad, wasn't altogether apolitical and young Nehru grew up in an intellectually stimulating environment, though his early life was cozy and privileged. Through Annie Besant, a family friend, Nehru as a teenager, for example, got an early exposure to the theosophical ideas of the universal brotherhood of humanity that eschewed distinction of race, creed, sex, caste or colour and emphasized the study of comparative religion and philosophy as well as science to understand the laws of nature and develop latent powers in humans.[39]

The political atmosphere must have kindled young Nehru's open and absorptive mind in the early years. In 1905, Nehru was sent to Harrow School, London, England, an independent boarding school for boys, whose alumni boasted of several British prime ministers including Robert Peel, Lord Palmerston, Stanley Baldwin and Winston Churchill. He later attended Trinity College, Cambridge, where he graduated with honours in natural sciences. After his graduation, he spent two years at the Inner Temple, London, to study law and become a barrister.

When he returned to India in 1912, after seven years of stay in England, he felt like 'a queer mixture of East and West, out of place everywhere, at home nowhere'.[40] He became a man in search of his roots and this led him to explore historical India, as many of his nationalist countrymen had been doing at the time. His mind was riddled with such questions as to why this great civilization had been subjugated and what was the path to freedom. During his intellectually formative years in England, he had taken a deep interest in the political occurrences in Europe and India. Once he settled, he began to practice law at the Allahabad High Court but he later found that 'the atmosphere was not intellectually stimulating and a sense of the utter insipidity of life grew upon me'.[41]

Sometime after his return to India in 1912, Nehru became actively involved with the INC, a party of upper class moderates such as Gopal Krishna Gokhale and Motilal Nehru. He soon became disillusioned when he saw that the bridge to freedom was far away and the path was not clear. During World War I, the Indian elites sympathized with the Allies and Nehru himself volunteered for the St John Ambulance Brigade. The contribution of India to British war efforts was immense, considering that,

> [Almost] 1.5 million Muslim, Sikh and Hindu men from regions such as the Punjab, Uttar Pradesh, Maharashtra, Tamil Nadu and Bihar volunteered in the Indian Expeditionary Force, which saw fighting on the Western Front, in East Africa, Mesopotamia, Egypt and Gallipoli...of these men, around 50,000 died, 65,000 were wounded, and 10,000 were reported missing, while 98 Indian army nurses were killed.[42]

In addition, 'the country also supplied 170,000 animals, 3.7 million tonnes of supplies, jute for sandbags and a large loan (the equivalent of about £2 billion today) to the British government... Having made huge sacrifices and demonstrated military valour equal to that of European soldiers, Indians widely expected a transition to self-government'.[43] But the British Indian government not only did not acknowledge the enormous sacrifices Indians had made for the British Empire but also enacted the draconian Rowlatt Act forbidding nationalistic activities and restricting civil liberties, which led to widespread protests all over the country and the resultant massacre of a peaceful gathering of people at the Jallianwalla Bagh in Amritsar on 13 April 1919.[44] The Butcher of Amritsar, Colonel Reginald Dyer, went unpunished.

Even before the Amritsar massacre, Nehru's views had begun to take a radical turn and he talked of non-cooperation and civil disobedience and joined Annie Besant, one of his childhood mentors, and others who demanded Home Rule, self-governance, for India as was enjoyed by Australia, Canada, South Africa and New Zealand. But the times were changing. Gandhi, after his long and successful non-violent struggle for the rights of Indians in South Africa, returned to India in January 1915, and gradually began to transform the INC into an all-encompassing mass social and political movement that left no Indian untouched. This was also the beginning of the most remarkable spiritual and political relationship between the agnostic Nehru who trusted science and rationalism and the devoutly religious and politically innovative Gandhi who believed in intuition, moral force and Satyagraha.

Nonetheless, both Nehru and Gandhi shared their faith in the essential goodness of humanity and dedication to India's freedom. Their bond became unbreakable, and their growing dominance over the INC was unchallenged. Nehru began to see that the road to freedom—for which he had to spend more than nine years in imprisonment spread over a period of 24 years, from 1921 through 1945—was not too far. And he used this period of incarceration for writing some of the most remarkable books, including *The Discovery of India, Glimpses of World History, Letters from a Father to His Daughter* and *An Autobiography: Toward Freedom*, leaving an unparalleled intellectual legacy. During the period when he was not in jail or busy with political activities, he travelled to Europe to seek friends and influence people to promote the cause of India's Independence.

Particularly significant was his visit to the Soviet Union during 1926–27, which, according to noted journalist Frank Moraes, was the:

> watershed in his political and economic thinking... Nehru's
> real interest in Marxism and his socialist pattern of thought
> stemmed from that tour, even though it did not appreciably
> increase his knowledge of communist theory and practice. His
> subsequent sojourns in prison enabled him to study Marxism
> in more depth. Interested in its ideas but repelled by some of
> its methods—such as the regimentation and the heresy hunts
> of the communists—he could never bring himself to accept
> Karl Marx's writings as revealed scripture. Yet from then on,
> the yardstick of his economic thinking remained Marxist,
> adjusted, where necessary, to Indian conditions.[45]

In the Madras session of the INC held in 1927, Nehru's resolution
for a complete break from the British Empire was heralded. As a
first step, in 1928, the INC asked for a dominion status for India,
which the British government rejected. When Nehru took over as
the president of the INC at the Lahore session in 1929, he introduced
the famed resolution 'The Declaration of Independence', which,
passed by the party, stated,

> We believe that it is the inalienable right of the Indian people,
> as of any other people, to have freedom and to enjoy the fruits
> of their toil and have the necessities of life, so that they may
> have full opportunities of growth... if any government deprives
> a people of these rights and oppresses them the people have a
> further right to alter it or abolish it. The British government
> in India has not only deprived the Indian people of their
> freedom but has based itself on the exploitation of the masses,
> and has ruined India economically, politically, culturally and
> spiritually...India must sever the British connection and attain
> Purna Swaraj or complete independence.[46]

There was no going back on the idea of the dominion status for India.
Also at the Lahore session, Nehru emerged as the supreme leader
of the INC and the Independence movement, a natural successor
to Mahatma Gandhi. On 31 December 1929, Nehru hoisted the

Tricolour flag on the banks of River Ravi in Lahore, the grand Mughal city that ironically would go to Pakistan because in the background was the rising power of the Indian Muslim League and its leader Mohammed Ali Jinnah who had kept away from the INC and Mahatma Gandhi's non-violent non-cooperation civil disobedience movement for India's independence.

Jinnah negated everything that Nehru and Gandhi had stood for. The Muslim League leader had a different idea of what India ought to be and planned an alternative future for the subcontinent. On 3 March 1940 in Lahore, Jinnah told his audience that the Muslims were a separate entity and must have their own homeland. After his call for the do-or-die Direct Action Day on 16 August 1946, which let loose communal furies that killed, wounded and made homeless thousands upon thousands, Jinnah would soon attain his goal of creating Pakistan, the homeland for the Muslims. And thus unchain India from the chains of the two-nation theory.

Unbound and free from the burden of Pakistan, India under Jawaharlal Nehru was free to make its 'tryst with destiny' and become a nation that would love and learn to play the game of democracy.

2

INDIA BEGINS THE GAME OF DEMOCRACY

Where the mind is without fear and the head is held high...
Into that heaven of freedom, my Father, let my country awake.

—Rabindranath Tagore

Three Articles of our Constitution, and only three, stand
between the heaven of freedom into which Tagore wanted his
country to awake and the abyss of unrestrained power.

—Late Chief Justice Yeshwant Vishnu Chandrachud

As you proceed to the Central Hall of Parliament, you see a Sanskrit *sloka* (stanza) about *vasudhaiva kutumbakam*:

Ayam nijah paroveti ganana laghuchetasam,
Udaracharitanantu vasudhaiva kutumbakam

This verse, which appears in the Maha Upanishad, embodies the most secular and lofty Indian philosophical thought: 'That one is mine and the other a stranger is the concept of little minds. But to the large-hearted, the world itself is their family.'

'As we begin every work with Divine blessings...'[1] thus spoke Acharya Jivatram Bhagwandas Kripalani, when the Constituent Assembly met on 9 December 1946, in the Constitution Hall— now known as the Central Hall of Parliament House—which was brilliantly decorated for the occasion. The front rows were occupied by some of the most erudite scholars, legal luminaries, and tenacious freedom-fighters including Jawaharlal Nehru, Maulana Abul Kalam Azad, Sardar Vallabhbhai Patel, Acharya Jivatram Bhagwandas

Kripalani, Rajendra Prasad, Sarojini Naidu, Hare-Krushna Mahatab, Govind Ballabh Pant, Bhimrao Ramji Ambedkar, Sarat Chandra Bose, Chakravarti Rajagopalachari and M. Asaf Ali. There was the press and there were visitors in the gallery above.

The magnificent building, a coliseum-style colonnaded, circular edifice with 144 pillars spread over six acres, was designed by two British architects, Sir Edwin Lutyens and Sir Herbert Baker. The construction of the building, which started in 1921 and was completed in 1927, was part of the newly developed New Delhi capital complex, the imperial city of the British Raj that had moved its seat of governance from Calcutta to Delhi in 1912.[2] The political purpose of building the Parliament House was to co-opt various self-rule movements of the early twentieth century in the subcontinent by channelling them into legislative participation under the British imperial order. More importantly, the British tried to rule over India by building institutions they were familiar with in their own country; including civil service and bureaucracy; a judicial system based on English jurisprudence; universities and an education system that would mimic British schools; structure of the armed forces; and a top-down chain-of-command administrative system similar to what was prevalent in Britain. Two years after the Parliament House was inaugurated to contain Indians' rising democratic aspirations, the INC issued a clarion call for *Purna Swaraj* (Sanskrit: full freedom and complete independence) from British rule as its goal; and in 1947, it had the opportunity to create the constitutional framework for federal parliamentary democracy that everyone had yearned and passionately fought for.

How they created a supple, expandable and yet steely constitutional framework to hold India together, with its mind-boggling cultural, racial and linguistic diversity, is a tribute to the genius of the founders of the Indian Republic, leaders of the Indian freedom movement and the Indian people. At its genesis, the Constitution of India had 395 Articles and 12 Schedules that covered all aspects of Indian life—from governance to the rights of minorities, with a special focus on the lowliest of the low, and the tribals (Adivasis). The final document left no one untouched, left no one behind. The Constituent Assembly, through lengthy debates, public participation and discussions via the news media, worked its way through committees and subcommittees. It took about three years to create an eclectic document to build a federal-parliamentary system of government with multiple levels of checks and balances. It was a document born of the Enlightenment, the European intellectual movement whose prominent proponents included Immanuel Kant, Johann Wolfgang von Goethe, Voltaire, Jean-Jacques Rousseau and Adam Smith. The Constitution and the English language would eventually make India an Indo-European civilization, with tremendous geopolitical consequences.

Although they were nationalists and many of them were revivalists of the ancient glory, the Assembly members unhesitatingly borrowed the building blocks from everywhere: for example, the parliamentary system and single citizenship from the United Kingdom, and the federal state system along with the supremacy of the Constitution, separation of powers and fundamentals rights from the US. Other building blocks came from the Irish, Canadian, Australian and French Constitutions. The idea of fundamental duties was borrowed from the Soviet Union Constitution. One of the most noteworthy, necessary and notorious constitutional ideas, Emergency Powers, came from the Weimar Constitution (the Constitution of the German Reich).

The debates in the Constituent Assembly were free, unfettered and robust. Through their ramblings and discursiveness, the debates captured historical actualities and laid bare the fears, the hopes and the aspirations of the people—of what India might become, what India ought to become. The discourses, debates and commentaries of the period were more like the collective streams of consciousness and free associations of thoughts of the people in search of themselves. It must have been a great time to be alive and witness the materialization of a democratic India, an indivisible India, emerging through open public dialogue during which leaders listened to each other and the public. They bargained, cooperated, collaborated, compromised and finally, created a dynamic self-renewing system that would weather any storm, face any abuse and bounce back from any knock.

There were 299 members of the Constituent Assembly, including nine women—members representing all castes and creeds and all shades of the political spectrum, philosophies and economic programmes. Added to this assemblage were the princely states' representatives that made the Constituent Assembly a kaleidoscopic portrait of India. One could see in this hodge-podge landscape the seeds of the emergence of regional and cultural identities and caste group rights, which would become a driving force in Indian politics and how Indians play the game of democracy. While the Assembly was building a constitutional future, the governments at the Centre and the states were struggling with the task of settling millions of refugees from Pakistan, managing food rationing due to perennial shortages, and stopping religious communal clashes here and there. Some princely states were beating their own drums and singing their own tunes and getting their militia battle-ready.[3]

It wasn't all that dark and gloomy. Consider this: the Hindi film industry or Bollywood, as it is known today, was emerging as India's cultural habitat; a national, secular and creative hub that would charm and attract the best and the brightest from all over and bind India in its cultural soft power just as the Constitution would steel India in its legal framework. R.K. Narayan published another comic-realistic novel in his inimitable, delightful Indian English, *Mr. Sampath—The Printer of Malgudi*, the imaginary idyllic South Indian town. While some ultra-nationalistic Indians, as the Constituent Assembly debates (conducted mostly in English) abundantly showed, were dubious and even hostile about the continuing use of English, deemed as a sign of slavish mentality, India's passionate love for the Englishman's language, literature and most of all his sports, especially cricket, remained undiminished. The Indian eyes, ears and hearts were lit with high expectations because this was the season of great cricketers, including Lala Amarnath, Rustomji Sheriyar 'Rusi' Modi, Vijay Hazare, Vinoo Mankad, Dattu Phadkar and Ghulam Ahmed, when the West Indies cricket team was visiting India. Bollywood, cricket and the Constitution-making processes showed how open and assimilative the Indian mind was, as it is today, through its slogan: vasudhaiva kutumbakam.

Four days after the preliminaries were over, on 13 December 1946, Jawaharlal Nehru moved the Objectives Resolution for the Constituent Assembly to declare 'its firm and solemn resolve to proclaim India as an independent sovereign republic and to draw up for her future governance a Constitution', that will guarantee and secure 'to all the people of India justice, social, economic and political: equality of status, of opportunity, and before the law; freedom of thought, expression, belief, faith, worship, vocation, association and action, subject to law and public morality', providing adequate safeguards 'for minorities, backward and tribal areas, and depressed and other backward classes', while maintaining 'the integrity of the territory of the Republic and its sovereign rights on land, sea, and air according to justice and the law of civilized nations'.[4] He was describing the core principles of the nascent document that would be developed into the supreme law of the land, the Indian Constitution: a structure of ordered freedoms, a generative mechanism that stabilizes as it creates and transforms a complex ancient civilization.

The Constituent Assembly passed the Objectives Resolution unanimously on 22 January 1947. On the eve of 14 August 1947, the Assembly met in the Constitution Hall, and 'at the stroke of midnight' when India had a 'tryst with destiny', it transformed itself into the Legislative Assembly of Independent India. The Phoenix had risen from the ashes. India was born again from the deep philosophical founts of the vedas to Mahatma Gandhi's story of *My Experiments with Truth*.

On 29 August 1947, a constitutional drafting committee was established under the chairmanship of the most eminent jurist Dr. Bhimrao Ramji Ambedkar, an alumnus of Columbia University, London School of Economics and Gray's Inn, to prepare a Draft Constitution for India. During the three years of deliberations upon the constitutional draft, the Constituent Assembly debated upon 2,473 amendments out of a total of 7,635 amendments that were proposed. Drafting the Constitution was a herculean task, of course, but making it acceptable to the Assembly, which, most of the time during the debates seemed like a house divided against itself, required different kinds of political and people skills. In the ultimate analysis, constitution building and acceptance was an act of conversion, a form of secular evangelism, a most zealous advocacy for the nation-building cause that required the exercise of all the available means of persuasion. This is what Aristotle called ethos, character and trustworthiness of the leaders; logos, their appeal to reason; and pathos, their ability to move passions. To direct and guide the heterogeneous Assembly in its humungous task of preparing a consensual and comprehensive sociopolitical nation-building document that would be permanent and stand the test of time, there were a number of prominent and highly regarded national leaders who, along with legal experts, kept the proceedings going progressively from session to session.

Apart from the visionary aura of highly personable Jawaharlal Nehru, there was Sardar Vallabhbhai Patel, an integrationist and synthesizer, an expert dealmaker, negotiator and tireless committee man; and Rajendra Prasad, the president of the Assembly with the unenviable task of keeping the day-to-day proceedings orderly and progressive. The Constitutional Draft Committee under the chairmanship of Ambedkar also included Govind Ballabh Pant, a freedom-fighter, a foremost leader of the United Provinces and a Hindi proponent; K.M. Munshi, scholar, writer, educator and former home minister of Bombay; Alladi Krishnaswamy Iyer, former Advocate General of Madras state; N. Gopalaswami Ayyangar, former prime minister of Jammu and Kashmir, who would later on play a significant role in drafting the Constitution of Jammu and Kashmir; Madhav Rao, legal advisor of the maharaja of Baroda; Syed Muhammed Saadulla, former chief minister of Assam, a Muslim Leaguer who supported the Lahore Resolution for the creation of the Muslim Homeland but decided to opt for India rather than Pakistan; and T.T. Krishnamachari, an economist and entrepreneur. Sir Benegal Narsing Rau, another brilliant judicial mind, was the constitutional advisor to assist the Constitutional Draft Committee.[5]

After shedding the burden of the Muslim League, the Indian

National Congress party had emerged as the most dominant political force in India, and it became incumbent upon its leaders to draw into the Constituent Assembly all shades of opinion and demographic representations. 'The Constituent Assembly,' Granville Austin observed, 'was a one-party body, in an essentially one-party country. The Assembly was the Congress and the Congress was India. There was a third point that completed a tight triangle: the government (meaning the apparatus of elected government both provincial and national), for the Congress, was the government too.' Instead of silencing 'dissent and confine policy and decision-making to the hands of the select few...the Congress in the Constituent Assembly and outside, held social, economic and political views ranging from the reactionary to the revolutionary, and it did not hesitate to voice them. The leaders of the Assembly, who played the same role in the Congress and in the Union Government, were national heroes and had almost unlimited power; yet decision-making in the Assembly was democratic. The Indian Constitution expresses the will of the many rather than the needs of the few.'[6]

MAJOR CONSTITUTIONAL CONTROVERSIES

For thousands of years, in spite of the presence of a multitude of languages and dialects, Indians have always found ways of communicating with one another and therefore have never felt handicapped in establishing relationships. Without being a nation, India has always been a nation, though not in the Westphalian (Treaty, 1648) sense. From the times of the vedas, Gautama Buddha, King Asoka, Adi Sankara, and other saints and philosophers, Indians have invariably transcended the language barrier. But in the Constituent Assembly, some members felt that India would not be India without a common national language and that language must be Hindi-Hindustani, the most widely spoken and understood in the country. The passion with which some champions of 'one nation, one language' spoke about the absolute necessity of making Hindi the national language and the lingua franca gave the Assembly a foretaste of the linguistic turmoil that would rock the nation in the future.

Consider the linguistic intolerance when Representative Raghunath Vinayak Dhulekar from the United Provinces, the sprawling Hindi region, said that those who did not know Hindi-Hindustani (a blend of Hindi and Urdu in which Bollywood movies are made) had no business to be members of the Constituent Assembly and should leave India. He resented that the proceedings of the Assembly were not being conducted in Hindi. He resented that members—instead of talking about Indian history—were so enamoured with America, Japan, Germany, Switzerland and the United Kingdom, from whose constitutions they were borrowing ideas. But Dhulekar was not alone in his support for Hindi chauvinism. Several other members urged that the Constitution should be primarily drafted in Hindi. It was during the debate on language that India discovered that there is South India's brainpower, the people whose uncompromising demand that English continue forever as a co-equal official language would enable the country to become a global digital power. The Muslim League had broken up India on the basis of religion. Would India break up on the question of language too? T.T. Krishnamachari of Madras talked of Hindi imperialism, warning that the choice was between a whole-India and truncated Hindi-India.[7] Acceptance of Hindi as the official language along with English, albeit until 1965, was the final compromise. But compromises are never final, as India would discover in the coming times.

WHAT'S THE CONSTITUTION ABOUT?

The Constitution of India, apart from being an important 'social document,' is above all, the absolute law of India—the supreme law—which means that all other laws, whether enacted by the Parliament, state legislatures or local bodies, cannot undermine its authority.[8] Since the Constitution created the Parliament, along with other institutions such as the Supreme Court, it cannot be subverted or lessened by an act of the Parliament or by a Supreme Court judicial review. The Constitution could be enhanced and adapted but it could not be diminished. The Constitution, as its

Preamble says, lays down fundamental democratic principles under which to determine the structure, procedures, powers and duties of government institutions at all levels from the Parliament to panchayats (village councils), in accordance with the fundamental rights of the people.[9] At birth, the Constitution of India—besides the Preamble—had 22 Parts containing 395 Articles and eight Schedules. Since then, it has been growing and evolving. Today, it has 25 Parts containing 448 Articles, 12 Schedules, and five Appendices. The Preamble embodies the aspirations and the vision of a secular democratic India. In lofty and majestic tones the Preamble proclaims:

> WE, THE PEOPLE OF INDIA, having solemnly resolved to constitute India into a SOVEREIGN (SOCIALIST SECULAR) DEMOCRATIC REPUBLIC and to secure to all its citizens:
> JUSTICE, social, economic and political;
> LIBERTY of thought, expression, belief, faith and worship;
> EQUALITY of status and of opportunity;
> and to promote among them all;
> FRATERNITY assuring the dignity of the individual and the unity and integrity of the Nation;
> IN OUR CONSTITUENT ASSEMBLY this 26th day of November, 1949, do HEREBY ADOPT, ENACT AND GIVE TO OURSELVES THIS CONSTITUTION.[10]

Although democratic socialism and secularism were implicit in the original Preamble, in 1976, during the times of Prime Minister Indira Gandhi, the Preamble was amended to include the term 'Socialist Secular' under the Forty-Second Amendment Act, 1976. The Constitution does not prescribe or promote any religion and guarantees all citizens the right to religious freedom. Since India is a democratic state, the authority of the government rests upon the sovereignty of 'we the people,' who enjoy equal political rights, participate freely in the processes of politics to elect their government, based on free and fair elections held regularly on the basis of adult franchise conducted by an independent, autonomous body, the Election Commission of India (ECI). As a republic, India has an elected head of the state, the president of India, who exercises limited constitutional power for a fixed term of five years.

Article I of the Constitution declares India to be a 'Union of States,' which means that the Indian Union, except for Jammu and Kashmir, is not the result of voluntary agreement among sovereign states, and the states of India, including Jammu and Kashmir, do not have the right to secede from the Union. The Indian Union, its states and union territories, together form a federal structure with a unitary bias, making India 'quasi-federal', 'a union of states under a central government rather than the individual governments of the separate states'.[11]

Like in a federation, the Constitution of India stipulates division of powers and responsibilities between the Centre and states based on union, state and concurrent lists of subjects; an independent judiciary headed by the Supreme Court, the guardian and the final interpreter of the meaning of the Constitution, with the power to adjudicate Centre–state disputes; and separate central and state administrations with parallel political and legislative structures. Nonetheless, with a single Constitution, common citizenship, provisions for a national emergency, federal election commission, merit-based all-India administrative and defence services and many other integrating features, the Constitution of India was designed to be a parliamentary federation, unitary in functions and spirit, albeit with distributed centres of power and responsibilities, depending upon circumstances.

This was necessitated by the pluralistic nature of society, regional diversities, fissiparous and centrifugal tendencies, and most of all due to the need for ensuring unity and integrity of the nation so that no one in the future could ask for a separate homeland and split India, like Jinnah, the sole spokesman for Pakistan and the Muslim League, had done.[12] The Constitution has made India into a dynamic equilibrium system, a self-renewing democratic structure that, after internal or external turbulence, regains its equilibrium state and continues its dynamics into the next evolutionary state.

Under Article 368, the Constitution can be amended in two steps. First, Parliament has to pass the Amendment Bill by a majority of total membership and a two-thirds majority of members present and voting in both Houses of Parliament. Second, the Bill goes to state legislatures for ratification, where not less than a half of the members must approve the amendment. Every bill that becomes law is subject to judicial review.

Fundamental Rights and Directive Principles of State Policy, which reflect and derive their energy from the Preamble, are the heart and the soul of the Constitution. Part III C Articles 12–35 of the Constitution guarantee fundamental rights to every Indian citizen. Originally there were seven fundamental rights, but keeping with the spirit of the Constitution, the Right to Property was dropped from the list of fundamental rights vide the Forty-Fourth Amendment Act of 1978, under the Indira Gandhi administration.

Fundamental rights, which are justiciable and enforceable, include the Right to Equality: equality before the law, end of discrimination, equality of opportunity, abolition of untouchability and abolition of titles. The Right to Freedom encompasses the freedoms of speech and expression, freedom to form associations, freedom to assemble peaceably without arms, freedom to move freely in India, freedom of residence in any part of India, and freedom of adopting any profession or trade or occupation. It protects the freedom of life and liberty, which cannot be limited or denied except under the due process of law.

Article 21A grants the right to education for children between the ages of 6 and 14 years. Article 22 protects citizens against arbitrary arrest and detention. The Right against Exploitation under Articles 23 and 24 prohibits the sale and purchase of human beings, forced labour, and employment of children in hazardous conditions. The Right to Freedom of Religion, under Articles 25–28, ensures the freedom of conscience, religion and worship, and freedom to establish and maintain one's religious institutions. The state shall not levy a tax on any religion. State-funded schools and colleges are prohibited from imparting religious instruction. Cultural and Educational Rights protect the rights of the minorities to maintain and develop their languages and cultures, including the right to establish, maintain and administer their educational institutions. Right to Constitutional Remedies (vide Article 32) makes fundamental rights enforceable by the courts. It endows the Supreme Court and High Courts with the power to issue writs for the enforcement of fundamental rights. For the overall protection and enforcement of fundamental rights as comprehensive human rights, the National Human Rights Commission (NHRC) was established in 1993 vide the Protection of Human Rights Act of 1993. The Act also provided for the creation of the State Human Rights Commission at the state level.

DIRECTIVE PRINCIPLES OF STATE POLICY

An extraordinary feature of the Constitution (Part IV) is the inclusion of guidelines in the form of Directive Principles of State Policy for the Union and state governments to create socio-economic developmental goals through their policies, to provide citizens with adequate means of livelihood; fair distribution of wealth; equal pay for equal work; protection of children, women, labour and youth; old-age pension and social security; local self-government; protection of the interests of the weaker sections of society; promotion of cottage industries; rural development and most of all a common civil code. These directives are aspirational goalposts to create a just and equitable society. The government could be admonished for not doing enough, but the directives, unlike the fundamental rights, are not enforceable. There's a dynamic tension between fundamental rights and directive principles that surfaced during the time when Prime Minister Indira Gandhi imposed the Emergency, which led to revisiting the constitutional principle of the basic structure of the Constitution.

TWO-HOUSE UNION PARLIAMENT

At the federal level, the Constitution provides for a bicameral legislature, the Union Parliament, consisting of the Lok Sabha and the Rajya Sabha. The Lok Sabha represents the people of India and its members, 543 out of a maximum 550, are directly elected on the basis of adult franchise and the first-past-the-post electoral system, which means that a candidate with the plurality of votes is the winner of the seat. Though the minimum voting age is 18, a candidate has to be 25 years of age in order to seek election for the Lok Sabha, where each state sends elected representatives proportionate to its population. Uttar Pradesh elects most members—80 including 17 from scheduled castes and scheduled tribes—while Tripura, a small northeastern state, sends only two, including one member from the scheduled castes. Although the formal tenure of the Lok Sabha is five years, the president of India, under the advice of the prime minister, can dissolve the Lok Sabha and order new elections.

While the Lok Sabha represents the people of India, the Rajya Sabha, as the representative body of the states, protects the states' interests vis-à-vis the Union; and it elects its members indirectly by state legislative assemblies. Out of its 245 state elected members for a maximum of 250, the legislative assemblies of states and union territories (UT) elect 233 members based on proportional representation through a single transferable voting system. The president of India nominates 12 members; people who have distinguished themselves in the fields of arts, science and literature; and people who wouldn't otherwise stand the hustle and bustle of electoral politics but whose voices must be heard. The Rajya Sabha has a rolling membership, with one-third of the members retiring after every two years; however, each member's tenure extends to six years. Except in financial matters, which is the exclusive domain of the Lok Sabha, the Rajya Sabha provides necessary democratic checks and balances, especially when the ruling party does not have a majority. Unlike the Lok Sabha, the Rajya Sabha is not subject to dissolution, though the president can prorogue it. In rare cases, joint sessions of both Houses can be held to resolve conflicting legislations.

The prime minister of India, first among equals, *primus inter pares*, with the union council of ministers, wields the executive power, and the council is collectively beholden to the Lok Sabha for all its actions. Through the practice of no-confidence motions, the

Lok Sabha holds the council of ministers accountable for its acts of omission and commission. The states, more or less, mimic the parliamentary system, except it is the president of India who, on the advice of the union council of ministers, appoints the nominal head of the state, the governor. In case of political instability, a state government could be dissolved and under Article 356 president's rule could be imposed for a period of six months, when a new state election must be held to form a new government. The extent of a state's autonomy depends upon how stable the ruling party's majority in the state assembly is, in the absence of which the puppeteer at the Centre could pull the strings and change the political scenario in the state. It's noteworthy that the Supreme Court of India can restrain the central government from an arbitrary and blatant imposition of president's rule on a state vide its landmark decision in the 1994 Bommai case.[13]

THE POWER OF JUDICIAL REVIEW

The Supreme Court of India, a public institution created by the Constitution of India, is the guardian and protector of the Constitution. Through its interpretation of the Constitution and through its scrutiny of the actions of the legislative and executive branches, it exercises its power as the final arbiter. Thus, in a limited sense, it becomes a co-equal in power, though not as much as the Supreme Court of the United States. The Supreme Court of India not only protects the fundamental rights of the people as guaranteed by the Constitution but also adjudicates when the fundamental rights come into conflict with each other; or conflict with the paramount obligations of the Union government or the states. The Supreme Court adjudicates disputes between the Centre and the states; or when two or more states have conflicting interests. As the final protector, interpreter and adjudicator of disputes, the independence of the Supreme Court and the judiciary is (and should be) absolute in the sense that no amendment or executive order could diminish it.[14]

The power of the Supreme Court as the final authority on the meaning of the Constitution of India comes from its power of judicial review, a doctrine adapted from the United States' Constitution. The constitutional basis of judicial review, as is the case with India, however, comes from Articles 13, 32, 226 and 227, which in totality proclaim that all laws, whether pre-constitutional or laws and amendments made after the adoption of the Constitution, must be compatible with the Constitution's basic structure, its foundational principles or otherwise they will be deemed null and void. In conflicting situations, it is only the Supreme Court, not Parliament, that interprets the Constitution to decide if a law or an amendment is in conformity with the foundational principles of the Constitution and if not, the law or the amendment will be deemed as unconstitutional.[15]

Nonetheless, after the adoption of the Thirty-Eighth Amendment Act, 1975, the Supreme Court was deprived of the power of judicial review to scrutinize laws made during an Emergency. For example, laws that infringed upon the fundamental rights vide Article 32 that specifies Right to Constitutional Remedies, went out of the Supreme Court's purview.[16] Furthermore, the passing of the Forty-Second Amendment Act, 1976 further diminished the judicial review powers of the Supreme Court under Articles 368(4) and 368(5) of the new amendment, which stated that any law passed by Parliament couldn't be challenged in the Supreme Court on any ground. After Emergency was lifted in 1977, the Constitution of India reasserted itself. In the Minerva Mills v. Union of India case, the Supreme Court ruled that judicial review was part of the 'basic Structure of the Constitution' and, therefore, cannot be eliminated, thus nullifying Article 368(4), 368(5) and 31C.[17]

Based on a government report that Minerva Mills was being 'managed in a manner highly detrimental to public interest,' the Union government authorized the National Textile Corporation Ltd. to take over the management of Minerva Mills after nationalizing it under the provisions of the Sick Textile Undertakings (Nationalization) Act, 1974. Several other textile mills had been nationalized and were being run by government bureaucrats primarily to protect the interest of the workers. But Minerva Mills stood up against the sweeping wave of nationalization that had taken over the country, and took the matter to the Supreme Court, raising some fundamental questions regarding the constitutionality of the Forty-Second Amendment Act, Sections 4 and 55: whether these sections are beyond the amendment power of Parliament; and whether the Directive Principles of State Policy (non-enforceable social justice goals) can have primacy over the (legally enforceable) Fundamental Rights conferred by the Constitution of India.

Declaring Sections 4 and 55 of the Forty-Second Amendment as unconstitutional, the Supreme Court ruled the following:

> Since the Constitution had conferred a limited amending power on the Parliament, the Parliament cannot, under the exercise of that limited power, enlarge that very power into an absolute power. Indeed, a limited amending power is one of the basic features of our Constitution and therefore, the limitations on that power cannot be destroyed. In other words, Parliament cannot, under Article 368, expand its amending power so as to acquire for itself the right to repeal or abrogate the Constitution or to destroy its basic and essential features. The donee of a limited power cannot be the exercise of that power (to) convert the limited power into an unlimited one.[18]

Keeping in mind what the American historian of the Constitution of India, Granville Austin, had written—that the Constitution was 'first and foremost a social document'—the Supreme Court paid close attention to the importance of the Directive Principles, considering them 'fundamental in governance of the country,' therefore, to destroy the guarantees of the Fundamental Rights (Part III) 'in order purportedly to achieve the goals of Part IV is plainly to subvert the Constitution by destroying its basic structure'. Describing Fundamental Rights as 'transcendental', 'inalienable' and 'primordial', the court said that the Directive Principles and the Fundamental Rights, 'together constitute the core of commitment to social revolution and they, together, are the conscience of the Constitution...Parts III and IV are like two wheels of a chariot, one no less important than the other. You snap one and the other will lose its efficacy. They are like a twin formula for achieving the social revolution which is the ideal which the visionary founders of the Constitution set before themselves. In other words, the Indian Constitution is founded on the bed-rock of the balance between Parts III and IV. To give absolute primacy to one over the other is to disturb the harmony of the Constitution. This harmony and balance between fundamental rights and directive principles is an essential feature of the basic structure of the Constitution.'[19]

AMBEDKAR'S FOREBODINGS

Much before Justice Chandrachud's warning about constitutional dictatorship, Dr Ambedkar had anticipated the danger of democracy being dissipated. In his final speech to the Constituent Assembly, he asked, 'What would happen to her democratic Constitution? Will she be able to maintain it or will she lose it again?' The operative word is 'again,' but when was India democratic? According to Dr Ambedkar, India once upon a time was 'studded with republics, and even where there were monarchies, they were either elected or limited. They were never absolute. It is not that India did not know Parliaments or parliamentary procedure.' He was referring to the Buddhist Bhikshu Sanghas, who, he surmised, must have borrowed their procedures from 'the rules of the Political Assemblies functioning in the country in his (the Buddha) time.' And that was the democratic system that India lost. Then he asked,

> Will she lose it a second time?... But it is quite possible in a country like India—where *democracy from its long disuse* (emphasis added) must be regarded as something quite new— there is a danger of democracy giving place to dictatorship. It is quite possible for this newborn democracy to retain its form but give place to dictatorship in fact. If there is a landslide, the danger of the second possibility becoming actuality is much greater.[20]

The fascination and obsession with the intellectual, political, spiritual and cultural treasures of ancient India and their recovery was not limited to Ambedkar. Many other members of the Constituent Assembly expressed similar sentiments, with some referring to the village panchayat system as grassroots village democracies. The impulse to reclaim the mythical and historical glory would take many forms, from rebuilding the Somnath Temple in Dwarka and the Ram Temple at Ayodhya to the rebuilding of the Buddhist Nalanda University, with which some of the most prominent Indians would be associated.

Ironically and most interestingly, Ambedkar as the foremost constitutionalist of the Constituent Assembly, had lauded the emergency provisions in the constitution, which Prime Minister Indira Gandhi would use to place the legislative acts of Parliament beyond judicial review. Admonishing the Constitutional Assembly and the country of the dangers of the ultra-constitutional methods, the Grammar of Anarchy, as he called it, Ambedkar advocated three measures to preserve democracy. 'The first thing in my judgement we must do is to hold fast to constitutional methods of achieving our social and economic objectives,' which means giving up the Gandhian methods that were used during the struggle for Independence, including civil disobedience, non-cooperation and Satyagraha. 'The second thing we must do is to observe the caution which John Stuart Mill has given to all who are interested in the maintenance of democracy, namely, not "to lay their liberties at the feet of even a great man, or to trust him with powers which enable him to subvert their institutions".' More than any other people, Indians are prone to hero-worship. The bhakti attitude can be very dangerous to democracy because in India, as Dr. Ambedkar said:

> Bhakti or what may be called the path of devotion or hero-worship, plays a part in its politics unequalled in magnitude by the part it plays in the politics of any other country in the world. Bhakti in religion may be a road to the salvation of the soul. But in politics, Bhakti or hero-worship is a sure road to degradation and to eventual dictatorship.[21]

Political democracy, he warned, is not good enough in a caste-ridden hierarchical society, therefore, 'The third thing we must do is not to be content with mere political democracy. We must make our political democracy a social democracy as well. Political democracy cannot last unless there lies at the base of it, social democracy.'[22]

MAINSTREAMING RELIGIOUS MINORITIES

The Constituent Assembly discussed on 27–28 August 1947, the issue of protecting the political interest of the minorities—Muslims, in particular—through population-based reservation in legislatures; but in light of how religious separatism had led to the bloody Partition of the country, the Assembly members including Muslims, fell in line with the advice of Govind Ballabh Pant, when he said, 'Your safety lies in making yourselves an integral part of the organic whole which forms the real genuine state.'[23] Home Minister and Deputy Prime Minister Sardar Patel was more blunt in his warning:

> If the process that was adopted, which resulted in the separation of the country is to be repeated, then I say: Those who want that kind of thing have a place in Pakistan and not here. Here, we are building a nation and we are laying a foundation of One Nation, and those who choose to divide again and sow the seeds of disruption will have no place, no quarter, here and I must say that plainly enough.[24]

The Advisory Committee on Minority Rights came to the same conclusion and decided 'that the system of reservation for minorities other than SC in legislatures be abolished.' When the Assembly considered the recommendations of the Advisory Committee on 25 May 1949, Sardar Patel spoke once again and said that 'time had come when the vast majority of the minority communities have themselves realized after great reflection the evil effects in the past of such reservation on the minorities themselves and the reservation should be dropped.' Echoing Sardar Patel, Tajamul Hussain, a Muslim lawyer from Bihar, vehemently condemned the idea of reservation:

> The term minority is a British creation. The British created the minorities. The British have gone and the minorities have gone with them. Remove the term minority from your dictionary. There is no minority in India...I would like to tell you that in no civilized country where there is parliamentary system on democratic lines, there is any reservation of seat...We want to merge in the nation.[25]

Of the 23 Muslim members of the Constituent Assembly, 13 were totally opposed to reservation, while, of the remaining 10, some wanted separate electorates, and others wanted reservation. Condemning the evil of separatism and supporting the motion, Prime Minister Nehru said,

> It is a motion which means not only discarding something that was evil, but turning back upon it and determining with all our strength that we shall pursue a path which we consider fundamentally good for every part of the nation...Now all of us here, I believe, are convinced that this business of separatism, whether it took the shape of a separate electorate or other shapes, has done a tremendous amount of evil to our country and to our people.[26]

After two days of prolonged debate, 25–26 May 1949, the Constituent Assembly rejected the system of reservation for religious minorities.

MAINSTREAMING SPECIAL MINORITIES

While the overwhelming majority of Constituent Assembly members were hostile to the idea of legislative reservation for religious minorities and were totally indifferent to reservation for women, they could not escape the collective guilt of what India had done to the Dalits, the Untouchables and the Scheduled Castes: the people at the bottom of the Hindu caste-by-birth-driven hierarchical society that had persisted for millennia. Embracing them and raising awareness about their plight, Mahatma Gandhi called them Harijans, the children of God, and condemned untouchability as a curse. In one of his letters he wrote, 'Untouchability is a soul-destroying sin. Caste is a social evil...'[27] This was not a passing thought. It was Gandhi's lifelong mission and passion. On 11 February 1933, while he was in Yerwada jail under the British rule, he published a weekly journal, *Harijan,* in English, Hindi and Gujarati. But in the course of time, Gandhi's passionate, sincere and benign efforts towards the eradication of untouchability, first and foremost by changing the minds of the people, by renaming untouchables as Harijans, was misunderstood as too condescending.[28] Today, the term is officially banned and is regarded as offensive. Dalit is the preferred word now.

The Constituent Assembly had no alibi for not taking serious and meaningful legislative action to alleviate the suffering and oppression of the Dalits. On 25 November 1949, Ambedkar told the Constituent Assembly that India was a society 'based on the principle of graded inequality,' not only in terms of wealth but also in the sense that '...political power in this country has too long been the monopoly of a few and the many are only beasts of burden, but also beasts of prey. This monopoly...has "sapped" [these down-trodden classes] of what may be called the significance of life.'[29] Following Ambedkar's lead, member after member expressed concerns that without special legislative provision, scheduled caste communities would never be able to gain social justice.

T. Channaiah, a Scheduled Caste member from Mysore, said, 'These backward communities suffer from two disabilities, namely, social disabilities and educational disabilities... I want this reservation for 150 years which has been the period during which opportunities have been denied to them.'[30] Moving the amendment resolution for reservation, V.I. Muniswami Pillai of Madras said:

> Sir, in the great upheaval of making a constitution for this country, I feel that the communities that have not enjoyed the loaves and fishes of the services should not be left out...unless there is an assurance that these communities—I especially mean the scheduled castes—are given a chance, unless there is an assurance that these communities will at all times be

taken into account and given enough and more chance in appointments, their uplift will still stand over...I may tell this House that it is not the object of any of the leaders of the Harijan community to perpetuate the communal bogey in this land for ever, but so long as they remain so backward in getting admission into the services it is highly necessary that they must be given some protection.[31]

Consequently vide Article 17 of the Constitution, 'Untouchability is abolished and its practice in any form is forbidden. The enforcement of any disability arising out of Untouchability shall be an offence punishable in accordance with law.'

And then there was another forgotten community, the aborigines, the Adivasis, the people of the forests, whose lands were being misappropriated for some vested interests. The Constitution accordingly recognizes the special rights of the Scheduled Tribes (Adivasis) as set out in Article 21 and under Schedules V and VI. Besides, Article 338 enjoins the President of India to appoint a Special Officer for the Scheduled Castes and Scheduled Tribes to report upon the working of the safeguards provided for them, which will be presented to the Parliament. Apart from receiving reservation and political representation in the Parliament and state legislatures, the Constitution lays down general rules for affirmative actions for government jobs and for admission in educational institutions for Scheduled Castes and Scheduled Tribes, who constitute about 25 per cent of the population of India. Scheduled Castes and Scheduled Tribes were the greatest long-term beneficiaries of the partition of the subcontinent. While struggling with Jinnah and the Muslim League, the Indian political leaders were also able to focus their attention on the deplorable conditions of the people at the bottom of the pyramid whom the hierarchical Brahmanistic religious order had left irredeemable.

The three-year-long Constituent Assembly debates, in spite of sharp differences over many subjects, were held by and large in utter civility that behoves a great ancient civilization reflected in the spiritual and humanistic deeds and thoughts of Gandhi, Nehru,

Ambedkar and others. Parliamentary procedures were meticulously observed. Debates were free, frank and vigorous. All voices were heard and recorded for posterity. For a historian, these debates are a rich gold mine for thematic and textual analysis of the collective mind of the leaders of India who represented all strata of society, all political thoughts, all castes and creeds, all corners of India— from tribal and Dalit leaders to Oxbridge intellectuals, lawyers and Sanskrit scholars. Two important points are worth noting. First, the INC, an umbrella political organization, dominated the Constituent Assembly. Second, the absence of the Muslim League with its toxic two-nation theory made the Constituent Assembly more cohesive, more determined and more focused on India's massive problem of governance and its deep social divisions.

As political scientist Richard Leonard Park, commented:

> First, few will deny the excellence of India's formal constitutional order: many liberal Western parliamentary traditions have been adapted to local conditions in the Constitution; in addition, certain specifically Indian institutions have been drawn upon to reflect the multiplicity of local and regional differences in political tradition that characterize village India and its centuries-old experience with local government. From the formal point of view, the Constitution, though young and subject to future corrections, compares favorably with any genuinely democratic structure of government in the world. [32]

The Constituent Assembly members, however, realized in the course of time what Walt Kelly, the creator of the comic strip 'Pogo,' would say, 'We have met the enemy and he is us.'[33] Partition and the subsequent separation of Pakistan from the subcontinent did not purge India of its problems, but rather made them more glaring during the Constituent Assembly debates as if India were lying on a psychiatrist's couch listening to its own fears and nightmares, its ancient dreams and future aspirations of what India had been and what India ought to be.

On 26 November 1949, the Constituent Assembly ratified the Constitution of India, which was signed by 284 members on 24

January 1950, and two days later it came into effect. And that was the day—26 January 1950—the Constituent Assembly of India metamorphosed into the Provisional Parliament of India until after the first general elections held in 1951–1952, when a new Parliament was elected. And that was the day when India began to play the game of democracy—a game of grand strategy, alliances and coalition-building, generating leverages, anticipating moves and countermoves, and creating motivational and persuasive narratives for mass mobilization. Indians love the spectacle of democracy as much as they love cricket and the Kumbh Mela; and chess or chaturanga or shatranj, which they invented.

GENERAL ELECTION CHURNS UP INDIA

Indians suspended their disbelief and plunged into the general election as naturally as a duck takes to water. Millions and millions of people—a majority of them illiterate—discovered for the first time that they were somebody; that the newly claimed freedom had endowed them with a special right—the right to vote for a symbol, a party or a person. They would exercise their right to vote in the seclusion of a voting booth in a public place, where they would see and be seen by others, under protective friendly official eyes, where they would feel themselves to be individual persons and they would be marked and counted, so rhapsodized historian Ramachandra Guha. And those who did not have a name would discover that they had a name and identity instead of being somebody's mother, grandfather, sharecropper or cattle-herder.[34] Based on adult franchise, the first general election mobilized Indians as Gandhi had mobilized them during the Dandi March and Satyagraha. In the course of time, they would be courted by politicians, they would begin to feel the dynamic power of the ballot, and discover how to exercise it to bring about a much-needed transformation in their lives. Long before Gandhi appeared on the political scene, India had a tradition of self-driven mass mobilization. Consider, for example, the once-in-12-years, self-organized massive Hindu pilgrimage gathering, the Kumbh Mela, the largest congregation in the world that has kept India rejuvenated for millennia regardless of whoever the political rulers were, Mughals or Mlechchas. Indians are capable of self-discipline. Just like the Kumbh Mela, India's first general election, conducted in the most orderly manner, showed that Indians are not only capable of doing the impossible but are also capable of self-discipline. It was, in a manner of speaking, a manifestation of this ancient tradition.

The general election spread over a period of four months between 25 October 1951 and 21 February 1952 was a collective experiential learning exercise for 173 million eligible voters. The eligibility to vote began at 21. Though 85 per cent of the voters were illiterate, they were nonetheless not ignorant and proved to be quick learners. India has always been an oral culture where itinerant storytelling, public discourse, open-air theatre and word-of-mouth dissemination of knowledge have been the dominant modes of shared experiences. It was the power of orality and the oral cultural tradition of India that Gandhi understood and appreciated the most and used it to organize the mind-boggling Indian diversity into a political force for freedom.[35]

Democracy in ancient Greece was born of the oral tradition. The vedas were born of the oral tradition. Few other cultures love the sound of the word, spoken and chanted, sacred and profane, as do the Indians. Democracy as an endless dialogue and cultural discourse fits into India's oral cultural tradition. For the Indians, it was as fascinating as going to the Kumbh Mela, Ramlila or a cricket match.

It must be kept in mind, nonetheless, that the steel framework consisting of the bureaucratic infrastructure, from the top Indian Administrative Service (formerly known as Indian Civil Service [ICS]) to the local level postmasters, patwaris (village land recorders) and the law enforcement machinery along with the nationwide railroad and communications systems, which the British had created and bequeathed to India, was used by the government to successfully carry out the general election. Throughout the independence movement, the Indian bureaucracy had remained obedient, always listening to its master's voice. So, when the Government of India appointed a senior ICS Officer Sukumar Sen (a scion of a Bengali family of intellectuals, graduate of the prestigious Presidency College and the University of London) as the chief election commissioner in 1950, he was tasked with organizing the first general election that would leave no one behind, from an isolated hamlet on a remote hill in Himachal Pradesh to densely populated Bombay. Sen, with the help of two other commissioners, took the levers of bureaucratic machinery in his hands and set the country in motion. The freedom and the challenge, and most importantly, the trust Prime Minister Nehru placed in him, galvanized Sen to complete 'mission impossible.' One might say that if Ambedkar was the architect of the Constitution of India, Sen was the builder who laid the foundation of electoral democracy.

The Election Commission of India (ECI) was established by the Constitution of India under Article 324 of the Constitution.[36] Like the Supreme Court of India, it is an autonomous organization and has the constitutional authority and responsibility of administering and controlling electoral processes in India. The ECI conducts elections for the Lok Sabha, the Rajya Sabha and state legislative assemblies, as well as for the offices of the president and the vice president in the country. Based on the principle of adult franchise, under the provision of the Representation of the People Act, the ECI undertook and successfully carried out the gruelling task of organizing the 1952 election for the Parliament and state legislative assemblies.[37] The colossal task included the making of the electoral roll for 173 million eligible voters, most of whom were illiterate and had to be educated about the election; and preparing foolproof ballot boxes and special ballot papers that would enable voters to identify the candidates of their choice through unique party symbols.

India is a nation representing a symbolic culture. Symbols have always moved Indians, whether it's Nandi the bull, Goddess Durga riding a tiger, Ganesha the elephant god, Hanuman the monkey god, Shiva the lingam, Krishna the charioteer, or the bhagwa colour (saffron) of Hindutva. In the general election, keeping in mind India's secularism, the ECI eschewed religious symbols and approved 14 distinct symbols for national parties along with separate symbols for state parties and independent candidates.[38] To prevent voter fraud, indelible ink was used. Whatever was being done for the parliamentary election had to be replicated for state legislature assembly elections. In 1952, at the national level there were 489 seats (out of 500) in 401 constituencies, representing all Indian states. Of those 401 constituencies, 314 had one seat, 86 had two seats and one had three seats.[39] Consider the magnitude of the task:

> About a million officials supervised the conduct of the polls... In all, candidates of over fourteen national and sixty-three regional or local parties and a large number of independents contested 489 seats for the Lok Sabha and 3,283 seats for the state assemblies. Of these, 98 seats for the former and 669 for the latter were reserved for the Scheduled Castes and the Scheduled Tribes. Nearly 17,500 candidates in all stood for the seats to the Lok Sabha and the state legislatures.[40]

The biggest challenge was to educate the electorates about how democracy functioned through elections based on adult franchise. The Press Information Bureau and the ECI made election information readily available to the media. The press, both English and regional languages, played a major role in spreading the news and educating people. And as the elections progressed, the thirst for election news increased. 'As many as 397 newspapers were started during the period of the elections, and most of these ceased to exist after the elections were over,' according to an ECI report.[41] Since most of the electorate could not read, reaching them through documentaries in regional languages was another way that government press bureaus tried to educate the people. Radio as an aural medium has a low threshold of reaching audiences regardless of their level of education, but in the first general election, it proved to be a very powerful means of mass education. The chief election commissioner, as well as the chief electoral officers took to All India Radio to explain to the people the importance of the general election as the essence of democracy, the importance of holding the polls and the responsibility of citizens as voters.[42]

Chipping away and splintering from the Congress party was inevitable, and it was also necessary from the point of view of national polity in order to test the participating political parties' strengths in the open marketplace of ideas that the general election provided. Ambedkar, one of the foremost constitutionalists, revived the All India Scheduled Caste Federation, believing that the INC, dominated by contrarian forces, would never do justice to the poor and downtrodden. In the first general election, the Scheduled Caste Federation contested 34 Lok Sabha seats from Bombay, the Central Provinces and Berar, Madras, Punjab, the United Provinces, Hyderabad, Rajasthan, Delhi, Himachal Pradesh and Vindhya Pradesh, but won only two seats. Ambedkar, who contested from Bombay from a reserved (North Central) constituency, lost to a relatively unknown Congress Scheduled Caste candidate; however, he was later elected to the Rajya Sabha. In the state legislative assemblies, the Scheduled Caste Federation won 12 seats out of 215 contested. It must have been a hard lesson and a humbling experience for Ambedkar, who once again lost the election in 1954 when he fought a by-election from Bhandara (Maharashtra) for the Lok Sabha. In 1956 he founded the Republican Party to create a broad-based political party. Indian leaders would later discover that democracy respects few heroes.

Many other prominent political personalities and freedom fighters would learn similar hard lessons. Freedom fighter and Gandhian, Acharya Kripalani, formed the Kisan Mazdoor Praja Parishad, but the party did not make much headway in the election. Acharya Kripalani himself lost the election, though the party won nine seats. Ram Manohar Lohia and Jayaprakash Narayan formed the Socialist Party, which also did not fare too well, winning only 12 seats in the election, and later merged with the Kisan Mazdoor Praja Parishad to form the Socialist Praja Party. Syama Prasad Mookerjee, a Hindu nationalist politician, orator, barrister and academician, who had served as minister for industry and supply in Nehru's cabinet, developed serious differences with him, quit the INC and founded the right-wing nationalist party, the Bharatiya Jana Sangh, the predecessor to the BJP of today. The Bharatiya Jana Sangh won only three seats. Some diehard ideologies mutate and evolve. In some sense democracy represents the Darwinian amoral world of struggle for existence, and survival of the fittest. It is also the marketplace for ideas where sometimes falsehood drives out truth, contrary to the optimistic faith of John Milton who said, 'Let her [Truth] and Falsehood grapple; who ever knew Truth put to the worse in a free and open encounter? Her confuting is the best and surest suppressing.'[43]

One of the most significant impacts of the general election was the surfacing of the CPI from its underground revolutionary sewers and rat holes onto the open political stage to fight elections and play the game of democracy, where one day, CPI, along with its splinter groups, would be defeated and become politically marginalized. With 16 seats, the CPI was the second-largest party to go to the Lok Sabha. The emerging political scene was fascinating. The left-leaning parties, including the communists, won 42 seats. Hindu nationalist parties won 10 seats. There was not much presence of regional parties in the Lok Sabha except for the Akali Dal with four seats, the party of the Sikhs that would become a permanent presence on the Punjab political scene. The INC the leftists of all shades, the Hindu nationalists, and regional-ethnic-caste-based parties, would form the emerging political pattern that would shape India.

The INC was still Jawaharlal Nehru's party and there was no challenge to its power. During the preceding several months of the election, Nehru took a whirlwind tour of the country, travelling thousands of miles, covering almost all regions to address public meetings. In each meeting, he propounded his vision of building a new India founded on science and technology, massive dams and canals for irrigation, and universal education. He conjured up a future that India had been dreaming about.

I was in high school when I attended a meeting in Hisar, a vast agricultural town, formerly in Punjab and now in Haryana. Dressed in white and his signature jacket with a red rose and the Gandhi cap, Nehru looked tall (though he was a short man), agile and handsome on the dais. There was a sea of people assembled on a bright sunny day. He spoke in conversational Hindi, often searching for a proper word that people could understand. He talked about irrigation canals by building new dams such as the Bhakra-Nangal Dam, about which everyone was talking. At one point, when he was talking about wheat crops, he halted for a moment to search for a proper word for wheat and looked at Sardar Partap Singh Kairon, a prominent state Congress leader, who promptly said, 'kanak'—the Hindi-Punjabi word for wheat. I had the impression that Nehru was perhaps first thinking in English and then translating his thoughts into Hindi; and hence the halting and sometimes out of syntax speech. He did not seem as fluent in Hindi as in English. Like the rest of the audience and my classmates, I had gone to see him, feel his presence, and listen to his voice. I felt his presence very comforting, reassuring and inspiring, as did the rest of India, I believe. I watched Nehru as he had imagined himself in 1937 in a cautionary tale published in the *Modern Review*, pseudonymously bylined 'Chanakya', India's ancient political philosopher, as to how one day the Indian people might view him as a human-god to be revered.[44] A similar apprehension about Indians' bhakti-devotional predilections, detrimental to democracy, was also expressed by Dr. Ambedkar.

The INC, with 45 per cent votes, achieved a landslide victory, winning 364 seats out of 489. The rest of the 55 per cent voters of India did not vote for the Congress party, but that is how multiparty democracy based on the first-past-the-post plurality voting method works. Similarly, with 42.4 per cent votes, the Congress party won 68.6 per cent of the state legislative assembly seats, and the party formed governments in all the 22 states, though, in West Bengal and three southern states, including Madras, Hyderabad and Travancore-Cochin, the Communist Party's strong showing was a harbinger of things to come.[45] There was another straw in the election winds. Congress party stalwart Morarji Desai, a puritan, self-righteous, pro-business politician, failed to win from his Bombay constituency. By defeating two prominent national figures, Ambedkar and Morarji Desai, the city of Bombay was speaking up: in elections, there are no sacred cows. Nonetheless, the Congress dominance over the country seemed unquestionable for the time being, and Jawaharlal

Nehru became the prime minister of the first democratically elected government of India.

The successful holding and the outcomes of the first universal adult franchise election transformed India—from what Winston Churchill, due to his profound ignorance about Indian civilization and culture, compounded by his deep racism, had called 'a mere geographical expression'—into an abiding political state. Instead of leaving India to the rule of the upper classes, which would have been, as Churchill had warned, 'an act of cruel and wicked negligence,' the first general election sent candidates—most of whom, no doubt, came from upper classes—from railway station to railway station, bus stop to bus stop, street to street, and door to door to solicit votes from the people whom earlier they might have despised.[46]

Democratic elections can be a frustrating and chastening experience, as many discovered. What Churchill had said in the 1930s persisted in various forms and shapes in the minds of Indians and foreigners during the elections. In the midst of the election campaign, according to Guha, even Nehru had developed doubts whether direct election based on adult franchise was suitable for selecting men of quality because 'the noise of propaganda,' and 'the sound and din' of electioneering would drive away the righteous and push up to the stage 'a dictator or a dumb politician who is insensitive.' Guha, then, unselfconsciously drops a sarcastic bombshell saying that when the final election results were declared showing that 'the Congress had emerged as the unchallenged ruling party, his (Nehru's) doubts had disappeared.' It is the moral responsibility of a historian to ask a 'what if' question. What if the results were a mixed bag and the Congress party had to share power with the CPI, the Bharatiya Jana Sangh or the Socialist Party to form a coalition government, as it normally happens in a parliamentary democracy? But this did not happen in the Lok Sabha election and Nehru's 'respect for the so-called illiterate voter' went up and all his doubts about the suitability of adult suffrage in India suddenly disappeared.[47]

With the landslide victory that the Congress achieved, Nehru was not the only person whose faith had been restored in the direct universal election based on adult franchise. Immediately after the first general election, political scientist Richard Park optimistically observed:

> As for implementation of the formal constitutional order, the general election itself demonstrates a serious intent to fulfill the spirit as well as the letter of the Constitution. Beyond the confines of the election process, gradual improvement of economic and social conditions throughout the country, framed in legislation and administered for the common good, should strengthen popular faith in the efficacy of democratic institutions and methods as opposed to their totalitarian counterparts.[48]

But more importantly it was the British newspaper, the *Daily Express* that asked an interesting question, 'What will Mr. Nehru now do with his immense power?'[49] Jawaharlal Nehru had the power of Caesar without being Caesar.[50]

POLITICAL PARTIES AND THE GAME OF DEMOCRACY

The dominance of the INC under the leadership of Nehru played a crucial role in stabilizing India as a federal-parliamentary, separate-but-together, political system. Under its broad and benign umbrella, nonetheless, the multiparty system too began to grow. The Indian people heard other voices too including the Socialist Party, the CPI, the Kisan Mazdoor Praja Party and the Bharatiya Jana Sangh; and most importantly, the regional state parties concerned with their local economic, cultural, and political interests. This would eventually lead to the development and evolution of a dynamic system of competitive and cooperative federalism of mutually dependent and interacting semi-autonomous states that would shape the federal government as well as the states.

Unsurprisingly the national opposition parties had their sympathizers even within the Congress party because the party under Gandhi's leadership had led the all-inclusive freedom movement; therefore, for historical reasons, it was not ideologically monolithic in spite of Nehru's dominant socialistic view. Despite their seemingly marginal presence in the political system, the opposition parties, national and regional, remained distinct political entities with divergent political and economic programmes. Since 'all politics is local,' the opposition parties played a more significant role at the state level rather than at the Centre. For example, in the first three state assembly elections, the opposition parties collectively got 35 per cent seats in 1952; 35 per cent seats in 1957 and 40 per cent seats in 1962. At the Centre, in the Lok Sabha, during the first three general elections, they had an average of about 26 per cent seats. It was through their significant electoral presence at the state level that the opposition parties began to exert influence at the Centre.

In the course of time, the opposition parties, as they gathered strength, began to explore commonalities, which would eventually lead to coalition governments first at the state level, and later at the Centre. But it is noteworthy that this entire democratic bloom began in the time of Nehru, who did not venture to suppress any opposition even if it was personally hostile to him. The developing democratic culture was bolstered by the freedom of the press, which became increasingly bold and assertive in its criticism of the government's policies and programmes. Tolerance of dissent developed into a democratic norm and became institutionalized as an indispensable opposition, an alternative home for those who differed fundamentally from the beliefs and ideals of the Congress party. This was seen in the case of Acharya Kripalani, a highly regarded Gandhian socialist and freedom fighter, who differed with Nehru on many issues and eventually left the Congress party to establish the Kisan Mazdoor Praja Party, as mentioned earlier.

But before splitting from the Congress, Acharya Kripalani raised a serious political and constitutional issue as to what should be the relationship between the parliamentary wing of the Congress party led by the prime minister and the party headed by its president. Acharya Kripalani, who was the post-Independence Congress party president, asked that the government be run in consultation with the party leadership. Nehru, Sardar Patel and others disagreed with Acharya Kripalani, arguing that while the Congress party could lay down broad principles and guidelines, however, in the parliamentary system of government, the council of ministers headed by the prime minister was answerable to the Parliament. The disagreement led to Acharya Kripalani's resignation as the party president in November 1947, and his successors Rajendra Prasad and B. Pattabhi Sitaramayya did not raise the question of organizational preeminence.

But in the 1950 Congress party organizational elections, the conservatives in the party led by Purushottamdas Tandon made a bid to control the party and assert its control over the government. Tandon, like Nehru, was born in Allahabad, Uttar Pradesh, and was a member of the bar of the Allahabad High Court before he joined the freedom movement led by Gandhi and the Congress party, of which he was a member since his student days. A staunch supporter of Hindi as the national language, in his political and religious views, he was closer to K.M. Munshi and Sardar Patel rather than to Nehru's agnostic secularism. The 1950–51 party organizational elections brought to the fore the schism between the conservatives and secular socialists of the party.

The Congress party was getting ready for the first general election and naturally whoever controlled the party would ultimately exercise the power over the selection of candidates, both for the Parliament as well as state assemblies. In other words this was an opportunity to assert the Congress party's supremacy over the government, an issue that was raised earlier by Acharya Kripalani in 1947. Ironically, Acharya Kripalani, who had earlier resigned over the issue of organizational supremacy, was now himself a candidate for the president of the Congress party position. Nehru supported him against Tandon, who was backed by Sardar Patel. It was internal democracy at its fiercest and a most serious challenge to Nehru's leadership. In the three-way contested Congress party election held on 29 August 1950, Tandon won against Acharya Kripalani and a third marginal candidate, Shankarrao Deo. The victory of the right-wing conservatives and their dominance over the party apparatus provoked a number of socialist Congress party members led by Acharya Kripalani, as mentioned earlier, to leave and form their own political party, the Kisan Mazdoor Praja Party in 1951.

With the rise of the conservatives and their organizational views that the party should control the government, Nehru's lifelong mission of establishing a socialist, secular society came under a serious threat and he decided to give a do-or-die internal battle to the party's conservative leadership. Believing that the Congress party was indispensable to India and he was indispensable to the Congress party, especially at a time when the country was getting ready for the first general election, Nehru asked the party to choose between him and Tandon. In a bold political move, he submitted his resignation from the Congress Working Committee and the Central Election Committee. Having seen the writing on the wall that the All-India Congress Committee would not support him, Tandon resigned from the Congress presidency on 8 September 1951. Nehru was elected as the Congress party president in spite of his innate conviction that the office of the party president and of the prime minister should be kept separate. Caesar-ism takes many forms. Or one might say, desperate situations need desperate measures and this was one of them.

With the passing away of Sardar Patel in December 1950 and the conservative challenge contained, Nehru remained the supreme leader of India until his death in 1964. Tandon, along with other right-wing conservative members, in spite of the setback, continued with the Congress party. In fact, Tandon was invited by Nehru to work with him in the Congress Working Committee, which he did without apparent rancour. Indians have a high tolerance for cognitive dissonance. This was aptly proven when thousands and thousands of Indians like Tandon would go along with the flow, the Nehru flow, in spite of internal conflicts and contradictions.

In order to retain its all-India character as the party of governance as well as the party of mass movement for nation building, the INC had to maintain its all-embracing historic character of ideological openness, a loose modular structure held together by the strong charismatic leadership of Nehru. In the course of time, keeping in view Nehru's own predilection, party commitment to social justice and socialism, the Congress party began to move toward the left and became a centre-left party. The centre-left Congress party accommodated the socialists without however alienating the capitalist class, landlords, merchants and industrialists, who not only balanced the leftists in the party but provided financial backing, which was important for the party.

Apart from accommodating the class aspirations, the Congress had to be cognizant of caste, communal and regional interests while maintaining its secular ideology and framework. The all-embracing holistic outlook and attitude of the Congress party—be all that you can be to all and sundry—made it absorptive and assimilative to the opposition parties' ideas and programmes and thus compelled them to become more distinctive. It was not enough for the opposition parties to proclaim that they were not the Congress party; but who they were and what they stood for became important, as was the case, for example, with the CPI. Those parties who couldn't become distinguished and distinct from the Congress party became vituperative and censorious. For example, Jayaprakash (J.P.) Narayan, who accused Nehru of taking the capitalist road to reach the socialist goal, warned him of 'an ugly example of Indian fascism,'[51] in regard to the bill outlawing strikes in essential services in 1949. He urged the Congress party to adopt his 14-point socialistic agenda, including land reforms, nationalization of banks, insurance and mines as a condition for his cooperation.[52] What J.P. Narayan's Socialist Party with a small political base couldn't do, he wanted the Congress party to do for him.

SOCIALISTIC PATTERN OF THINKING

Nehru needed the support of the socialists outside the Congress to buttress his socialist agenda within the party. But he wanted to do so at a pace acceptable to the party at large, preferably based on consensus. Nonetheless, he did not hesitate to use coercive persuasion to get his way, as it happened in January

1955 at the Avadi session of the All India Congress Committee (AICC), which declared, 'Planning should take place with a view to the establishment of a socialistic pattern of society, where the principle means of production are under social ownership or control, production is progressively speeded up and there is equitable distribution of the national wealth.'[53] By adopting the vaguely defined socialistic pattern of society doctrine, the Congress party defanged the socialists and the communists in India. But the Congress party overreached itself at the Nagpur session in January 1959 when it adopted cooperative joint farming, service cooperatives, a ceiling on landholdings, and state trading in food grains as its core socialistic programme. Except for the ceiling on landholdings, other programmes were abandoned as unworkable, but the commitment to the socialistic pattern of society was reaffirmed at the Bhubaneswar session of the Congress party in January 1964, which, by suppressing people's entrepreneurial spirit, would leave India paralyzed for a long time.

The socialistic policies of the INC had burdened India with what one of its most ardent admirers, economist Raj Krishna,[54] called the 'Hindu rate of growth,'[55] which he blamed on India's cultural inertia rather than Nehru's vision of democratic socialism. Regardless of the fact that the socialistic policies had failed to stimulate economic growth, the intellectual establishment at India's top universities, think tanks, the news media as well as the policymaking bureaucracy at national and regional levels had been totally transformed by Nehru's mode of thinking. Few intellectuals could escape the socialistic mindset of the era. In spite of Nehru's commitment to liberalism and diversity of thought, there was soft and invisible but systematic purging and cleansing 'of all non-Left thinkers since the 1950s. One of its early victims was liberal economist B.R. Shenoy, who questioned Nehru's economics. He was squeezed out of the establishment and persecuted, but continued to write against socialist planning... The result of the systematic cleansing was that there were no non-Left academics remaining in the social sciences field in India by the early 1990s.'[56] Even when the Soviet Union collapsed, the Indian mindset remained left-oriented. Because of the socialistic model of protectionist thinking, Indians were not ready to embrace the freedom and the challenges of the competitiveness of the open marketplace, at home and abroad. Even today, Indians shrink from competition.

But India's economic failures did not damage Nehru's reputation. What hurt him the most was something beyond his control. India had gone through the terrible trauma of defeat in the Himalayas. This was the first time since Independence that there was a loss of faith in Nehru's leadership. 'Who after Nehru?' became a painful question because of his lengthy dominance over the Congress party and the nation at large. There was no second tier of leadership because Jawaharlal Nehru had not let other leaders grow to challenge and replace him. Sadashiv Kanoji (S.K.) Patil, a senior cabinet minister, in response to a British journalist's question about Nehru's successor, said, 'Who can say? The prime minister is like the great banyan tree. Thousands take shelter under it, but nothing grows.'[57] So furious was Nehru that he grounded Patil to the back benches for his audacity to call a spade more than a spade. The Congress party had become a bandwagon for all kinds of opportunists seeking political power, influence and patronage. It had become a party of the licence-raj crony capitalism, though it kept uttering its shibboleth of socialistic pattern of society, which had lost its meaning for most people. The Congress party was moving away from its constituencies and yielding ground to opposition parties, including regional state parties.

To stop the rot and to rejuvenate the party, Madras Chief Minister K. Kamaraj, in consultation with Nehru, proposed the Kamaraj Plan, under which senior leaders at the Centre and states would resign from their positions and take up party organizational work. In order to clean up the stables, Nehru was to decide who would be shuffled out of the government to do the party work, from a total of 300 resignations received, including some top politicians such as Morarji Desai, Lal Bahadur Shastri, S.K. Patil, Jagjivan Ram, B. Gopala Reddy and K.L. Shrimali, as well as six state chief ministers. But the Kamaraj Plan came too late to rejuvenate the

Congress. Jawaharlal Nehru was tired and sick. He suffered a mild stroke and collapsed at the Bhubaneswar Congress session. The Himalayan war had drained Jawaharlal Nehru's energies and killed the beautiful illusion of India's greatness that he had built on his policy of nonalignment. It would be left to his indomitable daughter Indira Gandhi to restructure and rejuvenate the Congress party and give India a new direction. But Nehru's legacy of socialism would keep India shackled for a long time.

3

____

FREEDOM TRAIL RUNS
THROUGH PRINCELY STATES

*By common endeavour we can raise the country
to a new greatness, while a lack of unity will expose
us to fresh calamities.*

—Sardar Vallabhbhai Patel

*By far the most important achievement of the present
government is the unification of the states into the Dominion
of India. Had you failed in this, the results would have been
disastrous... Nothing has added to the prestige of the present
government more than the brilliant policy you have followed
with the states.*

—Lord Mountbatten

After the breakup of the Mughal Empire, which began soon after the death of Emperor Aurangzeb in 1707, India had become a vast pick-me-up-slice-by-slice conglomeration of warring princely states. This turn of events was being watched hawk-eyed by the Dutch, the French and the British trading companies to protect the commercial privileges that the Mughal emperor had granted them. They erected fortresses and recruited natives to raise their private militias, in addition to building their navies in order to protect their colonial possessions. Under Robert Clive, one of the most innovative and ruthless political and military geniuses, the East India Company metamorphosed from a trading firm into a great conqueror and colonizer, especially beginning with the Battle of Plassey, at which Siraj-ud-Daulah, the nawab of Bengal who had the richest kingdom in India, was defeated in 1757.[1] A puppet ruler, Mir Jafar, a general of the nawab, betrayed the nawab and was subsequently installed as the new ruler.

That was the beginning of the direct and indirect colonial rule by the East India Company, under which, for the next hundred years, the Company gradually began to control the entire Indian subcontinent, either directly or through multiple and complex chains of subsidiary alliances with puppet princely states based on pensions; and the Doctrine of Lapse, under which any princely state, under the paramountcy of the British East India Company, would automatically be annexed if the ruler either died without a male heir or if the heir was found to be incompetent.[2] Every native ruler under the East India Company's suzerainty lived under the Sword of Damocles. But their day of reckoning came soon.

The British Empire was shaken up in 1857 when disinherited princes and their allies under the titular Mughal Emperor, Bahadur Shah Zafar, carried out a massive rebellion—the so-called Sepoy Mutiny or the First War of Independence, which was mostly limited to northern and central India. However, with the help of the Sikhs in Punjab along with the newly emerging technology of the telegraph, the disorganized rebellion without a central command-and-control was soon crushed. The victorious East India Company forces brutalized the losers. The Mughal Emperor was exiled to Burma (now Myanmar), where he spent his life writing mournful poetry that Indians today love to recite. Most importantly, India had reached a point of inflexion. The East India Company was taken over by the British government, and India came under the direct control of the British Crown in 1858.

The idea of India as a geocultural conglomeration was later transmuted by Mahatma Gandhi into a mass movement through the INC, the khadi and the white cap, which Jawaharlal Nehru tried to rediscover through his book, *The Discovery of India*. Nehru did not create the idea of India, nor did he reinvent the idea of India.[3] Only after India had become the most precious British crown jewel, that the West was amazed to discover the Sanskrit language, the vedas, the upanishads and the Buddha. Indians, too, began to rediscover themselves once the West had begun to wonder at the ancient glory of India. Thus spoke some of the brightest minds of the West:

> India was the motherland of our race, and Sanskrit the mother of Europe's languages: she was the mother of our philosophy; mother, through the Arabs, of much of our mathematics; mother, through the Buddha, of the ideals embodied in Christianity; mother, through the village community, of self-government and democracy. Mother India is in many ways the mother of us all.
>
> —Will Durant, *The Case for India (1930)*

> India is the cradle of the human race, the birthplace of human speech, the mother of history, the grandmother of legend, and the great-grandmother of tradition. Our most valuable and most instructive materials in the history of man are treasured up in India only.
>
> —Mark Twain

> We owe a lot to the Indians, who taught us how to count, without which no worthwhile scientific discovery could have been made.
>
> —Albert Einstein

Under the British Crown, beginning in 1858, the colonial relations with the princely states underwent a fundamental change. The policy of annexation was given up. Under the paramountcy of the British Crown, each princely state entered into some form of subsidiary alliance with the Crown. Based on each state's individual treaty, some states retained more internal autonomy than others while giving up control over external relations. Through this new pattern of dependency relationship that assured the Indian princes of their power and rule over their kingdoms, the rulers—rajas, maharajas, nawabs and nizams—became the most loyal followers of the British Crown. As Lord Canning boasted, 'The territories under the sovereignty of the Crown became at once as important and as integral a part of India... Together they form one direct care and the political system, which the Moghuls had not completed and the Mahrattas never contemplated is now an established fact of history.'[4]

Thus, the British Crown had a dual system of rule over India, the princely states under the British suzerainty and the rest of India under the viceroy. To bring princely India and British India together, the Chamber of Princes was established in 1920 as an advisory body so that the princely states could voice their opinions and concerns to the British India government under the Viceroy.[5] In response to the growing movement for independence under the INC, the Government of India Act, 1935 contained a scheme for a federation including British India and the princely states, but because of the events of World War II in 1939 and growing differences between the INC and the Muslim League, the Act went nowhere.[6] It's notable, nonetheless, that the admiration between the British Royalty and the Indian Royalty, the princes, was mutual until 1947 when the question arose about the place of the princely states in independent India.

On the morning of 15 August, when India stood up free at the world stage, it had only 52 per cent of its territory under its sovereign control. The rest of India was a congeries of 565 princely states that had existed under the suzerainty of British India but now found their status had become undetermined and their future uncertain. Since the paramountcy and subsidiary alliance arrangements between the British Crown and the princely states could not be transferred to the Indian Union, each princely state, in theory, would become independent and sovereign, which would have led to a fragmented India, with princely fragments scattered within the body of India, except for those fragments lying outside its borders on the west and east (Pakistan). The vision of a united India that was firmly held by the INC would be negated. It would be freedom half won.[7] The princely states were more important to India than the territories that went into the making of Pakistan. The INC government insisted that the princely states must accede to India with the same rights and obligations as the rest of the British provinces joining Independent India, without which the network of trade, commerce, communications, railroads, transportation, ports, irrigation and other undertakings vital to the economic activities of India would become non-operational.

On this vital point, Lord Mountbatten, the viceroy who became the first Governor General of Independent India (from 1947 to 1948), fully supported the Congress party and the Indian government's aspirations, despite the fact that, while some princely states had serious reservations about joining the Indian Union, others, especially Bhopal, Travancore and Hyderabad, were completely hostile to the idea of giving up their princedoms.[8] Although they had a forum, the Chamber of Princes, the princely states were unable to present a united front to the Indian government and thus had little political leverage and manoeuvrability left. Most of them saw the writing on the wall and negotiated for favourable terms for accession to the Indian Dominion with the Congress party and the Indian government.

Apart from gentle to coercive persuasion from Sardar Vallabhbhai Patel, home minister and minister of states, and Vappala Pangunni (V.P.) Menon, administrative head of the States Department, many princely states faced popular pressure from their own subjects who, having been part of the freedom struggle led by Mahatma Gandhi and Nehru, insisted on integration with India. Lord Mountbatten played a key role in the integration of the princely states with the Indian Union. In this endeavour, the Congress leaders trusted him implicitly. So did most of the princes who believed that he would be a fair umpire during the accession negotiation with the Indian government. Lord Mountbatten made it clear to those reluctant to join the Indian Union that there was no possibility of the British Crown protecting them from external aggression, or from their own subjects if they rose against them, or enabling them to join the British Commonwealth as sovereign independent states. His personal relations with the nawab of Bhopal, whose majority subjects were Hindus and who would have preferred to remain independent or even join Pakistan, enabled the nawab to finally sign the Instrument of Accession to India.[9] While Lord Mountbatten used personal diplomacy with princes, Congress leaders played hardball and left no doubt that the end of the British paramountcy would not make them automatically independent; rather, it would leave them footloose and vulnerable and in their mutual interests, they needed to sincerely negotiate their relations with India.

The integration of the states was a herculean task indeed. Despite the soft power wielded by Lord Mountbatten and the tough rhetoric of some Congress leaders—especially Nehru, who had no sympathy with feudal rulers—the major burden of accomplishing the state integration, the footwork from state to state, endless negotiations and retaining the confidence of the rulers and their subjects fell on the shoulders of Sardar Patel and his tireless associate V.P. Menon. Rather than act as bullies and tail twisters, they conducted themselves with dignity as benevolent diplomats, giving the impression of dealing with equals.

Negotiations began with the Standstill Agreement that confirmed the status quo, that is, the existing relationships, agreements and treaties, which a princely state had with British India. This was followed by the Instrument of Accession, under which a princely state would accept accession to the Indian Union and cede certain specific subjects to be administered by the Indian government and the rest by the princely state, depending upon the existing arrangement per the terms of the Standby Agreement. Some states that had internal autonomy, for example, surrendered defence, external affairs and communications while keeping control over the rest of the administrative areas. Other states that had a different degree of autonomy under the British Crown now had the same degree of control under the Instrument of Accession. In other words, the Instrument of Accession was nothing but a process of legitimizing and transferring through fresh treaties, the princely state–British Crown relationship to the Indian Union.

To soften the blow and make the princes comfortable, the Instrument of Accession included several friendly provisions; for example, it assured the princes that they would not be obliged to accept the Constitution of India when it was ratified. The Instrument also guaranteed a princely state autonomy in administrative subjects that were not conceded to the government of India. Other privileges of the princely rulers, such as exemption from customs duty and immunity from prosecution in Indian courts, would be honoured. They would be eligible for British honours and decorations as well. They would choose their own pace of democratization in their respective states. At its face value, the Instrument of Accession granted the princely states as much autonomy as they had before, except that now, instead of being beholden to the British Crown, they would deal with the government of India as the paramount power. The states were warned, however, that the Standstill Agreement, which confirmed the existing arrangement and their present status, was only a first step and must be followed by the Instrument of Accession.[10]

The soft-and-hard kid-glove approach of the Instrument of Accession that assured the princely rulers their existing autonomy without encroaching upon their personal privileges persuaded a vast majority of them to join the Indian Union by 15 August 1947, when India became an independent nation. A few states, nevertheless, were reluctant to sign the document, especially Jodhpur and Jaisalmer, sandwiched between India and Pakistan, who had received a tempting, open-ended offer from Pakistan to join them. But being Hindu-majority states, whose rulers too were Hindus, they finally signed the Instrument of Accession with India.[11] Others like Travancore, Junagadh, Hyderabad and Jammu and Kashmir envisioned themselves as future sovereign independent nations and brought India much grief.

When the Dewan of Travancore, Sir C.P. Ramaswamy Iyer, declared that Travancore, one of the most progressive and turbulent princely states in southern India facing the Arabian Sea, would not join the Indian Union and would become an independent state, the announcement aroused bitter anger and controversy in the state. The maharaja's government resorted to repressive measures leading to violence that killed many, including a student. On 25 July 1947, when Iyer was attending a function in the Swathi Thirunal Academy of Music (now the Swathi Thirunal College of Music) at Trivandrum, he was attacked by a socialist activist; he survived with non-life-threatening injuries. Soon after the violent event, the maharaja saw the light of day and hastened to sign the Instrument of Accession—and that was the end of the dream of an independent Travancore.[12]

THE STRANGE CASE OF JUNAGADH

Junagadh was a princely state facing the Arabian Sea in the western state of Gujarat, whose overwhelming majority of the population in 1947 was Hindu. But the state had a Muslim ruler, the nawab of Junagadh, Muhammad Mahabat Khanji III, whose ancestors had ruled the state and some other feudatories in the region for the past 200 years, in fact, since the disintegration of the Mughal Empire. The state's communications, railroad, transportation and economy were interconnected with the rest of the region of Kathiawar, now part of Gujarat. Except for the port of Veraval that connected it to the Arabian Sea, the rest of the state was surrounded by territories of the Indian princes who had already joined the Indian Union. Junagadh was not contiguous with Pakistan, but the state's Veraval port was not far away from Pakistan's Karachi port.

In the early stages after the declaration of the Indian Independence Act, 1947, when the princely states were left to make their own choice whether to join India or Pakistan, the constitutional advisor to the nawab of Junagadh, Nabi Bakshi, and the state's chief administrator, Dewan Abdul Kadir Mohammad Hussain, had assured Lord Mountbatten and Indian leaders that the state would accede to India, which seemed a natural thing to do. But soon, the story took a different twist when the state Dewan was replaced by a Muslim League politician from Karachi, Sir Nawaz Shah Bhutto, who changed the nawab's mind, and the state decided to join Pakistan without informing Indian leaders. In spite of the visit of V.P. Menon to the state to persuade the nawab to rethink his decision, the nawab, regardless of the dire consequences that Menon had forewarned him about, remained firm. He signed and sent the Instrument of Accession to Pakistan, which the Constituent Assembly of Pakistan accepted and the Governor General of Pakistan, Mohammed Ali Jinnah, countersigned it. Junagadh's accession to Pakistan became a fait accompli and legal on 15 September 1947. If West Pakistan and East Pakistan, with 1,372 miles of Indian territory between them, could be one country, there was no reason for Junagadh not to become part of Pakistan, especially when Veraval was only 367 nautical miles from Karachi.

But Sardar Patel and Nehru thought otherwise. They had other plans regardless of the legality of the issue. The final decision on the country to join should be decided by the people of Junagadh. Moreover, it would be 'intolerable that pockets of Pakistan should be created inside Indian territory.'[13] The first step was to form, with the blessing of the Indian government, a provisional government for Junagadh, which was formed on 25 September 1947 by Samaldas Gandhi in Bombay and which received wide support from the All India States Peoples' Conference as well as from the Bombay-based Gujarat States Organization. Samaldas was a nephew of Mahatma Gandhi. Morarji Desai was the chief minister of Bombay. When Pakistan protested against the provisional government's destabilizing activities, India responded that this was nothing but a popular expression by the people of Junagadh against the decision of the nawab to join Pakistan.

During the extensive diplomatic exchanges and consultations between the two countries, Pakistan kept reminding India that Junagadh's accession to Pakistan within the law of the Independence Act of 1947 was final. While the Indian government maintained the facade of negotiations, India imposed a total blockade on the state. The situation deteriorated and became untenable for the nawab and what he did was nothing but shameful, and his action revealed his dissolute and immoral character. As V.P. Menon wrote: 'The nawab realized that events were not going as he had anticipated; and he decided on flight... The nawab took with him the entire cash balances of the State and all the shares and securities in the treasury.'[14]

With the ignominious flight of the nawab, the state's Dewan, Sir Shah Nawaz Bhutto, wrote to Mohammed Ali Jinnah that '...I should therefore suggest that you immediately arrange for a conference of the representatives of the two Dominions to decide the Junagadh issue.' Without waiting for a definitive response from Pakistan,

Dewan Sir Shah Nawaz Bhutto was authorized by the Junagadh State Council to negotiate with Indian authorities to take over the state administration. The nawab too had encouraged Bhutto to use his 'judicious discrimination as the situation demanded.' [15]

On 8 November, Sir Shah Nawaz Bhutto wrote to Nilam Buch, the regional commissioner, Western India and Gujarat States, to take over the state administration 'pending an honourable settlement of the several issues involved in the Junagadh accession. The Junagadh Government, therefore, has requested that in order to avoid bloodshed, hardship, loss of life and property and to preserve the dynasty, you should be approached to give your assistance to the administration.'[16] On the same night, Bhutto left for Pakistan. On 9 November 1947, Captain Harvey Johnson and Chief Secretary Gheewala handed the administration over to Nilam Buch.

Pakistan never accepted the decision, arguing that since Junagadh had already acceded to Pakistan, neither the dewan nor the erstwhile nawab had the authority to enter into any negotiation with India for any settlement. In response to Pakistan's feeble and impotent protest, India played the game of democracy. And as it had promised, a plebiscite was held in Junagadh in which 99.95 per cent of the population voted to join India.[17]

On 13 November 1947, Sardar Patel visited Junagadh where, as was expected, he received a rousing reception at a mammoth gathering on the grounds of the Bahauddin College. V.P. Menon recounted:

> Sardar then visited the famous Somnath temple at Prabhas Patan. He was visibly moved to find the temple, which had once been the glory of India looking so dilapidated, neglected and forlorn. It was proposed then and there to reconstruct it so as to return it to its original splendour... This was my first visit to Somnath. As a schoolboy, the story of the sack of Somnath by Mahmud Ghazni had made a profound impression on me. I never even dreamt that I should one day visit this temple. The decision to reconstruct Somnath was an act of historic justice that warmed my heart.[18]

But what happened in Junagadh was a prelude to the perilous and perfidious events of the princely state of Hyderabad.[19]

CREATIVE DESTRUCTION IN HYDERABAD

The princely state of Hyderabad, which spread its wings like dark clouds over 86,000 square miles of the Deccan Plateau of India, stood in the way of the dreamers of democracy whose time had arrived. The Nizam, Mir Osman Ali Khan Asaf Jah VII, a Muslim potentate, once a vassal of the Mughals and later of British India, ruled over a population of 16 million with an overwhelming Hindu majority, who wanted the state to accede to India. The Muslim minority who controlled the levers of power in the state had become radicalized under the political organization Majlis-e-Ittihadul-Muslimeen (MIM) and its militant wing, the Razakars. The Razakars, under its fanatic leader Qasim Razvi, wanted Hyderabad to accede to Pakistan and terrorized the Hindu population, especially in the countryside.

The nizam, one of the richest people in the world, was a legendary figure. *Time* magazine, in its 22 February 1937 issue, featured the nizam of Hyderabad on its cover page. With a wealth of over $2 billion, the nizam was worth twice the total value of the Indian treasury at the time of Independence. Queen Elizabeth II's exquisite diamond necklace collection includes the 'Nizam of Hyderabad Necklace' that was given to her as a wedding present by the nizam. The nizam's 173-piece jewellery collection, including the Jacob Diamond, the world's fifth-largest diamond, was estimated at £200 million. Apart from having several wives, he had countless concubines and mistresses, 34 legitimate children and innumerable illegitimate children.[20]

The nizam was hell-bent on turning his subservient British state into an independent nation that would keep its ties with the British Crown and establish relations with the Indian Union only as a sovereign nation. The nizam had many admirers in Britain, especially among the Conservatives, including, Winston Churchill, who wanted to keep 'a little bit of India' with them, but they had no leverage, especially when Lord Mountbatten had firmly joined hands with Congress leaders Nehru and Patel to bring about the integration of princely states with the Indian Union.[21]

Nor did the nizam realize the onslaught of the raging storm—religious and political—within the state. The MIM and the Razakars could give him limited protection. There were other powerful political forces storming the centre stage, including the Hyderabad State Congress party, the Hindu Mahasabha–Arya Samaj and the CPI. While the local Congress party demanded that Hyderabad merge with the rest of India, as did the Hindu organizations, the CPI, on the other hand, was committed to speedy distributive justice, especially in the vast swath of the countryside where its writ ran large and the cadre had forcibly distributed the land among the landless and abolished bonded labour.[22] Whereas the communists were running their own parallel government in some parts of the countryside, the Razakars were ravaging other vulnerable areas and terrorizing the Hindu population. According to a survivor account:

> About 25 to 30 Razakars came on horses and gathered several people. They took villagers to the outskirts and made them stand in a circle before shooting them dead. They burnt haystacks and threw those injured and surviving into the fire... The Razakars raided our village three times in six months in 1947 and 1948. I was caught alive and hanged upside down. They tortured me seeking the whereabouts of Thumma Seshaih, the commander of armed squad in this area. I was sent to jail for one and half years at Warangal, Gulbarga and Jalna. I was released after six months of police action that led to Telangana liberation and merger with Indian Union.[23]

Out of fear, many Hindus began to leave the state to look for safe havens in neighbouring states, a strange phenomenon of internal migration based on trepidation. Similarly, many Muslims from other parts of India who could not go to Pakistan migrated to Hyderabad, thinking that the nizam and the Majlis would give them protection.[24]

In anticipation of an attack by the Indian Army, the nizam hatched plans to import guns and ammunition from international suppliers, bought in the name of Pakistan (for which it received £2 million), and to be airlifted and dropped by an Australian World War II veteran turned fortune hunter-mercenary, Sidney Cotton. Limited engagement with the Indian Army would give Hyderabad enough time to hold on until the United Nations' (UN) intervention, a cockamamie plot that had the blessings of Jinnah and other Pakistani leaders. Beginning 4 June 1948, Cotton and his men, flying over the Indian Territory, airlifted and delivered to the nizam more than 3,000 tons of small arms and ammunition.[25]

Apart from war preparations, the nizam's government and the Majlis had unleashed venomous propaganda against the Hindus and India via the state-controlled radio, newspapers and other available avenues. Qasim Razvi, the Razakar supremo, asked Muslims to have the Quran in one hand and sword in the other and march forward and cut the enemy to pieces, and establish Islamic supremacy over stone and monkey worshipping Kafirs.[26] While the nizam's anti-India propaganda and clandestine war preparations were going on, Hyderabad Prime Minister Laik Ali kept on endless negotiations with V.P. Menon, Sardar Patel's right-hand man, agreeing to some terms one day and backing out the next day. Laik Ali's tactics caused so much frustration and consternation that Nehru felt pushed to the edge and he warned Laik Ali that he would reduce Hyderabad to smithereens if it did not accede to India.[27] The last appeal of Lord Mountbatten, before his return to Britain after the expiry of his term as India's Governor General, to the nizam was to ask him to see reason and accept the accession to India; but his advice went unheeded.

All along, the Indian resident agent K.M. Munshi and his informants were watching with alarm the terror Qasim Razvi's storm troopers, the Razakars, had been perpetrating on the innocent people. Munshi sent regular reports to Delhi as to how increasingly impossible the ground realities had become in Hyderabad. The Iron Man of India Sardar Patel was left with no choice. The richest and the most vainglorious prince of British India had become a cancerous tumour and had to be removed. On 28 February 1948, Munshi, India's Agent-General to Hyderabad, wrote a scathing letter to the nizam's Prime Minister Laik Ali about the most serious threat posed by the Majlis and the Razakars, obviously patronized by the Nizam's government, to the peace of the state. The Majlis, Munshi wrote, 'provides a fertile source of recruitment to the State Army and Police Forces. Its volunteers, Razakars, operate throughout the State in close collaboration with the State Army and Police Forces. They spread a reign of terror amongst the non-Muslim population of the State and it is common knowledge that, although they have been inflicting widespread injury on person and property, they are generally immune from the processes and penalties of the law. Assisted by the State Police, they frequently conduct raids on the neighbouring provinces of the Dominion.'

With a volunteer force of 150,000 and further recruitment being stepped up, Kazim Razvi 'has openly declared again and again that Hyderabad is an Islamic State and that sovereignty therein vests in the Muslims of Hyderabad. He has called upon the Razakars to liberate the Muslims of India from the Government of India... these pronouncements come from the President of the Party to which majority of the Ministers in your present Government owe allegiance, and are calculated to inflame the Muslims of the State and in the whole of India against the non-Muslims and Dominion of India...'[28]

It took the Indian Army, under the command of Major General Jayanto Nath Chaudhuri, hardly four days to wipe out the Nizam's 200-year-old Muslim kingdom situated in the heart of free India. On 17 September, the Nizam surrendered and accepted Hyderabad's unconditional accession to India. Apart from his personal wealth, which he was allowed to keep, the nizam was rewarded with the title of *Rajprumukh*, or the Governor, of the new state of Hyderabad. The Razakars were banned. Qasim Razvi found a safe haven in jail.

But unfortunately, the Muslim population of Hyderabad was left unprotected and became victims of communal violence that erupted after the Nizam's army was defeated. The report of anti-Muslim violence reached Nehru, who promptly appointed a committee led by Pandit Sundarlal to investigate the grim situation in Hyderabad. The committee, consisting of Pandit Sundarlal, Kazi Abdul Ghaffar and Moulana Abdulla Misri, conducted its 'goodwill mission' from 29 November through 21 December 1948, visited most of the state districts, interviewed more than 500 people, addressed several public meetings, and had a private audience with people from all strata of Hyderabad State.

The committee observed that out of 16 districts of the Hyderabad State 'only three districts remained practically, though not wholly, free of communal trouble which affected the state first during the activities of the Razakars and then during the reprisals that followed the collapse of that organization.' While the Hindus were left with their weapons, the Muslims were disarmed. Some of the soldiers were either indifferent or participated in violence against the Muslims. Most of the violence took place in the countryside. According to the report, an estimated 27,000–40,000 people were killed, while unofficial estimates run up to 200,000.[29] That's too many killings in a short period of time, which would have required a mass burial of the Muslims. The districts worst affected by the Hindu communal violence were earlier the main strongholds of Razakars, the goons who had terrorized the Hindus of these districts. The findings of the report were so alarming that the report was not made public until 2013. In spite of the fact that the committee found Major General J.N. Chaudhari 'a man without any tinge of communal prejudice, a firm disciplinarian and thorough gentleman,' the general had lost control over some of his troops who, along with communal forces, went on a rampage. In the end, the committee tried to create a fairly balanced picture by concluding:

> This communal trouble followed close upon the heels of the police action and the consequent collapse of the Razakar organization, which had stood in the Muslim mind, as an effective barrier against the establishment of responsible government which was synonymous, to the average Hyderabadi Muslim, with Hindu Raj, because it would be based on the will of the Hindu majority. Muslim masses were generally slow to realize that their sufferings were the inevitable repercussions of

the atrocities committed on the Hindus only, a few days before, by the Razakars. The Razakars movement had the sympathy of a good number of Muslimans in Hyderabad. Such of them as dared publicly to oppose that madness paid heavily for their temerity, so much so that one of them fell before the bullet of an assassin. Like the Razakars the perpetrators of crimes against the Muslims encouraged the belief that they had the backing of the authorities...[30]

After spending about a decade in jail, in 1957, the Razakar leader Qasim Razvi was let go to Pakistan, where he sought and was given asylum. But India did not ban his Islamist organization, which today has a new avatar, the All India Majlis-e-Ittehadul-Muslimeen (AIMIM), led by an articulate conservative Muslim cleric with a telegenic face, Asaduddin Owaisi, who, as a member of the Lok Sabha from Hyderabad, plays the game of democracy deftly and swears by the Constitution as the best protector of Muslims in India. While most Indian Muslims have been reticent about Kashmir, Owaisi is outspokenly nationalist, calling Kashmir 'an issue of sovereignty of our country... I will oppose Prime Minister Narendra Modi till my last breath, but when it comes to the country, we support the government whichever party is in power.'[31]

Hyderabad, now the capital of the state of Telangana, is a high-tech cosmopolitan city with some of the top business schools and universities. The booming city is home to India's major IT companies and business enterprises. And with Hyderabadi Biryani and other Mughlai cuisine, the legacy of the nizam culture, Hyderabad is forever. Hyderabad was not destroyed just like that. It went through creative destruction.

HOW PAKISTAN TOOK THE WRONG BUS TO KASHMIR

Until 31 October 2019, when the state was split into two Union Territories, Ladakh and Jammu and Kashmir, after the Jammu and Kashmir Reorganization Act passed by the Parliament in August 2019, Jammu and Kashmir was the only state in India that had its own Constitution.[32] The state regulated its relations with the Indian Union through Article 370 of the Indian Constitution. The accession to India was not imposed upon the people of the state; nor upon its ruler, Maharaja Hari Singh, who could have chosen to accede to Pakistan, especially when the latter's hoards and well-armed tribal militia commanded by some of its best battle-hardened British trained officers had let loose the terror through infiltration, and ravaged and pillaged the state, and were almost knocking at the maharaja's palace in Srinagar in October 1947.[33] The constitution that the people of the state gave themselves was a voluntary act of union with India and embodied the secular values of the nation. It was because of their constitution that the people of Jammu and Kashmir played the game of democracy through multiparty alliances, political horse-trading and bargaining, indulging in violent as well as peaceful street protests and as a last resort knocking at the door of the Supreme Court of India, as do the rest of Indians.

The Preamble to the now-defunct Jammu and Kashmir Constitution was a transparent document and was a total rejection of the Muslim League's two-nation theory, in spite of the fact that the state had, and even today has, an overwhelming Muslim majority. Along with the Sikh majority state of Punjab and the Christian majority states including Nagaland, Mizoram and Meghalaya in the Northeast, Jammu and Kashmir as a Muslim majority state strengthened India's multireligious and multicultural secular democracy. As the Preamble declared:

> We, The People of The State of Jammu And Kashmir, having solemnly resolved, in pursuance of the accession of this state to India which took place on the twenty-sixth day of October 1947, to further define the existing relationship of the state with the union of India as an integral part thereof, and to secure to ourselves
>
> JUSTICE, social, economic and political;
>
> LIBERTY of thought, expression, belief, faith, and worship;

EQUALITY of status and of opportunity; and to promote among us all

FRATERNITY assuring the dignity of the individual and the unity of the nation;

IN OUR CONSTITUENT ASSEMBLY this seventeenth day of November, 1956, do HEREBY ADOPT, ENACT AND GIVE TO OURSELVES THIS CONSTITUTION.[34]

Unlike the post-war Japanese constitution, which was imposed on the nation by the United States and the Allies, the Jammu and Kashmir Constitution was created by the representatives of its own people. In spite of its special status, which no other Indian state had, and in spite of Pakistan-sponsored militancy, Jammu and Kashmir, more or less, synced with the Indian Union.

EARTHLY HEAVEN, TURBULENT HISTORY

Jammu and Kashmir has a fascinating history. Since 1846 the princely state of Jammu and Kashmir, which also included Ladakh in the northeast, bordering Tibet as well as Gilgit–Baltistan in the northwest bordering (now) China's Xinxiang Province, was ruled by a Rajput Dogra dynasty. The composite state was partly clubbed together by the East India Company, who, after the First Anglo–Sikh War in 1845–1846, annexed Kashmir from the Sikh rulers and transferred the territory to Raja Gulab Singh of Jammu under a subsidiary alliance arrangement that included an indemnity payment of 7.5 million rupees. As the hereditary ruler of Jammu, Gulab Singh's kingdom was a tributary of the Sikh Durbar, but after the East India Company transferred Kashmir to him, the maharaja as the ruler of Jammu and Kashmir acknowledged the paramountcy of the East India Company; and then after 1858, the British Crown.

The maharaja ruled over a vast and ruggedly beautiful region of valleys, lakes and mountains covering 85,806 square miles. From the southern plains and low hills of Jammu, there rises a range of mountains called the Pir Panjal that leads one to the Kashmir Valley drained by the Jhelum River. Through the uplands of Bhadarwah and Kishtwar runs the deeply gorged Chenab River. Further north and northwest are located Baltistan and Gilgit, while Ladakh sits on the eastern plateau between the Kunlun mountain range and the Himalayas. The Indus River originating from the Lake Mansarovar region in Tibet runs through Ladakh and onwards to Baltistan and Gilgit; and then to the south draining along with its tributaries the vast region of Pakistan before it merges with the Arabian Sea. Jammu and Kashmir sits under the awe-inspiring, majestic, protective shadow of the colossal mountain ranges from the Hindu Kush, the Palmir, the K2 (near the Godwin-Austen Glacier) and the Karakoram Range to the Kunlun Mountains and the Himalayas.[35] 'Gar firdaus bar-rue zamin ast, hami asto, hamin asto, hamin ast' (If there is a heaven on earth, it's here, it's here, it's here!), said the awestruck Mughal Emperor Jahangir when he visited Kashmir in the seventeenth century. And the Mughals loved Jammu and Kashmir.

Until 1947, Jammu and Kashmir had better transportation links with the southwest region, what became Pakistan, than with India. One could travel from Kohala near Murree to Leh in Ladakh; and also from Rawalpindi via Kohala to Muzaffarabad and Baramulla to Srinagar in Kashmir. It was through these multiple routes that Pakistan's tribal militias poured into the Kashmir Valley in October 1948.

In 1947, Jammu and Kashmir had a Muslim majority (more Sunnis than Shias) population of 76.4 per cent, Hindus 20.1 per cent, and Sikhs and Buddhists 3.49 per cent. Ethnically the population mix-up included Punjabis, Gujjars, Arains, Jats, Sudhans, Rajputs, Pandits, Tibetan-Mongolians and Dards. Over this motley population of disparate ethnicities, religions, languages and dialects, and cultures spread over the plains, the valleys and the mountains ruled the Hindu Maharaja Hari Singh who had led, by and large, a sheltered life under the tutelage of the British Crown.[36]

Like the nizam of Hyderabad and the nawab of Junagadh, Maharaja Hari Singh toyed with the idea of wanting Jammu and Kashmir to become an independent country, the political status that the state did not have under the British Crown, the Sikh rulers or the Mughals. To keep trade, transportation and communication links open for the landlocked state and maintain the status quo, the maharaja offered Standby Agreements to both India and Pakistan. Pakistan accepted the Standby Agreement expecting that Jammu and Kashmir being a Muslim majority state, would accede to Pakistan. India, on the other hand, refused to accept the Standby Agreement. Jammu & Kashmir National Conference (JKNC), a secular party in the image of the Indian National Conference, led by a popular leader Sheikh Mohammed Abdullah, wanted the state to join India. The maharaja's prime minister, Mehr Chand Mahajan, too advised the maharaja to accede to India.

In this environment of uncertainties and indecisiveness, Pakistan was hatching military plans to knock the state out of the royal hands of the maharaja. First of all, Pakistani irregulars called Gilgit Scouts, under the command of sympathetic British officers, staged a revolt in Gilgit and Baltistan, and the region was annexed by Pakistan. Soon after, Northwest Frontier tribals, mostly Pashtuns, Mehsuds and Afridis, from Pakistan's badlands—the same tribals who since then have been subjecting Pakistan and Afghanistan to lethal doses of Jihad—were let loose like bloody hounds into the Kashmir Valley. The maharaja cried for help from India; but Lord Mountbatten wouldn't budge unless the maharaja signed the Instrument of Accession, which he did on 26 October 1947. With the formal acceptance of the state accession by the Governor General of India Lord Mountbatten on 27 October 1947, Jammu and Kashmir became a part of India, and the state's defence became India's obligation.

In a short time, India called forth the best of its military and organizational forces, and liberated most of the territory and pushed back Pakistani hoards to what became known as Azad Kashmir. Under coercive persuasion from India, the maharaja released Sheikh Abdullah from jail, where he had been locked up for his opposition to the maharaja's rule, and appointed him as the state prime minister. Subsequently, the maharaja appointed his son Karan Singh as the prince regent until 1952, when the Constitution of India came into effect, and the Dominion of India became the Republic of India.[37]

WAR AND THE DRAMA OF ACCESSION

Within weeks of gaining Independence, Pakistan hatched a plan to launch a seemingly clever scheme of invading and annexing Jammu and Kashmir. That was the time when Indian leaders were busy settling millions of brutalized, ravaged, sick and hungry refugees who were pouring into India from East and West Pakistan while at the same time protecting the left behind vulnerable Muslims. As the top-secret strategic plan Operation Gulmarg was getting ready to be rolled out, perchance the blueprint fell into the hands of Major Onkar Singh Kalkat of the Bannu Brigade, a military cantonment in Pakistan's Northwest. Major Kalkat opened the envelope marked 'top secret' from Pakistan's British Commander-in-Chief General Frank Messervy addressed to the Brigade Commanding Officer C.P. Murray, who at that time was away.

Being a non-Muslim military officer, who should have gone to India along with other military officers, Major Kalkat came under suspicion for having seen the top-secret plan and was jailed; but he escaped and reached Delhi on 18 October 1947. When he told the story to his military bosses in the defence ministry, no one believed him until after the invasion had actually begun on 24 October.[38]

By the first week of September, as per Operation Gulmarg, 20 tribal militias, each with a strength of 1,000 tribesmen, were to be enlisted from various Pashtun tribes and made battle-ready at brigade headquarters at Bannu, Wanna, Peshawar, Kohat, Thall and Nowshera, with a timeline of reaching the launching pad at Abbottabad on 18 October and breaking into Jammu and Kashmir on 22 October 1947. With a pincer movement, ten militias were to attack through Muzaffarabad to advance to Kashmir Valley, a stronghold of Sheikh Abdullah's National Conference and another ten militias to advance to Poonch, a stronghold of the Muslim Conference, the town whose population was sympathetic with Pakistan, in order to advance to Jammu. The meticulously detailed plan of attack prepared by the British commanders of the Pakistan Army obviously had the approval and blessings of Pakistan's top leadership, including Prime Minister Liaquat Ali Khan and Governor General Mohammed Ali Jinnah.

By 1 October, the regiment, Prince Albert Victor's Own (PAVO) Cavalry, in charge of executing the military plan, with the South Wing based in Gujarat (a military cantonment in Pakistan), the North Wing based in Abbottabad and the Central Wing based in Rawalpindi had completed the task of arming and training the tribals.[39] With so much preparation going on in tribal areas for the recruitment, arming and mobilization of 20,000 militiamen, Pakistan's streets must have been abuzz with stories of something momentous happening. But the grapevine scuttlebutt did not reach India. And when Major Kalkat, who had stumbled upon the attack plan and escaped to India, wanted to brief his superiors, there was no one who would listen to him.[40]

Poonch, a principality of Jammu and Kashmir, offered Pakistan the most encouraging prospects because its restive population, mostly Muslim, felt closer to the neighbouring state of Punjab (Pakistan) than to the Muslims of Kashmir Valley under the influence of Sheikh Abdullah's secular National Conference Party. Poonch was also a major recruiting area for the British Army during World War II. When, after the war was over, Poonch soldiers returned home with their arms on their shoulders, the maharaja was alarmed and he ordered them to be disarmed.[41] With fewer job prospects for thousands of discharged soldiers and high taxes, the discontent roiled the people of Poonch and turned them into a rebellious militia, which, though soon crushed by the state troops, nonetheless frightened the maharaja.[42] He decided to reorganize his administration, and on 25 August 1947, he invited a pro-India jurist Justice Mehr Chand Mahajan of the Punjab High Court as prime minister. The Muslim Conference, the party that was committed to Pakistan, exploited the situation and accused the maharaja's troops of committing indiscriminate atrocities on innocent people, and in a message to Pakistan Prime Minister Liaquat Ali Khan, urged him to take action before it was too late.[43]

Pakistan wasted no time, and soon, essential supplies including petrol, sugar and salt for which Jammu and Kashmir depended upon Pakistan were cut off, apart from the suspension of train services to Jammu. In order to assess the political situation and the ground realities in Kashmir, Prime Minister Liaquat Ali Khan sent Mian Iftikharudin to Srinagar. On his return in September, he reported to the prime minister that the National Conference, under the leadership of Sheikh Abdullah, had an overwhelming following and influence in Kashmir and there was little prospect of fomenting a popular revolt in the Kashmir Valley. Nor was there any prospect of the maharaja succumbing to the economic and trade embargo and acceding to Pakistan. Armed invasion was the only choice. On 12 September, Pakistan prime minister, Liaquat Ali Khan met with Mian Iftikharudin, Colonel Akbar Khan and another Punjabi politician, Major Shaukat Hayat Khan, to consider Pakistan tribal supported 'popular uprising' against the maharaja. Because of his unwillingness to join Pakistan, there was no other choice except to mobilize the frontier tribes as liberators of their brethren in Kashmir.

With the simmering rebellion in Poonch and economic blockades, the maharaja was in desperate straits and once again asked Mehr Chand Mahajan to hasten his decision to assume the state's prime ministership, promising reforms and accession to India, which Prime Minister Nehru, however, would not accept unless the National Conference leader, Sheikh Abdullah, was released from prison and allowed to participate in the government.[44] Consequently, upon further negotiations, Sheikh Abdullah, a friend and admirer of Nehru, was released and received a rousing welcome in Kashmir Valley, where he was hailed the Lion of Kashmir. With Sheikh Abdullah's release, Jammu and Kashmir's accession to India became closer and war with Pakistan more imminent, even though Nehru declared, 'wherever there is a dispute in regard to any territory, the matter should be decided by a referendum or plebiscite of the people concerned. We shall accept the result of this referendum, whatever it may be.'[45]

But Pakistan was too impatient to wait for the referendum to test the will of the people of Jammu and Kashmir and punched a massive blow through Poonch around 3–4 October 1947, gaining control of the district and cornering and laying a choke on the maharaja's garrison.[46] By 8 October, the Mirpur district was captured by the rebel militia, which included deserters from the maharaja's army, World War II discharged servicemen, and some Pakistan soldiers on leave in that area.[47] The Pakistan Army supervised the entire operation, including radio communications. The Indian Army was deaf and blind to what was going on. It had neither the intelligence in Jammu and Kashmir nor in Pakistan, which was rather surprising.[48]

When the country was partitioned, the Indian Army, the Royal Indian Navy and the Royal Indian Air Force too were divided between the two dominions on a more or less religious basis. However, all the commanders-in-chief, including those of the Army, the Navy and the Air Force, three for each dominion, were British. Field Marshal Claude Auchinleck, the last Commander-in-Chief of undivided India, was appointed as the Supreme Commander for the purpose of completing the division of the Armed Forces. Consequently, when the British Commander-in-Chief of Pakistan Army Headquarters General Frank Messervy informed Field Marshal Auchinleck, the Supreme Commander, about the tribal raiders' advance towards Jammu and Kashmir, he must have passed on the information to Governor General Lord Mountbatten, Commander-in-Chief of the India Army Headquarters General Rob Lockhart, and the Government of India.[49] But no one was listening.

MAHARAJA PLEADS FOR HELP

On 24 October 1947, Srinagar was waking up in a festive mood, unselfconscious of what was happening on the state's western borders. The capital was getting ready for the annual gala celebration of Dusserah, the day of victory of good over evil, in the traditional pomp and glory of the royalty of Maharaja Hari Singh who, perhaps, hoped against hope that the approaching Pashtun militia, which had already overtaken Muzaffarabad and were knocking at Uri, would dissipate or would be thwarted by the counterattacks carried out by his brave Dogra soldiers. Perhaps chants and prayers of the priests and invocation to God would help; perhaps some miracle would occur as most Indians think when faced with deep crises. He had not made up his mind between Independence and India. It was time to hail Goddess Durga as the maharaja sat with the best of his jewels and regalia under a golden canopy in the brightly lit Durbar Hall, receiving homage from the state nobility. Suddenly, the entire Kashmir Valley went dark. The festivities in the Durbar Hall nonetheless continued as a standby generator kicked into power and relit the flickering chandeliers. The invading militia had knocked out the power plant at Mahura that supplied electricity to Srinagar. The gods did not help, but India could. When the maharaja got the message that the Pashtun militias were not far away, he sent an SOS to the Government of India asking for troops to save Kashmir.[50]

Due to the fact that the intelligence coming from Pakistan, official and unofficial, had gone unheeded, the tribal militia attack came as an unexpected development and caused tremendous consternation in Delhi. Lord Mountbatten wouldn't entertain the idea of sending British troops to the rescue of the maharaja as was recommended by Supreme Commander of the Joint Command, Field Marshal Claude Auchinleck, to whom both Indian and Pakistan Army commanders-in-chief reported. Governor General Mountbatten did not want British troops to be involved in the military conflict between two dominions, especially when the maharaja had asked for help from the Government of India without making any commitment regarding the state's accession. Lord Mountbatten demanded that the maharaja must sign the Instrument of Accession before Indian troops would be sent to fight back the invaders.[51] While the negotiations were going on, Indian troops were nonetheless put on alert.

Most shocking was the revelation during the Defence Council of India meeting to discuss the Kashmir situation that General Lockhart, the Commander-in-Chief of the Indian Army, had been informed by his counterpart the Commander-in-Chief of the Pakistan Army General Frank Messervy that Pakistan tribal militia had already captured Muzaffarabad and, furthermore, reinforced by troops from the Northwest Frontier tribal area, the invaders were heading towards Srinagar. Regardless of whether this was duplicity or stupidity, General Lockhart was directed to prepare for the military operation and issue deployment orders at short notice. It was a matter of moments before the Indian troops were to be landing in Srinagar. Since Maharaja Hari Singh had given up any hope of saving his kingdom on his own, he had agreed to sign the Instrument of Accession. On the advice of V.P. Menon—who, along with Sardar Patel, was the single most important shaker-and-maker of the princely state integration—the maharaja accompanied by his family along with precious family heirlooms, had packed up to move to Jammu, the summer capital of the state.

Brigadier Samir Bhattacharya, in his book, *Nothing But! Book Three: What Price Freedom* has given a fascinating narrative of the meeting between Prime Minister Mehr Chand Mahajan of Jammu and Kashmir, who was accompanied by V.P. Menon and Sheikh Abdullah, and Prime Minister Nehru, at his residence in Delhi the morning of 26 October 1947. After the formalities and pleasantries were over, Prime Minister Mahajan, who had already been advised by the maharaja to use his discretion, asked in desperation, 'Please give us the military forces we need. Take the accession and give whatever power you desire to the popular party, but the Indian Army must fly to save Srinagar today and by this evening or else I will go to Lahore and negotiate terms with Mr Jinnah.'[52] This outburst was too much for Nehru to bear, and he said angrily, 'If you favour an agreement with Pakistan then leave at once.' Sardar Patel and Sheikh Abdullah, who assured Nehru that his party, the National Conference, was in full support of the accession to India, brought the situation under control; and the consensus to send the troops was reached which the same morning was approved by the Cabinet.

However, Governor General Mountbatten, before he signed the Instrument of Accession, directed that as soon as Pakistan raiders were driven out of the state and normal conditions returned, the people of Jammu and Kashmir must approve the accession of the state to India. Menon and Mahajan flew back to Jammu to have the maharaja's signature on the Instrument that he had already approved. The maharaja had 'given specific instruction to his ADC that in case Mr Menon did not return, he should be shot with his own revolver while he was asleep because he knew by then everything would have been lost.'[53] The same evening V.P. Menon returned to Delhi with the Instrument of Accession, which was now fully and finally signed and ratified by both Maharaja Hari Singh and the Government of India. After a most contentious meeting of the Defence Council, with the legal force of the accession, albeit subject to the will of the people after normalcy returned as well as the full support of Sheikh Abdullah, the undisputed leader of the National Conference, Indian troops were ordered to beat back Pakistani raiders from Jammu and Kashmir.[54]

CRISIS PUSHES INDIA

In this moment of great crisis facing the newly independent nation, the Indian Armed Forces, enriched by their experience in many theatres of World War II, displayed some of the most imaginative, innovative and ingenious methods of fighting battles after battles until Pakistan Pathan tribals were driven out of the Kashmir Valley. Late at night on 26 October, Major S.K. Sinha, a staff officer, received orders from Army Commander Lieutenant General Dudley Russell to expeditiously dispatch a battalion by air to Srinagar using a combination of Air Force and civilian aircraft, and a brigade by road to Jammu.[55] The responsibility of carrying out the operation and leading the Sikh Regiment (1 Sikh) was conferred upon Commanding Officer Lieutenant Colonel Ranjit Rai. Brigadier J.C. Katoch's formation was responsible for operations in the Valley, while the Jammu Sector was under 50 Parachute Brigade commanded by Brigadier Paranjape. Rescue Kashmir, ordered Lieutenant General Russell with the instructions:

a) Secure Srinagar airport and civil aviation wireless station;
b) Take such action, as your first task and available troops allow, to:
   i.   Drive tribesmen away from Srinagar.
   ii. Aid the local government in the maintenance of law and order in Srinagar.[56]

It seemed that the lesser the instructions, the more innovative the commanders became because they planned en-route as they went along. The airlift of the military personnel to Srinagar coordinated and carried out by the Air Force, the Civil Aviation and the Army was exemplary. On 27 October 1947, Air Force and Civilian Aviation aircraft conducted twenty-eight flights carrying fully-equipped battle-ready soldiers, besides supplies, arms and ammunitions. By 10:00 a.m., the first wave of Indian troops was in Srinagar, and the operation to rescue Kashmir had begun. The airlift of troops, supplies and equipment continued flawlessly thanks to the superb coordination of operations conducted by not only the Air Force and the Army but also by the civilian pilots and the ground staff, which drew accolades from Lord Mountbatten, who wrote that '... in his war experience, he had never come across an airlift of this order being successfully undertaken with such slender resources, and at such short time'. [57]

Before the Indian forces could launch their operation on the battlefront, however, the Jammu and Kashmir State Forces' 4 Kashmir Infantry had suffered a setback when some of its troops defected to the invaders and threatened the safety of the road to Srinagar. But due to the extreme courage displayed by Brigadier Rajinder Singh, Commander-in-chief of the Jammu and Kashmir State Forces, his gallant men blew up the bridge and held back the invaders at Uri, thus delaying their march to Baramulla until 24 October. But once the Pakistan-Pathan invaders entered Baramulla, a city on the Jhelum River, they let loose their bloody thirst for lust and loot on the people of the city, heedless of whom they were raping and robbing, Muslims, Hindus, Christians or Sikhs. One such Kashmiri was Maqbool Sherwani, a 19-year old National Conference activist whose refusal to help the raiders led to his being tortured. He was nailed to a cross.

By this time, Lieutenant Colonel Ranjit Rai of 1 Sikh had advanced to Baramulla, where he discovered, to his shock, that the invaders were not a disorganized rabble but, in fact, they were well-armed men led by Pakistan military officers. Their well-planned pincer movements forced Lt. Col. Rai to retreat to Pattan, during which he was fatally wounded. But his men delayed the advancement of Pakistani troops, the valuable time during which Indian forces had gathered their strength to save the Valley. Lt. Col. Rai was the first commanding officer who died for Kashmir and India, and the grateful nation awarded him the Maha Vir Chakra (MVC). He was replaced by Major Harwant Singh, and under his command, 1 Sikh held fast and thwarted the invaders' efforts to get past the defences at Pattan (Baramulla), and by 2 November, the tide had begun to turn in the Indian forces' favour, thanks to the courageous performance of 1 Sikh.

According to military accounts, Jinnah was furious at the military setback, and he ordered Lt. General Douglas David Gracey, Chief of the Pakistan Army, to undertake an all-out invasion of Jammu and Kashmir, but the British General, with the backing of Field Marshal Auchinleck, refused to comply with his orders. Field Marshal Auchinleck explained to Jinnah the danger of such a move to the security of Pakistan, especially when Indian forces had already become well entrenched in the Valley. Besides, he threatened to withdraw 500 British officers from the Pakistan Army, which would cripple it.[58] Stupefied by the betrayal of the British generals, Jinnah rescinded his orders to General Gracey and decided not to commit regular Pakistan Army troops, hoping against hope that the Pakistan tribal militia would do the job. The failed operation prompted a Muslim League leader to say, 'Sir, we missed the bus.' To which the founder of Pakistan, the homeland for the Muslims of the Indian subcontinent, Quaid-e-Azam Jinnah quipped, 'No, sir, we got in the wrong bus.'[59]

Perhaps a Pakistani historian's assessment is more to the point:

Two tricks of fortune conspired to cheat the Quaid-I-Azam (Jinnah) of the Kashmir gaddi (throne); the loss of a day and a half in pillaging at Baramulla, and the reckless bravery of an Indian officer, who with no reserve of men or ammunition made an attack on the invading forces as if he had the whole Army Division at his disposal, dashed down the Baramulla road... He seized the airfield, delayed the raiders advance by 36 hours, and

> enabled reinforcements sent by air to reach Srinagar. He saved
> Kashmir though he gave his life in the effort.[60]

On 1 November, when the war was raging on fiercely between Pakistan-backed tribal militias and Indian Forces in the Kashmir Valley, Lord Mountbatten flew to Lahore to meet with Jinnah to find a way of ending the conflict between the two dominions. He proposed that in case of disputed accession of princely states including Jammu and Kashmir, Hyderabad and Junagadh, the accession should be decided by the will of the people determined impartially through a plebiscite. Jinnah's focus was on Jammu and Kashmir, and he accused India of grabbing the state accession through fraudulent means.[61] He wasn't sure that with Indian troops being in the Valley and Sheikh Abdullah and the National Conference supporting the accession to India, whether a plebiscite would make any sense. He insisted that since Kashmir had a Muslim majority, it should naturally accede to Pakistan and for which, therefore, he was willing to give up the claim on Junagadh. Jinnah also rejected Mountbatten's suggestion that a plebiscite could be conducted under the auspices of the UN. Jinnah was a tough and tenacious bargainer, but sometimes he overplayed his hand and lost, as in the case of Kashmir thinking wishfully that 'as the tribes were then in the ascendant, for the time being, he thought he would hold out a bit longer for better terms.'[62] In any case, the removal of Sheikh Abdullah, the most popular leader committed to secularism, from the politics of Jammu and Kashmir, as Jinnah demanded, would have been unacceptable to India.

After visiting Srinagar on 3 November 1947 to assess the military situation, Sardar Patel and Defence Minister Baldev Singh reported to the Defence Committee and recommended that the military strength be enhanced. Consequently, a separate Jammu and Kashmir Division was established under the command of Major General Kalwant Singh with instructions to repulse invaders from Baramulla and recapture the city—the gate to the Kashmir Valley. Major General Kalwant Singh couldn't wait. His forces recaptured Baramulla and when the troops entered the city, they were shocked.

It 'had been stripped by the tribesmen of its wealth and its women... The devastation by the raiders was indeed ghastly, reminiscent of Nadir Shah's sacking of Delhi. A number of foreign correspondents bore testimony to the arson and pillage, loot and rape which had been indulged in by the tribesmen in Baramula.' [63]

By 11 November, Indian troops had taken control of Uri, Tanmarg and Gulmarg without much resistance. While India and Pakistan, amidst increasing hatred and mutual recriminations, continued their on-and-off talks of settling the Kashmir issue by the will of the people as soon as peace prevailed and conditions were conducive to holding a plebiscite, fighting continued in the southern and northern regions of the state. Finally, Indian forces, after a yearlong siege, recaptured Poonch. While Gilgit and Baltistan remained under the occupation of Pakistan forces, Ladakh was secure for India. Both armies had reached their maximum level of competence or their level of incompetence, as the Peter Principle would say, and were no longer able to break into each other's held territories. With the occupation of one-third of the strategic northern area, Pakistan someday would open the door for China to reach the Arabian Sea and turn itself into a dependent client state, a form of twenty-first-century neo-colonialism.[64]

SEEKING UN INTERVENTION

When India had recovered most of Jammu and Kashmir from Pakistan-backed militia and further military action seemed unproductive, and negotiations between Mountbatten and Jinnah as well as between Nehru and Liaquat Ali had brought forth no results, India decided to take the issue to the UN. The United Nations Security Council (UNSC) set up the UN Commission for India and Pakistan (UNCIP), and on 21 April 1948, passed a resolution that called for an immediate ceasefire. It asked the Government of Pakistan 'to secure the withdrawal from the state of Jammu and Kashmir, of tribesmen and Pakistani nationals not normally resident therein who have entered the state for the purpose of fighting.' Furthermore, it asked the Government of India to reduce its armed forces to the minimum essential for maintaining the peace and law and order so that necessary conditions could be established for holding the plebiscite 'on the question of Accession of the state to India or Pakistan.'[65]

Ironically, it fell on the shoulders of two British Generals, Commander-in-Chief Douglas Gracey of Pakistan and Commander-in-Chief Roy Bucher of India, to sign the ceasefire agreement that came into effect on 1 January 1949. The ceasefire agreement, however, did not lead to any immediate reconciliation of the question because of the presence of Pakistani troops and the so-called Azad Kashmir Army, as well as the strength of Indian troops needed to keep the peace, among other procedural issues. After visiting the region and assessing the ground situation, the UNCIP reported to the Security Council in 1948 that in the present conditions, no plebiscite could be held. Only after the complete withdrawal of Pakistan troops and Pakistan nationals from the part of Jammu and Kashmir under Pakistan control, and the subsequent reduction of Indian troops to a reasonable level from the territory under its control, could a plebiscite be held. India's response was positive, but Pakistan huffed and puffed and 'attached to its acceptance so many reservations, qualifications and assumptions as to make its answer "tantamount to rejection".'[66]

India thought that it stood on a high legal and moral ground because since the state had already acceded to India, and the National Conference and Jammu and Kashmir's most popular leader Sheikh Abdullah had fully backed the accession, the holding of the plebiscite would affirm the existing actualities. Pakistan as the aggressor and in illegal possession of Indian Territory must cease its aggression. Pakistan argued that the people of Jammu and Kashmir had revolted against the maharaja who ran away from the capital and lost his authority, and therefore, Pakistan's assistance to the people was morally justified. Moreover, the maharaja had signed the Standstill Agreement with Pakistan, not with India, which was, of course, a poor excuse for invasion.

As time passed and negotiations dragged on, and none of the demilitarization proposals was acceptable to India and Pakistan,

India's original complaint against Pakistan's aggression became more of a dispute between two equal contending parties to be mediated by international powers, especially the US and the UK, who began to calculate their own interests in the emerging post-World War II Cold War scenario. Even Lord Mountbatten began to regret that the UN wasn't the impartial forum he thought it would be and protested to Prime Minister Clement Richard Attlee that he was 'convinced that this attitude of the US and the United Kingdom is completely wrong and will have far-reaching results. Any prestige I may previously have had with my Government (of India) has of course been largely lost by my having insisted that they should make a reference to the UN with the assurance that they would get a square deal there.'[67]

In 1950 the UNCIP appointed Sir Owen Dixon, an Australian jurist, to pursue the plebiscite plan based on its previous demilitarization proposal, but when he failed to achieve any agreement, he came up with his own scheme, the Dixon Plan. According to him, disparate people populated the state of Jammu and Kashmir, and therefore, a different approach was needed. Under this plan, the plebiscite should be limited to the Kashmir Valley. Azad Kashmir, Gilgit and Baltistan should go to Pakistan, while Jammu and Ladakh should remain with India. The plan included a neutral administration, which meant the Sheikh Abdullah administration would be put in suspended animation during the time the plebiscite was to be held in the Kashmir Valley. The plan also included the withdrawal of troops by both sides. This was an impractical scheme, which was rejected by India.[68] Dixon blamed India for its obduracy because he 'became convinced that India's agreement would never be obtained to demilitarisation in any such form, or to provisions governing the period of the plebiscite of any such character, as would in my opinion permit of the plebiscite being conducted in conditions sufficiently guarding against intimidation and other forms of influence and abuse by which the freedom and fairness of the plebiscite might be imperilled.'[69]

In two years of squabbling and haggling, with one peacemaking commission after another, the Government of India lost its faith in the UNSC's ability to bring about demilitarization and plebiscite on terms acceptable to it. India saw itself as the victim of Pakistan's aggression, for which it had taken the issue up with the UN. Neither the British Commonwealth proposal for plebiscite, including the stationing of a joint India–Pakistan force in Kashmir, nor the US–UK arbitration proposal was acceptable to India.[70]

Disappointed with the UN, India finally decided to take away the dispute from the international forum and asserted that the Jammu and Kashmir dispute was between two countries of the subcontinent and no third-party interference would be acceptable; nonetheless, maintaining that Pakistan was in illegal occupation of one-third of the state. This was the beginning of another phase of struggle with Pakistan. With the convening of the Constituent Assembly for Jammu and Kashmir in July 1950 and the successful passage of the state constitution in 1957, modelled on the secular democratic Indian Constitution, it seemed that Jammu and Kashmir had finally become an inseparable and integral part of India. Except that during this period, Sheikh Abdullah began to dream a different dream, a nightmare for India.

TEMPTATIONS AND TRIBULATIONS OF SHEIKH ABDULLAH

The most difficult thing in life is what to do with one's friends when they 'go to wrong hands,' said Nehru in desperation when he found that Sheikh Muhammad Abdullah, once-upon-a-time his friend and secularist-in-arms, was scheming to sever (the rest of) Jammu and Kashmir from India.[71] A part of Jammu and Kashmir, including Gilgit-Baltistan, which India was unable to liberate from Pakistan's tribal raiders in 1947, was under the occupation of Pakistan. Although the maharaja of Jammu and Kashmir had signed the Instrument of Accession to India, the majority Muslim population of the state was at best uncertain about its future with India. Looking at the history of India that led to Partition, it wouldn't have been difficult for a populist demagogue like Sheikh Abdullah to emotionalize and radicalize the Kashmiri Muslims to change their loyalty and opt for independence—not altogether a new idea because Maharaja Hari Singh too had for a long time nurtured such ambitions and had held back his state's accession decision until he found that Pakistan tribals were knocking at his palace gate. Just as anti-Indian forces, including Western as well as Chinese, were plotting with Angami Phizo to separate Nagaland from India, some foreign interests, especially Anglo-American, saw the geopolitical importance of Kashmir from their own global perspectives.[72] An independent Kashmir could become a Himalayan launching pad and watchtower for reconnaissance over the Eurasian communist landmass and South Asia. The Anglo-American-concocted witches' brew was too tantalizing for Sheikh Abdullah and he could not resist the temptation of being the ruler of Kashmir as an independent nation, an Asian version of Switzerland under the US–UK umbrella. The claim of Sheikh Abdullah seeking foreign collaboration primarily rests on limited but credible sources, especially the one, an interview with US ambassador Loy Henderson on 29 September 1950; and the other, a meeting with Adlai Stevenson II, former Democratic Illinois governor who had lost twice, in 1952 and 1956, to a World War II decorated general, Republican Dwight Eisenhower, in the US presidential election.

An Ivy League silver-tongued polished egghead, Stevenson visited Kashmir in the summer of 1953 and held long conversations with Sheikh Abdullah. Beguiled by Stevenson's disarming charms, Sheikh Abdullah was reported to have said that an overwhelming majority of Kashmiris wanted independence; they had their own culture and language; the Kashmiri Hindus were different from Indian Hindus and so were Kashmiri Muslims who were different from Pakistani Muslims; despite the state's Hindu minority, Kashmir was a homogenous state. Even some of Azad Kashmir's (Pakistan-controlled) leaders, he said, preferred an independent Kashmir.[73]

Either Sheikh Abdullah did not know the culture and demography of Jammu and Kashmir or he was being duplicitous with his conniving and sympathetic American listeners. The people of Jammu and Kashmir are no more homogenous than are the people of Uttar Pradesh or West Bengal, for example. The people of the Jammu region, constituting a Hindu majority speak Dogri, a dialect of Punjabi; the Ladakh region Buddhists speak a Tibetan dialect; a majority of Azad Kashmir people speak Punjabi/Saraiki dialects; Gilgit-Baltistanis speak Dardic, Tibetan and other Central Asian dialects; it's only the people of Kashmir Valley who speak the Kashmiri language, which the state has disowned in favour of Urdu. In 1975, Sheikh Abdullah and his entourage visited Ahmedabad, and during a meeting with local journalists, which I attended as the editor of a monthly magazine, *People's Times*, I asked him about the status of the Kashmiri language.

While Sheikh Abdullah kept close-mouthed, one of his companions, a Kashmiri journalist, said that Kashmiris spoke Urdu, which of course was not true. Sheikh Abdullah's statement that Jammu and Kashmir State was a homogenous state was a dangerous half-truth. The wily American politician Stevenson, who promised millions in aid once Kashmir became independent, outmatched Sheikh Abdullah's 'truthiness'.[74] In pursuit of the American Cold War diplomacy where 'Fair is foul, and foul is fair', Stevenson promised the gullible 'Lion of Kashmir' the moon and stars, that 'the Valley would have a permanent population of at least 5,000 American families...that within three years every village in Kashmir would be electrified and so on and so forth'.[75] Since there's no recorded evidence left for a historical review, the journalistic reporting needed to be taken with caution. Nonetheless, based on Sheikh Abdullah's several other public statements, it's fair to say that Macbeth had succumbed to the witches' temptations.

Just two years before he met with his American tempters and puppet-masters, Sheikh Abdullah, while addressing the Kashmir Constituent Assembly in 1951, had rejected the idea of a sovereign independent Kashmir as geopolitically absurd, and keeping in mind the lust of the Pakistani invaders, he warned his people that what happened in 1947 could happen again.[76] He wanted Jammu and Kashmir to be part of India and yet keep its autonomous status with its own flag and political nomenclature such as prime minister instead of chief minister, and with limited control over its sovereignty.

But this separate-but-together status under the domination of the National Conference was not acceptable to the Hindus of

Jammu and Kashmir, represented by the Jammu Praja Parishad, who insisted upon complete integration of the state with India. Balraj Madhok, Prem Nath Dogra, Hari Wazir and others, who were earlier associated with the RSS, an ultra-nationalistic organization, founded the Jammu Praja Parishad in 1947. The Parishad turned out to be an albatross around Sheikh Abdullah's neck and the undoing of his subliminal dream of making Jammu and Kashmir an independent nation. In order to suppress the Parishad-led agitation for complete integration of the state with India, Sheikh Abdullah's National Conference government incarcerated hundreds of Parishad members, including its top leaders, who were, however, let go after the intervention of Congress leaders. During the Jammu and Kashmir Constituent Assembly elections in 1951, fearing that the National Conference would rig the election outcomes, the Parishad, many of whose candidates were rejected on minor technicalities, withdrew from the elections, thereby giving the National Conference a total victory, without any opposition.[77]

Sheikh Abdullah failed to realize that Indians play the game of democracy not only in legislative assemblies but also on city streets. The National Conference under the 1952 Nehru–Sheikh Delhi Agreement had won much greater autonomy than the Indian Constitution had accorded to any other state of the Indian Union.[78] The Jammu Praja Parishad's demand for total integration of the state with India was encompassed in the slogan: *'Ek vidhan, ek nishan, ek pradhan* [One Constitution, One Flag, One Prime Minister, for the whole country]'.[79] When on 15 January 1952, students sympathetic with the Parishad protested against the state flag being hoisted along with the national flag, they were harassed, arrested and expelled from their colleges. A few weeks later, a 72-hour curfew was imposed in order to control the ongoing agitation during which several Parishad leaders were also arrested.

Central intervention quietened the streets of Jammu for some time, but the muffled voices that Sheikh Abdullah was not sincere in his commitment to India became louder and louder, especially when on 10 April 1952, during a public address at Ranbirsinghpura, he questioned the rationality of the state joining India terming it immature and unrealistic, and that Kashmir should wait until such time that 'we are satisfied that the grave of communalism has been finally dug…of that we are not sure yet.'[80] What would happen to his people, the Kashmiris, the Kashmiri Muslims, he asked, if Jawaharlal Nehru passed away? If there was any doubt about his intention of splitting from India, he made it clearer on 13 July 1953 when he said in a public meeting that, 'Kashmir should have the sympathy of both India and Pakistan… It is not necessary for our state to become an appendage of either India or Pakistan.'[81]

While Sheikh Abdullah's mind was being preyed upon by foreign carpetbaggers and goodwill hunters, some advocating that Kashmir would be better off being independent, others convinced that the state's natural and cultural affinity lay with Pakistan, there entered another firebrand politician into the Kashmir fray, Syama Prasad Mookerjee, the founder of the Bharatiya Jana Sangh.

Born in 1901, Mookerjee came from a distinguished intellectual family of Bengal. Like his father, Syama Prasad Mookerjee was a jurist, having studied law at Lincoln's Inn where he was called to the Bar, and at the young age of 33, he was appointed the vice-chancellor of Calcutta University. From the very beginning of his chequered political career, he had been associated with Hindu national organizations such as the Hindu Mahasabha and the RSS. In 1952 with the encouragement and support of M.S. Golwalkar, the leader of the RSS, Dr Mookerjee founded the Bharatiya Jana Sangh, the progenitor of the modern-day BJP that rules India under Prime Minister Narendra Modi.[82]

Espousing the cause of the Jammu Praja Parishad, one nation under the constitution, Mookerjee raised the issue in the Lok Sabha attacking the impotence of the government in dealing with the challenge of Sheikh Abdullah's dubiousness and deviousness regarding Kashmir's integration with India. When the government declined to negotiate with the Parishad's leaders unless they gave up the agitation, Mookerjee decided to give the movement greater visibility by extending the agitation to the streets of Delhi, in which he was joined by the volunteers of the Jana Sangh and other sectarian parties including the Hindu Mahasabha and the Ram Rajya Parishad.

The Jammu and Kashmir issue was too important to be left between Nehru and Abdullah, or to the Jammu and Kashmir Constituent Assembly, or at the floor of Parliament. Hundreds of protesters shouting slogans were arrested for defying the prohibitory orders, but they did not go unnoticed. The message had a national appeal regardless of the ideology of the messenger. Indian secularists and constitutionalists have contempt for Hindu national parties and street democracy in spite of the fact that they have played a big role in developing India's political culture. Indians play the game of democracy at several levels, any which way they can: through massive election participation; parliamentary debates and no-confidence motions; coalition forming and horse-trading; hartals, bandhs and dharnas; fast-unto-death; and finally, when nothing else works, they knock at the doors of the Supreme Court of India with a PIL.

Like most Indians, Mookerjee thought that Article 370 and Article 35A, which inter alia, barred Indians from buying properties and settling down in Jammu and Kashmir, posed a serious threat to national unity and demanded its annulment. Fearing trouble, the Jammu and Kashmir government issued a prohibitory order against Dr Mookerjee entering the state, which he defied on 11 May 1953. As he entered the state en route to Srinagar, he was arrested and jailed. Within the next few weeks, his health took a sudden downturn, and he was diagnosed with pleurisy, a disease characterized by the inflammation of lungs, chest pain, etc. On 22 June 1953, he suffered a severe heart attack and died the next day, in what some considered to be under mysterious circumstances.[83] His body was flown to his hometown Calcutta, where his funeral received the send-off of a great national hero.

Mookerjee's death did not help the already inflammatory situation prevalent in Jammu and the rest of India, especially because there was a widespread suspicion that the Jana Sangh leader was done in by foul methods. This was, however, a most opportune time for Sheikh Abdullah, who could have joined forces with Jawaharlal Nehru in condemning religious communalism and strengthening the forces of secularism, but he turned away from his friend, and in fact, refused to meet with him in Delhi when Nehru asked him to do so. Sheikh Abdullah had the illusion that not only the entire Kashmir Valley but also the J&K cabinet would be with him when he, which meant Kashmir, would say a final goodbye to India as he told a National Conference workers' meeting on 10 July 1953 at Mujahid Manzil in Srinagar.[84] But before Sheikh Abdullah could do anything outrageous, destroy everything that Nehru stood for—the unity and integrity of India above all—and cause political havoc in the country, it was ethically justified and politically imperative, as Shakespeare's Flavius would say, 'These growing feathers plucked from Caesar's wing/Will make him fly an ordinary pitch...'

Sheikh Abdullah would be safer under house arrest rather than as a footloose politician mouthing political absurdities and spreading conspiracies of 'servile fearfulness,' and bondage with India. At a higher level, political ethics mean choosing the lesser evil. Sheikh Abdullah was out of touch with reality. His cabinet was divided. The people of the state were divided. The head of the state, Sadre-i-Riasat Karan Singh, the son of the former maharaja, was against him.[85] Like many Indian leaders, religious and secular, believing in the power of magical thinking, Sheikh Abdullah counted on the power of his rhetoric that when he would declare independence purported to be on 21 August 1953, Anglo-American carpetbaggers and bounty hunters would come to his rescue. No, they didn't. It was Bakshi Ghulam Mohammed, the deputy prime minister of Jammu and Kashmir and his cohort who accused him of corruption and divisiveness, and they had a ready and willing listener, the state governor, Sadr-i-Riasat Karan Singh, who summarily dismissed Prime Minister Sheikh Abdullah of Jammu and Kashmir on 9 August 1953 on the ground that he had lost the confidence of his cabinet.

And Sadr-i-Riasat Karan Singh invited Bakshi Ghulam Mohammad to form the government. To let the 'Lion of Kashmir' go free in the Kashmir Valley would have been suicidal, and therefore, he was caged and consigned for the next 11 years to a comfortable house arrest for his own safety as well as for the safety of the newly formed government of Bakshi Ghulam Mohammad. It's unthinkable that Sadr-i-Riasat Karan Singh would have taken such a colossal step and acted alone without the full support of Nehru, who, being a cautious man, wouldn't have taken the internationally fraught decision without the unquestionable and reliable intelligence provided by the Intelligence Bureau (IB) and the full support of his cabinet. Putting his misguided and once-upon-a-time trusted friend in jail was one of the most humane and ethical political decisions Jawaharlal Nehru ever took. An independent Kashmir would have been invaded by Pakistan as it was in 1947; or eaten piecemeal by China; or, if left alone, would have become another Syria or Yemen. In any case, Jammu and Kashmir had no greater claim to independence than Nagaland, Mizoram, Khalistan or Dravida Tamil Nadu. Kashmiri Muslims were no different from Hyderabadi, Bengali or Gujarati Muslims.

Bakshi Ghulam Mohammad was no political saint, but he accepted the political actualities and worked within the federal-parliamentary system without giving up Jammu and Kashmir's special status under Article 370 of the Constitution. On 5 October 1953, the state legislative assembly passed a unanimous vote of confidence in Bakshi as well as the dismissal of Sheikh Abdullah as the prime minister of Jammu and Kashmir. During the vote of confidence motion, Bakshi said that some members of the National Conference had repudiated what the party stood for and 'went to the length of openly advocating positive alternatives for the creation of an "independent valley" of Kashmir from the debris of a state shattered to pieces... So we decided to part from our colleagues as their approach and attitude was clearly inimical to the freedom and progress of the state...we sent a memorandum to Prime Minister Sheikh Abdullah...our considered opinion that under these conditions the government as constituted then could not be efficient or effective in handling the affairs of the state.'[86]

Having assumed power as the prime minister of Jammu and Kashmir as well as the National Conference president, the most important job for Bakshi was to assure India that the state's accession to India was final and absolute. On 15 February 1954, the state constituent assembly members (64 out of 75 present) unanimously voted to ratify the state's accession to India. Sheikh Abdullah in jail must have waited for some deus ex machina or a miracle to change his destiny. On 26 January 1957, the Jammu and Kashmir Constitution came into force with an explicit provision vide Part II, Article 3 stating, 'The State of Jammu and Kashmir is and shall be an integral part of the Union of India.' This provision cannot be tampered with or legally amended per the provisions of Part XII Article 147 of the Jammu and Kashmir Constitution.[87] Bakshi stated amidst cheers, 'We are today taking the decision of final and irrevocable accession to India, and no power on earth could change it.'[88]

Bakshi Ghulam Mohammad was not a flamboyant political personality, nor did he have the charisma of Sheikh Abdullah. Nonetheless, Jammu and Kashmir kept pace with the rest of India in economic development during his tenure as the state premier. He made education free from kindergarten through to university. The number of school-going children increased from 64,000 to 234,000. By 1963, women's educational institutions increased from 181 to 653 and their enrolment from 14,488 to 63,306. With the increase in technical education, the state's technical manpower increased from a mere 72 in 1953 to 4,770 by 1963. The number of hospital beds rose from 600 to more than 3,000. More than thirty thousand displaced refugee families from Pakistan-occupied areas were resettled. It was during the Bakshi regime that the Jawahar Tunnel was constructed at the cost of over ₹30 million to provide a permanent strategic and commercial roadway between the Kashmir Valley and the rest of India.[89]

But at the end of the Bakshi regime, an extraordinary event happened in the Kashmiri Valley. On 27 December 1963, the Moi-e-Muqqadas, the hair of the Prophet Muhammad, was found missing from the Hazratbal Mosque in Srinagar. In 1947 when Pakistani tribal invaders carried out death and destruction in the Valley, Kashmiris were defended by the might of the Indian Armed Forces. In 1953, when Prime Minister Sheikh Abdullah was fired unceremoniously and jailed, Kashmiris took it stoically by and large. But the disappearance of the Prophet's hair from the shrine provoked volcanic outrage, for which the government was totally unprepared. B.N. Mullik, director of the Intelligence Bureau, gave the following account:

> What I saw in the town was something which I had never seen before 35 years of executive service dealing with law and order. Everything was closed: offices, schools, shops, cinemas, restaurants. Langers (eating places) had been set up at various places in the town. Large crowds were coming from villages, carrying food, bedding and even fuel for warming their bodies. There was no end to the stream of people and the smallest procession was at least a mile long covering the entire width of the road including the footpaths.[90]

The relic did not belong only to Kashmiri Muslims. It was part of the Islamic sacred heritage. The Muslim world was shaken up. There was a communal flare-up in East Pakistan targeting the minority Hindu community, which led to the exodus of hundreds of thousands of Hindus to India. There were communal riots in Calcutta, and it was feared that the communal fire might spread to the rest of India. On 4 January 1964, the holy relic mysteriously reappeared in the shrine, which raised questions including whether the recovered holy relic was authentic and secondly, who did it? Home Minister Gulzarilal Nanda said that three Kashmiri Muslims, one of them suspected to have links with Pakistan, were arrested, while others involved with the disappearance would be named later.[91] While the question of crime and punishment receded into the background, establishing the genuineness of the holy relic was of utmost importance. Lal Bahadur Shastri, who had stepped down from his ministerial position under the Kamaraj Plan, was called back to the Nehru Cabinet as a minister without portfolio, and he took charge of the holy relic's authentication. A highly regarded and most trusted politician, Shastri went to Srinagar and confabulated with the state officials and politicians; and set up a panel of clerics who vouchsafed that the holy relic indeed was the hair of the Prophet Muhammad. The Valley regained peace. Ghulam Mohammed Sadiq, the newly appointed state prime minister (the title was changed to chief minister after 1965 in keeping with other Indian states' heads of government), was more committed to India than any other Kashmiri politician.

RETURN OF THE SHEIKH

Would there be lasting peace in Jammu and Kashmir without Sheikh Abdullah, who was in jail and undergoing trial for the Kashmir Conspiracy Case? The ignominious defeat in the 1962 Himalayan war, the explosive event of the holy relic's sudden disappearance-reappearance, and perhaps his failing health after the stroke might have persuaded Jawaharlal Nehru to think again about Sheikh Abdullah. After much deliberation with Jammu and Kashmir Prime Minister Sadiq and other leaders, Nehru, cautiously hopeful that Abdullah might behave better outside jail, set him free on 8 April 1964, dropping the Kashmir Conspiracy Case.[92] Thousands and thousands of frenzied people lined the beautifully decorated streets of Srinagar to see their much sinned against hero Sheikh Abdullah coming home from the Jammu house-arrest where he had spent 11 years.

Wherever Abdullah went, he talked about the wishes of the Kashmiri people and their right to self-determination, as if accession had never taken place, which alarmed not only many members of the Congress party but also everyone else on the right and the left, the Jana Sangh and the Communist Party. Only the socialist leader Jayaprakash Narayan and the Swatantra Party leader C. Rajagopalachari, in spite of their differences with Nehru on other issues, believed that given enough goodwill, Abdullah might bring about lasting peace not only in Kashmir but also between India and Pakistan.

In spite of the open hostility expressed by the Jana Sangh demanding that Article 370, which confers special status on Jammu and Kashmir, be abrogated and other Indian politicians demanding that the Lion of Kashmir be caged again, Abdullah remained unperturbed and imperturbable. It was remarkable that while in his public persona at least, he showed no rancour despite years of homey incarceration, but at the same time, he also seemed unpersuaded that Kashmir's final destiny had already been determined and that it was with India. Apart from his five-day stay at the prime minister's residence at Teen Murti and long conversation with Nehru, Abdullah also met with several Congress and opposition party leaders, including Jayaprakash Narayan as well as Rajagopalachari; the latter believing that greater autonomy or perhaps joint sovereignty between India and Pakistan over Kashmir might be the solution.

When Sheikh Abdullah visited Pakistan on 24 May 1964 at the invitation of President Ayub Khan, the army general who had seized power in 1958, he was apparently going as a peacemaker between the two nations with several proposals that he had already discussed with Indian leaders. But Abdullah never took his eyes off the prize for which he had spent 11 years in jail: an independent Kashmir Valley whose sovereignty would be guaranteed by both nations. Pakistan would keep what it had conquered: Azad Kashmir along with Gilgit-Baltistan, and India with Jammu and Ladakh. With the warm and rousing public receptions he received in Pakistan's national capital, Rawalpindi, and the two days of successful meetings with President Ayub Khan, the sheikh was brimming with optimism. The Pakistani president agreed to a meeting with Jawaharlal Nehru in Delhi in June. There was no joint statement of their meeting, but *Dawn*, a newspaper that was the voice of the authoritarian Ayub government, scolded Abdullah for being beguiled by the superficiality and pretentiousness of Indian secularism and being oblivious to the miserable plight of 60 million Muslims.[93] After his upbeat meetings with President Ayub Khan, Abdullah went to visit Muzaffarabad, the capital of Azad Kashmir, the Pakistani-occupied sliver of Kashmir, when he received a bolt from the blue: Jawaharlal Nehru was dead. Sheikh Abdullah cried. And so did millions of Indians on 27 May 1964.

SARDAR VALLABHBHAI PATEL: THE ROCK THAT INDIA LEANED ON

Christians believe that Jesus Christ was crucified because of the sins of humanity; and surprisingly, in a similar tone and mode of thought, Sardar Patel, on the death of Mahatma Gandhi, said on All India Radio that, 'the greatest man of the world has had to pay with his life for the sins which we have committed. We did not follow him when he was alive; let us at least follow his steps when he is dead.'[94] But two of the greatest statesmen of the era, who had laid the foundation of democratic India, Sardar Patel and Nehru, were also at odds with each other on several issues; and on many occasions, Mahatma Gandhi had to make peace between them. Gandhi's assassination brought them together and a few days after his death, in a spirit of genuine reconciliation, Jawaharlal Nehru wrote to Sardar Patel: 'With Bapu's death everything is changed... I have been greatly distressed by the persistence of whispers and rumours about you and me, magnifying out of all proportion any difference we may have.' To which Sardar Patel responded with utter sincerity: 'We both have been lifelong comrades in a common cause. The paramount interests of our country and our mutual love and regard, transcending such differences of outlook and temperament as existed, have held us together.' In spite of policy and temperamental differences, Sardar Patel never challenged Nehru's leadership. Addressing the Congress party in the Constituent Assembly, Sardar Patel said: 'I am one with the Prime Minister on all national issues. For over a quarter of a century, both of us sat at the feet of our master and struggled together for the freedom of India. It is unthinkable today, when the Mahatma is no more, that we should quarrel.'[95]

It is a tribute to Sardar Patel's greatness and his enduring legacy as a political leader and builder-integrationist of India that today, even the BJP considers him as one of its own. It's partly because Sardar Patel's high-order patriotism—India first and foremost—appeals to the BJP's nationalism, though Sardar Patel had nothing to do with the BJP's Hindutva ideology. Sardar Patel was a supreme nationalist and he wanted people to forgo their emotional attachments and affiliations with recalcitrant ideologies that had divided India. In April 1947, when he was the home minister in the interim government, Sardar Patel visited his home state Gujarat where a Hindu–Muslim communal flare-up had occurred. Asking people to maintain peace, in one of his meetings in Ahmedabad, he expressed his fear of India relapsing into old grooves:

> A snake grows a new skin to take place of the worn out one it sheds... We may become politically sovereign, but internally we lack the attributes of a free people, such as equality, cohesion and national character... Has India organised a new state and society to replace the old order which she wants to discard?[96]

Sardar Patel was a son of the soil, the hardscrabble soil of Gujarat, of the down-to-earth hardworking, pragmatic Patidar community, the people who are mostly agriculturists and merchants and are now becoming increasingly professionals and industrialists. Even those members of the Patel community who have emigrated abroad have never forgotten their traditional roots, their Patidar culture.

Sardar Patel was unencumbered with the British cultural finesse and the political baggage of Jawaharlal Nehru, though he too had gone to London and studied law at the Middle Temple Inn. And after returning to India, he settled as a successful barrister in Ahmedabad. But very soon, Sardar Patel washed his hands off of the remnants of the Englishness and in October 1917 he joined Mahatma Gandhi for the struggle for India's Independence.[97] From then on, the INC became Sardar Patel's entire life. His dedication to the cause of freedom transcended everything else and drew the best out of him as a community organizer, grassroots party builder, negotiator and political leader, nonetheless, all along committed to and practising Mahatma Gandhi's non-violence doctrine. As the American theologian-philosopher Reinhold Niebuhr said, 'God grant me the serenity to accept the things I cannot change, the courage to change the things I can, and the wisdom to know the difference.' That was Sardar Patel's attitude towards the emerging political realities in India regarding the Cabinet Mission Plan of an Independent India as a loose federation with a weak Centre and autonomous provinces. He persuaded the Congress Working Committee and its leadership to accept the proposal and form the government headed by Jawaharlal Nehru. But when the Muslim League, under Mohammed Ali Jinnah's leadership, launched the Direct Action Day for Pakistan on 16 August 1946 that let loose massive communal violence, Sardar Patel finally grasped the painful reality that a united India was not possible, that a majority of Indian Muslims were with Jinnah who was their sole spokesman.[98]

A feeble central government would weaken and fragment India further, keeping in mind that many princely states wanted independence.[99] There was no choice but to accept the partition of India as the price of freedom. Despite Mahatma Gandhi's rejection, the Congress Working Committee accepted Lord Mountbatten's Partition Plan. At the All-India Congress Committee meeting that was called to approve the Partition Plan, Sardar Patel explained that his nine months in the government as the home minister under the Cabinet Mission had completely disheartened him. 'Whether we like it or not,' he said, 'de facto Pakistan already exists in the Punjab and Bengal... I would prefer a de jure Pakistan, which may make the League more responsible. Freedom is coming. We have 75 to 80 per cent of India, which we can make strong with our own genius. The League can develop the rest of the country.'[100]

For the next three years, until his death on 15 December 1950, Sardar Patel faced some of the toughest and most challenging tasks he had ever undertaken: Stopping the Hindu–Muslim communal violence; the division of public assets and Armed Forces personnel between India and Pakistan; reconstituting the civil and law enforcement services as the Indian Administrative Service and the Indian Police Service; reorganizing the bureaucracy and setting up the government of Independent India under Prime Minister Jawaharlal Nehru; supervising the two-way migration of 14 million refugees between India and Pakistan; the resettlement of about seven million Sikh and Hindu refugees—bitter, homeless and brutalized—who were pouring in from both East and West Pakistan; and most of all the integration of 565 princely states with India.

Making India whole again through the integration of the princely states, which Sardar Patel—along with one of India's shrewdest and most capable political officers, V.P. Menon—accomplished by using all the available means of persuasion, diplomacy, rewards, coercion, and force whenever necessary, was his greatest service to India. Sardar Vallabhbhai Patel shaped India for Jawaharlal Nehru to build the India of his dreams: secular, democratic and global in outlook. On 18 December 1950, in one of his customary letters to state chief ministers, Nehru wrote a brief eulogy for his comrade-in-arms for the freedom of India:

> Three days ago, when I should have normally written to you this letter, a heavy blow fell upon all of us and upon India [Vallabhbhai Patel died on 15 December 1950]. We shall take a long time to recover from it and, even so, there will always be a sense of emptiness for those who had the privilege of knowing and working with Sardar Vallabhbhai Patel. The great ones pass, the warriors who led us in our struggle depart, and we all feel somewhat lonely and desolate. On those who remain, the burden and responsibility grow heavier. Sardar Patel was a strange mixture of single-mindedness in the pursuit of his objectives and many-sided activities. On all these activities, he has left his powerful impress, and both the central government and every state government have felt, during these three or four years, the mark of a strong and guiding hand. So, in your work, you will miss him as we will miss him from day to day in our work at the Centre. You will have to do without him, for there is no one to take his place.[101]

4

INDIA MARCHES WITH NEHRU

The entire world today is a huge question mark and a challenge... Perhaps it is true that a nation can only truly advance if it has to go through the fire from time to time.

—Jawaharlal Nehru to his chief ministers

Sometimes a film captures the truth and zeitgeist of the age more than a long historical account, as was the case with Bimal Roy's 1953 classic, *Do Bigha Zamin*. Shambu Mahato ekes out subsistence out of a parched piece of land that stands in the middle of land owned by a local landlord Thakur Harnam Singh, who plans to construct a mill on it. Thakur wants to buy Shambu's small parcel in exchange for the debt that the farmer has not paid back, but Shambu refuses.

He loses the case in court and is asked to pay back the amount in three months. Shambu goes to Calcutta to earn money to pay back the loan and get his land back from the landlord. After a series of misadventures in Calcutta, Shambu returns home only to find that since he had not paid back his debt, the land had been auctioned, and a factory is being set up on the piece of land he once owned. Shambu tries to scoop a handful of dirt from the land, but the security guard drives him out.[1]

Behind the heart-wrenching emotional drama of a debt-ridden subsistence farmer, there is the rise of new India: of factories that would need the land as much as the farmers did. Shambu had no one to help him to save his itsy-bitsy debt-ridden farmland, and in desperation, he tries his luck in the big city as millions more would try in the future. A half-century later, the CPI-M-led Left Front government of West Bengal, with Chief Minister Buddhadeb Bhattacharjee at its helm, resurrected the 1894 Land Acquisition Act to implement an eminent domain takeover of 997 acres of farmland in Singur to enable Tata Motors to build its factory for Nano cars.[2]

The unwilling displaced farmers, more than 9,000 of them, were supported by West Bengal's feisty and charismatic opposition leader Mamata Banerjee of the Trinamool Congress party. Under the 'Save Farmland' movement, Tata Motors was not only compelled to scuttle its project and move it to Gujarat, but more importantly for democracy, it also brought an end to the 34-year-long suffocating rule of the Communist Party in West Bengal. That's how India plays the game of democracy. In 1953, the fictional Shambu Mahato took his misfortune as his inevitable fate, his karma. But that had begun to change.

At the beginning of Independence, India was striving to become a nation hell-bent on giving up fatalism, an attitude of resignation; that people were powerless to do anything other than what they had been doing, that it's all in their stars, their immutable destiny. The long-drawn struggle for freedom from the early times to the Gandhi–Nehru era had started changing the fatalistic outlook of the people. There was great big hope in the heart of every Indian that events could be changed for the better if the nation as a whole worked hard. In fact, there was no choice. The only way the country could become really independent and have a place as a respectable nation in the world was to grow the economy and lift India out of abject poverty, massive illiteracy and abysmally low life expectancy.

At the time of Independence, 75 per cent of the population of India lived in villages, most of whom, like Shambu Mahato, were very, very poor. Agriculture contributed up to 60 per cent to the gross domestic product (GDP). Industry accounted for very little. The farmer was the backbone of the country, but the backbone was bent and weak due to centuries of oppression. Agricultural practices were primitive and unscientific, and consequently, productivity was low and crops that varied from region to region were of poor quality. Farmers grew their crops as they had been doing for centuries. In a manner of speaking, villages were self-sufficient, as self-sufficient as a homeless man living on a sidewalk, at the level of tolerable misery. Village life was also ridden with caste prejudices and superstition. Caste and fatalism were the two ruling visible forces in rural India. This unbroken centuries-old tradition was the biggest burden India faced. Food was scarce. Indians were physically emaciated. The biggest challenge was how to improve the agricultural practices of rural families that had no other opportunities except what they got from their hardscrabble lands, fragmented landholdings that always looked up to the skies for the mercy and bounty of the seasonal rainfall. Most of the agriculture in India depended upon the monsoon, which was uncertain and there was always drought in some region or the other of the country. Moreover, the pattern of ownership of land by the few deprived most of the rural people of their motivational stake in the system, creating a helpless dependency system. Landownership and property rights, instead of incentivizing innovation and prosperity, became a tyrannical stranglehold.

To solve this problem, India needed to be rapidly industrialized. Although agriculture and industrialization have a symbiotic relationship, industrialization on its own was an important aspect of economic growth, and therefore, the question was which industrial model should India adopt for its rapid growth? There was no advanced country in the world at that time, as it is even today, where the government did not play a significant role in the economy. In the Soviet Union, the state controlled all aspects of the economy. In the US, although by and large the government kept away from running the industry and business directly, all major infrastructural projects, highways, railroads and dams were either carried out or financed by the government. European countries followed mixed economy models. The Soviet Union model was based on centralized planning, which was very attractive to the Indian intelligentsia and political leaders, especially in the Congress party, albeit they disliked the authoritarianism associated with it.

By the time of Independence, a broad consensus had developed in the country that the state was indispensable to socio-economic development. Without government involvement in agricultural development and industrialization, it would be impossible to pull the country out of deep poverty, a legacy of two centuries of British colonialism, negligence and exploitation. Economic progress for the whole nation through central planning became a political necessity and a pillar of the Indian democracy. It was realized that the social justice goals of the Constitution embodied in the Directive Principles of State Policy could be achieved only through central planning, which would inevitably involve the participation of people in every walk of life. Nehru believed that when people cooperated to achieve collective and shared goals, they would transcend narrow-minded provincialism, communalism, casteism, separatism and all other disintegrating forces that threatened India.[3] National integration through central planning was a bold new political idea.

On 15 March 1950, the Government of India set up the Planning Commission, which, chaired by Nehru, included senior cabinet members, top civil servants and experts.[4] This was not a sudden development because in 1938, INC, under the presidency of Subhash Chandra Bose, had established the National Planning Committee, but due to the interruption by World War II and other political developments, the Planning Committee went into abeyance. The idea was revived in 1949 when the Government of India decided to establish the Planning Commission for the overall development of the Indian economy with a new sense of urgency linking it with the Directive Principles of State Policy of the Indian Constitution that enjoined:

> The state shall strive to promote the welfare of the people by securing and protecting as effectively as it may a social order in which justice, social, economic and political, shall inform all the institutions of the national life and shall direct its policy towards securing, among other things, (a) that the citizens, men and women, equally, have the right to an adequate means of livelihood; (b) that the ownership and control of the material resources of the community are so distributed as best to subserve the common good; and (c) that the operation

of the economic system does not result in the concentration of wealth and means of production to the common detriment.

Apart from the constitutional imperatives of equitable social and economic justice, it had become necessary that:

> With the integration of the former Indian States with the rest of the country and the emergence of new geographical and economic facts, a fresh assessment of the financial and other resources and of the essential conditions of progress has now become necessary. Moreover, inflationary pressures inherited from the war, balance of payments difficulties, the influx into India of several million persons displaced from their homes and occupations, deficiencies in the country's food supply aggravated by partition and a succession of indifferent harvests, and the dislocation of supplies of certain essential raw materials have placed the economy under a severe strain. The need for comprehensive planning based on a careful appraisal of resources and on an objective analysis of all the relevant economic factors has become imperative.[5]

The Planning Commission, chaired by Prime Minister Nehru, had a big burden on its shoulders and the whole world was watching whether—and how far—India's bold experiment of playing the game of democracy and centrally planned economy would succeed.

NATIONAL INTEGRATION THROUGH PLANNED ECONOMY

The First Five-Year Plan (1951–1956) laid heavy emphasis on agriculture, community development, irrigation and power; as well as industries, minerals, transportation, communications and social services. Although the major goal of the Planning Commission was to mobilize the resources of the country for a quick transformation of the economy, it also strengthened the political integration of the country through shared economic goals. Since all economic development projects were national projects, no state could lay exclusive claim on its resources. Job opportunities were open to all, thus, creating mobility and internal migration.

The plan included a total outlay of ₹2,378 crores aimed at seven broad categories, including irrigation and energy, agriculture and community development, transport and communication, industry, social services and rehabilitation of landless farmers, etc. The economy grew by 18 per cent, per capita income went up by 11 per cent and consumption by 8 per cent.[6] Partly this was due to the fact that India started from a low threshold. Successive good monsoons, too, helped. Indians began to see the future bright and beautiful from one five-year plan to another. It was not a trickle-down economy; rather, it was an economy based on distributive justice to be achieved through a socialistic pattern of society where the government would control the levers, the 'commanding heights', of the economy. Indians saw visions of massive dams, canals, power plants, steel plants, as well as world-class engineering and research institutions, schools and colleges, and roads and highways.[7]

Indians wanted more and rapid industrialization, which became the driving force behind the drafting of the Second Five-Year Plan based on what came to be known as the Mahalanobis Model developed by Prasanta Chandra Mahalanobis, the founder-director of the Statistical Institute of India, Calcutta. In a data-poor country, which was the condition at that time and perhaps even today, the establishment of the Central Statistical Organization (CSO) and the development of the National Sample Survey (NSS) was a compelling necessity because planning depended on the measurement of all available resources, natural, human and capital, which required prioritizing their planned use to achieve well-defined goals. Measurement entered into the Indian mode of thinking.

After experiential learning through his travels abroad where he held dialogues with experts in the United States, Europe, the Soviet Union and communist China about planned economic growth, Mahalanobis concluded that in order to materialize the vision of 'the Socialistic Pattern of Society', India needed to develop a heavy industry base on which would be built a superstructure of second and third tier of industries, including manufacturing and production of consumer goods. While the public sector would have the major responsibility for heavy industrialization—from the extraction of raw material to building power plants and steel plants, at the same time, downstream industrialization—from building machines that manufacture machine tools, which in turn manufacture consumer goods—the role of the private sector would be no less significant. The categorical emphasis upon placing capital goods industry under the control of the public sector was deemed necessary for making India economically independent, creating jobs. Also for equitable distribution of economic opportunities and rewards in order to realize the goals of social justice embodied in the concept of 'the socialist pattern of society.' Creating jobs is one of the best ways of creating social and distributive justice. A job feeds a family.

Although the Government of India aimed at controlling 'the commanding heights', of the economy, the economic planning goal was not to create total state capitalism; not only because India had a thriving though limited private sector that was expected to play a greater role as the public sector grew, but also because of the fact that India had another enduring economic player, the massive mom-and-pop corner store cash-based retail economy. The emerging three-tier economy included industries that would be the exclusive domain of the government, for example, atomic energy, defence, aircraft, iron and steel, electricity generation and distribution system, heavy electrical, telephones and extraction industry such as coal, etc.; the second category such as chemicals, pharmaceuticals, road transportation, etc., would be open to both public and private sectors; the third category, which meant the rest of the economy, would be open to the private sector. By the end of the Second Five-Year Plan, the economic portrait of India as a mixed economy under the protective umbrella of the government had been established and received wide acceptance both at home and abroad.

While technocrats, economists, politicians and the media were deeply engaged in debating the goals, the priorities and the feasibility of the Second Five-Year Plan, the common people saw the Plan in the shape of steel plants: one at Bhilai, Madhya Pradesh (now in Chhattisgarh) built with the aid and technology from the Soviet Union—a country for whom Indians had begun to develop high admiration—specializing in the production of steel rails, wide steel plates and other steel products apart from chemical byproducts; the second, an integrated steel plant at Durgapur, West Bengal, built with British aid and cooperation that reestablished relations between two sovereign nations; and the third at Rourkela, Odisha, with West German technology and know-how, a country that had become associated in the Indian mind with the freedom fighter Subhas Chandra Bose. Started in 1955, all three steel plants began to transform the landscape and lives of the people. Apart from producing steel that India needed for its rapid industrialization, the most important gain was in the form of technology and knowledge transfer because the steel plants used the state-of-the-art technology of the time. Establishing and strengthening diplomatic relations with two important European countries, Germany and the United Kingdom as well as the Soviet Union in the era of the Cold War, was important in itself. Besides, the steel plants offered Indian experts competing models of technology and plant management. It was a learning time for India and there was a lot to learn from the West and the Soviet Union, for which, as we would see, the policy of non-alignment would play a significant role.

The Mahalanobis planning model corresponded with the mode of consciousness and zeitgeist of the time. But neither Nehru the democrat-socialist, nor Mahalanobis the planner-statistician, realized the power of the competition of the open marketplace regarding product innovation, pricing and cost reduction, capital allocation and distribution efficiencies, which is the essence and the strength of free marketplace capitalism, the engine that created unprecedented prosperity first in the West followed by South Korea, Japan and Taiwan. The protective umbrella of self-reliance in the course of time would become a licence-raj closed system that would shackle the spirit of India. India would need another liberator.

INDIA'S NEW TEMPLES OF SCIENCE

As the common man in Indian saw the promises of modernization and industrialization of the country in steel, chemical and fertilizer plants, there was another tangible aspect, another manifestation of the Second Five-Year Plan, which enthralled them: the harnessing of the mighty Indian rivers for irrigation, electricity generation and flood control, that would enable farmers to manage periodic droughts and the vagaries of the monsoons. The abodes of gods and goddesses for millennia, the mountains and rivers would become temples of modern India, as the secular-agnostic Nehru described them while inaugurating the Bhakra-Nangal Dam on 8 July 1954. Of the several river dam projects that were being undertaken, including Hirakud, Damodar, Tungabhadra and Govind Ballabh Pant Sagar, the one on the Sutlej River captured India's imagination the most. Bhakra-Nangal Dam is a set of two dams built on the Sutlej River. One at Bilaspur in Himachal Pradesh is a concrete gravity dam that forms the 90 kilometres (56 miles) long Gobind Sagar Reservoir, spread over 168.35 square kilometres (66 square miles) and has the capacity to hold 9.34 billion cubic metres (247 billion gallons) of water. The 520 metres (1,700 feet) long dam rises to the height of 226 metres (741 feet)—one of the highest in the world. The hydroelectric project produces 1,500 megawatts of power, regarded impressive in those days, which is supplied to Punjab, Haryana, Rajasthan, Himachal Pradesh and Delhi. Eight miles downstream on the Sutlej River in Punjab is another dam, the Nangal Dam.

The Bhakra-Nangal multipurpose dam project was conceived and planned before Independence but was taken up systematically in the 1950s. Through four spillways, the excess dam water during the monsoon is regulated and prevents flood damage. The dam irrigates 10 million acres of agricultural land in Punjab, Haryana and Rajasthan.[8] Dedicating the project to the people of India on 22 October 1963, Jawaharlal Nehru said, 'Bhakra-Nangal Project is something tremendous, something stupendous, something which shakes you up when you see it. Bhakra, the new temple of resurgent India, is the symbol of India's progress.'[9]

But the new temples of India couldn't solve the problems of Shambu Mahato, the protagonist of *Do Bigha Zamin*. India of course needed steel plants, dams, power stations and chemical fertilizer factories, but more than that, it was the farmer, the tenant, the sharecropper who needed help regarding their unsustainable landholdings and the perpetual debt trap. Planners saw a twofold solution to the problem—opening up and upturning the virgin lands locked up in the forested foothills of the Himalayas, the Aravali range of central India and the Western Ghats running to the Arabian Sea, and making them cultivable and habitable through controlled deforestation. But this was a drop in the bucket for farmers hungry for land. Eliminating the exploitative zamindari or the absentee landlord system corresponded with an emerging consciousness—that in order to create a just society, India must move towards a socialistic form of society.

The tenant would become the owner, but again, the landholding must be limited so that the landless too could share the land through redistribution. By 1960, in spite of all these efforts at the recovery of virgin lands and redistribution of existing agricultural holdings, 41 per cent farmers in India had less than a hectare (2.471 acres) and cultivated only about seven per cent of the total available agricultural land; 41 per cent farmers cultivated 1 to 10 hectares that amounted to about 62 per cent of the agricultural land; and five per cent farmers had more than 10 hectares and cultivated about 31 per cent of the land. Another way of looking at the problem is that 63 per cent of farmers had no more than two hectares of land and cultivated less than 20 per cent of the arable land.[10]

But it highlighted a serious problem: too many people trying to make a living on too little land. Fortunately, the cultivable agricultural land share of the total landmass area in India is 60 per cent, 159.6 million hectares, the second-highest in the world next to the US. But with millions of farmers depending upon agriculture, the burden on rural India was simply too much, considering the agricultural practices and resources that were available in the first two five-year plan periods. In the US, there's no limit to agricultural land ownership and farming is mechanized and industrialized and is done on a massive scale. The Soviet Union developed collective farms, which created its own problems. Neither the US nor the Soviet model was feasible in India. The Indian farmer needed more than land.

STATE ENTERS THE RURAL LANDSCAPE

In 1952 the Government of India launched a pilot project, the Community Development Programme (CDP), a series of countrywide projects to help the rural population. CDP projects were designed to build rural roads, dig water wells, develop cattle breeding, and improve farming practices by the use of fertilizers and better-quality seeds. The key to this planned peaceful rural revolution was the village-level worker with a mission to change the mindset of the farmer and introduce him to rational thinking.[11] Of course, the programme had political objectives, too, because it reached millions of people more than any other economic programme. Under the First Five-Year Plan, for example, about 78 million people were covered under Community Development Programmes with an expenditure of about ₹460 million, which was symbolic of the fact that the Congress party under Nehru was dedicated to serving the rural people, of which the ballot was the ultimate test.[12] Farmers, however, needed more than advice from urban agricultural experts; they needed irrigation, fertilizers and affordable credit. But most of all, they needed land reforms that would give the cultivators a sense of ownership and security. Land reforms have been one of the greatest challenges for democratic India.

The land reform legislation affected four areas, including the abolition of intermediaries, zamindars or absentee landlords, who, under the colonial land revenue system, were rent collectors; improving and regulating the tenancy system that provided tenants security and a greater share in agricultural production; a maximum limit on landholdings in order to redistribute surplus land to the landless; and the consolidation of fragmented landholdings. The abolition of absentee landlordism by and large was successful. In other areas, the implementation of reforms was uneven because landowners exercised their political influence and used 'various methods of evasion and coercion, which included registering their own land under names of different relatives to bypass the ceiling, shuffling tenants around different plots of land, so that they would not acquire incumbency rights as stipulated in the tenancy law'. And consequently, the success of land reform was contingent upon the 'political will of specific state administrations, the notable achievers being the left-wing administrations in Kerala and West Bengal'.[13]

Thus, land reforms in India became not so much an economic necessity or an attempt at distributive justice but rather a politically contested area with mixed consequences. From an economics point of view, according to the research done by Maitreesh Ghatak and Sanchari Roy, 'The evidence suggests that land reforms had a negative effect on poverty, while the effect on productivity is mixed. In states where these measures were strongly implemented, the effect of land reform on productivity seems positive.'[14] Land reforms, however, must be understood in the light of the Congress party session held at Nagpur in 1959, at which the party passed the agrarian resolution under which the village panchayat would be the controlling centre of a village's economic activities, based on cooperatives.[15]

This was supposed to be a democratic alternative to collective farming as practiced in the Soviet Union and China. And as propaganda kept pouring from these two giants of socialist economy as to how collectivization had transformed their agriculture, Indians were mesmerized. A couple of delegations sent to China in 1956 to study the marvels of collective farming confirmed what they had already learnt from the communist propaganda channels. Now was the time to aggressively push socialism through joint cooperative farming and Panchayats. But the Nagpur Resolution created the fear of creeping communism and aroused strong passions and opposition from many prominent members of the Congress party, including C. Rajagopalachari, N.G. Ranga and the Uttar Pradesh farmers' leader Charan Singh. They protested that totalitarianism was being imposed upon the country. While Nehru could disregard the reactionaries outside his party, he could not ignore the divisions within the Congress party in spite of the fact that he was at the peak of his political power and the undisputed leader of the party. Heeding the voices of intense opposition to joint cooperative farming from his own party members as well as the news media, Nehru mellowed down.

In February 1959, he assured Parliament that although joint cooperative farming was a most desirable solution for rural India, including land reforms and agriculture, no legislation was being introduced on joint cooperative farming. In spite of his assurances, the Congress party was split because some highly regarded senior party members were convinced, especially after the Avadi (1955) and Nagpur (1959) sessions, that the Nehru-dominated party had taken a definitive left turn. Under the leadership of C. Rajagopalachari, Minoo Masani, N.G. Ranga, K.M. Munshi and other Congress party leaders, a liberal-conservative rightwing party, the Swatantra Party, was established in order to bring together under one umbrella various isolated political groups that advocated individual entrepreneurship and free-market economy. Nehru termed the new party as a political grouping of reactionary landlords, big businesses and princes.[16]

The founding of the Swatantra Party was an inflection point in Indian democracy for several reasons. It broke the monolithic socialistic thinking, the collective mindset of the nation that Nehru had created with his charming, sophisticated, dominant personality in which he was supported by the free but deferential news media as well as Indian intellectuals, especially from the South and West Bengal, who controlled top universities and research institutions. The Swatantra Party was founded on the idea of individual freedom and entrepreneurship believed to be strongly correlated with economic growth and prosperity.

Below the level of top industrialists and business houses, the Tatas, the Birlas, et al., there were millions of middle-level and small businesses scattered all over the country who loved Nehru but never subscribed to his socialistic mode of thinking. The Swatantra Party embodied the views of India's silent majority who believed in private property and were confident of getting ahead on their own if given opportunities, but the party did not make much headway because of the paucity of its grassroots organization. The party disappeared; nevertheless, the BJP, with a much better political organization, subsumed its economic philosophy.

But the ultimate blow to joint cooperative farming came

inadvertently from China, whose collective farming's spurious success stories had been an inspiration for the Indian political class. Chinese repression in Tibet, the flight of the Dalai Lama to India, the discovery of a Chinese-built road through Indian territory Aksai Chin in Ladakh (Jammu and Kashmir), and the encroachment into Indian territory south of the historically established McMahon Line in the east (now Arunachal Pradesh) not only shook up India but was also 'a personal loss of face and prestige for Nehru.' Moreover, to the public mind, it seemed that:

> any plan which smacked of the China model (was) automatically suspect and very difficult to push publicly. A further retreat became inevitable and the Congress party put forward a position in Parliament, which essentially argued for setting up 'service cooperatives' all over the country over the next three years and left the issue of setting up cooperative farms sufficiently vague. Cooperative farms were to be set up *voluntarily* wherever conditions became mature.[17]

Gradually, the joint cooperative farming programme went into the dustbin of history, thanks to the game of democracy the Indians had learnt to play since Independence. Democracy forces politicians to think in terms of what system scientists call 'equifinality,' which means that an open democratic system can reach the same goal by other potential means, paths or trajectories.[18] Democracy engenders plurality and flexibility of responses, and therefore, since joint cooperative farming failed, other efforts at mitigating the problem of rural poverty, inequality and landlessness were adopted in the course of time. But in spite of all the efforts, India is a land of small self-cultivating farmers and the picture has not changed substantially since 1976–77 when 'nearly 97 per cent of the cultivators had operational holdings of less than 25 acres and they operated 73.6 per cent of the total area... On the other hand, along with this vast mass there were the large landowners operating above 25 acres, though they constituted only 3 per cent of the holdings and 26.2 per cent of the operated area. Further, the share of the large landowners, both in the proportion of holdings and area controlled, kept declining steadily over time. Very large estates of over 100 acres were very few and rare, and they were generally run on modern capitalist lines.'[19]

MAKING INDIA SCIENTIFIC

Addressing the thirty-fourth session of the Indian Science Congress in Delhi on 3 January 1947, Nehru advised the scientific community that India needed a scientific, rational and planned approach to solve its problems. More than searching for truth, science must work for society at large. He expounded:

> For a hungry man or hungry woman, Truth has little meaning. He wants food. For a hungry man God has no meaning. And India is starving and to talk of truth and God and many of the finer things is mockery. We have to find food for them, clothing, housing, education and health are absolute necessities that every person should possess... So, Science must think in terms of the 400 million persons in India. Obviously, you can only think in those terms and work along those lines on the wider scale of coordinated planning.

Acknowledging that it's not easy to draw a line between scientific work for peace and war, he said that India could not ignore the great force, atomic energy, simply out of fear of war and therefore, 'obviously in India we want to develop it and we will develop it to the fullest. Fortunately, we have eminent scientists here who can do so, I hope, in cooperation with the rest of the world and for peaceful purposes.'[20]

In the 1958 Scientific Policy Resolution passed by the Lok Sabha, he once again emphasized the need for applied science because, in the modern age, it is 'the effective combination of three factors—technology, raw materials and capital, of which the first is perhaps the most important, since the creation and adoption of new scientific techniques can, in fact, make up for the deficiency in natural resources, and reduce the demands on capital.'[21] But it is applied science that is the source of technology, apart from 'the spirit of the people' that can be spurred further as the people see material progress taking place to meet their needs. It is 'the intense cultivation of science on a large scale, and its application to meet a country's requirements...which, for the first time in man's history, has given to the common man in countries advanced in science, a standard of living and social and cultural amenities', once limited to a privileged minority. Moreover, science has a social and cultural dimension in the sense that it gives humans new tools of thinking about the basic assumptions of life and thus providing new dynamism to society. After all one of the objectives of a democratic society such as India is social justice and welfare, which can be achieved 'only through scientific approach and method and the use of scientific knowledge that reasonable material and cultural amenities and services can be provided for every member of the community, and it is out of recognition of this possibility that the idea of a welfare state has grown.'[22] Thus in Nehru's vision of emerging India, science and technology were indispensable for achieving economic and social progress and for the establishment of a welfare state based on democracy. India needed new temples of learning, 'temples of science built for the service of our motherland.'[23]

As much as Nehru felt inspired by the masses, he also felt at home with scientists and intellectuals including S.S. Bhatnagar, Meghnad Saha, Homi Bhabha, J.B.S. Haldane, Sir C.V. Raman, Satish Dhawan, Nalini Ranjan Sarkar, J.C. Ghosh, Humayun Kabir and P.C. Mahalanobis, among others.[24] Although Nehru was a Hindu agnostic, he was proudly aware of India's intellectual tradition. As scholar David Arnold observed:

> With their remarkable capacity for abstract thought, Indians had pioneered the study of mathematics, algebra, and astronomy in ancient times; they similarly had the capacity to deploy this intellectualism to help shape modern science. Thus, inspiration might be found in 'the old Vedantic conception that everything, whether sentient or insentient, finds a place in the organic whole.' The career of the plant physiologist

Jagadish Chandra Bose (1858–1937) demonstrated for Nehru how India's philosophical and spiritual traditions could actively inform and supplement the work of modern science. The 'culture of science' gave India pride in its past, but also the intellectual authority and resources to be an active and equal participant in the present-day domain of science.[25]

During his lifetime as India's statesman, scores of national laboratories and scientific and technical institutes were established, including the National Physical Laboratory, which was founded before Independence on 4 January 1947. Later under the umbrella of the Council of Scientific and Industrial Research, several more laboratories were set up, including the Tata Institute of Fundamental Research specializing in physics and mathematics; and the Atomic Energy Commission in 1948 in the Department of Scientific Research. In 1954 the Department of Atomic Energy, under the direct control of the prime minister, was established with Homi Bhabha as the secretary. The goal was to harness the atom for electrical energy, for which the first nuclear reactor was set up in Trombay, Bombay that went critical in 1956. Many more nuclear reactors for peaceful uses were planned. Space exploration fascinated India, and a beginning was made with the establishment of the Indian National Committee for Space Research and a Rocket Launching Facility at Thumba, Kerala, in 1962. India also took the bold step, which seemed rather hazardous, keeping in mind the level of literacy at that time, of changing to the decimal system of coinage and metric system in measurements. Its success was a great tribute to the Indians' ability to adapt to rapid change.[26] It also proved that widespread illiteracy in India did not prevent people from experiential learning.

In order to support the topnotch scientific laboratories and research institutions with a continuous flow of highly trained brainpower, India established—modelled on the Massachusetts Institute of Technology—five major technological institutions, the Indian Institute of Technology (IITs), beginning at Kharagpur in 1951 followed by others in Madras, Bombay, Kanpur and Delhi, which in turn would become breeders and multipliers of similar technological institutions all over the country. By 1965, India was spending ₹850 million on research, 77 times more than in 1950, and with a scientific and technical research force of 731,500, four times more than in 1950. In the same year, enrolment in engineering, technology and agricultural sciences rose to about 93,000, six times more than in 1950.[27] But the catchment area of these intellectual streams was limited and poor.

Nehru and the Indian elite were enamoured with the new temples of learning that were being built to bring India into the modern age. They gave the urban elites an illusion of rapid scientific and technological progress taking place. The IITs, the Indian Institute of Management (IIM), the All-India Institute of Medical Sciences, the Sahitya Akademi, and various other cultural institutes along with research laboratories, nuclear reactors, space exploration initiatives, albeit necessary, were based on a narrow foundation of urban English medium schools and universities run by the government as well as private trusts and foundations.

Because of the unfortunate British colonial legacy, at the time of Independence, about 88 per cent of India's brainpower was locked up in illiteracy, according to census data. To liberate India's massive brainpower required imaginative planning, massive investment and training. The inaugurations of hydro dams and power plants by Nehru and other ministers, which were prominently front-paged on daily newspapers, broadcast on All India Radio and shown as newsreels in movie theatres, gave the people a sense of instant gratification and progress; nonetheless, setting up a primary school in a village, persuading parents to send their children to school, and most importantly, asking teachers to come and teach every day, was a humongous task, especially when education was primarily the responsibility of the states.

The Planning Commission, the agency for the Five-Year Plans, gave a glimpse into the magnitude of the stubborn problem of illiteracy that India faced in harnessing its human resources when it began to plan for economic growth:

At the primary stage quite a large number of pupils discontinue their studies even before obtaining a state of permanent literacy. Of the total number of students entering schools in 1945–46 only 40 per cent reached class IV in 1948–49. The expenditure on the remaining 60 per cent was largely wasted. The experiment of compulsion, which is generally regarded as the only remedy for improving the position, has not made much progress. In 1948–49, approximately 115 lakhs (11.5 million) pupils were under compulsion and most of the States expressed their inability to enforce it. The problem of 'stagnation', that is, where a pupil spends a number of years in the same class, is also serious. There is, moreover, incomplete utilisation of existing facilities, as is shown by the unsatisfactory results of a large number of students. This wastage is largely due to the poor quality of teaching as well as faulty methods of education.[28]

THE MANY CHALLENGES OF EDUCATION

The problem was vast and complicated, keeping in mind the mandate of the Constitution—that by 1961 the government should provide free and compulsory education to every child until the age of fourteen. It was an impossible goal to meet and required changing it to 1966, and later on, forgotten at best. Keeping other plan priorities in focus, the government nonetheless poured huge amounts of money for increasing education at all levels, primary, secondary, higher as well as technical education. By 1964–65, during the Third Five-Year Plan, the funding increased sevenfold to ₹1,462 million. Regardless of the quality, the outcome assessments in terms of raw data were impressive. For example, boys' enrolment in primary schools more than doubled, while girls' enrolment increased more than three times (1950–51 to 1965–66). In the same period, the number of secondary schools increased more than three times to 24,477, and the enrolment increased four times for boys and more than six times for girls, according to government sources.

The data for higher education expansion was equally impressive. During the Third Five-Year Plan period, there were 613,000 students enrolled in 54 universities and 2,500 affiliated colleges, of which 22 per cent were women.[29] But data could be deceptive. The population, too, had been steadily growing and thus increasingly putting pressure on educational facilities, resulting in lowering educational standards and turning out unemployable university graduates, or as they were derisively called, 'road scholars.' At the lower level of education, some of the problems that the Planning Commission observed at the beginning of the First Five-Year Plan continued in the 1960s. Apart from the fact that five per cent of the rural population had no schools at all, the majority of schools had mud buildings without blackboards and drinking water. About '40 per cent of primary schools had only one teacher to take three or four classes,' and consequently, about 'half of those enrolled in class I would have left school by the time they reached class IV and been rapidly reduced to virtual illiteracy again.' It was clear enough that 'there was no equal opportunity in education and therefore also hardly any equalization of opportunity in work and employment for the poor and those in the rural areas, who constituted the vast majority of the Indian people.'[30]

Even in 2019, when India entered the second five-year political term of Narendra Modi's much-heralded digital age, 75 per cent of primary school students dropped out before reaching the eighth grade, a massive workforce that could have been suitable for low-tech manufacturing. But as the Infosys co-founder N.R. Narayana Murthy said during a lecture at Presidency University, Kolkata, economists and planners never thought about the massive reservoir of untapped skill power since the 1950s, the times of Jawaharlal Nehru.[31] Nonetheless, elite schools such as St. Xavier's Collegiate School, La Martiniere, Doon School, Bombay Scottish and Modern School, to name a few, along with top colleges and universities, IITs, IIMs and Jawaharlal Nehru University, among others, that feed into and form the supply chain for the Nehru-built temples of learning, have been growing and continue to do well. This is a perverted form of the two-nation theory, or what Indians today call 'India and Bharat', one at the top echelons of the pyramid communicating with global elites and the other vast majority at the bottom of the pyramid, waiting for trickledown welfare doles and subsidies, which eventually factor into and change the game of democracy that Indians love to play. Indians find it much easier to build temples and attract millions of people to the Kumbh Mela than to send their kids to schools. Or for leaders to persuade rural people to use Prime Minister Modi's massive national programme for toilets to keep India clean.[32]

India needed a radical social change, but the question the Nehru generation faced was whether the new social order encapsulated in the catchphrase of the time 'the Socialistic Pattern of Society' could be accomplished with all the contending forces released by democratic freedoms and pluralism. Of course, Nehru had the constitutional sanction of Article 36 which has a section on the Directive Principles of State Policy that declares: 'The state shall strive to promote the welfare of the people by securing and protecting as effectively as may be a social order in which justice, economic and political, shall inform all institutions of the national life'. The Avadi Session (1955) of the Congress party had ratified the synthesis between the Directive Principles and the socialistic pattern-based welfare society, which became the guiding ideology of the Five-Year Plans. Some of these objectives could be achieved through the expansion and overarching dominance of the public sector, which would open employment and business/contract opportunities to all based on merit as well as other social considerations.

The rights of industrial workers—who mostly came from lower strata of society—including the right to form labour unions, collective bargaining and employment security, as well as the right to strike work were recognized through legislative actions. Since the public sector was purported to be the dominant form of industrial organization, it was assumed that labour rights would be taken care of; and the private sector would follow the lead of the public sector regarding the rights of the labour. But according to some scholars, it was a trickledown condescending attitude because the government gave sporadic attention to labour issues believing that 'a filtration process would carry general economic progress to the working classes and thus specific state action for labour welfare was of low priority, and he (Nehru) saw disciplined trade unionism as a legitimate civil right as well as a means of ensuring economic progress.'[33]

LOWEST OF THE LOW

The sweeper class, referred to as the untouchables in India, is the lowest of the lowest strata in the Hindu hierarchical caste system. On a purity-pollution measurement scale on which Hindu society has lived and thrived for ages, the untouchables have been regarded as the worst polluters. Even their shadow polluted the upper classes. There was a time, long, long ago, when an untouchable shouted the alert: Keep away, keep away, while walking the street. That was the case with Bakha, a teenager whose father was the head of sweepers of a fictional town Bulashah in Punjab, in Mulk Raj Anand's novel, *Untouchable*, published in 1935.[34] It tells the poignant story of a teenager born in ignominy and yet aspiring to escape his fate, somehow. He wanted to play hockey and go to school. In one scene, Bakha, who wants to see how worship is conducted in a temple, clandestinely climbs up the stairs to have a peep of the deities Ram and Krishna, about whom he has heard but never seen. Suddenly, there is a commotion and a temple priest comes out yelling, 'I have been polluted, I have been polluted,' and points to a teenage girl, Sohini, Bakha's sister, who is there to clean the temple latrines. The priest had tried to molest the untouchable girl but when Sohini resisted, he accused her of polluting him. Who would have believed the untouchable girl! A normal day in the life of Bakha turned into a day of utter humiliation.

During the debate on the Constitution on 25 November 1949, Ambedkar made a powerful speech, in which he pondered on the future of the free democratic Indian Republic, beginning on 26 January 1950, when political equality based on the principle of one man one vote, would contradict the actualities of social and economic life entrenched with inequalities. He admonished:

> We must remove this contradiction at the earliest possible
> moment or else those who suffer from inequality will blow
> up the structure of political democracy which this Assembly
> has so laboriously built up.[35]

While Article 17 of the Constitution had abolished untouchability, Parliament reinforced the constitutional provision by passing the Anti-Untouchability Law in 1955, making the practice of untouchability a cognizable and punishable offence.[36] But passing a law does not mean that the evil would vanish automatically. Although the Supreme Court is the final protector and interpreter of the Constitution, the judiciary cannot take action on its own. The victims of oppression must assert their rights, which they can do either by peaceful civic protests or by seeking justice in court. There have been several landmark cases regarding the rights of Dalits, especially in regard to access to sacred places, and in each case, the Supreme Court has reiterated the constitutional provision of equal rights for all. For example, in the Venkataramana Devaru versus State of Mysore lawsuit, regarding temple entry by a Dalit, Justice Aliyar J. Venkatarama of the Supreme Court ruled:

> A custom which denied to large sections of Hindus the right
> to use public roads and institution to which all the other
> Hindus has a right of access, purely on grounds of birth could
> not be considered reasonable and defended...on any sound
> democratic principle...[37]

The same democratic principles would apply to the question of Scheduled Castes, Scheduled Tribes and other weaker classes by giving them reservations in educational institutions and government jobs as well as providing them with educational scholarships, loans and grants and legal aid, etc. For the effective implementation of legal remedies, the Commissioner of Scheduled Castes and Scheduled Tribes was appointed. But the caste system has been so entrenched in the Hindu psyche that it has been impossible to abolish it, especially from rural India, where the oppressed classes constitute the landless classes. In the ultimate analysis, the failure of primary education, especially in rural areas, is linked with the caste system. Upper-class teachers would not stoop to teach Scheduled Caste children, nor would upper-class parents want their children to be taught by a Dalit teacher. For Mulk Raj Anand's Bakha or Sohini, or Bimal Roy's Shambu Mahato, the future would be technology and the bright lights of Kolkata, Delhi, Mumbai, Chennai and the rising new digital megalopolis. Indians would learn that technology changes people's minds and consciousness. [38]

CODIFYING THE HINDUS

Codifying the multifarious practices of Hinduism regarding its traditional personal laws into a uniform standard code and getting it passed by the Parliament in the face of serious opposition by many sections of the public was one of the greatest political achievements of Nehru. [39] Although the process was started during British rule, it did not gather much steam because the British followed the policy of non-interference in the personal law affairs of the Hindus and other Indians. But Indians had become aware that a uniform code was needed to unify the nation and the process must begin with the Hindus.

After Independence, the Nehru government undertook the process of codification, but because of the widespread opposition from various conservative Hindu politicians within and outside the Congress party as well as religious organizations, he moved slowly. He let the debate continue and all voices be heard. Finally, for political reasons, the original code bill was split into four separate bills: the Hindu Marriage Act, the Hindu Succession Act, the Hindu Minority and Guardianship Act, and the Hindu Adoption Act, which were passed separately in the 1952–56 sessions of the Parliament. [40] As a tactical approach, the piecemeal legislation aroused less opposition, and eventually, the unified Hindu code became the law of the land. The Hindu Code encased and knitted all castes, sects and denominations into a uniform whole, a valiant attempt to create social justice through legal equity. [41] In some sense, the Code uplifted the position of Hindu women, for example, by giving them property and inheritance rights as well as the right to divorce at par with men. [42]

The achievement was far from what Nehru had visualized: a uniform civil code for the whole nation, but he regarded it as a major step, as he wrote in a letter to state chief ministers: 'We have not only striven for and achieved a political revolution, not only are we striving hard for an economic revolution but that we are equally intent on social revolution; only by way of advance on these three separate lines and their integration into one great whole, will the people of India progress.' In another letter to state chief ministers about the revolutionary nature of the Hindu religious reform legislation especially with regard to women, he said, 'They have broken the barriers of ages and cleared the way somewhat for our womenfolk to progress... I have long been convinced that a nation's progress is intimately connected with the status of its women.'[43] Would the Hindu reform laws eventually become a source of inspiration for Muslim women who have been more oppressed than their Hindu sisters?

Unfortunately, a uniform civil code covering all religions could not be enacted because Nehru was not ready to confront the Muslim orthodoxy regarding polygamy, inheritance and the most unjust practice of triple Talaq. Following the British practice of non-interference in personal law matters regarding the Muslims, Nehru left the Muslim community, especially the women, far behind in comparison with Hindus. The misplaced emphasis upon secularism that Muslim sensibilities should not be hurt and that changes in the Muslim personal law should be enacted only when the Muslims would be ready for it would turn the Muslim community into a walled ghetto community, a voting bloc for the Congress party for a long time to come. The Constitutional promises of achieving Indian unity through the Uniform Civil Code would remain an unattainable goal.

LINGUISTIC HOMELANDS

The long struggle for Independence under Gandhi's leadership had been transformed into a mass movement that turned Indians into proud Indians, except for Muslim Leaguers who, along with Jinnah's two-nation theory, departed for their new homeland. But hardly had the blood-soaked streets in the aftermath of Partition dried up and the midnight furies bottled up, Indians began to look at themselves in different shades of culture. Culture and language are inseparable; therefore, the importance of one's mother tongue for education, administration, democratic participation and political accountability of leaders cannot be underestimated. Language thus became the driving force, the dividing force, as well as the uniting force of politics in the times of Nehru and later on through the 1960s and to some extent even today.

To bring the people into its fold and make the struggle for freedom a mass movement, in 1921, the India National Congress reconstituted its structure on the basis of its local branches based on regional languages. Gandhi ardently believed in the development of provincial languages though he warned against the fissiparous tendencies and asked Indians to be Indians first and foremost. Immediately after Independence, there were some serious concerns and urgent problems for the national leadership. Partition had caused severe economic dislocation with millions of refugees to be rehabilitated; and an unsettled warlike situation with Pakistan over Jammu and Kashmir. The security and stability of India were of paramount importance. While linguistic reorganization of the country was desirable, to which the Congress party no doubt was committed, the process could wait until urgent issues were taken care of.

The Linguistic Provinces Commission, appointed by the Constituent Assembly in 1948 under Justice S.K. Dhar, had cautioned that linguistic reorganization at that time might cause administrative disruption and threaten national unity. Consequently, the Constituent Assembly eschewed the issue of linguistic reorganization of India from its deliberations. But since the language issue, especially in the South, did not go away, the Congress party appointed a committee in 1948 consisting of Jawaharlal Nehru, Vallabhbhai Patel and Congress President Pattabhi Sitaramayya—together known as the JVP Committee, to examine the issue again.

The JVP Committee came to the same conclusion, as had the Dhar Commission, that the creation of linguistic states at the time was politically inappropriate and that national unity and economic development needed to be the primary national concerns. However, the JVP Committee acknowledged that a strong case did exist for the breakup of the Madras Presidency into Andhra State and Tamil Nadu but did not recommend any action because of the dispute over Madras city. In politics, inaction is a form of action, especially in India, when people become easily emotional over an issue.

However, Telugu-speaking people of the Andhra region could not wait on the vague promises of the future. On 15 December 1952, Potti Sriramulu, a devout disciple of Gandhi and an engineer who had given up his vocation to become a freedom fighter, died after 51 days of his fast-unto-death for the formation of Andhra Pradesh, a separate state for Telugu-speaking people, which at that time was part of the multilingual Madras Presidency. Telugu speakers, after Hindi and Bengali speakers, were the third-largest linguistic-cultural group in India, and they wanted to be on their own. For more than 300 years, the Telugu-speaking region was home to a great empire, Vijayanagara (1336–1646), that covered almost the entire Deccan Plateau. But after the British conquest, their identities had become subsumed into the larger Madras province where the Tamils were dominant. The demand for Andhra Pradesh was a struggle for the recovery of their lost sense of identity, part of which was in the Nizam's kingdom of Hyderabad and part in the Madras Presidency.

The recovery, consolidation and integration of Telugu identity was the mission of the Andhra Mahasabha, the socio-cultural organization established in 1921, which spearheaded the movement for Andhra Pradesh after Independence.[44] Although the Congress party in principle was committed to the formation of linguistic states, the process was fraught with disruptiveness and divisiveness. Rajagopalachari, the Chief Minister of Madras, was dead opposed to the idea of Andhra Pradesh. Nehru feared that linguistic divisions would threaten the unity of India, especially after India had undergone the tragedy of the religion-based division of the country. He was more interested in the consolidation of Indian polity than with regional languages and cultures without, however, totally relinquishing the concept of linguistic states. He believed that although in the future 'the formation of linguistic provinces may be desirable in some cases, this would obviously be the wrong time. When the right time comes, let us have them by all means.'[45]

What complicated the issue was the fate of the city of Madras on the Bay of Bengal, once the East India Company's trading post and military garrison, which in the course of time became home to diverse linguistic populations including Telugus, Tamils, Kannadigas and Malayalees; and a most important cultural, educational and intellectual centre of the South, which Andhra supporters demanded as part of the new state. But for Sriramulu, who played the game of democracy by resorting to the fast-unto-death strategy, the coercive persuasive political method that he had learnt from Gandhi, the Andhra case was morally and politically just and worth dying for. In 1946 when Sriramulu undertook his first fast-unto-death in support of opening Hindu temples to Harijans in Madras, he was persuaded by Gandhi to give up the fast, which he did. Now, this was the second time he had undertaken the fast-unto-death and this was for a much larger cause and there was no one to stop him. Sriramulu was the first language martyr. His martyrdom caused havoc; nonetheless, from a historian's point of view as to how Indians play the game of democracy, he was a prime political mover and shaker. His death made the law-and-order situation uncontrollable and Madras Chief Minister Rajagopalachari and Nehru bowed to the violent wishes of the Telugu people.

Sriramulu set an example that would become a political pattern in India. The Telugu-speaking people got Andhra Pradesh but not Madras, which they desperately wanted. From another perspective, the struggle for Andhra Pradesh was, in fact, a struggle between Tamil-speaking and Telugu-speaking people. Long before Independence, 'Telugu leaders and newspapers started to complain that the "progress of Dravidians overshadowed" that of the Andhras (Telugu speaking) and the creation of a separate province would "cure this handicap".'[46] This fear of dominance by 'the other' would become a constant theme in Indian politics and how Indians play the game of democracy. In January 1953, the Government of India set up a committee led by Justice Kailas Nath Wanchoo of Allahabad High Court to demark the boundaries of Andhra Pradesh, which the Wanchoo Committee established without the inclusion of Madras. However, Madras, now Chennai, remained with Tamil Nadu. A similar struggle took place in the city of Bombay. Later on, with the integration of the Telugu-speaking areas of Hyderabad state, Andhra Pradesh decided to establish Hyderabad as its capital. Ironically the Telugu language could not keep the state together. In 2017, Telugu-speaking Telangana, after a long struggle and protest against neglect by 'the other', became its own separate state with Hyderabad as its capital, forcing Andhra Pradesh to build a new capital.[47] Thus Telugu-speaking Andhras became divided by their common language, as did the vast Hindi-speaking people of middle India.

The case of the reorganization of the sprawling Bombay Province was equally complex and fascinating. In the final analysis, it was centred on Bombay City, which, even at the time of Independence, was the most cosmopolitan metropolis, the everyman city, positioning India in a dominant commercial, financial and strategic position in the Indian Ocean and the Arabian Sea.[48] There was no religious, linguistic or cultural group that Bombay did not boast of. Some of the most driven, aggressive, ambitious and entrepreneurial people, the Sindhis, Punjabis and others, had moved to Bombay after Partition, along with the pre-existing legacy-rich businessmen and industrialists, including the Gujaratis, Parsis, Khojas, Bohras and Marwaris. Besides, it was home to the burgeoning film industry, later to be known as Bollywood, whose melting pot amalgamated talent and merit-based culture, of the Khans and the Kapoors and the Chopras and everybody else, would shape the culture of India in many ways.

Where to put this everyman's dream city on the linguistic homeland map of India, the city that kept the whole country energized, was the biggest challenge before the States Reorganization Commission, which the Government of India appointed in 1954, tasking it to make recommendations on the broad modalities that should govern the restructuring of India. The challenge was whether language and culture could be the only organizing political and administrative principles without keeping the larger view of the unity of India, the financial viability of states and national development plans, along with other factors. The task was much more complex and arduous than that of the Radcliffe Boundary Commission that had split British India into Pakistan and India by drawing lines on the map. The retired Chief Justice of India Fazal Ali headed the States Reorganization Commission with parliamentarian H.N. Kunzru and historian-diplomat K.M. Panikkar as its members.[49] Considering 'factors bearing on reorganization' the States Reorganisation Commission came to the conclusion that 'it is neither possible nor desirable to reorganize states on the basis of the single test of either language or culture, but that a balanced approach to the whole problem is necessary in the interest of our national unity.'[50] The SRC recommended the reorganization of the vast Hindi region into Uttar Pradesh, Bihar, Madhya Pradesh and Rajasthan. The demand for tribal states carved out of Assam and Bihar was rejected. Punjab, which has a largely bilingual population that speaks both Hindi and Punjabi, was enlarged by the addition of Patiala and East Punjab States Union (PEPSU), thereby rejecting the Sikh demand for a Punjabi-speaking state or the Punjabi Suba. After adjustment and exchange of territories, four southern states, based on Telugu, Tamil, Kannada and Malayalam languages, Andhra Pradesh, Tamil Nadu, Karnataka and Kerala, respectively, were recommended. The SRC recommended the formation of a separate Marathi-speaking state, Vidarbha, while at the same time recommending the enlargement of the bilingual Gujarati and Marathi Bombay State by adding Saurashtra State and Kutch State.[51]

The passing of the States Reorganisation Act 1956 shows how parliamentary democracy and direct (street) democracy interact and condition each other. Through the long tradition of civil disobedience, including petitions, protests, strikes, shutdowns, fasts and sometimes street violence, the people of India limit the power of Parliament and the government and force them to seek alternative solutions. The three-member States Reorganisation Commission spent 18 months collecting data and listening to the people, mostly the elites, since the members did not know all local languages and based on their observations and prior assumptions, they made recommendations, of which the Government of India rejected some parts and the people, especially in Bombay and Punjab, rejected some other parts. The proverbial wisdom of the crowd is not always guaranteed and like the government, the crowd could go wrong. But that's how the game of democracy is played out in India.

Channelling the crowd power in India has been one of the greatest challenges for politicians in the country. Breaking up Bombay State and Punjab in the ultimate analysis was based on the wisdom and the might of the crowd. Once a person feels secure in his language and culture, he opens up to others, thus resulting in the course of time in the acceptance of 'the other.' That's what the Maharashtrians, the Gujaratis and the Sikhs were seeking. Out of fear, neither the States Reorganisation Commission nor the Government of India understood them.

When the SRC Report was discussed in Parliament, the focus was the bilingual Bombay State; and the contest was about the city of Bombay, the crown jewel of India.[52] If the Samyukta Maharashtra Samiti, speaking for the Marathi speakers, had given up its demand that Bombay be included and become the capital of Maharashtra State, the Bombay State would have been easily bifurcated into linguistic states of Maharashtra and Gujarat. If Bombay City were contiguous to both Maharashtra and Gujarat, as Chandigarh would later become to Punjab and Haryana, it would have been a different case and the city could have been considered a joint capital. While some Maharashtrian/Bombay politicians such as S.K. Patil, Yashwantrao Chavan and Nehru himself liked its cosmopolitan character to continue and wanted it to be a separate city-state (based on the trifurcate proposal), other Maharashtrian parliamentarians were adamant that the city must be part of Maharashtra.

N.V. Gadgil, for example, warned that if the linguistic principle were rejected in the case of Marathi-speaking people, the democratic struggle would move to the streets of Bombay.[53] Delhi seemed far away from Bombay, the contested city where the political storm had been gathering with the Jana Sangh, socialists, communists and even B.R. Ambedkar, the prominent constitutionalist, throwing their weight behind the movement for Maharashtra with Bombay. On 16 January 1956, Jawaharlal Nehru announced the government's decision to create separate states of Maharashtra and Gujarat, however, with Bombay City as a separate union territory.

That was like a red rag to a bull. The situation became highly emotionalized and as a preventive measure, the police arrested hundreds of people, including top leaders of the Samyukta Maharashtra Samiti, which fueled the simmering fire of anger and the people went on a rampage and rioted, bringing the fast-paced city to a grinding halt. The riots continued for about a week, during which 80 people were killed.[54] Morarji Desai, a Gujarati politician, was the chief minister of Bombay State, and he became the most hated person in the city.

The violent street protests were reflected in the ballot box when the second general election was held in 1957. The Samyukta Maharashtra Samiti and the allies won 101 of the 133 seats in the Marathi-speaking region, while the Congress party won only 32 seats. In the Gujarat region of Bombay State, the Congress managed to eke out 57 out of 89 seats, while in Bombay City, it just got 13 out of 24 seats.[55] Overall, the Congress party won 234 out of 396 seats in the enlarged Bombay State, and Yashwantrao Chavan was elected leader of the Congress party, replacing Morarji Desai as the chief minister of Bombay State. Chavan, however, saw the writing on the wall. The wobbly Gujarat-Maharashtra Bombay State was not sustainable because not only did Maharashtrians want their own state, Gujaratis too, under the banner of the Mahagujarat movement led by Indulal Yagnik and others, demanded separation. In the hostile environment, the political prospects for the Congress party in the state would be in jeopardy. Chief Minister Chavan, with his Gujarati-Maharashtrian cabinet, was able to impart to Nehru and the Congress party's President Indira Gandhi the political wisdom of bifurcating the state.

On 4 December 1959, the Congress Working Committee recommended the formation of two separate linguistic states of

Gujarat and Maharashtra.[56] On 1 May 1960, Chavan became the first chief minister of Maharashtra, with Bombay its capital. This is how democracy works in India. Today Bombay is still the everyman city, more than ever, though it's now called Mumbai. It is a cosmopolitan city, a global city that draws entrepreneurial talent and capital from all over the world. A journalist, in a nostalgic tone, commented on the occasion of the 50th anniversary of the Maharashtra state:

> In fact, the battle to include what was then known as Bombay City in a Marathi state was split along class lines. The business class that funded the Congress wanted the city to become a Union Territory that it could control while the predominantly Marathi working class wanted it to be the capital of a progressive Maharashtra.[57]

Today Maharashtra is the most progressive state but in a different sense: it is the richest state in India. With $430 billion GDP and 12 per cent growth in 2018–19, it ranked first in the nation. The Marathi language in Bombay (Mumbai) shares cultural space with Hindi and English, a cultural phenomenon that's taking place in varied shades and degrees in all major cities, including Delhi, Kolkata, Pune, Bengaluru, Hyderabad, Chennai and Goa, thanks to industrialization-driven internal migration and Bollywood.

With the merger of Patiala and East Punjab states into Punjab on the recommendation of the States Reorganisation Commission, the case became a festering linguistic and communal issue. Neither the SRC nor Nehru and the Congress party were in favour of a state being formed on the basis of religion. Although the Sikhs suffered the most during Partition, they also gained the most. Forced migration aggregated them into Punjab, where they formed a substantial plurality in comparison with the Hindi-speaking region of Haryana and the Hindi-Pahari-speaking people of the Himachal region. Into this bizarre linguistic mix-up was added another perplexing shade of political colour.

The Punjabi-speaking Hindus of the state disowned their mother tongue. Under the influence of the Jana Sangh, they claimed Hindi to be their mother tongue. Nowhere else in the world have a people willingly disclaimed their own mother tongue, which has made the Hindu Punjabis culturally the most rootless but also easily adoptable and assimilative people. So, the struggle for a Punjabi-speaking state became a communal cause championed by the Sikh religious-political party, the Shiromani Akali Dal, under the leadership of Master Tara Singh, a first-generation Sikh convert from Hinduism, whose demand for the Punjabi Suba was a ruse for Khalistan, so claimed the Hindus. Standing tall over the communal and political divisions was an American educated (University of California, Berkeley and University of Michigan), astute, secular Sikh Congressman Partap Singh Kairon, the chief minister of Punjab, a confidant of Nehru, who kept both the Akali Dal and the Jana Sangh under his and the Congress party's political dominance. After the death of Nehru, the political climate changed in Punjab. Sikh militants killed Kairon in 1965, and a year later, Prime Minister Indira Gandhi finally came to grips with the issue and trifurcated the state into Punjab (with a Sikh majority), a Hindi-speaking Haryana state, and Hindi-Pahari-speaking state, Himachal Pradesh. Chandigarh remained the joint capital of Punjab and Haryana.[58]

A decade of controversies, political debates, mass agitations, street violence, fast-unto-death endgames and assassinations finally brought forth a stronger nation, united despite different languages, nonetheless in search of a lingua franca that would transcend linguistic identities.

MAINSTREAMING TRIBALS WHO SPEAK A THOUSAND TONGUES

Nothing was beyond the empathy and compassion of Gandhi, who wrote in *Hind Swaraj*:

> My idea of village Swaraj is that it is a complete republic, independent of its neighbours for its own vital wants, and yet interdependent for many others in which dependence is a necessity... this panchayat will be the legislature, judiciary and executive combined to operate for its year of office...perfect

democracy based upon individual freedom. The individual is
the architect of his own government. The law of non-violence
rules him and the government. He and his village are able to
defy the might of a world.[59]

His views were in sharp contrast to Nehru's, who thought that 'A
village, normally speaking, is backward intellectually and culturally
and no progress can be made from a backward environment.
Narrow-minded people are much more likely to be untruthful
and violent.'[60] Ambedkar was equally pessimistic about rural
India and wondered, 'What is the village but a sink of localism, a
den of ignorance, narrow-mindedness and communalism?' [61] But
beyond the romanticized and vilified rural India, there was another
invisible India, the tribals, the aborigines, the Adivasis, with whom
anthropologist Verrier Elwin had fallen in love and wondered, 'Is
it eccentric to live in beautiful scenery in the hills among some of
the most charming people in the country, even though they may
be ignorant and poor?'[62]

According to the 1951 Census, the first census conducted after
Independence, the tribal population of India, as defined by the
Constitution, was 6.23 per cent of the total population of the country.
The Census of India includes 573 tribes spread all over the country
but since a tribe's population may be present in several states, the
actual number of distinct tribes may be much less. Tribals are mostly
concentrated in Madhya Pradesh, Chhattisgarh, Jharkhand, Odisha,
West Bengal, Maharashtra, Gujarat, Rajasthan and Andhra Pradesh,
where they constitute substantial minorities. Over the centuries,
subservient and exploitative relationships developed between them
and the surrounding non-tribal populations.

The case of tribals in the Northeast, however, is different
because in that vast, rugged mountainous region, they constitute
overwhelming majorities and have been struggling to establish
separate identities through autonomy or outright secession, which
has been the strongest and the greatest challenge to what we
might call the 'India Constant': The Unity of India, above all and
at all costs. It is in this broad parameter of the 'India Constant'

that the Gandhi–Nehru–Ambedkar–Elwin contradictions can be comprehended. The challenge for India has been how to preserve the indigenous cultures while exposing them to progressive forces of modernization and integrating them with the rest of India. It's a fascinating political phenomenon, from a historical perspective, that the tribalism of tribal India has been emerging and reincarnating in the rest of India in various masquerades such as regionalism (Assam for Assamese), the sons-of-the-soil, caste-based quota claims, and states claiming a special status to exclude others because of their special histories such as Jammu and Kashmir special status vide Articles 35A and 370 of the Constitution of India. There's a constant refrain in India: we're different; therefore, we're special.

But the tribals in India, the most exploited and oppressed people, do deserve special care, which the Constitution guarantees them vide Schedule V and Schedule VI. The British colonialism broke the isolation of the forest-dwelling tribal communities by letting loose, according to anthropologist Verrier Elwin, missionaries who destroyed 'their art, their dances, their weaving and their whole culture,' and 'merchants and liquor-venders, cajoling, tricking, swindling them in their ignorance and simplicity until bit by bit their broad acres dwindled and they sank into the poverty in which many of them still live today.'[63] The poverty outside the Northeast tribal region has been increasing due to the fact that the forests on which tribals have depended for all their needs have been dwindling because the outsider-settlers have denuded them for farming; and moreover, forest conservation laws of the British era had limited the tribals' access to their traditional natural commons and communal assets.

Besides, some of the forested areas are rich in minerals, including coal, iron, bauxite and other raw materials that India needs for industrialization. The conflict between the interests of tribals in protecting their traditional ways of life and the state interests in reclaiming forest land for expanding agriculture and mining operations, in the course of time, led to widespread conflicts.

Nehru's ardent efforts to help the tribals to get out of their protective forest walls and join the mainstream at their own pace, without giving up their culture, was based on the Congress party's long-standing policy towards tribals inspired by Gandhi's Ashram and Sewagram activities in the tribal areas of Gujarat and other places. To give the policy structural support, Article 46 of the Indian Constitution directs the government to adopt legislative and administrative measures to promote the educational and economic interests of the tribal people and protect them and their lands from exploitation and social injustices. As in the case of Scheduled Castes, the Constitution provides Scheduled Tribes with seat reservations in legislative assemblies and job quotas in administrative services. The Constitution mandates the setting up of Tribal Advisory Councils in all states for tribal welfare. The commissioner for scheduled castes and scheduled tribes, appointed by the president of India, watches over Tribal Advisory Councils' activities.

Compared to the surrounding non-tribal rural and urban areas, the pace of education in tribal areas has been rather slow. In spite of hurdles, nonetheless, the tribal community has increasingly become aware of its rights. The spread of literacy, higher education, job reservations, and political participation in the panchayat, state and national elections have raised demands in the growing tribal middle classes for a fair share of the economic development, resulting in protest movements against outsiders that have turned violent sometimes. Through transportation, communications, infrastructure, digital technology, economic developments, and most of all, through political participation, tribals are opening up to outside influences and becoming assimilated into mainstream India along with the conflicts that result from integration.

THE SPECIAL CASE OF NORTHEAST HILL TRIBALS

Since long, tribals of the Assam hills had been living isolated lives due to the difficulty of the terrain, legends of fierce warrior culture, and later on due to the British colonial policy of preserving their cultures and protecting them from exploitation by outsiders, who were not allowed to buy land or other properties. Although hill tribals were kept isolated from the rest of India, they were exposed to the outside world through the activities of Christian missionaries who established churches, schools and hospitals. The British colonial policy and the missionaries' proselytizing activities created a sense of separateness among the hill tribes of the Northeast region who felt no sympathy with the long-drawn freedom struggle that went on in the rest of India. The long cultural indoctrination by the missionaries and the British colonial policy left them not only isolated but also hostile towards India. Consequently, after Independence, it became a herculean task to re-educate and persuade them to become part of India while maintaining their traditional culture and autonomy. The Constitution of India takes special notice of the Assam tribal people and Article 244 of the Sixth Schedule provides them with special protection. To give the provision an administrative and political force, the Government of India carved out from the state of Assam the Northeast Frontier Agency (NEFA) in 1948 as a union territory under a separate administration. Special development policies were implemented without disturbing their traditional way of life. But the NEFA did not cover other hill tribes of Assam, including the Nagas, the Mizos and others. The hill tribals resented being part of Assam, especially during the linguistic reorganization of states, when Assamese, under the Assam Official Language Act of 1960, became the state official language. Nevertheless, the hill tribals willy-nilly were becoming part of the political process and, in their own ways, had begun to play the game of democracy.

For example, various hill tribal parties combined to form the All-Party Hill Leaders Conference (APHLC) in 1960 and demanded a separate state, which led to protests, demonstrations and strikes as was happening in other parts of the country. Through a long-drawn-out democratic process of special commissions and their reports followed by negotiations, discussions and compromises, the Government of India, through a constitutional amendment, created a new state of Meghalaya (1972). In the same period, Manipur and Tripura transitioned from Union Territories to full states. The NEFA, a Union Territory, too became a full state, Arunachal Pradesh (1987). But some northeast hill tribals, the Nagas and the Mizos, supported by China, Pakistan and some misguided foreign church clergies, broke out into prolonged violent insurgencies that led to widespread atrocities, drained India's military resources and drew international attention. Eventually, the insurgent Nagas and Mizos put down their arms and joined the democratic processes of political and economic development, as did other separatists, for example, in Punjab. Without nation-building, whether through persuasion or pressure, which is a continuous process, the idea of India, the India Constant, would remain a mere illusion.

THE NAGA CHALLENGE: THE INDIA CONSTANT

For a long time, the Northeast has been associated with the Nagas, though the region has 220 ethnic groups who speak innumerable dialects. The region never captured the imagination of India until the Nagas, under the unrelenting and vicious leadership of Angami Zapu Phizo, began to fight for an independent Naga nation. What made the Nagas look ferocious was the legend of headhunting, a celebratory ritual for manhood,[64] which was abolished in the late nineteenth century. Though barbaric, it's important to keep in mind that severing the head of an enemy and bringing it home to the ruler or showing it to the public on a charger as a trophy was not an uncommon practice among some people in earlier ages. Even the Bible mentions the severed head of John the Baptist. The Baptist Christian missionaries transformed the Naga culture, but instead of bringing them closer to India, they polarized them and indoctrinated them with a sense of separate identity. The British, too, left them to their hills, to their traditions and customs, and moreover, they kept the Nagas segregated from the rest of the country during the movement for Independence.

At the time of Independence, as mentioned earlier, the Naga territory was part of a vast sprawling province of Assam. The region is comprised of mountains and plains, drained by the mighty Brahmaputra, borders with Bhutan and Tibet to the north, and Burma (now Myanmar) and East Pakistan (now Bangladesh) to the east. Besides the Nagas, Assam included several other tribes who would fight for their own independent nations. Acculturating the violent tribes of Assam and the Northeast into the national democratic mainstream, the India Constant, has been a prolonged struggle and by and large a success story. Today the region, now known as 'the seven sister states' including Assam, Arunachal Pradesh, Nagaland, Mizoram, Meghalaya, and the former princely states of Manipur and Tripura, plays the same game of democracy as does the rest of India, that is, multiparty electioneering, political horse-trading, coalition governments, question hours, no-confidence motions, street protests, and formation and reformation of governments, with all the noise and chaos and random violence of Indian democracy.

The political transformation of 'the seven sisters' of the northeastern region began with the Nagas, who said they were not Indians. India insisted that the Nagas must become part of the Indian family, separate but together. To be separate and yet together has been a constant theme as well as an obsession in India since Independence. In this sense, the Nagas have been no different from the Khalistan-minded Sikhs, the Muslim Kashmiris and the Dravidian Tamils. Conjeevaram Natarajan Annadurai (Anna), Jarnail Singh Bhindranwale, Sheikh Muhammad Abdullah and Angami Zapu Phizo had similar dreams. During World War II, when Phizo was in Burma, he had collaborated with the invading Japanese army, a kind of goodwill, in case the Japanese won. Due to British India's indulgence, Phizo was not treated as a traitor.

The Naga tribes' demand for their homeland began with the establishment of the Naga National Council (NNC) in 1946. Apparently united under one banner, they were actually divided into two major factions, one seeking maximum autonomy through negotiations, and the other faction led by Phizo was vehemently bent on complete independence from India. The radicals under Phizo prevailed and on 14 August 1947, a day before India's Independence, nine members of the NNC declared their own Independence. Later on, the NNC claimed that based on their door-to-door conducted referendum in May 1951, an overwhelming majority (99 per cent) of the people of the Naga Hills wanted Independence.[65] Of course, the Indian government refused to acknowledge the Naga self-conducted referendum as a legitimate expression of the Naga tribes.

The NNC boycotted the 1952 election, independent India's first general election that would have covered the Naga Hills' tribals. The call for an independent Nagaland began to snowball, and the Nagas rallied around Phizo and the NNC for an independent state that would include the Nagas on both sides of the India–Burma border. In several meetings with Phizo and other NNC leaders in 1951–52, Nehru, while assuring them of maximum autonomy within the Constitution, nonetheless, categorically rejected their demand for an independent Naga nation. Nehru's every gesture of sympathy and goodwill was rejected by Phizo and the NNC, and they began to talk in a language reminiscent of Jinnah that Hindus and Muslims had nothing in common and were two separate nations. In fact, Phizo and the NNC went further and said that the moment they saw Indians, 'a gloomy feeling darkness creeps into our minds'. [66]

The point of no return occurred in March 1953 when Prime Minister Nehru and Burmese Prime Minister U Nu visited Kohima (now the capital of Nagaland) to address a public meeting to assure the Nagas, since they were spread over on both sides of the India–Burma border, that their future in India and Burma would be secure. Some Naga leaders wanted to make a representation to Nehru, but the deputy commissioner of Kohima announced to the gathering that no meeting or delegation of any kind would be allowed. According to a retrospective eyewitness account, the deputy commissioner's announcement, when translated into the Nagamese language to the audience, was 'enough to stir up a huge commotion amongst the Nagas gathered at the Kohima local ground that day...the whole crowd rose up at once shouting and expressing their annoyance and anger in their own traditional manners and walked out of the local ground leaving behind only heaps of dust.' The unexpected event 'left both Nehru and U Nu completely stunned and numbed,' and caught them both 'completely unaware and unprepared... a total humiliation and disgrace for both Nehru and U Nu... something they had never experienced before and would not witness again anywhere in their lives.' After this humbling experience at Kohima,

'Nehru and U Nu travelled by road to Imphal,' a long trip, during which, 'Nehru did not utter even a single word.' [67]

Now onwards, it was another long insurgency for the Indian Army and the Assam Rifles to handle. The NNC leadership went underground and turned into a ferocious guerrilla force. The Federal Government of Nagaland and the Naga Federal Army were formed. The jungle guerrilla warfare between the Indian Army and the Nagas under Phizo and the NNC continued with increasing intensity spreading over hills and dales. When T. Sakhrie, an NNC leader, sought compromise and accommodation with the Government of India, he was brutally murdered by Phizo's men in January 1956.[68] Phizo, who had escaped via East Pakistan (now Bangladesh) to London, continued guiding the secessionist insurgency with the support of some of the sympathetic and misguided British clergy who too believed that the Nagas had nothing to do with India. While the insurgency and the Army operations continued, the Government of India took some definitive administrative and legislative measures to give the Nagas a separate political and cultural identity.

In 1957, after discussion with Naga tribal leaders, the Indian government consolidated the Naga territories into a single administrative unit of the Naga Hills Tuensang area, a Union Territory with substantial autonomy, directly administered by the central government. Because of Phizo guiding the insurgency from London, the local tribal leaders had little influence over the underground insurgents, and the attacks on Army posts, government institutions and banks continued unabated. But the solution ultimately had to be political. In July 1960, Nehru and the Naga People's Convention (NPC) reached a 16-point agreement under which Nagaland would become a state within the Indian Union.[69] Parliament passed the Nagaland Act in 1962. Nagaland, with Kohima as its capital, became a full-fledged state on 1 December 1963. Nagalanders elected their first Legislative Assembly in January 1964 and formed their first democratically elected government on 11 February 1964. With the political structure in place, it was now a matter of a long-drawn-out process of persuasion and coercion, carrot and stick, which would eventually bring the people of Nagaland to the Indian democratic fold. It must be said that Angami Zapu Phizo never gave up on his dream of a free Nagaland until his death on 30 April 1990, in London, where he had lived as a stateless citizen on the sympathy and the goodwill of strangers.

5

INDIA DANCES WITH NEHRU ON THE WORLD STAGE

The only alternative to coexistence is co-destruction.

—Jawaharlal Nehru

Where freedom is menaced or justice threatened or where aggression takes place, we cannot be and shall not be neutral.

—Jawaharlal Nehru

So important to all of us, that if he did not exist—as Voltaire said of God—he would have to be invented. ...One of the most difficult men with whom I have ever had to deal.

—Dean Acheson on Jawaharlal Nehru

One of the greatest and most enduring achievements of the Nehru era was the establishment of the Indus Waters Treaty with Pakistan. The landmark agreement for river water sharing was mediated by the World Bank and signed by Prime Minister Jawaharlal Nehru and Field Marshal Ayub Khan, the President of Pakistan, on 19 September 1960 in Karachi. The treaty gave India control of the water flowing in the three eastern rivers, the Beas, the Ravi and the Sutlej, while Pakistan got control over the three western rivers, including the Jhelum, the Chenab and the Indus. The Indus River originates in the Tibetan plateau near Lake Mansarovar and flows through the Union Territory of Ladakh (formerly part of the state of Jammu and Kashmir) before it enters Pakistan, where in the southerly downstream direction, it is joined by five major tributary rivers originating in India before it empties itself into the Arabian Sea near the Karachi port. Beginning in the Himalayan, Karakoram and the Hindu Kush ranges, and fed by snow, glaciers and several tributary rivers apart from the five aforementioned tributaries from the Indian side, the Indus, with a total drainage area of 450,000 square miles and annual water flow of 58 cubic miles, is one of the largest rivers of the world. Like the Nile and the Tigris, it has been the cradle of a great ancient civilization, the Indus Civilization, vedic India and Sanskrit. The mighty river was known in ancient India in Sanskrit as Sindhu, and flowed along with explorers and itinerants through ancient Persia, Greece and Rome, and returned as the Indus to give the country its name, India.

THE INDUS WATERS TREATY

The question was how the river waters of the Indus basin, which originate in India but ultimately merge with the Indus River in Pakistan, were to be shared between the two countries after Partition. Under the provisions of the treaty, India was allowed to use the eastern rivers, before they flow into Pakistan, for limited irrigation purposes and unrestricted use for non-irrigation purposes such as power generation, navigation, floating of property, fish culture, etc. based on specific regulations for building such projects. Since Pakistan's Punjab was also dependent upon the three eastern rivers allotted to India, Pakistan was to receive from India in ten instalments, £62,060,000 for constructing canal and irrigation systems in Pakistan. For dispute resolution, the Indus Waters Treaty established the Permanent Indus Commission having officials from both countries, for the implementation of the goals and objectives of the treaty, data exchange, cooperation for the development of the basin and the resolution of potential disputes. Either country must inform and provide data to the other about any project that might affect the other country. Disputes may be submitted to the Permanent Court of Arbitration or Neutral Technical Expert.[1]

The treaty's provisions were very generous to Pakistan, keeping in mind that, while India was allotted about 20 per cent of the river's water, Pakistan was given the right to 80 per cent. Reaching an amicable river water-sharing agreement between two countries that had fought a bitter war over Jammu and Kashmir was imperative for economic survival, especially of Pakistan, but it wasn't easy. Outside involvement was deemed essential. Based on the thoughts of David Lilienthal, the chairman of the Tennessee Valley Authority and the US Atomic Energy Commission, that the Indus basin river system dispute should be viewed as an engineering problem for the economic development of both countries rather than a political one, the World Bank and its president, Eugene Black, took the lead to work with India and Pakistan to resolve the dispute as to how best to develop and utilize the resources of the Indus basin. After two years of protracted discussion, the World Bank proposed in 1954 that instead of river water sharing, the rivers should be divided between the two countries; the three eastern rivers going to India, and the three western rivers going to Pakistan with the provision that the international community should take the responsibility of financing the construction of canals and storage dams needed by Pakistan for the development of its three western rivers to compensate for the loss of water from the three eastern rivers to be allotted to India.

The consortium countries including Australia, Canada, West Germany, New Zealand, the UK, the US, along with the World Bank, entered into an agreement with Pakistan and established the Indus Basin Development Fund Agreement to fund the project. The Indus Waters Treaty, with the goodwill of the World Bank, which meant the United Sates primarily, became effective in September 1960 and since then has been in operation without any major hurdles.[2]

NON-ALIGNMENT WITH MALICE TOWARDS NONE

Nehru was first and foremost a nationalist albeit with an international outlook. The pursuit of an independent foreign policy was founded on enlightened domestic necessity so that India could build its economy based on the principles of democracy and socialism, which required functional and purposeful friendship with both the West and the Soviet bloc. There's continuity and consistency between Gandhi's freedom struggle based on nonviolence and Nehru's foreign policy based on non-alignment. Gandhi's whole life, in South Africa as well as in India, and the struggle for human rights and freedom was grounded on breaking down the walls and on the firm belief that people with different ideologies and religious beliefs could and must live together with mutual respect. India's non-alignment policy was the expression and projection of India's nonviolent freedom struggle on the international stage.

It's a tribute to Nehru's political genius and innovative thinking that he turned India's non-alignment policy into an international movement embraced by most of the newly liberated countries. As an ancient civilization now on its own after centuries of domination, India needed a platform to speak its mind and be heard, and so did other newly independent countries. And the spadework that was done by the India-led non-alignment movement provided an alternative platform to the ideologies and the military blocs of the two superpowers, the Soviet Union's Warsaw Pact and the US-led North Atlantic Treaty Organization (NATO), Southeast Asia Treaty Organization (SEATO), Central Treaty Organization (CENTO), Baghdad Pact and others.

India, as the most important leader of the Non-Aligned Movement, coupled with Nehru's personal charisma, gave the platform high seriousness and respectability. The Non-Aligned Movement was not a passive withdrawal or immoral neutrality, but an active engagement and fight against 'evil forces of fascism, colonialism and racialism or the nuclear bomb and aggression and suppression' and therefore as Nehru said, 'we stand most emphatically and unequivocally committed against them,' and furthermore, 'We are unaligned only in relation to the cold war with its military pacts' as well as objecting 'to all this business of forcing the new nations of Asia and Africa into their cold war machine...we are free to condemn any development which we consider wrong or harmful to the world or ourselves and we use that freedom every time the occasion arises.'[3]

As a community of independent countries, in the course of time, the non-aligned bloc evolved into a third force on the international fora; and consequently, the bloc introduced an informal democratic system of checks and balances in the West dominated UN. With the non-aligned bloc's activism, the world seemed a safer place instead of being a mutually destructive bipolar world.

Although China under Mao Zedong, advocated a policy of confrontation against the West, calling the US a paper tiger, believing that in a nuclear war most of China's huge population would survive, Nehru, on the other hand, advocated a policy of peaceful coexistence between nations with different political systems and ideologies. To operationalize the concept of peaceful coexistence into a practical system, Nehru used the Buddhist concept of *Panchshila*, widely understood in Asia, and reformulated it into five guiding principles, Panchsheel, which was the basis of the Sino–Indian Agreement 1954, regarding China's suzerainty over Tibet in 1954.[4] The five principles of Panchsheel included:

1. Mutual respect for each other's territorial integrity and sovereignty
2. Mutual non-aggression
3. Mutual non-interference in each other's internal affairs
4. Equality and cooperation for mutual benefit
5. Peaceful coexistence

It was out of firm conviction, not a mere political necessity, that Nehru advocated at every international forum that a pluralistic world with different ideological systems was essential so that the possibility of mutual nuclear destruction could be avoided. Greater and more varied the grey area, that is, the distance between the West and the Soviet bloc, better the chances of world peace. India and the newly liberated countries needed global peace so that they could get out of the colonial legacy of massive poverty. The approach was in sharp contrast to Chairman Mao's political doctrine of confrontation against the West of which armed coexistence was only an initial phase.[5]

Between March and April in 1947, six months before Independence, more than 20 Asian countries' representatives assembled in New Delhi for the Asian Relations Conference hosted by Nehru, who, at that time, was the head of the provisional government of India. The purpose of the conference was to bring together Asian leaders 'to study the problems of common concern to the people of the continent, to focus attention on social, economic and cultural problems of the different countries of Asia, and to foster mutual contact and understanding.'[6] India was going to be an independent nation soon and needed to build up diplomatic relations with other rising leaders in Asia. Inspiring and eloquent, with a sweeping view of history, Nehru told the gathering of Asian leaders:

> We stand at the end of an era and on the threshold of a new period of history. Standing on this watershed, which divides two epochs of human history and endeavour, we can look back on our long past and look forward to the future that is taking shape before our eyes. Asia, after a long period of quiescence, has suddenly become important again in world affairs...It was here that civilization began and man started on his unending adventure of life. Here the mind of man searched unceasingly for truth and the spirit of man shone out like a beacon, which lightened up the whole world.[7]

In pursuit of active non-alignment, India, in December 1948, raised its voice and, along with several Asian countries as well as the support of the US, thwarted the Dutch attempt to reassert its colonial control in Indonesia. The Security Council passed a resolution in January 1949 asking the Netherlands to stop hostilities and restore the Indonesian President Sukarno's republican government in Yogyakarta.[8] A major milestone of the non-alignment movement, the Bandung Conference, took place in 1955 at a gathering of 29 Africa–Asia nations, of all political shades and ideologies, held in Bandung, Indonesia. The delegates, including those from India, Burma, Ceylon and Pakistan, represented a total of 1.5 billion of 54 per cent of the global population at that time.

The participant countries had different experiences in their struggle against colonialism to regain their independence. During his speech to the Bandung Political Conference, Nehru made it crystal clear that India was not part of either of the two blocs asserting that:

> If we have to stand alone, we will stand by ourselves, whatever happens (and India has stood alone without any aid against a mighty Empire, the British Empire) and we propose to face all consequences...We do not agree with the communist teachings, we do not agree with the anti-communist teachings, because they are both based on wrong principles.[9]

His attention was focused on colonial powers. China's expansionist ambitions and the creeping threat in the Himalayas were not even in his peripheral vision when he said, 'We will defend ourselves with whatever arms and strength we have... *I am dead certain that no country can conquer India* [emphasis added]. I know what my people are. But I know also that if we rely on others, whatever great powers they might be if we look to them for sustenance, then we are weak indeed.'[10]

Nehru's idealism of stand-alone self-reliance, especially in military affairs, would be seriously tested by China's aggression in 1962 when India realized that conventional and asymmetrical warfare by an intrepid enemy was more dangerous than the threat of nuclear warfare. But until then, India played a large role on the world stage, a remarkable achievement that was totally disproportionate to its economic and military strength.

The Bandung Conference, where the Panchsheel was expanded to a 10-point declaration for the promotion of world peace and cooperation, was also a call for post-colonial countries to band together and cooperate with each other by sharing technologies and knowhow for economic development and reduce their dependence upon industrialized nations of the West, the former colonial powers. The theme of world peace and the perils of nuclear weapons were taken up again at the Belgrade Non-alignment Conference in 1961, where Nehru joined hands with President Josip Broz Tito of Yugoslavia, a communist country that had broken away from the Soviet bloc, and President Gamal Abdel Nasser of Egypt, an acclaimed Arab leader, whose nationalization of the Suez Canal had led to the invasion of Egypt by the UK, France and Israel.

It is important to keep in mind that India played a truly constructive role in bringing about the resolution of the Suez Canal crisis. Nehru, apart from condemning the dastardly aggression, sought the US intervention to end the conflict in which Egyptian forces could not match against the UK–France–Israel forces. Under US sponsorship, the UN Security Council passed a resolution asking for a ceasefire and pullback behind the armistice lines. Subsequently, India worked with Asian–African nations to pass a resolution in the General Assembly for full compliance of the UN ceasefire resolution. Another UN resolution provided for the formation of a UN peacekeeping force in the Suez Canal zone, for which India was requested to send armed troops for peacekeeping.[11] It is with this backdrop that the Belgrade Non-alignment Conference must be seen. The important point is that although India was non-aligned, it did not hesitate to seek American intervention to end the crisis in a country that was a member of the non-aligned group of nations. Working with the US and being active in global affairs for world peace was a form of positive non-alignment policy. In the background of the Belgrade Conference, however, another conflict was brewing. India was facing its own low-level crisis with China on the Himalayan border. Would India seek the West's help if the crisis blew out of proportion?

India's interest in multinational forums, as we have seen, began before Independence, which also included its association with the Commonwealth, an intergovernmental organization of 53 nations, former British colonies that had developed commonalities of shared values including English language, democracy, free speech and the rule of law. In spite of some opposition that the continued association with the Commonwealth might impact India's standing as an independent nation, Nehru, the internationalist, thought it would serve the national interest. India needed international exposure for trade, commerce and economic development that necessitated international networking.

Although the Indian military had played an active role during World War I and World War II under the British military command, as an independent nation, it was now time to play a different role, the role of peacekeeping under the auspices of the UN; a different facet of the non-alignment policy, which was a learning experience for India. The first stress test for the non-alignment policy came during the Korean War. Korea had been a Japan ruled territory since 1910, but after World War II and Japan's defeat, Korea was split between the Soviet Union and the US at the 38th parallel. The Soviet Union and China backed communist North Korea and the West supported non-communist South Korea lived uneasily in the Cold War tension of the era.

Nonetheless, emboldened by the expansionist policy of the Soviets and the Chinese, North Korea crossed the 38th parallel and invaded South Korea on 25 June 1950. Although India supported the US-sponsored Security Council resolution condemning the North Korean aggression, it declined to support another resolution calling for the setting up of a UN command to defend South Korea. Since India's vote as a non-permanent member of the Security Council did not count and the Soviet Union had abstained from voting, the UN Command was set up with General Douglas MacArthur as the head of US forces, who not only drove back North Korean forces beyond the 38th parallel but also continued marching to its northern border with China.

Since Mao's China did not have diplomatic relations with the US, it used the office of the Indian ambassador in China, K.M. Panikkar, to warn the US that it would retaliate. But General MacArthur wasn't listening, and China sent wave after wave of Chinese troops to push back the American forces to the south of the 38th parallel. At the UN, India refused to denounce China as the aggressor, though China was also invading Tibet, which we will discuss later. India's Left-leaning vitriolic Defence Minister V.K. Krishna Menon eagerly played the role of a peacemaker giving Indians a false sense of international prestige. But it was only after the death of Josef Stalin in June 1953 that a ceasefire was actually established, and repatriation of the prisoners of war (POWs) began. In some sense, it was a glorious moment for Indian diplomacy and its active non-alignment foreign policy, especially when Indians learnt that the UN had set up the Neutral Repatriation Commission with Army Major General K.S. Thimayya of India as the chairman.[12] The 38th parallel, the actual line of control, became the frontier between China supported communist North Korea, which would eventually become a nuclear power, from an authoritarian South Korea that would develop, in alliance with the US, into a dynamic democratic economy.

INDIA'S DIMINISHING VALUE ON WORLD STAGE

Whatever limited success in peacemaking and diplomatic reputation India had earned during the Korean War dissipated when the US and China entered into the most brutal and inhuman war in a divided Vietnam, a French colony that France could no longer control due to Ho Chi Minh's guerrilla fighting force, the Viet Minh. At the end of World War II, the Viet Minh forces under the leadership of Ho Chi Minh, the founder of the Indochinese Communist Party and later the Viet Minh, seized the northern Vietnamese city of Hanoi and declared the establishment of the Democratic State of Vietnam, which however was limited to North Vietnam. With the full military support of China and the Soviet Union, North Vietnam, in its attempt at the unification of the whole country, continued its struggle against South Vietnam, an anti-communist regime supported by the US.

In the prolonged conflict between the US and Vietnam, which also involved Laos and Cambodia and lasted until the fall of Saigon in 1975, India had little role to play except constantly berating the US, whose help it would later need on many occasions and on many fronts. India's support for the struggle of Vietnam, however, was legitimate and consistent with its anti-colonial policy. The ultimate victor of the Vietnam War was China. Flying from Pakistan in 1971, Henry Kissinger, the US National Security Adviser, paid a secret visit to China that paved the way for President Richard Nixon to make a week-long visit in 1972. Normalizing relations with China was deemed necessary as leverage against the Soviet Union and, more importantly, to end the Vietnam War that had dehumanized America. American diplomat Winston Lord observed:

> By dealing with Russia and with China we hoped to put pressure on Hanoi to negotiate seriously... we sought to persuade Russia and China to encourage Hanoi to make a deal with the United States and give Hanoi a sense of isolation because their two, big patrons were dealing with us. Indeed, by their willingness to engage in summit meetings with us, with Nixon going to China in February 1972, and to Moscow in May 1972, the Russians and Chinese were beginning to place a higher priority on their bilateral relations with us than on their dealings with their friends in Hanoi.[13]

In this big global diplomatic game, India had receded into the background. India was nowhere. Nehru had become a distant historical memory. The non-alignment had become a policy of firm national interest when Indira Gandhi ruled India.

INDIA AND THE SOVIET UNION

Even before India achieved Independence, Nehru had been a great admirer of the Soviet Union, its system of planned economy, massive industrialization, and the humane treatment of workers, peasants, women and children. On the 10th anniversary of the Bolshevik Revolution, when he visited the Soviet Union, he found the spirit of the revolution still alive though Lenin had died a few years before. Perhaps like most other people who admired the Bolshevik Revolution from the outside, he too was unaware of its aftermath, the forced collectivization, corrective labour camps, and Gulag prison camps for political prisoners under both Vladimir Lenin and Josef Stalin. Aleksandr Solzhenitsyn, a Gulag survivor and winner of the Nobel Prize for literature, gave a chilling account in his 1973 eyewitness-based fictionalized account, *The Gulag Archipelago: An Experiment in Literary Investigation.*

Impressed by a communist Soviet Union's achievements, Nehru, a committed democrat, wanted to accomplish the same socio-economic goals through democratic socialism. The Soviet Union was a superpower and India needed its goodwill and help. Developing friendly relations with the Soviet Union would become the cornerstone of India's foreign policy. But the Soviet Union under Stalin viewed India as a lackey of western imperialism, in spite of having achieved Independence. The decision to continue its membership of the British Commonwealth added to the misperception.[14] The Soviet Union was committed to the global communist revolution and the Soviet Communist Party had great hopes from the CPI to carry out its revolutionary agenda. The CPI was conducting an insurgency in Telangana, Hyderabad, which, however, failed.[15] Gradually Stalin's attitude began to change, though not his ultimate revolutionary goal, so he 'cautioned the CPI leaders that the Nehru government was not a puppet government. It had a social base and mass support and could not be overthrown easily.'[16] According to an impressionistic account of the Indian ambassador to the Soviet Union K.P.S. Menon (1952–1961), Stalin had 'almost rustic simplicity…spontaneous humour…single-mindedness… perspicacity…vision of the world as divided into black and white— *with a lonely grey, India, standing in between* [emphasis added]'. He commented upon Stalin's 'utter ruthlessness, and his cynical and thoroughly Marxist disregard of morals which he made no attempt to hide.'[17] The *'lonely grey area, India,'* created space for Indian diplomacy. Much was at stake. Although Stalin did not care much about India's first ambassador Vijaya Lakshmi Pandit, who was also Prime Minister Nehru's sister, he warmed up to Dr Sarvepalli Radhakrishnan, the philosopher diplomat who would later go on to become President of the Indian Republic. In the January 1950 meeting with Stalin, Dr Radhakrishnan expressed the 'hope that good relations between two countries would be strengthened… affirmed India's anxiety to do everything possible to work for peace which was essential to enable her to build up the country and improve living standards.' Dr Radhakrishnan expounded what Nehru had affirmed at the Colombo Powers meeting (1954) that,

'India's policy of neutrality was real and positive,' and India was anxious 'to avoid cold war tactics and anti-Communist pacts.'

The brief exchange aroused Stalin's interest in India, which is captured in the official diplomatic summary and is worth reading:

> Stalin asked several questions regarding India's position in Commonwealth and seemed anxious to know if she was more or less independent than, say, Canada. Ambassador explained position especially in light of India's forthcoming declaration as a Republic. Stalin asked if India was entitled to have her own army without any restriction and also if there is a navy, He NODDED approval when informed that was case; Commander-in-Chief was Indian and there was also an Indian Air Force. He enquired if relations with Pakistan were still bad and about language they spoke there. He was told that relations were rather strained as Pakistan was of the view that wherever there were Muslims they must be with them. Of the languages of India he enquired which was dominant and expressed satisfaction that Hindi was PHONETIC and NOT HIEROGLYPHIC as it would thus be easier to liquidate illiteracy, unlike the position in China where even to read a newspaper it needs five years of study.[20]

Before his return to India, S. Radhakrishnan had another meeting with Stalin, which showed that Stalin had begun to see India in a different light and was eager to help any which way that was doable. Though it was a minor irritant, Stalin agreed to recall the *Tass* correspondent in New Delhi whose coverage about India was perceived to be unfair. When Dr Radhakrishnan expressed that India had a strong desire and anxiety for preserving Indo-Soviet friendship, Stalin replied:

> Both you and Mr. Nehru are persons whom we do not consider to be our enemies. This will continue to be our policy and you can count on our help... The United States and Britain look on Asian peoples as backward and look down upon them. We treat all Asians as equals. It is this which helps us to conduct

a correct policy. The Americans and the British treat them superciliously [sic]. Our policy helps us to have very different relations with the Asian peoples.[21]

K.P.S. Menon, who replaced Radhakrishnan as the next ambassador to the Soviet Union, however, had a different impression about Stalin, whose political philosophy, as he expressed to Menon, was encapsulated simply as: 'The peasant is a very simple man but very wise. When the wolf attacks him, he does not attempt to teach it morals but kills it. And the wolf knows it and behaves accordingly.'[22] Coming from a Gandhian background, K.P.S. Menon perhaps failed to comprehend Stalin's shrewdness and ruthlessness until India would confront the wolf that came over from the Himalayas.

Developing friendly relations with the Soviet Union, apart from serving India's larger goal of the national interest, would also co-opt the CPI. The defanged party would eventually join mainstream Indian politics and play the game of democracy like any other political party, rather than looking to the Soviet Union for instructions. The positive role played by India, based on its active non-alignment policy during the Korean War, possibly changed Stalin's misperception that India was a western puppet. In 1951–52 India suffered one of its periodic droughts and asked for food aid, but before the US could make up its mind, the Soviet Union agreed to send a shipment of 50,000 tons of wheat to tide over the crisis. The crisis must have also convinced the Indian leaders that the country needed a wider network of friends and the non-alignment policy needed to be flexible. Pursuant to this policy, India signed its first trade agreement with the Soviet Union in 1953.[23]

THE EMERGENCE OF NIKITA KHRUSHCHEV

The mellowing of the relationship was further hastened after Stalin's death. His departure was followed by de-Stalinization and a period of brutal power struggle, after which Nikita Khrushchev emerged as the Communist Party Secretary. After denouncing Stalin's crimes, Khrushchev took modest steps in opening up and liberalizing the

Soviet Union, however, without giving up on Marxism–Leninism on which he had grown up. Khrushchev wanted Soviet citizens to see western achievements and believed that the Soviet Union could compete with the West. Bold enough to meet the challenge, he allowed Soviet citizens to travel abroad and foreigners to visit the Soviet Union.[24] To compete with the western world, the Soviet Union had to go beyond the Soviet bloc in order to establish trade relations with the emerging Third World countries to let them see how good the Soviet technology and its products were. This further required, for practical reasons, the dumbing down or softening of hardline Stalinist ideology so that international relations through commerce and trade could be enhanced. In other words, the Soviet Union was coming out of its protective shell and was ready to compete on its own terms, for which India and other emerging countries provided a platform.

Diplomatic relations with India during the Stalin era, however limited, had shown an opening for both countries. India was eager to take advantage of the Soviet Union's changed view of the world under Khrushchev and needed to balance American assertiveness in Asia (CENTO and SEATO) by developing relations with an alternative competing global power. Competition between two superpowers, if managed well, could be beneficial to India in acquiring technology and economic assistance from both blocs for industrial development. Since the Soviet Union had accepted the peaceful coexistence of different political systems, India's democratic polity and domestic policy would not be adversely affected. Moreover, close and managed relations with the Soviet Union would domesticate the extremists in the CPI. Although there were political limits to what India could accept from the Soviet Union, the Indian ambassador in Moscow recommended, 'it was worth pursuing the possibility of the Soviet Union establishing a tractor factory in India first and perhaps a steel factory and oil refinery later on.'[25]

India's non-alignment policy was evolving into a policy of realpolitik in search of competitive advantages without giving up its role as a world peacemaker. The challenge for India would be how to integrate the technology and economic aid received from two different systems, one based on state-controlled economy and the other anchored in democratic capitalism, into India's five-year planned economy within a federal-parliamentary system. It was a test of Indian political genius. But the system was flexible, and India adapted and assimilated the virtue of the two systems. India was beginning to embark upon the Second Five-Year plan that emphasized heavy industry under the public sector and consumer goods, mostly in the private sector, along with the goal of increasing agricultural production. The nation was attempting a state-run industrial revolution based upon developmental needs rather than market forces. It needed technology and economic aid for steel plants, oil exploration, coal production, fertilizer factories, and railroad and transport infrastructure. The Soviet Union had built a massive industrial base and was ready to help. Once the Soviet Union entered India's economic development plans, it was only a matter of time before western countries too would enter the Indian economic space, which they did. Five steel plants, for example, were built during the Second Five-Year Plan with technology and economic aid from the Soviet Union, Britain and West Germany. And most of all, with no strings attached. Most importantly, developing friendly relations with the Soviet bloc helped India in establishing trade and commerce in the rupee exchange with the bloc rather than in pound sterling or the dollar, of which India did not have enough reserves. This was a most shining facet of the non-alignment policy.

It was in this changed environment that in 1955 Nehru paid a highly acclaimed visit to the Soviet Union, including to some Soviet Republics in Central Asia, and to Czechoslovakia, Poland, Yugoslavia, the UK, Egypt and some other countries. Mikhail Gorbachev, who was a young student at that time, would later on write in his memoir that Jawaharlal Nehru's visit to Moscow was an 'unexpected stimulus' and opened his eyes to see beyond the Communist Party propaganda of the world being black-and-white, and that 'This amazing man, his noble bearing, keen eyes and warm and disarming smile, made a deep impression on me.'[26] Despite the absence of civil liberties and the Soviet sense of paranoia of being surrounded by hostile forces, Nehru was impressed by the immense progress being made in the field of science, technology, athletics, infrastructure and children's education. He was keenly interested in adapting the Soviet planning approaches to Indian democratic planning methods. He also did not hear any war drums against the West. But whatever countries he visited, Nehru asserted India's independent foreign policy and opposition to military pacts.[27]

The new leaders of the Soviet Union Communist Party, Secretary Nikita Khrushchev and Prime Minister Nikolai Bulganin, heartily reciprocated the gesture by visiting India for three weeks in November–December 1955. The welcome the visitors received was spontaneous and totally unexpected, for which the Indian security was unprepared. For example, in Calcutta, 2 million Indians gathered to greet the Soviet leaders, which worried the Indian and Soviet security so much that the visitors were transferred from an open car to an enclosed protected van. As an American reporter observed,

> 'It was the biggest, noisiest greeting ever received by Soviet leaders outside their own country. 'A feast of friendliness,' Indian Prime Minister Jawaharlal Nehru called it. The visit was also a watershed for the Soviet Union's relations with India and, in fact, with the rest of the developing world. In the three decades since, the Soviet Union and India have formed one of the strongest, if oddest, partnerships between nations.'[28]

As a parting gesture, the Soviet leaders announced the donation of equipment for a 30,000-acre new mechanized farm in Suratgarh, Rajasthan. But there was a hefty matter that seriously concerned Nehru—the treacherous behaviour of the CPI. It was widely believed that the CPI was seeking and following instructions from the Soviet Communist Party. Khrushchev, however, denied the charge and assured his host that the Soviet Communist Party had no connection with the Indian Communist Party.

But later research, including the communist leader Mohit Sen's autobiography, *A Traveller and the Road, the Journal of an Indian*

Communist, showed that the CPI indeed was a running dog of the Soviet Communist Party.[29] Perhaps Nehru did not realize fully that the Soviet leaders did not visit India to give a free lunch; that they were Stalinists with kid gloves (consider the Cuban nuclear brinkmanship); that they were proselytizers; and that most of all, the CPI was one of their assets. Later on, Mao's China would use various shades of Indian communists and other similar hidden assets for their own military and political purposes.

In spite of the perfidious dealings of the CPI and the Soviet leaders' soft power and hard sell during their visits, the strengthening of Indo-Soviet relations raised India's international prestige. But at the same time, it also created the impression that India's non-alignment was tilting towards the Soviet Union, which became obvious during the Hungarian Revolution (or the Hungarian Uprising) in 1956 when Soviet tanks rolled through Budapest and crushed the uprising. At the UN, India refused to condemn the Soviet brutality though at home, Indian commentators were very sympathetic with the Hungarians' aspirations for freedom, and there was a popular cry against the ruthless Soviet actions.[30] India's UN representative, Defence Minister Krishna Menon, regarded by some at home and abroad as crypto-communist, abstained from the UN resolution that asked the Soviet Union to withdraw its forces from Hungary. He wouldn't have done it without Nehru's approval.

India's muted criticism of the Soviet action was in sharp contrast to its bitter condemnation of the UK–France–Israel invasion of Egypt during the Suez Canal crisis, giving the impression that Nehru was 'falling for the Moscow line—buying their entire bill of goods.' Subsequent diplomatic reports regarding the Soviet brutal suppression and rising domestic criticism from Acharya J.B. Kripalani and Jayaprakash Narayan, however, 'brought into question Nehru's own ambivalence on Russia's interventionism,' and convinced him that 'the Hungarian uprising was of a nationalist character, and not organized by fascist elements,' making him openly critical of the Soviet military action in Hungary.[31] In an attempt at being even-handed between the East and the West, he 'advocated a mutual withdrawal of Warsaw Pact and NATO forces from Central

Europe.' When the leader of the Hungarian uprising Imre Nagy was executed in June 1958, Nehru was shocked and 'expressed his feelings of dismay' at the 'cold-blooded act.' He expressed deep and genuine disappointment that a 'succession of foolish actions' had spoiled the international environment and 'almost put an end to the idea of real peace in our generation.'[32] But the damage to India's reputation as a non-aligned power at home and in the West had been done.

INDIA, TIBET, CHINA

India needed the Soviet Union more than it needed the West, especially when its relations with China were deteriorating due to the discovery that China had built a road through Aksai Chin in Ladakh, Jammu and Kashmir, which had led to a military conflict along the border. It would become increasingly difficult for India to indulge in its high-toned, moralistic and open denunciation if either of the Cold War superpowers took actions that endangered international peace. Complicating the geopolitical equation was the brewing ideological split between the Soviet Union and Mao's communist China in dealing with Asian-African nations, particularly India. Consider the following exchange that took place between Communist Party Secretary Nikita Khrushchev and the Chinese leaders, Mao Zedong and Zhou Enlai in October 1959 after the Soviet leader had returned from a two-week visit to the US:

> Khrushchev: We may say that Nehru is a bourgeois statesman. But we know about it. If Nehru leaves, who would be better?… We believe that the events in Tibet are the fault of the Communist Party of China, not Nehru's fault.
>
> Mao: No, this is Nehru's fault…
>
> Khrushchev: Why did you have to kill people on the border with India?
>
> Mao: They attacked us first…

Zhou: Whose data do you trust more—Indian or ours?

Khrushchev: Comrade Zhou Enlai. You have been Minister of Foreign Affairs...for many years and know better than I how one can resolve disputed issues without spilling blood.[33]

INDIA RECLAIMS BUDDHIST HERITAGE TO EMBRACE THE DALAI LAMA

Though India is a secular republic, Buddhist symbols are integrated into its political culture. The Indian flag incorporates the Asoka Chakra, the Wheel of the Law of Dharma, in perpetual motion. The official seal of the Republic of India is the four-headed lion, the symbol of Emperor Asoka, who proclaimed Buddhism to the four corners of the world. The 2,500th anniversary of the Buddha's birth offered India an opportunity to reclaim its Buddhist heritage and renew its cultural bonds with Asia. Nehru, a secular agnostic Hindu Brahmin, was deeply enamoured with India's Buddhist heritage, and for him, Emperor Asoka was an iconic symbol of the Indian civilization. He took a personal interest in the celebration of the Buddha Jayanti. S. Radhakrishnan, the philosopher-statesman and then the vice president, was in charge of organizing the international celebration, which lasted for the entire year through 1956. At the time of the celebration, a new commons, the Buddha Jayanti Park, was created in New Delhi; and ancient Buddhist pilgrimage sites including Sarnath, Bodh Gaya, Kushinagar, Lumbini and other places were brushed up for international Buddhist pilgrims. The high seriousness of the celebration could be gauged from David Geary's account:

Part of the nationwide programme included: physical improvements made at Buddhist sites; the publication of dozens of government-sponsored books and pamphlets on Buddhism and Buddhist places (such as the book, entitled *2500 Years of Buddhism*, produced by the Publications division of the Government of India Information and Broadcasting Ministry); the broadcasting of numerous features, talks, and dramas about Buddhism by All India Radio; the convening of an International Buddhist Conference; the erection of the Buddha Jayanti Monument in Delhi; a Buddhist art exhibition; the issuing of a special commemorative stamp; the making of a government-sponsored film on the life of Buddha; the publication of the complete Pali Tipitaka in a number of Indian languages; railway concessions for pilgrims; the declaration of the Buddha Jayanti day—the *vesak purnima*—as a public holiday for the whole of India; and the organization of thousands of Buddha Jayanti cultural events and cultural progammes on the life and teachings of the Buddha.[34]

One of the most important visitors for the celebration was the 21-year-old Dalai Lama, the spiritual-political head who was revered as the god-king of Tibet. The Panchen Lama and a large entourage of Tibetan Lamas also accompanied him. Although he was coming to India under the shadow of communist China that had invaded and occupied the country in 1950, the Dalai Lama was received as a head of state and was offered the Indian guard of honour. Nehru and Dr Radhakrishnan received him at the airport. When he visited Bodh Gaya, 'thousands of people thronged the seven-mile route from Gaya to Bodh Gaya as the entourage drove through numerous welcome arches that had been erected in honour of their visit. Upon reaching the temple, with an international reception of Buddhist monks and visitors, the Dalai Lama and the Panchen Lama presented sets of Tibetan Buddhist Scriptures to the temple management committee along with a gold lamp to be used in daily worship.'[35]

Three years later, the Dalai Lama would escape the Chinese-occupied Tibet and thus change forever relations between India and China. Tibet and the Dalai Lama would enter into the global consciousness. The Dalai Lama's Dharamsala abode and the headquarters of the free Tibetan Government would draw millions of visitors from all over the world. Ironically, while the geographical Tibet would remain an occupied territory of communist China, the spiritual Tibet would remain free, a free agent with a message that would keep China sleepless. China would always be afraid of the free Tibet beyond its borders, beyond its control, in India and abroad. For about 400 years, Tibet, from the mid-fourteenth century through the eighteenth century, had de facto independence. The Ming Dynasty did not impose any direct control in spite of the fact it had nominal claims on the Tibetan territory.[36] In the eighteenth century, Tibet came under the suzerainty of the Manchu Qing dynasty that lasted until 1912. But after the fall of the Qing dynasty, Tibet was free with Dalai Lama XIII as the ruler. Chinese troops were expelled from Tibet. In 1913 Dalai Lama XIII issued a proclamation stating that the relations with China were not based on subordination and Tibet was an independent nation:

> During the time of Genghis Khan and Altan Khan of the Mongols, the Ming dynasty of the Chinese, and the Ch'ing Dynasty of the Manchus, Tibet and China cooperated on the basis of benefactor and priest relationship. A few years ago, the Chinese authorities in Szechuan and Yunnan endeavoured to colonize our territory. They brought large numbers of troops into central Tibet on the pretext of policing the trade marts. I, therefore, left Lhasa with my ministers for the Indo-Tibetan border, hoping to clarify to the Manchu emperor by wire that the existing relationship between Tibet and China had been that of patron and priest and had not been based on the subordination of one to the other.[37]

TIBET'S STRUGGLE FOR FREEDOM

Until 1950, Tibet enjoyed de facto independence while China underwent, through the era of its warlords, the civil war, and the humiliation at the hands of Japan during World War II. In fact, Tibet had gotten de jure independent after the Tibet–Mongolia Treaty of 1913. Mongolia had been recognized by Russia as an independent country. *The Times* of London commented that 'the analogy between the Tibetan and Mongolian cases is close. Over both territories,

Chinese claims were shadowy... Great Britain and Russia have both said practically the same thing in regard to Tibet and Mongolia respectively—no interference with their autonomy.'[38] Under the Tibetan–Mongolian Treaty of January 1913, both countries agreed to recognize each other as independent.[39] Though the independence of Tibet was not formally recognized, the British, after the military expedition of Sir Francis Younghusband in 1903–04, had already established trade and diplomatic missions in Tibet.

In 1914, Tibet and the British government signed the Simla Agreement that established the McMahon Line as the international boundary between Tibet and India, the agreement that China initialled but did not sign due to differences over the Tibet–China boundary.[40] The Tibetan government made no serious efforts in seeking diplomatic recognition, and its contacts with the outside world remained limited to India, Great Britain and the US. Nor was Tibet militarily prepared to defend itself against the rising tide of communist China, whose troops had begun to carry out an incursion into its territory.[41]

In 1950 Tibet was a divided, feudal, theocratic state with a vast area, with no foreign allies and friends, and a poorly equipped, ill-trained military force to defend its de facto independence. When Tenzin Gyatso became the fourteenth Dalai Lama, he was only 15 years old. Before his ascension as the spiritual and political leader of Tibet, a controversial Regent, Ngawang Sungrab Thutob, ruled the country. His rule had created divisions and instability in Tibetan society.[42]

One of Tibet's top religious leaders, the Panchen Lama, for example, was already with the People's Republic of China. On 31 January, he asked Mao for 'the prompt liberation of Tibet' by the People's Liberation Army since 'It is recognized by the whole world that Tibet is the territory of China, and all the Tibetans think that they are one of the nationalities of China.' In a spirit of complete surrender and supplication, Panchen Lama admonished:

> The act of the Lhasa authorities today undermines the integrity
> of the national territory and sovereignty and runs against the

will of the Tibetan people. We, on behalf of the Tibetan people, beseech you to rapidly send righteous troops to liberate Tibet, cleanse the reactionary elements, drive out the imperialist forces in Tibet, solidify the national defence in the Southwest, and liberate the Tibetan people.[43]

The Tibetan monk's admonishment was unnecessary because China under Mao Zedong claimed that Tibet was part of China and was determined to conquer and integrate it in any which way it could. With a battle-hardened combat army that had vanquished the Kuomintang in the civil war, Mao's troops were ready to move into Tibet to negotiate and persuade the Tibetan government for the peaceful liberation of the country.

A LONE BATTLE FOR INDEPENDENCE

Tibet was there for the taking in 1950. The British had begun to retreat to their 'scepter'd isle,' the 'other Eden,' when they saw that the sun was finally setting on their empire. India was preoccupied with Kashmir, Pakistan, refugee resettlement and had no clue what to do about Tibet.

After World War II and the defeat of Japan, the Soviet Union supported the Republic of Mongolia as an independent country, albeit under their sphere of influence. But since Tibet isn't geographically contiguous with Russia, Stalin showed little interest in Tibet. India under Nehru had been romancing with China long before Mao's People's Liberation Army (PLA) seized control from the Chiang Kai-shek government. The PLA's seizure of Tibet from the Dalai Lama was a cakewalk in comparison with the long-drawn military struggle against the Kuomintang. If Tibet had the same support from the Soviet Union as Mongolia had, or if it had a defence arrangement similar to what Chiang Kai-shek's Kuomintang government in Taiwan had with the US, or if India had been farsighted and muscular enough, the story of Tibet would have been different. After all, communist China did not dare invade Hong Kong. It felt persuaded for a negotiated settlement with the UK over the return of Hong Kong to the Mainland, though it still does not know how to control its freedom-loving people. And Taiwan is a free and prosperous democracy.

During the negotiations between two delegations in Delhi in September 1950, while Tibet looked for some reasonable accommodation with China, the Chinese representative, on the other hand, was not interested in anything except for Tibet to accept China's sovereignty proposal, including the part where Tibet would become part of China; and that Tibet's defence, foreign relations and trade would be under China's control. To which the Tibetan delegate Tsepon W.D. Shakabpa responded with empty bravado, 'Tibet will remain independent as it is at present, and we will continue to have very close "priest-patron" relations with China. Also, there is no need to liberate Tibet from imperialism since there are no British, American or Guomindang (Kuomintang) imperialists in Tibet, and Tibet is ruled and protected by the Dalai Lama (not any foreign power).'[44]

On 7 October 1950, the PLA attacked the Tibetan forces at the border town Chamdo, captured the Tibetan commander Ngabo and the local governor Ngapoi Ngawang Jigme. The PLA sent the captured commander and the governor to negotiate with the Dalai Lama and his Regency government in Lhasa for accepting the Seventeen Point Agreement, under which Tibet would become part of China. On 23 May 1951, the Tibetan government representative in Peking (now Beijing) signed the agreement, which was ratified by the Dalai Lama in October 1951. But China did not live up to its promise of internal autonomy for Tibet and began to force changes on the Tibetan people, who eventually revolted in 1959.[45] The Dalai Lama escaped to India, where he was received as a most honoured guest and allowed to reconstitute his religious establishment and government-in-exile in Dharamsala. It seemed as if it would be the end of the history of Tibet. But it turned out to be the beginning of the rise of the Dalai Lama as a most admirable international iconic figure of peace and the spokesman for Tibet and human rights. Tibet became divided, its geopolitical body with China, and its spiritual life with India.

CHINA'S ATTACK ON INDIA TO CONTROL TIBET

The 1962 war between India and China was inevitable. It was a war between two incompatible political and cultural systems: one, a conformist throughout its history, viewing the world as a perpetual ideological battlefield; and the other, holding a post-modernistic humanistic view that chimes with its ancient mores, believing that various incompatible systems can co-exist in spite of cognitive dissidence and dissonance. Indians feel comfortable living—in fact, they flourish working through unorthodoxies and discords. The India–China War was a civilizational war, and it was a necessary war, and it is still going on albeit in a different mode. The war opened India's eyes to a phenomenon that it had never experienced before: an open, pluralistic democratic system with freedom of the press and fiercely articulated public opinion against a massive monolithic militarized closed system run by a singularity—a supreme helmsman and a coterie of self-referential ideological oligarchs answerable to no one.[46]

The apparent cause of the war was the strategic road that China had built through Aksai Chin in Ladakh—a high mountain desolate region that had been historically part of the Indian state of Jammu and Kashmir—which China desperately needed in order to connect its restive Muslim Xinjiang with its newly conquered Buddhist Tibet. In order to dispute India's claim on Aksai Chin, China asserted that since the entire border between Tibet and India extends from the McMahon Line in the east to the tri-junction of Tibet–Xinjiang–Kashmir in the west was the legacy of British imperialism, it was therefore unacceptable to them. Historically Aksai Chin had been part of the princely state of Jammu and Kashmir since the Dogra rulers of the state, which was part of the Sikh empire, and had integrated Ladakh into the state in 1834. Trade routes through Aksai Chin and the mountain ranges connected Kashmir–Ladakh with Central Asia.[47] After the British established their suzerainty over Jammu and Kashmir and carried out the survey of the region, they established the Ardagh–Johnson Line along with the Kunlun Mountains range as the northern boundary of the region.[48] Despite the shifting British boundary lines, neither the Qing nor the Kuomintang ever seriously challenged or contested the Ardagh–Johnson Line boundary, which independent India under Prime Minister Jawaharlal Nehru accepted—until communist China under Mao Zedong after the occupation of Tibet built the highway in 1956–57 between the Kunlun Range in the north and Karakoram Range in the south.[49]

In the eastern region, the boundary between British India, Tibet and China was concluded under the Simla Agreement in 1913–14. While the Tibetan and the British Indian representatives signed the Simla Agreement, the Chinese representative only initialled the document but did not sign it because of the disagreement about the China–Tibet boundary. Consequently, the accord became a bilateral agreement between British India and Tibet.[50] However, in spite of the uncertainty about the validity of the Agreement, British India began to use the McMahon Line as the official boundary between India and Tibet. The McMahon Line runs through the highest elevation in the Himalayan range. In the south of this border is the Buddhist monastery at Tawang, which paid religious obeisance to the Dalai Lama but, nonetheless, after the Simla Agreement, the monastery came under the geopolitical jurisdiction of British India. This was the border that independent India inherited along with other historical borders, including the Aksai Chin region.[51]

From 1950 when China occupied Tibet until 1956, China did not raise any dispute about the Himalayan border, but once it had completed the construction of the strategic road connecting Xinjiang with Tibet, the border became radioactive. China claimed 46,000 square miles of the Indian Territory in Aksai Chin in the west and rejected the McMahon Line in the east. Chinese maps began to show the Northeast Frontier Agency region (NEFA, now Arunachal Pradesh) and Aksai Chin as part of China.[52] The relations between India and China deteriorated precipitously in 1959 when the fourteenth Dalai Lama, after a failed Tibetan revolt against Chinese occupation, escaped Lhasa and was accorded a warm, sympathetic welcome and asylum in India along with other Tibetan escapees. Having created new border actualities in Aksai

Chin, China was confident that it would muscle its way through negotiated settlement; but Nehru repudiated the idea of conducting any negotiation until the complete withdrawal of the Chinese troops from Aksai Chin. Regardless of the firm stand and fierce public opinion in India about Chinese duplicitous behaviour, several meetings took place between Chinese Prime Minister Zhou Enlai and Prime Minister Nehru, followed by meetings of the officials of the two countries to settle the boundary dispute, but they turned out to be futile.[53]

To strengthen its claim up to the historic McMahon Line, India adopted 'the forward policy', a defensive policy to push back the aggressor, China, from India's territory, and began sending troops to patrol and establish outposts in the region to which India claimed sovereignty. Perception of where some of the outposts were located, whether north or south of the McMahon Line, led to clashes with the Chinese troops who were pursuing their own version of 'the forward policy'.[54] The difference was that while India's 'forward policy' was mostly empty rhetoric without much substance, China's 'forward policy' was based on solid military planning and logistics. Lt. General B.M. Kaul, the newly appointed General Officer Commanding (GOC) of the Northeast region, did not anticipate war taking place between India and China and therefore did not enhance military preparedness. India was blindsided by its ancient habit of magical thinking and chanting mantras whenever it faced any calamity. Communist China, on the other hand, followed the policy of what American political scientist John Mearsheimer termed as offensive realism, which it is still pursuing as seen in the South China Sea.[55]

China, once it felt confident that the National Republic of China (Taiwan), under the protection of the US, wouldn't attack the mainland, moved its heavy artillery onto Tibet. Surprisingly, India did not know when China used the Calcutta port to send a large amount of non-military equipment to Tibet.[56] While India pursued its 'forward policy' timidly and ineffectively—'Willing to wound, and yet afraid to strike'[57]—China was ready for a major military assault, especially when Mao Zedong felt assured that the

October 1962 brewing Cuban Missile Crisis between the US and the Soviet Union would keep them occupied,[58] and therefore a massive shock-and-awe crippling strike would be good enough to bring India to the negotiating table and make it accept the border settlement based on the present militarized actualities that China had created with its aggressive forward policy under the barrage of diplomatic communications.

The June 1962 confrontation at Thag La Ridge, which began with the establishment by the Indian forces of a strategic outpost at Dhola, on the southern slopes of the 14,000-ft. ridge that constituted the McMahon Line, gave India a foretaste of how well prepared the Chinese were. Or rather, more appropriately, how poorly prepared the Indian forces were. By 18 October, the Chinese forces had pushed back the Indian forces from the south of Thag La Ridge and were ready to launch a massive attack simultaneously on the eastern and western sectors more than a thousand miles apart.[59]

The Chinese troops knew the terrain like the back of their hands, thanks to their intelligence gathering through their spy network. Apart from 'their great superiority in manpower and fire-power,' the Chinese, according to the Indian Defence Department account, 'also enjoyed important geographical and logistical advantages, namely:

1. they were attacking downwards from the mountain heights, whereas the Indian defenders were having to fight uphill;
2. as the Chinese military build-up had been in progress for a long period, the Chinese were much better acclimatized to the bitter cold, atmospheric conditions, and the mountainous terrain than the Indian forces who had had much less time for acclimatization; as regards transport, the Chinese were within easy reach of their Tibetan bases through a network of military roads extending to the McMahon Line, whereas Indian troops in forward areas were dependent for supplies on air drops by transport planes.'[60]

This was in sharp contrast to what Jawaharlal Nehru, in his address to the Lok Sabha on 25 November 1959, had said:

I can tell this House that at no time since our Independence, and of course before it, were our defence forces in better condition, in finer fettle, and with the background of our far greater industrial production...to help them, than they are today. I am not boasting about them or comparing them with any other countries, but I am quite confident that our defence forces are well capable of looking after our security.[61]

In every encounter on the eastern McMahon Line border from 20 October through 24 October, the Chinese troops outflanked, outmanoeuvred, encircled and ambushed Indian troops, cut off their telecommunications and forced them to retreat from the Namka Chu River south of the McMahon Line. The next assault was on Walong, an easternmost town 15 miles south of the McMahon Line, where the Chinese troops, with wave after wave of troop reinforcement, overpowered the undermanned and poorly equipped Indian troops and forced them to withdraw to safer positions. The town of Tawang, which has the famed Buddhist Monastery, fell into Chinese hands without much resistance. By 25 October, the Chinese troops controlled the commanding heights of the North-East Frontier Agency (NEFA, now Arunachal Pradesh), and the region was there for them to take.

In the Aksai Chin region, where China already controlled most of the disputed territory north and south of the Tibet–Xinxiang highway, the Indian defences, outpost after outpost, crashed like mud houses when the Chinese troops launched their attack on 20 October and took over Chip Chap Valley, Galwan Valley and Pangong Lake. The only redeeming feature in the dark war saga was the tough fight the Indian troops put up to control Rezang La Ridge to safeguard the nearby airfield at Chushul.[62] By 24 October 1962, the Chinese troops were in command of the territories they had coveted, thereby giving China diplomatic leverage to dictate terms to India for settlement.

In a letter to Nehru, Chinese Prime Minister Zhou Enlai proposed that in order to have a negotiated settlement, Chinese and Indian troops should withdraw twenty kilometres from the present line of actual control in NEFA that would take back the Chinese troops north of the McMahon Line. In Aksai Chin, the proposal included maintaining the present, actual line of control. What Zhou Enlai was proposing was swapping of the territories: the Chinese newly acquired territory in the eastern Himalayan McMahon Line sector with its previously controlled Aksai Chin territory in the western sector. China would accept the McMahon Line in exchange for India accepting the McCartney–McDonald Line in Aksai Chin, which would have legitimized the strategic Tibet–Xinxiang highway. The 1899 McCartney–McDonald Line, rejected by China, was buried in the dustbin of history, but now since it suited China's strategic needs, it became a bargaining chip.

The difference between the Johnson Line that India regarded as its Aksai Chin border and the McCartney–McDonald Line that China claimed as its traditional border would have been easily rectified before the hostility had begun. But once China occupied so much of the Indian territory, the news media and the public opinion in India began to see it as an existential threat from China. The Indian Parliament declared a national emergency and passed a unanimous resolution on 14 November 1962 that summed up India's deep sense of anguish, betrayal and determination to fight back:

> This House notes with deep regret that, in spite of the uniform gestures of goodwill and friendship by India towards the People's Government of China on the basis of recognition of each other's Independence, non-aggression and non-interference, and peaceful coexistence, China has betrayed this goodwill and friendship and the principles of Panchsheel which had been agreed to between the two countries and has committed aggression and initiated a massive invasion of India by her armed forces... *this House affirms the firm resolve of the Indian people to drive out the aggressor from the sacred soil of India, however long and hard the struggle may be.* [emphasis added][63]

During the three-week lull period since 25 October, while China kept extending the fake olive branch, its troops were doubling down on their preparation to launch a massive attack. In the northeast, for example, the Chinese had constructed 'in an extraordinarily short time' vehicle roads that enabled the Chinese 'to bring up strong reinforcements preparatory to launching their latest offensive.' Indian commanders had no clue. They were simply reacting to the Chinese new offensive initiatives without anticipating what would be their next move. On 14 November, the Chinese forces began their offensive by outflanking the Fourth Indian Division at the 14,000-ft Sela Pass and launched a 'pincer' movement that cut off the pass from the strategic town of Bomdila, which was captured by the Chinese on 19 November. The fall of Bomidila was catastrophic and decisive. As the Indian forces retreated from one defensive position to another, the Chinese troops kept advancing into the south until they reached the threshold of the Assam plains. The battleground situation in the northeast after the fall of Bomdila was irredeemable.

In the Ladakh–Aksai Chin sector, after the lull, the Chinese's major focus was Chushul Valley and its nearby airstrip. Chushul is a narrow sandy valley at an altitude of about 14,229 feet. It's bound on the north by the Pangong Tso Lake and on the east and west by 18,700 ft. mountain ranges, including the strategic Rezang La pass, where a fiercely contested engagement took place. The Chushul airfield with advanced landing ground airstrip is to the south of the valley. Under 'the forward policy' a number of posts were established around Chushul, which lies on the road to Leh, the capital of Ladakh.

On 18 November, the Chinese forces launched a heavy infantry attack near Chushul, but in spite of heavy casualties, the Indian forces held on to the strategic area and the nearby airstrip, which was shelled heavily by the Chinese. Indian troops, although outnumbered by ten-to-one 'fought with considerable elan and tactical skills, inflicting horrendous casualties on the Chinese... Peking radio admitted to having suffered its worst casualties at Rezang La. Ironically, it could have also been an indicator of things to come. The Indian Army was just coming to grips with this war. Barely a fraction of the Army had been involved. It was possible that the Battle at Chushul was a sign that the remainder of the war was going to be much harder and a notice to us that if the country had not lost its nerve the end of this war could have been on better terms.'[64] In spite of their inability to wrench the strategic Chushul Valley from the Indian forces, the Chinese had under their control more area in Ladakh than what they had been claiming. The Indian forces had vacated Daulat Beg Oldi, but it wasn't in Chinese possession.

When the Chinese announced the ceasefire on 21 November, its forces were not far from Assam's tea plantations and the Digboi oilfield. The Indian Army moved its headquarters from Tezpur to Guwahati. Thousands of civilians were evacuated from the NEFA region to the plains of Assam.

CLOAK-AND-DAGGER CEASEFIRE

On 19 November 1962, to the surprise and relief of Indians and many others, Zhou Enlai announced a unilateral ceasefire beginning 21 November stating:

> Beginning from 1 December 1962, the Chinese frontier guards will withdraw to positions 20 kilometres behind the line of actual control which existed between China and India on 7 November 1959. In the eastern sector, although the Chinese frontier guards have so far been fighting on Chinese territory north of the traditional customary line, they are prepared to withdraw from their present positions to the north of the illegal McMahon Line, and to withdraw twenty kilometres back from that line. In the middle and western sectors, the Chinese frontier guards will withdraw twenty kilometres from the line of actual control.[65]

The date of the announcement for the line of actual control, 7 November 1959, was nothing but linguistic chicanery. After pushing the line of actual control post by post to where they claimed the boundaries, China simply labelled it 7 November 1959, much like a deceptive bottler would change the label on the wine bottle to make it look vintage. It's worth considering the 25 November 1962 response of the Indian external affairs ministry to the Chinese ceasefire announcement:

> A certain amount of confusion has been caused by the deceptive Chinese proposal on the question of the withdrawals of Chinese and Indian troops to what the Chinese call the 'line of actual control as on November 7, 1959.' This is in contrast with the Government of India's position that if Chinese professions of peace and a peaceful settlement of differences are really genuine, at least the *status quo* which obtained before Sept. 8, 1962, when the Chinese committed fresh aggression in the North-East Frontier Agency, should first be restored... In other words, this is the Peking Government's usual method of causing confusion by perverting the meaning of words and making statements which bear no relation to reality.[66]

The non-aligned nations remained non-aligned between India and China during the Himalayan war. The Colombo Powers, including Egypt, Burma (Myanmar), Cambodia, Ceylon (Sri Lanka) and Indonesia met in Colombo, Ceylon, on 10–12 December 1962, and offered a peace proposal that specified withdrawal of the Chinese troops in the Ladakh sector by 20 kilometres creating a demilitarized zone where the Indian civilian posts could be established; and in the Northeast region (NEFA), the Indians, troops and civilians, could go back to the south of the McMahon Line, except for the Dhola (Thagla Ridge) and Longju whose location vis-à-vis the McMahon Line was to be determined later. India accepted the proposal. But China, after accepting it in principle, virtually killed it through its habitual quizzing. Since the Colombo proposal was only a proposal, argued China, full adherence was unnecessary, and differences could be settled during meetings.[67]

A DESPERATE NEHRU

During the war, when Chinese troops had overrun the NEFA and reached the edge of Assam, a desperate Jawaharlal Nehru requested

President John F. Kennedy for air support, including 12 squadrons of fighter jets and a modern radar system, to which the US responded feebly. The US Air Force provided non-combatant support to Indian forces and planned to send its aircraft carrier USS Enterprise to the Bay of Bengal. The US also let it be known to China via Warsaw (Poland, a Soviet satellite) that it intended to help India.[68] The US was involved with the Cuban Crisis and couldn't have offered more than the minimum assistance to India without turning it into another nuclear crisis.

In May 1963, the US National Security Council, which included Defence Secretary Robert McNamara and General Maxwell Taylor, chairman of the joint chiefs of staff, considered the US response if China attacked India again. McNamara, according to declassified tapes, said, 'Before any substantial commitment to defend India against China is given, we should recognize that in order to carry out that commitment against any substantial Chinese attack, we would have to use nuclear weapons. Any large Chinese Communist attack on any part of that area would require the use of nuclear weapons by the US, and this is to be preferred over the introduction of large numbers of US soldiers.' To which President John F. Kennedy responded, 'We should defend India, and therefore we will defend India.' Highlighting the overall threat of China, General Taylor told President Kennedy: 'This is just one spectacular aspect of the overall problem of how to cope with Red China politically and militarily in the next decade. I would hate to think we would fight this on the ground in a non-nuclear way.'[69]

India was not South Korea and the US wouldn't have rushed to put its boots on the ground to help India to fight China as it did in South Korea. The very fact that the extreme option of the use of nuclear weapons crossed their minds showed how seriously the US looked at the global threat from communist China, as it did from the Soviet Union having just pulled back from the brink of the Cuban Missile crisis. Nonetheless, the prospects of the US' active involvement, if China attacked India again, might have been one of the factors that persuaded China to halt and withdraw from the NEFA. If China's objective was to force India to come to the negotiation table to accept the package deal, including swapping the McMahon Line border in the eastern sector with the Aksai Chin Line of Actual Control (the Chinese version) in the western sector, even as of today it hasn't happened. The fear of another attack from China hasn't persuaded India to legitimize what China achieved on the ground in 1962. If the objective was to drive India to the West, it did not happen because after the initial rush of military aid and sympathy from the Unites States and the UK, another supplicant, Pakistan, a member of the SEATO and CENTO, entered into their geopolitical calculations, and the new conditions became unacceptable to India.

Ironically, Indian leaders never gave up their illusion of India's abiding friendship with the Soviet Union. When the Soviet Union was planning to install missiles in Cuba, at the same time,

> 'Beijing, in a show of residual trust between the ideological rivals, notified Moscow on 8 October of China's imminent strike against India. Forced to choose between his two 'peaceful' friends, Khrushchev left no doubt about his choice. Returning Beijing's confidence, he affirmed solidarity with China. He assured the PRC ambassador, Liu Xiao, that the Soviet Union would not side with India in the coming confrontation and offered to delay the delivery to India of the promised MiGs. Khrushchev confided in the envoy his 'most cherished dream... to get rid of the cold current [that] is separating us.'[70]

Keeping this shift in policy, *Pravda*, the Soviet Communist Party newspaper, not only criticized India's border dispute assessment and sided with China but also 'went as far as providing sensitive intelligence about India to the PRC.'[71] India never felt so alone and deserted.

The war with China had a transformative impact on India. India's non-alignment policy that had a tilt towards the Soviet Union, especially during Krishna Menon's ascendancy in Indian politics, now seemed to move towards pragmatic realism. The dependency relationships with the Soviet Union, especially in its efforts at militarization, continued, nonetheless. Even after fifteen years of Independence and two Five-Year Plans, India was nowhere near a manufacturing nation. It had no muscle power.

INDIA'S STRUGGLE TO STRENGTHEN ITS DEFENCES

The India-first security-state populist mentality that was reflected in Parliament in the post-war period began to trump other developmental priorities. India needed to raise six to 10 additional mountain armoured divisions for modernizing the army, which necessitated doubling the defence budget to ₹867 crores for the 1963–64 budget year without however relinquishing the essential development plans. In order to avoid excessive dependence upon western foreign aid and without pressuring limited foreign exchange reserves, India had to depend upon domestic sources, which meant resorting to deficit financing. The increased defence budget from 15–17 per cent to 28 per cent of the total national budget in 1963 left no sector or class untouched and would become a permanent feature in future budgets. Raising and making the additional mountain armoured divisions operational and battle-ready required not only rigorous military personnel training but also necessitated improving infrastructure, road building, communications, transportation, and most of all, the acquisition of cold weather, mountain military equipment.

The manufacture of the Soviet MiG-21 supersonic jet fighters in India had been on the planning board for quite some time, but it was only in 1963 that Hindustan Aircraft, which would become Hindustan Aeronautics Limited (HAL), rolled out its first squadron of MiG-21s for the Indian Air Force. The National Aeronautic Laboratories, Research and Development in Electronics, and Bharat Electronics were given defence orientation and would eventually spawn the Digital India of today.[72]

During the war, China's People's Liberation Army (PLA) carried out surveillance on the Himalayan region with its superb intelligence-gathering abilities. Its troops moved in the NEFA as familiarly as a snake moves from lair to lair. While India depended upon its rhetoric of the mislabelled 'forward policy' in terms of intelligence, it was in the dark. One of the major post-war tasks was to improve India's intelligence-gathering capacities, and it would be left to Indira Gandhi to establish the Research and Analysis Wing (R&AW), the external spy agency. India also began to look again at the Tata Institute of Fundamental Research, the Bhabha Atomic Research Centre, and its nuclear reactors Apsara and CIRUS, whether they could serve India's new defence paradigm.[73]

All things considered, the post-India–China war militarization psychology that gave rise to the India-first national security state of mind in 1962–63 would transform India in the course of time into a most dominant military power in South Asia and the Indian Ocean.[74] Instead of giving up on the Himalayas, India began to double down its efforts to embrace it and to defend it not only as a natural fortress but also as the abode of its gods. Since the Himalayan war had brought Pakistan and China closer, Jammu and Kashmir assumed a new strategic significance. Some of the highest mountain roads and airfields would be constructed in Ladakh, which would also become one of the most frequently visited tourist destinations for Indians and foreigners.

FAMOUS GUILTY MEN

The ignominious end to the India–China War proved to be the graveyard of the reputations of many prominent Indians, especially Krishna Menon, the Defence Minister, who had misread the Chinese intentions and underestimated the might of the PLA. Menon had spent many years as Nehru's roaming spokesman and advocate for India's non-alignment policy, sanctimoniously lecturing the West at every international forum about its imperial legacy and the continued sins of colonialism. Abhorred in the West, Menon was admired by the Indian elites and the media, as well as many Asian–African countries for his fierce intelligence and acerbic tongue. His haranguing, moralizing, endless rhetoric against the West created the illusion of virtuous strength of the Indian non-alignment policy.[75]

Although Menon enjoyed his role as a diplomat, he proved incompetent as the defence minister. While the Chinese had established a network of intelligence in the NEFA and knew every ridge, crest and valley, India was totally unaware of the Chinese military build-up across the McMahon Line. The Chinese attack was not due to any sudden provocation, such as the Aksai Chin 'forward policy' of establishing outposts in the disputed territory. The Chinese aggression was three years in the making and there was nothing unknown or unknowable, except that some politicians, particularly Menon, thought that the Chinese preparedness did not mean intention to commit aggression and, furthermore, that Pakistan was a much greater peril and needed closer military vigilance. He underplayed the Chinese menace to India due to 'ideological bias in favour of China and other Communist Countries...', stating on 10 January 1962 in Tezpur in Assam that 'the India-China border dispute was not of such a magnitude as could precipitate a war.'[76] It was a failure of imagination. Menon failed to contextualize the Chinese war preparedness in the broader ideological framework of the Soviet–China contested worldviews regarding the fate of the Communist Revolution. Most importantly, to secure its hold on Tibet, India had to be taught a lesson, according to Chinese planners. Attacking India, thus, was killing two birds with one stone, denouncing Khrushchev for his apostasy of peaceful coexistence with the US and settling 'accounts with Indians.'[77] As a top diplomat, Menon should have known how the seemingly monolithic communist bloc was cracking up and its global consequences.

Menon was not easy to get along with. In 1959 the Chief of the Army Staff, General K.S. Thimayya, a World War II veteran who had also played a peacekeeping role after the Korean Armistice, resigned from his position but was persuaded by Nehru to keep going, which he did until his retirement in 1961.[78] But Menon's fate was sealed when the Indian Army got its first beating in October 1962, and Nehru desperately appealed to Kennedy for help. Menon, provocative, much admired and controversial in India, was one of the most hated men in America because he had the habit of calling a spade more than a spade; and he had to go as the price for American aid.

At his funeral in October 1974, Krishna Menon, much admired and also much hated, received the most well-deserved gesture of gratitude when two diplomats got down from their car and 'placed a huge floral wreath on the body,' and a red banner that proclaimed: 'On behalf of the freedom-loving people of the world to the memory of the great Indian who struggled for the independence of Vietnam.'[79] No Vietnamese ever expressed such sentiments about Henry Kissinger, 'the peacemaker of Vietnam.'

Along with Krishna Menon, top generals, including the newly appointed Chief of the Army Staff, General Pran Nath Thapar, and Lieutenant General Brij Mohan Kaul, who was chief of the general staff and general commanding officer in the Northeast, were held responsible for the debacle and had to resign. Both generals, graduates of the most prestigious military academy, the Royal Military College at Sandhurst, had distinguished military careers, having fought as mid-level officers in many battles during World War II. It is worth keeping in mind, however, that during World War II, they saw action under the overall general command of British officers and shared their glory. But in the India–China war, they were on their own and their responsibility for the entire war operation was absolute.

One of the most important responsibilities of top military generals in a democracy is to educate their political bosses so that they can make informed decisions. General Thapar and General Kaul either did not know enough or they did not have the courage to confront their Defence Minister Krishna Menon with facts regarding the extent of the Chinese capabilities and their intentions. When a country is at war, ignorance is no excuse; it is a crime. Indians righteously condemned the guilty men, the politicians and generals who, having created a rhetorical illusion of India rising and shining on the international stage, let the nation suffer a most mortifying defeat.

Besides the famous guilty men whose lifelong achievements were pulverized in the 1962 war, who else was held responsible for India's defeat? The suspicion fell upon Chinese-Indian community members who came to India during the British colonial times and had been living mostly in Kolkata and some in other places such as Chennai and Mumbai since the eighteenth century. One of the most peaceful and industrious communities, the Chinese-Indians ran small businesses and manufacturing outfits such as tanning, shoemaking, Chinese restaurants, salons and beauty parlours. When the war was lost, Chinese-Indians were treated as traitors and accused of Chinese espionage in India.

The Chinese-Indians Association in Kolkata openly and vociferously condemned the Chinese aggression, but no one trusted them. On 25 October, the Government of India issued the Foreigners Order under the Defence of India Act of 1962 under which the people of Chinese descent were not allowed to leave their homes for more than 24 hours without permission; a later order authorized the arrest of any person of foreign (Chinese) origin whose country was at war with India; and the worst tragedy fell on the community on 3 November when under another Foreigners Order (Internment), the people of Chinese descent from the Northeast, Assam and West Bengal were taken to an internment camp in Rajasthan. Apparently, their situation was no different from the internment of the Japanese-Americans in the US during WWII, except for the fact that after the war the Japanese-Americans were let go free as American citizens, and later on, they were compensated with a due apology. In the case of Chinese-Indians, 2,395 were repatriated to China in 1963; another 7,500 left India in subsequent years for Hong Kong, Taiwan and other countries. Only in 1998, the remaining Chinese were given Indian citizenship.[80]

The most consequential casualty of the defeat was Jawaharlal Nehru's reputation at home and abroad. The grand edifice that Nehru had built, stood on four pillars, including democracy, secularism, non-alignment and socialism. It did not include a strong military and national defence system and only after the crushing defeat did Nehru realize that, 'We were getting out of touch with reality in the modern world and we were living in an *artificial atmosphere of our own creation* [emphasis added].'[81] When Nehru asked Kennedy for military help, and planeloads of arms began to pour into India, the non-alignment seemed unsustainable.

At home, too, the media and the people were unforgiving. The seriousness of public criticism and personal attacks on Nehru found political expression in the Congress party's loss of three parliamentary by-elections in 1963, which however, from the national point of view wasn't such a disaster because it strengthened the democratic opposition. Besides, for the first time in its history since Independence, the Indian parliamentary opposition used a very powerful tool of the game of democracy, the 'no-confidence' motion to put the Nehru Government on the floor and make it answerable to the people regarding the fiasco of the India–China War. Imagine if Nehru had listened to Sardar Patel's perceptive warning in 1950 for the need to bolster India's national defence vis-à-vis China because communism did not necessarily immunize a country from imperialistic ambitions. Especially keeping in mind that China not only coveted, he warned, 'the Himalayan slopes on our side but also included important parts of Assam... Chinese irredentism and Communist imperialism...has a cloak of ideology which makes it ten times more dangerous.' It's imperative for India to be cognizant of the new kind of threat because 'In the guise of ideological expansion lies concealed racial, national or historical claims.'[82]

In 1958 Nehru had come to similar conclusions per his conversation with an Indian diplomat heading for China:

> I don't trust the Chinese one bit. They are a deceitful, opinionated, arrogant and hegemonistic lot. Eternal vigilance should be our watchword. You should send all your telegrams only to me, not to the Foreign Office. Also do not mention a word of this instruction of mine to Krishna (Menon). He, you and I all share a common worldview and ideological approach. However, Krishna believes, erroneously, that no Communist country can have bad relations with any Non-Aligned country like ours.[83]

Was Jawaharlal Nehru under the spell of Krishna Menon's 'Evil Genius'? Long before his death in 1964, attributed to the staggering events of the war during which for the first time Nehru had felt helpless and hopeless and seemed to have lost his grip on reality, his health had been gradually declining. During the visit to the US when Nehru met with President Kennedy on 5 November 1961, Kennedy sought Nehru's views on international hotspots such as Vietnam, Berlin and the disarmament. Nehru listened but did not respond, leaving Kennedy 'puzzled and uneasy', who later on said that, 'It was like trying to grab something in your hand, only to have it turn out to be fog.'[84] A subsequent meeting with President Kennedy's New Frontier Policy elites turned out to be equally disappointing. Historian Arthur Schlesinger, the author of *A Thousand Days*, who attended the meeting, said that 'I had the impression of an old man, his energies depleted, who heard things at a great distance and answered most questions with indifference.'[85] India's ambassador to the US, B.K. Nehru, too, realized that the aging Prime Minister was tired and ailing and affirmed 'that Kennedy "wrote Nehru as finished"'.[86]

THE INDIA THAT NEHRU LEFT

When Jawaharlal Nehru died on 27 May 1964 at the age of 75, the freedom house that he had built assiduously and imaginatively, with deep faith and great hopes, based on a dynamic federal parliamentary system, was standing on strong foundations. Multiparty elections, centrally planned public sector, inclusive economic growth based on cooperative federalism and distributive justice, and social and agricultural reforms had strengthened the secular, democratic and nationalistic foundation of India. And not least, the external aggression from across the Himalayas that threatened the integrity of India had brought India closer as a nation.

As a democratic nation with checks and balances provided by the bicameral parliament, the independent judiciary, semi-autonomous states, active forms of street democracy, unionism, a robust free press and a self-confident intellectual class, India moved slowly and steadily. Jawaharlal Nehru gave the nation a sense of purpose and direction and an abiding vision of greatness to come. Due to his 17-year-long perseverance and endurance as the most dominant political figure, personal charisma, humanism, lofty idealism, poetic eloquence and international stature, Jawaharlal Nehru made Indians feel, regardless of their religion, caste or ethnicity, that India was their country; and he was their supreme leader and the prime minister; and that India was forever united and unbreakable. The non-alignment policy, the chimeric dream that India could be a bridge and bridge builder, would become, in the course of time, a policy of pragmatic realism in pursuit of national interest, reinforced by the hard power of military strength.

The socialistic-welfare mode of thinking—that the state-controlled economic heights create and enable equality of opportunity and distributive justice, and most of all that people at the bottom of the pyramid must be taken care of regardless of the imperatives of the GDP-driven, market-oriented reforms—is Jawaharlal Nehru's enduring legacy. The socialistic mode of consciousness has entered into India's bloodstream and has become the nation's DNA, which has been manifesting itself in many forms of federal welfare schemes; for example, the Mahatma Gandhi National Rural Employment Guarantee Scheme (MGNREGS), cooking gas and toilets for everyone and much more. All political slogans in India are socialistic slogans aimed at the welfare of the masses.

Could India have taken another path in 1947, other than the non-aligned democratic socialism? Would India have become a 'different kind of country' if another leader had been at the helm of affairs or if Jawaharlal Nehru were a different kind of person?[87] This is an erroneous historical hypothetical because Nehru was the progeny of his age, the age when the global political and economic order was being redesigned and restructured in fundamental ways and modes. The US had been rising to become an unparalleled superpower and had established, along with its European allies, the institutions of global governance, including the UN and the Bretton Woods institutions such as the World Bank and International Monetary Fund; the Soviet Union was emerging as an alternative centre of global power with the goal to socialize the whole world with its slogan, 'Workers of the world, unite'; communist China under Mao Zedong was spreading its neo-imperialistic hegemonic wings on Southeast Asia, and the European colonial empires were dissipating and taking shelter under NATO. Most of all, Nehru had grown under the moral influence of Mohandas Karamchand Gandhi, the Mahatma, who identified himself with the poorest of the poor and had shaped and led India's nonviolent independence movement for decades until his assassination.

It would have been impossible for Nehru or any other leader of his generation to free himself from the milieu and the system into which he was born and grew up, and think outside the box. Nehru found it much easier to understand European socialists and Marxists rather than the Fords and Rockefellers of America. As he wrote in his autobiography:

> Russia apart, the theory and philosophy of Marxism lightened up many a dark corner of my mind. History came to have a new meaning for me. The Marxist interpretation threw a flood of light on it... It was the essential freedom from dogma and the scientific outlook of Marxism that appealed to me. I turned inevitably with goodwill towards communism, for, whatever its faults, it was at least not hypocritical and not imperialistic. It was not a doctrinal adherence, as I did not know much about the fine points of communism, my acquaintance being limited at the time to its broad features. These attracted me, as also the tremendous changes taking place in Russia.[88]

The admiration for Marxist dialectical philosophy held him back from comprehending the evils of Mao's communist China, for which he and India paid very dearly. Nehru's passionate interest in developing a gentler and kinder form of Marxism and Communism that he packaged as democratic socialism and his fervent desire to see India as a socialist nation prevented him from understanding the goodness and the strength of the US, an individualistic, entrepreneurial nation, a perpetually self-renewing society that has defied the curse and the paradigm of 'the downfall of civilizations.'

There was nothing in Nehru's elitist education at Harrow School in London, Trinity College at Cambridge or Inner Temple Inn, where he went to become a barrister, that would have opened his eyes to the creative and generative dynamism of American society, its prosperity, its innovativeness, and its economic power predicated on a free, open and competitive marketplace.[89] Perhaps change would have come, and he would have seen America in a different light if he had lived longer. Jawaharlal Nehru had a beautiful mind. He brought to India the spirit of the European Enlightenment in the form of a secular constitution and democracy that the people of India have embraced with passion. Only a great civilization can bring forth on earth such sweetness and light as Jawaharlal Nehru.

PART TWO

Creator and Destroyer

6

THE LITTLE MAN SHASTRI, WHO COULD

*I tremble when I am reminded of the fact that I have to be in
charge of this country and Parliament, which had been led by
no less a person than Jawaharlal Nehru.*

I am not as simple as I look.

—Lal Bahadur Shastri

On 27 May 1964, India lost its jewel. The nation sank into profound grief following the death of its charismatic leader, Jawaharlal Nehru. But the biggest question was: Who would succeed Nehru, the giant whose moral stature among the people, rational scientific outlook, political courage, and vision of grandeur and statesmanship had shaped India in its most dangerous decades.[1]

At this difficult juncture, the Congress Working Committee chose someone who would not rock the boat and do no harm. When Gulzarilal Nanda was installed as an interim prime minister, no one objected because he was not a contender. An unassuming Gandhian politician, originally from Sialkot, Pakistan, Nanda wholeheartedly participated in the freedom struggle. Beginning his public life in 1922 in Bombay as a Satyagrahi, Nanda later served in many capacities: as labour minister of the Bombay Government, secretary of the Hindustan Mazdoor Sevak Sangh, president of the Indian National Trade Union Congress, secretary of the Ahmedabad Textile Labour Association, deputy chairman of the Planning Commission, and minister for planning, irrigation and power in the Union Cabinet, also, as the home minister. As a member of Parliament, he represented Bombay, Gujarat and Haryana constituencies at various times in his long political career—something extraordinary, because normally in India, politicians calculate their fortunes based on caste, language, regional and religious identities.[2] Gulzarilal Nanda was an all-India man, but he was not overly aggressive and ambitious.

The search and the struggle for a permanent replacement for Nehru began immediately. Congress party president Kumaraswami Kamaraj assumed the responsibility of finding a replacement for the colossus who had brought to India secular democracy, federal-parliamentary constitutionalism and the idea of planned development. Kamaraj was an embodiment of the simplicity, astuteness and brainpower of the South, as well as the region's considerable penetration and intellectual domination in the nation's life after Independence. Once again, his role would show the impact the South was going to have in national politics.

Born in 1903 in a humble family of lower-caste people, the Nadars, Kamaraj rose to political prominence through the struggle for independence under the leadership of Mahatma Gandhi. And at a most crucial time in Indian history, in 1964, he played a decisive role. A self-educated man, a bachelor by choice, Kamaraj lived a quiet, hardworking life and ascended the ranks to the highest position in the most important political party in the country: the INC. He was the chief minister of Madras State (now Tamil Nadu) before he took up the powerful position as the president of his party on 9 October 1964. Kamaraj always dressed in the traditional southern style. Due to a lack of formal education (he educated himself in prison during the independence movement), his knowledge of English was limited, so he spoke a few words; nonetheless, he was highly respected.[3]

He did not speak much but listened a lot to party members and came to the conclusion that the man from Gujarat, Morarji Desai, would not be the best person to take over the helm of the country. Morarji Desai, finance minister in Nehru's cabinet, gave the impression of being too rigid and self-righteous. He was suspected to be less of a socialist and rather too friendly with the business community, which was probably a half-truth. Morarji Desai was a strict Gandhian, a self-disciplinarian, though those who did not like him called him sanctimonious and inflexible. Desai was perhaps too ambitious, so he was passed over.

Another prospective candidate, Lal Bahadur Shastri, a diminutive humble man from the most populous state, Uttar Pradesh, was selected to head the government of the largest and most turbulent democracy in the world. Somehow, at that time, it seemed that the Syndicate, consisting of party bosses and chief ministers of some important states, including Atulya Ghosh of Bengal, S.K. Patil of Maharashtra, N. Sanjiva Reddy of Andhra Pradesh, and S. Nijalingappa of Mysore (Karnataka), might take India towards a collective leadership. It was assumed that the Syndicate would control the country through this little man, Lal Bahadur Shastri. In fact, Shastri was so small (five feet tall or so) that people laughed at him when he stood upon the stage to address the public. But as it turned out, he was indeed a strong man. And in his limited span of leadership, he let India function as a federal-parliamentary system of democracy. The glow of the Nehru era had passed away, and now it was the beginning of the time when many feared that India would go through years of turmoil into an unknown future.

It might give the impression that the Syndicate was a kind of collective authoritarian body, but this was not the case because the Congress party President Kamaraj consulted everybody who mattered. But more than anything else, it was important that someone from the vast sprawling Hindi belt should emerge as the leader of the nation. Reluctantly, Morarji Desai listened to his better nature and withdrew from the leadership contest though he never gave up his dream of becoming the prime minister. There would always be a future for him, he believed. The continuity and stability of the country were more important than the personal ambitions of individuals at this inflexion point of history. The smooth political transition improved the image of India as a unified democratic country, albeit poor and fragile. The Congress Working Committee unanimously approved the choice of Lal Bahadur Shastri as the parliamentary leader, and the next day the Congress Parliamentary Party ratified him as the leader. On 9 June 1964, Shastri was sworn in as the second prime minister of India.

Contrary to expectations, Shastri straightaway began to assert his authority in the formation of his cabinet. Morarji Desai could not secure a berth because he insisted on becoming the deputy prime minister, which was not acceptable to Shastri or leaders of the party, the Syndicate. Indira Gandhi, who would eventually emerge as a most consequential person in India's long history, was included in the cabinet on the insistence of many party members, but Shastri gave her a position that wouldn't challenge him—the information and broadcasting ministry. India had very little experience in broadcasting and had no sense of the power of information. Interestingly, Indira Gandhi insisted that the Teen Murti House, which Nehru had occupied, should be turned into a memorial. The Nehru family was not going to give up its legacy.[4]

Kamaraj and other political bosses thought that this was the beginning of collective leadership in India. But looking at the political landscape and culture of India, divided but struggling to be together, it would have been impossible that India could become a collective leadership. A diverse and segregated society in a perpetual conflict mode would require a strong hand at the Centre of the political federation built on linguistic and regional cultures. Although soft-spoken and unassuming, Shastri—a follower of Mahatma Gandhi and later Jawaharlal Nehru, in whose cabinet he served as the railway minister—turned out to be a determined man and solid as a rock. Some people had doubts over his ability to hold the country together. Many thought that a country as large as India, from Nagaland and Kashmir to Tamil Nadu, and with so many languages, castes, races and ethnicities, could not be held together without a strong authoritative Centre, especially when the country had been experiencing troublemakers and territorial nibblers from China in the north and Pakistan in the west.

INDIA SHALL SPEAK BOLLYWOOD HINGLISH

Prime Minister Shastri faced two major problems during his short tenure, and for the time being, he seemed to have successfully solved both problems. But in India, problems never get completely resolved. Shastri celebrated India's Republic Day on 26 January 1965, as had been done annually since the times of Jawaharlal Nehru. Nevertheless, the year 1965 was different because the time for the fulfilment of the long-promised proposal of making Hindi the sole national language of India had arrived. But since non-Hindi-speaking states, especially in the South, were not at all ready to accept Hindi as the sole national language, what was to be done?

In 1949, the Constitution Assembly had accepted Hindi as the official language of India, and the Constitution went into effect on 26 January 1950. But keeping in mind the strong sentiment of the South against the imposition of Hindi as the sole national language, a grace period of 15 years was accepted. Now the time had come, and Hindi states were eager to see its implementation. The constitutional provision and political assurances notwithstanding, people in the South were terribly upset that making Hindi India's exclusive official language would deprive them of everything, from participation in the central government political processes, better paying prestigious government jobs and more importantly, the vast and growing public sector employment opportunities. The Academy of Tamil Culture had passed a resolution in 1956, demanding that English must continue to be the official language of the Union as well as the language for communication between the Union and state governments.

Although Tamil Nadu's Dravida Munnetra Kazhagam (DMK) organized the campaign, it had massive public support as well as the backing of some of the well-known politicians, lawyers and freedom fighters. Prominent public personalities who opposed the imposition of Hindi included T.T. Krishnamachari, a member of the Constituent Assembly and a cabinet minister who held several portfolios, including finance and commerce. Other noticeable Hindi opponents included T.A. Ramalingam Chettiar, a law graduate from

Madras Presidency College, who came from a wealthy merchant banker family; N.G. Ranga, parliamentarian and farmer leader, the founder-president of the Swatantra Party; N. Gopalaswami Ayyangar, once the prime minister of Kashmir who later was instrumental in crafting Article 370 of the Constitution that granted Jammu and Kashmir autonomy; S.V. Krishnamurthy Rao, Deputy Speaker of the Lok Sabha; and C. Rajagopalachari, lawyer, writer, statesman, the last governor general of India, founder of the Swatantra Party.[5] Their voices could not be ignored.

For a long time, the DMK had wanted the Tamil-speaking region to secede from India and to make the Tamil region into a separate nation. But after the India–China War in 1962, the party dropped the demand. Nonetheless, it wanted to protect the culture of the Tamils. C.N. Annadurai, the DMK supremo, was a fiery orator and much respected by the people of the state. For both the DMK and Annadurai, Hindi was no better than any other Indian language except for the fact that a large number of people spoke the language. For them, this was no merit. According to Annadurai, the numerical superiority of the Hindi language was not a sufficient reason for making it a dominant language that might put the non-Hindi-speaking people at a disadvantage.[6]

Nehru had been sensitive to these sentiments. In 1963, he had tabled the Official Languages Bill in Parliament, which said that even after 1965, English may still be used along with Hindi as an official language. There was a big debate about the word 'may', and non-Hindi-speaking people in the South feared that 'may' would pretty soon turn into 'may not'. So, they insisted that 'may' should be replaced with 'shall'—that is, English shall be used as an official language of the Indian Union.[7]

So, as the nation began to get ready to celebrate Republic Day on 26 January 1965, the question of language arose again. Annadurai wrote to Prime Minister Shastri, seeking that the matter of a change to Hindi as the official language be postponed. But Shastri and the Union Government stood by their decision to switch over to Hindi as the sole national language (along with the continuous use of English). This led to massive protests by people in the South. It took violent form at times. Hindi was demonized, Hindi books and even copies of the Constitution were burned. Hindi signs and billboards in the South were blackened. Students were angry everywhere because this would have deprived them of their future, which could be assured only if the English language continued for official purposes. All forms of protests that were perfected during the struggle for Independence, were used to fight against the imposition of Hindi.

On that Republic Day, some students took extreme measures. Two men set themselves on fire. Another person in Tiruchi (or Tiruchirappalli) took his life by swallowing insecticide. Self-immolation and suicide by insecticide were not only forms of protest against Hindi, but they were also in the service of the Tamil language, according to the suicide notes. The extent and the ferocity of protests in the South shook up the central government. The country was once again divided on the question of language. Many members of the ruling Congress party were deeply concerned about the situation and asked the government to stop the imposition of Hindi on non-Hindi-speaking people. The protesting Congress leaders included some high-ranking politicians such as S. Nijalingappa, chief minister of Mysore; Atulya Ghosh of West Bengal; Sanjiva Reddy, former Union minister; and K. Kamaraj, the Congress president. However, Congress leader Morarji Desai, speaking to the press in Tirupati, said that if Tamil people learned Hindi, they would increase their chances of playing a bigger role in the political life of the people, and their influence would increase. Desai regretted that India did not make Hindi the official language of India from the beginning. He argued regional sentiments should not come in the way of national unity, and Hindi was the only way for integrating the nation.

Although Prime Minister Shastri was strongly in favour of Hindi, he was also concerned about the unity of India. Two union ministers, C. Subramaniam and O.V. Alagesan, resigned from the cabinet in protest against the move, which made matters worse. The prime minister had to take some action. Speaking to the nation through All India Radio, Shastri expressed his deep distress over the tragic events and assured the people of the South that he would honour the assurances given by Nehru—that Hindi would not be imposed and that English would continue as long as the people wanted. Not only would English continue as a link language, but the all-India civil service examinations would be held in English along with Hindi. The all-India administrative services, including the Indian Administrative Service (IAS), the Indian Foreign Service (IFS), the Indian Police Service (IPS) and the growing central government public sector jobs, some of the most integrating forces in India, were done through merit-based examinations in which the South had fair dominance due to its competence in the English language. So were the Services Selection Board examinations of the Indian Armed Forces.

There was a long and heated debate in Parliament about the government's surrender to the violent anti-national protests in the South regarding the English language. But parliamentary members from the South said that they had made enough sacrifices and that they would not accept Hindi as the sole official language or the link language. Many members from the east, especially from West Bengal, such as Hiren Mukherjee and N.C. Chatterjee, from the left and the right, said that national unity was more important than language. Although both Nehru and Shastri were in favour of Hindi, keeping in mind the unity of the country and the Congress party, they accepted the compromise that both Hindi and English would continue as the official languages of India. And as it has turned out, the compromise has been paying India well. The English language has not only kept the country united but also has become an immense source of wealth creation and advancement in international affairs. Without the English language, perhaps IT companies would not have dominated the world of technology. Most importantly English language as a window to the European Enlightenment would not let India slip into medievalism. A historian might venture to say—in so many ways—the South rules. If the partition of India had not occurred, the South would have remained India's backyard. The brainpower would have been locked up in the outer ménage, as it were.

PAKISTAN LAUNCHES OPERATION GRAND SLAM

On 11 January 1966, Prime Minister Shastri's body was flown back to New Delhi in a Soviet aircraft from Tashkent (Uzbek Soviet Socialist Republic, now Uzbekistan), where Shastri had gone to sign the peace declaration that ended the 1965 war between India and Pakistan. He had died of cardiac arrest, though conspiracy theorists cried foul play.

The India–Pakistan war of 1965 was, in a manner of speaking, a war not only between the two decrepit armies of the subcontinent but also a puppet war among the countries that had supplied their leftover outmoded armaments to their clients. [8] The US, the UK and the Soviet Union had been selling their redundant weapons of war, including Centurions, Shermans, Pattons, Chaffees, ZMX, PT-76s, Hawker Hunters, de Havilland Vampires, EE Canberra and B-57 Canberra bombers, MiG-21s, F-86 Sabres, F-Starfighters and other sundry weapons to India and Pakistan. In the seven-week-long war (5 August–22 September), India and Pakistan lost 6,800 men, 300–490 tanks and 80–95 aircraft and other war ammunition, which created fresh markets for the arms suppliers and further deepened the subcontinent's dependency relationships with them. The war ended when the arms suppliers and cold war global puppeteers found that the conflict had gone too far, and neither side would win, and that it might drag them into the conflict.

In 1965 General Mohammad Ayub Khan of Pakistan, who had seized power in a military coup in 1958, planned an ingenious manoeuvre called Operation Gibraltar. The operation was designed to infiltrate irregular forces into Jammu and Kashmir, hoping to precipitate a local insurgency in the Kashmir Valley against Indian rule, especially when the wily lion of Kashmir, Sheikh Abdullah, was put in jail again for hobnobbing with China's Prime Minister Chou Enlai in Algiers.[9] It was presumed that the Kashmiri resentment would scale up to popular insurgency, which, however, did not happen.

Why did Pakistan code-name the attack Operation Gibraltar? It has a historical significance for the Muslim world because, in 711, the Umayyad Caliphate in North Africa invaded Spain from the port of Gibraltar and established Muslim rule in Europe. Pakistan purposely chose the name Operation Gibraltar to draw a parallel to the Arab conquest of Spain. Since the founding of Pakistan in 1947, its ruling classes have been trying to establish a distinct historical identity for the nation going back deep into Islam's great past.[10]

Also, there's an illusion in Pakistan, especially among the Pashtuns and Punjabis, about Muslims being a martial race; therefore, they are better fighters than the Indian soldiers (Hindus and Sikhs) who had suffered a humiliating rout at the hands of Communist China in 1962. As President Ayub Khan, egged on by his Foreign Minister Zulfikar Ali Bhutto, wrote to his Army Chief General Musa, 'As a general rule, Hindu morale would not stand for more than a couple of hard blows delivered at the right time and the right place. Such opportunities should therefore be sought and exploited.'[11] In early August, a group of irregulars crossed the ceasefire line and slipped into the Kashmir Valley. The plan was to blow up bridges and destroy government buildings hoping the confusion would create unrest. At the same time, when the irregulars were ravaging the Kashmir Valley, Radio Pakistan announced that the Valley was in uproar and the people of Kashmir had risen against the Indian rulers. This was a misleading statement because most of the information that came to the Indian police and the military came from the local people.

But when the uprising did not take place, and Operation Gibraltar collapsed, General Ayub Khan ushered in plan B, Operation Grand Slam. Pakistani troops crossed the ceasefire line in the Jammu sector using heavy artillery and made quick progress. The Indians fought back hard, especially in the Uri sector and captured the strategic pass, Haji Pir, which is an overlook point from where they could watch the infiltrators. The gloves were off. The war was in full swing. The Pakistani army, with two divisions of Patton tanks, started a major offensive in the strategic region of Chhamb-Akhnoor. Within a short time, Pakistani troops made swift progress and were deep into the Indian territory aiming to capture a bridge to break up the link between Jammu and Kashmir Valley as well as sever the region from Punjab. The Indian Army called in the Air Force, and soon Indian Vampires and Pakistani Sabres were engaged in intense aerial dogfights. The Pakistani Army failed to capture Akhnoor, the strategic fulcrum that proved to be a decisive turning point especially when India opened up the attack deep into the Pakistani Punjab, forcing the Pakistani Army to scramble and relocate its troops in order to defend its major city Lahore. Kargil, another area of strategic importance, was under Indian control, although Pakistan controlled the highlands overlooking Kargil and the Srinagar–Leh road. To force Pakistani troops out of the strategic area, the Indian Army launched a massive operation. With Akhnoor and Kargil in secure hands, India made a bold move and opened a new front in the west and on 6 September, the 15th Infantry Division crossed the international border with the aim of moving toward Lahore which became an existential threat to Pakistan. So alarmed was the US that it asked for a ceasefire in order to evacuate its citizens from Lahore.

The Pakistani Army launched a counter-attack and took Khem Karan from the Indian forces, with the intent to capture Amritsar and Jalandhar. But these manoeuvres and thrusts proved to be ineffectual pipe dreams. The Pakistani 1st Armoured Division never made it beyond Khem Karan, and by 10 September, it lay crushed at the Battle of Asal Uttar. The area became a graveyard of Sherman and Patton tanks, and with approximately 97 Pakistani tanks destroyed or abandoned, the place came to be called 'Patton Nagar.' On the other hand, the Pakistani 6th Armoured Division had routed the Indian 1st Armoured Division. The hostilities in the Rajasthan sector began on 8 September. The Pakistan Desert Force and the local militia attacked and captured some Indian villages in Rajasthan and launched an assault on the Kishangarh fort, which was recaptured by Indian troops after several days of bitter fighting. The war, nonetheless, was going nowhere. The Indian Army lost 3,000 men, while Pakistan suffered a loss of 3,800 men. The Indian Army took control of 759 square miles of Pakistan territory, while the Pakistan Army captured 210 square miles of Indian territory.

The US and the Soviet Union used pressure diplomacy to persuade India and Pakistan to cease the hostilities and since both countries mostly depended upon them for aid and trade as well as for weapons and war ammunitions, they had little choice but to agree. On 22 September 1965, the UNSC unanimously asked for an unconditional ceasefire. Both sides accepted the UN-brokered peace that culminated with the Tashkent Declaration, under which India and Pakistan agreed to return each other's conquered territories and go back to the 1949 line of actual control in Kashmir. The Soviet Union took the lead, and Premier Alexei Kosygin invited Prime Minister Lal Bahadur Shastri and President Ayub Khan to Tashkent to sign the Tashkent Agreement on 10 January 1966 that stipulated the parties to withdraw their forces to the pre-war boundaries by 25 February 1966.

During the war, both countries had been fed with fake news and euphoric propaganda that each side had been winning the war. But the sudden death of Prime Minister Shastri stilled the euphoria and plunged India into grief and uncertainty. Some writers such as Stanley Wolpert argued that India had the upper hand and could have won the victory. He put it succinctly,

Ayub was a giant of a man, as tall and sturdy as India's Prime Minister Lal Bahadur Shastri was small and physically frail. But India's army was four times larger than Pakistan's and quickly dispelled the popular Pakistani myth that one Muslim soldier was 'worth ten Hindus'. Operation Grand Slam ground to a halt as soon as India's tanks rolled west across the Punjab border to the environs of Lahore. In three weeks, the second Indo-Pak War ended in what appeared to be a draw when the embargo placed by Washington on U.S. ammunition and replacements for both armies forced cessation of the conflict before either side got a clear victory. India, however, was in a position to inflict grave damage to, if not capture, Pakistan's capital of Punjab when the ceasefire was called, and controlled Kashmir's strategic Uri-Poonch bulge, much to Ayub's chagrin.[12]

While the US and the Soviet Union, through diplomacy and arms embargo, brought the war to an end, hawk-eyed China swooped to Pakistan's defence, rhetorically speaking, condemning India as a warmonger. Since the India–China war in 1962, China had been supporting Pakistan. In 1965 China gave Pakistan $60 million in development assistance. During the war, China warned India, strongly condemning its 'aggression.' However, China did not intervene in the war because it had received a tough admonition from the US and the Soviet Union warning against expanding the conflict by any foreign intervention. Pakistan also did not show a keen interest in accepting the Chinese offer, fearing that this would complicate the problem. Because of global pressure, China's reckless behaviour was restrained.[13]

Once again, it was the failure of an early awareness system that foresees and projects possible threats from an enemy. Once again, it showed that India did not care much about intelligence gathering. In 1965 the Indian military intelligence had no clue that Pakistan was preparing to attack. The failure to be aware of the presence of Pakistan's heavy artillery in Chhamb was the reason that India was surprised by the attack. Had India collected enough intelligence, it could have taken steps in preventing the war in the first place, either through military manoeuvres or through diplomatic channels. According to the official account, on 22 September, when the Security Council was pressing both countries for a ceasefire, at that time, Prime Minister Shastri asked General J.N. Chaudhuri, the chief of the army staff, whether India could possibly win the war if the ceasefire were delayed. General Chaudhuri responded that most of the frontline ammunition had been exhausted, and moreover, the Indian Army had suffered heavy tank losses.[14]

Later it was found that hardly 14 per cent of the frontline ammunition had been used. India had twice the number of tanks that Pakistan had. The Pakistan Army had used up its frontline ammunition. If this information were available to Prime Minister Shastri, perhaps he could have delayed the ceasefire and been in a better bargaining position. Worse than that, it was felt after the war that there was poor coordination between the three military services.[15] Jeremy Black, in his book *War in the Modern World Since 1815,* came to a similar conclusion, stating:

> India's chief of army staff urged negotiations on the ground that they were running out of ammunition and their number of tanks had become seriously depleted. In fact, the army had used less than 15 per cent of its ammunition compared to Pakistan, which had consumed closer to 80 per cent, and India had double the number of serviceable tanks.[16]

But as mentioned earlier, the end of the 1965 war was decided by the superpowers, not by how much ammunition, tanks or airplane fighters were left on either side.

INDIA INTERRUPTED AND FUTURE DISRUPTED

Had the war of 1965 not interrupted the nascent Shastri administration, it was possible that Lal Bahadur Shastri would have pried opened India's closed socialistic economy and made it gradually more liberal. At the beginning of his administration, he tried to reduce the importance of the Planning Commission and its control over the economy. The National Development Council involving state-level leaders received more power. Some of the top industrialists, such as G.D. Birla, became close to the prime minister. As a small step towards liberalization, the government decontrolled steel and cement industries. And it was decided during this time that the rupee should be devalued so that exports could be encouraged. It's surmised by some economists that the push towards a more export-oriented economy would have been a new beginning for India. The country might have taken a little more private sector and trade-oriented approach as was happening in the East Asian tiger countries of Taiwan, South Korea and Japan.[17]

Unfortunately, at that time, when Prime Minister Shastri was planning to take tentative steps to embrace new ideas, a serious economic crisis was hanging over the nation. There were droughts from 1964 through 1966 and the 1965 war aggravated the financial situation. India became all the more dependent upon food shipments under the US PL 480 Food for Peace wheat programme. The government of India needed substantial external financial help to fund the Fourth Five-Year Plan. The financial condition was so desperate that India had to take a planned holiday for 1967–68. The food situation was so grave and the consequent strained financial situation so compelling that India had to ask the US for greater financial assistance and subsidized wheat supplies. This was also the time when Shastri gave a new slogan, '*Jai Jawan, Jai Kisan!*' (Victory to the soldier, victory to the farmer).

In the White House, there was a different kind of man. President Lyndon Johnson used wheat shipments as a diplomatic tool to subdue India's self-righteous voice of arrogant non-alignment. A beggar teaching morality of war and peace to the US to end the war in Vietnam was intolerable to the hurly-burly Texan. This era was different from the Kennedy years when the regime was more liberal towards India. Subsequently, India had to devalue the rupee due to external pressure.[18] The financial crisis of 1966 and the half-baked liberalization of the economic policy demonstrated that India was clueless and a country divided in a time of crisis. There was no consensus about how to promote India's international trade and competitiveness. The Indian business community was opposed to the devaluation of the rupee because imports and import substitution would be expensive for manufacturing. The intellectual class that was raised on the hallowed diet of socialism and non-alignment somehow regarded the devaluation of rupees as demeaning to the dignity and self-image of India, a country never bowing to external pressures.

Partly because of the unanticipated war, Lal Bahadur Shastri left the economy in a greater mess than he had inherited. If India had valued the necessity of keeping a watch on across-the-border based intelligence resources, the country could have preempted the war. The Pakistani attack could have been prevented. Failure of imagination was compounded by the failure of intelligence. On the brighter side, India was a robust democracy, poor but proud.

THE WOMAN WHO RESHAPED THE SUBCONTINENT

My father was a statesman, I am a political woman.
I am not a person to be pressured—by anybody or any nation.

—Indira Gandhi

Indira Gandhi is very tough.
She suckered us...this woman suckered us.

—Richard Nixon

During her long tenure as India's prime minister—from 1966 to 1977 and then 1980 to 1984—Indira Gandhi incorporated Sikkim into the Indian Union; created six new states; broke up Pakistan and helped create a new nation, Bangladesh; initiated the Green Revolution that liberated India from the US food dependency as well as from moving pockets of recurrent famines; experimented with authoritarianism by imposing the Emergency, and after 18 months, restored democracy; and finally, she crushed the Khalistan militants holed up in the Golden Temple of the Sikhs, for which she paid with her life. It was a glorious life. Her death was tragic and spectacular. India burned in anger and hatred. But India remained one and indivisible.

In a November 1999 millennium series poll, BBC Online readers chose Indira Gandhi as the greatest woman of the last thousand years—ahead of Queen Elizabeth I, Mother Teresa, Marie Curie, Margaret Thatcher, Joan of Arc, Emmeline Pankhurst, Aung San Suu Kyi and Eleanor Roosevelt. Some of the respondents said: 'Indira Gandhi was a strong-willed woman who led one-fifth of the world's population, democratically, non-aligned in a bi-polar world... Indira Gandhi was a dynamic leader and worked for the uplifting of India and its women... Indira Gandhi's boldness during the Emergency period is commendable, and at that time, a lot of changes and improvements took place in the great nation of India.'[1]

As fate would have it, the sudden death of Lal Bahadur Shastri once again catapulted the suave and unassuming Gandhian, Gulzarilal Nanda, into the position of an interim prime minister. And this gave time to the Kamaraj-led Syndicate to find an acceptable successor who could win the confidence of the people and the Congress party. While theoretically, the field was open for contest, the Syndicate was in favour of Indira Gandhi for several reasons. Although she had limited administrative experience, having served only as minister of information and broadcasting in the Shastri administration, she was young, attractive and had a winsome personality. She had the glow and aura of her illustrious father, Jawaharlal Nehru, which mattered a lot because Indians tended to believe that talent runs in the family. Indira Gandhi was the heir to a great man and his legacy. Most of all, she was a secular-minded person. There was another reason for the Syndicate to select her—they thought, perhaps, that she would be amenable to their collective views and run the country in consultation with them.[2]

Although most of the chief ministers consulted by the Syndicate supported Indira Gandhi as the prime minister, Morarji Desai believed that he was made of the right stuff and declared his candidacy. There was an open and democratic contest and, as it happens in many elections, there was much talk about horse-trading and other tall promises made by both the contesting parties. Desai was no doubt an experienced politician and also had a reputation of possessing high moral standards. He was the chief minister of Bombay and Jawaharlal Nehru's finance minister. When the elections were held, the Congress Parliamentary Party voted overwhelmingly for Indira Gandhi, who got 355 votes against Morarji Desai's 169.

Besides, prompted by Kamaraj and the Syndicate, Indira Gandhi had the support of the majority of the state leaders as well. With the overwhelming support of the Congress party parliamentarians and regional leaders, Indira Gandhi became the prime minister of the largest democracy in the world. More importantly, this also showed that the federal system had begun to assert itself in the sense that state leaders asked to be counted in such a vital national decision-making process. But before Prime Minister Indira Gandhi could deal with the aspirations of state leaders and manage the Syndicate bosses, she had to confront a threat to India's integrity from the tribals of the Northeast, the Mizos and the Nagas, who never thought of themselves as Indians and wanted a separate country for themselves.[3]

TRIBALS AND THEIR TRIBULATIONS

In India, the struggle by linguistic and ethnic groups to establish their identities sometimes took extremely violent forms; but eventually, they settled down to accept a separate state status in the Indian Union. Mizoram was one such state which witnessed such violence in an unmitigated form. Mizoram, the southernmost landlocked region in the sprawling Northeast, shares borders with several other states collectively called the seven sister states. Besides, it has a long border with Bangladesh and Myanmar, and in fact, on the map, it looks like a dagger driven between the two countries. At the time of Independence in 1947, Mizoram was part of Assam until 1972, when it became a union territory. But it took another decade and a half of bloodshed before it became the twenty-third state of India in 1987 when Rajiv Gandhi was the prime minister.

The population of Mizoram, as per the 2011 census, was more than a million people, but in 1966, when Indira Gandhi took over as the prime minister, the population was merely 300,000. About more than 90 per cent of the state is forested. Most of the people are Christians, making it the second Christian majority state in India. Mizoram is a highly literate society, more than 90 per cent, due to its long contact with Christian missionaries. But it had been suffering from what is called slash and burn shift cultivation and poor crop yield. Mizoram was the first regional conflict that Mrs Gandhi faced as soon as she took over as the country's top leader.

The Mizo conflict started with the famine of 1958–59 when the great flowering of bamboos, which occurs once in 40–50 years, led to an explosion in the population of black rats that feed on the abundant protein of the bamboo leaves. The rats ravaged the land, crops, and hoarded grains in silos and warehouses, causing tremendous shortage of food for the Mizo people. The response from Assam and central governments was inadequate. The Mizo people formed an organization, the Mizo National Famine Front, to protest against the poor response of the government to the suffering of the people. Later on, the Mizo National Famine Front was changed to a political organization, the Mizo National Front (MNF), which, under the leadership of the Mizo politician Laldenga, asked for a separate state in the Union but later on, he demanded a separate country.[4] Laldenga knew India's vulnerabilities, its conflict with its neighbours, and the possibility of getting weapons from East Pakistan (now Bangladesh) and China.

Since Mizoram is a deeply hilly, forested area, it was not difficult for Laldenga and his men to hide arms and ammunitions and fight from their position of strength. In February 1966, the MNF began its violent campaign by attacking government offices, supply lines and distribution systems. They cut off communications, raided banks, blocked roads and prevented the government forces from entering the territory. The Indian government's response was brutal. It was the first time that the army and air force had begun bombing their own people and foreshadowed the future.

Indira Gandhi did not hesitate to send armed forces to quell the insurgency. It was the beginning of a pattern that would become the national policy, the 'India Constant', the Indian State above all, not to give in to insurgencies at any cost. Later on, the same hardened attitude and aggressive policy were used to annihilate and eliminate Khalistani militants from the Golden Temple. From the Mizoram insurgency and the Khalistan militancy, it would become clear that India Gandhi was not a sit-back non-violent, peaceful politician who would give in to unreasonable demands upon the Indian State. To her, as we would see, the integrity of the nation, the India Constant, was extremely important. Nothing else mattered.

Of course, the Mizoram problem was not solved with the quelling of insurgency in 1966, but eventually, it would be. In 1972, Mizo Hills became a union territory directly governed by the Centre, but the festering problem continued until 1986 when finally, during Rajiv Gandhi's administration, Mizoram became a separate state. A journalist observed in a celebratory tone:

> For former insurgent and Mizo National Front (MNF) strongman, Laldenga, the ballot has proved more powerful than the barrel of a gun. At the end of his first essay in electoral politics, he found himself holding a prize he has coveted for more than three decades: command of the rugged 21,081 sq. kilometres territory of Mizoram and its six-lakh people. Laldenga is not just Mizoram's fourth chief minister; for his supporters he is the 'Hnampa' (father of the nation).[5]

India is one nation though many claim its fatherhood. And this is how the genius of India's federal system has been assimilating diversity, keeping people together by letting them be separate.

THE NAGALAND PROBLEM

In July 2017, a unique political drama took place in Kohima, the capital of Nagaland. Governor P.B. Acharya dismissed Chief Minister Shurhozelie Liezietsu. When challenged by a group of MLAs, Liezietsu failed to turn up to prove his majority in the state assembly. The governor swore in T.R. Zeliang as chief minister of Nagaland. Only five months earlier, Zeliang had resigned as chief minister because of the statewide protests against his decision to hold urban local body elections with 33 per cent seats reserved for women. Both Zeliang and Liezietsu, albeit coming from different Nagaland tribes, belonged to the same political party, the Naga People's Front, so this was an intraparty fight, which was resolved by the state governor, supported by a decision of the state high court.[6] Today, Nagaland is like any other messy democratic state in India. But it wasn't always so.

In many ways, Nagaland is a unique state in India. Located in the corner of northeast India with borders with Myanmar in the east and with the states of Assam, Manipur and Mizoram on the west, it has a population of about 2 million people and is home to 17 tribes, each with its distinctive culture, custom, language, dress and rituals. The English language and Christianity unite these diverse tribal people in this extraordinary beautiful state.[7] Nagaland is one of the three states in India, along with Meghalaya and Mizoram, with a predominantly Christian population. Most of them are devout Baptists.

On 1 December 1963, Nagaland became the sixteenth state of India. Becoming a state does not necessarily mean a peaceful coexistence. Since independence and, in fact much earlier, Nagaland had been experiencing insurgency as well as intra-tribal ethnic conflicts that became more intense in the beginning of the 1950s. However, in the course of time, the state began to settle down, and today, there is less violence than there used to be. Economically it began to grow rapidly and showed remarkable growth for a decade, touching 9–10 per cent.

Even before the coming of the British, the Naga Hill tribes had been living an isolated existence. The Nagas had no contacts with the Mughals or earlier rulers. But when the British came to India, under the British East India Company, contacts with the Nagas began to take shape. By the end of 1922, the British colonial administration had established complete sway over the Naga Hills and incorporated them into the sprawling Assam region. Most importantly, the British colonial administration introduced the Indian currency, the rupee, into the Naga tribal region and began to integrate the region economically with the rest of India. Also, Christian missionaries from the US and Europe started making inroads into the territory and gradually converted the tribal people, who were mostly animistic, to Christianity, especially of the Baptist Church.[8]

For a long time beginning in 1929, the Nagas have been asking for some kind of self-rule based on their own traditions. In June 1946, the Naga National Council submitted a four-point memorandum to British officials discussing the independence of

India from British control and their place in the subsequent political arrangement, asking for some form of autonomy.

Jawaharlal Nehru, in response to the memorandum for local autonomy, welcomed the Naga people to join the Indian Union after independence. He promised them local autonomy and cultural safeguards. At that time, the Naga National Council (NNC) wanted to become an autonomous part of Assam in a free India with local autonomy and safeguards for their way of life. They also wanted a separate electorate for Nagas. However, it was only after 1946 that the NNC began to assert that they had an absolute right to become a separate and independent nation. After the independence of India in 1947 nonetheless, Nagaland remained part of the vast sprawling province of Assam. But Nagas were unhappy with the arrangement, and strong nationalistic sentiments arose among a section of the Naga people.

Led by Angami Zapu Phizo, the NNC demanded a separate political union of their ancestral and tribal groups. And that was the beginning of a long bloody insurgency under his leadership, in which thousands of Nagas and Indian troops were killed. The Union sent the Indian Army in 1955 to restore order. In 1957, an agreement was signed between Naga leaders and the Indian government for the creation of a separate region of the Naga Hills. The region became a union territory directly administered by the central government, with a large degree of autonomy. But Nagas were not reconciled, and violent agitation continued, during which insurgents attacked the army and government institutions and banks. In July 1960, Prime Minister Nehru and the NNC reached a 16-point agreement under which the Government of India agreed to the formation of Nagaland as a full-fledged separate state on 1 December 1963 with Kohima as the state capital.

In January 1964, Nagaland had the first democratically elected Legislative Assembly, which soon after began to function, but it did not bring an end to the insurgency, and Naga rebels continued pillaging and attacking government and private properties of rival tribes. Once again, a ceasefire was announced, and negotiations were resumed, but the violence didn't stop. In March 1977, Prime

Minister Indira Gandhi imposed president's rule in the state. In the same year, leaders of the largest rebellious group decided to lay down their arms and accept Nagaland as an integral part of the Indian Union. However, a small group of insurgents continued with their activities. Throughout the long conflict, the Nagaland Baptist Church Council, no doubt, played a big role in the peace negotiations. But it was only in 2012 that Naga leaders finally contacted the central government, seeking a solution for lasting peace. The Nagaland Legislative Assembly elections were held in February 2013 to elect members of the legislative assembly for 60 assembly seats. The Naga People's Front was elected to power with a 37-seat majority. It would seem that Nagaland, like Mizoram, had finally merged its identity with India as a separate-but-together part of the nation.

THE GREENING OF INDIA

On a hot summer day of 8 June 2017, the 47-year old grandson of Indira Gandhi, Rahul, vice president of the Congress party, went to Mandsaur in Madhya Pradesh to sympathize with farmers, with the same dashing spirit for which his great-grandfather, Jawaharlal Nehru, was known. The farmers not only in Madhya Pradesh but also in Maharashtra, Tamil Nadu and elsewhere, had been producing too much food and had been agitating for higher minimum support prices (MSP) of their agricultural products, which had glutted the markets. They were feeling crushed under their debts and demanded waiver of farm loans. Their agitation, blocking highways, disrupting traffic, attacking government buildings, turned into a bloody confrontation, as usually happens in India, which killed five people.

More than the farmers' indebtedness and the vagaries of nature, it's the lack of political imagination and poor management that's the cause of the farm crisis in India, albeit it must be said that India has learnt how to produce enough food for its 1.3 billion people. According to a study:

Even when the average seasonal monsoon figure appears to be normal, fluctuations in rainfall in a country with 56 per cent of sown area rainfed [sic], can cause extreme wet and dry local conditions with wide economic, employment and social implications: about 600 million Indians depend on agriculture in India. A wide range of reasons—including low productivity of land, market failures, debts, pests and uncertain weather—have led to a farming crisis in India, and farmer's suicides have become a serious humanitarian and political issue for more than a decade.[9]

In spite of the fact that India faces occasional bouts of droughts that hit various regions from time to time, India today is not a hungry nation as it was until 1966 when Indira Gandhi doubled up with the Green Revolution. The Green Revolution saved India from being a nation with a begging bowl, preaching morality to the world. Driven by economic and political necessity, the Green Revolution was predicated upon the availability of agro-technological resources such as a robust variety of seeds and chemical fertilizers. However, the underlying factor of the greening of India, water, which in spite of the variable bounty and capriciousness of monsoons, accounts for 85 per cent of India's precipitation, is a serious problem, not only for farming but also for the holistic health of more than a billion Indians. Holistic health needs not only plentiful clean drinking water available on tap but also water for indoor plumbing and changing people's toilet habits in pursuit of the vision of making India clean.

Water, in this sense, is truly the life and blood of India and therefore needs multidimensional resource management so that not only farmers but also the increasing urban population can live a healthy and productive life. More than farming, it is the urbanization that's a most compelling reason for India not only to manage its water resources but also to increase them manifold. According to a water expert, 'We must recognize that the fundamental problem India has is not of actual shortage of water but of its wasteful and unsustainable management.'[10] India consumes massive amounts of groundwater for both agricultural and domestic purposes. It had

30 million groundwater extraction systems in place by 2017 that adversely affect water tables and the quality of water because the recharge of groundwater is much slower than its extraction.[11] Six hundred and thirty million people living in rural areas do not have access to clean water, without which people become victims of diseases such as cholera, malaria, dengue and blinding trachoma, according to a WaterAid report.[12]

The Green Revolution was begun and had been perfected by American agronomist Norman Borlaug and his team in the research centres and agricultural fields of Mexico under the Cooperative Wheat Research Production Programme, supported by the Rockefeller Foundation and the Mexican Ministry of Agriculture. The decades-long research involved genetics, plant breeding, plant pathology, entomology, agronomy, soil science and cereal technology, which eventually developed disease-resistant wheat varieties capable of adaptation to diverse growing climates with remarkably high yield potential.

Agro-technology was already a success in many food-deficit countries, including Mexico, before C. Subramaniam, minister of food and agriculture in the Lal Bahadur Shastri's administration, took up its initial implementation under the leadership of agriculture secretary B. Sivaraman and geneticist Dr M.S. Swaminathan, now famously called the Father of Green Revolution in India.[13] But it was the political will and the trust Lal Bahadur Shastri, and later on, Indira Gandhi placed in C. Subramaniam that made India eventually self-sufficient in food production. The agro-scientific revolution could have died in the lab unless it was widely disseminated and propagated by the political leadership. And there was no better way of doing it than C. Subramaniam turning his own backyard into an experimental field for growing the new variety of wheat. Lest it was thought to be a gimmick, he initiated a new programme to sell hybrid seeds, pesticides and fertilizers at highly subsidized rates.

These bold policy measures and their whole-hearted implementation enabled India to overcome chronic food deficiency as well as shameful dependency on the import of wheat from the US. In 1965–66, India imported 30 million tons of American wheat under the United States Public Law 48 scheme. And since there was a paucity of foreign exchange, India could not buy food in the open global market, and therefore, the American wheat shipment done under rupee payment was the only plausible way. But food scarcity had been there for very long. Jawaharlal Nehru, too, struggled, on the one hand, with India's self-chosen role of a global moral leader condemning the western and American imperialism, and on the other hand, expecting food aid on generous terms.

When the food aid was denied or delayed, Jawaharlal Nehru burst out in anger, 'We would be unworthy of *the high responsibilities with which we have been charged* [emphasis added] if we bartered our country's self-respect or freedom of action, even for something we need badly.'[14] And yet there was no escape from drought and famines that rolled across the country until the Green Revolution, of course, an American imported technology, changed the agricultural landscape. India works the best when it is under siege.

Today, India has a robust economy. It's a top destination for foreign direct investment, has foreign exchange reserves of more than US$634 billion, and a manageable current account deficit of 1.3 per cent of GDP (January 2022). That's a long way from 1966 when Indira Gandhi, due to acute shortage of foreign exchange, was forced to devalue the rupee from ₹4.76 to ₹7.5 to the US dollar, hoping that it would stimulate exports, build up foreign exchange reserves and let loose the floodgates of foreign aid into India.[15] Devaluation, which was strongly recommended (some say forced upon) by the World Bank, International Monetary Fund and the the Aid-India Consortium, did not open up the centrally controlled five-year-plan steel-framed rigid economy, nevertheless.[16] India was distrustful of FDI and preferred foreign aid—actually, low-interest loans—to finance its economic growth, import oil, machinery, food grain, and arms and armaments. The mortifying war with China in 1962 and the euphoric 1965 war with Pakistan had dwindled India's foreign exchange reserve to a low of US$625 million.

The 1966 devaluation was met with a tremendously hostile reception from almost all political parties in India. The government failed to get sufficient support even from its own Congress party members. The Syndicate that had put Indira Gandhi into office thought she was becoming too independent. Some of the criticism came from members who were concerned about the forthcoming election in 1967, while others were offended at the secrecy. The leftist parties who had supported Mrs Gandhi for the prime ministership also were against the devaluation, arguing that it was a surrender to the international aid consortium and India could no longer control its own policies to serve its national interest. The political weakness of Mrs Gandhi was compounded by the failure to explain to the people why the devaluation was necessary at this juncture. Even her own cabinet was divided.

The support for the devaluation came from a limited number of economists and some industrial groups who thought the role of private enterprise might increase, and there would be less socialism. Some export groups also thought they might benefit from the move. On the whole, most people believed that the government had succumbed to foreign pressure. The only party that supported Mrs Gandhi was the Swatantra Party, which was at that time a laissez-faire and industry-friendly party, a political party before its time.[17]

During the first two decades of Independence the World Bank and other international financial institutions played a very significant role in India's centrally planned economic development programme. The superpowers of the Cold War era, the US and the Soviet Union, took a keen interest in India's development lest it should lean too far to the other side. India's five-year plans in the 1950s and 1960s were substantially underwritten by western-dominated financial institutions. India depended on others not only for development assistance but also, as mentioned earlier, for food imports. This was despite the fact that at the time, India was pursuing a centrally planned socialist economic strategy, which, though chimed with the Soviet Union's central planning, was anathema to the US private free enterprise system.[18]

Indians enjoyed political freedom without economic freedom. The central government and the Planning Commission exercised complete control over key heavy industries in the public sector as well as infrastructure and dominated the private sector industry through extensive licensing procedures. Although the majority of the people lived in rural India and depended upon agriculture, the government did not pursue agriculture modernization. But the economic crisis that hit India in the 1960s was primarily due to the aggregated impact of two wars, with China in 1962 and Pakistan in 1965, as well as droughts and food shortages, which made India weak and vulnerable to outside pressures. The US and international financial institutions pressured India to alter its economic policies so that western capital could gradually get into its economic system. Not until the success of the Green Revolution, which eventually ended India's need for outside food aid and India began to build up its foreign exchange reserves to solve its balance of payment problem, was India able to avoid the crisis that had led to the 1966 devaluation.

In 1964 the World Bank sent its economist Bernard Bell on a mission to examine the economic situation in India and report back with policy recommendations to help the country. India apparently resented this outside scrutiny, but the World Bank assured India that, as the Consortium Coordinator, the bank would be in a better position to organize financial assistance of the donor countries for India. The Bank report called for a total structural reform of India's highly centralized economy. The problem was serious because India had a very low level of foreign exchange reserves and essential imports could not be maintained, especially in agricultural products and fertilizers. The Bell Report recommended the devaluation of the rupee, de-emphasis upon heavy industry, a greater focus on agriculture and modification in its extensive licensing programme for the industry. Moreover, the report also recommended increased private investment as well as direct foreign investment. The World Bank told the Indian policymakers that these recommendations, if implemented, would encourage substantial development assistance from financial institutions and the foreign exchange requirements of the country would be met.[19]

Although India was a non-aligned country, proud of its independence, always vowing not to kowtow to outside powers, India's planning minister Asoka Mehta, nonetheless, presented its

Fourth Five-Year Plan draft to the World Bank for review, and in response, the bank assured that the Aid Consortium would be generous enough to give aid amounting to US$1.2 billion for 1966 and 1.5 billion for 1967. However, the most significant recommendation was the devaluation of the rupee, which would ensure continuity of foreign aid.

President Lyndon Johnson's generosity towards India when Indira Gandhi visited him in 1966, was transactional. He asked the US Congress to approve 3.5 million tonnes of emergency food aid for India. But Johnson was also terribly annoyed at India's critical view of the Vietnam War in which America was involved in a life-and-death struggle. After the enforced devaluation of the rupee, Indira Gandhi visited Moscow and issued a joint statement with the Soviet Union leader Leonid Brezhnev in which the military action of the US in Vietnam was condemned. Since India needed its help, the US expected something in return rather than the Indian leader preaching like a moralist, à la the Pope or the UN secretary general, who didn't need American food aid.[20]

Lyndon Johnson had an overbearing personality and gave the impression of being erratic at times. Nonetheless, he got things done, but at the same time, he also expected something in return; so, his transactional behaviour was not unusual as per the American political standards of 'you scratch my back and I'll scratch yours'. Indians thought America to be a big bully, a country that had blood on its hands, so perhaps they thought that the guilt complex might make the US a little more generous.[21] Perhaps under some different circumstances, if the meaning and the importance of the rupee devaluation had been discussed and explained to the Indian public, it might have been better received.

The Indian news media, albeit less flabbergasted by the sudden announcement of devaluation than the general public, 'was a little more evenly distributed between approbation and criticism. This may be partly because some newspapers preserve a degree of editorial independence, so that the reactions to an economic issue, in particular, may be dictated by who happens to be the editor... (and) the political orientation of the papers and journals.'[22]

Agriculture Minister C. Subramaniam and some economists and right-wing politicians did believe that industrial reforms and currency devaluation would benefit the country. However, it must be said that the set of economic reforms advocated by the World Bank, considered as a whole, would have meant a basic shift on the consensus established by Jawaharlal Nehru on the fundamental principles of economic development in India: the state must control the economic heights.[23] The Syndicate members headed by K. Kamaraj were totally opposed to the devaluation, thinking it would lead to anti-Nehru policies in spite of the fact that some of them were pro-business, and if they had been consulted, they might have supported it. Adding to the confusion, the planning minister Asoka Mehta had also assured Parliament that devaluation was not under consideration.[24]

Amidst this confounding and conflicting environment of economic advice from economic experts and politicians, Mrs Gandhi took her own counsel. Her major political interest was to break out of the bondage of the Syndicate and to strengthen her position as the prime minister. But equally important to her was to resolve the foreign exchange crisis, the biggest external threat from which there was no escape, which made the devaluation of the rupee a necessary evil.[25] Only the West could help India to recover its economic equilibrium.

The reaction against the devaluation announcement was massive and intense, and it came from the left and the right, both the Congress party and the opposition of all hues. Everyone had their own reason for being against the devaluation. The left said that India had bowed down to the pressure from the World Bank that had acted as an agent of American imperialism. Only the pro-business Swatantra Party supported the measure, hoping that it would lead to further liberalization of the economy. Within days of the devaluation announcement and the liberalization of foreign exchange controls, the US resumed economic aid to India, which provoked the reaction that devaluation was conditional. The foreign aid was predicated upon Mrs Gandhi accepting the World Bank's economic package. There was no doubt in people's mind, that the government had to devalue the rupee under pressure from the aid-giving consortium of nations, which meant the US. Indians thought that the West and the World Bank were being highly intrusive into India's economic sovereignty.

The devaluation of the rupee did not result in the liberalization of the economy because it came from outside sources.[26] Since she was under attack from all sides, Mrs Gandhi became more radical. She abandoned liberalization. Rather, in the course of time, she began a more aggressive expansion of the public sector and more severe licensing requirements to have greater control over private industry. Eventually, she nationalized the banks. One consequence of the devaluation was that the World Bank's relations with India reached a nadir of distrust. Indians developed a strong resentment against the World Bank, especially when it failed to get additional foreign aid from the Aid Consortium. The Bank itself did not fulfil its US$1.2 billion commitment as it had promised. Instead, India had to be satisfied with only US$900 million. India felt besieged by internal and external forces. It was realized that India should not have become so vulnerable and dependent upon foreign aid. It was important, therefore, to build up foreign-exchange reserves, which couldn't be done without a robust export industry for which India needed liberalization of the economy and foreign direct investment. It would take another 25 years and another serious financial crisis before Prime Minister Narasimha Rao and his finance minister Manmohan Singh would find a way to get India out of the foreign exchange doldrums and set India in a new economic direction and on the road to prosperity.

GENERAL ELECTION: 1967

The 1967 general election in India for the Lok Sabha was a historic event, not because of the fact that it was a massive democratic game, as it had been in the previous such elections, but because it took place at a time when India was passing through grave multidimensional crises. It had just devalued the rupee amidst much controversy. There were fires everywhere, caste, class, communal and linguistic. To a casual outside visitor, India seemed to be a country more chaotic than an orderly civilized democratic nation based on the rule of law. Many outside observers wondered how long it would take for India to go the way of Pakistan, which had come under a military dictatorship. They wondered whether India could survive, whether it could hold itself in a democratic framework, India with its huge population and limited resources, and perpetual linguistic–caste–class conflicts.

Was the nation ripe for a steamrolling authoritarian regime? To the Indians, an alternative was not visible. Nor were they looking for one. They had not lost faith in the electoral democracy. What the outside observers didn't realize was that democratic elections had become part of India's political and socio-economic culture, the way to assert their distinctiveness and celebrate their inseparableness. Two decades after Independence, India was becoming a nation of many semi-autonomous states with their own cultural identities. Since states were separate and also part of a larger mutually dependent and interacting dynamic system, it became possible for India to continue as a democratic nation. In fact, what outside observers failed to notice was that it was during election times that India displayed a high level of political and social intensity.

It was during election time that Indians of all kinds, at all levels of existence, from Dalits to the most privileged high-caste people, spoke their minds. It was only through democratic elections that the people of India understood that they could play the game of democracy, genuinely exercise their rights and change the government.

Although the Congress party had ruled the country since the times of Jawaharlal Nehru, there were other parties that were asserting themselves, including the Communist Party, the pro-business conservative Swatantra Party, the Hindu nationalist Jana Sangh as well as regional parties, for example, the Akali Dal in Punjab and the Dravida Munnetra Kazhagam (DMK) in Tamil Nadu. India had also begun to learn American methods of mass marketing campaigns, high-powered sloganeering, toxic negative advertisements against opponents and political horse-trading.

Thanks to the independence of the Election Commission and its commitment to enable voters even living in the remotest part of the country to exercise their right to vote, the 1967 election was a remarkable achievement, regardless of the electoral results. The Congress won only 283 seats against its previously held record of 361, but good enough to give it a comfortable majority to form the government at the Centre.

Along with the general election for the Lok Sabha, state assembly elections were also held, which proved to be a setback for the Congress party. The most spectacular electoral defeat for the Congress party was in the south, particularly in Tamil Nadu, where the DMK won a resounding victory getting 137 seats out of the 234 assembly seats. The Congress party, in spite of its fairly good record in the state, won only 51 seats.[27] C.N. Annadurai, the DMK leader, was elected as the chief minister of Tamil Nadu. The DMK had risen on the political foundation that Tamil Nadu was a separate culture and Tamil movie stars played a big role in energizing the people in asserting their separate cultural identity.

One reason that played a significant role in the rise of the DMK in Tamil Nadu was the feeling that Hindi protagonists might impose the language on southern people, which energized and antagonized the people in Tamil Nadu against the Congress party. But as mentioned, many popular leaders in Tamil Nadu rose from the film industry. People like M. Karunanidhi, M.G. Ramachandran, M.R. Radha and many others had attained fame/popularity because of their roles in Tamil films, in which they played swashbuckling heroes, fighting against the evil forces. And people loved them. The Congress, too used film personalities such as Shivaji Ganesan, Nagesh, Padmini and others, but they could not counter the DMK propaganda.

The rise of linguistic-cultural regionalism gave political control to the DMK, and since then, either the DMK or its breakaway party, the All India Anna Dravida Munnetra Kazhagam (AIADMK), has controlled the political power in the state. In the neighbouring state of Kerala, which has a unique balance of Hindus, Christians and Muslims living in harmony, regionalism did not assert itself.

Kerala was a left-leaning state where the communists had been in power since 1963. The Congress lost in Kerala also. In 1963 the CPI broke up into two factions, the CPI and the CPI(M). The new party, the CPI(M), under the leadership of E.M.S. Namboodiripad, won 52 seats out of 133 in the state assembly. The Congress party won only 30 seats. The CPI, the original parent party, won 19 seats, which enabled both communist parties to form the government with E.M.S. Namboodiripad as the state chief minister.

Another interesting outcome of the election was in West Bengal, where the Congress party lost its long-held sway. West Bengal had a long tradition of its politics being dominated by leftist parties. The 1967 election threw upfront an alliance of the leftist parties, the United Front (UF), consisting of the Left Front and the Bangla Congress, a splinter group from the Congress party. The Congress party won 127 seats out of 280. The CPI(M) won 143 seats and the Bangla Congress won 34 assembly seats. The United Front, including the Bangla Congress, the CPI(M) and some other leftist groups had enough seats to form the government. Ajoy Mukherjee of the Bangla Congress was elected as the chief minister with Jyoti Basu of the CPI(M), a London educated barrister, becoming the deputy chief minister. Jyoti Basu was one of the savviest politicians in the country and eventually he became a dominant political figure in West Bengal. Although his influence was limited to West Bengal, his rise showed the affirmation and assertiveness of federalism in India.

As in Kerala, the Communist Party in West Bengal too had split into two separate parties, the CPI and the CPI(M). The CPI owed its allegiance to the Communist Party of the Soviet Union. The CPI(M) was beholden to Mao's China. The ideological differences between the two factions of the Communist Party were not very significant but they looked at different outside powers for inspiration and support. Nonetheless, both parties were committed to use democratic processes to gain political power and lead the state's economic and social development programmes based on their respective ideological platforms. Unfortunately, that turned out to be a mirage. It was during the political dominance of the CPI(M) under Jyoti Basu that West Bengal gave birth to one of the most virulent extremist leftist movements, the rise of Naxalites, the scourge that spread to many parts of India.

In West Bengal the coalition government did not last long, which necessitated the imposition of President's rule in the state in 1969 followed by new elections after a period of six months. After the elections, the CPI(M), with 80 seats, became a major force in the new alliance with the Bangla Congress and other parties. Ajoy Mukherjee was once again elected as the chief minister, but the CPI(M) kept the most important portfolios, Home and Labour, which gave it the real power in the state. This was the worst of times in West Bengal. There was little law and order. The legislative assembly proceedings were frequently interrupted. Even the governor was not allowed to address the assembly.

Although the CPI(M) was a major partner in the government, it did not hesitate to encourage street protests and violence to gain its ideological objectives. Workers laid siege on factories, many of which consequently closed down, resulting in a massive flight of capital, and professionals and intellectuals from the state. Chief Minister Ajoy Mukherjee was so helpless that he undertook a fast to protest against the abuses of his own government, the inability of his own government to establish law and order in the state.[28]

Most importantly it was the conflict between the CPI(M) and the Naxalites that led to frequent and bloody confrontations with the police. The Naxalites now formed their own party, CPI (Marxist-Leninist), which received vociferous support from China. The leader of CPI (ML), Charu Majumdar, advocated the total elimination of landlords and the feudal system in rural West Bengal through violent means. Landlords were the class enemies. In the rural areas, the Naxalites beheaded landlords and, in the cities, they attacked the police. The movement also spread to state colleges and universities, which led the police to raid college campuses and dorms where, in many cases, the police found homemade bombs. Jhumpa Lahiri's novel *The Lowland* gives a glimpse of how the Naxalite movement was tearing apart families and Bengali society.

While the Naxalites were ripping the state apart, in other parts of India, especially in the northern Indian states of Uttar

Pradesh, Madhya Pradesh, Bihar and Haryana, where there were non-Congress coalition governments, corruption and nepotism had skyrocketed. Political crossover from one party to another was so frequent that many people began to call their governments '*Aya Ram Gaya Ram*', or come-and-go, governments. Many united front opportunistic alliance governments consisting of the Jana Sangh, the Socialists, the Swatantra Party and local parties, who had nothing in common, were formed and dissolved.

There were other trouble spots raising their heads in India. In Hyderabad, Andhra Pradesh, the demand for a separate Telangana State led to processions, train stopping and strikes that turned violent sometimes. A new state, Meghalaya, was carved out of Assam to appease the hill people led by the All-Party Hill Leaders Conference, fearing that the rebels might turn to China for military succour. In Punjab, the Sikhs insisted that Chandigarh must exclusively be the capital of Punjab. A Sikh political leader, Darshan Singh Pheruman, died after a prolonged fast demanding that Chandigarh must be part of Punjab. But he died in vain since Chandigarh even today remains the capital of both Punjab and Haryana. Bombay, the financial and industrial hub of India, saw the rise of a new extremist pro-Maharashtrian political party, the Shiv Sena, started by cartoonist Bal Thackeray, enabling Bombay to regain its status of the maximum city, the city of extremes, once again.

After the 1967 elections, India looked like a congeries of disorderly political states with a weak Centre. India that was held together by Jawaharlal Nehru's grand vision of a democratic secular socialist India was disappearing. That was the biggest challenge that Prime Minister Indira Gandhi faced at the time. On the one hand, there was a recalcitrant Congress Syndicate that wanted to exercise political control and on the other hand, the states were gaining power by asserting their own separate identities. In these particularly chaotic conditions, Prime Minister Gandhi began to forge a new political identity for her and for the country. She began to use the levers of power to reshape the politics in India and thus began one of the greatest political experiments in India. Indira

Gandhi picked up where Jawaharlal Nehru had left off. She began to talk increasingly about socialism in concrete terms, a nation that controlled the economic heights of the economy, a country where the state-controlled enterprises would dominate every aspect of people's lives so that the people would identify with one well-defined ideology, socialism, rather than with regionalism and casteism.

RADICAL SOCIALISM

To rally the country to her new vision, Indira Gandhi, in May 1967, presented to the nation a 10-point programme of socialistic reforms that included social control of major banks, nationalization of general insurance and export-import trade, abolition of the privileges and privy purses of the princes, minimum wages for rural and industrial workers, public distribution of food grains, checks on monopolies and concentration of economic power, limits on urban incomes and property, and more effective implementation of land reforms. The 10-point programme appealed to her supporters, especially the Young Turks, the radicals of the Congress party, but the Syndicate was not very responsive. Indira Gandhi and the Young Turks believed that the new revolutionary programme would rekindle the people's imagination and revive enthusiasm for the Congress party. She emphasized the problems of a landless labourer, showed her concern for the minorities in India, and also defended the public sector, stating that the function of the public sector was not to make profits but to create a broad industrial base for further economic development.[29]

The old guard of the party, the Syndicate, presented to Mrs Gandhi an existential threat, not only to her political career but also to her father's legacy. She had a feeling of being cornered and had no other way out except to fight back and assert her supremacy as the prime minister and the leader of the party and the country. In 1969, an extraordinary chance opened up for her to assert her primacy in the Congress party. The President of the Republic of India, Zakir Hussain, died in office. The Syndicate wanted to replace Dr Hussain with one of its own candidates, N. Sanjiva Reddy, a seasoned political leader, former speaker of the Lok Sabha and chief minister of Andhra Pradesh. In a head-on confrontation, Mrs Gandhi decided to propose the name of the Vice President V.V. Giri, a labour leader who had excellent relations with the prime minister. At the All-India Congress Committee in 1969 that met in Bangalore, Mrs Gandhi opposed Sanjiva Reddy's candidacy for the presidency, but the Congress Working Committee (CWC) overruled her. When she returned to Delhi, Mrs Gandhi took an extraordinary political step. She took away from Morarji Desai, a member of the Syndicate, who was also Deputy Prime Minister in her cabinet, one of the most coveted portfolios, Finance. Once Desai was out of the way, she immediately announced the nationalization of 14 major banks. On All-India Radio, she said that a few rich companies could not be allowed to dominate the socio-economic and political system of the country. Banks should not be only socially controlled, but they should also be publicly owned. Nationalized banks would advance loans to millions of unbanked people in rural and urban areas, including farmers, small businesses and self-employed people. The bank nationalization was challenged in the court, which the Supreme Court upheld. But under the Constitution, the President of India can issue an ordinance, which V.V. Giri, as the acting president, did, so the bank nationalization was final. The nationalization of the banks galvanized the country and made Mrs Gandhi extraordinarily popular among the masses and the intelligentsia who had become mostly left-leaning since the early days of the Nehru era. Although bank nationalization, in the course of time, increased the number of branches, especially in rural India, the question remained whether the nationalization stimulated economic growth, lessened poverty and added to the wealth of the nation.

As mentioned earlier, Mrs Gandhi challenged the Syndicate by proposing the name of Vice President V.V. Giri as the president of India against the CWC-nominated official candidate Sanjiva Reddy. With clandestine support from Mrs Gandhi and her supporters, Giri decided to run as an independent candidate. Eventually, she openly supported Giri's candidacy in violation of the party discipline while the President of the Congress party, S. Nijalingappa, asked

Indira Gandhi to support the official candidate, Sanjiva Reddy. The internal struggle continued until a week before the election was held when Mrs Gandhi finally spoke up and told Congress MPs and MLAs that they should vote according to their conscience. This was actually a clarion call to the Congress party legislators to disregard the decision of the Congress party high command, which they did and voted for V.V. Giri, who won the presidency. Since she had defied the party's decision, on 12 November 1969, the Congress party president S. Nijalingappa expelled Mrs Gandhi because of the breach of discipline. Expelling the prime minister, the leader of the country, from the party was an extraordinary step. The split of the Indian Nation Congress into two separate parties, the Congress (O) controlled by the Syndicate and the Congress (R) led by Mrs Gandhi, proved to be a momentous event with far-reaching consequences.[30] The same year the Congress (O) and the Congress (R) had a show of their respective support among Congress party members by meeting in Ahmedabad and Bombay, respectively. Mrs Gandhi and the support group presented themselves as standing for socialism and secularism, a party for the poor that stood for the economic development of the nation as a whole. Mrs Gandhi denounced the Congress (O) of the Syndicate as the party of capitalists.

The Congress party (R) attracted a majority (446 out of 705) of the All-India Congress Committee members. In the Lok Sabha, however, Mrs Gandhi's Congress (R) had a shortfall of 45 seats to become the majority party. To form a majority in the Lok Sabha Mrs Gandhi and her party sought the support of independents and the CPI. The CPI jumped upon the opportunity to join Mrs Gandhi's socialistic bandwagon and become a little more respectable and acceptable, especially when India was developing friendly relations with the Soviet Union. The CPI calculated that by joining forces with Mrs Gandhi's new left-leaning party and publicly supporting her programmes from outside, it might eventually play a bigger role in the country's political fortunes. The CPI strengthened Mrs Gandhi's socialistic credentials as genuine rather than politically opportunistic. The Congress alliance with the communists made them respectable and politically acceptable and eventually made it easy for the CPI(M) to take political control of West Bengal for three decades.

After bank nationalization, Indira Gandhi turned her attention to the abolition of the privileges of the hereditary princes. At the time of Independence, the princely states were persuaded to merge with the Indian Union, and in lieu of it, the princes were given a guarantee that they would retain their princely titles, jewels and palaces apart from being paid privy purses commensurate with their state revenues. But as time passed, the Congress party and the general public began to feel that in a country of teeming poor, it was improper that princes should continue having these luxurious lifestyles. In 1967, the All-India Congress Committee passed a resolution that asked for an end to the princes' privy purses and titles. In May 1970, Parliament debated a bill amending the Constitution to annul the privileges of the princes. The Lok Sabha approved the bill, but the Rajya Sabha rejected it by a single vote, which prompted a presidential ordinance derecognizing the princes and their titles. However, the presidential ordinance was challenged in the Supreme Court, which ruled that the ordinance was arbitrary and unconstitutional. It became clear to the prime minister and her supporters that not only the old Congress party but also the Supreme Court was protecting feudal interests and opposing her programme of socialism. There was no better way of seeking support for her socialistic programme than dissolving Parliament and asking for a new mandate from the people.

CREATIVE DESTRUCTION

In terms of Indian mythology, Indira Gandhi could be compared to god Shiva, the destroyer and the creator, more than to goddess Durga, the invincible. Shiva is associated with creative destruction, a term borrowed by Joseph Schumpeter in 1942, who applied it to capitalism, which requires periodic destruction so that it can be re-created. Indira Gandhi broke up the grand old party of the independence movement into two warring factions and eventually refashioned the breakaway Congress party (R) to become a most dominant and dynamic force in the country for a long time to come. Thereafter she took a bold step of calling for general election in 1971 in order to get a massive mandate to put into practice her progressive socialist agenda as well as to fight recalcitrant forces in Parliament as well as outside. Keeping in mind the struggling small farmers, daily-wage landless labourers, unbanked small businessmen, and petty entrepreneurs, Mrs Gandhi's election manifesto embodied her socialistic vision for rapid economic and social development. The election manifesto also paid attention to the condition of the lower castes and minorities, reestablishing her secular credentials. The manifesto, however, polarized the nation between the progressive forces and what Mrs Gandhi called reactionary forces.

The Grand Alliance of the opposition parties, including the Jana Sangh, the Swatantra Party, the Congress (O), the socialists and many smaller regional parties, led by the old guard C. Rajagopalachari, Morarji Desai and other Syndicate members, coined a catchy slogan, '*Indira Hatao, Desh Bachao* [Hindi: Remove Indira, Save the Country]'. In response to which Mrs Gandhi's controlled party, the Congress (R), came up with a more memorable slogan, '*Garibi Hatao* [Hindi: Eradicate Poverty]'. This was the stuff of a heated general election that saw India coming together despite all its divisions and fragmentations. The Grand Alliance could not compete with the progressive vision and energy of Mrs Gandhi, who campaigned from one corner of the country to the other, explaining her programme and persuading people that her party was the real Congress party. She talked about the nationalization of banks and the removal of princes' privileges in order to assure her audiences that she was on their side. Her personal charm and, furthermore, the fact that she was the daughter of Jawaharlal Nehru with a progressive agenda and the slogan '*Garibi Hatao*' electrified the audience wherever she went.

The victory in the election was spectacular: her party Congress (R) won 352 out of 518 parliamentary seats. Riding on the coat-tails were the communists, the CPI and the CPI(M), which together got the next highest number of seats, 48, in the Lok Sabha. The Congress (O) was brutally beaten, getting only 16 seats. Even the

Tamil regional party, the DMK, with 23 seats, did better than the Congress (O). With the massive victory, the Indian National Congress (R) was recognized as the genuine Congress party. Despite some electoral malfeasance, the fifth general election was an extraordinary successful achievement. [31] People's faith in democracy was restored. The electoral democracy had come to stay in India. With so much power in her hands and the party and the people behind her, Mrs Gandhi began to reshape the Indian subcontinent as had never been done before.

THIS IS WHY BANGLADESH HAPPENED

The process of the creation of Bangladesh was no less gruesome and horrendous than the creation of Pakistan. Twenty-four years after the independence of India and the creation of Pakistan, Mujibur Rehman made a similar argument as Jinnah had done for the Muslim Homeland, that the Bengalis of East Pakistan, although (mostly) Muslims, have a separate language, separate culture, and therefore are a separate nation, and that they could not live together with the people of West Pakistan. On 25 March 1971, the War of Bangladesh Liberation began when the military rulers in Pakistan under President General Yahya Khan decided to launch Operation Searchlight to crush the separation movement led by the Awami League and the intelligentsia of East Pakistan.[32] The Pakistan Army units from West Pakistan began systematic destruction and elimination of civilians, university students and intellectuals as well as the Hindus who made up 20 per cent of the population, a military mission which, in the words of a courageous hawkeyed Pakistan journalist Anthony Mascarenhas, was a well-executed pogrom. Writing in *The Sunday Times*, he said, 'I have witnessed the brutality of "kill and burn missions" as the army units, after clearing out the rebels, pursued the pogrom in the towns and villages. I have seen whole villages devastated by "punitive action".'[33]

The military rulers cancelled the results of the 1970 election, the first national general election since Pakistan's founding, and arrested Sheikh Mujibur Rehman, who should have become the prime minister of Pakistan since his party, the Awami League, had won a majority of the seats in the National Assembly. The Pakistan Army, which was supported by extreme elements, including the Islamists-created religious militias, the Razakars, al-Badr, and al-Shams, started massacring the local populations selectively to terrorize them into submission. The military campaign and the terror let loose by the militia included mass murders, internal displacement, deportation and rape. More than 10 million people fled to India, apart from 30 million internally displaced people. Those were the days of the vulture.[34]

The Mukti Bahini, the national liberation army, which was formed by voluntary civilians, defected soldiers from the Pakistan Army, the East Bengal Regiment and the East Pakistan Rifles, played a crucial role in fighting against the atrocities committed by the Pakistan Army. The Mukti Bahini carried out widespread sabotage, including 'Operation Jackpot' against the Pakistan Navy.[35] By November 1971, the Mukti Bahini had taken control over a wide area of the country, especially the countryside. On 7 April 1971, the provisional government of Bangladesh was formed in exile. Many Pakistani Bengalis, including top military and diplomatic personnel, joined the provisional government in Kolkata. The widespread genocide caused tremendous outrage all over the world, thanks to the reporting done by the Western press. India, under the leadership of Indira Gandhi, gave massive diplomatic, economic, and military support to the Bangladesh nationalists.

President Richard Nixon, an anti-India racist and his coldblooded realpolitik minion, the White House National Security Advisor Henry Kissinger, fully supported Pakistan's genocidal military generals, especially because Pakistan had helped open the door to China. To understand Henry Kissinger's mind and his twisted logic, recall a most notorious quote of this Jewish refugee who had escaped Nazi Germany: 'And if they put Jews into gas chambers in the Soviet Union, it is not an American concern. Maybe a humanitarian concern.'[36] Senator Ted Kennedy, on the other hand, led a brave campaign demanding an end to the genocide by Pakistan's military.[37]

On 3 December 1971, Pakistan launched airstrikes on northern

India. This jolted India, who had been a passive observer thus far, and compelled it to launch a counterattack on both Pakistan fronts, the west and the east. While the Indian forces held back Pakistan's pre-emptive attack on the Western front, the Indian forces on the Eastern front, based on the logistics and strategic information provided by the Mukti Bahini, made rapid advances into East Pakistan. On 16 December 1971, the Pakistan Army surrendered in Dacca (now Dhaka), and by 1972 most of the nations recognized Bangladesh as a sovereign independent nation.

Pakistan was a divided nation at its birth, the two parts of the country divided by a thousand miles of unfriendly India. The populations of West Pakistan and East Pakistan were almost equal, but all the resources and the power were concentrated in the West. East Pakistani Bengalis felt they were being exploited economically and their grievances and concerns were being ignored. Apart from the geographical monstrosity that was Pakistan, the administration of the two regions from Islamabad was an unprecedented challenge. Since the formation of Pakistan as a new nation, the country had never been continuously under democratic governance. The cultural and linguistic disparity of the two regions, the violence and unruly behaviour of political parties, the absence of strong civil society and institutions tempted the military, again and again, to seize power until the generals messed up and reluctantly restored power to a democratically elected civilian government, who in turn would mess up the country again.

The seeds of the destruction of Pakistan as the home for Indian Muslims were laid by Jinnah, who, in 1948, while on a visit to Dacca, declared categorically that Urdu and only Urdu would be the national language of Pakistan.[38] But in East Pakistan Bengalis felt that their language, with its long literary history and illustrious literature, was superior to any other Pakistani language and must have its rightful place. For them, Bengali language and culture were more important than Pakistan as a homogeneous religious nation; therefore, the movement for a separate country of the Bengali-speaking people actually started long before the War of Liberation began. It started in 1952 with what is called the Language Movement

Day.[39] It's remarkable that the language and the feeling of being a Bengali transcended religious-solidarity-based Pakistan as the pre-Independence Muslim League had imagined.

But after the humiliating defeat in the war, General Yahya Khan resigned on 20 December and handed over power to Zulfikar Ali Bhutto. As president, commander-in-chief and the civilian chief martial law administrator, Bhutto's first and foremost job was to get 93,000 Pakistan prisoners of war (POWs) back to West Pakistan. Although India treated the POWs with utmost humanitarian care according to the Geneva Conventions, they were a great financial liability and India couldn't have kept them for long. Nor could Pakistan have kept Mujibur Rehman in prison, awaiting the death sentence when the game was over. Mujibur Rehman was released on 8 January 1972, and two days after his return to Dacca, he took charge as the prime minister of Bangladesh. On 2 August 1972, India released 93,000 Pakistani POWs under the Shimla Agreement signed between Indira Gandhi and Zulfikar Ali Bhutto. Although some commentators have suggested that there was a quid pro quo between the release of Mujibur Rehman and the POWs, there was no other way.[40] Apart from international pressure, Indira Gandhi had other things to do. So did Zulfikar Bhutto.

AS PEACEFUL AS THE SMILING BUDDHA

In May 1974, Raja Ramanna, the director of the Bhabha Atomic Research Centre (BARC), called Prime Minister Indira Gandhi and said, 'The Buddha has finally smiled'. Amidst all the chaos and civil commotion going on all over the country, Indira Gandhi had authorized the country's first nuclear bomb test in the Pokhran Test Range in Rajasthan, the first nation to do so outside the five permanent members of the UNSC. Calling it an implosion, the nuclear test was said to be for peaceful purposes. The peaceful nuclear narrative was the continuation of what Jawaharlal Nehru had said in 1948, 'We must develop this atomic energy quite apart from war—indeed I think we must develop it for the purpose of using it for peaceful purposes... Of course, if we are compelled as a nation to use it for other purposes, possibly no pious sentiments of any of us will stop the nation from using it that way.'[41] The nuclear programme had remained in peaceful suspended animation until the times of Lal Bahadur Shastri, but when Indira Gandhi took over as the prime minister, the programme got a shot in the arm, especially after the India–Pakistan War of 1971. To intimidate India, President Richard Nixon dispatched the USS Enterprise into the Bay of Bengal, to which the Soviet Union responded by sending a nuclear missile submarine to shadow the USS Enterprise. India needed a nuclear deterrent, and in 1972 Prime Minister Indira Gandhi sanctioned BARC to develop a nuclear device, code named the Smiling Buddha, which was successfully tested in the desert of Rajasthan on 18 May 1974.[42]

The successful test, which came three years after the victory over Pakistan for the establishment of Bangladesh, strengthened Indira Gandhi's reputation at home as an intense nationalist apart from the fact that it catapulted India into the ranks of the five nuclear powers. The top nuclear scientists Homi Sethna, Raja Ramanna and B. Nagchaudhari were deservedly awarded Padma Vibhushan awards, India's second-highest civilian honour. On 22 July 1974, Mrs Gandhi told Parliament that 'activities in the field of a peaceful nuclear explosion are essentially research and development programmes... No technology is evil in itself: it is the use that nations make of technology which determines its character. *India does not accept the principle of apartheid in any matter and technology is no exception* [emphasis added].' Like Jawaharlal Nehru, she remained equivocal about 'weaponization of India's nuclear capability,' stating, 'If our scientists have the basic know-how, without which we couldn't have done this, then any government could have directed them to make a bomb if they had so desired.'[43] But India's peaceful declarations were accepted with a pinch of salt and in reaction to India's test, the Nuclear Suppliers Group (NSG) was formed to prevent nuclear proliferation by controlling the export of nuclear materials, equipment and technology, from which India was excluded and she remained a nuclear pariah until the US–India Civil Nuclear Agreement in 2008.[44]

SHEIKH ABDULLAH REHABILITATED

In 1975, Sheikh Abdullah, once known as the Lion of Kashmir, was brought out from the cold dungeon and rehabilitated after 22 years of political wilderness under the Indira–Sheikh Accord and reinstated as the chief minister of Jammu and Kashmir, the strategic Muslim majority state that he had helped bring under the Indian Constitutional umbrella, strengthening India's credentials as a secular democracy, albeit, later on, he became conflicted and confused. Indira Gandhi reshaped the Indian subcontinent in the aftermath of the 1971 victory, the breakup of Pakistan and the creation of Bangladesh. As an absolute nationalist, she would brook no challenge to the integrity of India, the India Constant.

The question of giving Jammu and Kashmir the right of self-determination through plebiscite was as dead as a dodo. Even the idea of restoring the state to its pre-1953 autonomous constitutional status in the Indian Union was inconceivable because during the last two decades, Article 370, that gave Jammu and Kashmir a special status, had been eroded to nothing, though the accord stated that 'The State of Jammu and Kashmir which is a constituent unit of the Union of India, shall, in its relation with the Union, continue to be governed by Article 370 of the Constitution of India.' Although the residual power will remain under the purview of the state, 'Parliament will continue to have the power to make laws relating to the prevention of activities directed towards disclaiming, questioning or disrupting the sovereignty and territorial integrity of India or bringing about the cession of a part of the territory of India or secession of a part of the territory of India from the Union or causing insult to the Indian National Flag, the Indian National Anthem and the Constitution.' Whatever 'provisions of the Constitution of India already applied to the State of Jammu and Kashmir without adaptation or modification are unalterable.' And even those provisions that had been applied with modification could not be altered or repealed except by the president under Article 370. The accord provided that 'the state government can review the laws made by Parliament or extended to the state after 1953 on any matter relatable to the Concurrent List and may decide which of them, in its opinion, needs amendment or repeal, for which the president's assent to such legislation would be imperative'.

In regard to 'laws to be made by Parliament in future …the State Government shall be consulted regarding the application of any such law to the State and the views of the State Government shall receive the fullest consideration,' but the supremacy of Parliament would remain unchallenged. Furthermore, 'no law made by the Legislature of the State of Jammu and Kashmir…relating to such matters as the appointment, powers, functions, duties, privileges and immunities of the governor' or 'the matters relating to elections namely, the superintendence, direction and control of elections by the Election Commission of India, eligibility for inclusion in the electoral rolls without discrimination, adult suffrage and composition of the Legislative Council…unless the Bill, having been reserved for the consideration of the president, receives his assent.' Sheikh Abdullah demurely and deceptively accepted the Faustian bargain.

In other words, the Indira–Sheikh Accord, under the all-but-dead Article 370 put a steel framework over Jammu and Kashmir as never before. As Sumantra Bose wrote:

> In return for Abdullah's release and appointment as IJK's [Indian-controlled Jammu and Kashmir] chief minister, his ever-faithful associate, Mirza Afzal Beg, signed another 'Delhi accord' with the government of India whose terms verged on capitulation to New Delhi and Indira Gandhi. The agreement reaffirmed, virtually without modification, the terms of IJK's incorporation into India since 1953. A patently hypocritical clause stated that 'Jammu and Kashmir, a constituent unit of the Union of India, shall continue to be governed under Article 370.' In reality, between 1954 and the mid-1970s, 28 constitutional orders 'integrating' IJK with India had been issued from Delhi, and 262 Union laws had been made applicable in IJK… The Delhi-determined circumstances of an emasculated Abdullah's return to office amounted to a clever evasion of the Kashmir conflict rather than a substantive solution to it.[45]

The accord restored Sheikh Abdullah to power and helped establish the Abdullah political dynasty in the state, keeping in pattern with political dynasties in other states; but it did not restore peace to the state. While many Kashmir leaders believed that Sheikh Abdullah, for the sake of power, 'had relinquished the Kashmiris' right of self-determination,' on the other hand, the Hindu party, 'The Jana Sangh in Jammu and Delhi protested against this accord. As always opposed to the special treatment meted out to the valley in preference of Jammu, Jana Sangh supporters wanted Article 370 to be abrogated and the whole state included in the Indian Union, like all the other states... Opposition to the Kashmir accord continued and a new educated class was being drawn into the political arena.'[46]

A BRIEF EXPERIMENT WITH AUTHORITARIANISM

Like Partition, the Emergency was a necessary evil and once it was over, India emerged a much stronger democracy than ever before. Today democratic checks and balances are so strong that it would be extremely difficult for even the most powerful prime minister to do what Prime Minister Indira Gandhi had done on 25 June 1975.

By 1971, Mrs Gandhi was at the acme of her political power. Her faction of the INC had a massive majority (68 per cent) in the Lok Sabha. In the cabinet of ministers, she was not the first among equals but she was the cabinet, the supreme leader. She was advised by a dedicated coterie of British trained socialist thinkers and counsellors, including Parmeshwar Narayan Haksar and other Kashmiri pandits, who believed that, as in the Soviet Union, the bureaucracy should be committed and loyal to the supreme leader and the Congress party's ideology. But unfortunately, Mrs Gandhi's Congress party (I, for Indira) at that time had no well-structured ideology and vision, therefore, Mrs Gandhi was the party's ideology, which was cunningly summed up by an aspiring sycophant, Dev Kant Barooah of Assam: 'India is Indira, and Indira is India. Who lives if Indira dies?'[47] She struck fear and commanded loyalty, it was said, by keeping dark dossiers, what is called 'opposition research' in the US, on her rivals and troublemakers. She handpicked state chief ministers who became her minions. Federalism had receded.

Her left-leaning populist postures, bank nationalization, abolition of princely privy purses, the electrifying slogan *'Garibi Hatao'*, and her quick and spectacular victory against Pakistan that enabled the becoming of Bangladesh and transformed the geopolitics of the Indian subcontinent forever, had endeared and bonded her with India's teeming poor, Dalits and minorities as well as left-leaning intellectuals who had been dominating university campuses and the news media. Moderate communists, wolves in sheep's clothing, became her allies and some of them donned the Congress cap and infiltrated her party. Some like Rajni Patel, lawyer and trade unionist, joined her inner circle of advisors whose derivative aura of political power created its own circle of toadies, including businesses and industrialists in Bombay who wanted to get things done quickly in Delhi. Much later, a commentator observed:

> As a brilliant barrister and Mrs Indira Gandhi's eyes and ears and a conduit to business in Mumbai, Rajni Patel held unimaginable power: ministers would supplicate before his desk at his Cuffe Parade office, there would be lines of favour seekers and daily the phone would ring from 'headquarters in Delhi' with matters of national import to be discussed.[48]

But when Rajni Patel fell out of favour with Indira Gandhi, the light went out of his life.

While Indira Gandhi reduced the original Congress party and the Syndicate to ineffectual rubble and co-opted and muffled the leftists and communists, she did not know how to douse the raging inflation and fulfil the rising expectations among the young and the restless, the educated unemployed and unemployable that were annually churned out in hundreds of thousands by poorly funded colleges and by poorly educated college and university teachers. Most of all, she had a hard time controlling the judiciary, which eventually did her in.

In the Golaknath Case (1967), a case about property (land) ownership, the Supreme Court of India ruled that Parliament could not amend the Constitution if it affected fundamental rights guaranteed under the Constitution. Mrs Gandhi, with her Congress party's brute parliamentary majority, passed the 24th Amendment in 1971, overruling the Supreme Court's judgement. Similarly, the 26th Amendment (1971) overruled the Supreme Court's decision regarding the abolition of the princely privy purses. It was, however, the 1973 landmark Kesavananda Bharti case, a case about the management of a Hindu religious institution Edneer Matha's property, that questioned the constitutional validity of the 24th Amendment; and a 7–6 court majority ruled that Parliament could not alter the basic structure of the Constitution, thereby, reaffirming its previous Gokalnath decision. The Basic Structure Doctrine gives the Indian Supreme Court the power to review any amendment passed by the Indian Parliament that alters or conflicts with the foundational elements, the fundamentals of the Indian Constitution.[49]

After the Kesavananda Bharti case, in order to make the judiciary listen to its master's voice, the voice of Parliament and its leader, in 1973 Indira Gandhi appointed Ajit Nath Ray, an Oxford-educated barrister, as the Chief Justice of the Supreme Court superseding three senior justices of the court.[50] Unlike in the US, the chief justice of the Supreme Court of India is appointed by seniority. Justices retire at 65. Justice Ajit Nath Ray was amenable to Mrs Gandhi's political and economic ideology and it came in handy when she declared the emergency.

DISORDER, DISORDER EVERYWHERE

A no-confidence motion against the government is a most distinguished feature of the Indian parliamentary democracy, which enables the opposition to question the conduct of the government and its ministers and vote it out of power if it could muster a majority. But between 1966, when Indira Gandhi became the prime minister and the declaration of the Emergency in 1975, the government faced ten no-confidence motions in the Lok Sabha, which indicated how frustrated the Opposition was. In spite of the fact that she had forged a powerful political machinery to control her party and the government, the country at large wasn't peaceful. From 1973 through 1975, there was a crescendo of political unrest against Indira Gandhi across the country. Some thought the parliamentary system was not suitable for a diverse country like India. The country needed a more authoritarian presidential system that could assure political stability, without which social and economic progress was difficult to accomplish. Some people thought a cadre-based Soviet-style Congress party would be much better suited for India. 'Make [her] president for life and nothing more need be done,' said one of her most loyal sycophants.[51]

Indira Gandhi's fear about her assassination and her family were not totally unfounded, keeping in mind what had happened to Sheikh Mujibur Rehman and his family members in Bangladesh in 1975; and her own Railway Minister Lalit Narayan Mishra in January 1975. The hitmen, their ideological goals and their victims may have been different but assassination as a tool of regime change was used by many agencies, including the CIA and the KGB. Foreign friends and sympathizers such as British Deputy Prime Minister Michael Foot and Cuba's Fidel Castro had warned her about the danger to her personal life. Soviet intelligence reports too alerted her about the CIA's intent to eliminate her and install a US-friendly regime in India. At home, her enemies ranged from a religious cult like the Ananda Marg, Gandhian socialist Jayaprakash (J.P.) Narayan and socialist-anarchist revolutionary George Fernandes, whose hatred against Indira Gandhi was so intense that he would not have hesitated to make a bargain with the devil, especially after she brutally crushed the railway strike that would have crippled coal supply to the nation's power plants.[52] Added to this was the devastation caused by successive droughts and the OPEC oil price shocks that had emaciated the Indian economy. India seemed hopeless. The euphoria of victory over Pakistan for the liberation of Bangladesh had dissipated and the cost of the war had set in.

The government's inability to meet the challenge of growing expectations among the Indian youth and widespread labour unrest across the country for better wages and working conditions led to violent confrontations with the police. Jayaprakash Narayan's

Total Revolution Movement had got a shot in the arm by the Gujarat University students protesting against the rise of the cost of dorm food, that turned into a massive popular agitation, the Nav Nirman, against Chief Minister Chimanbhai Patel, an amoral political carpetbagger who was notorious for buying politicians and widespread corruption. Morarji Desai's fast-unto-death demanding the dismissal of the Chimanbhai government eventually led to its dissolution and the imposition of President's rule in Gujarat in March 1974. And if that could happen in Gujarat, why not in Bihar, Jayaprakash Narayan's home state, the platform at which he called for the ouster of Indira Gandhi. Violent strikes, fasts-unto-death, shutdowns and countrywide general disorder became the order of the day. The widespread student agitation led by Chhatra Sangharsh Samiti in Bihar in early 1974 received full-throated support from Jayaprakash Narayan, who envisioned a non-violent transformation of society through his brand of undefined Total Revolution. Mrs Gandhi refused to accept his demand for dissolving the Bihar Legislative Assembly. George Fernandes, socialist labour leader of the All-India Railwaymen's Federation, the largest trade union in the country, launched a nationwide railways strike paralyzing the nation. The government's response was ferocious. Thousands of railway employees were arrested and evicted from their government-provided living quarters. A bomb killed the railway minister L.N. Mishra. Several other political figures escaped assassination attempts.

Raj Narain was a stormy petrel of Indian politics. A socialist and colourful, rowdy political buffoon who wore a red head bandana, someone who claimed descent from the royal family of Varanasi, Raj Narain had lost the 1971 parliamentary election to Indira Gandhi by a wide margin in the Rae Bareilly constituency in Uttar Pradesh. Being a perpetual political fighter since the days of the independence movement when he was a student, he filed a lawsuit in the Allahabad High Court accusing Mrs Gandhi of election fraud and misuse of state machinery for election purposes. Indira Gandhi was subjected to cross-examination in the High Court for five hours, which strengthened the impression that in democratic India, no one was above the law. On 12 June 1975, Justice Jagmohanlal Sinha of the Allahabad High Court absolved Mrs Gandhi of serious charges such as bribing voters and election malpractices. Nonetheless, he ruled that Mrs Gandhi was guilty of the charge of misuse of government assets and personnel for her election campaign. Yashpal Kapoor, a government officer, for example, was found to have helped her in the election campaign before he had resigned from his government job, the court ruled. The state law enforcement was used to erecting a dais for her. Her campaign did not pay for the electricity. And so on.

On these minor technicalities, instead of letting her off with a reprimand, the court nullified her election, unseating her from the seat in the Lok Sabha—an example of punishment being totally out of proportion to the crime. More egregiously, the court also debarred her from contesting any election for six years, another example of the judiciary gone over the top. Indira Gandhi appealed against the High Court's decision to the Supreme Court of India. As a quirk of destiny, Chief Justice Ajit Nath Ray, whom she had appointed to the post suppressing three other senior judges, was on vacation along with 11 other Supreme Court justices. On 24 June 1975, Justice V.R. Krishna Iyer, the vacation judge, upheld the Allahabad High Court's decision and ruled that she be debarred from voting as a member of the Lok Sabha, thereby suspending all her parliamentary privileges. Nonetheless, she was allowed to continue as prime minister until alternative arrangements were made. Justice V.R. Krishna Iyer's order was temporary, valid until the court finished reviewing Mrs Gandhi's appeal of her conviction by the Allahabad Court on charges of electoral fraud, a process, Justice Iyer stated, that might take another two or three months. The Supreme Court's 12 vacationing judges, including the Chief Justice A.N. Ray, were to return on July 14 when the chief justice would have named a panel of three or five justices to review the original decision of the Allahabad High Court. But Mrs Gandhi couldn't wait. Nor did the Opposition who had taken up the verdict of the man—a vacation judge who had become the sole judicial power of the Supreme Court of India at the nation's most critical moment—Justice V.R. Krishna Iyer and his decision (to-be-reviewed) as final. Consequentially and most importantly, the Supreme Court of India annulled the popular electoral will of the people of India and actively began to participate in how India plays the game of democracy.

India was shaken up. Led by the winner of the court verdict Jayaprakash Narayan, a sanctimonious Gandhian with a wobbly idea of Total Revolution, and Morarji Desai who thought of himself to be the true heir to the legacy of India's Deputy Prime Minister Sardar Vallabhbhai Patel in the Nehru era, protesters surrounded Parliament and the prime minister's residence. J.P. Narayan staged a massive rally in Delhi and asked that the police reject the orders of government if they were immoral and unethical, as was Mahatma Gandhi's dictum during the freedom struggle.

Narayan had assumed the moral authority of Mahatma Gandhi but Narayan was no Mahatma. Nor did he understand the statecraft and the necessity of force to govern a complex country like India. In the aftermath of China's 1962 aggression, Narayan came to a college in Jamnagar, Gujarat, to address a public meeting mostly consisting of students, during which he went on spinning a khadi charkha and nonchalantly talked of meeting the Chinese aggression non-violently. The audience found his response of passive resistance to the dragon breathing on India's neck shockingly impotent and repulsive. Someone in the audience stood up and yelled that China would regard India as a nation of cowards (a nation of Banias, traders, the protester said). The crowd cheered but Narayan had no answer.[53] Yet in 1975, he talked of Total Revolution without spelling out what he meant.

Summing up the conundrum, P.N. Dhar, Indira Gandhi's former principal secretary and a member of her inner circle, said in his book *Indira Gandhi, The 'Emergency' and Indian Democracy*:

> What led Indira Gandhi to take such a drastic step? Did she have to pick up the gauntlet thrown down by J.P. on the Ramlila grounds? There is no simple answer. Her problem was much more complex than his, for whom what was happening in

the country was like a medieval morality play in which all the angels were on his side. He had no dilemmas; his mind was full of certitudes. He was more attuned to the rhetoric of revolution than to the complexities of administering a difficult country. Indira Gandhi's situation, on the other hand, was agonizing for her.[54]

India was aflame. On the evening of the day of the Supreme Court verdict, Indira Gandhi, without consulting the Union Cabinet, requested President Fakhruddin Ali Ahmed to take a drastic constitutional step. On 25 June 1975, before the clock struck midnight, the president of India proclaimed a state of internal emergency on the advice of the prime minister, citing threats to national security arising from internal disturbances, including the Indian Railways strike, student protests, widespread deterioration of law and order and the breakdown of authority across the country.[55] Within hours, all major newspapers' offices went dark, and most of the political opposition was jailed.

The cost of war against Pakistan for Bangladesh liberation, the 1973 oil crisis and the drought had put the country in the economic doldrums. India seemed ungovernable. In a political crisis such as India faced at that time, the situation was ripe for a military coup, but the Indian Armed Forces had remained apolitical. The path of least resistance for Mrs Gandhi could have been to resign after the Supreme Court verdict and hand over the power to Jagjivan Ram, the senior-most cabinet member, but Mrs Gandhi was not a Gandhian given to renunciation, especially when she had a massive electoral verdict from the people. On the advice of her inner circle, especially the brilliant and suave Siddhartha Shankar Ray, the chief minister of West Bengal, she was persuaded that since the security of India was under threat, as provided in the Constitution, fundamental rights could be suspended for six months.[56] It was a bold political move that rattled India, and eventually, when democratic liberties were restored, India emerged as a much more fortified democracy with stronger democratic and institutional checks and balances.

WHATEVER HAPPENED DURING THE EMERGENCY?

The emergency provisions of the Constitution, Part XVIII Articles 352 to 360, are a unique feature of India's political system. They empower the central government to confront and control any anomalous or extraordinary situation that poses an existential threat to the sovereignty, unity, integrity and security of the country. During an emergency the country becomes like a porcupine, with a ferocious, protective, self-defensive outer shell. The central government becomes omnipotent. The states' autonomy goes into suspended animation until normalcy returns. This innovative feature of the Indian Constitution transforms the federal structure of shared power into an authoritarian unitary system during an emergency. Talking about the flexibility and elasticity of the Indian Constitutional system, Dr B.R. Ambedkar, a jurist and guiding light among the framers of the Indian Constitution, said in the Constituent Assembly that:

> The framers of our Constitution, profiting from the experience of the working of other Constitutions, have inserted suitable provisions in the Constitution to assure the rigour of legalism and rigidity, which are inherent in all federal Constitutions. All federal systems, including the American, are placed in a tight mould of federalism. No matter what the circumstances, it cannot change its form or shape. It can never be unitary. On the other hand our Constitution can be both unitary as well as federal, according to the requirements of time and circumstances.[57]

The Constitution specifies three types of emergencies, including national emergency proclaimed because of war, external aggression or armed rebellion vide Article 352; emergency due to a breakdown of the constitutional apparatus in a state vide Article 356 that enables the Centre to impose 'president's rule' on the state; and financial emergency caused by threats to the credit and financial stability of India vide Article 360.

Since Independence, no financial emergency has ever been

declared in spite of the fact that there was indeed such a crisis in 1991 due to the depletion of foreign exchange reserves. From 1951–2000, the imposition of president's rule on states occurred 108 times, leaving no state untouched one time or the other, and hardly anyone ever protested against it. In fact, in most cases, people welcomed the imposition of president's rule on a state in trouble. National emergency has been proclaimed three times. The first proclamation of national emergency was made in October 1962 due to China's aggression in the northeast and continued until January 1968, which included the war against Pakistan in 1965. At the time of the aggression by Pakistan in December 1971 during the Bangladesh Liberation, the second proclamation of national emergency was issued.

On 25 June 1975, even though the second national emergency was in force, the president, under the advice of Indira Gandhi, announced a new state of national emergency based on the threat of 'armed rebellion' and 'internal disorder,' in light of the fact that some opposition leaders such as Jayaprakash Narayan had exhorted the police and armed forces to abandon the discharge of their duties if they thought the orders were illegal. Though the national emergency proclaimed in 1975 was unusual in the sense that it was meant to control internal disturbances rather than an external threat and has proved to be extremely controversial, most of the people in India took it in their stride, nonetheless. Most people did not see the difference between the imposition of president's rule on a state and the internal national emergency imposed on the whole country. No doubt, emergency powers were misused, for which there was widespread criticism all over the world.

But what did Indira Gandhi do with so much power that the Emergency gave her? In order to justify the Emergency as a much-needed politico-economic necessity, she formulated a 20-point economic programme to uplift the conflict-ridden country, which included increasing agricultural and industrial production, improving public services, and fighting poverty and illiteracy, among other efforts that would transform India into a dynamic, productive nation. Emergency promised a new era of government efficiency, including trains and buses running on time, government employees working and observing office hours, schools and colleges working per schedule, teachers teaching, and everything else that a decent civil society expects, which unfortunately was not happening in India.

When Sanjay Gandhi, Indira Gandhi's impetuous and ambitious son who was running the Maruti Auto Company, began to take centre stage, he declared his own five-point programme, including literacy, family planning, tree planting and the abolition of the curse of caste and dowry. Initially, the populist veneer put on the emergency made the bitter medicine palatable to the masses, except for journalists, opposition political leaders, and some trade unionists and campus intellectuals, most of whom retreated into silence. The Emergency gave Mrs Gandhi extraordinary powers and thus, she became unafraid of the consequences, she launched a massive crackdown on civil liberties and the political opposition.

Under the provisions of the Maintenance of Internal Security Act (MISA), the government used police force across the country to put thousands of protestors and strike leaders under preventive detention, notwithstanding the habeas corpus. Some of the most notable people, including the former queen mother Vijayaraje Scindia of Gwalior, Jayaprakash Narayan, Raj Narain, Morarji Desai, Charan Singh, Atal Bihari Vajpayee, Lal Krishna Advani, Arun Jaitley, Satyendra Narayan Sinha, the erstwhile glamorous Queen of Jaipur Gayatri Devi and many other protest leaders were immediately arrested. Of all people, it was J.P. Narayan who evoked worldwide sympathies from foreign media and politicians, partly because of his long association with Mahatma Gandhi, Jawaharlal Nehru and the independence movement. And most of all, it was his perilous health; he was a diabetic who needed regular dialysis. As Dhar observed:

The fact remains that both J.P. and Indira Gandhi, between whom the politics of India was then polarized, failed democracy and betrayed their lack of faith in the rule of law... it was not a contest between a revolutionary leader leading the hosts towards a new social and political order and a wily politician anxious to impose her personal dictatorship on the country. The actual outcome, on both sides of the barricades, was much less spectacular. J.P. proved an ineffectual revolutionary and Indira Gandhi a half-hearted dictator.[58]

The Rashtriya Swayamsevak Sangh (RSS) and the Jamaat-e-Islami as well as some political parties, were banned. Some communist leaders, who opposed Mrs Gandhi, too were arrested. Congress leaders, who disagreed with the emergency proclamation and amendment to the constitution, including Mohan Dharia and Chandra Shekhar, resigned from the government and the Congress party. They were placed under detention. In Tamil Nadu, the Karunanidhi government was dismissed and the leaders of the DMK were imprisoned. Chief Minister Karunanidhi's son M.K. Stalin was arrested under MISA. Although several state high courts decided that even after the declaration of the emergency, a person could challenge his detention, the Supreme Court of India, under Indira Gandhi's appointed Chief Justice A.N. Ray, overruled their decisions. The state could suspend a person's habeas corpus rights and detain him without any obligation to inform him of the grounds of his arrest and suspend his personal liberties. Many political leaders, for example, George Fernandes, escaped arrest and went underground and continued organizing protests, but it was not long before they were apprehended and detained.

THE WORST OF IT

One of the worst occurrences of the Emergency was the widespread and forced sterilization campaign to limit India's runaway population growth. The programme was initiated in September 1976 by Sanjay Gandhi to carry out his five-point plan. Those who followed his diktat had a missionary zeal. For example, Rukhsana Sultana, one of Sanjay Gandhi's close associates who gained notoriety for the sterilization campaign in the Muslim inhabited areas of old Delhi, might have pleased some Hindu nationalists who thought that

Muslims were breeding too fast. But the sterilization campaign was not aimed at religious minorities; rather, on the whole, it was aimed at the poorer sections of society. On 8 March 1977, according to a newspaper report,

> The villagers of Uttawar (in Haryana) were shaken from their sleep by loudspeakers ordering the menfolk—all above 15—to assemble at the bus-stop on the main Nuh-Hodol road...the police went into the village to see if anyone was hiding... the men on the road were sorted into eligible cases...to be sterilized.[59]

Government officials worked hard to achieve their vasectomy quotas. The campaign had limited impact beyond the northern states, including U.P., Haryana, Punjab, Himachal Pradesh and Rajasthan. But the psychological impact of sterilization was pan-India. In 1975–1977, the campaign carried out 11 million sterilizations, but not all were voluntary and peaceful. Many people died in violent protests against forced sterilization, while innumerable others perished because 'The sterilizations were performed in assembly-line fashion, in great haste, and in unhygienic conditions. There was no "follow-up care" offered whatsoever. Many men and women died from subsequent infections. Some 1,800 families filed wrongful death lawsuits on behalf of deceased relatives, but the actual death toll was much higher.'[60]

The Turkman Gate slum clearance programme was part of Sanjay Gandhi's plan to beautify Delhi, which ended on a devastating note when the police shot and killed the residents of the area who protested against demolition of their houses in 1976. The Turkman Gate residents, mostly Muslims, refused to move out of the area since, for their work and trade, they would have to commute daily to come to the city. The bulldozing of the slums that began on 18 April 1976 aroused violent resistance and confrontation with the police. The police opened fire on protesters killing hundreds, but because of the media censorship, few people knew what had happened. Only after the emergency was lifted, some reporters began to reconstruct the tragic events of the Turkman Gate. John Dayal and Ajoy Bose, in their book, *For Reasons of State: Delhi Under Emergency*, gave an extremely disturbing account of a horrific scene that made one wonder whether the Indian police were capable of such brutalities. According to their dramatically reconstructed eyewitness account:

> Razia Begum had been waiting for her husband for over an hour in her house but still no sign of him. There was a knock at the door and she eagerly went to open it. She found the figure of a police constable instead of her husband.
>
> 'Take off your earrings,' he ordered. Razia gave him her earrings.
>
> 'Where do you hide your other jewellery?' Helpless, Razia directed him to the little box where her jewellery was and their accumulated saving over the years.
>
> 'And now your clothes.' Razia pointed to the suitcases beside the bed. 'Not the clothes in your suitcase. The clothes on your body.' The constable showed his betel-stained teeth. Razia's eyes widened with terror. With a wild lunge, she managed to dodge the constable's grasping arm and ran out onto the verandah.
>
> Below lay a 40-foot drop to the ground.[61]

THE POST-PARTITION MIGRATION

The partition of India resulted in a massive migration of refugees, which increased the population of Delhi from 700,000 to 1.4 million by 1950. There was no open space left in metropolitan Delhi; there were people everywhere, putting immense pressure on civic services. In order to plan Delhi and to regulate its rapid and haphazard growth, on 30 December 1957, the central government set up the Delhi Development Authority (DDA) for a well-planned, orderly and rapid development of the capital city for a new and rising India. The biggest challenge for the DDA has always been to provide ample residential and commercial infrastructure facilities to its growing millions. Apart from the refugees from Pakistan, the capital and the metro region have been a magnet for immigrants from the neighbouring states. The challenge, therefore, has always been how to transform Delhi metro region into an orderly organic city that is hospitable for all and many more to come. The DDA Master Plan, established in 1962, aimed at a well-organized and structured development of the Delhi metropolis. The plan necessitated identifying and acquiring new lands that would be developed into residential properties and made into self-reliant settlements, which would also include commercial offices and retail outlets. In many ways, the DDA had been successful in accommodating the constant flood of people into Delhi, but along with authorized colonies, there was also a concomitant growth of hundreds of unauthorized colonies and slums.

In 1975 when the Emergency was promulgated, the population of Delhi had grown to more than 4.4 million. Every authorized colony had a support structure of slums and unauthorized settlements, where the servant classes lived, who in turn needed their own commercial and retail spaces. These creeping slums also penetrated the old city, for example, the Turkman Gate, Karol Bagh and other surrounding areas that made Delhi an eyesore for an ambitious city planner Jagmohan Malhotra, himself a Pakistani refugee, someone who was frustrated by the burden of democracy. Jagmohan found not only a kindred spirit in Sanjay Gandhi but also someone who had become a most important centre of power and was willing to delegate the authority to get things done.

Most scholars blame Sanjay Gandhi for the horrendous excesses of the Emergency, including bulldozing and demolitions of slums around the Turkman Gate and other places in Delhi as well as the sterilization programme. But there were other true believers of the Emergency, those who were Sanjay Gandhi's close associates— including city planner Jagmohan, top cop P.S. Bhinder, Youth Congress leader Ambika Soni, the socialite Rukhsana Sultana, and political hangers-on such as Navin Chawla, R.K. Dhawan, V.C. Shukla and Bansi Lal. They gravitated towards Sanjay Gandhi and built a cult around him because he embodied their blazing tunnel vision of transforming India rapidly. Growing population and growing slums were the two aspects of the same festering problem that needed forced sterilization and bulldozing. Any structure that stood in their way must be demolished. Any Indian who stood in their way must be silenced. But Sanjay Gandhi and his henchmen had no long-term vision, plan or ideology for governing a vast and complex country like India.

The Emergency was too long. It became counterproductive and destructive and degenerated into a kind of domestic, state terrorism. That was not what Prime Minister Indira Gandhi had envisioned when she chose the path of the Emergency to tame political chaos and reset India on the path of economic growth. She failed to transform the Emergency into a sustainable political structure. The experiment in total authoritarianism failed and it was this realization that there was no alternative to democracy that persuaded her to lift the Emergency and go for the general election. Like the rest of India, Indira Gandhi needed fresh air and needed to breathe freely.

INDIA REVERTS TO FREEDOM AND TURMOIL

*Freedom became one of the beacon lights of my life and it has
remained so ever since. Freedom with the passing of years
transcended the mere freedom of my country and embraced
freedom of man everywhere and from every sort of trammel—
above all, it meant freedom of the human personality, freedom
of the mind, freedom of the spirit...*

—Jayaprakash Narayan, 1957

In her announcement in January 1977, Indira Gandhi said that the Emergency had become necessary 18 months ago because the country was at a point of inflexion, in great danger; in fact, it was on the brink of disaster. The Emergency had been lifted, she said, because the country had been nursed back to health and had returned to normalcy. Simultaneously, when she was speaking to the nation about the lifting of the Emergency and the announcement of the Lok Sabha in March 1977, opposition leaders were being released from prison all over the country.

Immediately after their release, prominent opposition leaders met in Delhi and decided to form a coalition to contest the election against the Congress party. The parties included the Jana Sangh, the Bharatiya Lok Dal, the Socialist Party and the Congress (O), headed by Morarji Desai. They chose a common name for the coalition, the Janata Party, and at a press conference that followed, it was announced in the presence of Jayaprakash Narayan that they would redeem the country from Indira Gandhi's dictatorship. There was nothing else on the Janata Party's platform except to get rid of Indira Gandhi to save the nation, in spite of the lofty manifesto declaring that the election was 'a choice between freedom and slavery; between democracy and dictatorship; between abdicating the power of the people and asserting it; between the Gandhian path and the way that has led many nations down the precipice of dictatorship, instability, military adventure and national ruin'.[1]

The most stunning political news came a week and a half after the announcement of the formation of the Janata Party. Veteran Congress leader Jagjivan Ram, who had initially supported the Emergency and remained loyal to Indira Gandhi, announced that he was quitting the party along with H.N. Bahuguna and Nandini Satpathy. He not only represented the Scheduled Caste that constituted a substantial vote bank for the Congress party but was also highly regarded as a suave Indian politician. After the resignation, he formed his own party, Congress for Democracy (CFD), hoping to forge electoral arrangements with the Janata Party and its allies, the DMK, the Akali Dal and the CPI(M), to present a united front and prevent the Congress (I), (where 'I' stands for Indira) and its allies, the CPI and the AIADMK, from gaining electoral advantages through splitting the opposition.

It was one of the most exciting elections ever held in India. For the first time, the people were clear in their minds as to how much their votes mattered to them. They began to realize what the Emergency had done to them. It was the first time that the power of negative campaigning was amply demonstrated in an Indian election. The portrayal of the Congress party as a party that did forced sterilization, castration and demolition of houses of the poor, worked well, especially in northern India.

INDIRA HATAO, DESH BACHAO

As the results of the elections began to be announced on the night of 20 March 1977, the nation was shocked and awed. The Congress party was losing and losing so badly that even Indira Gandhi, as well as her younger son Sanjay Gandhi, had lost their seats. The outcome hit her like a thunderclap. She was defeated by her old nemesis, Raj Narain, the rowdy socialist politician who had won a judicial victory against her electoral malpractices, which had unseated her from Parliament and prompted her to declare the Emergency. However, while the Janata Party–CFD alliance won a resounding victory, taking 298 seats out of 542, its sway was limited to the north, where the excesses of the Emergency had been deeply felt. The South stood by Indira Gandhi's Congress party, giving it 92 seats out of the total 154 it won.[2]

With about 55 per cent parliamentary seats and 43 per cent popular votes, the Janata Party's victory, keeping in mind the horrendous excesses of the Emergency, was spectacular, but it wasn't a national mandate, especially when the South had kept aloof from the alliance party. Nor had the hastily formed coalition the time to deliberate and develop a coherent ideology, a collective mind, a new vision for the country, in the absence of which personal ambitions trumped the national interest. It was nevertheless a great experiment in coalition government.

The morning of 24 March 1977 seemed to call a new dawn for India after the 18-month turmoil and dark nights of the Emergency. The formation of the Janata Party (including CFD and allies) government, the first non-Congress government since Independence, began with the invocation of Mahatma Gandhi and his lofty ideals enshrined at his final resting place at Raj Ghat. Led by Jayaprakash Narayan and J.B. Kripalani, both Gandhian freedom fighters, the newly elected Janata MPs pledged to serve the nation above all. However, three major Janata Party leaders, Morarji Desai, Jagjivan Ram and Charan Singh, who had their own loyal followings among the MPs and their pre-merger parties, never wavered their eyes from the prize—becoming the prime minister of India. The fear that a leadership contest would divide the alliance parliamentary party and threaten its majority before it took power led the leadership selection to the deference of Jayaprakash Narayan and JB Kripalani, who on 24 May chose Morarji Desai, the Janata Party–CFD parliamentary leader and hence the prime minister, notwithstanding some hesitation and reservation from Jagjivan Ram and George Fernandes.

Prime Minister Morarji Desai played his hand deftly. Although he kept for himself the ministry of finance, he judiciously offered important posts to the alliance's other prominent leaders, especially his rivals, the Jat leader Charan Singh and the Dalit leader Jagjivan Ram, who were made deputy prime ministers. Besides, Charan Singh was given the portfolio of the minister of home affairs, the most powerful position next only to Desai himself. Jagjivan Ram became the minister of defence. Jana Sangh leaders Atal Bihari Vajpayee and Lal Krishna Advani were also give key positions in the cabinet as the minister of external affairs and the minister of information and broadcasting, respectively. Raj Narain was put in charge of the ministry of health, while Madhu Dandavate headed the ministry of railways. Trade union leader George Fernandes was appointed the minister of communications. Perhaps the most significant appointment to the cabinet was that of Shanti Bhushan, who, as minister of law and justice, restored the constitutional balance upset by Indira Gandhi. Congress (O) veteran leader Neelam Sanjiva Reddy, who had lost to V.V. Giri in the presidential election, too had his day. He became the sixth President of India on 25 July 1977.[3]

THE JANATA RULE

As expected, the first and foremost action undertaken by the Desai government was to repeal the contentious executive decrees issued during the Emergency that had made the Parliament supreme and the judiciary subservient to the will of the executive branch, the prime minister and his cabinet. The Constitution was amended to make it harder but not impossible for any future government to declare a state of emergency, mess with fundamental freedoms and the independence of India's judiciary. Since Indira Gandhi's Congress party, along with its allies, was holding 163 seats out of a total of 250 seats in the Rajya Sabha, the Janata Party could not get the repeal of the emergency executive orders passed. Ironically, this was the first time that the Rajya Sabha had asserted its autonomy rather than being a rubber stamp of the Lok Sabha. Nonetheless, in

1977–78 the Janata Party government was successful in getting the 43rd and the 44th Amendments passed, to restore the Constitution to the pre-Emergency status, albeit not fully.

The most controversial action of the government was to withdraw all charges against the 25 people accused in the Baroda Dynamite case, which included the new minister of industry, George Fernandes. In 1976, the Central Bureau of Investigation (CBI) had charged Fernandes and others of smuggling dynamite to blow up government offices and railway tracks in protest against the Emergency. A presidential pardon would have been better rather than decriminalizing the case. However, the reinstatement of the railway employees who had been bamboozled by the union leaders and were fired after the May 1974 strike, was a wise decision.

In a populist move, the Janata Party government hastened to establish several inquiry commissions to investigate the allegations of corruption and human rights abuses by the Indira Gandhi government, members of the Congress (I) and law enforcement. The Shah Commission, however, drew the most public attention in the beginning but during its prolonged hearings, Indira Gandhi and other accused bogged it down in procedural details as well as with legal challenges to its authority, and consequently, the Commission lost its high seriousness in the public mind.[4] The Commission published its three-volume report on the illegal activities of the government during the Emergency and the major actors responsible for it. The report dealt with the events that led up to the declaration of the Emergency and the gagging of the press; the hand of Sanjay Gandhi at the Turkman Gate confrontation in which the police fired on a crowd protesting against the demolition of their homes; and finally, the horrific conditions, torture and forced family planning sterilizations that mostly affected the poor and the disenfranchised.

But how do you punish the guilty? Some leaders of the Janata Party asked for special courts to be established to warrant a speedy trial of the cases related to the Emergency. In response, the Lok Sabha passed an Act, establishing two Special Courts on 8 May 1979; but a little after two months, on 16 July 1979, Charan Singh, the Jat leader, struck a Machiavellian bargain with Indira Gandhi's parliamentary group and withdrew his bloc's support from the Janata government. Morarji Desai struggled for a while to keep up the government but having found that the ground had sunk underneath him, he resigned and retired from politics. The long political career of a self-righteous, holier-than-thou politician ended up as a flash in the pan. Charan Singh had a few inglorious months of being India's prime minister until the next general election ended the chaos. Indira Gandhi returned to power, and the Shah Commission Report was forgotten. In January 1980, the Supreme Court of India ruled that the Special Courts established by the Janata government had no legal validity and hence no trials were held. The new political order under the resurrected Indira Gandhi government decriminalized the emergency crimes and the criminals, as had the Janata government, for example, in the Baroda Dynamite case.

The political antics of the Janata government were no different from the Indira Gandhi Congress. Disregarding the states' autonomy, the Janata government manoeuvred ten states that had Congress governments to disband and hold new elections in June 1977. The AIADMK, led by a popular film actor M.G. Ramachandran, won a resounding victory in Tamil Nadu. He parleyed his matinee idolatry into political capital. Six Hindi-speaking northern states, including Uttar Pradesh, Bihar, Haryana, Madhya Pradesh, Rajasthan and Himachal Pradesh, voted the Congress party out of power and established Janata governments, as did the eastern state of Orissa. The Punjab election catapulted into power the Akali Dal–Janata coalition government. Perhaps the most spectacular outcome of the turmoil was the political rehabilitation of Sheikh Abdullah, who was dismissed from power in 1953 for plotting to establish an independent Jammu and Kashmir state. The National Conference won a decisive victory in Jammu and Kashmir, while the Janata Party won 13 seats to the Congress party's 11. With a massive majority in Parliament and 1,246 seats in the state legislative assemblies, the Janata Party seemed to have political supremacy all over the country, but it was a broken house perching on a sandy foundation.

FOREIGN POLICY RESET

The hostile stance taken by the Nixon Administration during the Bangladesh Liberation War had driven the Indira Gandhi government closer to the Soviet Union, resulting in the Indo-Soviet Treaty of Peace, Friendship and Cooperation signed in August 1971 with emphasis on mutual strategic cooperation.[5] The Indo-Soviet Treaty though a significant departure from India's position of non-alignment in the Cold War, had become a compelling necessity keeping in view the developing Pakistan–China–America axis.

But much had changed since then, and Prime Minister Morarji Desai and the Minister of External Affairs Atal Bihari Vajpayee decided to reset India's foreign policy regarding the two superpowers and the immediate neighbours Pakistan and China.[6] In 1979, Vajpayee visited Beijing to re-establish diplomatic relations that had been cut off due to the Sino-Indian War of 1962. India and China decided to hold regular dialogues to expand trade, enhance border security and resolve long-standing trans-Himalayan territorial disputes. Unfortunately, Vajpayee's visit was cut short due to the breakout of hostilities when China attacked the northern border of Vietnam, India's long-standing ally. India protested and Prime Minister Desai 'expressed his profound shock and distress at the outbreak of hostilities on the northern borders of Vietnam... (which) created a situation endangering international peace and security... The prime minister expressed his earnest hope for the immediate restoration of peace and as a first step, stressed the urgent need for the withdrawal of Chinese forces from Vietnam...'[7] This should have been a wake-up call for India that China believed and practised aggressive realism in international relations. Friendship is an alien word in China's diplomacy.

Although distrust about the United States had not disappeared from the Indian mind, especially among the elites, the Desai government pursued diplomatic means to improve relations with the US in order to reset its foreign policy to genuine Nehru-era non-alignment. In January 1978, President Jimmy Carter made an official visit to India to improve trade relations and expand cooperation in science and technology. A village in Haryana changed its name to Carterpuri in honour of President Carter and his wife Rosalynn, who visited the village.[8]

There was change in the air. In 1977, speaking in Hindi, the first Indian diplomat ever to do so, Minister for External Affairs Vajpayee addressed the UN General Assembly (UNGA) stating that India stood firmly 'for peace, non-alignment and friendship with all countries.' A year later, addressing the UNGA, he talked about disarmament being a distant goal: 'the probability of a nuclear war looms over us like a menacing shadow,' that would not go away by simply creating 'zones free of nuclear weapons comprising the nuclear "have-nots".'[9]

ECONOMIC GROWTH UNDER THE JANATA PARTY

The Janata coalition government, a motley crowd that rode on a wave of extreme fury that forced sterilization and slum demolition had aroused in the north, had no cohesive economic vision. It was a political hodgepodge, a conglomeration of disparate political parties from the extreme Left to the extreme Right that had banded together to remove Indira Gandhi from power. The coalition government abandoned the idea of launching the Fifth Five-Year Plan and instead introduced a rolling Five-Year Plan.[10] The rolling plan consisted of three kinds of plans that would dovetail with each other as the economy developed. The first phase of the plan was for the current year that comprised the annual budget; the second phase extended to a number of years, maybe three, four or five. The second phase of the plan was to be kept altering as necessitated by the changing Indian economy. The third phase of the plan was 'a perspective plan,' which looked at the economy for ten, fifteen or twenty years. The rolling plan was thought to be adaptable and capable of overcoming the inflexibility of rigidly targeted five-year plans by amending targets, projections and resource allocations as the country's economy developed. Unfortunately, the rolling plan with its constant adjustment to the moving economic targets lacked the overall arching perspective of a fixed five-year plan as to where the country was heading. Although many constituents of the Janata Party were pro-free enterprise, they did not have the courage to trust the market forces. The concept of the government controlling the commanding heights of the economy still dominated the Janata Party and planners' minds.

In actuality, the rolling plan aimed at boosting agricultural production and indigenous industries to promote economic self-reliance. The government asked multinational corporations to enter into partnership with Indian corporations, perhaps with the idea of technology transfer but more so out of fear of dominance by foreign capital. Although India could do without Coca-Cola, the departure of IBM from India was a setback.[11] But the Janata government failed to grasp why the people of India had turned against Indira Gandhi in the first place. As they say, it's economy, stupid!

The global and domestic economic forces were beyond the government's control. Inflation skyrocketed; fuel shortages persisted; unemployment and poverty remained unchanged. Unruly trade unions struck, again and again, crippling industry and economic production.[12] India returned to chaos.

THE UNRAVELLING

The fall of the Janata government did not come too soon. The Janata Party was not only a house divided against itself, the house had no foundation. Socialists, trade unionists and pro-business leaders couldn't agree on the direction of the economy, making major economic reforms hard to achieve. Sometimes personal ambitions took the garb of political and ideological divisions. Socialists and secular Janata politicians could not stand the Jana Sangh members Atal Bihari Vajpayee and Lal Krishna Advani, whose association with the Rashtriya Swayamsevak Sangh (RSS) was unacceptable to them; consequently, Vajpayee and Advani stepped down from the government in 1979 rather than disassociating themselves from the RSS. The Janata government's failure to bring to a conclusion the prosecution of Emergency-era abuses and their perpetrators added to its incompetence. For lack of evidence, the legal cases against Indira Gandhi plodded on endlessly. The impression in the public mind of Mrs Gandhi being continuously subjected to harassment and prosecution began to arouse sympathy for her. Instead of seeking justice, the government gave the impression of vindictiveness and a witch-hunt.

Two forces unravelled the prime ministerial era of Morarji Desai. First, the economy stagnated, inflation surged, thus hitting the poor and the middle class, the foreign exchange reserves dipped sharply, the oil prices went up, and the prime minister, in spite of his experience in finance and industry, had no clue as to what to do about it. Secondly, his self-righteous attitude and contemptuous disregard for other people's opinions created ill tempers all around. Jat leader Charan Singh found it difficult to get along with the prime minister, whom he thought to be an undeserving rival. As a protest against Desai's high-handedness and abrasive leadership style, Charan Singh resigned from his position as a cabinet member. Desai also gave the impression of being sympathetic with the members of the Hindu party, the Jana Sangh, which exasperated the secular and socialist members of the Janata Party. Jayaprakash Narayan, the moral leader of the coalition, passed away on 8 October 1979, leaving the helter-skelter party undone.

In the meantime, Indira Gandhi had been regrouping her political forces. In January 1978, when a number of her party members led by some senior leaders of the Congress, including Y.B. Chavan and Brahmananda Reddy, left the organization, she revamped the party with a new name Congress (I). A month later, when the state assembly elections were held in Karnataka and Andhra Pradesh, the Congress (I) beat both the Janata Party and her other rivals. Neither the news media, which was still biased against her because of the Emergency excesses, nor the Janata Party leaders who were engrossed in their political infighting, could see the changing mood of the public. It must have come as a revelation when Indira Gandhi won with a large margin, a parliamentary by-election from the Chikmagalur constituency in Karnataka in November 1978, in spite of several commissions of inquiries and court cases against her regarding the crimes of the Emergency.

But the Janata Party could not stand her presence in the Lok Sabha and expelled her from Parliament for breach of privilege and contempt of the House on a minor charge and jailed her for a week.[13] Increasingly many people began 'to view Indira Gandhi's persecution not as justice but as revenge and vendetta and an effort to disgrace her. They felt she had already been punished enough by being voted out of power. Moreover, deep down, the rural and urban poor, Harijans, minorities and women still considered Indira Gandhi as their saviour; their Indira Amma or Mother Indira.'[14]

Indira Gandhi, a shrewd and calculating politician, never to be defeated or underestimated, offered Charan Singh the support of her party, the Congress (I), which after some attrition, had remained cohesive and loyal to her. The hungry and ambitious Jat leader Charan Singh took the bait. The temptation of occupying the highest political leadership position, becoming the prime minister of India, was worth paying any price, morals be damned. With only 64 members of Parliament out of 529 supporting him, he staked his claim to the office and President Neelam Reddy asked him to form the government and prove his majority on the floor. However, the Congress (I) backed out of its assurance to support the ailing but aspirational Charan Singh, who had refused to withdraw the Emergency related court cases against Indira Gandhi as the price of her political support. Jagjivan Ram and his supporters also quit the teetering alliance. And consequently, only three weeks in the prime minister's chair, Charan Singh gave up his claim to the high office and resigned; but was asked to stay until further arrangements.

With the withdrawal of support from the Jana Sangh, the collapse of the government and the retirement of Morarji Desai to Bombay, the Janata Party had dwindled into a spent force. With no other party who could hold a majority in Parliament, the president had no choice but to dissolve the Lok Sabha and call for a fresh election for January 1980. A perceptive Indian journalist observed reflectively that within months of Morarji Desai taking power:

> Naked ambition, corruption, cynical manipulation of caste and community became the abiding symbols of 1979... From

his deathbed, the architect of the great Janata experiment, Jayaprakash Narayan, watched the shattering of his dream.[15]

Having seen the chaotic behaviour of the mishmash of political parties forming a coalition to govern this vast and complex country, the people of India once again turned to Indira Gandhi for giving them a stable government. She apologized for the excesses committed during the Emergency and asked the people to vote for the party that would function and work for them. As a remorseful pilgrim, Indira Gandhi had a long conversation with a living legend, the highly revered Gandhian leader Vinobha Bhave in his ashram at Wardha to seek his blessings, which made her seem less sinning than sinned against. Indians love the penitent. The splintered Janata Party was humiliated and routed in the election, gaining only thirty-one seats. Charan Singh's faction of the Janata Party won only 41 seats. Indira Gandhi's Congress (I) won a resounding victory bagging a strong majority, 353 seats, in the Lok Sabha. Her much-maligned son Sanjay Gandhi who had brutalized the nation with his excesses during the Emergency also got elected from Amethi in Uttar Pradesh. Another era had begun. Indira Gandhi's political resurrection was a strange case of crime, punishment and quick redemption.

WHEN INDIRA GANDHI RETURNED

A woman so closely tuned to the country and its people; so complex, so skilful, so farseeing, so concerned, so capable of an insightful listening, so moved by beauty; and yet, at times, so primaeval, so obsessive, so brittle, even trivial—a woman who refused to be measured, who laid her own ground rules.

—Pupul Jayakar, Biographer

Indira Gandhi was neither a moral giant like Gandhi nor an intellectual giant like Nehru.

—Balraj Puri

In May 1968, Indira Gandhi wrote to Jayaprakash Narayan, the Sarvodaya leader and the protagonist of the Total Revolution Movement, that not every political party or individual in India was committed to the democratic framework, that in many cases, the exercise of democratic rights took the form of not the freedom to dissent but rather to disrupt and destroy.[1] Seven years later, Indira Gandhi declared the Emergency, partly to restore law and order and establish a sense of peace, although many scholars rightfully talk about the fact that the real reason behind this draconian measure was her being dislodged by the judiciary from her elected position as a member of Parliament. Politicians, especially those in positions of power and responsibilities, have complex motives for their actions.

SOME TRIUMPHS, MORE TRAGEDIES

Even if the Supreme Court of India had affirmed her as a properly elected member of Parliament, Indira Gandhi would have had a hard time facing the chaotic conditions prevailing in India. Indian politicians, including Indira Gandhi, didn't realize that freedom makes people aspirational; and that the basis of democracy is a healthy pace of economic growth that keeps up with the growth of population. The Soviet-style Five-Year Plan, based on state capitalism, and operationalized through the Planning Commission that had developed under Jawaharlal Nehru, continued under her premiership too—but had not proved to be productive in terms of growth in jobs or growth in the GDP. Nor did the Janata Party comprehend the fact that, in a poor, developing country, democracy at best is aspirational and can only survive if there's a vision, a shared collective dream as concrete executable policies and steady programmes for socio-economic progress that lifts all boats.

The Janata Party was a hastily clubbed together conglomeration of divergent parties without any coherent economic plan to face the problem of controlling rampant inflation and shortages of consumer goods for daily necessities for the common people, which prompted the demand for higher wages by trade unions and led to strikes all over the country. The Janata Party, which had promised the moon, was bewildered and overcome by continuous nationwide protests. To disrupt and destroy probably gives Indians a sense of empowerment. The so-called rolling five-year plan of the Janata Party was, in reality, no plan to rejuvenate the economy. While India twisted and turned in chaos after the fall of Morarji Desai's short-lived government, for the caretaker Prime Minister Charan Singh 'it was the ultimate ecstasy. For the remaining millions watching the death-throes of the Janata Party, the moment was devoid of agony or ecstasy but consumed by wholesale indifference. Few tears were shed over Morarji Desai's political demise. There were no laurels to welcome Charan Singh into office.'[2] Of course, Jayaprakash Narayan, with his nebulous concept of the Total Revolution Movement, was dead and gone, without leaving any structure of political morality.

J.P. was an exemplar of what Matthew Arnold said about Percy Bysshe Shelley, 'A beautiful and ineffectual angel beating in the void his luminous wings in vain.'

The epitaph for the Janata Party was not that it discredited itself; rather, the party made an experiment in democratic coalition politics and failed. From its failure rose the possibility of creating better working models for future coalition politics, with which some states had been already experimenting. Nonetheless, the federal system struggled under the brief Janata rule. Neither the Janata Party nor the Congress realized how indispensable the federal system was for containing and controlling the disparate and centrifugal forces that threatened to tear the nation apart, as Indira Gandhi discovered in her second coming when she paid with her life.

India falling apart or exploding like a big bang is a national paranoia, which leads the Centre to impose its will on the states by hook or crook. With 353 Congress (I) seats in the Lok Sabha, Indira Gandhi should have felt supremely powerful and confident, but she wasn't. The opposition dominated the Rajya Sabha, the Upper House, and except for Andhra Pradesh and Nagaland, most of the state governments were out of her party's control. However, through political manoeuvres, her troubleshooters were able to contrive political defections in four others, Karnataka, Sikkim, Haryana and Himachal Pradesh. Without the control or the compliance of the state legislatures, Indira Gandhi would not have been able to implement her election promises of re-establishing law and order, restoring industrial peace and exercising control over the economy to stabilize consumer prices: the major reasons why India had brought her to power again in spite of the horrendous excesses of the Emergency. The standing of Congress (I), which was in the minority in the Rajya Sabha, would be further diminished if the opposition-dominated state legislatures succeeded in electing 84 new members slated for the election in that year.

By dissolving nine state assemblies under presidential orders, a unique feature of the Constitution, Indira Gandhi wanted to make certain that the Congress dominated most of the states. She believed that the country needed a firm hand to rule and that the states must listen to and obey the Centre so that her programmes and policies were not flouted. The authoritarian streak had not disappeared even after the travails of the Emergency and the chaotic interregnum of the Janata Party rule.

On 17 February 1980, the Centre dismissed the opposition-controlled state governments of nine states, where the Congress (I) had won the parliamentary elections, including those of the Akali Dal in Punjab; the Janata Party in Bihar, Gujarat, Madhya Pradesh and Rajasthan; the Lok Dal in Orissa and Uttar Pradesh; the AIADMK in Tamil Nadu and the Congress (O) coalition in Maharashtra. It seemed like a political tit-for-tat. After all, the Janata Party too had dismissed nine Congress-ruled governments in 1977, reasoning that they did not reflect the popular will that had brought the Janata Party to power, and therefore, these state governments had lost their mandate. Indira Gandhi's gamble paid off. The Congress (I) and the allies won in all nine states. The twisted constitutional logic buttressed the political expediency and the necessity that the Centre's writ must run all over the country. The governments of West Bengal and Tripura, controlled by the CPI(M), were, however, left alone because the party had supported the Congress (I). Besides, the CPI (M), with 37 parliamentary seats, was an important political force. The Jammu and Kashmir government ruled by Sheikh Muhammad Abdullah's Jammu and Kashmir National Conference (JKNC) was spared because the reconciliation process was a work in progress.

Dismissing unfriendly state governments and holding new elections held the possibility of changing the balance of power in the Rajya Sabha, which was to elect 84 new members. Under the Indian Constitution, state assemblies elect the Rajya Sabha members. The Rajya Sabha cannot veto financial bills, but otherwise, it can checkmate the Lok Sabha in many ways. The Rajya Sabha could block any non-financial bill. Indira Gandhi not only succeeded in getting pliable state assemblies and the Rajya Sabha but also state governors of her choice, who though ceremonial in duties, still could create problems for the Centre. Moreover, Mrs Gandhi's return to power brought about an extensive transfer of top government officials, including some of the Emergency-era officials holding prominent positions of power.[3] By the middle of the year in 1980, it seemed that Indira Gandhi had become once again the undisputed leader of India; and she had as much power as she had during the Emergency except that now she had the democratic mandate to wield power.

But the gods of India were against Indira Gandhi. So were the endemic regional, communal, ethnic fissiparous undercurrents that surfaced to rock the boat and wrought her plans to rejuvenate the country to nothing. Her favourite son, Sanjay, whose activist goons and stormtroopers had caused so much havoc in the country through involuntary sterilization, demolitions and forced slum clearance, media censorship and the internment of political dissenters, died on 23 June 1980 in a fiery crash when he was flying a single-engine airplane over Delhi, the city he had tried to beautify through brutality. With him died the hopes of Indira Gandhi to groom him as the heir to the Nehru political dynasty. To his credit, Sanjay, in spite of his inhumane excesses of the Emergency, had more or less rehabilitated himself not only by winning the parliamentary election from Amethi, Uttar Pradesh but also through the stoic acceptance of the humiliation of the 30-month rule of the Janata Party. He correctly saw that India's exploding population—what is today euphemistically called the demographic dividends and the aspirational slumdogs becoming millionaires—led to poverty, 'slummification' and environmental degradation. His problem-solving methods were abominable. But he was a quick study, matured and became wiser, as the post-Emergency Janata Party interregnum showed. He could have had a bright political future. In his fatal crash, there was a whisper of destiny, perhaps.

Indira Gandhi, the charismatic, shrewd, tenacious and ruthless politician, was above all a mother. The loss of a child is the fount of perpetual pain for any woman. It's difficult to surmise what role the subterranean grief played in her political decision-making; nonetheless, for the remainder of her life, she was a driven woman despite the fact that she had another son, Rajiv, to comfort her and to lean on. But she needed more from Rajiv, who until then was more interested in distinguishing himself as a commercial pilot than dealing with the treacherous whirligigs of Indian political life. In spite of his initial reluctance and aversion to politics, he felt persuaded to enter the political arena for his mother's sake, and perhaps, India's sake, to give a sense of steadiness and dynastic political continuity, keeping in mind that Indira Gandhi was in her sixties and anything could happen. He got himself elected in 1981 as a member of the Lok Sabha from Amethi, the seat left vacant by his younger brother's demise.[4] The post-Emergency Janata Party experiment in coalition politics and the resulting chaos made the Nehru–Gandhi dynasty more relevant than ever.

THE STATE OF THE UNION

In spite of the concentration of political power at the Centre and the subservience of the state governments and the bureaucracy, democracy in India creates enough spaces for multiple centres of power, local, linguistic-regional or religious, to challenge the government. To disrupt and destroy is a political norm, the way India plays the game of democracy. While the Indira Gandhi administration was doing its utmost to rebuild and refurbish the Emergency-sullied image of India abroad through state visits and cultural programmes, assuring the people, especially the elites of the English-speaking world, the Anglosphere, that India was committed to democracy, secularism and socialism—as it was during the times of Jawaharlal Nehru—there were bushfires all over, some occasionally threatening to engulf the entire country.

One such bushfire could be seen in the case of trade unionist Datta Samant, who had some significant success with comparatively small industrial units workers, for example, Bharat Gears, Amar Dye-Chem, Rallis India's pharmaceutical division, Britannia, Fit Tight Nuts and Bolts and others.[5] But his aggressive trade unionism crippled and almost destroyed the Bombay textile industry in early 1982.[6] There were 62 textile mills that employed 250,000 organized workers, who were represented by the Rashtriya Mill Mazdoor

Sangh (RMMS), the officially recognized union of the textile mills. But in 1982, the new combative union leader, Datta Samant, a physician by training, who had tasted success elsewhere descended on the textile scene and promised workers the higher wages they deserved. His success in getting major wage increases for workers of Premier Automobiles, once the manufacturer of Fiat, Padmini and Premier, had emboldened him that his methods of coercion would work with the textile mill owners, mostly Gujaratis and Marwaris, if the workers held long enough.

The textile mill workers abandoned the Indian National Trade Union Congress (INTUC)-affiliated RMMS, which had represented them for decades and chose to follow Datta Samant in their wage struggle against the Bombay Mill Owners Association. Samant led a massive strike forcing the entire textile industry of the city to be shut down. What George Fernandes had done to the Indian Railways through his extreme violent methods of disruption and destruction, Samant was trying to do to the textile industry.

Samant demanded not only wage hikes but also stipulated that the government must nullify the Bombay Industrial Act of 1947. He also demanded that the INTUC-RMMS would no longer be the only official union of the Bombay textile industry. Ironically, he was a prominent member of INTUC before he decided to carve an independent path in trade unionism. In 1972 he was elected on the Congress platform as a member of the Maharashtra state legislative assembly (Vidhan Sabha) and was interned during the Emergency. The wage increase demand was important but was incidental to Samant's personal goal of establishing a power base in Bombay's industrial scene. He had his political ambitions.

The Congress government of Maharashtra was dubious about him. It did not want to be seen as sympathizing with the textile mill owners, though their support was important to the party. But so was that of the textile labour. Some politicians saw Samant as a political threat. His challenge to the INTUC-affiliated RMMS was unacceptable. Samant's power over the city's mill workers made the Congress apprehensive, lest his tentacles spread to the port and dockworkers, and even beyond, to the city's poorly paid law enforcement personnel, some of whom had rebelled in sympathy.[7] Giving him control of India's commercial capital was unthinkable. To fight him out was the only way out. He had become a national threat, a threat to Indira Gandhi that she could not ignore. Mumbai and the textile industry suffered tremendous economic losses but refused to give in to his outrageous demands. It turned out to be a test of wills. Supported by the government, the textile industry owners dug in. Negotiations failed.

Many textile mill owners started moving their plants outside the city. Some moved their operations to Gujarat. Disputes and disenchantment over the way the strike was being conducted, the failure of negotiations, the workers' perilous conditions due to lack of money and the Shiv Sena's hostility towards the Samant-led strike had begun to create a state of hopelessness. The strike dissipated and crumpled. The textile workers received no wage concessions from the Bombay textile mill owners, for whom it was a pyrrhic victory. The rising costs and union aggressiveness compelled the textile industry to move away from Mumbai, eventually rendering tens of thousands of mill workers unemployed.

In the course of time, Datta Samant, the physician-turned-labour leader, overcame his humiliating defeat and gradually re-established his credibility with the Mumbai working class, leading them subsequently to many small and big successes in labour disputes. He was opposed to the Shiv Sena and the Jana Sangh, grew closer to the communists, and was elected to the Lok Sabha in 1984 as an independent; nonetheless, he had no ideology, no political base. He was assassinated in 1997 by Bombay's underworld mafia, a perpetual danger to the city that the government had not been able to eliminate.[8]

While the year-long Bombay textile strike drew international attention, myriad other fires were smouldering in several other parts of India, some of which later engulfed the whole country and altogether changed the political landscape of India. Communist militant groups such as the Naxalites, suppressed during the Emergency, raised their heads again in the forest-dwelling tribal people of Andhra Pradesh and the landless Harijans of central

Bihar. There were violent agitations for separate states for Jharkhand (Bihar), Chhattisgarh (Madhya Pradesh) and Uttarakhand (Uttar Pradesh), where, in spite of millions of rupees being spent on public welfare schemes, many sections of the population were left behind and felt dispossessed by forces beyond their control. The fires were extinguished, but they would flare up again until these backward regions would become separate states.[9]

THE NAGAS AGAIN

On 19 February 1982, the Naga underground insurgents led by T. Muivah bushwhacked an Indian military convoy on the Imphal-Ukhrul road, during which, according to a news report, 21 soldiers, including a major of the 21 Sikh Regiment, were killed by the National Socialist Council of Nagaland guerrillas. The Army unit had indulged in acts of extreme barbarism and was later questioned by the Supreme Court for the disappearance of two citizens, a retired school teacher and a village pastor, whom they had taken into custody. In reprisal, 'the 21 Sikh Regiment was sought out, stalked and annihilated in an ambush believed to have been led by V.S. Atem, who later became "commander of the Naga Army"'.[10]

During the Emergency, the government signed the Shillong Accord with the Naga underground rebels of the Naga National Council fighting for a separate homeland to lay down their arms. The 1975 Accord included that the underground Naga rebels unconditionally accepted the Constitution of India, would surrender their underground arms, and in the course of time would 'formulate other issues for discussion for final settlement.'[11]

Though they inhabited the same hilly tracts in the Northeast, the Nagas were not a single united tribe; rather, there were many tribal groups with intense rivalries. A radical group headed by Muivah, who had once established contacts with the People's Liberation Army of China (PLA), broke away from the Naga National Council, calling them traitors, and established its separate outfit, the Naga National Socialist Council of Nagaland (NSCN). Like many other misguided separatist groups such as the Pakistan-supported militant

Kashmiris, the militant Khalistani Sikhs, the Mizos and others who wanted to break away from India, T. Muivah thought that if India broke up, there would be a greater possibility of the Nagas getting independence from India. Aware of these treacherous developments in the Northeast, the Indian government increased the military force in the rebel areas. When the Indian convoy was ambushed, the Army hit back savagely, indiscriminately, searching for rebels, village after village, which did not bring about a peaceful settlement.

In August 1997, after decades of engaging in fighting with Indian armed forces, the NSCN, under the leadership of T. Muivah and Isak Chishi Swu, signed a peace agreement with the Government of India. Nonetheless, it took another 16 years before the final settlement was reached between the Nagas and the Government of India under Prime Minister Narendra Modi.[12] Today, Nagaland, tribal, picturesque and Christian, is a state just like any other Indian state. Soon the militants in Assam and Punjab would learn the same bloody lessons before they settled down into the federal system.

ASSAM FOR ASSAMESE ONLY?

Assam, a beautiful state known for wildlife and tea plantations, is geographically situated south of the eastern Himalayas. The mighty Brahmaputra runs through it. It is more than twice the size of Bhutan, the Buddhist country that borders it in the north along with the state of Arunachal Pradesh. Assam is wedged in by restive states, including Nagaland and Manipur to the east and Meghalaya, Tripura and Mizoram to the south. The Siliguri Corridor, a 14-mile strip of land also called the Chicken Neck, connects the state to the rest of India.

Known for its distinctive black Assam tea and a variety of Assam silks, the state is home to the one-horned Indian rhinoceros along with the wild water buffalo, the Asian elephant, pygmy hog and four species of the big cat. The biodiversity of Assam is immense; for example, it's home to 450 species of Asiatic birds. Wildlife tourism of the Kaziranga National Park and the Manas National Park, World Heritage sites, is a unique attraction of the state. Assam's abundant rainfall feeds the Brahmaputra River, although the river originates in Tibet. Its tributaries and lakes provide the region with a unique hydro-geomorphic landscape. The first oil well in Assam was drilled in 1867, and the first refinery was established in Digboi in 1901.

This vast expanse of abundant beauty, massive natural resources and fertile land has been in violent political turmoil for a long time because the native people, the Assamese, resented the outsiders, especial the Bengalis, who have been migrating to the state from West Bengal and Bangladesh for several decades, changing the demographics of the state. In the course of time, the outsider, the Bengali intellectual class dominating teaching, professions and bureaucracy; the Marwari dominating the trade; and the rich tea gardens controlled by big business in Kolkata created collective paranoia, a sense of loss over their culture and economy, making the Assamese feel that they were not masters of their own land. Although there have been periodic riots in Assam since before Independence, the situation began to take a serious turn in the 1970s and 1980s when the All-Assam Students' Union (AASU) took the lead in organizing statewide protests, which frequently took a violent turn, demanding that infiltrators be deported. Sometimes the clashes became anti-Bengali, sometimes anti-Muslim, which created a diffused sense of fear, distrust and a siege mentality among the minorities.

The trigger point came in 1980 when during the preparations for the Lok Sabha election, the Chief Electoral Officer decided that all names from the previous voters' list be included in the electoral roll. This prompted the AASU to mount a statewide agitation against the inclusion of illegal immigrants in the voters' list and admonished the political parties to boycott the election unless the electoral rolls were revised and the names of illegal immigrants deleted. In 1979, led by the AASU, the All Assam Gana Sangram Parishad was established, which included, apart from the AASU, the Assam Sahitya Sabha, the Purbanchaliya Lok Parishad as well as the Asom Jatiyabadi Dal, the Asom Yubak Samaj and other groups. It was a mass movement and thousands of people were arrested daily, protesting against illegal immigrants from Bangladesh who, they claimed, posed serious threat not only to the people of the state of Assam but in fact to the entire northeastern region, by altering its demography.[13]

In 1983 Assam saw one of its most horrendous communal and ethnic conflagrations since the sprawling state was split into seven separate states in the 1970s. The massacre that took place in Nellie was the result of an outcome of the decision to hold the Assembly election in 1983 in spite of strong opposition from several organizations in the state, including the AASU, who had given a call to boycott the election. Despite the fact that the police, under the capable leadership of Assam Inspector General of Police K.P.S. Gill, was fully cognizant of the most dangerous and troublesome electoral constituencies, and despite the fact that the elections were held under a heavy security shield provided by the Central Paramilitary Force (now Central Armed Police Forces) as well as Indian Army units, communal violence burst out in Nellie that killed, on the morning of 18 February 1983, more than 5,000 (official figure, 2,191) people, mostly Bengali Muslims, some of whom had lived there since generations.[14] Chief Minister Hiteswar Saikia, whose party Congress (I) had won the controversial election, appointed a commission of inquiry into the Nellie Massacre. But the Tiwari Commission report was not made public, and in the course of time, all criminal cases were dismissed as part of the 1985 Assam Accord.

Under the Indira Gandhi government, Parliament enacted the Illegal Migrants (Determination by Tribunals) Act, 1983 (IMDT Act), to establish procedures to detect illegal immigrants who had continued to come to Assam from Bangladesh even after 1971 and expel them from the state.[15] In fact, the major goal of the Act was to provide special protections against excessive harassment to the minorities, especially the Muslims from Bangladesh, who were adversely affected by the Assam anti-immigrant campaign. The Act made it difficult to deport illegal immigrants from Assam, which, according to some observers, was responsible for the brisk rise of the Muslim population and the consequent demographic change in Assam. The Supreme Court of India struck down the IMDT Act in 2006 in Sarbananda Sonowal v. Union of India.[16]

In 1985, the central government under Prime Minister Rajiv Gandhi signed the historic Assam Accord in an attempt to resolve the long-burning crisis. With the agitation coming to an end with the electoral victory of the Asom Gana Parishad to the state legislative assembly and its leader Prafulla Kumar Mahanta assuming the chief ministership of the state, it seemed all quiet in the state, at least for a while. The central government nevertheless did not implement the Accord entirely. As per the provisions of the Assam Accord, anyone who migrated to Assam from East Pakistan after 1951 and before 1971 was to be awarded citizenship. But in spite of the Accord, a large number of illegal immigrants who had come to Assam even after 1971 (the year Bangladesh was created) were given voting rights, thereby violating Clause 6 of the Accord, which was supposed to protect the constitutional rights of the Assamese. Even today, the Assam problem remains intractable.

THE PASSION OF THE SIKHS

The Sikh community occupies a very special place in the country. But Indira Gandhi did not know the community in spite of the fact that her son Sanjay was married to a Sikh woman. Maneka Gandhi was the daughter of Amardeep Kaur Anand and Lt Col Tarlochan Singh Anand. Since her husband's tragic death, the good widow had been playing a quieter social and political role for the welfare of women and the poor. Manmohan Singh, the Sikh gentleman and a refugee from Pakistan, played a key role as finance minister in rebuilding India's shattered economy in the 1990s. Uncorrupted and incorruptible, Dr Singh was a prime minister for two full terms (1994–2014), the highest office of which the young Indian dreams are made of. Prime Minister Narendra Modi has been building upon the economic foundations that Dr Singh laid. Another secular Sikh politician, Amarinder Singh, a retired Army officer, scion of an erstwhile royal family of Patiala, founder of the Punjab Lok Congress and a former member of the Congress party, was the chief minister of Punjab. Jagmeet Singh, son of Sikh Indian immigrants, a lawyer from Toronto, became the first non-white leader of a major political party, the New Democratic Party of Canada, in 2017. It's unimaginable to think about the Indian Armed Forces without the Sikhs. Between the comic litterateur and historian Khushwant Singh and the suave political economist Manmohan Singh there is no field of human endeavour where the Sikhs have not distinguished themselves in India and abroad. The remains of Sikh soldiers of World War I and World War II are scattered in several theatres of war.

The passion of the Sikhs comes from their deeply devotional religion born at the confluence of diverse religious beliefs in the fifteenth century under Nanak Dev, the first guru and founder of Sikhism. In the course of time, the religion grew up in the crucible of pain and suffering at the hands of the Mughals, which steeled its devotees, turned them into a warrior race, and gave them their unique identity under Gobind Singh, the tenth and the last guru. During Partition, they suffered the most and also gained the most because the forced migration aggregated them into political dominance in Punjab. Having reclaimed the Punjabi language from neglect and oblivion (since the Punjabi Hindus had accepted Hindi as their mother tongue), the Sikhs claimed the language as their own and built their identity around the language and the religion. By and large, the Sikh political aspirations have been no different from those of the DMK (the Annadurai era), the Nagas, the Assamese, the Kashmiris and others, seeking autonomy from India's federal system.

The Anandpur Sahib Resolution of 1973 was not a demand to break away from India; it was a call for autonomy as inscribed in the Constitution, though out of paranoia state autonomy has never been fully allowed in practice. Though some Sikhs did call for an independent Khalistan, just as some Kashmiris have been asking for an independent Kashmir, by and large, the Sikhs did not want to give up on India and shrink into a landlocked Khalistan on the edge of a hostile Pakistan. The paranoia about India breaking up makes the central government blind to local aspirations. Lack of peripheral vision and the inability to anticipate crises creates political blindness that leads to brutality, as happened during Operation Blue Star.

Operation Blue Star was launched at the Sikhs' holiest shrine—the vast sprawling complex of the Golden Temple (Sri Harmandir Sahib)—to drive out Jarnail Singh Bhindranwale, who along with his followers had turned it into a heavily armed fortress. Former Major General Shabeg Singh Bhangu, who had fought in the 1971 India–Pakistan War and trained the Mukti Bahini volunteer army during the Bangladesh Liberation War, was the strategic brain behind the Sikh militants who had holed up in the temple complex.

Once in the good books of Indira Gandhi, who used him as a blunt wedge to split the Sikh political party, the Akali Dal, Jarnail Singh Bhindranwale became increasingly disillusioned with the Akali Dal leadership for its inability to follow through the Anandpur Sahib Resolution; and also, its inability to deal with a dissident Sikh religious group, the Nirankaris. The Nirankaris do not believe in the tenth Sikh Guru, Gobind Singh, as being the last one; nor do they accept the Sikh sacred book Adi Granth as the last word. They neither bury nor cremate their dead; instead, they give the dead a water burial by letting the body into a river. Mainstream Sikhs do not accept the Nirankaris as true Sikhs.

In April 1980, Bhindranwale was accused of the assassination of the Nirankari religious head Baba Gurbachan Singh at a Nirankari convention in Amritsar. To escape prosecution, he, along with a couple of hundred followers, took shelter in the precincts of the Golden Temple. Later, the charges were dropped against him due to lack of evidence, as often happens in the Indian judicial system, when the accused is too political to be prosecuted.

Having tasted blood with impunity, Bhindranwale saw his religious and political clout growing, as some of the Sikhs, especially the young, became increasingly radicalized. By 1983, Bhindranwale and militants had turned the Golden Temple into a well-defended fortress with light machine guns and semi-automatic rifles. [17] When the Punjab Police Deputy Inspector General Avtar Singh Atwal visited the temple as a devotee, perhaps to gather first-hand knowledge of the situation, he was shot dead as he was leaving the compound. Bhindranwale was asked to move out of the Guru Nanak Niwas, part of the Golden Temple complex, but he refused. There was no way out for the militants, however. Nor did the government know how to negotiate with Bhindranwale and the militants. Surprisingly enough, no one in the Army knew how to touch base with one of their own, former Major General Shabeg Singh Bhangu, who was the organizing brain and muscle behind the insurgency. After having sidelined the reluctant General S.K. Sinha, who thought that the cost of launching an attack on the holiest place of the Sikhs might be too high, Operation Blue Star was conducted by his replacement, Army Chief General Arun Shridhar Vaidya and the Vice Chief Lt. General Krishnaswamy Sundarji.

On 3 June 1983, Punjab was turned into a mute and blind state. A 36-hour curfew was imposed on the entire state. Public travel was suspended. Communications were cut off. The electric supply was interrupted. When the army units under the command of Lt. General Kuldip Singh Brar stormed the Golden Temple, Operation Blue Star was expected to be over in 36 hours, but it took more than a week. Lt. General Brar was not only fighting Bhindranwale and his well-armed, kill-or-be-killed militant followers but also one of the Indian Armed Forces' own, the ex-soldier, Shabeg Singh, a veteran of many wars as mentioned earlier.[18] On 4 June, Gurcharan Singh Tohra, former head of the Shiromani Gurdwara Parbandhak Committee (SGPC), was tasked to negotiate with Bhindranwale, at which he failed. Shockingly, no one in the army knew how to break through the fog and reach Shabeg Singh.

With tanks, heavy artillery, helicopters and armoured vehicles, it took the Indian Army troops, with a variety of regiment nomenclatures including 10 Guards, 1 Para Commandos, Special Frontier Forces, 26 Madras, 9 Kumaon, 12 Bihar, 9 Garhwal Rifles, et al., three days, from 5 June to 7 June, to secure the Harmandir Sahib complex.[19] Both Bhindranwale and Shabeg Singh were killed along with 700 Indian military personnel, 500 militants, and thousands of innocent civilians all across the state.[20] It was a horrendous war in the most sacred spot of Harmandir Sahib, to keep India unbroken, to maintain and uphold the 'India Constant,' so that everyone embraced India as their own.

But India had a long way to go before everyone felt India as their own. This became amply clear after Prime Minister Indira Gandhi was assassinated on 31 October 1984 at her residence at Safdarjung Road by her two Sikh bodyguards, Satwant Singh and Beant Singh. It was revenge taken in retaliation for the attack on the Sikh holy temple. Her assassination was followed by several days of brutal massacre of Sikhs by Hindu mobs aided and abetted by some of the Hindu political leaders of the Congress party that killed, according to one account, more than 3,000 in Delhi and 8,000 or more in 40 other cities, where the Sikhs were a vulnerable minority.[21] Hindu mobs rampaged through Sikh neighbourhoods using whatever weapons they could lay their hands on, iron rods, knives, clubs, hacking Sikhs to death, using kerosene and petrol to set their houses on fire, dragging them from trains and buses and lynching them.

The worst-hit areas were where some of the poor Sikhs lived, including Sultanpuri, Mangolpuri, Trilokpuri and several other areas across the Yamuna River in Delhi. For the Sikhs, it was a reminder of the horrific time of Partition. It felt as if someone had once again proclaimed the Muslim League Direct Action Day, but this time it was only against the Sikhs. The central government and the law enforcement authorities just stood by and let the massacre happen, as they would let it happen again in the 2002 Gujarat riots. Since the massacre, subsequent governments have appointed ten commissions to investigate the anti-Sikh riots. Nothing conclusive or politically acceptable emerged from the first nine commissions, so consequently, the government appointed the Nanavati Commission in 2000 headed by Justice G.T. Nanavati, a retired Judge of the Supreme Court of India.[22] The commission submitted its report in February 2005, which implicated, apart from law enforcement officers who failed to control the riots, several Congress leaders, especially H.K.L. Bhagat, Jagdish Tytler and Sajjan Kumar, in organizing concerted attacks against the Sikhs.

The Nanavati Commission reported that although in the beginning the attacks against the Sikhs were sporadic, from the morning of 1 November, however, the scenario changed:

> [S]logans like 'Khoon-Ka-Badla-Khoon Se Lenge' were raised by the mobs... Male members of the Sikh community were taken out of their houses. They were beaten first and then burnt alive in a systematic manner... The shops were identified, looted and then burnt. Thus what had initially started as an angry outburst became an organized carnage...[23]

It must have come as a great relief when the Commission absolved Rajiv Gandhi and other top Congress party members of any connection with the massacre of the Sikhs. During the massacre, Rajiv Gandhi, who had just been made the prime minister of India, said thoughtlessly and uncaringly, 'When a big tree falls, the earth shakes.'[24] The earth shook up but killed only the Sikhs. Throughout the rioting, the police 'remained passive and did not provide protection to the people,' a situation very similar to what happened in the Gujarat riots of 2002 when Atal Bihari Vajpayee was the prime minister of India and Narendra Modi was the chief minister of Gujarat. [25]

WHAT A WONDERFUL LIFE IT WAS!

A few days before she was killed in a blast of gunfire, Indira Gandhi told her friend and biographer Pupul Jayakar, 'Whatever happens to me—I feel I have paid all my debts.'[26] While Jawaharlal Nehru integrated the nation through a federal parliamentary constitutional system and democratic secular socialism based on a centrally planned economy, Indira Gandhi strengthened India through the Green Revolution that made the country self-sufficient in food grains, thus freeing India from its pathetic dependence on food imports, especially from the United States. Most importantly, she reshaped the Indian subcontinent by helping the birth of a new nation Bangladesh, thereby not only making nonsense of Mohammed Ali Jinnah's two-nation theory but also creating new geopolitical possibilities for India at the global stage.

The idea of India, the 'Indian Constant', is, in the ultimate analysis, based on hard power, which she used unhesitatingly but cautiously not only for breaking up Pakistan but also for domesticating the Nagas, the Khalistani militants and militant trade unionists. The Emergency, whose compelling rationale Dr B.R. Ambedkar, India's foremost constitutionalist, had presented in the Constitutional Assembly debates, was a drastic measure imposed to control the growing anarchy let loose by forces beyond democratic controls. Making the Emergency a permanent one-party rule, à la the Soviet Union or the Chinese Communist Party model, as some wanted and others feared at that time, would have been for Indira Gandhi tantamount to killing her father Jawaharlal Nehru and his historic democratic legacy.

Indira Gandhi was an authoritarian democrat, perhaps Machiavellian, perhaps Chanakyan, but a democrat nonetheless. She never lost her faith and commitment to democratic elections and won and lost them justly. Her strength, like her father's, came from the passionate love she had for India and its people. But unlike Jawaharlal Nehru, she was down-to-earth and more pragmatic, believing that the end sometimes justifies the means, especially in regard to national interests, the India Constant. As she said, she was a politician, not a statesman, like her father; and she was a shrewd politician, the likes of which India has yet to see. She transformed non-alignment into assertive and aggressive realism to serve the national interest long before American political scientist John Mearsheimer turned the practice into a theory.

Although she had good counsellors and advisers and lent her ears to everyone worth listening to, she was the final decision-maker. Once she took a decision, she pursued it resolutely and ruthlessly and bulldozed anyone who stood in her way, as it happened in 1969 when she split the Congress party and shoved the Syndicate into the dustbin; and in 1971, during the creation of Bangladesh, fully aware of the Nixon–Kissinger decision to send the Seventh Fleet to the Bay of Bengal to intimidate India.

The greatest test of her endurance came during the Janata Party rule 1977–79 when she was subjected to endless harassments, inquiry commissions and lawsuits, but she survived and fought her way back into power, putting the inglorious Emergency past behind.

To her, personal loyalty and the commitment to her vision were imperative in all political relations. Her vision of India as a strong, self-dependent, secular socialist democracy was the motivating force both for her domestic policies and international relations. The decision to test the nuclear weapon on 18 May 1974 had the same rationale as the Green Revolution, that is, India must be self-dependent for food, energy and national security.

With her death, Indira Gandhi 'became a martyr to the cause of unity and integrity of the country...her ideas became irresistible. Urge for national unity, stability and strong government superseded the urge for freedom, equality and ethnic and caste loyalty. The era of Indira Gandhi continued with added vigour after her death... Indian nationalism—excluding the alienated minorities—characterised by monolithic and populist tendencies is the most outstanding legacy of the era of Indira Gandhi.'[27]

Three decades after her death, Narendra Modi of the BJP, embodying the same spirit of extreme nationalism as Indira Gandhi had demonstrated, would transcend the divisiveness of casteism and provincialism to give India a new sense of destiny.

THE ASCENT OF PRINCE CHARMING, RAJIV GANDHI

I am young, and I have a dream. I dream of an India—strong, self-reliant, and in the front rank of the nations of the world in the service of mankind.

—Rajiv Gandhi in his address to the US Congress, 13 June 1985

You are young. You are the future. We are receding into history. There is a new generation of leaders now and a global desire to live in peace and end conflict and tension. It lies in your hands to shape the destiny of the new world order. Use it wisely.

—Deng Xiaoping to Rajiv Gandhi in Beijing 22 December 1988

When Indira Gandhi died at the hands of her assassins on 31 October 1984, there was no second-in-command to succeed her. She had made no provisions for it, although she knew that in the aftermath of Operation Blue Star, her days were numbered. Perhaps she had some premonition when she said, 'If I die a violent death, as some fear and a few are plotting, I know that the violence will be in the thought and the action of the assassins, not in my dying.'[1] She couldn't have nevertheless imagined the well-organized massacre of the helpless Sikhs living in Delhi and other places across India. But in the deep recess of her mind, Indira Gandhi must have had her son Rajiv in mind to succeed her, in spite of his own reservations:

…I had no love for politics. I treasured the privacy of my family life. My mother respected both these sentiments. Then my brother, Sanjay was killed in the prime of his life. It broke a mother's heart. It did not break a prime minister's will… There is a loneliness that only a bereaved mother can know…she called to me in her loneliness… At her instance, I left my love for flying at her instance I joined her as a political aide. From her I learned my first political lessons. It was she who urged me to respond to the insistent demand from the constituency and the part to take my brother's place as Member of Parliament for Amethi. With her blessings I was made General Secretary of my party asking me to accept the challenge of stepping into her shoes. In accepting this challenge I fulfilled a national duty and a filial duty of a son to a mother.[2]

Within hours of her assassination, Rajiv Gandhi flew back from West Bengal. Union Cabinet Minister Buta Singh and President of India Zail Singh, two of Indira Gandhi's firm loyalists and prominent Sikh politicians, who had supported the bloody Operation Blue Star, had no difficulty in persuading Rajiv Gandhi to step into his mother's shoes as the prime minister of India. A massive tide of sympathy that rose after Indira Gandhi's death endeared the son to the people of India, who saw in him the continuity and stability that India needed. Apart from the charisma of his mother that rubbed off on him, albeit temporarily, he was indeed a good-looking, charming young man with a winsome smile.

Like any other children of the privileged classes, Rajiv Gandhi went through some of the best schools for the rich and famous in India and later on to Cambridge and London, where at best he was an indifferent student and ended up with no degree to his credit and no accountability for not having one. Perhaps his best achievement during his years in England was his marriage with a beautiful Italian Catholic girl, Sonia, who, after coming to India, adopted the country as her own and has played an extraordinary role in Indian politics. No Indian is more Indian than Sonia Gandhi.[3]

Rajiv Gandhi had three years of parliamentary experience when destiny plucked him from semi-obscurity and made him the leader of the most tumultuous democratic nation in the world. In spite of his blundering remark about the anti-Sikh riots ('When a big tree falls, the earth shakes') and his negligence to call the troops to quell the riots soon after he became the prime minister, he was seen entering the Indian political scene as Mr Clean. However, in the course of only the next few years, his image became sullied with political expediencies, damaging compromises, corruption scandals and general incompetence for managing national crises.[4] Unlike his mother, Rajiv Gandhi was not a politician. He was a gentleman who was shoved into a den of wolves, and in an attempt to become one of them, he was eaten up by them.

Since Parliament had completed its five-year term, Rajiv Gandhi advised President Zail Singh to dissolve it and hold fresh elections. Riding on the wave of fear and sympathy after Indira Gandhi's death, the Congress (I), of which Rajiv Gandhi was now the president, won 404 seats in a 533-seat Lok Sabha. But the greater surprise was the electoral performance of the Telugu Desam Party (TDP) of N.T. Rama Rao of Andhra Pradesh. With 30 seats, TDP became a major opposition party on the national stage, foreshadowing the coming power play of the regional parties at the Centre to impact national politics. It also signalled the rise of regional power centres and their leaders, who would not be ignored. India was emerging as a nation of nation-states with their own competitive interests. But India's problems are recurrent and intractable, and only a strong central leadership could solve them, as Indira Gandhi had demonstrated in her long political career.

SMOULDERING AND BLEEDING PUNJAB

Negotiations to solve Punjab's haemorrhaging problems, which Operation Blue Star had aggravated, took place in the shadow of another dark tragedy that happened beyond India's border and beyond India's control.[5] India was vulnerable everywhere and its vulnerability affected many innocents abroad.

On 23 June 1985, Air India Flight 182 Kanishka, operating on the Toronto–Montreal–London–Delhi route, was destroyed by a bomb at an altitude of 31,000 feet and crashed into the Atlantic Ocean, killing 329 people (including 268 Canadian, 27 British and 24 Indian citizens). It was the deadliest terrorist attack involving an airplane that portended the 11 September 2001 terrorist attacks, but global terrorism had not yet caught the American imagination. The Canadian law enforcement determined that the Sikh militant group Babbar Khalsa carried out the bombing in retaliation against India for Operation Blue Star. India was shocked and grieved but gave it up as a Canadian problem. The Canadian Commission of Inquiry, under the former Supreme Court Justice John Major, concluded in its 2010 report that the terrorist attack was due to a failure of intelligence and lack of coordination between the government, the police and the security intelligence.[6]

THE PUNJAB ACCORD

Like other agreements reached between the government and insurgents, dissidents and rebels, the Punjab Accord reached between Prime Minister Rajiv Gandhi and the Akali Dal president Harcharan Singh Longowal was much heralded as a beacon of peace to the long-standing bloody conflict that had poisoned the waters of Punjab. The agreement, signed on 24 July 1985, acknowledged the Sikh grievances and accepted the demands of the Akali Dal, who claimed to represent the Sikhs. Several conservative and extremist Sikh leaders in Punjab and abroad opposed the Accord. Haryana's political leaders, who were not consulted, also opposed the deal. Sikh militants opposed to the Accord, assassinated Harcharan Singh Longowal.

The Accord included compensation to the families of people killed in the Sikh agitation and recompense for property damages. The Army recruitment would be based on merit, which nullified the 1974 edict by the defence minister Jagjivan Ram in order to reduce over-representation from Punjab, Haryana and Himachal Pradesh. Sikh soldiers discharged from the Indian Army for desertion during Operation Blue Star would be rehabilitated and/or provided employment. The All-India Gurdwara Act of 1925 would be updated. Notifications for disturbed areas under the Armed Forces (Special Powers) Act in Punjab would be withdrawn. Chandigarh would be given to Punjab, overriding the Shah Commission's recommendation that it be given to Haryana. Instead of Chandigarh, Haryana would get the Hindi-speaking villages of Punjab, for which a commission would determine which areas would go to Haryana. A tribunal headed by a Supreme Court judge would ascertain the river water claims of Punjab and Haryana and its outcomes would be binding on both the states. [7]

The Punjab Accord promised too much and could not fulfil the expectations raised, especially regarding the transfer of Chandigarh to Punjab and the resolution of the river water sharing issue. The assassination of the Akali leader Sant Longowal generated a massive surge of political support for the Akali Dal, which put the party in power in the state after the 1985 election with 60 per cent votes and 73 out of 115 of the Assembly seats.

But the Akali Dal control of the levers of power in Punjab did not quench the thirst for Sikh militancy altogether. On 26 January 1986, at a global meeting of the Sikhs, a committee to draft the constitution of Khalistan was formed, and a few months later, the Khalistan Commando Force was formed at Akal Takht at the Temple Complex. To flush out extremist Sikh militants who once again had occupied the Golden Temple, the Akali Dal chief minister Surjit Singh Barnala launched Operation Black Thunder.[8]

The first phase of Operation Black Thunder was launched on 30 April 1986 when 300 National Security Guards along with 700 Border Security Force troops stormed the Golden Temple. After eight hours, about 300 Sikh militants surrendered. But that was not the end. Only two years later, in May 1988, when Punjab was under the president's rule, the militants once again controlled the Temple complex and the situation turned very grave. It took the Director General of the Punjab Police K.P.S Gill, a veteran of the anti-Naga insurgency, ten days to finish the job and clean out the Temple complex from the insurgents. More than firepower, he used the blockade strategy to break the militant siege.[9] Later on, Harinder Baweja wrote in a tribute to K.P.S. Gill:

> He earned his spurs during Operation Black Thunder in 1988 when he allowed the media to witness the entire operation that involved flushing out terrorists who had once again—after the 1984 Operation Blue Star in which Jarnail Singh Bhindranwale was killed—fortified the Golden Temple and taken shelter.[10]

The damage to the Golden Temple was very little, much less than it was during Operation Blue Star in spite of the fact that forty-one militants were killed and another two hundred surrendered.[11] Soon after, Sikh devotees resumed their religious activities and the temple was open to the general public, including the media. It's worth noting that, although the government—as part of its strategy to fight Sikh militant extremism in Punjab—banned the use of religious places for political and military purposes,[12] it did not stop Hindu extremists from using public places and streets to launch their campaign for claiming and rebuilding the Ram Temple in Ayodhya at the place where a dilapidated, sixteenth-century mosque, Babri Masjid stands. Random insurgent ambushes continued even after the success of Operation Black Thunder. A senior police officer was killed in 1990. On 16 June 1991, Sikh extremists killed eighty people on two trains after the end of the Assembly elections, which brought the Congress to power. On 31 August 1995, the Congress chief minister of Punjab, Beant Singh, was killed in a blast, a reminder that the Sikh militant threat was not over, although it had been dissipating.

THE IMPORTANCE OF BEING SHAH BANO

The Shah Bano case was a most fascinating legal case that not only aroused communal passions in India but also brought into conflict the power of the Parliament against the power of the Supreme Court of India, the ultimate authority on the interpretation of the constitutional law and protector of the people's fundamental rights enshrined in the Constitution. The Parliament in India is supreme so long as its acts do not violate the foundational principles of the Constitution, the basic structural doctrine that was propounded by Justice Hans Raj Khanna and reaffirmed after the Emergency.

In the case of Shah Bano, the question was whether a Muslim husband, Mohammed Ahmad Khan, a lawyer from Indore, Madhya Pradesh, could, under Islamic law, throw his divorced wife on the streets without providing her and her children reasonable maintenance, the alimony. As per Islamic law, Khan took a second wife and after living together with both wives, he divorced Shah Bano, 62, and threw her out along with her children, with a maintenance allowance of ₹200 per month, which he nonetheless stopped paying in 1978. Since Shah Bano had no means to support herself and her five children, she petitioned the court, under Section 125 of the Code of Criminal Procedure (1973), demanding from her ex-husband a maintenance amount of ₹500 for herself and her children. Khan claimed that under Islamic Law, he was under no obligation to support his ex-wife except give her a one-time payment of ₹5,400. The lower court decision enjoined Khan to pay Bano a paltry amount of ₹25 per month as maintenance, which on appeal was raised to ₹179.20 per month by the Madhya Pradesh High Court.

When on Khan's appeal, the case went up to the Supreme Court, the question was whether Section 125 of the Code of Criminal Procedure applied to Muslims also. One might say that the maintenance provision under Section 125 of the Code of Criminal Procedure is one of the most humane laws ever passed by the Indian Parliament with the sole objective that 'this provision is to provide a summary remedy to the dependent wife, children, and parents from destitution and to serve a social purpose. The right under these provisions cannot be defeated by anything in the personal law of the parties.'[13]

The bench, a five-judge panel, unanimously decided on 23 April 1985 that 'there is no conflict between the provisions of section 125 and those of the Muslim Personal Law on the question of the Muslim husband's obligation to provide maintenance for a divorced wife who is unable to maintain herself.'[14] The law applies to everyone regardless of religion, caste or creed and the court ruled that Mohammed Khan must provide his ex-wife Shah Bano monthly maintenance money, thereby upholding the decision of the state High Court. The Supreme Court went further and pointed out that the constitutional provision of the Uniform Civil Code in India, which has remained a dead letter, would help national integration by eliminating adherence to incongruent laws that have conflicting principles. In later Muslim divorce cases, the Supreme Court reasserted the principle that the right to post-divorce maintenance is absolute.[15]

The Supreme Court's decision provoked protests from the Muslim community, who feared that the state was encroaching upon their personal rights protected under the Muslim Personal Law. Fundamental Sunni Islamists of the most conservative Islamic school, the Barelvi, and the All India Muslim Personal Law Board were at the forefront of the media, fuelling a raging storm. The plight of the destitute old divorcee, mother of five children, was forgotten. The Congress (I) had an absolute majority, and the Supreme Court judgement provided Prime Minister Rajiv Gandhi with an opportunity to reassert the secular state especially given what had happened during and after Operation Blue Star. Despite such authority and keeping in mind the forthcoming general election and the power of Muslim voting banks, especially in northern states with substantial Muslim populations, he succumbed to the pressure from the conservative Muslim lobby. The Muslim Women (Protection of Rights on Divorce) Act 1986 that the Parliament passed invalidated the Supreme Court's judgement in the Shah Bano case.

The Act sanctioned the maintenance amount to a divorced Muslim woman only during the period of iddat (the waiting period), or until 90 days after the divorce, as per the provisions of Islamic law. Ironically the language of the Act left enough loopholes for the courts to interpret the law in future cases in a way that wouldn't substantively nullify the provision of Section 125 of the Criminal Procedure Code of 1973. Parliament makes laws, but it is within the domain of the judiciary to interpret those laws. The power of the judicial precedent and decision law is immense, as demonstrated by some later cases such as Danial Latifi & Anr. v. Union of India, 2001, which challenged the legality of the Muslim Women (Protection of Rights on Divorce) Act.

Since the Muslim Women (Protection of Rights on Divorce) Act did not supersede the provisions of Section 125 of the Criminal Procedure Act, the Supreme Court, in future cases, interpreted the law in such a manner that it did not violate the equality principles enshrined in Articles 14 and 15 of the Constitution of India. Thus the court held that the provision of the Muslim Women Act that 'a reasonable and fair provision and maintenance to be made and paid to her *within* [italics added] the *iddat* period by her former husband,' means that maintenance is not limited for the *iddat* period and goes beyond and protects the divorced woman until she remarries. It's difficult to know the original intention of the lawmakers, but the word 'within' has given the court latitudes of interpretation that by and large protects the rights of Muslim women.[16] The Muslim Women Act and Section 125 of the Criminal Procedure Code modify but do not nullify each other.

The political fallout of the case was loud and fierce. But sadly, it was not because of any sympathy for the poor old discarded divorced woman Shah Bano; the situation was best used as an opportunity to batter Rajiv Gandhi and the Congress, who were accused by a wide section of Indians, including some prominent Muslims, of pandering to the Muslim community for political gains. A prominent Muslim politician Arif Mohammad Khan, then the minister of state in the Ministry of Home Affairs, who resigned in protest, had later on this to say:

> The crucial role was played by typical senior Congressmen like N.D. Tiwari and Arjun Singh. Their argument was that if the Muslims want to lag behind and languish, why should they [Hindus] meddle in their affairs? ...They said it wasn't their responsibility to hold the hands of the Muslims and drag them into the twenty-first century.[17]

It would be for the BJP of Narendra Modi to liberate Muslim women from another social curse, the triple talaq, for which there is no basis in the Quran or the Constitution.

BHOPAL TRAGEDY: WORSE THAN CHERNOBYL

Wake up, people of Bhopal,
you are on the edge of a volcano!

—Journalist Rajkumar Keswani in Jansatta

It was the night of 3 December 1984. The Union Carbide pesticide plant in Bhopal, Madhya Pradesh, spewed a toxic gas methyl isocyanate (MIC) into the atmosphere that turned the surrounding areas, mostly inhabited by workers and hut-dwellers, into a gradually swelling and enveloping toxic gas chamber from which there was no escape. More than half a million people were exposed to the lethal gas, which killed, according to the government records, 3,787 people; others assessed the toll to be much higher at 8,000–10,000, in the first two weeks. And those who survived the immediate deadly exposure died later, a lingering death due to gas-related injuries. Those who did not die sooner or later existed like zombies, the living dead with permanent disfigurement and infirmities, and their number ran into thousands.

Sloppy management, tardy maintenance, a poorly trained workforce and an absence of disaster planning gradually built up an unstable, explosive state at the pesticide plant. Routine pipe maintenance produced a back-flow of water that entered a supposedly impenetrable MIC tank, thus building unsustainable heat and pressure, which caused the deadly gas to leak. And there was no way to stop it. The plant was not technologically equipped to control the ever-expanding gas cloud that began to envelop the city of more than a million people.[18] Indra Sinha, the author of the novel, *Animal's People*, writing on the occasion of the twenty-fifth anniversary of the disaster, describes the plight of Aziza Sultan, a young mother of two with her third child on the way:

> When the panic began, her entire family ran out of their house. They were in night clothes and it was bitterly cold, but nothing mattered except to run... A thick gas cloud enveloped everything, reducing the streetlights to brown pinpoints.

Indra Sinha continues, now with Aziza Sultan's first-person horrific narrative:

> I had a miscarriage right there in the middle of the street, my body was covered with blood.[19]

The Union Carbide Corporation (UCC), now a subsidiary of Dow Chemicals, owned a 50.9 per cent stake in the Union Carbide India Limited (UCIL) at the time of the disaster, while the government-controlled state banks and Indian shareholders controlled the rest. In 1989 Union Carbide paid a paltry sum of US$470 million to settle claims arising from the disaster. The UCC CEO Warren Anderson and some former employees, including the former UCIL chairman Keshub Mahindra, were convicted in Bhopal of causing death by criminal negligence and sentenced to two years imprisonment and a fine of about US$2,000 each. Anderson made a brief visit to India after the disaster but never returned to face any judgement. He died in 1994 still believing that the disaster was sabotage caused by a disgruntled plant employee, which, to date, remains the company's (Dow Jones) official claim.[20]

This is how a global corporation, hungry for foreign direct investment, treated India. Even after the disaster, when the UCC ceased its pesticide operation, it had not cleaned up the contaminated industrial site completely. According to a National Institute of Health study, 'The plant continues to leak several toxic chemicals and heavy metals that have found their way into local aquifers. Dangerously contaminated water has now been added to the legacy left by the company for the people of Bhopal.'[21]

Apart from the futile attempt to fight a foreign industrial behemoth in the aftermath of the industrial calamity that, in its effect, was no different from what happened at Chernobyl, the only other action the government took was to pass the Environment Protection Act in 1986. The Act created the Ministry of Environment and Forests, purporting to strengthen India's commitment to the environment by integrating environmental strategies into all economic and industrial development plans. But look at the results: in 2019, the air in major cities and industrial areas was unbreathable for most of the year. In the race for economic growth, India keeps huffing and puffing for breath like an asthmatic patient. A Lancet Commission on Pollution and Health report shared that, in 2015, India accounted for 2.5 million of the total 9 million worldwide in pollution-related deaths. These deaths are not as tragically spectacular as caused by the toxic plumes of the Union Carbide Bhopal gas chamber. You cannot sue anybody for the slow death of your dear ones.[22]

THE SMOKING GUNS OF BOFORS

By all accounts, the Swedish 155 mm Howitzer gun (Fälthaubits 77) developed and manufactured by Bofors AB was an excellent choice for the Indian Army, as the 1999 Kargil War testified. But the way the deal was done, through bribery and kickbacks involving Indian politicians and European operatives, showed that even top Indian politicians were susceptible to greed and international pressures. The scandal also showed the power of the free press in India and international whistleblowers long before the era of WikiLeaks.

The US$284 million Bofors gun deal, done on 24 March 1986, that soon turned into a scandal, shocking and rocking India, surfaced during V.P. Singh's tenure as defence minister (1989–1990). However, before he could act on it, Prime Minister Rajiv Gandhi dismissed him. But the free press in India and abroad could not be gagged. Tipped off by a Swedish radio report that Bofors had bribed Indian politicians and Swedish operatives, Indian journalist Chitra Subramaniam, working for *The Hindu*, pursued the lead based on hundreds of documents that Sten Lindstrom, former chief of Swedish police, had leaked to her.[23] When *The Hindu's* investigative zeal petered out under political pressure, two other newspapers, *The Indian Express* and *The Statesman*, one of the most courageous newspapers in India (for which I wrote a weekly column during 1998–2013), took up the publication of the Bofors revelations. The scandal-ridden Rajiv Gandhi administration lost the 1989 Lok Sabha elections—one might say, thanks to the robust free press. The scandal revealed that Ottavio Quattrocchi, an Italian businessman who had access to some of the high and mighty, was the facilitator between European and Indian big businesses and the Indian government.

On 18 July 1989, a Joint Parliamentary Committee that was set up under B. Shankaranand, to investigate the allegations of kickbacks, submitted its report to Parliament. In October 1999, based on the report, the Central Bureau of Investigation (CBI) filed a case against Quattrocchi, Win Chadha (who was a representative of the Swedish arms manufacturer), the Hinduja brothers and Defence Secretary S.K. Bhatnagar. On 10 June 2002, the Delhi High Court terminated the case, but on 7 July 2003, the Supreme Court of India reversed the High Court's decision for reconsideration. Nonetheless, on 4 February 2004, the Delhi High Court dismissed all charges against the Hinduja brothers that they had bribed Prime Minister Rajiv Gandhi and the former Defence Secretary S.K. Bhatnagar.

Pronouncing the judgement, Justice J.D. Kapoor ruled:

> The facts of the case itself show that so far as the public servants—Rajiv Gandhi and S.K. Bhatnagar—are concerned, 16 years of investigation by a premier agency of the country— the Central Bureau of Investigation—could not unearth a scintilla of evidence against them for having accepted bribe/ illegal gratification in awarding the contract in favour of A.B. Bofors...[24]

The Delhi High Court, nevertheless, upheld the decision of the special court regarding the charges of cheating and conspiracy against the Hinduja brothers, and per the court order, the Chief Metropolitan Magistrate was directed to frame charges against the Hinduja brothers, Martin Ardbo, then chief of Bofors, and Quattrocchi. Since Quattrocchi and Ardbo were absconding, they would face trial when they appeared before the court. In fact, having failed to get Quattrocchi back to India for trial in spite of spending ₹250 crores towards the probe, the CBI on 4 March 2011 dismissed the case. Quattrocchi died in 2013.[25]

The ghost of the long, tortuous legal case occasionally reappeared. On 14 July 2017, the CBI said it would reinvestigate the Bofors case if the Supreme Court or the Centre ordered it. Responding to private detective Michael Hershman's allegations that the Rajiv Gandhi Administration had sabotaged his investigation, the CBI, on 18 October 2017, once again said that it would look into the 'facts and circumstances' of the Bofors scandal.[26] It is indeed sad that when foreign corporations are involved in legal cases in India, as the Bhopal Gas and the Bofors Gun cases show, there's no respite in sight. The cases would eventually disappear into India's collective forgetfulness, the nation's historical amnesia.

RAJIV GANDHI'S FOREIGN FORAYS

Addressing the nation after he was installed as the prime minister, and setting the tone of his administration, Rajiv Gandhi pledged continuity in foreign affairs, stating:

> Jawaharlal Nehru bequeathed to us a foreign policy which Indira Gandhi so creatively enriched. I shall carry it forward... We highly value the wide-ranging and time-tested relationship with the Soviet Union, based on mutual cooperation, friendship and vital support when most needed...With the United States of America, we have a multifaceted relationship. We attach importance to our economic, technological and cultural cooperation with them... We have always been friends with both the East and the West, as they are called, and we want better relations between them.[27]

According to a declassified report, Rajiv Gandhi was genuinely interested in refashioning India's foreign policy in order to have access to high technology and military relations with the US and Western Europe.

During his Washington visit in 1985, 'he focused on new technologies most applicable to India, such as biotech developments, and showed less interest in a robotics demonstration, suggesting that the national prestige aspects rank below practical applications in his scale of values.'[28]

During his five-year tenure, Prime Minister Rajiv Gandhi

made 58 foreign trips, including the Soviet Union, the US, France, the UK, Japan and West Germany and the neighbours Pakistan and Sri Lanka, among others. His foreign policy was change-in-continuity, maintaining the independent non-alignment foreign policy of Jawaharlal Nehru, however, with a newer and more pragmatic approach to the US and West Europe, the ultimate source of innovation and high technology, which he believed was indispensable for India's growth.[29]

Addressing the joint session of the US Congress on 13 June 1985, he said, 'Our task today is to bring India to the threshold of the twenty-first century... [which] means the absorption of modern technology... Our Governments have recently reached an understanding on the export of high technology from the US to India.'[30] While Jawaharlal Nehru wanted India to cultivate a scientific temper and fight poverty through socialist planning, and Indira Gandhi had ushered in the Green Revolution to free India from food dependency, Rajiv Gandhi was the first technocrat prime minister of India who saw the future of the nation through the application of technological innovations of which the US and Western Europe, with their free-market economies, were the main sources.

Without giving up on India's long-standing friendship with the Soviet Union, Rajiv Gandhi showcased India as an independent emerging power. The conversation between Rajiv Gandhi and Ronald Reagan, and their advisers, during the 1985 US visit covered a wide range of issues, including the US arms sales to Pakistan that could be used against India, differing views about the Soviet presence in Afghanistan, and Rajiv Gandhi's 'impressions of Soviet leader Mikhail Gorbachev during his recent visit to Moscow.'[31] In spite of their differing views about the international situation, especially Afghanistan and the Soviet Union, Ronald Reagan, in his public remarks, assured Prime Minister Gandhi that despite 'areas of disagreement' there 'are opportunities to prove our goodwill by discussing our differences forthrightly...'

In response, Rajiv Gandhi said that 'the United States and India have a tradition of working together. If my visit strengthens that tradition, I shall feel that it has been worthwhile.'[32] He assured his

American hosts at the Washington Press Club that India's friendship with Moscow was not an expression of hostility towards the US, adding:

> I don't think we are more attracted to the Soviet Union than to the US...we look to see what's beneficial for us and the developing world. We make decisions on principles that we hold dear. We are not going to be tied to the apron strings of any major power.[33]

Rajiv Gandhi was given the honour of being invited to address the joint session of the US Congress, a rare American diplomatic gesture to a visiting statesman, which his grandfather Jawaharlal Nehru too was offered in 1949.

When Mikhail Gorbachev, General Secretary of the Communist Party of the Soviet Union, came to India on a four-day visit in late November 1986, the Soviet Union was still a superpower and Ronald Reagan had yet to tell him, 'Mr. Gorbachev, tear down this wall.'[34] The Soviet supremo had been talking of things hitherto unheard of, such as Perestroika (reformation) and Glasnost (openness), which seemed, to many observers, as ideological bombshells, and they did cause geopolitical tremors. But his visit to India was nothing but a confirmation of old military ties between the two countries. As an Indian national magazine observed:

> ...the defence relationship between the two countries were quickly dispelled with the Soviets offering—and India accepting—a virtual carte blanche for the procurement of the latest military hardware... the Indian Government used the visit to let the world know that, in a changing security environment, India was no longer embarrassed about holding the Soviet bear's hand in public. [35]

This was only a year after Rajiv Gandhi had visited the US and received a warm embrace from Ronald Reagan and the American media.

The Soviet Union was embroiled with its puppet Afghanistan government's war against the Islamic Mujahideen, who were financed and supported by the United States, Saudi Arabia and Pakistan. A few weeks before the Soviet leader's visit, US Defence Secretary Casper Weinberger had stopped by in New Delhi on his way from China to Pakistan when he met with Rajiv Gandhi and offered to sell supercomputers and military equipment while assuring India that the US arms to Pakistan, the AWACS, the latest M1 Abrams tanks and the F-16, and much more, were meant to fight the threat posed by 115,000 Soviet troops occupying Afghanistan. India's exuberant welcome to Mikhail Gorbachev must be seen in the larger geopolitical context and India's security interests, keeping in mind that 'The border intrusion by China, the threat of the Pakistan bomb, the AWACS and the militarization of the region had created a tangible sense of insecurity in the country.'[36]

Of course, Gorbachev made no other commitment except to sell weapons, nonetheless, assuring India without mentioning Pakistan or China, that 'We shall not take a single step in our foreign policy that could damage India's real interests... The Soviet Union strongly condemns all those intrigues and plots against your country as well as any attempts to undermine India's integrity and unity.'[37] In 1962, when China was breaking through the Himalayas to overrun the plains of Assam, it was the US and not the Soviet Union that had come to India's rescue. Indians did not realize that the Afghanistan War had hollowed out the entrails of the Soviet Union from within and the system was on the verge of collapse. The Delhi Declaration, a proposal for setting up an international convention for banning the use or the threat of the use of nuclear weapons, also included the Soviet Union's promise to provide India with high technology, supercomputers, submarines, and long-range naval aircraft as well as help build an international space station to launch satellites. But for all that, India would have to wait until the nation learned to do the stuff on its own or explore other avenues for such acquisitions.

MEETING CHINA'S DENG XIAOPING

Rajiv Gandhi's visit to China from 19 to 23 December 1988 at the invitation of Prime Minister Li Peng thawed the frigid relations between the two countries. Thirty-four years before his visit, his grandfather Prime Minister Jawaharlal Nehru had visited China, met with Chairman Mao Zedong and Premier Zhou Enlai, and signed the Five Principles of Peaceful Coexistence, the Panchsheel, giving up and giving away India's interests in Tibet, which however did not save India from the 1962 calamitous war. Since then, China had not yielded an inch of the Indian-occupied territory. Nor had China lost its fear of the Dalai Lama and thousands of Tibetan refugees living in India.

The highlight of Rajiv Gandhi's visit was his meeting with the legendary Chinese leader Deng Xiaoping in the Great Hall of the People, who was reported to have told Rajiv Gandhi 'to shape the destiny of the new world order...'[38]

Deng was suggesting to his Indian visitor to forget the past and look to the future as China was doing by opening out to the world. Breaking with the past, Deng Xiaoping had started an economic revolution in China. The US, Japan and Western Europe had begun to invest in China and opened their markets to Chinese-made goods, which eventually would transform China into a global manufacturing hub.[39] China's GDP at the time of Rajiv Gandhi's visit was US$312 billion, and India with US$293 billion was not far behind; but in 2019, China's GDP was five times larger than that of India. While Rajiv Gandhi was soliciting American and West European modern technology to transform India, China was taking the capitalist road for development, and the West, led by the US, through collaboration and foreign direct investment, had opened the flood gates of modern technology transfer to the communist nation.

Rajiv Gandhi could not see how the global marketplace, which essentially meant the US, Japan and Western Europe, was transforming China and whether India could follow a similar trajectory. The highlight of the 1988 visit was the decision 'to set up a Joint Working Group (JWG), with the twin function of ensuring peace and tranquillity in the border areas and making concrete recommendations for an overall solution of the boundary question within a definite time frame...'[40] With China, as India would discover, no agreement was ever final because each breach of an agreement created newer possibilities for diplomatic leverage for China. On the other hand, India was so circumspect in its relationship with China that it refused to condemn the Tiananmen Square massacre of 4 June 1989, while the whole wide world was aghast to see a young Chinese man standing in defiance against the advancing Army tank.

DANGEROUS LIAISON WITH PAKISTAN

General Muhammad Zia-ul-Haq, after deposing Zulfikar Ali Bhutto and later executing him by hanging after a phoney court trial, assumed the presidency of Pakistan in 1978 and began to play a pivotal role in the Soviet–Afghanistan War. Armed to the hilt and fully financed by the US and Saudi Arabia, General Zia, a devout Muslim, helped raise a lethal guerrilla Islamist force, the Afghan Mujahideen, who, after a prolonged war, forced the Soviet withdrawal in 1989. While Pakistan's relations with the US and China improved, its relations with India deteriorated because of its clandestine support to Khalistani militants and conflict in Siachen in the northern Kashmir mountain ranges.

Away from the disputed region of Kashmir, India was conducting a mock war exercise called Operation Brasstacks in the desert of Rajasthan, November 1986–January 1987, a show of massive troop mobilization of the Indian forces near the Pakistan western border. The integrated war exercise 'involved two armoured divisions, one mechanized division and six infantry divisions. The stated objective of Operation Brasstacks was to test new concepts of mechanization, mobility, and air support...'[41] The brainchild of a dangerously flamboyant infantryman General Krishnaswamy Sundarji, the purpose of Operation Brasstacks was 'to integrate India's [sic] special weapons, including tactical nuclear into day-to day field maneuvers of the troops.'[42] Pakistan viewed the overwhelming conventional military exercises as an existential threat. Apart from moving its armoured units to the front in Punjab and Rajasthan, it also let it be known that in case of India's attack, Pakistan would use all the available means at its disposal, including nuclear weapons.

Pakistan had always been denying that it was developing a nuclear bomb. Nevertheless, in January 1987, a 'prominent Pakistani nuclear scientist Abdul Qadeer Khan stated in an interview with a visiting Indian journalist, Kuldip Nayar, that Pakistan possessed nuclear weapons and that they could be used to defend Pakistan against an Indian attack'.[43] Ironically, amidst all the tension and massive deployment of troops at the border, President General Zia invited himself to the India–Pakistan cricket match in Jaipur, saying that 'Cricket for peace is my mission, and I have come with that spirit.' Nevertheless, at the time of his departure, General Zia said to the Indian prime minister, as quoted in *India Today*:

> Mr Rajiv, you want to attack Pakistan, do it. But keep in mind
> that ...this will not be a conventional war but a nuclear war.
> In this situation, Pakistan might be completely destroyed, but
> Muslims will still be there in the world; but with the destruction
> of India, Hinduism will vanish from the face of this earth.[44]

General Zia was prompted to deliver the nuclear threat directly to Rajiv Gandhi based on the information delivered to him in a confidential letter written by President Ronald Reagan on 12 September 1984, which said that 'it is likely that at some point India will take military action to pre-empt your nuclear programme... an Indian attack on Pakistani nuclear facilities would almost certainly prompt retaliatory strikes against Indian nuclear facilities and probably lead to a full-scale war'. [45]

Whether it was General Zia's nuclear threat or his bold efforts at peacemaking through cricket diplomacy and media charm offensive, something worked. Both countries agreed to withdraw 80,000 troops from their borders and they also established modalities to withdraw another 150,000 from Kashmir.[46] In the news conference, smiling and praising each other, Rajiv Gandhi and General Zia-ul-Haq vouchsafed not to attack each other's nuclear facilities and take a step-by-step approach to mend relations.[47] General Zia-ul-Haq, the most significant Pakistani leader after Mohammed Ali Jinnah, was killed in a mysterious airplane crash on 17 August 1988. Once again, sham democracy was restored in Pakistan and Benazir Bhutto of the Pakistan Peoples Party, the daughter of Zulfikar Bhutto, whom General Zia had hanged, was installed as the prime minister. On 21 December 1988, in Islamabad, Rajiv Gandhi and Benazir Bhutto signed the Non-Nuclear Attack Agreement which, apart from barring the destruction of each other's civilian and military nuclear facilities, included confidence-building measures such as exchanging lists of nuclear facilities sites.[48]

SRI LANKA ACCORD, DEADLY DISCORD

Sri Lanka's independence from Britain in 1948 exposed deep ethnic fissures between the Buddhist Sinhalese majority and the Tamil Hindu minority. The Sinhala Only Act (1956), recognizing Sinhala as the sole official language, posed an existential threat to the Tamil language and culture. The island Tamils demanded a separate state, Tamil Eelam, in the northeastern region. The 1983 amendment to the Sri Lankan Constitution, making separatist movements illegal, led to the emergence of a militant organization, Liberation Tigers of Tamil Eelam (LTTE) and a prolonged and horrendous civil war.[49]

The Tamils of Sri Lanka share their language, culture and religion with the people of Tamil Nadu, and India could not have ignored their plight. Indira Gandhi and later Rajiv Gandhi offered overt and covert support to Sri Lankan Tamils by providing them with sanctuaries and facilitating training camps for Tamil insurgents who eventually, under Vellupillai Prabhakaran, turned into the most brutal force that any country had ever seen. Following the anti-Tamil riots in July 1983 that caused untold loss of life, made thousands homeless, destroyed countless businesses and properties, and drove out many Tamils abroad to seek refuge, there was no stopping the LTTE.

Sri Lanka was made aware of, by the Indira Gandhi government, the fact that armed intervention in support of the Tamil movement was a possibility, which India would consider if the Tamils' legitimate aspirations were not met. But after Indira Gandhi's assassination, the Indian support for the militant movement diminished. Rajiv Gandhi initiated a new policy of re-establishing friendly relations with India's neighbours. Although the covert aid to Tamil rebels continued, Rajiv Gandhi made serious diplomatic efforts to find a solution to the conflict. India's regional security interests that aimed at reducing the scope of clandestine foreign intervention, especially those linked to Pakistan and China, necessitated a peaceful resolution of the Sinhala-Tamil conflict.[50]

Nonetheless, with support from some foreign governments, especially Pakistan, the Sri Lankan government intensified its anti-insurgent campaign and launched Operation Liberation, a full-scale attack against the LTTE stronghold in Jaffna, using heavy artillery, helicopter gunships and aircraft, causing massive civilian casualties and creating unprecedented humanitarian crises.[51] In June 1987, India sent an unarmed convoy of ships to provide humanitarian assistance (food and medicine) to the civilian population of the besieged Jaffna city but the convoy was intercepted and returned. Subsequently, India used its Air Force to drop supplies to the beleaguered population. As reported by an American journalist:

> Not since 1971 when India invaded what was then East Pakistan to help it become the nation of Bangladesh, has New Delhi so directly intervened in the internal affairs of a neighbour. India's action was seen as a reflection of Prime Minister Rajiv Gandhi's anger over the blocking of the flotilla, which turned back after a tense five-hour confrontation...[52]

Fearing India's intervention, Sri Lankan President J.R. Jayewardene lifted the siege of Jaffna and proposed to hold talks with the Rajiv Gandhi government for a possible solution to the conflict, which eventually led to the ill-fated India–Sri Lanka Accord on 29 July 1987.

In a declassified CIA report on the Sri Lanka conflict, Jayewardene told Peter Galbraith, a visiting American diplomat, that he was forced to accept the India–Sri Lanka Accord because his generals advised him against the military campaign, Operation Liberation, fearing that the casualties would be too high and unacceptable.[53] As *The Hindu* reported from the unclassified document:

> He [Mr. Jayewardene] made clear that he shared the GOI'S [Government of India's] implacable hostility toward Prabhakaran, calling the LTTE leader 'a mad fellow'...He stressed, though without obvious bitterness, that none of his outside friends would help him, so he had no choice but to make a deal with India...[54]

Jayewardene's assessment, as he conveyed to Galbraith, was totally different from what Sri Lanka's topmost military officer, General Cyril Ranatunga, GOC, wrote in his autobiography, *Adventurous Journey—From Peace to War, Insurgency to Terrorism*.[55] According to General Ranatunga, the Sri Lankan military was ready:

> Finally, he (President Jayewardene) nodded and said, 'You can flatten Jaffna if this menace can be eradicated and I will build a new Jaffna!'...The morale of the ground troops was high and we were sensing a prize catch... The following day, President Jayewardene called me and ordered a temporary halt of the Operation as the Indian Air Force was bringing in food supplies. When I protested, a visibly angry President retorted that we could not fight India.[56]

An ominous event occurred on the eve of the signing of the India–Sri Lanka Accord. At the Guard of Honour held for Rajiv Gandhi in Colombo at the President's House, a Sri Lankan naval sailor, Vijitha Rohana, pivoted and smacked his ceremonial Lee-Enfield rifle on the back of the Indian prime minister's neck. Rajiv Gandhi ducked and missed the full force of the blow. Many Sri Lankan Sinhalese shared Rohana's rage against India's support for the LTTE and interference in their country's affairs. It seemed that besides the Sri Lankan Sinhalese majority, the powerful Buddhist clergy too was not happy with the concessions offered to the Tamils. Nor were the Tamil extremists happy with the settlement; they wanted an independent Tamil nation.

Under the Accord, the Sri Lankan Government accepted the Tamil demands, including the transference of power to the provinces, the merger of the northern and eastern provinces, and reaffirming the official status of Tamil language.[57] To enforce the Accord, the Indian Peace-Keeping Force (IPKF) was to be stationed in Sri Lanka.

But in the course of time, the IPKF could not hold the peace between the LTTE and the Sri Lankan Forces. India decided to withdraw, and this was a humiliating blow to the nation's prestige as a regional power. By March 1990, India withdrew the last of its troops from Sri Lanka. *Los Angeles Times* commented wryly:

> But, as the last few hundred of India's 50,000-member 'peacekeeping force' withdrew from its neighbour, it was clear that the world's fourth-largest army had learned the lessons of Vietnam and Afghanistan the hard way... South Asia's principal power failed to crush a guerrilla force of Tamil separatists that was less than one-twentieth the size of the Indian force.[58]

The fighting between the LTTE and the government forces resumed and turned into a full-fledged civil war. At an election rally held in Chennai in 1991, a female LTTE suicide bomber, Thenmozhi Rajaratnam, blew Rajiv Gandhi up while bowing to touch his feet in obeisance. India plunged into grief. The LTTE forfeited its support in India. In 2009 when the Sri Lankan army carried out a major military offensive in the north against the LTTE, India stood by and watched the annihilation of the LTTE and thousands and thousands of civilians nonchalantly. In fact, the Sri Lankan military campaign was not only unopposed by India it received India's silent support in spite of the international denunciations of Sri Lanka's human rights violations. What Sri Lanka had done in 2009 was no more brutal than Operation Blue Star against the Khalistani militants, which was followed by the massacre of innocent Sikhs after Indira Gandhi's assassination.

THE STATE OF THE STATES

In his five-year tenure as India's prime minister, Rajiv Gandhi tried to resolve several long-standing political and ethnic conflicts, including Punjab, Assam and Mizoram, of which only the Mizoram problem found an enduring solution. The accord signed between the Government of India and the Mizo National Front (MNF) leader Laldenga on 30 June 1986, which granted Mizoram statehood in the Indian Union with two parliamentary seats and ended two decades of insurgency, has stood the test of time and is a tribute to Indian federalism.[59] Aizawl, Mizoram's capital, which saw the first air raid by the Indian Air Force on a civilian area within the country in 1966, today hosts a football stadium in the name of Rajiv Gandhi. Within federalism, everything is negotiable and there are many possibilities, as Punjab, Assam and other groups in West Bengal and Andhra Pradesh would discover in the course of time. This is the way the people play the game of democracy in India, where religion, caste, language, race and ethnicity play a very important part in how political decisions are made.

Consider the Nepali-speaking people of West Bengal, mostly concentrated in the Darjeeling hills. Under the leadership of Subhash Ghisingh, who founded the Gorkha National Liberation Front (GNLF), they began to demand a separate state of Gorkhaland using all kinds of coercive methods, including bandhs and hartals, as well as extreme violence. The Gorkhas, a hardy martial race of Nepali origin, have provided both the Indian and the British militaries with some of the finest fighting soldiers. It was during the British era that they migrated to Darjeeling and became the dominant Nepali-speaking ethnic group, surpassing the local Lepchas. After many days of bandhs and strikes and clashes with the security forces as well as with the ruling communist party cadre of Jyoti Basu's West Bengal CPI(M) government, negotiations were held to resolve the issue. Ghisingh and the GNLF agreed to drop the demand for a separate state and instead settled for the Darjeeling Gorkha Hill Council, a semi-autonomous administrative body, which was set up with limited powers. The accord would, however, prove to be temporary as insurgency would flare up in the future to be doused by the state with force and makeshift accommodations.[60]

Just as the Assamese have been fighting to throw out the non-Assamese, first the Bengalis and subsequently the Bangladeshis, the indigenous Bodo tribals of Assam too demanded a separate state. The Bodos, a distinct ethnolinguistic group, one of the Indo-Mongoloid groups belonging to the Tibeto-Burman branch of the Sino-Tibetan family in the Northeast, are said to be one of the earliest inhabitants of Assam.[61] And under the All Bodo Students Union (ABSU), their violent agitation followed the familiar pattern of other insurgencies, including bandhs, hartals, damage to roads and bridges apart from attacking and killing the police and civilians. Finally, nevertheless, the Bodos signed a carrot-and-stick-based accord with the government.

The same pattern of violence was also followed in the neighbouring state Tripura where the locals resented the Bengali immigrants and killed thousands of people during the eight-year-long insurgency. In 1988, the government under Rajiv Gandhi signed the Tripura Accord, under which the rebels agreed to give up their weapons and work under the Indian Constitution. The government lifted the ban on the Tripura National Volunteers, pledged to rehabilitate the guerrillas and assured to undertake measures for tighter security on its border with Bangladesh to prevent illegal immigration.[62] All these insurgencies and petty mutinies not only challenged the Indian state where citizens have the constitutional right to live and work anywhere, but also showed how individual states in India failed to uphold law and order to protect the rights of citizens.

Apart from the endemic violence in the Northeast and Punjab and the deadly conflict in Sri Lanka, India under Rajiv Gandhi saw new political forces rising in the states that would make governance more challenging as well as make federal polity more dynamic. For example, while the Congress party ruled with an overwhelming majority at the Centre, the Asom Gana Parishad held power in Assam, the Telugu Desam Party (TDP) in Andhra Pradesh, the DMK in Tamil Nadu and the Akalis in Punjab. One of the most remarkable political developments was the wholehearted acceptance of communist rule in West Bengal. Under the suave but ruthless leadership of Jyoti Basu, a Middle Temple (London) trained barrister; the CPI(M) had been in power in West Bengal for more than a decade. During this period, it crushed the Naxalite movement, carried out land reforms and maintained communal peace in the state, especially during the dangerous time after Indira Gandhi's death that provoked the anti-Sikh riots and later on after the demolition of the Babri Masjid. While the rise of the state and regional leaders was expected and showed the maturing of the Indian political system, India also saw the beginning of the rise of the Hindu-nationalist party, the Jana Sangh, into prominence, the party that under a different avatar would rule India in the future.

BURN AYODHYA, BURN!

Some scholars contend that since Rajiv Gandhi was reproached for slouching in appeasement towards the Muslim community for the Shah Bano divorce decision and the enactment of the Muslim Women (Protection of Rights on Divorce) Act, the prime minister, in mistaken belief, tried to do a balancing act by siding with the rising popular movement for building the Ram Temple in Ayodhya. The government ordered that the locks on the Ram Janmabhoomi–Babri Masjid be removed so that access to the birthplace of Lord Ram was open to all Hindus. Before that, once a year, a Hindu priest was allowed to offer puja to the idols that were surreptitiously installed in 1949.[63]

The rise of Hindu nationalism and the Jana Sangh that later on would become the BJP began inadvertently with Rajiv Gandhi's decision to allow the foundational ceremony or 'shilanyas' for the construction of the Ram Temple by the Vishva Hindu Parishad (VHP) and the Jana Sangh in Ayodhya on 10 November 1989 at the disputed site where the sixteenth-century Babri Masjid stood.[64] Pranab Mukherjee, president of India, 2012–17, in the second volume of his memoir, *The Turbulent Years: 1980–96*, called the opening of the Ram Janmabhoomi temple in Ayodhya not only an 'error of judgement', but he also questioned Prime Minister Rajiv Gandhi's secularism, stating that:

> The prime minister—having won an overwhelming mandate in
> 1984 primarily owing to consolidation on communal lines in

aftermath of his mother Indira Gandhi's assassination—and his prime strategist Arun Nehru found Hindu consolidation as a readymade recipe for electoral victory... The Shah Bano case and the government's capitulation before Muslim fundamentalists provided a context. A beleaguered Gandhi now tried to win over Hindus by playing the temple card at Ayodhya... The story of Ayodhya is replete with stealth, illegality and abdication of responsibility by successive Congress regimes, not only at the centre, but at the state level as well ...India's first prime minister Jawaharlal Nehru was able to gauge its sinister potential and was in favour of removing the idols stealthily placed in the mosque on 22 December 1949. However he was thwarted by the then chief minister G.B. Pant. In sharp contrast to Nehru, who steadfastly opposed use of religion in politics, Gandhi unlocked the temple to play the religious card to consolidate his support base following the revolt by V.P. Singh.[65]

VISHWANATH PRATAP SINGH AS PRIME MINISTER

Vishwanath Pratap (V.P.) Singh was the seventh prime minister of India from 1989 to 1990. Born in a Rajput family of landowners called zamindars, he was, in many ways, a very successful politician. From the very beginning of his political career, he was a member of the Congress party. He got elected to the Lok Sabha in 1971 and joined the cabinet of Indira Gandhi as deputy minister of commerce, and later on as minister of commerce from 1976 to 1977. When Indira Gandhi was re-elected as the prime minister in 1980, after a brief Janata Party interlude, he was asked to take over as the chief minister of Uttar Pradesh. And as the chief minister of the largest and politically the most significant state in India, V.P. Singh confronted the problem of crime and developed a reputation as a politician who could get things accomplished.[66]

When Rajiv Gandhi became the prime minister after the assassination of his mother and was re-elected after the 1984 general election, V.P. Singh joined the cabinet as finance minister. Both V.P. Singh and Rajiv Gandhi wanted to break away from the stranglehold of the license raj and liberalize the economy by reducing the burden of unnecessary regulations that were choking the economy. Apart from the firm steps that V.P. Singh took against gold smuggling, his more controversial action, which made him popular with the general public in India, was the use of the Enforcement Directorate of the finance ministry to crack down on big tax evaders. His excessive enthusiasm and well-publicized raids on top industrialists, including Dhirubhai Ambani and famous Bollywood actor Amitabh Bachchan, for example, rattled the political establishment that depended upon the largesse of the rich and famous.

Looking at the high public esteem in which V.P. Singh was held because of his integrity and popular actions against the wealthy and notorious, Rajiv Gandhi could not throw him out in the cold as he had done with Pranab Mukherjee. Instead, he reshuffled the cabinet and moved V.P. Singh to another important ministry, Defence, in January 1987. And as soon as he assumed his new office, he smelled a rat. His sharp hawk-eyed focus on what was going on in the Ministry of Defence brought him to the shady world of defence procurement. Most of the Ministry of Defence procurement was imported from abroad, which created opportunities for some well-connected and networked officers, politicians and businessmen to take advantage of the multimillion-dollar defence deals. One of the most glaring infractions that came into focus was the information about the Bofors guns procurement deal, which ultimately turned out to be the death knell for Prime Minister Rajiv Gandhi. But before Singh could take a step about the corruption case, he was forced to resign from the cabinet. Later on, he resigned from the Congress party as well as from the Lok Sabha.

Along with other dissidents, including Arun Nehru and Arif Mohammad Khan, Singh formed a new party called the Janata Morcha. Soon after, he was re-elected to the Lok Sabha in a by-election from Allahabad. As an opposition leader, he displayed great organizing skills by bringing all centrist parties together, including his new party, the Janata Morcha, the Janata Party, the Lok Dal and the Congress (Socialist) Party, to form the Janata Dal. To fight the forthcoming general election in 1989, the Janata Dal at the national level formed a coalition with regional parties, including the DMK, the Telugu Desam Party and the Asom Gana Parishad. The new coalition was called the National Front with V.P. Singh as the convener, which fought the 1989 general election after reaching an electoral agreement with the BJP and leftist parties in order to present a united front to fight the Congress (I) of Rajiv Gandhi.

The National Front and its allies won a simple majority to form the government. The BJP, the CPI(M) and the Communist Party of India did not join the government but committed nonetheless to support the government from outside. V.P. Singh was sworn in as the seventh prime minister of India on 2 December 1989. This was India's second experiment with a coalition government but much shorter than the first one after the Emergency under the Janata Dal with Morarji Desai as the prime minister.

As was the case with Morarji Desai during the Janata Dal interregnum, V.P. Singh's government did not last for long because the coalition wasn't ideologically coherent. There was no common economic and social platform. The communists and the Hindu nationalists had different agendas. V.P. Singh was a competent politician and a man of integrity but his cabinet was a cabinet of rivals, not a team with visionary leadership. He spent his short tenure of ten months in putting out fires here and there, some small, some big. His most urgent task was to close down the military operation and withdraw troops from Sri Lanka. The poorly planned operation was a disaster.

The Singh government's first major crisis was in Jammu and Kashmir. On 8 December 1989, Rubaiya Sayeed, daughter of India's Home Minister Mufti Mohammed Sayeed, an internist at the Lal Ded Memorial Women's Hospital, Srinagar, was kidnapped at gunpoint by Jammu and Kashmir Liberation Front militants. The kidnappers demanded the release of jailed separatists, including Abdul Hamid Sheikh, Sher Khan, Noor Mohammad Kalwal, Altaf Ahemed and Javed Ahemed Jargar, in exchange for her release. In spite of opposition from Jammu and Kashmir Chief Minister Farooq Abdullah, the Singh government accepted the militants' demand and released the prisoners to get Rubaiya Sayeed back to her parents.[67] Jagmohan Malhotra, notorious for Emergency excesses, was appointed the governor of Jammu and Kashmir, but he was rudderless. Kashmir Islamic militants fully armed and supported from across the border from Pakistan were beyond anyone's control.

THE DESCENT OF KASHMIR VALLEY INTO CHAOS

'We want Pakistan along with Hindu women but without their men' (Kashmiri language: *'Assi gacchi panu'nuy Pakistan, batav rostuy, batenein saan.*)', thus proclaimed the masked men flaunting AK-47s in the streets of Srinagar, heralding a new bloody dawn in the Kashmir Valley.[68]

If Rubaiya Sayeed were a Kashmiri Pandit, she might have met a different fate, perhaps, been gang-raped and cut into pieces and thrown on the wayside as was done to many Pandit women, including Girija Tickoo, a schoolteacher, who after being gang-raped was put under a chain saw; the wife of Border Security Force Inspector M.N. Paul, who was kidnapped, raped and murdered; nurse Sarla Bhat who after being repeatedly raped was killed and dumped on the roadside; Prana, the wife of Professor K.L. Ganjoo, who was raped and killed along with her husband; Babli Raina whose family members watched her being raped and killed before their eyes and so on.[69]

The killing of Kashmiri Pandits—lawyers, jurists, professors, teachers, doctors, nurses, businessmen, farmers and orchard growers, government officers, journalists, and innocent women and children—close to 1,341, according to a Panun Kashmir report, a political group that strives for the rights of Kashmiri Pandits, set the stage for the total elimination and the 'ethnic cleansing' of Kashmiri Pandits from the Valley. What began under the watchful eyes of Jammu and Kashmir Chief Minister Farooq Abdullah, however, took the shape of a mass exodus on 19 January 1990. It was a grim reminder of the gruesome days of Partition when thousands and thousands of Hindu and Sikh refugees—beaten, broken and brutalized—staggered along the road to India. Kashmiri Pandits were reliving the bloody history of 1947.

When Sheikh Mohammad Abdullah returned to political power in Jammu and Kashmir after the 1975 accord with Indira Gandhi, the accord that had included the Sheikh giving up his plebiscite demand besides making Jammu and Kashmir's autonomy under Article 370 virtually null and void, the state was not what he had left behind during his incarcerations and political wilderness. Kashmiri Muslims no longer lionized him. His roar and thunder had become the whimpering of a self-seeking, compromised politician. He was returned to power in Jammu and Kashmir, per the political arrangement, as its chief minister. He gave his allegiance to the Congress party before the 1977 Assembly elections when he revived his original party, the National Conference. But he was no longer the unquestionable leader of the people of Jammu and Kashmir. Other political groups, including pro-Pakistani extremist militants, were emerging on the political stage and the streets of Srinagar. Most importantly, the cadre-based Islamist-political party, Jamaat-e-Islami, with its tentacles in madrassas, and Pakistan supported Jammu and Kashmir Liberation Front operating from Pakistan occupied Kashmir, the so-called Azad Kashmir, were the rising political forces that had begun to capture the imagination of the Muslim youth.[70]

Sheikh Abdullah began to bend before the prevailing communal winds in the state. The Muslim character of Kashmir was being reinforced through political speeches and Friday sermons in mosques. Hundreds of village names were Islamized. On 28 May 1982, the Sheikh gave a fiery speech at the Hazratbal Mosque warning his cheering audience that Hindu communalists 'had always sought to reduce the Muslim majority in Kashmir,' and that 'a north Indian Hindu cabal [was] poised to strip his state of its Muslim character.'[71] Sheikh Abdullah's contorted religious-political paranoia was in response to the changing mode of consciousness of the Valley. *India Today*, in its report, warned:

> ...to protect Kashmiri Muslim interests, the Sheikh might play into the hands of Muslim communalist bodies like the Jamaat-e-Islami and the Jamaat-i-Tulaba... the organizations

reportedly wield enormous influence in the state's educational institutions. Moreover, youth organizations like the Mahazi Azadi, a militant 'liberation front', the People's League, and the Tulaba have been working up popular sentiment against an all-devouring Hindu India.[72]

Even when nearing his death, Sheikh Abdullah was no less bitter about India under Indira Gandhi than he was when he was arrested in 1953 under Jawaharlal Nehru. During the three decades of his off-and-on comfortable house confinements, the Valley had progressively descended into the deep dark night of anti-India militancy and communal hell. Sufism, a benign version of Islam, had been swallowed up by a rabid jihadist version of the Saudi-financed and Pakistan's ISI-supported Wahhabism. Democratic secular India and its intelligentsia wedded to political correctness and afraid of calling a spade a spade had no clue what to do when the Valley was spiralling down into militant Islamism. Regardless of whatever happened in the Valley, Sheikh Abdullah, to his credit, left a well-endowed political dynasty. In this sense, he was just like any other Indian politician.

When Farooq Abdullah succeeded his father Sheikh Abdullah as the state's chief minister following the latter's death in 1982, Jammu and Kashmir's Muslim population had become increasingly alienated from India.[73] As such, it was being indoctrinated by virulent pro-Pakistani Jamaat-e-Islami, and supposedly, a pro-independence party, the JKLF, fuelled propaganda. Terrorism was on the rise. Kashmiri Muslims celebrated Islamist terrorists as martyrs, as happened in February 1984 when Maqbool Bhat, a founder member of the JKLF, was hanged in Tihar jail.[74] Among the many decades' long terrorist activities that he either committed or backed, there included the masterminding of the hijacking of the Indian Airlines plane to Lahore in 1971 and in 1976; and the kidnap and murder of an Indian diplomat, Ravindra Mhatrae, in the UK by Maqbool Bhat's Kashmir Liberation Army members. As militancy arose in Kashmir, the Indian security forces' reprisal became increasingly brutal.

The political situation in the state did not improve when after the 1983 Assembly elections, Farooq Abdullah was appointed as the National Conference–Congress party alliance chief minister. Only a year after, in July 1984, Farooq Abdullah fell out of favour with Indira Gandhi. His brother-in-law Ghulam Mohammad (G.M.) Shah, who had defected to the Congress, toppled him to form the government. Since the political turncoat G.M. Shah had little support of the Kashmiri population, he too, like his father-in-law Sheikh Abdullah did in his sunset days, began to appeal to Muslim sentiments to gain community support. The construction of a mosque in Jammu in the New Civil Secretariat in 1986 led to Hindu–Muslim riots, which were subsequently followed by a series of attacks against the Hindus in Sopore, Vanpoh, Lukbhavan, Anantnag, Salar and Fatehpur, during which Muslim mobs killed several Hindus, in addition to destroying their properties and temples.[75] It was a foretaste of the horrific events to come. Chief Minister G.M. Shah, who, along with other Kashmiri politicians, had shown a soft, kid-glove, accommodative attitude towards Islamists for political advantages, had willy-nilly pushed further and pitted the Kashmir Valley Muslim population against India. However, both the National Conference and the INC, political rivals and coalition partners, did vouch for secularism and were determined to keep their hold on power.[76]

In 1987, Jammu and Kashmir had its Assembly elections with a voter turnout of 75 per cent. In spite of its seemingly growing popular support among the Muslim majority of the state, the Muslim United Front, led by the Jamaat-e-Islami Party, won only four seats out of 76. By all accounts, it looked like a rigged election. Even Farooq Abdullah, according to historian Paul Brass, admitted to these elections being rigged, although he denied being behind the rigging.[77]

The Jammu and Kashmir National Conference won 40 seats, enabling it to form the government with Farooq Abdullah as the chief minister in coalition with the INC that had won 26 seats. The BJP won only two seats in the predominantly Hindu Jammu. The election results created a facade of secularism in Jammu and Kashmir, while the ground realities had been changing.

The Muslim United Front that included the Plebiscite Front, the Jamaat-e-Islami, JKLF and other Muslim religious groups, won 31 per cent votes, which was not reflected in the handful of seats they won. Scholars have contended that fair elections would have led to power-sharing and compromises, perhaps, thus giving the parties a stake in the future.[78] It's argued that after being cheated at the ballot box because of the widespread electoral malpractices, the Islamist parties resorted to armed struggle and militancy that finally led to the exodus of the Kashmiri Pandits, whom they had begun to perceive as traitors to their cause.[79] It's a specious argument. On the contrary, the Islamists' victory at the ballot box would not have led to peace in the Valley because not only did Pakistan's ISI control the levers of the militancy but also the fact that nowhere in the Muslim world had the Shariat Law or the Caliphate ever been established through the ballot box, which was the ultimate goal of the jihadist parties under the umbrella of the Muslim United Front.[80] In July 1988, the Jammu and Kashmir Liberation Front launched a bomb attack in Srinagar.[81] There was no going back.

THE EXODUS OF KASHMIRI PANDITS

The reign of Islamist terror for expelling the Hindus of Kashmir Valley began on 4 January when Hizbul Mujahideen declared jihad through *Aftab* and *Al Safa*, Srinagar Urdu newspapers, and proclaimed that the infidels, Pandits and all, quit the Valley. Chief Minister Farooq Abdullah and the ruling National Conference failed to stem the rising tide of militancy, and the government collapsed. Jagmohan Malhotra, who took over as the state governor after president's rule was imposed, failed to control the chaos in spite of the imposition of curfew in the city.

According to media accounts, Hindu homes were marked red for destruction and their walls were splashed with posters and handbills telling Pandits to leave Kashmir. Hindu women were told to put on tilak, the identifying mark, on their forehead, not to give them protection but to objectify them for kidnapping and rape. Roaming the streets of Srinagar were masked men carrying

AK-47s telling people to reset the time to Pakistan Standard Time. According to an article in *The Sunday Guardian*:

> The scene was reminiscent of Nazi Germany, only the yellow arm bands damning the Jews were missing... Then on 19 January 1990...the pressure reaches its zenith. As dusk approaches and Hindu families, women and children included, cower inside their homes, behind the false security of their doors, outside the spine-chilling exhortations to leave the Valley become louder and shriller.[82]

Here are snatches of a chilling exchange and banter recounted by Rahul Pandita in his memoir *Our Moon Has Blood Clots*:

> 'Let's distribute these houses,' one of them shouts. 'Akram, which one do you want?' he asks. 'I would settle for this house any day,' he points to a house. 'Bastard,' shoots back another, 'how you wish you could occupy this house with their daughter!' There is a peal of laughter. They make obscene gestures with their fists ...[83]

The horrific sufferings and brutalization of Kashmiri Pandits were dramatized in a recent Bollywood film, *Shikara*, which is based on author and journalist Rahul Pandita's book. He lamented that the problem, the miserable plight of the uprooted Pandit communities, can be attributed to:

> ...the apathy of the media and a majority of India's intellectual class who refuse to even acknowledge the suffering of the Pandits. No campaigns were ever run for us; no fellowships or grants were given for research on our exodus. For the media, the Kashmir issue has remained largely black and white—here are a people who were victims of brutalization at the hands of the Indian state. But the media has failed to see, and has largely ignored the fact that the same people also victimized another.[84]

Excessive display of sympathy and advocacy for Kashmiri Pandits by the dominant English language media and the ruling intellectual classes would be tantamount to indirect criticism of the Kashmir Valley Muslims, which in secular India is regarded politically incorrect. Indian journalists, writing for foreign media, who show and tell Hindu atrocities against Muslims are upheld as the guardians of Indian secularism, but not vice versa. In the ultimate analysis, Kashmiri Pandits became helpless and hopeless victims of the endless brutal war between the Indian security forces determined to crush the militancy and Pakistan-supported Kashmiri jihadist militants determined to break away from India to join Pakistan or to establish the Caliphate and the law of Shariat. Since the insurgency began in 1989–90, the Valley became a killing field for the militants as well as for the Indian security forces. Thousands and thousands of Kashmiri Muslims disappeared or were killed with no accountability. The ethnic cleansing of the Kashmiri Pandits and their exodus from their homeland—once the land of Panini, Patanjali, Charaka Samhita and Sanskrit philosophers—is part of the larger arch of the Kashmir tragedy. To bring peace to the Valley, India needs a paradigm shift.

HOW THE V.P. SINGH GOVERNMENT FELL APART

In Punjab, V.P. Singh tried to make peace with the Sikhs. He visited the Golden Temple and apologized for the ravages of Operation Blue Star. He replaced the governor Siddhartha Shankar Ray with another bureaucrat Nirmal Kumar Mukarji, tasking him with a plan to hold elections. The V.P. Singh administration's decision to implement the recommendations of the Mandal Commission, upheld by the Supreme Court, which recommended that a fixed quota of all jobs in the public sector be reserved for members of the historically disadvantaged Other Backward Classes (OBC), led to widespread riots among the upper caste youth in northern India.[85] The BJP, which supported the Singh government from outside, had its own agenda. The Ram Janmabhoomi movement, which served as a platform and rallying force for several radical Hindu organizations, had begun to gather new momentum. On 25 September 1990, the movement leaders Lal Krishna Advani and

Pramod Mahajan, choosing the Hindu sacred symbol of 'Rath,' the chariot associated with Lord Ram, began the procession. The Rath Yatra marched towards Ayodhya for the purpose of building the new Ram Temple at the disputed place where the Babri mosque stood. L.K. Advani and other leaders were arrested at Samastipur, Bihar, before they reached the disputed spot, which was protected by troops.

In retaliation against the arrest of its leaders, the BJP withdrew its support to the National Front government. V.P. Singh resigned on 7 November 1990. A hastily put up coalition government organized by 64 MPs of the Janata Dal and led by Chandra Shekhar as the prime minister lasted for a few months before the president called for a new general election.

11

NARASIMHA RAO TURNS
THE SHIP AROUND

[He] was a ship that sailed out every day into a storm.

—Biographer Vinay Sitapati

There are some periods in the history of a nation that leave eternal trails on its collective psyche. This was the case in India from 1991 through 1996, when India took bold measures to change its course, as it were, to pull itself up by the bootstraps. In the process, it challenged and strengthened democracy through bloody social conflicts and rapid economic growth. The period saw the rise of regional leaders who would transform the hidebound static federalism into a dynamic political system.

A month after Sonia Gandhi and the INC, chose a pliable southern polyglot scholar-politician Pamulaparthi Venkata (P.V.) Narasimha Rao as its leader and the prime minister, another powerful leader, had sprung up in the South—J. Jayalalithaa, a remarkable politician who was sworn in as chief minister of Tamil Nadu and who would become a reverential icon until her death in 2016.[1] Meanwhile, Sikh militancy was dissipating. An internationally known economist, Manmohan Singh, a Sikh gentleman who had stoically transcended the pain, suffering and humiliation of his brave community during the ravages of the Golden Temple, gathered a brilliant group of technocrats to manage India's new industrial policy.

This marked the beginning of India's economic reforms that would become unstoppable, keeping in mind the gravity of the situation that the Indian rupee exchange rate had collapsed, and the rupee had plunged in its value against the US dollar from 20 rupees for a dollar to 30 rupees in just one year. India was airlifting planeloads of gold to London as loan collateral, just as an Indian woman would pawn her jewellery to feed her children and send them to school, hoping that the sun would rise again and there would be a better tomorrow.

In the same year, the Rapid Action Force (RAF) was established by the Union Home Ministry to deal with riots, crowd control, rescue and relief operations, and other contingencies. However, one might wonder as to what the RAF was doing when Ayodhya was set on fire. The Bhopal Union Carbide gas tragedy kept haunting India in spite of the fact that the Chief Judicial Magistrate of Bhopal Court had declared Warren Anderson, the CEO of Union Carbide, a fugitive under the Indian law for declining to appear in the case. The Indian government had no leverage and did not seriously press for extradition of the absconder. While illegally brewed liquor killed hundreds of people in Odisha, a most feared handlebar moustachioed gangster Veerappan and his goons were causing havoc from their jungle hideouts in Karnataka, Tamil Nadu and Kerala.

But the worst was yet to come. On 6 December 1992, supporters of the VHP tore down a sixteenth-century mosque located in Ayodhya, Uttar Pradesh. The Hindus have always believed that the mosque built by the Mughal Emperor Babar was erected on the site that was the birthplace of Lord Ram, the Ram Janmabhoomi. The whole world watched the ensuing communal conflagrations in India that killed thousands of people. A few months later, on 12 March 1993, a series of bomb blasts, planted by Muslim underworld dons as vengeance against the demolition of Babri Masjid, rocked the country's commercial capital Mumbai, killing, by some estimates, 257 people and injuring 713. During the same time, coincidentally, perhaps, the All Parties Hurriyat Conference was formed in Kashmir. While Indians were killing one another, nature, too, was busy killing Indians. A massive earthquake of 6.4 magnitude rocked Maharashtra and claimed around 10,000 lives on 30 September 1993.

Some scholars say that India, under the Narasimha Rao administration, was either thwarted in its efforts by the United States or was unready to test nuclear weapons.[2] India nonetheless rolled out the Prithvi missile at the 1994 Republic Day Parade in New Delhi, which was rather ironic because, although India could make tactical surface-to-surface short-range missiles, it couldn't make field guns—otherwise, it would not have gone abroad to purchase the controversial Swiss Bofors 40 mm guns that had derailed Rajiv Gandhi's political career. During this time span, India saw the assassination of Punjab Chief Minister Beant Singh. And arms being dropped from an Antonov An-26 aircraft in Purulia district in the CPI(M)-ruled state of West Bengal, allegedly intended for the socio-spiritual organization Ananda Marga.[3]

CHANGING INDIA'S ECONOMIC DIRECTION

Since neither V.P. Singh's nor Chandra Shekhar's minority governments could hold on to power after the 1989 election, the Lok Sabha had to be dissolved after 16 months. The consequences of the implementation of the Mandal Commission's recommendations and failure to handle the Ram Janmabhoomi–Babri Masjid issue had rocked the nation with pervasive violence. Although the 1991 general election was held in a highly divisive and acrimonious environment of class, caste and communal conflicts or what's called 'Mandal-Mandir' issues, few politicians realized that India was perching on an existential economic precipice.[4] Since the Mandal Commission Report recommendations executed by the V.P. Singh government gave 27 per cent reservation to the Other Backward Castes (OBCs) in government jobs, the comparatively more privileged caste members, especially the youth, took to the streets in violent protests, mostly in the urban centres all over the country. V.P. Singh's good intentions for social justice were not the cause of his undoing.

His apparent success in preventing the march to Ayodhya for the Ram Temple building activities by the BJP and the VHP volunteers had instead galvanized the Hindu nationalists. This was the beginning of the rise of the BJP as a national party and the building of the Ayodhya Temple was used as the party's major platform. V.P. Singh's National Front fell apart. The Congress under Rajiv Gandhi's leadership, as recounted earlier, was muddling along when on 20 May 1991, a day after the first round of polling took place, Rajiv Gandhi was assassinated while campaigning in Sriperumbudur, Tamil Nadu. The suicide bomber, belonging to the Liberation Tigers of Tamil Eelam (LTTE), blew herself up while standing near Gandhi as an act of revenge against him for sending Indian troops to Sri Lanka in 1987.

The remainder of the election was suspended until the middle of June. And although the assassination generated massive sympathy for the Congress (I), when the election was resumed, the Congress (I) failed to get a majority. With 244 seats, the Congress (I), nevertheless, formed the government under P.V. Narasimha Rao, who, albeit not the first choice of Rajiv Gandhi's grieving widow Sonia Gandhi and the Congress Working Committee (CWC), was regarded as 'a man of great ability who had served as a senior minister in the cabinets of both Indira and Rajiv Gandhi, was generally considered a suitable successor to Rajiv... On 21 June 1991, exactly a month after the brutal assassination of Rajiv, Rao was sworn in as prime minister. In keeping with the practice established in Indira Gandhi's time, he held on to both the offices of PM and the Congress president...'[5] That was a smart move. Rao would be his own master, not beholden to the puppeteers of the old Nehru–Gandhi establishment, especially when political and economic challenges were massive and he needed to be creative.

Equally important was the fact that the Ayodhya Ram Temple issue had paid off well for the BJP, which won 120 seats. In the 1989 Lok Sabha, the BJP had 85 seats, while in the 1984 election, it had only two seats. For Prime Minister Narasimha Rao, the Ram Temple–Babri Masjid conundrum became an albatross around his neck that blinded historians to his greatest achievement, the Indian economy. Narasimha Rao turned the gigantic ship around, liberalized the state-controlled static economy and set India on the path of globalization. Others would challenge him and yet follow him.

THE ECONOMIC CRISIS

India's 1991 economic crisis was essentially a crisis of foreign exchange reserves, which had hit rock bottom. India was importing a lot more than it was exporting, which led to an unsustainable current account deficit. Some external factors also contributed to India's large current account deficit in 1990–91. The first shockwave came from events related to the Gulf War in the Middle East in 1990 that led to a spike in world oil prices. This worsened the balance of payment situation, which was further aggravated by a partial loss of export markets due to the Middle East crisis and the turmoil in the Soviet Union, the communist Leviathan that was on the verge of breaking up. Not only did the Indian expatriate workers' remittances decline from the Gulf countries, but thousands of them had to be repatriated from the war zones and rehabilitated back at home. The deterioration of the current account was also accentuated by the slow growth in export markets, especially the US. If the foreign exchange reserves had been as solid as they are today (US$634 billion as of January 2022), India would have smoothly sailed through the storm.

Export or perish, they said, but to do so, India's product must be competitive in the international market, as Manmohan Singh would tell the paralyzed nation. In spite of all the five-year plans, India had not become a manufacturing nation. India was rich in brainpower, poor in muscle power. Besides the shocks from external factors, the domestic political situation created tremendous uncertainty and loss of faith in India's ability to manage its affairs.

According to an analysis by International Monetary Fund (IMF) economists Valerie Cerra and Sweta Chaman Saxena:

> The widening current account imbalances and reserve losses contributed to low investor confidence, which was further weakened by political uncertainties and finally by a downgrade of India's credit rating by the credit rating agencies... The post-crisis adjustment programme featured macroeconomic stabilization and structural reforms. In response to the crisis, the government initially imposed administrative controls and

obtained assistance from the IMF.[6]

In 1991, India had just enough foreign exchange to import three weeks of essentials. Jawaharlal Nehru's socialist India was on the verge of defaulting on its external balance of payment obligations. India pledged 67 tons of gold reserves as collateral to secure an emergency loan of US$2.2 billion from the IMF, who recommended (read: imposed) certain measures to enable the country to outgrow its crisis on the path to recovery. The nation was incensed that the government had to pledge the country's gold reserves against the loan. Chandra Shekhar, who had succeeded V.P. Singh as an interim prime minister, authorized the gold liftoff to London before his government too skidded off the ground and went into oblivion. As a goodwill gesture, since the US controlled the IMF and, perhaps, a courageous step seeking new directions in foreign affairs, Prime Minister Chandra Shekhar also permitted fuelling facilities to US aircrafts during the Iraq Gulf War, much to the chagrin of the Congress whose support he needed to sustain his flimsy minority government. After six months, however, in February 1991, the refuelling permission was withdrawn. Whatever Chandra Shekhar did or failed to do, pushed India into a survival mode and created a sense of urgency for Prime Minister P.V. Narasimha Rao's economic reforms and other initiatives.

SOMEBODY'S GOT TO DO IT

Selecting an Oxford–Cambridge economist and the Reserve Bank of India governor Manmohan Singh, a soft-spoken, non-controversial, non-politician, as finance minister was an act of shrewdness and sagacity on the part of Prime Minister Rao. It enabled Singh to lead from behind and carry out fundamental structural reforms in the economy, ones that became irreversible. The reason India got into such a big mess was that Indian politicians had a poor understanding of how a complex economy embedded in a global economic network functioned. Non-alignment was neither an economic programme nor a philosophy. Indian politicians did not understand the political power of international commerce and trade. Unlike Narasimha Rao and Manmohan Singh, most Indian politicians in 1992 seemed to be paranoid about opening the windows unto the world, fearing that fresh wind and fresh ideas would be an interference in India's sovereignty.

The Singh–Rao economic salvage plan included opening up the Indian economy to foreign institutional and direct investment in order to build up foreign exchange reserves (which was the immediate cause of the economic crisis), reforming capital markets, deregulating domestic business and reforming the trade administration. Apart from the immediate goal of reducing the fiscal deficit, stabilizing the external debt and building foreign exchange reserves, structural changes were required for long-term economic growth to make the Indian economy open and globally competitive. Along with opening equity markets to foreign investors, the new policy allowed Indian firms to raise capital on international markets by issuing global depository receipts (GDRs).

Tariffs were reduced from an average of 85 per cent to 25 per cent. The rupee was made convertible on a trade account. The foreign direct investment (FDI) maximum limit on the share of foreign capital in joint ventures was increased from 40 to 51 per cent. In priority sectors, 100 per cent foreign equity was allowed. FDI approval procedures were streamlined. The National Stock Exchange entered the digital age by computerizing its trading system. The Security and Exchange Board (SEBI) regulatory authority and its watchdog role over security markets were enhanced by the Securities and Exchange Board of India Act, 1992. All these measures helped increase foreign investment, including the FDI, the portfolio investment as well as the capital raised on international capital markets. In a matter of a few years, India was out of the economic dark hole.[7]

The economic crisis was not a sudden volcanic eruption. The crisis had been building up since 1985, and political leaders and economic experts were cognizant of it. There were plenty of ideas floating around on how to tackle the problem, but no one knew how to take the bull by the horn. Prime Minister Narasimha Rao's choice of Manmohan Singh was a clever move because Dr

Singh, discreet, reticent and diplomatic, knew the crisis, knew the priorities and knew how important it was to put together a brilliant team of experts who could work with the IMF and the World Bank to create trust in the marketplace and to turn the ship around to a new direction. According to Arunabha Ghosh, a policy specialist in the United Nations Development Programme (UNDP), 'devaluation, involvement of the IMF, partial liberalization of the domestic financial sector, and gradual opening up of the external sector' were the building blocks of the new policy and there was no better person who could have accomplished it than the Oxbridge economist Manmohan Singh. But how did Singh do it? It was a masterly concert conducted by the technocrats, including economist Arvind Virmani, Montek Singh Ahluwalia, formerly of the World Bank; Ashok Desai, Oxford-trained academic, Raja Chelliah, a public finance expert; C. Rangarajan, RBI governor and Shankar Acharya of World Bank.[8]

In fact, it needed much more than merely the gathering of like-minded stars, clinical experts, policymakers and deciders to bring the paralyzed elephant back to life. Parliament had to be persuaded. The leftist intelligentsia and the cognoscenti who dominated the universities, the think tanks, the news media and the political-economic discourse in India since the times of Jawaharlal Nehru had to be persuaded. And that was the job of the new finance minister. Manmohan Singh's 1991 budget speech to Parliament was a great performance in economic diplomacy and political persuasion. As Aristotle would have said, Dr Singh used all available means of persuasion to coax Parliament into accepting his new economic plan as if it were their own plan waiting to be executed. Reading the 1991 budget speech, again, one gets the impression that Dr Singh was assuring Parliament that he was simply building on the foundation already laid by Jawaharlal Nehru and Indira Gandhi—that his economic plan was not a deviation, abandonment or disruption; but a continuation of the work where Rajiv Gandhi had left off. Making generous references to the Nehru–Gandhi establishment, he said:

> Thanks to the efforts of Pandit Jawaharlal Nehru, Indira
> Gandhi and Rajiv Gandhi, we have developed a well-diversified
> industrial structure. This constitutes a great asset as we begin
> to implement various structural reforms... I do not minimize
> the difficulties that lie ahead on the long and arduous journey
> on which we have embarked.[9]

Narasimha Rao trusted his finance minister Manmohan Singh, who, with his team of internal and external financial and economic experts, and deft handling of the domestic political opposition to the reform measures, brought the dire economic situation under control; and took bold steps to rejuvenate the economy by restructuring it and opening it to the market forces. Instead of keeping India in a protective shell of swadeshi self-reliant socialism and repeating the dead past, Manmohan Singh's approach was essentially a challenge-and-response approach of a quiet, self-assured wrestler: look into the mirror (for self-examination), pump up the iron, get out and fight; and as a flamboyant American professional boxer Muhammad Ali said, 'Float like a butterfly, sting like a bee'. No self-pity! Manmohan Singh succeeded because he hid the Muhammad Ali in him, and walked and talked like a statesman. This was the face that would launch a thousand ships in the future.

LOOK EAST, LOOK WEST, LOOK ALL AROUND

The economic liberalization policy undertaken to rescue India from its immediate foreign exchange crisis, an outcrop of a deeper structural disorder, wouldn't have been successful without India opening its closed doors, seeking new frontiers and building new trade routes. Prime Minister Narasimha Rao's 'Look East' policy was forged to build newer economic, strategic and cultural bonds with the vast Asia–Pacific region.[10] Desperate India in a challenge-response mode looked east, west and all around to build bridges. During his tenure, Narasimha Rao visited several Association of Southeast Asian Nations (ASEAN) countries, including Thailand, Indonesia, Singapore, Vietnam and Malaysia, to claim India's rightful place in a region that for many millennia had been a second home to Hinduism–Buddhism culture and traditions. The 'Look East' policy enabled India to become an active participant in various ASEAN organizations, 'a Sectoral Dialogue Partner of ASEAN in 1992, a full ASEAN Dialogue Partner in 1996, and also a member of the ASEAN Regional Forum (ARF) in 1996.'[11]

The 'Look East' policy captured the imagination of the foreign policy establishment and became one of the building blocks for the successive governments led by Deve Gowda, I.K. Gujral, Atal Bihari Vajpayee and Manmohan Singh to pursue and strengthen the India–ASEAN relations, which gained critical mass from the late 1990s through the early 2000s. The Atal Bihari Vajpayee government initiated the concept of 'extended neighbourhood,' which declared, '...our concerns and interactions go well beyond South Asia. They include other neighbours and countries immediately adjoining this region—our "extended neighbourhood"'.[12] Since then, India has never looked back, never turned its back on its neighbours.

THE HIMALAYAN NEIGHBOURS

In December 1991, Chinese Prime Minister Li Peng visited India, during which Indian leaders and intelligentsia were excessively deferential, hoping to build upon the optimism that Rajiv Gandhi's 1988 visit had generated. While such visits provoked Indians to think about long civilizational and philosophical bonds between the two countries, China's focuses were on its economic, strategic and geopolitical interests. As a commentator remarked:

> But falling between the twin stools of Chinese disinterest and Indian expectation, it seemed like a necessary chore, undertaken not to offend. The honoured guest politely went through the motions. But from the first quiet handshake with Indian Prime Minister P.V. Narasimha Rao, it was obvious that the benefits are likely to accrue only in the long term.[13]

It was important to assure the visitor that Tibet belonged to China, and therefore, the Dalai Lama and his followers were kept out of sight.

Two years later, when Narasimha Rao visited China in September 1993, hoping to establish improved relations, the visit ended up in the signing of the 'Agreement on the Maintenance of Peace and Tranquility along the line of actual control in the India–China Border Areas,' and setting up a separate mechanism to resolve the long-standing dispute based on sectoral approach aimed at defusing tensions. Keeping in mind the intractable relations that had arisen since the 1962 War, the treaty was good enough to keep the peace to enable the two nations to grow trade relations and compete in the international marketplace.[14] But according to some observers:

> Prime Minister Narasimha Rao's 1993 visit complicated the border resolution by adding an additional military line to the PLA's advantage. Rao went back to the Nehru approach of minor territorial (sectoral) adjustments instead of a 'package deal' for border resolution. China responded by saying that the entire border should be called the Line of Actual Control, without prejudice to the border positions of the two sides.
>
> China told India that with the LAC in place, troops could be withdrawn sector-wise instead of waiting for the entire LAC and border agreements. The agreed sectors could then have 'mutual and equal security' as agreed by the two sides. The hand of the PLA was evident in the Chinese offer, while India—much like during the Nehru years—did not consult its army while making its border policy.[15]

The most disappointing part of the China visit was that once again, Narasimha Rao failed to meet with China's supreme leader Deng Xiaoping, who did not think much of him. In 1988, when he accompanied Rajiv Gandhi to China, he was dropped from the visit when Prime Minister Gandhi was invited to see the supreme leader.

The Rao administration took other small steps to improve trade and diplomatic relations, of which the most significant was the treaty with Nepal, the Mahakali Treaty for the generation of hydroelectricity and its export to India.[16] In 1995, along with other countries of the South Asian Association for Regional Cooperation (SAARC), India too signed the South Asian Preferential Trade Agreement (SAPTA) to promote mutual trade and economic cooperation within the SAARC region with the eventual goal of establishing a free trade zone.[17] In 1994, India initiated the establishment of several joint ventures with Sri Lanka and this new thrust of economic diplomacy continued.[18]

OPENING UP TO ISRAEL

One of the boldest decisions Narasimha Rao took was to establish full-fledged diplomatic relations with Israel in 1992, which was necessitated by the new dynamics of economic liberalization. But it wasn't an easy one because owing to its perpetually hostile relations with Pakistan since Independence, India's foreign policy had become tied up with the Arab–Muslim world and the Palestinian cause. In 1947, Albert Einstein wrote a letter to Jawaharlal Nehru pleading with him to recognize the Jewish state:

> It is time to make an end to the ghetto status of Jews in Palestine and to the pariah status of Jews among peoples. I trust that you, who so badly have struggled for freedom and justice, will place your great influence on behalf of the claim for justice made by the people who for so long and so dreadfully have suffered from its denial.[19]

Nehru's response, in spite of his admiration for Einstein whom he met at Princeton in 1949, was evasive and unconvincing. It was burdened by the existing political actualities of realpolitik, not enlightened non-alignment.[20]

Nehru did not realize that three Jewish intellectuals, including Albert Einstein, Karl Marx and Sigmund Freud, shaped what is called the modern era. Einstein deserved a more sympathetic response from Nehru.

Although the struggle for freedom and independence for Israel and India had different genesis and took different trajectories to achieve their goals, both nations had similar aspirations: they both sought global acceptance. Israel was created by a resolution of the UN on 29 November 1947; India was created by an act of bloody Partition of the subcontinent on 15 August 1947. India could have embraced Israel at the time, but it didn't because of the domestic situation and the need to establish functional relations with the Arab–Muslim world.

Nevertheless, India never gave up on Israel and kept the channel of communications open. In 1950 India recognized Israel without establishing full diplomatic relations except allowing Israel to set up a small consulate office in 1953 in Bombay to help the Indian Jews who wanted to migrate to Israel. In 1956 when Egyptian President Gamal Abdel Nasser nationalized the Suez Canal and Israel forces invaded Egypt, India, along with other nations, played a peacemaking role. Israeli foreign minister Moshe Sharett visited India during the Suez Canal crisis and the contacts established during the visit must have helped India in 1962 when the Chinese invasion put India in a vulnerable situation. When Jawaharlal Nehru wrote to Israeli Prime Minister Ben Gurion requesting arms and ammunition, Israel responded without hesitation. In the 1971 India–Pakistan–Bangladesh liberation war, once again, Israel came to India's rescue when Indira Gandhi asked Israeli Prime Minister Golda Meir for arms. The 1977 meeting between Foreign Minister Moshe Dayan and Prime Minister Morarji Desai in Delhi was another step towards deepening strategic relations.

In 1985 Rajiv Gandhi met with Israeli Prime Minister Shimon Peres in New York during the UNGA meeting, but India was not ready to establish full diplomatic relations with Israel because of its commitment to the Palestinian cause and its warm relations with Yasser Arafat, leader of the Palestine Liberation Organization (PLO).

On 19 January 1992, the Indian Council of World Affairs conferred upon Yasser Arafat a unique honour—the Indira Gandhi Award for International Justice and Harmony. The award citation praised his unparalleled 'fortitude, courage and sacrifices' for the cause of the Palestinian people as well as 'humanity itself.' Arafat had come to India to drum up support for the ongoing Mideast negotiation for the Palestinian cause but was asked during the press conference whether India's diplomatic relations with Israel would strengthen India's hand in advancing the cause of the peace. In spite of his strong reactions, he accepted that it was India's sovereign right to do so.[21] There was nothing haphazard about Narasimha Rao's foreign policies initiatives. Having assured Yasser Arafat and the PLO that India was an unwavering friend, he went ahead to establish full diplomatic relations with Israel, a country most Indians have never stopped admiring.

NARASIMHA RAO'S SONG AND DANCE WITH THE US

The 1990s was a decade of triumph for the Americans, which was feted in Francis Fukuyama's scholarly treatise *The End of History and the Last Man*, in which he argued that the end of the Cold War—the end of the Soviet experiment—was the culmination of mankind's ideological development and the final triumph of Western liberal democracy and its manifestation in the democratic form of government. Ironically India's liberal democracy, the federal-parliamentary form of government, encased in the state-controlled planned socialistic economy, had leaned heavily on the Soviet Union, the anchor that disappeared in December 1991, leaving democratic socialist India unmoored. India realized that in order to liberalize the economy and give it a new direction and momentum, the country needed to build bridges with the United States.[22] And when Narasimha Rao visited the US in June 1994, corporate America saw another market opening up. India had come out from the Soviet cold. But could India withstand and adopt the American freedom, its fierce democratic form of capitalism of the open and competitive marketplace, the crucible of American innovation?[23]

Narasimha Rao was the third Indian leader since Independence to address a rare joint session of the US Congress, and he made the most of it. It was a well-integrated and flawlessly delivered speech, during which Narasimha Rao brought together the ideals of the two nations in a framework that seemed as if they were natural allies. In sum, Rao said:

Christopher Columbus in search of India, stumbled upon America, remarking that 'the more you go east, the more you are assured to come upon the West'. But it was Thomas Jefferson who inspired India and 'we accepted these fundamental freedoms and looked to the Declaration of Independence and the Bill of Rights while formulating the constitution of the world's largest democracy', and thus sharing forever the spirit of America's Declaration of Independence and 'values of secularism, political pluralism and the rule of law', which moved Swami Vivekananda so much that he embodied it in a poem 'To The Fourth of July'.

Narasimha Rao then moved on to the global chain of ideas of non-violence as to how Henry David Thoreau, inspired by Indian philosophical thought, wrote his famous essay on 'Duty of Civil Disobedience', which influenced Mahatma Gandhi in South Africa, which influenced South African leader Nelson Mandela and later Martin Luther King Jr who wrote, 'Gandhi was probably the first person in history to lift the love ethic of Jesus above mere interaction between individuals to a powerful and effective social force on a large scale. It was in this Gandhian emphasis on love and non-violence that I discovered the method of social reform that I had been seeking for so many months.'[24] Narasimha Rao acknowledged India's debt to 'Franklin Delano Roosevelt for his role in pleading with the British for India's independence.'[25]

After this paean to India–US historical togetherness, Narasimha Rao came to the real purpose of his visit and began to pitch like a suave salesman assuring his audience that:

After decades of centralized economic policies, India recently embarked on a reform programme designed to modernize our economy, liberalize trade and realize our economic potential. We welcome private investment and competition and encourage free-market growth... India's vast domestic market, huge educated, skilled and semiskilled workforce, sound financial institutions and time-tested and democratic system offer tremendous investment opportunities for forward-looking companies.[26]

More than anything else, Americans love the open marketplace because trading goods means trading American ideas and values. So, he asked the US Congress to lower the trade barriers, especially in regard to dual technology because, 'Many special materials and complicated computer processes found in missile control systems are also found in hospital intensive care units and global telecommunications system'.[27]

India pivoted to the United States, never to turn back. Narasimha Rao must have had in mind Jammu and Kashmir as an integral part of India when he invoked Abraham Lincoln's first inaugural address on the 4 March 1861, in which Lincoln had said, 'the union of these states is perpetual. Perpetuity is implied, if not expressed, in the fundamental law of all national governments. It is safe to assert that no government proper ever had a provision in its organic law for its own termination. Physically speaking, we cannot separate this in connection with the so-called self-determination slogans that are being raised today'.[28]

He then quoted the US Supreme Court 1868 decision about Texas entering into an 'indissoluble relation. All the obligations of perpetual union and all the guarantees of republican government in the union attached at once to the state. It was the incorporation of a new member into the political body, and it was complete and final'. 'India,' said Narasimha Rao, 'accepts this statement as truly characteristic of a multicultural, multiethnic and multireligious republic like India or the United States and as totally unassailable... It is the responsibility of nations to preserve the life and liberty of all their citizens under the law, regardless of race, religion and ethnicity. We in India, like you here in this great democracy, are determined in our assertion that the rights of minority groups must be protected vigorously under the rule of law... The task that confronts democratic governments today is to maintain protection of human rights in the face of the most dangerous threat to the violation of human rights—namely, the bullets of terrorists'.[29]

COMMERCIAL DIPLOMACY

Narasimha Rao's US visit was essentially an enterprise in commercial diplomacy, which required presenting a new facade of India where the state and private sectors worked together. The Indian delegation, apart from Finance Minister Manmohan Singh, the pioneer of economic reforms, included some of India's top business and corporate heads. The economic, diplomatic group found it easy to communicate with American businesses led by the newly formed India Interest Group of American investors that included top corporate giants such as AT&T, Coca-Cola, IBM, General Electric and General Motors, among others. The group had the political support of senators and congressmen close to President Bill Clinton, for example, Senator Patrick Moynihan and Congressman Lee Hamilton.[30] With such meticulous preparations and goodwill on both sides, Narasimha Rao succeeded during his six-day visit in convincing his American hosts that India was entering the era of the marketplace economy that would welcome American investors. As a consequence of the visit and economic liberalization, the United States identified India as one of the 10 big emerging markets.

The Indian government set up a government–industry task force in order to establish a long-term strategy to facilitate trade and investment, which required not only working with the private sector but also with state governments explaining to them how the inflow of capital and technology would create jobs and enhance revenue. The impact of trade and capital inflow became visible in the following years. According to analysts, 'Inflows to India rose steadily through the 1990s, exceeding $6 billion in 1996–97. The fresh inflows were primarily as portfolio capital in the early years (that is, diversified equity holdings not associated with managerial control), but increasingly, they have come as foreign direct investment (equity investment associated with managerial control).'[31]

WAR AND PEACE AT HOME

Kashmiri militants kidnapped K. Doraiswamy, an executive director of the Indian Oil Corporation, in Srinagar on 28 June 1991. After spending 54 days in captivity, Doraiswamy was finally freed in exchange for nine terrorists. But when Israeli tourists, who were abducted by Muslim militants from their houseboat in Dal Lake in Srinagar on 26 June 1991, tried to escape from their captors, they ended up in a gun battle with the militants. One Israeli and two abductors were killed. Of the eight Israeli tourists, two were women who were released by the captors. Kashmiri militants, who demanded the release of their jailed companions, were still holding two Swedish engineers who were kidnapped in March.[32] In July 1995, a Kashmiri militant group Al Faran kidnapped six foreign hikers in exchange for the release of 20 militants, but the government turned down their demand in a reversal of its previous exchange practice. On 13 August, the beheaded body of one of the Norwegian hikers, Hans Christian Ostro, was discovered and later, the remaining hostages were given up as dead. The government soon faced another incident of kidnapping, but this time involving a diplomat, Liviu Radu, the Romanian charge d'affaires in India, who was kidnapped by the Khalistan Commando Force on 9 October 1991, but was released on 26 November. It was perhaps the last hurrah of the dying Khalistan movement.

On 23 April 1993, the second year of the Rao administration, India was riveted by another hijacking drama, the fourth hijacking in just three months. A gun-toting Islamic militant Mohammad Yusuf Shah hijacked a domestic flight Boeing 737 en route from New Delhi to Srinagar and threatened to kill 140 passengers one by one unless the jetliner was flown to Kabul after refuelling. The hijacker, a Kashmiri Muslim, claimed that he was the commander of Hizbul Mujahideen, one of the Pakistan-backed Islamic fundamentalist groups fighting for the freedom of Kashmir. Having been refused to land in Lahore, the plane landed in Amritsar, where the Indian Black Cats elite commandos of the National Security Guard stormed the plane, shot the hijacker with all the passengers and the crew safe.[33]

A most sensitive political-communal challenge was the occupation of the Hazratbal Mosque, the holy shrine that is believed to hold a hair of the Prophet Muhammad, in Srinagar, by Kashmiri militants in October 1993. After a siege of 14 days and protracted negotiations, the crisis ended when the militants, instead of being starved to death as the government had threatened, were given a safe passage out of the mosque.[34] It was an occasion for festivity for the Kashmiris, as an American journalist reported, 'Spirits rose over the weekend when Indian troops completed their pullback from 13 sandbagged bunkers that ringed the Hazratbal mosque in Srinagar... Muslims thronged the streets around the mosque and marched in celebration through Srinagar after senior Indian officials joined Muslim religious leaders in ceremonies that reopened the mosque to worshippers.'[35]

THE SACRILEGE OF BABRI MASJID

Narasimha Rao had no one of the calibre of Finance Minister Manmohan Singh to help him in the troublesome domestic affairs. The campaign of the BJP and the VHP, to build a Ram Temple at the Babri Masjid site in Ayodhya was timidly handled and perhaps based on political calculations, initially tolerated if not encouraged by Prime Minister Rajiv Gandhi. His successor V.P. Singh, on the other hand, had the campaign forcefully stopped and paid for it when the BJP withdrew its support and the V.P. Singh government collapsed like a castle of sand. But each confrontation at the Ayodhya Temple–Babri Masjid site strengthened the Hindu right and revitalized the political fortunes of the BJP.

For India, 6 December 1992, was a profoundly tragic day. For the BJP, it was a momentous day because this was the day when the BJP, the VHP and other Hindu organizations began their ceremonial beginning for building the temple, albeit symbolic only, as they had assured the authorities that no damage would be done to the mosque. At the head of a crowd of 150,000–200,000 were top Hindu religious and political leaders, including the future prime minister of India Atal Bihari Vajpayee, Lal Krishna Advani, Murli

Manohar Joshi and others. There were barriers around the disputed mosque protected by the police, but according to an eyewitness account of a journalist, some of the saffron headband-wearing Kar Sevaks (volunteers) broke through the barriers, clambered up the mosque's central dome and began hacking it away, while the police outnumbered and fearful, retreated; and 'stood by and watched', protecting themselves with their shields from the stone-throwing crowd.[36] The Uttar Pradesh Chief Minister Kalyan Singh of the BJP was naïve enough to imagine and believe that a police battalion wielding non-lethal weapons, batons and shields, would be able to control an emotional crowd of two hundred thousand high-strung youth, sadhus and their patron politicians. In politics, naiveté is complicity in the crime.

Since 1987, the Hindu collective imagination had been seized by two extraordinary TV programmes, Ramanand Sagar's 78-episode series the *Ramayan*, the series that had turned every household television set into a shrine and every restaurant television set into an agora; and later, in 1988–90, B.R. Chopra's 94-episode series the *Mahabharat*, the war of righteousness, where each episode began with the Hindu charioteer god Lord Krishna's verse from the Bhagavad Gita at the Kurukshetra battlefield. These two epic television series, whose stories children learnt in schools and every village and town street-theatres through Ramlila had a transformative effect upon the Hindu psyche. Indian secularism is like an icing on the cake. Under the charmingly attractive frosting of secularism, India is a majorly Hindu nation, as much as the United States is a majorly Christian nation, where minorities, especially Indians, do very well. The BJP measured the impact of the changing mode of consciousness by counting the number of parliamentary seats won during the following general elections.

To a vast majority of Hindus, the Babri Masjid in Ayodhya represents a sense of loss, the historical loss that could not be redeemed. Many secular Hindus have the same feeling of a sense of loss about the ancient university that was founded in 472 AD at Nalanda, the seat of learning associated with Aryabhata, Dharmakirti, Dharmapala, Nagarjuna, Xuanzang, Yijing and many others, which was completely destroyed by the Turkish Muslim invaders under Bakhtiyar Khilji in AD 1197. The reconstructive nostalgia about Nalanda's ancient scholarly glory as the centre of global learning is no different from the spiritual longings of the Hindus who want to reconstruct the ancient temple at Ayodhya.[37] Both have been driven by a deep sense of loss, the recovery of which, according to their protagonists, is possible and most desirable. Nobel laureate Amartya Sen's secular campaign to rebuild Nalanda and the Advani-led BJP–VHP campaign to rebuild the Ayodhya Ram Temple have the same psychological genesis: the sense of loss. The Somnath Temple—which was destroyed by the Turkish invader Mahmud of Ghazni in 1026, and later by other Muslim rulers—rebuilt on the orders of Home Minister Sardar Vallabhbhai Patel in 1951, was an attempt at recovery from the sense of loss.[38] What the religious imagination seizes as beauty becomes the truth, to paraphrase John Keats.

The consequences, however, of how a society deals with its collective sense of loss can have different and multiple impacts. In the case of Nalanda, an Act of Parliament, the Nalanda University Act of 2010, brought about a resolution and a beginning to recover the past, though the controversy would continue.[39] Parliament did not have the courage to face the Ayodhya Temple–Babri Masjid conundrum though the courts have been fumbling and muddling through it. From the times of Jawaharlal Nehru through Indira Gandhi, the Ayodhya–Babri Masjid controversy had remained dormant. The mode of consciousness began to change during the times of Rajiv Gandhi when Indian society became increasingly fractious, on which the BJP capitalized by offering an alternative vision of India, one united under its umbrella, one reinforced by the Bollywood generated mythical visions of the Ramayana and Mahabharata.

Prime Minister Narasimha Rao inherited the Ayodhya Temple–Babri Masjid problem from Rajiv Gandhi and V.P. Singh; as he had inherited from them the economic problems, which he solved with extraordinary courage and initiative, putting India on an irreversible path of economic progress. Economic transformation necessitated new initiatives in foreign policy that broadened India's network of international alliances, which in turn fed into economic development, technology transfer and new areas of growth. But why couldn't Narasimha Rao, one of the shrewdest and smartest politicians of his time, foresee the brewing trouble at Ayodhya and outsmart and preempt the motley BJP–VHP crowd? Did his association with Hindu sadhus and godmen cloud his political judgement?

According to his biographer Vinay Sitapati, Narasimha Rao was cognizant of the dangers and options available to him to deal with the situation.[40] Madhav Godbole, the home secretary, prepared 'a secret contingency plan', containing 'the modalities for Central forces to take control of the mosque'. The plan specified that Article 356, the imposition of president's rule on a non-functional state, might have to be invoked. There would be danger to the security of the Ram Janmabhoomi–Babri Masjid structure for 'a period of a few hours when the structure would be quite vulnerable'.[41] Ground realities would prevent any failsafe operative plan to avoid destructive eventualities. The Intelligence Bureau reports had warned of the serious preparation being made to 'blow up the mosque on 6 December'.[42] But Narasimha Rao was conflicted as to the constitutional propriety of invoking Article 356, asking his secretary P.V.R.K. Prasad, 'How could a democratically elected Government be dismissed as a precautionary measure without any valid reason? Would it be constitutional? Won't we attract the odium of having resorted to a blatantly unconstitutional act?'[43]

Nor had he the support of the Cabinet Committee for Political Affairs (CCPA) to dismiss the BJP state government in Uttar Pradesh led by Kalyan Singh (who was as trustworthy as a fox guarding the henhouse) to impose president's rule. Without any support from his cabinet colleagues and the Congress party high command and apprehensive about the constitutionality of dismissing the government for an anticipatory catastrophic event, he turned to negotiations with the Hindu organizations in order to persuade them to leave the Babri Masjid alone, hoping that being a Hindu Brahmin had put him the same spiritual wavelength as the sants, mahants, sadhus and astrologers. In November 1992, he held discussions with the BJP leadership including L.K. Advani, Atal Bihari Vajpayee and Kalyan Singh seeking and getting assurances from them that the Babri Masjid would be left untouched.

But these leaders, whose fire and brimstone-scorching rhetoric had radicalized the Hindu zealots—a massive milling crowd of hundreds of thousands who had surrounded the Babri precincts—were unable to hold back the crowd; and very soon one karsevak clambered up the dome, and then another, and then another, until the heinous deed was done. The police retreated in the face of the conflagration. The Rapid Action Force was nowhere in sight. Here is a look-back, reflective, eyewitness account of journalist Sajeda Momin:

> [T]housands of saffron-clad 'kar sevaks' clambering atop the sixteenth-century mosque...what did bring tears to my eyes was the room full of petrified Muslims at Ayodhya Police Station, not knowing whether they would get out of there alive—this was the human face of what the Mosque's demolition meant to me... but today's India is beyond tears.[44]

Law and order fall under a state's jurisdiction; nevertheless, national security is the Government of India's responsibility. The Centre never hesitated to send the armed forces to control insurgencies in Nagaland, Mizoram, Punjab, Jammu and Kashmir and the Naxalite-infested areas. Calling up the army to safeguard the Babri Masjid precincts would have been an extreme option, a compelling necessity. Narasimha Rao was a smart, erudite man but not a bold, confrontational politician. He was too timid to take an audacious action, such as dismissing the state government or sending a deterrent force. Narasimha Rao was no Indira Gandhi, who could have protected the monument any which way in spite of her strong Hindu identity.

The winds of communal hate ignited by the Babri Masjid destruction fanned the flames far and wide, the flames of avenge and revenge leaping to other communal tinderboxes, especially Mumbai. Large-scale protests by Muslims, which were initially peaceful but eventually spun out of control and turned violent, were in reaction to the Babri Masjid demolition. From 6 December 1992 through 20 January 1993 the Hindu–Muslim riots killed 900, mostly Muslims. The violence in Mumbai was reported as having been pre-planned and carried out by the Shiv Sena, a Hindu-nationalist political party in Maharashtra.[45] The government response to the riots, as usually happens in India, was to appoint an inquiry commission. The findings and recommendations of Justice B.N. Srikrishna of the Bombay High Court submitted in 1998, were found to be politically motivated and therefore unacceptable by the Shiv Sena government of Manohar Joshi.[46] Hardly anyone was prosecuted or punished.[47] Justice denied led to further terrorism.

Until the 1993 Mumbai bombings, most Indians had never heard of Dawood Ibrahim, leader of the Mumbai-based international organized crime syndicate, the D-Company. Like the chief executive of a global corporation, Dawood Ibrahim coordinated a series of 12 bomb explosions in Mumbai on 12 March 1993.[48] The blasts covered entire Mumbai, 'the Maximum City', including the Bombay Stock Exchange Building, Fisherman's Colony in Mahim Causeway, Zaveri Bazaar, Plaza Cinema, Century Bazaar, Katha Bazaar, Hotel Sea Rock, Terminal at Sahar Airport (now Chhatrapati Shivaji International Airport), Air India Building, Hotel Juhu Centaur, Worli Passport Office and Masjid–Mandvi Corporation Bank Branch. The serial bomb blasts, carried out in a single day in revenge for the post-Ayodhya Bombay riots, were one of the most unique events in the history of global terrorism. Nothing of this kind had ever happened, not even during the horrific days of the partition of India. By the end of the day, 257 people were dead and 710 injured. Today, Dawood Ibrahim reportedly lives in a Pakistan sanctuary city, from where he carries on his global operations. Some of his henchmen have been prosecuted and jailed in India. One of the perpetrators, Yakub Memon, was sentenced to death.[49] As of today, some top gangsters including, Dawood Ibrahim and Tiger Memon, have not been arrested.

As a historian, I could not but admire the entire well-coordinated military-style operation carried out by a non-state actor that shook up India. But India never learns from its history. It would happen again on 26 November 2008, a seaborne terrorist attack that the whole world would witness from the luxury of their living room TV sets. Nonetheless, from a historical perspective, the 6 December 1992, Ram Janmabhoomi–Babri Masjid conflagration was not a turning point; nor was it a political game-changer. It simply fell into the pattern of Indian history where firestorms occur and are done with, much like the California fires that happen periodically and are gone. In 1994, Narasimha Rao visited the US, and after his highly acclaimed address to the joint session of the US Congress, President Bill Clinton and Narasimha Rao held a press conference, during which not a single reporter asked any question about the Babri Masjid or the Mumbai bomb blasts. India has a tremendous capacity to suffer pain and humiliation, thanks to the power of its historical amnesia.

THE WAY IT ALL ENDED

In a short period of just two years, it seemed Narasimha Rao had turned everyone into his enemy. There were serious allegations of corruption against him. The miscalculation and poor handling of the Babri Masjid controversy that turned into a bloody disaster had cleaved an unbridgeable chasm between Muslims and Hindus. His economic revival plan was deemed as a sell-off to capitalists and the betrayal of democratic socialism. Narasimha Rao was never so vulnerable. His party, the Congress (I), had no parliamentary majority. Nor did the prime minister have a countrywide populist constituency that he could appeal to for support. A sense of paralysis had overtaken the country in spite of the fact that economic reforms had begun to pay dividends.

The opposition, although fractured and disunited, saw a definitive opportunity to topple his government through a no-confidence motion, one of the many ways India plays the game of democracy. The opposition, the Right-wing Hindutva Bharatiya Janata Party and the Left socialist parties led by the CPI(M), tabled a no-confidence motion on 25 July 1993, charging Narasimha Rao with incompetence, corruption and failure to help the poor and needy. He was accused of clandestinely collaborating with Hindu fanatics and fundamentalists for the destruction of Babri Masjid. The government was criticized for its tardy response to the floods in July 1993 that killed hundreds of people in several states. A Mumbai stockbroker, Harshad Mehta, claimed that he had personally given ₹10 million to Narasimha Rao, which, of course, the prime minister denied. In response to the no-confidence motion, Narasimha Rao defended his economic policies that had saved the country from economic disaster without however agonizing over the charge of corruption. After three days of acrimonious debate, the Narasimha Rao government defeated the no-confidence motion with a vote of 265 to 251, a surprising victory.[50] The victory nonetheless did not stop the opposition from charging him with vote-buying fraud, the charge that was pursued under a Public Interest Litigation (PIL) lawsuit in February 1996 by the Rashtriya Mukti Morcha.[51] The PIL was based on a public confession made on 26 February 1996 by a BJP MP, Shailendra Mahato, who said that he and three other MPs were given ₹40 lakh individually in July 1993 to rescue the Narasimha Rao government.[52]

At that time, all the four plaintiffs belonged to the Jharkhand Mukti Morcha. The case lingered on and ran its own course and haunted Narasimha Rao even after he stepped down as the prime minister, and for which, in fact, he was sentenced to jail for three years.[53] In 2002, the Delhi High Court reversed the lower court's decision due to the lack of credibility of the main witness, Shailendra Mahato. Both Narasimha Rao and his co-accused Buta Singh were found not guilty.

There were two other cases against him, one regarding a forgery in which Narasimha Rao, along with his associates K.K. Tewary, godman Chandraswami and K.N. Aggarwal, were indicted for forging documents that showed that Ajeya Singh, son of former Prime Minister V.P. Singh, had opened an authorized bank account in the First Trust Corporation Bank in St. Kitts, a Caribbean Island nation, and deposited US$21 million in his father V.P. Singh's name as the beneficiary.[54] The forgery charge was made to sully V.P. Singh's reputation and although it occurred in 1989, the Central Bureau of Investigation did not take up the case until after Rao had stepped down as the prime minister in 1996. The other case was based on charges laid by an Indian-British businessman Lakhubhai Pathak that Narasimha Rao, along with Chandraswami and K.N. Aggarwal, had cheated him of US$100,000, the amount he had given them in exchange for allowing him to get paper pulp in India. Eventually, both the cases were dropped due to a lack of evidence.

During the five years of continuous political turmoil, India moved from one crisis to another, some resolved, others worsened. When India went for the 1996 general election, the people had forgotten Narasimha Rao's achievements, especially in economic development and foreign relations, which had transformed the country. They remembered the pain and the sufferings of Babri Masjid; and the riots, bombings, hijacking, kidnapping and rising prices. The Indian electorate voted Narasimha Rao and the Congress (I) out of power. Five years is a long period for an open democratic society where people's rising expectations for social justice, law and order, peace and prosperity must be met. Narasimha Rao had not been able to generate an overarching captivating vision of India, a new narrative in which Indians, all Indians, could believe. Narasimha Rao, in many ways, was a clever politician, but he was more of a skilled chess player rather than a man of the people, someone who could feel their pulse and touch their hearts. A scholar who could speak many languages, he lacked empathy and imagination. He spoke, but the Indian masses could not hear him. He felt more comfortable in the company of sadhus, sants and astrologers than with the dreamers, the aspirational Indian youth.

In his unhappy retirement, Narasimha Rao tried to salvage his diminished reputation by writing an autobiographical novel, *The Insider*, apart from fighting lawsuits against the long-simmering charges of bribery and corruption. None of the charges was proved and Rao was absolved. Narasimha Rao died a free man. Some of his contemporaries who knew him intimately thought that he was a beautiful person. On Narasimha Rao's ninety-first birthday, former External Affairs Minister K. Natwar Singh summed up his life exquisitely:

> Jawaharlal Nehru and P.V. Narasimha Rao do not have much in common except that both were intellectuals. P.V. Narasimha Rao... came from a humble home. His intellectual centre was India. Unlike Nehru, his knowledge of Sanskrit was profound... His roots were deep in the spiritual and religious soil of India. He did not need to Discover India.[55]

So tolled the bell for the man who showed India an alternative path of economic progress and political possibilities, reinforced the concept of 'India Constant' by fighting terrorism, and ushered in new diplomatic initiatives to raise India's global profile. His shortcomings and failures were many; nonetheless, as the Bard said, 'the good men do is oft interred with their bones.' The ungrateful Congress leadership, instead of performing the *antim sanskar* [last rites] in Delhi, Narasimha Rao's *karmabhoomi,* sent the *mrit sharir* [earthly remains] of the scholar-politician, the erudite multilinguist southern Brahmin, to be cremated in Hyderabad.[56]

PART THREE

As the Millennium Turned

ATAL BIHARI VAJPAYEE TAKES THE BULL BY THE HORNS

If India is not secular, then India is not India at all.

—Atal Bihari Vajpayee

*I am Hindu... However, my Hindutva is not constricted,
it is not narrow.*

—Atal Bihari Vajpayee

Atal Bihari Vajpayee, regardless of his public persona and 'inclusive' rhetoric, made possible the rise of Narendra Modi as the undisputed leader of the world's largest democracy. Through trials and errors and fire-and-brimstone nationalistic rhetoric, Vajpayee and the Bharatiya Janata Party (BJP) learned the political ropes—ways to bend and stand firm so that a coalition government could work successfully in the fragmented, motley, kaleidoscopic polity of India. Vajpayee was the first Indian politician outside the Indian National Congress (INC) who served for a full five-year term as the prime minister. A founding member of the BJP in 1980, he had been a leader of the Jana Sangh, the BJP's predecessor, and a long-time parliamentarian from Uttar Pradesh. He was minister for external affairs in the post-Emergency Janata Party cabinet of Prime Minister Morarji Desai (1977–79). A passionate orator, a Hindi poet, sometimes a populist rabble-rouser, given to grand theatrical gestures, Vajpayee had the gumption to address the UNGA in 1977 in Hindi, the first Indian politician to do so.[1]

By becoming the fierce political face and strident voice of the Ram Janmabhoomi Mandir movement in Ayodhya, where a dilapidated early Mughal-era mosque stood on the ancient site, Vajpayee and the BJP attempted to unabashedly assert the supremacy of India as an ancient Hindu civilization, from which the elite Indians had timidly shied away under the lovey-dovey secularism of the INC since the times of Nehru.[2] The BJP made political fortunes out of the Ram Janmabhoomi Mandir movement and broadened its political catchment area and its electoral base that eventually helped to establish the two-party coalition-based system in India.

POLITICAL MERRY-GO-ROUND

In 1996, when Indians went to the general election to elect the 11th Lok Sabha (the Lower House) members, the cauldron of political coalitions had begun to churn around two major parties, the Congress (I) and the BJP. The election was fought in the background of the sound and fury that erupted after the Ram Janmabhoomi Mandir movement's direct action at the Ayodhya Babri Masjid, Pakistan-supported militancy in Kashmir and ethnic violence in Punjab. Since the chances of a single political party winning a majority in the 545-member House seemed remote in the general election, the two major all-India parties, the Congress (I) and the BJP, began to seek alliances with regional parties based on ideological kinship, minimum commonly agreed programme, power-sharing or whatever horse-trading would work to win the electoral seats to form the government.

The third all-India political grouping was formed by the National Front (NF) and the Left Front (LF), who, too, sought to build coalitions with regional and state parties. There were 21 regional and state parties in the fray. The election result threw up a hung Parliament, with the BJP winning 161, the Congress (I) 140, and the NF/LF 131 seats.[3] The regional and state parties nibbled into the political territorial map of the national parties and consequently 'the fragmentation of seats among a large number of diverse regional and state-level parties' ushered in a 'period of unstable coalition governments, creating an air of political and economic uncertainty' as the nation entered 'the post-Congress era', of 'region-based multiparty system' that would give the BJP and the Congress the challenge of governance at the Centre as well as in the states.[4] In many different ways, the competitive multiparty system of coalition forming in the states was mirrored in the political fragmentation at the Centre, which Vajpayee managed adroitly when he became prime minister for a full five-year term (1999–2004).[5] But most importantly, it was during Vajpayee's earlier 13-month brief stint as prime minister (1998–99) that India transformed itself politically, economically and militarily, and found a new space in international affairs.

As the 1996 general election produced no clear mandate for any national party, the BJP being the largest single party was invited by President Shankar Dayal Sharma to form a government, as the established parliamentary traditions and practices mandated. It was asked to prove its majority in the Lok Sabha within two weeks. Because of the BJP's alleged association with the Ayodhya Temple–Babri Masjid 1992 riots and its extremist nationalistic ideology, the parties and its allies could muster the backing of only 196–200 parliamentarians against the 273 needed. Instead of facing defeat on the floor of the House, Vajpayee resigned. But he did so only after a stormy debate, in which the party was accused of damaging the secular foundation of the country that the Nehru generation had built. The Congress was the second-largest party, but it declined to form the government and instead supported the NF-led 13-party coalition government headed by H.D. Deve Gowda, the Janata Dal chief minister of the southern state of Karnataka. He was the second South Indian politician, after P.V. Narasimha Rao, to head a Union Government, becoming the 11th prime minister of India on 1 June 1996. However, because of the internal contradictions and his inability to deal with differences with coalition partners, the Deve Gowda government collapsed on 21 April 1997, when the Congress withdrew its support.

The United Front, once again with the support of the Congress, elected Inder Kumar Gujral of the Janata Dal to form the government on 21 April 1997. Gujral was a seasoned politician who, earlier as a member of the Congress, had worked in the cabinet of Indira Gandhi as minister for Information and Broadcasting during the emergency interregnum; he had resigned due to disagreement with Sanjay Gandhi over the issue of media censorship. Later on, he was sent to the Soviet Union as an ambassador. In the 1980s, Gujral broke away from the Congress, joined the Janata Dal, and worked as minister of external affairs in Prime Minister V.P. Singh's cabinet (1989–90). In the 11-month administration of Prime Minister Deve Gowda too, Gujral held the same portfolio, external affairs, during which he developed the now forgotten 'The Gujral Doctrine', of establishing good neighbourly relations, especially with Nepal, Bangladesh, Bhutan, Maldives and Sri Lanka, as a counterweight to the Pakistan–China axis. The policy was based on the rationale that 'since we had to face two hostile neighbours in the north and the west, we had to be at "total peace" with all other immediate neighbours in order to contain Pakistan's and China's influence in the region.'[6]

But working out a foreign policy doctrine was different from working with coalition partners, some of whom had dubious credentials and wanted to use their political position as leverage for personal gains or getting out of legal troubles and criminal pasts. One of the supporters of Gujral was the Bihar Janata Party leader, Lalu Prasad Yadav, an example of the 'criminal-as-politician' in India. Yadav, as the chief minister of Bihar, the poorest state in India, was the prime mover and benefactor of the Fodder Scam, an embezzlement scheme involving the theft of ₹9.4 billion from the Bihar State Treasury. The embezzlement did not occur overnight; rather, it was spread over a period of 20 years, and the funds were stolen from the agricultural support programmes for poor farmers.

Chaperoned by Yadav, a populist rabble-rouser with an atrocious sense of humour, Bihar's politicians and senior officials generated fictitious livestock herds' accounts and credited them with amounts meant for fodder, animal husbandry and sundry farm equipment. Besides being the political boss of Bihar, Yadav was also the president of the Janata Party, the largest component of the NF and the main supporter of Prime Minister Gujral.[7] Based on prima facie evidence, the Central Bureau of Investigation (CBI) sought and received authorization from the Bihar State Governor A.R. Kidwai to prosecute Yadav and his accomplices. The case was so blatant that several NF leaders called for action against Yadav and asked him to resign. Gujral, instead of taking action against his criminal-supporter Yadav, transferred CBI Director Joginder Singh and replaced him with R.C. Sharma, who was asked to go easy on the case.[8] But Gujral's manoeuvre did not help Yadav, who, after being expelled from the Janata Dal, formed his own party, the Rashtriya Janata Dal, in 1997.

Gujral's NF coalition government recommended President K.R. Narayanan to dismiss the BJP government in Uttar Pradesh and impose the president's direct rule under Article 356 of the Constitution. In an unusual step, President Narayanan declined to accept the recommendation and sent it back to the government for reconsideration. When the Allahabad High Court took up the case, it too ruled against the Gujral government and termed the imposition of president's rule unconstitutional.[9] As the constitutional head of the republic, the president of India has the power to say no to a government proposal that he deems unconstitutional, which reinforces the democratic checks-and-balances system, further buttressed by an independent judiciary. This presidential power was also available even before Indira Gandhi imposed the Emergency, but it wasn't exercised. Nonetheless, the Uttar Pradesh affair also showed how unstable a coalition government could be and raised questions about whether law and order and economic progress could be maintained in the absence of political stability.

But the NF–Gujral government came undone because of the report of the Jain Commission that was set up to investigate the conspiracy regarding the assassination of Rajiv Gandhi. A 26-year-old female operative of Sri Lanka's terrorist organization, the Liberation Tigers of Tamil Eelam (LTTE), had killed Rajiv Gandhi in May 1991 at a political election rally in Tamil Nadu. The Jain Commission report, submitted to the government on 27 August

1997 and subsequently leaked to the media, alleged the involvement of the Dravida Munnetra Kazhagam (DMK) as well as the party boss Muthuvel Karunanidhi in supporting the LTTE. The DMK was part of the ruling NF coalition and the Gujral government, but it also had the support of the Congress from the outside. On 20 November, the Jain Commission report was presented to the Lok Sabha, and amidst heated exchanges, the Congress demanded the dismissal of the DMK cabinet ministers. Prime Minister Gujral refused to fire his DMK cabinet ministers, which led to the withdrawal of the Congress support for the NF government, leading to Gujral's resignation on 28 November 1997.[10]

Paying tribute to his former colleague, Pranab Mukherjee, India's former president wrote in his memoir that Gujral, in spite of the political instability created by a hodgepodge coalition, refused to be pressured by the Congress and 'left the office of the prime minister with his head held high'. [11]

Nonetheless, Gujral left the nation's head in the doldrums. This was India's third government in eighteen months since the 1996 Lok Sabha general election had thrown up a splintered and disjointed parliament to govern the nation of almost a billion people struggling to get out of poverty, crime, violence and corruption. But it also showed that India's political dynamism and vitality would come from its federal pluralism, the system where the states strengthen the Centre, and they are in turn strengthened by it.

This was the year of the golden jubilee of Independence, but what a 'tryst with destiny!' Self-seeking politicians turned India's tryst with destiny into a travesty! India had descended from Nehru's vision of a united country on the path to everlasting progress to a country of political chaos and economic wilderness. Although the Indian Armed Forces wisely kept away from politics, the business and industry associations had the courage to raise their voice in dismay and frustration, asking the politicians to shutter the unseemly revolving door 'political drama' and end the 'political expediency and competitive populism', which was 'draining business confidence and pushing the economy backward'.[12] The two-year-long political instability also made it clear that to keep the heterogeneous country in a state of dynamic equilibrium, India would need a leader with mass appeal and strong organizational abilities such as Jawaharlal Nehru or Indira Gandhi; or someone politically Machiavellian to form coalitions and hold them together.

For weak politicians such as Deve Gowda or Gujral—regardless of their high personal values and sense of morality—to become a failed prime minister was a crime against India. There's no forgiveness in history. India cannot survive merely as an idea. Nation-building is an unending process, a massive challenge, especially when it has to be built with the building blocks of democratic freedoms.

President Narayanan, instead of following the path of least resistance and asking someone of the stature of Sitaram Kesri of the Congress to try his hand at another merry-go-round, announced the general election to be held in 1998. But the election results were once again indecisive, with the BJP-led coalition, the National Democratic Alliance (NDA), gaining 254 seats and the Congress and allies winning only 144 seats. Nonetheless, with the support of the AIADMK, the BJP-led NDA formed the government with Vajpayee as the prime minister again. The coalition government lasted hardly more than a year because the AIADMK, under the leadership of Tamil Nadu's Chief Minister J. Jayalalithaa, withdrew its support and the Vajpayee government fell by just one vote short (272–273) in a vote of no-confidence in the Lok Sabha on 17 April 1999.

A BRIEF BUT SIGNIFICANT STINT OF THE VAJPAYEE GOVERNMENT

Although short-lived, Vajpayee's BJP–NDA's 13-month rule was historic for the country. For one, Prime Minister Vajpayee took a bus journey to meet with Pakistan Prime Minister Nawaz Sharif, which resulted in the Lahore Declaration for a peaceful resolution of disputes and good neighbourly coexistence. Ironically, and more importantly, while the Vajpayee–Sharif diplomatic dialogue was going on in Lahore, General Pervez Musharraf, chief of the Pakistan Army, was preparing for the Kargil War, apparently without the knowledge and explicit approval of the civilian government.

India would learn, though not for the first time, that two parallel governments were operating Pakistan—the civilian and the military, with the latter having the upper hand. The Lahore Declaration was lost in the fog of the Kargil War.

The second historic moment was when India conducted a series of five nuclear bomb tests in the Thar Desert of Rajasthan at the Pokhran Test Range. This memorable event took place in May 1998, two months after Vajpayee took over as prime minister. The first underground nuclear test was conducted in 1974 when Indira Gandhi was the prime minister. Under her leadership, the nuclear explosion or 'implosion' was code-named the 'Smiling Buddha', indeed, an inappropriate and ill-chosen name, which now is called Pokhran I. Under Vajpayee, the 11–13 May 1998 nuclear tests were fittingly called 'Operation Shakti', the primordial cosmic energy associated with Shiva, the god of creative destruction.[13]

Even before Independence, Indian scientists—nuclear physicist Homi Bhabha and others—had begun to take an active interest in building the infrastructure for nuclear energy research. Thanks to their efforts, the Tata Institute of Fundamental Research was established in 1945 in Bombay. The Government of India, under the authority of the Atomic Energy Commission, established the Bhabha Atomic Research Centre in Bombay in 1954, with the avowed goal of developing peaceful applications of nuclear energy for power generation, under which several nuclear reactors were set up.

In the aftermath of the Himalayan debacle in 1962 and China's entry into the nuclear club in 1966, India couldn't have let itself fall behind and live under China's nuclear shadow, especially after Indira Gandhi became the prime minister. Besides, there was Pakistan's clandestine nuclear bomb programme that Zulfikar Bhutto, Pakistan's prime minister (1973–77), had vowed to pursue subsequent to the breakup of the country after the Bangladesh Liberation War of 1971. Although there was a pause in the nuclear programme development and testing due to international pressure, the programme never went into a deep freeze. Prime Minister Narasimha Rao was on the verge of conducting a nuclear test in 1995, but after American spy satellites spotted testing preparation at the Pokhran Testing Range, US President Bill Clinton put immense diplomatic pressure on India to scuttle the testing plan.

India was passing through dire financial straits, the forex level had hit rock bottom, and it needed international aid in overcoming the crisis. Ties between Pakistan and India had touched another periodic low and Pakistan was once again raising the Kashmir issue with the UN. Coming under extreme pressure, Prime Minister Rao froze the nuclear test plan.

BEING A NUCLEAR POWER

By the time Indian scientists conducted the Pokhran II tests, India had acquired the knowledge and technology to develop not only nuclear fuel for power generation but also to weaponize it for its Integrated Guided Missile Development Programme under the leadership of aerospace engineer A.P.J. Abdul Kalam, who would later become the president of India (2002–2007).[14] After the completion of the Shakti I–V Pokhran II tests, Prime Minister Vajpayee, addressing the media at the lawns of his official residence, said in a matter-of-fact tone, 'India conducted three underground nuclear tests in the Pokhran range...with a fission device, a low yield device and a thermonuclear device. The measured yields...in line with expected values...have also confirmed that there was no release of radioactivity into the atmosphere. These were contained explosions like the experiment conducted in May 1974.' [15]

Unlike in 1995, when US surveillance spy satellites spotted nuclear preparedness in the Rajasthan desert testing ground and India was pressured to halt the test, this time the CIA failed to fully grasp the import of the upsurge in activities in the Indian desert, beamed down by the US 'photo-reconnaissance and electronic eavesdropping satellites' to the agency's intelligence gatherers and readers.[16] The US spy satellites functioned flawlessly, but they saw what they were programmed to see. Political ground realities had changed. India had a different government, stridently nationalistic; one committed to break out of the big power imposed nuclear isolation and join the nuclear club.

It's doubtful whether anything would have stopped India from weaponizing its nuclear programme. India saw its destiny as being a global power. As Francine Frankel, director of the Centre for the Advanced Study of India at the University of Pennsylvania, putting the American dilemma in perspective, said, 'We are now faced with a question of whether we want to have a hostile relationship with India.'[17]

The United States condemned India's action and, under the 1978 Nuclear Non-Proliferation Act, the Clinton Administration imposed economic sanctions, including a ban on defence equipment and technologies' sales, and restricted access to US credit and financial institutions. Japan, along with some other nations, too imposed limited economic sanctions by freezing future loans and grants as well as suspending foreign aid and government-to-government credit lines. The sanctions impacted defence-related research and development laboratories, public and private companies, research institutes, Indian and US corporations engaged in joint research and defence-related scientists visiting the United States. US high-tech companies doing business with India were also impacted. Although not negligible, the sanctions were not unbearable.[18] The sanctions were eventually lifted in 2001 under President George W. Bush, which was a turning point in India–US relations.

IT'S FOR CHINA, STUPID!

A week before the underground nuclear tests, India's Defence Minister George Fernandes, on a national television programme, called China India's 'potential enemy No. 1'. The undiplomatically expressed views by a top government minister shook up the timid foreign policy establishment and unsettled China, but as a media expert in security and foreign affairs observed, 'Since the early '80s, the Ministry of Defence annual reports have been guardedly articulating the view that China was India's most potent threat', and therefore foregrounding 'national security before foreign policy, Fernandes was applying a long-overdue corrective which the BJP has been publicly demanding for quite some time;' and perhaps the socialist defence minister was '"articulating the silent majority's" views on national security.'[19] Not only the 'silent majority', but also the Ministry of Defence reports, 1985 through 1997, offered similar analysis about China's duplicitous game. Apart from improving its logistics in Tibet and overall military modernization programme, including nuclear arsenal and missile development, it has been helping Pakistan to acquire advanced weapons systems, which would add to regional tensions.[20] The views of Defence Minister Fernandes, albeit undiplomatically uttered, were more clearly expressed by Prime Minister Vajpayee in his letter to President Bill Clinton in which he explained India's rationale for going nuclear, while at the same time assuring him that India would continue to work with the United States in a 'multilateral or bilateral framework to promote the cause of nuclear disarmament', and affirming India's 'commitment to participate in non-discriminatory and verifiable global disarmament measures.' Nevertheless, Vajpayee gave a final admonishment about China helping Pakistan to become 'a covert nuclear state':

> At the hands of this bitter neighbour (Pakistan) we have suffered three aggressions in the last 50 years. And for the last ten years we have been the victim of unremitting terrorism and militancy sponsored by it in several parts of our country, especially Punjab and Jammu & Kashmir.[21]

Two weeks after India's Pokhran II tests, Pakistan too carried out its own underground nuclear tests code-named Chagai-I and Chagai-II, six in all, which received condemnation from the United States and the international community fearing the nuclear race in South Asia was on. But before the Chagai tests, Pakistan vociferously condemned India's perfidy and instead of cowering in fear, Defence Minister Ayub Khan said, 'We are in a headlong arms race...' and vowed to match India in every aspect. It was a livid gut reaction that was affirmed by Prime Minister Nawaz Sharif, who said, 'We are watching the situation and we will take appropriate action with regard to our security.'[22]

In 1967, three years after China exploded its first nuclear device and gatecrashed into the exclusive nuclear club consisting of the United States, Russia, France and the United Kingdom, the UN Committee on Disarmament negotiated the Treaty on the Non-Proliferation of Nuclear Weapons (NPT) to prevent non-nuclear states from acquiring such weapons and with the further aim of promoting peaceful uses of nuclear energy and achieving nuclear disarmament. Although Pakistan and Israel had their own reasons for not signing the NPT, India considered the treaty discriminatory, creating 'nuclear haves' and 'nuclear have-nots' and refused to be relegated into a 'nuclear apartheid'.[23] The five exempted nuclear states under the NPT have not lived up to their 'disarmament commitment...to put a permanent ban on nuclear-weapon testing in place... (Although) the Comprehensive Test Ban Treaty (CTBT) was finally opened for signature in 1996...it is unlikely to come into force in the foreseeable future (because) the political value of nuclear weapons remains as high as it was during the Cold War.'[24]

Twenty years after the underground nuclear explosion, India once again celebrated its nuclear state status in a 2018 Bollywood movie, *Parmanu: The Story of Pokhran*, which, according to its actor-protagonist John Abraham, is 'an ode to the Army and scientists, who although ordinary people, truly accomplished extraordinary feats in the face of adversity to ensure that India finds its due place on the world nuclear map'.[25]

THE BUS TO LAHORE THAT WENT NOWHERE

On 20 February 1999, less than a year before the two countries rattled the world with their underground nuclear explosions, Vajpayee disembarked from the Delhi–Lahore Bus, euphemistically named 'Sada-e-Sarhad' (Urdu: The sound of music of goodwill from the frontier) on Pakistani soil across the Wagah border that Cyril Radcliffe had drawn on the map to split India. Vajpayee said to a beaming Sharif that 'It is with a sense of elation that I find myself on Pakistani soil after a gap of 21 years...I bring the good wishes and hopes of my fellow countrymen who seek abiding peace and harmony with Pakistan...'[26]

On such occasions, poetic eloquence never escaped Vajpayee, who promised his Pakistani host to carry out discussions on all unresolved issues, including Jammu and Kashmir, cautioning, however, that the 'solution of complex, outstanding issues can only be sought in an atmosphere free from prejudice and by adopting the *path of balance, moderation and realism* [emphasis added].' [27]

In a celebratory atmosphere of the sound of band music, the Indian Border Security Force and the Pakistan Rangers turned their traditional in-your-face mock performance into a spectacle of joy. The Wagah to Lahore road was festooned and adorned in the splendour of the Pakistan national flag. 'Welcome Vajpayee' read the flag-draped trees and the road signs. A visiting foreign journalist gushed, 'By crossing the border in a bus, Prime Minister Vajpayee achieved what the Indian Army could not do with all its might in the 1965 war.' [28] Indian celebrities in that journey included film actor Dev Anand, Shatrughan Sinha, danseuse Mallika Sarabhai, journalist Arun Shourie, Urdu poet Javed Akhtar, painter-sculptor Satish Gujral, journalist Kuldip Nayar and captain of the Indian team that won the 1983 Cricket World Cup, Kapil Dev. To make the high-power diplomatic visit a friendly and homey affair, the bachelor prime minister also took his family with him, including his adopted daughter Namita, her husband Ranjan Bhattacharya, and granddaughter Niharika. It seemed as if they were going on a family reunion to reclaim their long-lost relatives.

While the band played on and the hearts prayed for peace between the nuclear neighbours, Pakistan Army Chief General Pervez Musharraf was surreptitiously directing his commandos to clamber up the Himalayan slopes, capture the commanding peaks, and swoop down and capture Kargil, the strategic town that connects Srinagar in the Kashmir Valley with Leh in Ladakh. Top Pakistan military officers, including General Musharraf (Army), Air Chief Marshal P.Q. Mehdi (Air Force) and Admiral Fasih Bokhari (Navy), boycotted the reception for the Indian visitors. Instead, they chose to attend a banquet for the Chinese Defence Minister Chi Haotian, hosted by Foreign Minister Sartaj Aziz, who, however, joined the Vajpayee–Sharif talks the following day. By deciding to be absent at the reception, the military chiefs broke the normal diplomatic protocol in which the prime minister would have introduced them to the visiting dignitary to whom they would have offered the military salute. The split between the Pakistan civilian government and the military establishment could not be shoved under the red-carpet welcome that Prime Minister Sharif had rolled out for the Indians.

The high-powered summit between India and Pakistan resulted in a treaty, the Lahore Declaration, along with the Memorandum of Understanding, which was signed on 21 February 1999 and was subsequently ratified by the Parliaments of India and Pakistan.[29] First and foremost, the Lahore Declaration was a recognition of the fact that both India and Pakistan were nuclear powers, which created the most dangerous possibility of mutual destruction. The danger inherent in the development and possession of nuclear weapons, including accidental and unauthorized use by state or non-state actors, therefore, needed confidence-building measures such as open channels of communication and feedback through periodic meetings between the representatives of the two nations.

The treaty also included advance notification regarding missile tests and any accidental or unauthorized use of nuclear devices that might occur to avoid any misunderstanding about each other's intentions. Both parties agreed that previous resolutions regarding the Kashmir dispute, the post-Bangladesh-liberation 1972 Simla Treaty and the 1988 Non-Nuclear Aggression Agreement for nuclear safeguards signed by Prime Minister Benazir Bhutto and Prime Minister Rajiv Gandhi were essential to keeping the peace.[30]

THE KARGIL WAR

While the Vajpayee–Sharif song-and-dance of nuclear peace was going on in Lahore, Pakistan Army Chief General Musharraf and his underling, General Ashraf Rashid, were directing their troops, camouflaged and disguised as Kashmiri militants, to infiltrate and cross the Line of Control (LoC), the de facto border of the divided Jammu and Kashmir. For the Pakistan Army, regardless of the risks and steep barren mountain hazards, the time was most opportune, and the prize was too great not to fight for. The military posts located on the mountain ridges ranging 16,000 to 18,000 feet overlooked the most strategic landscape, including Kargil, Drass, Mushko Valley and Batalik—the terrain that provided connectivity between Kashmir Valley and the sprawling Ladakh region, part of which, Aksai Chin, was already occupied by China after the 1962 War. General Musharraf's covert plan, Operation Badr, was launched to seize a strategic tract of land in Indian Kashmir that could have severed the Kashmir–Ladakh artery and forced Indian troops to withdraw from the Siachen Glacier.[31] And the loss of the strategic Himalayan region would have brought India's two worst enemies, Pakistan and China, geopolitically together.

Once again, the failure of the Indian intelligence was brought to the fore, resulting in India not being aware of the Pakistani infiltrators supported by the elite Special Services Group and the Northern Light Infantry. These infiltrators set up posts on the ridges on the Indian side overlooking Kargil and the national highway (NH1) to Ladakh's capital city, Leh. It was a nomadic Bakarwal shepherd in the Batalik sector of Kargil Valley who alerted the troops. India responded by launching Operation Vijay, with a massive deployment of force, including troops from regular divisions and paramilitary forces estimated at 30,000—primarily an infantry-artillery mission but fully supported by the Indian Air Force. Naval operations, too, were readied and put on full alert from 20 May to forestall Pakistan's surprise attack and to limit the conflict from becoming a full-blown war. The Indian Navy mustered all its strategic assets and used its sea power to block the Arabian Sea trade and oil routes of Pakistan, leaving Pakistan with less than a week of fuel.[32]

Round-the-clock MiG airstrikes against infiltrators and ground-launched, shoulder-fired missiles against Pakistan troops fighting from their hilltop hideouts enabled Indian troops to recapture the strategic 16,500-foot Tiger Hill that overlooks Kargil and the National Highway to Leh. By the end of June, the Indian Forces had recaptured most of the vital posts, the ridges and the high grounds.

Finally, the United States came to Pakistan's rescue. On 4 July, Prime Minister Sharif flew to Washington DC to meet with

President Clinton to seek his intervention to end the war, which, as some feared, might spiral into a nuclear conflict. As a face-saving mechanism, Prime Minister Sharif agreed to withdraw Pakistan troops from Indian territory; in fact, he had no choice because Indian troops had already beaten them back from most of the sectors. The remainder of the Pakistani troops in the Kargil-Drass sector were mopped up by 26 July and the fighting finally ceased. Denouncing the agreement, Hafiz Muhammad Saeed, chief of Lashkar-e-Taiba, said, 'Pakistan may withdraw, but the Mujahedeen (holy warriors) will not withdraw... Pakistan should not accept any responsibility on behalf of the Mujahedeen because those peaks are not in Pakistani army or Pakistani government hands, *but in our hands* [emphasis added].'[33] True to his calling, Muhammad Saeed carried out his mission, including the attack on the Indian Parliament in 2001, the Mumbai train bombings in 2006 and the most horrific Mumbai terrorist attack in 2008 that killed 164 civilians, including many foreigners. In spite of being announced as a terrorist by the US in 2012 with a bounty of US$10 million on his head, Saeed remained free in Pakistan. China had been puzzlingly quiet and benign about Saeed's terrorist activities.

The Kargil War could have gone out of control because both India and Pakistan were prepared to launch nuclear strikes against each other.[34] India was set to strike Pakistan with five nuclear-tipped missiles loaded on four short-range Prithvi and one long-range Agni that would have covered the entire country. Pakistan's six medium-range nuclear warheads loaded on Hatf 2 missiles were on alert to attack India's economic and military installations. Since both countries were ready for the launch-on-command stage for the nuclear warheads delivery systems, it was obvious that both Islamabad and New Delhi had been actively engaged in weaponizing their underground 1998 nuclear explosions. The world was never so close to nuclear war since the 1962 Cuban Missile Crisis.[35]

Did the nuclear weapons give Pakistan a false sense of security and parity with India to embolden it to launch the Kargil War? Vikas Kapur and Vipin Narang wrote:

> Pakistan may feel emboldened with its nascent nuclear arsenal
> to conduct bold excursions into Indian territory with perceived
> impunity as it did in Kargil, and India may be encouraged
> to act more aggressively around the Line of Control, both
> violating international law and bringing the world that much
> closer to the brink of nuclear exchange.[36]

But since neither nuclear brinkmanship nor the covert-overt mode of Kargil War adventurism worked, Pakistan discovered a new potent weapon against India: state-sponsored terrorism under which, 'Pakistan not only assists militant passage into Indian occupied Kashmir but also funds, trains, and arms these militants,' allowing them to live with impunity and move freely in the country.[37] For Pakistan, terrorism, a cheap and asymmetrical warfare strategy, was the best way to maintain parity with India.[38] This is what General Systems theorists call the Principle of Equifinality, according to which a system, such as a nation-state, could achieve the same goal by many different paths. That's what Pakistan has been trying to achieve since its creation, to get Kashmir any which way it could be done; but the long-term costs and consequences have been too high.

Pakistan is not only a terrorist state; it too has become a victim of terrorism by the very forces it unleashed against India. Regardless of the domestic repercussions, Pakistan found that random acts of terrorism carried out in Kashmir by Pakistani and Kashmiri militants evoked retaliatory responses from the Indian security forces, which alienated Kashmiris from India, apart from raising an international hue and cry against India's violations of human rights in Kashmir. Pakistan-supported terrorism and militancy diminished Jammu and Kashmir's constitutionally guaranteed autonomy under Article 370. Its abrogation in 2019 by Prime Minister Modi's government was only a formality of a fait accompli.

VAJPAYEE GETS A NEW MANDATE, SORT OF

Just when Prime Minister Vajpayee had concluded his seemingly successful Lahore bus tour, his coalition government faced a serious political crisis. One of the coalition partners, the AIADMK, with 18 parliamentary seats, withdrew its support. In a vote on a no-confidence motion, the Vajpayee government lost by one vote, 269 to 270. During the formation of the BJP-led 1998 coalition government, AIADMK leader J. Jayalalithaa had not only bargained for and received key cabinet and other ministerial positions for her party but had also made some other irrational political demands—one of which was that the Tamil Nadu state government, led by her bitter rival M. Karunanidhi's DMK, be dismissed and president's rule be imposed in the state.[39]

When her dangerous game of political tantrums and brinkmanship failed to persuade Vajpayee, she withdrew her support and the coalition government fell apart, opening a new chapter in the complicated game of Indian democracy based on coalition-building. President Narayanan dissolved the Lok Sabha and asked Vajpayee to continue as the caretaker prime minister until the general election, to be held in three phases from 5 September 1999 through 3 October 1999, produced a new government. It was during the interregnum of Vajpayee's caretaker government that Pakistan had launched the Kargil War and was beaten back. The BJP basked in the glory of victory and the wind was at its back.

By and large, the 13th general election was contested between two broad coalitions, the BJP-led Nation Democratic Alliance (NDA) and Sonia Gandhi-led INC and its allies. Moreover, there was a nebulous third-front loose grouping of communist and socialist parties as well as some free-floating unaffiliated independent candidates who added colourful confusion to the electoral scene.

Thanks to good monsoons as well as economic liberalization and financial reforms ushered in by the Narasimha Rao government, agricultural and industrial growth had picked up, and the economy was expanding with inflation under control—factors which helped the BJP–NDA's image as a party that could provide a stable government. Besides, there was a strong nationalist wave of the Kargil victory that shed a bright light on the BJP–NDA. On the other hand, for the Congress, its leader Sonia Gandhi herself became an election issue due to her foreign origin. Born in Italy, Sonia married

Rajiv Gandhi, and in the course of time, she became absolutely Indian, wore the traditional dress, sari, and learned to speak and address the public in Hindi, which many Indian political leaders couldn't do.

The challenge to her leadership had first come from within the party. Some of the senior Congress leaders, including Sharad Pawar, a veteran Maharashtrian leader and former state chief minister, P.A. Sangma, former speaker of the House and Meghalaya chief minister, and Tariq Anwar, a Bihari parliamentarian, who asked that the Congress elect a native-born leader. Rebuffed by the Congress, they formed their own party, the National Congress party (NCP). The BJP used the *videshi-swadeshi* (Hindi: foreign-native) negative campaign slogan against Sonia Gandhi and the Congress with an indeterminate effect on the election outcome.

The BJP's victory, however, was based on a strong alliance it had built with regional parties.[40] Political carpetbaggers and opportunistic leaders like Jayalalithaa and her AIADMK party were kept at a distance. The BJP–NDA coalition norms, 'mutual trust, regular consultation, consensus building, and acceptance of a common approach', were touted as 'representative of both national interests and regional aspirations', presenting the NDA as 'the mirror-image of our nation's unity in multifaceted diversity, rich pluralism, and federalism.'[41] Since 1989 the BJP had been growing in strength by forming alliances with regional parties and delivering its message in local and regional terms, but it was in the 1999 general election that the BJP provided a steel spine to the NDA and brought it to victory.[42] The BJP-led alliance of 14 parties won 270 seats and with the support of 29 seats of the Telugu Desam Party, it gave India a stable government for a full five-year term (1999–2004). Sonia Gandhi's Congress won 114 seats, while its other six affiliated parties won only 21 seats.[43]

THIRD TIME'S THE CHARM

The 1999 general election was a pivotal point because India was entering into an era of stable coalition governments. The change in the voters' behaviour had begun to occur in 1967, when the Congress party, under Indira Gandhi, despite winning a Lok Sabha majority, had lost in several state Assemblies, including Gujarat, Tamil Nadu, Orissa, Rajasthan, West Bengal, Kerala and Delhi. Indians voted differently for state legislative assemblies and for the Lok Sabha, an emerging political phenomenon that would eventually strengthen the federal system by making national political parties seek the support of regional parties based on either common minimum programme, political horse-trading or power-sharing—any which way the coalition worked. With the first-past-the-post voting system, a party with less than the majority of the cast votes could win a majority of seats in a state assembly or the Lok Sabha and form the government. Even during the best of times (1952) when Jawaharlal Nehru was the supreme and most popular leader of India, the INC had obtained only 44.99 per cent votes but won a landslide victory with 364 seats out of 489. In 1967 the Congress under Indira Gandhi, with 44.78 per cent votes, won 283 seats out of 520, amounting to 54 per cent of the Lok Sabha seats.[44]

Later, despite the subsequent Indira wave and post-Indira Gandhi assassination sympathy vote for her son Rajiv Gandhi, the Congress party's monopoly over political power was breaking up because state voters had begun to go their own ways, choosing regional parties over national parties. Regional parties not only pioneered and formed coalition governments in their states but also captured seats in the Lok Sabha, and by their sheer weight could not be ignored by the national parties. The replacement of a one-party government with a coalition government became inevitable when the first-past-the-post voting system did not throw up a single party with an absolute majority in the Lok Sabha. Prime Minister P.V. Narasimha Rao's Congress government (1991–96), the first successful coalition government experiment, forecast the future of government formation of India. With the comfortable majority of 303 parliamentary seats, Vajpayee, the leader of the BJP-led NDA coalition, was sworn in as the prime minister for the third time on 13 October 1999. But it wasn't an ominous beginning.

PAKISTAN TERRORISTS STRIKE AGAIN AND AGAIN

As India was preparing for the new millennium, five terrorists, members of the Harkat-ul-Mujahideen (HUM), a Pakistan-based Islamic militant group, hijacked Indian Airlines Flight IC 814 with 176 passengers and 15 crew members en route from Kathmandu, Nepal, to New Delhi, on 24 December 1999. Threatening to blow up the plane, they asked the pilot to 'fly west'. After a brief landing in Amritsar for refuelling but suspecting a rescue counterattack operation from Indian commandos, the hijackers ordered the pilot to take off and land in Lahore for refuelling. Pakistan's airport authorities allowed the plane to take off after refuelling, which, after a short flight, landed at the Dubai Military Airport. And after releasing 27 sick passengers, one of whom was fatally stabbed by the hijackers and died later, the aircraft was finally flown to Kandahar, Afghanistan, which at that time was under the Taliban's control. The hijackers demanded the release of Pakistani Muslim cleric Masood Azhar, the founder of the terrorist group Jaish-e-Mohammed, and other terrorists from Indian prisons as well as US$200 million. Azhar was being incarcerated in India in 1994. The well-planned hijacking was meant to get 36 Pakistani-supported jihadists-terrorists out of Indian prisons.

It was a most difficult time for India. According to the deal struck with the hijackers through Taliban interlocutors, Minister of External Affairs Jaswant Singh flew with three terrorists, including Azhar, Mushtaq Ahmed Zargar and Ahmed Omar Saeed Sheikh to Kandahar in exchange for the remaining 149 passengers and the aircraft crew. The hijackers and the three freed Islamic jihadists disappeared into the badlands of Pakistan from where they would hatch and carry out plots that would shock-and-awe the United States of America.

Omar Sheikh was one of the planners of the 11 September 2001 New York Twin Towers' attack. And in 2002, he kidnapped *The Wall Street Journal* reporter Daniel Pearl in Karachi and beheaded him. The Indian Airlines hijacking was one of al-Qaeda's and Pakistani jihadists' planned millennium attacks.[45] Pakistan's invisible parallel government, the Inter-Services Intelligence (ISI), had begun to do what General Musharraf and his mountain battalions had failed to do during the Kargil War—to make India, with all its economic power and nuclear capabilities, look and feel helpless, incapable, incompetent and clueless to protect its citizens, its assets, its territory and its democratic institutions.

While General Musharraf could not seize Kargil from India, he was nonetheless successful in seizing power from the duly elected civilian government of Prime Minister Sharif, peacemaker and co-author of the Lahore Declaration, by staging a coup d'état on 12 October 1999.[46] Under the dubious 'doctrine of necessity', the Pakistan Supreme Court legalized the martial law declared by General Musharraf. Nawaz Sharif was tried by the judge advocate general of the military court and found guilty of endangering the life of the Chairman of the Joint Chiefs of Staff General Musharraf and others.[47] Nawaz Sharif was convicted and sentenced to life imprisonment, but later General Musharraf, who installed himself as the chief executive, pardoned the prime minister and let him go to Saudi Arabia, where he was granted asylum. In 2001, through an executive decree, General Musharraf declared himself the President of Pakistan, and all his deeds were validated through a fraudulent referendum, which he won by over 97 per cent votes.[48]

MUSHARRAF COMES TO INDIA

With absolute power in his hands as Pakistan's ruler, President Musharraf travelled to India for a summit with Prime Minister Vajpayee to discuss outstanding issues especially limiting nuclear weapons, resolving the Jammu and Kashmir dispute and ending cross-border terrorism. Musharraf had no intention of giving up Pakistan's newly acquired parity through nuclear weapons or its strength through asymmetrical cross-border infiltration and random hit-and-run warfare. India had a deep distrust of Musharraf, the architect and the perpetrator of the Kargil War.

The Agra Summit (14–16 July 2001) was doomed for failure, despite all-round optimism.[49] Jaswant Singh, minister for external affairs, who, along with his Pakistani counterpart Abdul Sattar had put together a working draft, wrote in his memoir, *Call to Honour*, that the order of priority for both sides was topsy-turvy. When Vajpayee and his cabinet considered the draft, the consensus was:

> ...that without sufficient and clear emphasis on terrorism, also accepting categorically that it must cease, how could there be any significant movement on issues that are of concern or are a priority only to Pakistan? And none that are in the hierarchy of priorities for India? How can we abandon Shimla or Lahore? Or forget the reality of Kargil?[50]

The Indian media lionized the Pakistani strongman as the blustery army general burst through the carefully cultivated diplomatic veneer of the man wearing the presidential suit. The media-induced 'grandstanding fever' prompted General Musharraf 'into a great deal of unrestrained comment in front of a select gathering of editors.' Thus feeling enthralled and self-righteous, Musharraf 'refused to accept the presence of terrorism as an issue, continued to emphasize only the centrality of Jammu and Kashmir; was also most dismissive of Lahore (Declaration); would not at all accept the reality of what Kargil was, what he had done; and he seemed almost to dismiss the Shimla Agreement.'[51]

Nevertheless, the visit did impress upon India that Musharraf was the legitimate head of the state and India had no choice but to deal with him. The question, however, remained: how much control did Musharraf have over Pakistan ISI-supported and independently operating non-state terror agents functioning from Pakistan's soil? When during one of the sessions of the Agra Summit, Home Minister L.K. Advani asked Musharraf whether criminal-terrorist Dawood Ibrahim, the perpetrator of the 1993 Bombay bombings that had killed 257, who was then living in Karachi, could be extradited to India, Musharraf told a bald-faced lie and said, 'Mr Advani, let me tell you emphatically that Dawood Ibrahim is not in Pakistan.'[52] Dawood Ibrahim was a military and diplomatic asset for Pakistan and so was Osama bin Laden who too was protected in Pakistan; and Musharraf knew about it.[53] Five months after the failed Agra Summit, India was given the answer to how Pakistan would use its terrorist assets in the asymmetrical warfare that it seemed to have been perfecting.

On 13 December 2001, five terrorists wearing military outfits and carrying AK-47 rifles, grenade launchers, pistols and grenades, drove in a car with fake home ministry and parliamentary officials' tags into the Parliament House and began shooting. Although the Lok Sabha had been adjourned, a large number of people, at least 100 by some account, including some MPs and top government officials, including Home Minter Advani, Minister of State for Defence Harin Pathak, and Vice President Krishan Kant, among others, were present in the Parliament complex.[54]

All five gunmen were killed, besides six security personnel and one civilian, after an hour-long shootout that was broadcast live on television. Denouncing the militants, Vajpayee said, 'This was not just an attack on the building, it was a warning to the entire nation. We accept the challenge.' Just two months earlier, a similar attack had taken place on the Kashmir State Assembly that had killed 38 people.[55] India seemed to be fragile, frail and feeble against Pakistan's meticulously planned, asymmetrical, randomly erupting, diversified war. The enemy combatant was no longer at the border only; he could be anywhere. It was much easier to fight the enemy in regular warfare, but India had no strategy in fighting the ingenious state-supported terrorism. India could not have done what President George W. Bush did by invading and occupying Afghanistan and Iraq after the 11 September 2001 attacks. Nor could India have done what President Barack Obama did to the terrorists in the badlands of Pakistan by simply droning them out of existence.

The post-attack manhunt and investigation apprehended four perpetrators, including Mohammad Afzal Guru, Shaukat Hussain Guru and his wife Afsan Guru, and Syed Abdul Rahman Geelani, who were tried and convicted under various Indian criminal justice procedure codes in a specifically set up Special Trial Court, which completed its judicial proceedings in a record time of six months. Afsan Guru was convicted of a lesser crime as a facilitator and sentenced to five years' rigorous imprisonment and fine. The remaining three perpetrators were sentenced to death. However, on appeal Geelani, a Delhi University lecturer of Arabic, was acquitted, and Shaukat Hussain Guru's death sentence was commuted to 10-year imprisonment.

On 12 January 2007, the Supreme Court dismissed Afzal Guru's plea for commuting his death sentence. The President of India, Pranab Mukherjee, turned down his clemency plea on 3 February 2013. With Afzal Guru's execution, the attack on the Parliament of India saw a judicial closure. But not everyone thought that justice was done, not Omar Abdullah, chief minister of Kashmir, who called the hanging a tragedy that would 'reinforce a sense of alienation and injustice among a generation of youth in the valley.'[56]

And not least, India's fiery-mouthed, liberal socialist critic and activist Arundhati Roy who argued that Afzal Guru's story was 'performed like a piece of medieval theatre on the national stage, in the clear light of day, with the legal sanction of a "fair trial," the hollow benefits of a "free press" and all the pomp and ceremony of a so-called democracy.'[57] Under the fig leaf of false piety and misplaced sympathy for the perpetrator of the crime as the victim of injustice, Arundhati Roy and other Indian public intellectuals failed to comprehend the truth about India, that the Parliament of India is the sacred body wherein resides the beating heart of modern India, the secular constitution, the idea of India, the India Constant. After the attack on the Indian Parliament, what forgiveness?

Apart from the slow motion, law-and-order, legal-judicial responses, including the passing of the controversial legislation, the Prevention of Terrorism Act (POTA) that was passed (425-296) by a joint session of Parliament in 2002, Prime Minister Vajpayee ordered a massive mobilization of Indian forces: a half-million troops, on the borders of Jammu and Kashmir, Punjab, Rajasthan and Gujarat facing about 300,000 Pakistani troops amassed in response to India's military build-up.[58] In the absence of any alternative military strategy for fighting a state-supported asymmetrical war by Pakistan's non-state agents, India indulged in senseless military brinkmanship that aroused global fears about two nuclear powers playing the game of mutually assured destruction. India charged that Pakistan-

ISI-supported Lashkar-e-Taiba and Jaish-e-Mohammed were responsible for the attack on the Parliament, which of course, Pakistan denied.[59]

After US Secretary of State Colin Powell's 'general to general' talk with Musharraf and British Prime Minister Tony Blair's intense diplomacy, as well as keeping in mind the United States' war against global terrorism after the September 11 attacks, Musharraf in a television address to the nation announced, on 12 January 2002, that Pakistan would fight against extremism and terrorism. He banned Lashkar-e-Taiba and Jaish-e-Mohammad, two groups that India had blamed for carrying out the attack, issuing a warning, 'No organizations will be able to carry out terrorism under the pretext of Kashmir... Whoever is involved with such acts in the future will be dealt with strongly whether they come from inside or outside of the country.' But at the same time, he asserted that Pakistan's position on Kashmir remained unchanged and the issue must be resolved as per the UN resolutions. [60]

Because of Pakistan's conciliatory promises and commitment to fight global terrorism as well as international diplomatic pressures, both India and Pakistan climbed down from their high horses and rhetorical bravado, and began to demobilize and withdraw troops from the borders in October 2002. There was something else, something very persuasive: Pakistan too had nuclear weapons and Musharraf would not give up their first use ('Use it or lose it'), despite India's no-first-use policy.[61] The five-month-long mobilization-demobilization confrontation under the Operation Parakram standoff cost India US$3.2 billion, according to some sources.[62] Distracted by the firestorm outside, India failed to see the fire engulfing its kitchen.

THEN THERE WAS THE UNHOLY MASSACRE

King Henry the Fourth's sleepless wail, 'Uneasy lies the head that wears the crown', was never truer than in the case of Vajpayee. Ever since he took over the reign of the country, he faced, in quick succession, one bloody crisis after another: the Kargil War; the hijacking of the Kathmandu-Delhi-Kabul Indian Airlines Flight; and Pakistan-based terrorist attack on the Indian Parliament followed by the massive build-up of troops that brought India and Pakistan to the brink of nuclear war (from December 2001 to June 2002). India was under a collective psychological siege. And then came the burning of the holy Ayodhya train from where the flames of hell leapt up from town to town, from one labyrinthine street to another, in a most horrific uncontrollable wave after wave of barbarism. It was all the more shocking that it happened in the most peaceful state, Gujarat, where one can find globetrotting traders, stockbrokers, diamond merchants, industrialists and dealmakers. These are people, who in their daily lives, live by the most humane ethical edict of absolute nonviolence, 'ahimsa parmo dharma', when, in a manner of speaking, they are not selling diamonds or playing the stock market. How did such beautiful people turn into killers?

In February 2002, Gujarat slipped into what Joseph Conrad called 'the heart of darkness'. Civilizational restraints collapsed. The policeman-chowkidar disappeared. The politician went into a deliberative passive-aggressive mode with his lips murmuring: let nature take its course. The repressed beast broke through the thin crust of civilization, dharma and sanskriti, and responded to 'the wakening of forgotten and brutal instincts...'[63]

Emboldened by the Hindu nationalistic BJP government at the Centre, led by avuncular poet-politician Vajpayee, thousands of volunteers, karsevaks, from Gujarat responded to the call of the Vishva Hindu Parishad and were drawn to Ayodhya to participate in the conclusion of the foundation laying ceremony of the temple to God Ram in a disputed place where earlier a Mughal-era sixteenth century inactive and uninhabited mosque Babri Masjid stood, and which had been already demolished on 6 December 1992. Having performed the ancient vedic fire sacrifice, the *Purnahuti Maha Yagna,* on 25 February 2002, the devotees from Gujarat took the Sabarmati Express to return to Ahmedabad, about 900 miles, that would take them more than 30 hours to reach their destination.

The train reached Godhra, a Muslim majority town in Gujarat, in the morning hours of 27 February 2002, and the devotees, as they had been doing at previous stopovers, shouted slogans, 'Glory to Lord Ram, Jai Sri Ram, Jai Sri Ram.' On the railway platform, a minor scuffle broke out between the *Karsevaks* and some tea stall peddlers, mostly Muslims. A little while after the train had left the station, someone pulled the manual emergency brakes from within a compartment and the train stopped near the outer signal. Of the nine compartments in the Sabarmati Express, coach number S-6 burst into flames. The conflagration charred 59 people, including women and children to death, while injuring 48 others.

According to the inquiry conducted by the Gujarat Forensic Lab, the fire originated within the compartment and was started by someone who had poured inflammable liquid and set it on fire. The train was heavily pelted from outside.[64] On 6 March 2002, the government of Gujarat appointed a commission of inquiry headed by retired Supreme Court Justice G.T. Nanavati who, after six years of investigation concluded that the Godhra train burning was pre-planned and masterminded by a Godhra Muslim cleric Maulvi Husain Haji Ibrahim Umarji, a former officer of the Central Police Force named Nanumiyan, and their accomplice Razzak Kurkur. Outside the signal area where the train was stopped, thousands of Muslims attacked the train, the report said.[65] The opposition parties, including the Congress and the CPI, condemned the findings of the report as partisan and politically motivated.

After the 2004 general election, when the United Progressive Alliance (UPA) government of Manmohan Singh took office, Railway Minister Lalu Prasad Yadav appointed former Supreme Court Justice Umesh Chandra Banerjee to investigate the Godhra train fire, whose committee's report rejected the findings of the Nanavati Commission and confirmed the Gujarat Forensic Lab report that the fire was set from within the compartment and it was accidental (the Banerjee Committee was subsequently declared illegal by the Gujarat High Court). The report makes a very telling observation:

> On the basis of available evidence, the Committee has found
> it unbelievable that 'Karsevaks' (to the extent of 90 per cent

of the total occupants) armed with 'trishuls', would allow to get themselves burnt without a murmur by miscreant activity like a person entering S-6 coach from outside and setting the coach on fire.[66]

'Curiouser and curiouser', as *Alice in Wonderland* would have said, the Gujarat High Court, in response to the Banerjee Report challenge filed by Nilkanth Tulsidas Bhatia, an injured passenger of the Godhra train, ruled the finding to be 'unconstitutional, illegal and null and void'. Not only that, but the High Court also asked the Government of India not to present the report to Parliament.[67] The trial court convicted 31 Muslims for the crime of whom 11 were awarded the death sentence. However, on appeal the High Court commuted the death sentence of 11 convicts to life imprisonment. The prime suspects, Maulvi Husain Haji Ibrahim Umarji and Nanumiyan were acquitted for lack of sufficient evidence. Thus, justice was done in the sense that all the judicial procedures and dictums were followed; nonetheless, the truth is yet to be known.[68] Argumentative Indians got lost in their arguments. In spite of *satyamev jayate*, Indians sometimes find it difficult to handle the truth, if it is politically incorrect, for example, if it violates their sense of secularism, if it involves minorities, especially Muslims.

THE THIRST FOR VENGEANCE

After the Godhra train burning, the inter-communal flames leapt to other towns, especially Ahmedabad, Vadodara and Surat, as well as several small towns and rural areas in the state.[69] The otherwise peaceful people of Gujarat, as psychologists would say, went into a state of post-disaster syndrome. And the angst-driven people, in their collective disturbed state of mind, yielded to mob fury that went on feeding on its own cascading intensity. One of the worst-hit localities was Naroda Patia of Ahmedabad, where some of the most gruesome, ghoulish, ghastly deeds were committed on 28 February 2002, a day after the Godhra train burning.

It's hard to say where the post-Godhra flame first hit the

tinderbox, but it is difficult to ignore the grisly murder of a Muslim Congress party Member of the Indian Parliament, Ehsan Jafri, in his home at Gulberg Society in the Chamanpura area of Ahmedabad, an upper-middle-class residential district, a mix of bungalows and apartments, inhabited by Muslim businessmen and professionals. As slogan-shouting Hindus broke through the walls of the gated community and began to set houses on fire, the residents took shelter in the house of the parliamentarian Jafri hoping that his political connections might protect them. Jafri made repeated telephone calls to the police, but no one heard his distress calls. During the six-hour-long attack, the mob hacked and burnt 69 people, including Ehsan Jafri, apart from leaving another 85 injured. Later a court judgement said that it was the 'darkest day in the civil society of Gujarat,' but, nonetheless, he added, 'it was the private firing by Shri Ehsan Jafri that acted as a catalyst and which infuriated the mob to such an extent that the mob went out of control...'[70]

Like a California wildfire, the post-Godhra flames jumped from one Muslim locality to another. Khalid Noor Mohammed Sheikh, who had lost nine family members in the massacre, told Human Rights Watch that the belly of his 30-year-old daughter Kauser Bano was 'cut open and the fetus was pulled out and hacked to pieces before she was killed'.

R. Bibi, whose 36-year-old son was killed by the police and her house completely destroyed, told the Human Rights Watch:

> The crowds came... Suddenly there was an attack. They were raping women. Then they were killing them, burning them and cutting them up into pieces. The police killed my son... My life was taken away when they shot my son. Everything has been taken away and now they want evidence, where will I get the body from?[71]

When the carnage eventually came to an end, there were 1,044 dead (790 Muslims and 254 Hindus), 2,500 injured and 223 missing. The riots left more than 900 women widowed and 600 children orphaned, according to official figures reported to Parliament.[72] The Concerned Citizens Tribunal Report and other independent sources put the death toll higher, 1,926–2,000.[73] Besides the human toll, there was widespread destruction of Muslim religious properties, including 230 mosques and 274 dargahs (Sufi shrines). The riots left more than 150,000 people homeless, including both Muslims and Hindus. Although the 2002 Gujarat riots predominantly hit the Muslims, the Hindus did not escape the communal fire.[74] According to the Human Rights Watch, 'In the weeks that followed the massacres, Muslims destroyed Hindu homes and businesses in continued retaliatory violence.'[75] This was corroborated by a story from *India Today* about a Hindu camel-cart owner Chhaganlal who was slashed to death by a Muslim mob in Sarkhej, a suburban town in the neighbourhood of Ahmedabad on 7 May, more than two months after the communal riots had hit the state:

> Unlike the first phase of the riots, now Hindus too have begun to suffer, thanks to a new belligerence of the Muslims who have been under siege for 10 weeks. The repeated recovery of huge caches of weapons from Muslim pockets forced some of the ministers to ask Modi about the steps the police was taking to flush out these armouries.[76]

Putting several accounts together, including judicial inquiries, official investigations, NGOs reports and media reportage, the picture that emerges after about two decades of historical retrospection is that the state had lost control, as had happened in 1947 and 1984. Muslims were more sinned against than sinning, but they were no sitting ducks. They were equally ferocious; and they fought back as they had done during the 1969 riots, the time of Congress Chief Minister Hitendra Desai. The 1969 riots were triggered by an attack on a Hindu temple and had killed 430 Muslims out of 512 deaths.[77] An unusual aspect of the 1969 riots was that they also occurred in the more or less integrated textile mills' shantytowns, called chawls, where Hindu Dalits turned against their Muslim neighbours, negating the theory that desegregated communities see less inter-communal violence, that 'Towns where Hindus and Muslims continue to be integrated—in businesses, political parties, unions, professional associations of lawyers, teachers, doctors and students, and clubs—are also towns where riots remain either absent or rare.'[78]

And then consider the 1985 riots during the chief ministership of Madhav Singh Solanki of the Congress, which originally began as inter-caste riots regarding the question of reservations but later developed into Hindu–Muslim riots killing 275 people, including Hindus, Dalits and Muslims.[79] Without understanding the deeper causes of communal riots in Gujarat and elsewhere in India, some NGOs, scholars and commentators have readily taken the path of least resistance and indulged in dangerous half-truths, clouding historical judgement.[80] The 2002 Gujarat riots were extremely vicious, but they were not organized or abetted by the state. Some politicians and officials might have either silently participated or turned a blind eye to the raging communal fires, and they should have been punished. In 2002 the Gujarat State was not deliberately negligent, but it was certainly grossly incompetent as it was in the 1969 and 1985 riots when the Congress was in power in the state.

Narendra Modi was appointed Gujarat chief minister by the BJP national high command on 7 October 2001. Only two days before the riots, Modi had won a by-election as an MLA from Rajkot to legitimize his position as the state chief minister. He was only five months into his new job when the riots erupted. Because at the time of appointment, he was not an elected state party leader, he had not established full dominance over the state's divided and feuding BJP. Nor had he established full control over the state administrative establishment.[81] Chief Minister Narendra Modi was no more responsible for *causing* the 2002 post-Godhra riots than was Prime Minister Rajiv Gandhi for *triggering* the 1984 anti-Sikh riots in the wake of Indira Gandhi's death. However, most people, including scholars, social activists, international observers and human rights watchdog groups in the collective mindset of an echo chamber have come to believe that much like the Congress government of Rajiv Gandhi in 1984, Chief Minister Narendra Modi's BJP government too did not do enough to stop the riots and was therefore legally, morally and politically responsible.

Against the plethora of emotionalized mass public opinion,

however, must be considered the Supreme Court of India appointed Special Investigation Team's (SIT) lengthy report that did not find 'any evidence of the chief minister having promoted enmity among various communities on religious grounds. According to their report, '...the SIT, on the contrary, claimed that the Chief Minister had repeatedly appealed to the people for peace and had also taken due care for the rehabilitation and medical facilities for the riot victims in the relief camps'.[82]

Of particular interest was the SIT's findings to the charge that Lok Sabha member Ehsan Jafri's 'frantic calls for help' from the Gulberg Society were ignored. Since the telephone company's incoming and outgoing call records are preserved for legal and security purposes, based on its scrutiny, the SIT report said:

> ...neither Mr Modi nor the then Ahmedabad city police commissioner, P.C. Pande, or his deputy, M.K. Tandon, and other senior police officers, had received any call from Mr Jafri for help...nor at any time of the crucial day were any of these mobile phones 'switched off'...[83]

Furthermore, in response to the allegation that the deployment of Army troops in the riot-affected area was unnecessarily delayed, the SIT found that because of the standoff between Indian and Pakistani forces post the Parliament terrorist attack, army personnel were deployed in the sensitive border areas. But the Centre did withdraw some troops from the forward positions and airlifted them for deployment in the riot-affected areas beginning 28 February 2002.

In the Anglo-Indian judicial system, there are some legal dictums that must be kept in mind. For example, there is the presumption of innocence, which means a person is innocent until proven guilty; in serious criminal cases, the proof of crime must be beyond reasonable doubt, which means 99 per cent proof of guilt; and then there are crimes of 'negligence', 'gross negligence' and 'criminal negligence'. Keeping these jurisprudential principles in mind, the Gujarat government acquittal was based on the principle that the benefit of the doubt must go to the accused, the Gujarat

State, which meant primarily Chief Minister Narendra Modi. There was no foolproof evidence, the evidence beyond reasonable doubt, of deliberate criminal wrongdoing and involvement. There was no intent. Incompetence is not intent. But for a politician in power, especially a state chief minister, incompetence is unforgivable.

The buck must stop somewhere, and in this case, the buck should have stopped at the door of Chief Minister Modi; but more so at the door of Prime Minister Vajpayee, because, ultimately, he, as *the prime minister of India*, was responsible for domestic peace and security. The ultimate test of a good society is not only the growth of GDP, which no doubt is of paramount importance, but the quality of life: especially for the people at the bottom of the pyramid, including the minorities for which law and order, the peace of the street, is the foundation. It wasn't helpful when on 12 April 2002, Prime Minister Vajpayee gave a speech in Goa in which he talked about Muslims' unwillingness or inability for peaceful coexistence with other communities.[84]

DEMOCRATIC SOCIALISM TO DEMOCRATIC CAPITALISM

India needed more than law and order and communal harmony. India needed jobs and growth. More than anything else, India needed dense connectivity through infrastructure and telecommunications, without which the vision of a strong united India, a vision shared by Indian leaders from secular Nehru through Hindu nationalist Vajpayee, would not be achievable. Nehru envisioned the future of India through non-alignment, planned economy, massive dams, steel plants, IITs and BARC. Vajpayee saw the future of India through free enterprise, nuclear and missile umbrella, telecommunications, and national highways and rural roadways. Just as President Dwight D. Eisenhower had laid the foundation of the Interstate Highway System for interstate commerce, Vajpayee planned the prosperity of India through interstate and rural connectivity by building the National Highways Development Project and the Pradhan Mantri Gram Sadak Yojana.

The National Highway Project included the four-to-six-lane,

3,625-mile-long Golden Quadrilateral (GQ) passing through 13 states and connecting four major metro cities, including Delhi, Bombay, Madras and Calcutta, built at the cost of US$6.8 billion. Besides, the project included the construction of North-South and East-West national highways connecting Srinagar in Kashmir to Kanyakumari in Tamil Nadu; and Silchar in Assam to Porbandar in Gujarat for a total distance of 4,438 miles at the cost of US$8 billion. The supplementary project, the Pradhan Mantri Gram Sadak Yojana (PMGSY), was begun on 25 December 2000, in order to link unconnected isolated villages, about 40 per cent of the inhabitants all over the country, with all-weather roads.

The passion for dense connectivity to keep India united was nothing new. The Mughals, too, had done it through highways (Lahore to Agra, for example) and waterways to connect their vast empire, which at its peak extended to central Asia and Afghanistan. And before the Mughals, there existed, since the days of Chandragupta Maurya (321 BCE–297 BCE) the Grand Trunk Road (Pataliputra to Takshashila), which was extended and rebuilt by King Sher Shah Suri in the sixteenth century.[85] Apart from upgrading the Grand Trunk Road and the Mughal era roadway infrastructure, the British enhanced it through railways, the telegraph and the postal system. For Vajpayee and the BJP's Hindutva ideology, the Golden Quadrilateral and the crisscrossing highways were imperative for strengthening the complex federal system of 36 states and union territories by breaking down India's geographical, multicultural and multilingual barriers, although the primary purpose was to speed up economic development.

Highlighting the importance of the national scheme, the government said:

> Rural Road Connectivity is not only a key component of Rural Development by promoting access to economic and social services and thereby generating increased agricultural incomes and productive employment opportunities in India, but also as a result, a key ingredient in ensuring sustainable poverty reduction.[86]

Keeping this primary objective in mind 'the PMGSY is to provide connectivity, by way of an all-weather road (with necessary culverts and cross-drainage structures, which is operable throughout the year), to the eligible unconnected habitations in the rural areas, in such a way that all unconnected habitations with a population of 1000 persons and above are covered in three years (2000–2003) and all unconnected habitations with a population of 500 persons and above by the end of the Tenth Plan Period (2007).'[87]

The scheme would also cover 'the hill states (Northeast, Sikkim, Himachal Pradesh, Jammu & Kashmir, Uttaranchal) and the desert areas...as well as the tribal (Schedule V) areas', in order 'to connect habitations with a population of 250 persons and above.'[88] Various state chief ministers, in the course of time, would start their own rural road projects to provide the remaining connectivity in their states. This all-embracing vision of India as a beehive, India as a 'vasudhaiva kutumbakam', protected by a nuclear umbrella, was one of the most transformative political acts of Vajpayee during his five-year administration.

The National Highways Authority of India (NHAI), which was originally established in 1988, was authorized to carry out the toll-operated National Highway Project (GQ); but to enable it to function without bureaucratic red-tapism, NHAI was made an autonomous body in 1995. Although the National Highway Project was a public sector project, Indian private sector companies and foreign corporations played a predominant role in its execution. The government bore the cost of project feasibility studies; shifting of utilities/services, environmental clearance, cutting of trees, etc.; and land for the right of way and wayside amenities. Apart from the provision of receiving limited capital grants from NHAI, private sector companies were privileged to collect tolls, develop and operate wayside amenities such as restaurants, motels/hotels, rest/parking areas, petrol pumps and workshops.

They were given corporate tax holidays, were allowed limited commercial borrowing privileges and were permitted to import high-capacity road construction equipment without import duties. NHAI bonds were exempted from the capital gains tax and 100 per cent foreign direct investment (FDI) was allowed.[89] Five years after the work began on the GQ project, an American reporter gave a glimpse of the transformative impact of the massive project:

> Where crops once grew along the Golden Quadrilateral, gas stations are sprouting... Reliance Industries Ltd, one of India's largest private conglomerates and a petroleum giant—has grasped the highway's commercial potential... Reliance has (made) itself the golden arches of the Golden Quadrilateral. Its...gas stations are identically bright and streamlined, with computerized billing and clean, airy dhabas...[90]

The Golden Quadrilateral National Highway Project was a major departure from Nehru's socialistic pattern of society. Vajpayee ushered India into the age of democratic capitalism that would liberate the pent-up entrepreneurial energies of India. Reposing his faith in the private sector for rapid economic growth, in spite of tough resistance from labour unions, Vajpayee took definitive steps in divesting some major iconic public sector units (PSU), including Bharat Aluminium Company (BALCO), Hindustan Zinc, Indian Petrochemicals Corporation Limited and Videsh Sanchar Nigam Limited (VSNL). Equally radical was the New Telecom Policy (NPT) proclaimed on 3 March 1999 that ushered in a digital revolution, which would turn India into a data and network mobile society and a major digital global player. Two decades after starting with a low teledensity of less than three per cent, 85–90 per cent Indians would own a smartphone and count it as an absolute necessity of life.

How did Vajpayee break up the old tired screechy music band and start a new one with fresh sound? On 1 October 2000, the government separated the service function of the Department of Telecommunications (DoT) and housed it in a new corporation, the Bharat Sanchar Nigam Ltd (BSNL). Separating the regulator and policymaker, Department of Telecommunications, from the service provider (BSNL) along with the establishment of the Telecom Dispute Settlement Tribunal, the government gave a big fillip to telecommunications growth. In spite of these structural reforms, the Indian Telecomm was still a government monopoly, which on

15 August 2000 was broken up by the introduction of free-market competition in domestic long-distance telecommunication services. Import duties on mobile handsets were reduced from 25 per cent to five per cent. The BSNL lost its monopoly over international telecommunications.[91]

Thus, liberated from the state stranglehold, Indian telecommunications began to embrace the competitiveness of the open marketplace resulting in an unprecedented development, growth, and innovation, much as it had happened in the United States when in 1984, AT&T's (Ma Bell) telecommunications monopoly was broken through divestment, creating seven 'baby Bells' that led to extraordinary growth, diversity and improvement in services.[92]

AMERICA'S SUPER SALESMAN COMES TO INDIA

After the harrowing events of the hijacking of the Indian Airlines flight, the terror attack on Parliament, the broken promises of the bus-to-Lahore peace journey, the Kargil War, and the brutal killing of 36 Kashmiri Sikhs by Islamic militants, the visit of President Bill Clinton, March 2000, brought hope and joy to the Indians. They liked him and his family. The Indian media was mesmerized by President Clinton's people-friendly touch-me-diplomacy that had made him a darling of the American people in spite of the scandals and the (failed) impeachment. 'He's cast such a spell', said an Indian columnist, that, 'even the sanest of people have lost their reason.'[93] In 1998 when India exploded the Pokhran II, Americans were taken by surprise, shocked and dismayed, and President Clinton had imposed sanctions on India. But the resentment, if any, wasn't uppermost on the Indians' minds. They just basked in his glorious larger-than-life presence in public meetings as well as when they saw him on their television sets. He seemed genuine and they wanted America's friendship. So did America, he said. Thousands and thousands of Indians were streaming to the United States as students and techies. He shared India's grief when he visited with Rachna Katyal, the widow of the 25-year-old newlywed Rupen Katyal, killed by the hijackers of the Indian Airlines flight in December 1999. On his visit to Nayla village, Jaipur, Rajasthan, he talked with women about computers and cooperative dairy farming and the need for clean water. And later on, he danced with them a Rajasthani folk dance, to the delight of television audiences across India.

On his visit to Agra and the Taj Mahal, while signing the environment agreement, he talked about pollution and the River Ganga and environmental degradation without being preachy. At the Mahavir Trust Hospital, Hyderabad, he celebrated India's success story regarding the complete eradication of polio, setting an example for the rest of the world. In Hyderabad, he held a teleconference with state district representatives. And to the business community of Hyderabad, he talked about the Information Age and how India was becoming a driving engine of the new economy. Highlighting the contributions of Indian-Americans, he said, 'Indian-Americans now run more than 750 companies in Silicon Valley alone…we're moving from brain drain to brain gain in India, because many are coming home.'[94] Wherever President Clinton went, whether visiting the Bengal tigers in the Ranthambhore National Park, the Mumbai Stock Exchange or in his address to Parliament, he said in so many different ways, 'We came as friends to a changing India, to gain a better understanding of your country, your views, in order to build a new partnership on a higher level than that which we have experienced over the last 22 years.'[95]

While giving the 'common vision into common progress' sentiment a concrete shape in the Vision Statement signed by Prime Minister Vajpayee and President Clinton on 21 March 2000, the joint statement tended to raise the relationship between India and the United States to a higher strategic level, hoping that 'In the new century, India and the United States will be partners in peace, with a common interest in and complementary responsibility for ensuring regional and international security.'[96] This was an acknowledgement of India's strategic role keeping in mind the rapid rise of China that had begun to become a major strategic concern for the US in the Asia–Pacific region.[97] It's in this light that the document acknowledged the *equivocality* over India's nuclear weapons:

> India and the United States share a commitment to reducing
> and ultimately eliminating nuclear weapons, but we have not
> always agreed on how to reach this common goal... Nonetheless,
> India and the US are prepared to work together to prevent the
> proliferation of nuclear weapons and their means of delivery.[9]

The Vision Document proposed to strengthen Indian-American partnership through high-level institutional dialogues, forums and joint working groups, including Foreign Policy Dialogue; Dialogue on Security and Non-Proliferation; Joint Working Group on Counterterrorism; and India–US Science and Technology Forum.[99] India had come a long way from the era of Soviet friendship and dependency. During the address to Parliament, President Clinton praised Vajpayee's visit to Lahore as a 'courageous journey', which made dialogue all the more necessary to solve mutual problems.

Not everyone was swept away by the super-salesman's song and dance for 'the new world order' dominated by the sole superpower, the United States of America. There were a series of demonstrations and protests in various parts of the country, including New Delhi, mostly by leftists and trade unionists. There were also other sections of unheard voices that had not forgotten the decades of deep-rooted mutual suspicions and conflicts of interests.[100] 'As India rushes into what it conceives will be a new economic and strategic partnership with the US...in its ardour for a new role in world affairs', wrote a commentator, 'the BJP-led government may well be disarming the country of all the defence mechanisms it has to cope with an increasingly uncertain global environment', especially, he cautioned, 'If India should go along with the new strategic posture of the US in Asia, it could conceivably endanger a slow but fairly sure-footed process of reconciliation with China.'[101]

MAYBE KOWTOWING TO CHINA

In 1965, about three years after China had beaten India in the Himalayas, there was a curious exchange of letters between the two countries: not over the crest of a misty ridge or a river running through a treacherous valley, but over something more sentient and animate. China accused Indian troops of stealing from their countrymen, Tibetan herders, 800 sheep and 59 yaks near the borders of Sikkim, at that time an Indian protectorate. China demanded the return of the animals, threatening serious consequences as it normally does when it makes any diplomatic demand on its adversaries. At that time, a young Indian parliamentarian, Atal Bihari Vajpayee of the Jana Sangh party felt his funny bone tickled and in an outrageous sense of hilarity, he gathered a group of peaceful protestors and took a herd of sheep to the Chinese Embassy in New Delhi carrying placards pouting, 'Eat me but save the world.' Nobody has ever accused the communists, not least the Chinese communists of the Maoist era, of having a sense of humour. China shot the Indian Embassy in Beijing an angry communiqué, saying that parliamentarian Vajpayee's protest was in fact backed by the Indian government of Prime Minister Lal Bahadur Shastri, who at that time was repulsing Pakistan's attack on Kashmir. China also accused Indian troops, as they have been habitually doing, of incursions, kidnapping and building military structures on Chinese territory.

In response, the Shastri government said that regarding 'the four Tibetan inhabitants allegedly kidnapped by Indian troops... they like other Tibetan refugees...had come into India on their own volition and without our permission and taken refuge in India. They are free to go back to Tibet at any time if they desire to do so.' Regarding the sheep and yaks, it's up to the herdsmen 'to take them to Tibet if and when they choose to go back to *their homeland* [emphasis added].' The Government of India, the note said, had nothing to do with 'a spontaneous, peaceful and good-humoured expression of the resentment of the citizens of Delhi against the Chinese ultimatum and the threat of war against India on trumped-up and trivial issues'.[102]

In 1959 when the Dalai Lama escaped to India, 80,000 Tibetans also followed him and since then, they have been trickling into India with their sheep and yaks. With the establishment of the Dalai Lama and the Tibetan Government-in-exile in Dharamsala, Tibet became a de facto divided country. Geopolitically, Tibet is under Chinese occupation or, as they claim, a part of China. But spiritually, Tibet, with its global presence in Dharamsala, will always be a part of India. As geopolitical scholar Brahma Chellaney observed, 'Insecure about its hold, and unsure of the validity of its claim, on a territory that was mostly independent in history, China sees India as the key to Tibet, whose traditional cultural and trade links were southward.' [103]

Until China makes peace with Tibet, it will be always fearful of India in spite of repeated assurances by Indian leaders that Tibet is indeed part of China, as Prime Minister Vajpayee did on his visit to China in June 2003; and that was 38 years after his sheep-led protest. The most important part of the Indo-China Joint Declaration signed on 23 June 2003 was India's reaffirmation that:

> The Indian side recognizes that the Tibet Autonomous Region is part of the territory of the People's Republic of China and ...it does not allow Tibetans to engage in anti-China political activities in India. The Chinese side expresses its appreciation ...that it is firmly opposed to any attempt and action aimed at splitting China and bringing about 'independence of Tibet.'[104]

In the 1954 Accord, India acknowledged China's suzerainty (overlordship) over Tibet as an autonomous region (with its own internal government) within the Republic of China. But the 2003 memorandum accepted China's sovereignty over Tibet, reducing it to any other province of China. G. Parthasarathy, an Indian diplomat and former high commissioner to Pakistan, echoing the views of Chellaney, said, 'This is the first time that we have "recognized" Tibet as being a part of China... implicit in this formulation is rejection of the Chinese claim that Tibet has historically been a part of China.' Regarding Sikkim, he said, 'The Border Trade Agreement signed during Mr Vajpayee's visit explicitly speaks of "Changgu of Sikkim State" and "Renqinggang of the Tibet Autonomous Region" as venues for border trade markets... thus [Sikkim was] explicitly acknowledged by China as being a "State" of India just as much as Tibet is acknowledged by us to be an "Autonomous Region" of China.'[105] A year later, China recognized Sikkim as an Indian state. Sikkim joined India in 1975 when the Assembly of Sikkim abolished the monarchy and resolved to join India as a constituent state through a referendum.

More optimistic than Chellaney's hard-nosed geopolitical realism, Parthasarathy wrote that 'China has recognized that peace and tranquillity along its borders with India makes sound strategic sense', nonetheless, hoping against hope that: 'Agreements signed during the visits of Prime Ministers Rajiv Gandhi and P.V. Narasimha Rao and the progress made during Mr Vajpayee's visit will not only help in promoting peace and tranquillity along the common borders and promote moves to settle the border issue but also set the stage for economic exchanges across land borders.'[106]

Far from peace and tranquillity, China had been instigating border skirmishes, rationalizing on flimsy excuses such as theft of sheep and yaks, to keep India in a constant state of submissive fear. What China could not accomplish through border micro-aggressions, it did so by providing its all-weather friend and client-state, Pakistan, capabilities for weapons of mass destruction. By providing Pakistan with fissile material, designs of nuclear weapons and components for nuclear enrichment facilities, added Parthasarathy, 'It would be no exaggeration to say that no country... caused more damage to Indian national security than China.'[107]

Not only were such hot-button controversial issues beyond the scope of Prime Minister Vajpayee's goodwill visit but also, even cross-border terror, of which India had been a victim since long, was not included in the joint memorandum. Historically speaking, the great merit of the 2003 visit lay in the fact that it kept the doors of negotiations open for exploring areas of cooperation, 'for India and China to work slowly but methodically toward solving their problems while engaged simultaneously in a range of cooperative and competitive ventures.'[108]

THEN CAME THE RECKONING

The general election, held in a staggered manner from 20 April through 10 May 2004, called upon 675 million eligible Indian voters to elect the 543 members of the 14th Lok Sabha. Three days after the last vote was counted, Prime Minister Vajpayee said in his address to the nation, 'Dear countrymen, we have given up office, but not our responsibility to serve the nation. We have lost an election, but not our determination.'[109] Another smooth political transition and change of government was in the offing in the world's largest democracy. Indians did to Vajpayee what the British had done to Winston Churchill in the post-World War 1945 election. That's the power of democracy. Democracy is for the people, not for the heroes when their time is up.

Vajpayee graciously continued, 'Victory and defeat are a part of life, which are to be viewed with equanimity.' Sidelining the fierce ethnic, caste, communal conflicts and terrorist attacks during his administration, he praised India as a diverse nation with many languages and ethnicities coexisting harmoniously.[110]

In his defeat, Vajpayee was a picture of ascetic nobility. But not all Indian voters, over 370 million who actually voted, had seen the five years of the BJP-led coalition administration the way the outgoing prime minister was portraying it—as 'India Shining'. Early in the campaign, a media report said that while campaigning for the forthcoming Lok Sabha elections:

> ...the Congress president, Sonia Gandhi...upped the ante on the political front here by undertaking a visit to the Holambi Kalan area in northwest Delhi where slum dwellers of Yamuna Pushta are being relocated. Pointing towards the slum clusters, Ms Gandhi took a swipe at the NDA Government, asking: 'Where is India Shining?'[111]

Echoing the sentiment, Mark Tully, a British reporter, said:

> During her (Sonia Gandhi) recent 'meet the people' campaign in rural Uttar Pradesh—the state which returns the largest number of MPs—large numbers of voters turned out to hear her claim the government had done nothing for women, youths and farmers.[112]

The Congress party had learnt the complexities of coalition

building. The UPA, which was clubbed together after the general election, had 335 members, including external support from the Left Front, the Bahujan Samaj Party (BSP), the Samajwadi Party (SP) and other smaller parties. India was developing a unique two-party coalition government system in which two major national parties, the INC and the BJP, sought a coalition with regional parties that would lead to cooperative federalism and the devolution of power to the states.[113] The BJP-led NDA could get only 181 seats, a loss of 89 seats from the 1999 general election. Based on their own electoral performances, the two major parties, the Congress with 145 seats and the BJP, with 138 seats, had little chance of forming a government. The Left Front consisting of the CPI(M), the CPI and others, gained 17 seats to increase its strength to 59.[114]

The country moved from the Centre-Right BJP-led NDA coalition to the Centre-Left Congress-led UPA coalition government, which gripped investors with fear and adversely affected the Bombay Stock Exchange. The Sensex fell from an all-time high of 6,250 to 4,300 in mid-May, with a 565-points loss in one day alone.[115] But the market felt reassured when it saw the face of the newly elected reformist-economist Prime Minister Manmohan Singh, who in the 1990s had pulled India out of a deep economic quagmire and set the country on a path to a global marketplace economy.[116]

Atal Bihari Vajpayee created political possibilities that never existed before. He practised politics as the art of the possible and showed that Indians could feel comfortable in dealing with political contradictions. He roped in more than a dozen headstrong and demanding regional party coalition partners and successfully completed a first non-Congress government at the Centre. On the economic front, interestingly enough, he built on the foundation of the economic reforms laid out by his predecessor Prime Minister Narasimha Rao. When Vajpayee handed over power to Dr Manmohan Singh after the general election in 2004, India's foreign exchange reserve stood at US$100 billion, inflation was less than four per cent, and GDP was growing more than eight per cent, according to the government data.[117]

The Vajpayee government took giant economic steps, including the Fiscal Responsibility and Budget Management Bill to bring down the fiscal deficit and make public sector companies more financially responsible; the establishment of massive Golden Quadrilateral all-weather highway connectivity projects; and the disinvestment and privatization of public sector companies, including Bharat Aluminium Company, Hindustan Zinc and Indian Petrochemicals Corporation. The New Telecom Policy comprising the establishment of the Bharat Sanchar Nigam and the Telecom Dispute Settlement Appeals Tribunal as well as the ending of the monopoly of the Videsh Sanchar Nigam (VSNL) over international telephony ushered in a communications revolution that, along with the mammoth highway and railroad connectivity projects, began to transform India economically, socially and politically.

The most socially transformative initiative of the Vajpayee government was the introduction of Sarva Shiksha Abhiyan, the universal, compulsory and free access to education for children aged 6–14 years, estimated to be costing ₹205 million when the programme was launched in 2002 under the 86th Amendment of the Constitution.[118] But India was not shining for everyone. Those left behind were drawn to the promises of the Congress party's *Congress ka haath, aam aadmi ke saath* (Hindi: Congress for the common man). There's always a democratic alternative that creates hope in India.

13

RISE OF THE SIKH GENTLEMAN AS PRIME MINISTER

Politics is the art of the possible—the art of the next best.

—Otto von Bismarck

On 13 May 2004, when the BJP-led Atal Bihari Vajpayee's NDA government, drunk on an American-style election campaign, 'Indian Shining', riding on the promise of the rebuilding of the Ayodhya Ram Temple, and a spectacular, ancient 'Rath Yatra' full of nationalistic fervour, was expecting a victory to rule for another five-year term, some 380 million voters sprung a dramatic surprise that can happen only in a democracy: They just said no. They voted for the re-energized and resurgent Congress party led by the Italian-Indian woman, Sonia Gandhi, daughter-in-law of one of India's most remarkable Prime Ministers, Indira Gandhi. After the death of her husband and former Prime Minister Rajiv Gandhi at the hands of an LTTE terrorist, Sonia Gandhi had, for some time, retreated into the silence of her Indian widowhood but gradually began to emerge on the political scene.[1] The Congress party, with its massive all-India organization and secular ideology, was too important for the country to let it wither away. So was the legacy of the Nehru–Gandhi family.

The Congress, realizing the new political realities of ethnically and regionally divided federal India, had forged strategic alliances with the power brokers of regional parties—an arrangement which, after the election, was turned into a formal political coalition, the UPA, under the leadership of Sonia Gandhi. During the election, the

NDA's negative campaign against Sonia Gandhi and the Congress suggested that turning over the nation's topmost leadership job to a foreign-born person, albeit thoroughly indigenized and Indianized every which way, nonetheless, carried security risks. The call had gone unheeded by the voters. But the opposition's clamour did not go away even after the Congress party's victory. As former President A.P.J. Abdul Kalam recalled in his memoirs, *Turning Points: A Journey Through Challenges:*

> I had a number of emails and letters coming from individuals, organizations and parties that I should not allow Mrs Sonia Gandhi to become the prime minister of our country. I had passed on these mails and letters to various agencies in the government for their information without making any remarks. During this time there were many political leaders who came to meet me to request me not to succumb to any pressure and appoint Mrs Gandhi as the prime minister, a request that would not have been constitutionally tenable. If she had made any claim for herself, I would have had no option but to appoint her.[2]

Instead of becoming a constant bait for the conservatives, Sonia Gandhi stunned the nation, and in fact, won the country's admiration by her act of renunciation and gave up her constitutional right under the parliamentary system to become the prime minister. More than anyone else, it was President Kalam who was astonished:

> ...The Rashtrapati Bhavan is ready for the swearing-in ceremony at the time of your choice. That is when she told me that she would like to nominate Dr Manmohan Singh, who was the architect of economic reforms in 1991 and a trusted lieutenant of the Congress party with an impeccable image, as the prime minister. This was definitely a surprise to me and the Rashtrapati Bhavan Secretariat had to rework the letter appointing Dr Manmohan Singh as the prime minister and inviting him to form the government at the earliest.[3]

On 22 May 2004, Dr Manmohan Singh took the oath as the 13th prime minister of India, which was not a happenstance.[4] Without being aggressive and self-seeking, he had always been in his own disarming ways a gentleman seeker, quietly assertive and ready to report for duty, as they say in military parlance, if something turned up. A lot of opportunities turned up in his life and he made the best of them. Sanjaya Baru, journalist and scholar who became Prime Minister Singh's media adviser and spokesman (2004–2008), claimed that he was the first farsighted journalist to think aloud about Dr Singh becoming the prime minister in 2004, leaving the management of the political affairs of the Congress party and the UPA to Sonia Gandhi.[5] After the 1999 general election too, when Vajpayee and Sonia Gandhi were herding and mustering MPs to form the government, Baru had cautioned in a newspaper column about the perils of Sonia Gandhi becoming the prime minister due to the political baggage of her being foreign-born, and instead advocated for Dr Singh. Even if the rest of India overlooked Baru's 1999 wild and magnificent proposal, five years was a long gestation period during which the idea might have become a practical possibility in Dr Singh's fertile mind. Like Wilkins Micawber in Charles Dickens' *David Copperfield*, Dr Singh was always ready 'in case of anything turning up.' It was rare to find a political leader who would be 'a reliable, trustworthy and capable head of government.'[6] And his natural self-effacing nonchalance notwithstanding, his early-morning-sky-blue trademark turban was so notable that even a satellite wouldn't have missed spotting Dr Singh.

From the Sikh Emperor Maharaja Ranjit Singh to Prime Minister Manmohan Singh, it had been a long journey when the Sikh would say, '*Raaj Karega Khalsa...*' (Only the pure would rule...and Singh was the purest of the pure). Commenting upon India's diversity and inclusion, a non-Hindu (Sikh) prime minister, Roman Catholic Congress party president Sonia Gandhi and Muslim president, A.P.J. Abdul Kalam, an American, would say:

> The gentlemanly Oxford-educated economist who saved India
> from economic collapse in 1991 and began the liberalization of

its economy, has been *appointed* [emphasis added] the country's next prime minister...the architect of the restructuring of the Indian economy after four decades of quasi-socialism, is an apt choice to lead India now, when it is fast rising as a global economic power.[7]

PROMISES TO KEEP

Beholden to the UPA and the outside support of the Left Front, as well as the Congress party's own election manifesto that enabled it to defeat Vajpayee's BJP-led government, Singh's administration (UPA-1) laid heavy emphasis on the welfare of the poor. Based on the alliance's Common Minimum Programme (CMP), it promised to do what the previous governments since independence, whether Congress or non-Congress, had not been able to accomplish. It promised 'to provide a government that is corruption-free, transparent and accountable at all times, to provide an administration that is responsible and responsive at all times, and all people are equal—there is no discrimination on any caste.'

Keeping in mind the BJP government's inability to ensure ethnic and religious peace in Ayodhya and Gujarat, UPA-1 promised to 'enforce the law without fear or favour to deal with all obscurantist and fundamentalist elements who seek to disturb social amity and peace'. While the BJP government was mostly pro-urban middle class, the UPA-1 government promised to 'enhance the welfare and well-being of farmers, farm labour and workers, particularly those in the unorganized sector, and assure a secure future for their families in every respect'. It made a commitment to 'fully empower women politically, educationally, economically and legally' and 'provide for full equality of opportunity, particularly in education and employment for the Scheduled Castes, Scheduled Tribes, OBCs and religious minorities'.

All these promises would become empty unless the economy 'grows at least seven-eight per cent per year in a sustained manner over a decade and more and in a manner that generates employment so that each family is assured of a safe and viable livelihood,' which meant that there was a need...to 'unleash the creative energies of our entrepreneurs, businessmen, scientists, engineers and all other professionals and productive forces of society'. [8] Thus the social welfare programme promises were predicated upon reform-based free enterprise economic growth under the government's watchful eyes. Moreover, the UPA-1 government pledged to de-communalize the school syllabi; spend at least six per cent of the GDP on education with an emphasis on pre-school, primary and secondary education; two to three per cent of the GDP on healthcare; and ensure the availability of life-saving drugs at affordable prices.

Without acknowledging the Vajpayee government's massive contribution to infrastructure, the Golden Quadrilateral, etc., the UPA-1 government vowed to augment the urban and rural renewal through comprehensive programmes. To put the Centre–state financial relations on a firmer footing and reduce regional developmental imbalances, the UPA-1 government proposed to 'make the National Development Council (NDC) a more effective instrument of cooperative federalism'. Against the BJP government's threat to do away with Jammu and Kashmir's special constitutional status, the UPA-1 government pledged 'to respecting the letter and spirit of Article 370 of the Constitution that accords a special status to Jammu and Kashmir,' apart from pursuing dialogue 'with all groups and with different shades of opinion in Jammu and Kashmir...on a sustained basis, in consultation with the democratically-elected state government'. [9] Unfortunately, the 1975 Indira–Sheikh Accord had already killed Article 370, and what remained was a skeleton of the past. Nonetheless, the promise to keep Article 370 alive made good politics.

Of vital importance was the government's commitment to economic reforms initiated since the era of Prime Minister Narasimha Rao, when Dr Singh was the finance minister. The UPA-1 government declared that it would 'take all necessary steps to revive industrial growth and put it on a robust footing through a range of policies, including deregulation, where necessary incentives to boost private investment will be introduced,' adding that FDI would 'continue to be encouraged and actively sought, particularly in areas of infrastructure, high technology and exports and where local assets and employment are created on a significant scale... Indian industry will be given every support to become productive and competitive'. To ensure free and fair competition in the marketplace, 'regulatory institutions will be strengthened'.[10]

In its commitment to the security and welfare of the labour force and the role of trade unions, it 'rejected the idea of automatic hire and fire... Rights and benefits earned by workers, including the right to strike according to law, will not be taken away or curtailed'. Pledging its commitment to 'a strong and effective public sector whose social objectives are met by its commercial functioning,' the CMP document said that all 'privatization will be considered on a transparent and consultative case-by-case basis,' except for the sacred cows—what it called the public sector's *navaratna* (Sanskrit: nine gems) companies such as Bharat Heavy Electricals Limited (BHEL), Coal India Limited, Gas Authority of India Limited (GAIL), Indian Oil Corporation Limited (IOCL), National Thermal Power Corporation Limited (NTPC Limited), Oil and Natural Gas Corporation Limited (ONGC), Steel Authority of India Limited (SAIL) and Bharat Petroleum Corporation Limited. In short, Dr Singh's government was not totally giving up on the state's control over the commanding heights of the economy on which the Congress party's socialistic doctrine was based.

Regarding national security, the UPA-1 government 'committed to maintaining a credible nuclear weapons programme while at the same time it will evolve demonstrable and verifiable confidence-building measures with its nuclear neighbours,' nonetheless, stating that it would 'take a leadership role in promoting universal, nuclear disarmament and working for a nuclear-weapons-free world'. Asserting that there would be no compromise in the fight against terrorism, the government stated that it had been 'concerned with the manner in which [Prevention of Terrorism Act] POTA has been grossly misused'. The UPA government would repeal it, while at the same time enforcing the existing laws strictly. Without invoking the policy of nonalignment, the government asserted that it would follow an 'independent foreign policy...to promote multi-polarity in world relations and oppose all attempts at unilateralism... reiterates India's decades-old commitment to the cause of the Palestinian people for a homeland of their own.'[11] The UPA called its Common Minimum Programme '*collective* [emphasis added] maximum performance,' which was the biggest challenge before Prime Minister Singh.

THE TRILLION DOLLAR CLUB

Though many observers said that he had just stumbled into the prime ministership of the largest and most complicated democracy in the world, in his first five-year term, Dr Singh had unparalleled accomplishments that would place him in the league of Nehru and Indira Gandhi.[12] His major undertakings and achievements included the National Rural Health Mission (NRHM), the National Rural Employment Guarantee Scheme (NREGS), the Unique Identification Authority of India (UIDAI), the Right to Information Act, and one of the most historic achievements—the civil nuclear agreement with the United States. It was during his tenure as finance minister in the 1990s under the Narasimha Rao administration that the Indian economy had entered a phase of speedier development. Fortunately, the Vajpayee government had carried forward the economic liberalization policies, and Prime Minister Singh continued the economic momentum resulting in impressive GDP growth of eight to nine per cent during 2005–2009, making India one of the fastest-growing economies in the world.[13] Continuing and expanding the infrastructure and highway building programmes (the Golden Quadrilateral), reforming the banking and financial sectors of the economy, reducing farmers' indebtedness, and overall pro-business policies resulted in accelerated economic growth. It was during Dr Singh's administration (UPA-1) that India joined the trillion-dollar GDP club.[14]

It's amazing that in the first year of his administration, Dr Singh had gradually moved away from Nehru's democratic socialism to a democratic free-market economy without, however, deviating from

Nehru's nonalignment foreign policy. Addressing the 2005 India Today Conclave, he said:

> If our commitment to remain an open society is one of the pillars of our nationhood, the other is our commitment to remain an open economy... that guarantees the freedom of enterprise, respects individual creativity, and at the same time mobilizes public investment for social infrastructure and the development of human capabilities... the principles to which all countries...want to adhere...[15]

TOWARDS UNIVERSAL HEALTHCARE

Initially, the National Rural Health Mission (NRHM), launched in April 2005, was focused on addressing the healthcare needs of the deprived rural population of the 18 states that were identified as having 'weak public indicators' and substandard health facilities. The scale of the systemic health system deficiencies 'included lack of holistic approach, absences of linkages with collateral health determinants, gross shortage of infrastructure and human resources, lack of community ownership and accountability, non-integration of vertical disease control programs, non-responsiveness and lack of financial resources.'[16] The scheme was extended to urban areas in May 2013 under the National Urban Health Mission (NUHM), which, along with NRHM, was placed under an umbrella body, the National Health Mission. Under the mission of the rural health scheme, the designated states were empowered to establish a comprehensive, integrated and decentralized healthcare delivery system, including, among other essentials, water, sanitation, education and nutrition for the deprived sections of the population.

The health outcomes of the National Health Mission were to be assessed based on the metrics of the national Public Health Standard. The National Health Mission included Accredited Social Health Activists (ASHAs), community volunteers tasked to bring the needy people to the services available at the Public Health System, including outpatient services, diagnostic facilities, in-patient care and nurse-midwives. Facilities such as National Mobile Medical Units, National Ambulance Services, and Janani Shishu Suraksha Yojana for pregnant women and infants, Child Health Screening and Early Intervention Services, and Mother and Child Health Wings in hospitals were purported to connect poor households into the Public Health System. All these decentralized rural health development schemes were to take place through panchayat-based Village Health and Sanitation Committees (VHSCs), which in turn were integrated into district plans.[17]

This was an ambitious national undertaking of which there's no end state, keeping in mind the needs of 640,867 villages accounting for about 69 per cent of the Indian population (2011 census data) as well as a massive urban population whose health needs had to be met. As the healthcare system began to expand and demands increased, the system exposed healthcare inequities based on unforeseen cultural and physical barriers, including factors such as gender, socioeconomic status, education and rural-urban distance from healthcare facilities. Keeping in mind the caste-and-creed based segregated nature of Indian society, the introduction of the universal state healthcare plans raised the question of priorities: who, what, when, where, why and how. Shouldn't tribals, Dalits and crowded urban poor have the same access to healthcare specialists as others? [18]

Unlike building a highway system such as the Golden Quadrilateral, the National Health Mission is not an end state. There would never be a sense of mission accomplished because, in an open democratic society, every development exposes inequities. There's no gainsaying the fact that in spite of all these efforts and the availability of 1.4 million doctors, India, by the end of the UPA's ten-year rule, was unable to meet its health-related millennium development goals.[19]

UPPITY URBANITES VS THE DOWNTRODDEN

In 2006 access to the institutions of higher and professional education became an extremely contentious issue when the Union

Government implemented the proposal to reserve for the Other Backward Classes (OBCs) 27 per cent seats in the nation's top schools, including the Indian Institutes of Management (IIMs), Indian Institutes of Technology (IITs), All India Institute of Medical Sciences (AIIMS), Indian Institute of Science (IIS), and other central government-funded and managed institutions of higher learning—meritorious establishments that attract the best of the Indian youth and produce top professional elites that run political and corporate India.

During the independence movement, while the INC was fighting against two fronts—fighting for freedom from the British Raj and preventing the Indian Muslim League from breaking up India—a large section of Indian reformers were struggling with the most degrading ills of Indian society, especially its caste system, that had kept the lower castes, the Shudras, the Untouchables, now known as Dalits, in dehumanized conditions of virtual slavery, in many ways worse than the American slavery, and the aboriginal tribal people in savage neglect. No other society had ever reduced humans to a state of nothingness as the Indian caste system had done to the Untouchables. The Shudras were barred not only from learning Sanskrit and the sacred Indian texts but, in fact, any form of learning. They could not enter temples, they could not worship the Indian gods, and even physically touching an upper-class person or looking at him or her was a most heinous sin.

In 1947, when the British rolled up their Indian Empire and the Indian Muslim League shrank and disappeared into Pakistan, Indians began to look deeply into the heart of India and discovered, that words of Walter Kelley, mentioned previously, rang truer than before. The enemy was the caste system, the invisible hierarchical multi-storeyed prison system that the ancient Indians had ingeniously devised as the divine mandate to maintain social stability and keep law and order regardless of the condition of the political state. Kingdoms appeared and disappeared but the ironclad caste system kept the people hierarchically bound and segregated.

To liberate India, it was imperative to liberate the most oppressed, the Dalits and the Adivasis, grouped as the Scheduled

Castes and Scheduled Tribes. The Indian Constitution took special note of them. To lift them up, the Constitution reserved 22.5 per cent seats for them, 15 per cent for Scheduled Castes and 7.5 per cent for Scheduled Tribes, in higher education institutions and public sector enterprises both at the Centre and states. But they were not the only ones left behind. There were many more, millions of them, historically deprived and backward people who, through decades of electoral politics and democratic processes, had gotten the voice to speak up and ask, What about us? In 1979, the Morarji Desai-led Janata Party, which had come to power after the defeat of Indira Gandhi's post-emergency general election, appointed the Mandal Commission to look into the grievances of the Indians who came to be labelled as the Other Backward Classes (OBCs), a class of people who lived between 'Upstairs, Downstairs,' between the upper classes who had flourished during the British Empire as well as the Nehru socialistic era, and the god-forsaken Dalits.

The Mandal Commission, headed by Bindeshwari Prasad Mandal, a parliamentarian from a wealthy landlord-zamindar Yadav family in Bihar, concluded in its 1983 report that based on several social indicators, including caste, education and economics, 52 per cent of India's population fell into the rank of the Other Backward Classes (OBCs), and recommended that 27 per cent jobs in the central government and the public sector companies be reserved for them. Thus the OBCs and Scheduled Castes and Scheduled Tribes would take up 49.5 per cent jobs.[20] It fell to the lot of the National Front-led government of V.P. Singh, India's prime minister (1989–90), to implement the Mandal Commission's recommendations; but it led to widespread student protests, self-immolations and deaths, and a subsequent temporary stay order by the Supreme Court.[21] On 16 November 1992, the Supreme Court nevertheless upheld the government order, and the same year, the recommendations for the OBCs reservations began to be implemented for the central government jobs.[22]

During the prolonged and bloody protests against the implementation of the Mandal Report, an important issue was raised regarding the merit and competency of the OBC aspirants for the reserved quota jobs in the government and public sector companies. Offering them jobs before they were educationally prepared was putting the cart before the horse. To obviate this dilemma, Dr Singh's UPA administration proposed to create reservation quotas for the OBCs in higher education. In a 2005 case, P.A. Inamdar & Others Vs. State of Maharashtra, which subsumed other similar cases, the Supreme Court of India ruled that starting an educational institution was like any other trade or profession to which everyone was constitutionally entitled and free to practice.[23] The seven-member Supreme Court bench, in its unanimous decision, ruled that the government could not impose its reservation policy on minority and non-minority unaided private colleges, including professional colleges, who were free to determine their own admission policies, fee structures and other administrative functions within the law.[24]

Under the Indian constitutional system, Parliament is the supreme legislative authority for making laws, while the Supreme Court is the final interpreter and arbiter of the meaning of the Constitutional law. The Indian Parliament can make any law so long as it does not challenge the basic structure of the Indian Constitution. In fact, in the Inamdar case, the Supreme Court called for a new comprehensive, well-thought-out legislation for admission policy as well as fee structure. In sharp contrast to the prevailing sentiment of the upper classes opposed to reservations of any kind, on 21 December 2005, the Lok Sabha almost unanimously (one opposed, one abstaining) passed the 93rd Amendment to the Constitution, which inserted Clause 5 in Article 15 of the Constitution:

> Nothing in this article or in sub-clause (g) of clause (1) of Article 19 shall prevent the State from making any special provision, by law, for the advancement of any socially and educationally backward classes of citizens or for the Scheduled Castes or the Scheduled Tribes in so far as such special provisions relate to their admission to educational institutions, including private educational institutions, whether aided or

unaided by the State, other than the minority educational institutions referred to in clause (1) of Article 30.[25]

The move by the government to reserve 27 per cent seats for the OBCs and the constitutionally ordained 22.5 per cent seats for Scheduled Castes & Scheduled Tribes would leave 51.5 per cent seats for the open general category. In spite of the government assurance that the number of seats available would be increased so that there would be little impact upon the total availability of the general category of seats, there were widespread protests, including some hunger strikes by upper-class students from medical schools, IITs and other institutions in Delhi, Roorkee, Mumbai and other places. Doctors too from various parts of the country opposed to the government reservation policy joined the protest movement.

Nonetheless, because of the political consensus, invocation of the Essential Services Maintenance Act, the Supreme Court directive asking resident doctors to resume work, and most of all, the lack of sympathy displayed by the public, the protests died down. It's noteworthy that when Parliament and street protests cannot solve a problem, the Supreme Court of India becomes the final arbiter, as it happened regarding the question about the OBC reservations. On 10 April 2008, a five-justice bench of the Supreme Court unanimously upheld the Central Educational Institutions (Reservation in Admission) Act (2006) beginning with the 2008–2009 academic year. It also validated the 93rd Constitutional Amendment that added Article 15(5) into the Constitution, authorizing the Centre and the states to enact laws regarding quota reservations. Justifying its decision, the Chief Justice of India said:

> Reservation is one of the many tools that are used to preserve and promote the essence of equality, so that disadvantaged groups can be brought to the forefront of civil life... Reservations provide that extra advantage to those persons who, without such support, can forever only dream of university education without ever being able to realise it. This advantage is necessary.[26]

But the Supreme Court took notice that the upper OBC segments, the 'creamy layer,' which have gotten out of the backwardness trap, be excluded from the quota reservations. A person who has already graduated with a college degree belonged to 'the creamy layer,' and wouldn't be eligible for any quota reservation for post-graduate schools or research institutions. The list of backward classes was subject to review after five years. The concept of 'creamy level' did not apply to Scheduled Castes and Scheduled Tribes.

BEGINNING OF THE DIGITAL REVOLUTION

The idea of unique identification numbers (UID) or Aadhaar, had its genesis in improving national security, an issue that, for the nationalists, especially the BJP, became tied up with the question: Who is an Indian?

After the 1998 Kargil War, the BJP-led Vajpayee government appointed Krishnaswamy Subrahmanyam, a highly regarded national security and strategic affairs analyst, to head the Kargil Review Committee. Based on its analysis and recommendations, the Government of India decided in May 2001 to start a National Identity Card Project beginning with border villages in order to check illegal infiltration and subsequently the ID project to be extended to cover the entire country. In December 2003, Home Minister L.K. Advani, in response to the demand of Overseas Indians, gathered to celebrate the Pravasi Bharatiya Divas earlier in the year in New Delhi, introduced in the Lok Sabha the Citizenship (Amendment) Bill 2003. The purpose was to provide the overseas people of Indian origin (PIO) from 16 countries the right of dual citizenship, including permanent visa and the right to purchase property and invest, however, without the right to vote. The Bill was passed with overwhelming support from major political parties, hoping that overseas Indians would contribute to India's economic growth and development.[27]

Included in the Citizenship (Amendment) Act 2003 is Clause 14-A regarding the national ID cards, stating:

The central government may compulsorily register every citizen of India and issue a national identity card to him. The central government may maintain a National Register of Indian Citizens and for that purpose establish a National Registration Authority... The procedure to be followed in compulsory registration of the citizens of India shall be such as may be prescribed.[28]

What began as a 'Who's Indian?' security question for the purpose of strengthening national security evolved into a most massive transformative programme 'to improve the delivery of government services, reduce fraud and corruption, facilitate robust voting processes' and much more.[29]

On 28 January 2009, the UPA government established the UIDAI and appointed entrepreneur and co-founder of Infosys, Nandan Nilekani, as the set-up's chairman with the rank of a Cabinet Minister.[30] On 26 April the 12-digit, identification abstract number to be assigned to each individual by the UIDAI was given a visual form and name, brand name and logo, Aadhaar (foundation), designed by Atul Sudhakarrao Pande, so that 'people can connect with both these instantly', thereby making the UIDAI plan and the ID number easily recognizable and to create trust in the system.[31]

The first Indian to get an Aadhaar number was Ranjana Sonawane, a tribal woman in Tembhli village in Nandurbar district in Maharashtra on 29 September 2010. Prime Minister Singh and the UPA alliance chairperson Sonia Gandhi inaugurated the scheme when the first ten people received their Aadhaar numbers. Welcoming Aadhaar as a definitive way of establishing a person's identity, Sonia Gandhi said:

> With this, Tembhli has got a special importance in the map of India. People of Tembhli will lead the rest of the country. It is a historic step towards strengthening the people of our nation... Starting from this tiny hamlet, the scheme will reach more than a billion people of this country.[32]

Nilekani explained that this was the first time that a tribal woman living at the bottom of society's totem pole had become somebody, somebody through a number, through a unique Aadhaar number that 'is the only universal identity available to all Indian *residents* [emphasis added], even those who do not possess any other form of identification, making them *visible to the state for the first time* [emphasis added].'[33] Since all residents are not Indian citizens, Aadhaar could eventually be used as a tool for identifying illegal aliens, which was the original intent after the Kargil War Report. Aadhaar 'is that rare government scheme that was not designed to address a single need…it is an open identity verification system that can be plugged into any application that requires an individual to prove who they are, whether they're enrolling for a rural job guarantee scheme or opening a bank account.'[34] The Aadhaar system is unique because 'no other identity scheme has used biometric identity verification—using a person's fingerprints and iris to validate their identity—on such a large scale.'[35] In spite of the uniqueness of a person's Aadhaar number supplemented by their eyes and fingers as the touchstone of identification, the hacker's challenge would be whether Ranjana Sonawane could be digitally cloned.

The first large-scale practical application and test of the India-spanning UIDAI infrastructure began on 1 January 2013. Dr Singh, announcing on 26 November 2012 the new system of Aadhaar-based distribution of welfare benefits, said, 'The funds that are provisioned for direct benefits like pensions, scholarships and health-care benefits must reach the intended beneficiaries without delays and leakages.' Besides the need for the efficient distribution of direct benefits to the targeted recipients, he said, 'the government also provides an amount of over ₹3 lakh crore (approximately US$35 billion) in subsidies' to people below the poverty line (BPL): each family getting ₹3,000–₹4,000 (US$55–US$78), which now would be transferred to the family's bank account based on its Aadhaar card. The success of the scheme, he added, would depend upon the distribution of Aadhaar cards, close cooperation between the finance ministry and the UADAI, as well as integrating the banking system with the postal network in the rural areas.[36]

It would be on this foundation later on that Narendra Modi would build the superstructure, Digital India.[37]

PRIVACY CONCERNS

The game-changing socio-economic scheme leveraging digital technology to alleviate poverty through distributive justice, create governance efficiencies, stimulate economic development, strengthen open democratic processes and fight corruption—the scheme that would leave no Indian untouched—would also require digitization and networking of databases raising many legal and privacy concerns. By 2013, UIDAI had enrolled 600 million Indians in Aadhaar, and there was no going back on this massive networked database system that enabled Indians to resolve several critical issues, as Nilekani claimed, including 'identity, financial inclusion, cash-less economy [cash transactions form the bedrock, globally, for fraud and corruption], direct benefit transfer and subsidy reform.'[38] However, he could not see legal and political challenges to such a revolutionary and transformative nation-building project.

The first contention was that the UPA Government had exceeded its authority by launching the UIDAI scheme without Parliamentary approval since the National Identification Authority of India Bill 2010 had been still pending before the Rajya Sabha. Secondly, the collection of the biometric data was a violation of the privacy protections as per Part III (Articles 12–35), especially Article 21 of the Constitution.

In its decision on a PIL filed by retired Karnataka High Court judge K.S. Puttaswamy and advocate Parvesh Khanna in November 2012, a two-judge bench of the Supreme Court issued an interim order on 23 September 2013, that since enrolment in Aadhaar was voluntary, 'no person should suffer for not getting the Aadhaar card in spite of the fact that some authority had issued a circular making it mandatory and when any person applies to get the Aadhaar Card voluntarily, it may be checked whether that person is entitled to it under the law and it should not be given to any *illegal immigrant* [italics added].'[39] The original intent of the ID scheme, which was triggered after the Kargil Review Committee report, as mentioned earlier, was to check illegal immigrants in the border areas.

The government had issued instructions that an Aadhaar card be issued to every resident regardless of their citizenship bonafide. If the government had issued orders that Aadhaar be limited to citizens only, the UIDAI would have never gotten off the ground. It was a bold but imperfect system, a work-in-progress, nonetheless absolutely essential for the welfare, economic development, national integration and security of India. The writ petition was referred to a Constitutional bench. The petitioners contended:

> There are no safeguards or penalties and no legislative backing for obtaining personal information, and the proposed law introduced by the government has been rejected by the Parliamentary Standing Committee on Finance. Provisions for collection and retention of biometric data have been held impermissible in the United Kingdom and France by their top courts.[40]

Several issues remained unresolved. The 2014 general election knocked off the UPA government from power. Nilekani, having lost the election for a parliamentary seat in spite of his global reputation and wealth, was savvy enough to persuade Prime Minister Modi that the UIDAI was in the national interest.[41] And thereby hangs a tale.

SOCIAL WELFARE FOR THE RURAL POOR

Since India did not have a large and growing manufacturing base that could draw the rural people to urban factory floors, as had happened in Communist China, India's rural population remained bottled up in more than 600,000 villages with little hope of getting out of the century-old poverty trap in spite of a series of Five-Year Plans since Independence. In 2005 the UPA-1 government initiated the National Rural Employment Guarantee Scheme in order to provide a minimum of 100 days of work annually to each rural household adult member to undertake manual labour. The right to work law passed by Parliament in 2006 initially covered 625 districts, but by 2008 the Act, renamed as Mahatma Gandhi National Rural Employment Guarantee Act (MGNREGA), was scaled up to cover all of rural India. The government patted itself on its back for creating the largest and most ambitious social security and public works programme in the world for rural development that would also create and enhance rural infrastructures such as roads, canals, water harvesting systems, and ponds and wells. Instead of giving cash doles to the rural unemployed, the entitlement programme created a mechanism for minimal wealth transfer to rural India through work programmes, thereby helping the recipient to maintain their individual dignity by doing gainful work. Since the programme is administered by Gram Panchayats, it increased opportunities for democratic participation at the local level.

The implementation of programmes, as invariably happens in large projects, fell short of the Planning Commission's objectives and goals. But according to the Ministry of Rural Development's Report (2012–13), MGNREGA's achievements had been noteworthy. Since its inception in 2006, for example, 12 billion man-days of employment were generated, resulting in wage payments to rural households amounting to ₹110,000 crores. On average, 50 million households have been provided employment every year since 2008. Eighty per cent of households were being paid directly through bank/post office accounts, and 100 million new bank/post office accounts were opened. The average wage per person-day went up more than 80 per cent since the programme's inception, albeit with state-level variations. Scheduled Castes and Scheduled Tribes accounted for 51 per cent of the total man-days' work generated and women for 47 per cent; well above the mandatory 33 per cent as required by the Act. Of the 14.6 million rural works taken up since the beginning of the programme, about 60 per cent had been completed and 120 million job cards had been given to the unemployed. The programme generated 90 million payrolls that were uploaded on the Management Information System (MIS), available for public scrutiny, along with all the details regarding the expenditure of the MGNREGA.[42] The official data painted a rosy picture of rural transformation, which, however, fell short of public scrutiny.

The Comptroller and Auditor General (CAG) of India carried out a survey of 3,848 gram panchayats in 28 states and four UTs for a period of five years, from April 2007 through March 2012, which documented shortcomings in the implementation of the MNREGA programme, including low rates of work completion of only about 30 per cent, poor planning of work at the panchayat level, insufficient public awareness of the programme, and paucity of trained staff leading to mismanagement, among other issues. The CAG audit also included the survey of 38,376 beneficiaries, including 26,115 males and 12,261 females, average age 41, who were interviewed from 3,837 gram panchayats spread over 27 states and three union territories.[43]

HEARING RURAL INDIA'S SILENCE

A very revealing portrait of rural India emerged from the survey. About one-third of the total beneficiaries were women, but they were less than 20 per cent in Gujarat, Jammu and Kashmir, Madhya Pradesh, Mizoram, Odisha, Uttar Pradesh and West Bengal. Forty-three per cent of beneficiaries were illiterate. More than 80 per cent of beneficiaries belonged to weaker sections of society, including Scheduled Caste, Scheduled Tribes and OBCs. At the all-India level, the number of adults in the household was three, with the highest of five in Nagaland and the lowest of two in Tamil Nadu, Puducherry, and Dadra and Nagar Haveli. The average household income was ₹20,047, ranging from ₹11,000 to ₹30,000. About 90 per cent of the beneficiaries were casual labourers or small marginal farmers. Seven per cent of the surveyed rural population did not have any ration card, but in some states, including Jharkhand, Manipur, Meghalaya and Odisha, 20 per cent of beneficiaries reported having no ration card. Regarding the housing, overall, 79 per cent of beneficiaries had temporary or semi-temporary, mud-thatch type dwelling units.

Sixty-five per cent of beneficiaries had electricity connections, 27 per cent had TV sets, 35 per cent had bicycles and six per cent had motorcycles in their household. *Sixty-three per cent of the respondent beneficiaries did not have toilets*. Sixty-five per cent of the beneficiaries were not fully aware of the full benefits of the MGNREGA scheme. In 55 per cent of the cases, job cards did not have complete information, including a photograph, among other shortcomings. The most poorly updated job cards were in Jammu and Kashmir. The payment of wage basis was not standardized in the sense that work performed was not the predominant criteria for work wages, though more than 80 per cent reported having received wages within 15 days. The mode of payment varied from cash to payment through bank and post office. The beneficiary survey also showed that Gram Panchayats and Gram Sabhas were not completely dedicated to the MGNREGA mission. The social audit of the MGNREGA work by Village Monitoring Committees and the block level officers was inadequately and poorly undertaken. The CAG Survey reported that more than 30 per cent of the beneficiaries felt that MGNREGA did not have much impact upon their lives. An overwhelming majority reported that MGNREGA saved them from migrating in search of work, while more than half the respondents said the scheme helped them to shun work they did not want to do. Most shocking, *75 per cent responded that MGNREGA had made only marginal or little difference to their family income.*[44]

Prime Minister Singh, in spite of the reported gaps in performance and outcomes, nevertheless, expressed deep satisfaction with the programme that had paid more than a trillion rupees in wages to rural people. The MGNREGA story, he said, 'is worth telling.... the scheme scores high on inclusiveness... *Wage disparities are being reduced and women are coming out more in the public sphere to take up work and interact with banks, post offices and government officials. This has done wonders for their self-confidence and given them a greater say in financial matters of the household* [emphasis added]'.[45]

If Gram Panchayats, tasked to play the central role, took their responsibilities seriously, MGNREGA could very well become a driving engine for India's rural regeneration, the prime minister said, putting too much trust in the panchayat system. MGNREGA is a bold welfare programme for rural job creation, asset transfer in the form of infrastructure building, financial inclusion and distributive justice. But it's a work in progress. Bold and ambitious; nonetheless, it's a poor alternative to urbanization and industrialization, which are necessary to siphon off and train the massive rural poor to a more efficient and skilled workforce.

BUILDING BRIDGES WITH CHINA

On the invitation of President A.P.J. Abdul Kalam, China's President Hu Jintao visited India 20–23 November 2006 for long-ranging negotiations between the two fastest developing global economies with growing bilateral trade relations touching US$20 billion—mostly in favour of China. In order to avoid any untoward incident, the police put restrictions on Tibetan activists. During Chinese Premier Wen Jiabao's visit to Bangalore earlier in April 2005, Tenzin Tsundue, born and raised in India, a poet and activist for Tibetan independence, had raised a 'Free Tibet' flag across the street where Wen was addressing an audience. With the growing importance of trade and diplomatic relations between the countries, the Indian government wanted to avoid any more such embarrassing incidents during President Hu's visit, which also included trips to Agra and Mumbai.

Since the last visit of Chinese President Jiang Zemin to India in 1996, China's economy had grown by leaps and bounds. In 2006, China's economy grew by 10.7 per cent with US$2.75 trillion GDP on tiptoe, to exceed Germany's economy in the next two years. With a 9.3 per cent growth rate in 2006 and US$950 billion GDP, India's economy was one-third of China's economy.

India celebrated the visit as India–China Friendship Day, with national media, China experts, geo-political strategists and academicians in New Delhi engaging in deep discussions about the rise of China on the world stage as a global economic power. Under the well-cultivated bonhomie, there was a diffused fear of China looming over the Himalayas. The fear was on the other foot too. The number of Tibetans who followed the Dalai Lama's escape to India in 1959 had grown to 150,000 living in India and abroad. The Dalai Lama had created global consciousness about Tibet as a unique culture under the Chinese occupation. In this sense, though

China controls Tibet, it's a divided nation. Geopolitically, it is part of China. Culturally and spiritually, it's part of India, thanks to Nehru's compassion and wisdom; and Tibet is not going away. China will always be apprehensive about India's intentions even when the Dalai Lama passes away. Since India's technological and economic growth is unstoppable in the framework of a federal-parliamentary dynamic system, it's difficult to say how the relations between the two countries would develop.

During all such visits by the head of a state, it's diplomatically savvy to say that the visit was successful. There's always the usual joint statement with some agreements about cooperation on many areas of common interests. During this visit too, both countries concluded wide-ranging agreements and protocols regarding

> 'the bilateral dialogue and consultation mechanisms between the two foreign offices (that) provides for the establishment of a hotline between the two foreign ministers... a framework for bilateral investment flows between the two countries... a mechanism to inspect trade... the exchange of scientific personnel (and) scientific literature... the development of contacts and cooperation between the educational institutions of the two countries... (preservation) of cultural heritage... joint scientific and academic research....'[46]

Brajesh Mishra, Prime Minister Vajpayee's principal secretary and National Security Adviser (1998–2004) and an astute strategic thinker, gave a balanced account of President Hu's visit at a roundtable conference held by a New Delhi think-tank, Observer Research Foundation. Characterizing the visit as a normal periodic routine, he said it would be unrealistic to expect any breakthroughs regarding border disputes, membership of UNSC or India's access to the NSG. The challenge is how India reshapes its relations with its neighbours, especially in the light of the active Chinese presence. He admonished:

- India needs to correct its own shortcomings and build itself, rather than go on complaining.

- Whether it was because of ahimsa or non-alignment policy, India has not thought of the use of power. *India has had no 'strategic thinking culture'* [italics added].
- Tawang is important to India not only strategically but also politically and culturally. India cannot give up on the issue.[47]

The best outcome of the visit was that it kept the government-to-government and diplomatic channels of communication open between the two countries, which paved the way for the Congress party president Sonia Gandhi and her son Rahul Gandhi to visit China (25–29 October 2007), perhaps to show that there was another centre of power. Prime Minister Singh reciprocated the Chinese leader's visit in 2008.[48] Two decades earlier, Sonia Gandhi had accompanied her husband, Prime Minister Rajiv Gandhi, on an ice-breaking state visit to China. Since then, diplomatic relations had been zigzagging between carefully cultivated warmth and cold uncertainty. In 2006, for example, India and China re-opened the ancient trading post at Nathula Pass connecting Sikkim with Tibet—it had been closed since the 1962 War. Later in 2006, a verbal war erupted between the two countries, with China claiming Arunachal Pradesh as its territory, with India asserting that China was illegally occupying 14,672 square miles of its territory in Aksai Chin of the Jammu and Kashmir region. An Indian Administrative Service officer from Arunachal Pradesh was denied a visa to visit China in 2007. China pressured the Asian Development Bank in 2009 not to approve the US$60 million loan for a flood management project in Arunachal Pradesh, which, however, the bank ignored. And again, when the Dalai Lama visited the famed Tawang Buddhist Monastery in 2009, China lodged a serious protest. That was a year after the much-heralded visit to China by India's prime minister, Manmohan Singh in 2008. When Dr Singh visited Arunachal Pradesh, two weeks after his China visit, the Chinese foreign ministry lodged a protest. Indians could never be sure how China would behave at any time.

On the occasion of Prime Minister Singh's visit, *The New York Times* carried an ironic headline about the visit, 'Two Giants Try to Learn to Share Asia'.[49] China had no such intentions. China had begun to use its growing economic and soft power to spread its influence all over Asia and tried to keep India away from joining any alliance with the United States and its Asian allies, including Australia, Japan and South Korea. Before his departure for Beijing, Prime Minister Singh was quick to say, 'I have made it clear to the Chinese leadership that India is not part of any so-called contain China efforts,' which he rephrased more diplomatically during his address at the Chinese Academy of Social Sciences in Beijing:

> ...our destinies are linked by geography and history. ... India and China seek tranquillity and stability in our immediate neighbourhood... We recognise that the world is evolving and developing features of multipolarity... major powers, bound together by economic interdependence... seek to cooperate with each other to mutual benefit. India and China must be part of this cooperative framework.[50]

To be an equal partner with China, India had to be equal to China in military and economic terms; and India wasn't. China had massive leverage against India, including its mounting military presence in the Himalayas from where at any time it could create controlled panic on the Indian collective psyche by asserting its claim on Arunachal Pradesh; Pakistan's growing economic-military dependency on China, the so-called all-weather friendship; overtures to Nepal, Bangladesh, Sri Lanka and Maldives; and its large but invisible strategic presence in Myanmar. The flare-up at the Himalayas was not far from his mind when Dr Singh reminded the Beijing audience that 'the boundary between us is peaceful. We are both determined to keep it so while our Special Representatives seek a settlement of the boundary question.'[51]

One area where both India and China wanted to see progress was in trade relations, and in this area, too, China was the dominant partner since the balance of trade was in its favour, which Dr Singh wanted to rectify. India wanted China's cooperation on the India–US Nuclear Deal, especially with the NSG, which China had been stalling because the denial added to its leverage against India. China, on the other hand, was more interested in investment opportunities in India. For example, in December 2010, Chinese Premier Wen Jiabao visited India, what the BBC called a 'bumper Indian trade' trip, leading a trade delegation of 400 business leaders.[52] By 2012 India–China trade had reached US$66 billion, mostly in China's favour; and to keep the relations tilted that way, China President Hu Jintao, at the 2012 BRICS (Brazil, Russia, India, China, and South Africa) summit in Delhi, assured Dr Singh that 'it is China's unswerving policy to develop Sino-Indian friendship, deepen strategic cooperation and seek common development... China hopes to see a peaceful, prosperous and continually developing India and is committed to building a more dynamic China–India relationship.'[53] While the trade relations between the two countries kept a steady growth, the Himalayan border remained quietly smouldering, albeit occasionally bursting here and there into flames that were diplomatically managed. When President Pranab Mukherjee, on his visit to Arunachal Pradesh in November 2013, proclaimed that the state was an integral and important part of India, China routinely protested, but the bilateral relations on other levels continued.

LANDMARK INDIA-US NUCLEAR ENERGY AGREEMENT

During his address to the US Congress in July 2005, when Dr Singh said, 'There is much we can accomplish together,' he was opening a new chapter in India's rocky relationship with the United States. Since the 11 September 2001 terror attacks, the United States' global outlook had been absolutely transformed. America had become a wounded lion. There was an axis of evil out there, America discovered, and an attitude of 'You're either with us, or against us,' had taken hold of the American psyche. The very openness of India and the US made them vulnerable, Dr Singh told his audience, and 'we must deal effectively with the threat without losing the openness we so value and cherish,' and, since both countries had 'suffered grievously from terrorism, we must make common cause against it'. He effusively acknowledged the US contribution to India's Green Revolution that not only lifted millions out of poverty but also enabled India to 'participate more fully in global agricultural trade.'

Time was most opportune, and he exhorted the lawmakers for India and the US to cooperate in another vital area—energy security. Since the world's reserves of hydrocarbons were limited and the demand was ever-increasing, it was necessary to tap new energy sources, especially nuclear energy, for which, he said, 'President Bush and I arrived at an understanding in finding ways and means to enable such cooperation,' assuring the Congress that 'India's track record in nuclear non-proliferation is impeccable;' India had 'adhered scrupulously to every rule and canon in this area... India, as a responsible nuclear power, is fully conscious of the immense responsibilities that come with the possession of advanced technologies, both civilian and strategic;' and India had never been, and would never be, 'a source of proliferation of sensitive technologies.'[54] Dr Singh was attempting a herculean task of bringing India out of the nuclear backstreet pariah status after the Pokhran I and II (1974 and 1998) nuclear tests to an acknowledged nuclear power on the world stage.

Recognizing 'the significance of civilian nuclear energy for meeting growing global energy demands in a cleaner and more efficient manner,' the Joint Statement between President George W. Bush and Prime Minister Manmohan Singh, signed on 18 July 2005, said that 'the two leaders discussed India's plans to develop its civilian nuclear energy programme,' while acknowledging that as 'a responsible state with advanced nuclear technology, India should acquire the same benefits and advantages as other such states.' Furthermore, according to the Joint Statement, President Bush assured the prime minister that he would 'work to achieve full civil nuclear energy cooperation with India as it realizes its goals of promoting nuclear power and achieving energy security.' In response, Dr Singh assured President Bush that India would take decisive steps in becoming a responsible nuclear power, including:

> Identifying and separating civilian and military nuclear facilities and programs in a phased manner and filing a declaration regarding its civilian facilities with the International Atomic

Energy Agency (IAEA); taking a decision to place voluntarily its civilian nuclear facilities under IAEA safeguards; signing and adhering to an Additional Protocol with respect to civilian nuclear facilities; continuing India's unilateral moratorium on nuclear testing; working with the United States for the conclusion of a multilateral Fissile Material Cut-Off Treaty; refraining from the transfer of enrichment and reprocessing technologies to states that do not have them and supporting international efforts to limit their spread; and ensuring that the necessary steps have been taken to secure nuclear materials and technology through comprehensive export control legislation and through harmonization and adherence to Missile Technology Control Regime (MTCR) and Nuclear Suppliers Group guidelines.[55]

In a conversation with *The Washington Post* editors and their concerns about nuclear proliferation, Dr Singh assured that India's peaceful nuclear programme was homegrown and not based on stolen technology. And, although 'we have nuclear assets, our programme is totally under civilian control. We are a democracy, there are enough checks and balances in our country, and we have an impeccable record of not contributing in any way to nuclear proliferation.'[56] In a similar vein, contesting the claim that access to uranium under the Bush–Singh agreement would enable India to increase its nuclear weapon stockpile, Ashley Tellis of the Carnegie Endowment for International Peace observed perceptively that President Bush's 'strategic overture toward India' is nothing but 'an effort to strengthen India's ability to expand its civilian nuclear power programme in order to increase the share of nuclear energy's contribution to India's large and rapidly growing electricity needs.'[57] One of the chief negotiators of the deal, under Secretary of State R. Nicholas Burns, said that the civilian nuclear cooperation agreement would 'help India's economy gain access to the energy it requires to meet its goal of growing at eight per cent and beyond over the long term while reducing competition in global energy markets.'[58] Although the promise of India's 'access to the only practically inexhaustible source of clean energy now known to man,' has yet to be fully realized, or one might say, it's a work in progress; there's no gainsaying the fact that India did get 'reliable access to this technology and others in partnership with the most powerful entity heretofore seen in the international system, namely the United States…Such opportunities to forge a critical geopolitical relationship do not come often in a lifetime'.[59]

From Nehru, who took a hesitant and fearful step in accepting the hand of friendship offered by John F. Kennedy after the Chinese Himalayan aggression, to Dr Singh's whole-hearted embrace of George W. Bush's Atoms-for-Peace overtures, India had come a long way. But many Indian political leaders, especially from the Left Front, which supported the Congress-led UPA coalition government, as well as many activists and intellectuals of the non-alignment era, did not see the US–India Civil Nuclear Agreement as a path-breaking diplomatic and strategic achievement. It was during the intense debates and discussions on the agreement that India saw the true steely character of Dr Singh—that he was no pushover, not a wayside 'accidental' politician who was picked up to lead the world's most dynamic and turbulent democracy. Rather, Dr Singh always kept his eyes on the prize, India's economic growth, which would need access to modern technologies and abundant sources of energy for which a strategic partnership with the US was paramount. Later on, Narendra Modi would follow the same path.

Trained as a socialist economist in Fabian England, Dr Singh became a pragmatist and a strategic communicator. He persuaded Congress President Sonia Gandhi that the civilian nuclear agreement was in the long-term national interest. It was reported that he was not keen on keeping his job and that he would resign if the party did not back him up on the nuclear deal.[60] Since the visit of President Bill Clinton during the time of Prime Minister Vajpayee, a pro-America business lobby had been growing who believed that a strategic partnership with the United States was vital for economic growth. They saw in the nuclear deal something more valuable; they saw other doors opening for collaboration. Dr Singh was in the fourth year of his successful tenure as the prime minister, during which the economy had grown more than eight per cent. But the nuclear deal was a landmark achievement, and despite widespread opposition to the deal, including from some members of the Congress party, it had to be saved. The deal was pivotal to the development of India–US geopolitical strategic relations. On 22 July 2008, the Congress–UPA government sought a vote of confidence in the Lok Sabha after the CPI(M)-led Left Front withdrew its support over the issue. The Congress–UPA government won by a narrow margin of 19 votes (275–256, with 11 abstaining), which showed how ambivalent and seriously divided the political establishment was over the issue.[61]

COMPLICATED DEAL

The India–US Civil Nuclear Agreement was a complex long-drawn-out process and took three years (2005–2008) to conclude, which included the passage of the Henry J. Hyde United States–India Peaceful Atomic Energy Cooperation Act of 2006 (Hyde Act); India's agreement for the separation of military nuclear facilities from civilian facilities that would be subjected to IAEA safeguard inspections; and the NSG's special exemption for India—since India was not a signatory to the Treaty on the Non-Proliferation of Nuclear Weapons, or simply the Non-Proliferation Treaty (NPT)—which would give India access to nuclear fuel for civilian nuclear purposes. According to the military-civilian separation plan, 35 civilian nuclear systems came under the IAEA inspection in August 2008, after which the NSG gave India a waiver for buying nuclear fuel for its civilian nuclear installations. On 10 October 2008, Pranab Mukherjee, India's external affairs minister, and Condoleezza Rice, the US secretary of state, signed the historic US–India Civil Nuclear Agreement also called the 123 Agreement for Peaceful Cooperation.

The NPT, signed on 1 July 1968, recognized five countries—the United States, the Soviet Union, the United Kingdom, France and China—those that had tested nuclear weapons before 1 January 1967 as the only nuclear weapons states. Under the treaty, non-nuclear state signatories of the NPT agreed never to acquire nuclear weapons in lieu of which the nuclear-weapon states would share with them nuclear technology for peaceful purposes. India did not sign the Non-Proliferation Treaty considering it as discriminatory. And since India exploded the nuclear device in 1974, it was excluded from the club of five nuclear powers. Moreover, in 1974 the NSG, a cartel of 48 nuclear fuel suppliers, was formed to exclude countries such as India from access to the nuclear fuel trade. Therefore, the significance of the NSG waiver must not be undervalued. It made India an outlier, the only nuclear-weapon state which though not a signatory to the NPT, was nonetheless allowed to do nuclear trade and commerce with other countries.

The Hyde Act and the waiver conditions of the NSG, however, do constrain India from carrying out nuclear tests. It would be another eight years before Westinghouse and Nuclear Power Corporation of India (NPCI) would sign an agreement to build six nuclear reactors in India. What had held back the full operation of the deal was the Indian nuclear liability law, the Civil Liability for Nuclear Damage Act of 2010, which would make the nuclear equipment supplier responsible for any accident.[62] Moreover, the Fukushima Daiichi nuclear meltdown following the 11 March 2011 earthquake and tsunami had made Indian states rather wary of the nuclear energy plants in their states.

On his visit to India in 2006, Bush paid a handsome compliment to India when visiting the Indian School of Business at Hyderabad. He stated that 'India is a great example of democracy... is very devout, has diverse religious heads, but everyone is comfortable about their religion. The world needs India.'[63] But with Obama in the White House in 2009, American global priorities changed. The US was hit with an unprecedented financial crisis in 2008 that threatened the world financial system and the global economy. To stabilize the US economy and the global financial order was a herculean task and that was Obama's top priority. Obama decided to get out of Iraq and Afghanistan, which had been bleeding the United States. He began to see India as part of the equation that included Pakistan and Afghanistan. The United States also announced its pivotal shift to (East) Asia to rebalance its Asia–Pacific relations in order to manage the rise of China, which included the establishment of the Trans-Pacific Alliance that excluded China. By default, it also excluded India because India was not geopolitically Asia–Pacific.

On 24 November 2009, Dr Singh visited the United States in order to reset and revitalize the India–US relationship that he had built with Bush. India believed that the US withdrawal from Afghanistan would lead to a Pakistan-supported Taliban victory, which would be disastrous for Central and South Asia. Nuclear nonproliferation and climate change were other weighty issues that concerned both countries.[64] By the time of Dr Singh's visit to the United States, which was followed by Obama's visit to India in 2010, the United States had become India's top military supplier, especially after the sale of eight P-8 Poseidon, 10 Boeing C-17 military transport aircraft, and GE F414 engines worth more than $7 billion. It's ironic, commented some scholars, that 'Even as nonmilitary trade and investment and social and cultural ties between India and the United States have advanced in recent years, Washington remains of two minds about its relationship with New Delhi,' and 'arms sales may be the best way for the United States to revive stagnating US–Indian relations.'[65]

On his visit to India in November 2010, a year after Obama visited China, where he had greeted China President Xi with a bow characteristic of a satrap paying homage and acknowledging a Chinese emperor, the American President told the Indian Parliament what it wanted to hear:

> The just and sustainable international order that America seeks includes a United Nations that is efficient, effective, credible and legitimate. That is why I can say today—in the years ahead, I look forward to a reformed UN Security Council that includes India as a permanent member.

Obama called relations with India one of the 'defining partnerships' of the twenty-first century, mentioning 'partnership' myriads of times during his address.[66] The high seriousness and authenticity of President Bush were missing.

In spite of all the rhetoric about 'defining partnership,' the

Obama Administration's decision to limit H-1B visas to India's IT professionals and other protectionist measures against outsourcing worried India. Although diplomatic and media spinners tried to downplay the remarks, India's IT industry felt uncertain about the future when Obama grumbled about the US tax policy, which according to him states, 'you should pay lower taxes if you create a job in Bangalore, India, than if you create one in Buffalo, New York.'[67] In spite of the unsettling remarks, India and the United States revived the Bush-era Strategic Dialogue initiative in Washington DC in June 2010, where the two countries undertook to 'deepen people-to-people, business-to-business and government-to-government linkages...for the mutual benefit of both countries and for the promotion of global peace, stability, economic growth and prosperity,' pledging to cooperate in several areas of mutual interest, including advancing global security and countering terrorism; disarmament and non-proliferation; trade and economic relations; clean energy and climate change; and agriculture, education, health, science and technology.[68]

INDIA AND RUSSIA STAY THE COURSE

Beyond the noise and chaos of India's difficult albeit indispensable relations with the United States, India's geopolitical relations with Russia have withstood all kinds of cataclysmic global tremors.[69] Ties with Russia, even after the breakup of the Soviet Union, remained at a steady level of cooperation, including at the UN, BRICS, G20, the Shanghai Cooperation Organization and the NSG. During his decade-long tenure, Prime Minister Singh visited Russia nine times, including for the Victory Day celebration. At the 14th Russia–India Annual Summit, 20–22 October 2013, Dr Singh held talks with President Vladimir Putin about important ongoing issues, such as increasing trade from a minuscule US$11 billion to US$20 billion by 2015, longstanding defence relations and most of all nuclear cooperation—especially about the Russian nuclear reactors for units 3 and 4 for the Kudankulam nuclear power project that had faced difficulties due to the Civil Liability for Nuclear Damage Act, 2010, passed by the Indian Parliament.

During his address at the Moscow State Institute of International Relations, Prime Minister Singh summed up India's long and enduring relationship with Russia, stating that 'over the past six decades, no country has had closer relations with India and no country inspires more admiration, trust and confidence among the people of India than Russia,' and the friendship 'enjoys complete political consensus and enormous public goodwill and support in India... Russia has stood by India at moments of great international challenge when our own resources were limited and our friends were few'. Calling Russia 'an indispensable partner for our defence needs,' Dr Singh said that the time had come for opening a new chapter for 'technology transfer, joint ventures and co-development and co-production...long-term plan of cooperation in nuclear energy' as well as in other areas such as oil and gas.[70]

President Putin, on his visit to India in December 2012, expressed similar sentiments of abiding friendship between the two countries. In an op-ed piece for *The Hindu*, he wrote, 'Political epochs changed but the principles of bilateral ties, such as mutual confidence and equality, remained the same. I would like to stress that deepening of friendship and cooperation with India is among the top priorities of our foreign policy... The Declaration on Strategic Partnership... became a truly historic step.'[71] Keeping in mind the ongoing progress regarding the Kudankulam nuclear power plant, he talked about future collaboration in the field of nuclear energy,

> 'steel industry, hydrocarbon production, car and aircraft manufacturing, chemical and pharmaceuticals industries, in the field of information and biotechnologies...the Integrated Long-Term Programme of Cooperation in the sphere of science, technology and innovation...The joint operation of the Russian global navigation satellite system...The licensed production and joint development of advanced armaments rather than just purchasing military products becomes a key area of activities...fifth-generation multifunctional fighter plane and a multipurpose transport aircraft...the "BrahMos" cruise

missile...joint prospects for strategic partnership between India and Russia in the twenty-first century.'[72]

President Putin must be a good salesman. On his day-long visit, he sold US$2.9 billion defence weapons to India, including 42 Sukhoi Su-30 fighter jets and 71 Mil Mi-17 helicopters. What's called defence cooperation with Russia was, in fact, nothing but India's dependence upon its major arms supplier, and indeed the foundation of its abiding friendship with Russia.

PROSPECTING FOR PEACE WITH PAKISTAN

A few months before his government was ousted from power in the general election, Prime Minister Vajpayee had held direct talks with President Musharraf at the 12th South Asian Association for Regional Cooperation (SAARC) summit held in January 2004 in Islamabad. Musharraf, who, as Pakistan's army general, had led a successful military coup against Prime Minister Sharif in 1999, was apparently in full control of the levers of power in Pakistan. While addressing a session of the UNGA in September 2003, he called for a ceasefire along the LoC, the defacto border that had separated the disputed state of Jammu and Kashmir since 1947. After the SAARC Musharraf–Vajpayee meeting, the foreign secretaries of the two countries met later in the year to establish a platform for a multilevel Composite Dialogue process that would include foreign ministers, foreign secretaries, military officers, border security officials, anti-drug enforcement officials and nuclear experts.

Carrying forward the confidence-building process of his predecessor, Dr Singh met with Musharraf on 24 September 2004, on the sidelines of the 59th UNGA session in New York at the Roosevelt Hotel where the two leaders were closeted without aides for an hour after which they issued a joint statement reiterating their 'commitment to continue the bilateral dialogue to restore normalcy and cooperation between India and Pakistan... agreed that confidence-building measures (CBMs) of all categories under discussion between the two governments should be implemented keeping in mind practical possibilities...addressed the issue of Jammu and Kashmir and agreed that possible options for a peaceful, negotiated settlement of the issue should be explored in a sincere spirit and purposeful manner... agreed that CBMs will contribute to generating an atmosphere of trust and mutual understanding so necessary for the well-being of the peoples of both countries.'[73] It was the first meeting between the two leaders after the first round of the Composite Dialogue Process had been concluded between the officials of the two countries.

Some goodwill gestures had already taken place, including an agreement on the establishment of a hotline between maritime security agencies to enable the exchange of information regarding detained fishermen who unintentionally drift into the other side's territorial waters; giving advance notice about ballistic missile tests; protocol for the exchange of prisoners; expert-level meeting on drug trafficking and terrorism; expert-level meeting for the establishment of a communication link between Indian Coast Guard and Pakistan Maritime Security Agency; and exchanging lists of nuclear installations and facilities. India had also made getting a visa easy for some Pakistani citizens, including academics, business people and the elderly. And most significantly, Prime Minister Singh and the Congress party president Sonia Gandhi inaugurated the first bus service from Srinagar to Muzaffarabad on 7 April 2005, in spite of the fact that only a day before the launch of the service, terrorists had attacked the Srinagar tourism office. [74]

Lest the warm spirit between the two countries dissipate, Musharraf expressed an ardent desire to visit India for the one-day India–Pakistan cricket matches, which would give him an opportunity to continue the dialogue through cricket diplomacy.[75] Dr Singh responded wholeheartedly, extending him an invitation to visit India, the land of Musharraf's ancestors before he had migrated from Delhi to Pakistan in 1947. This was Musharraf's second visit to India after the 2001 Agra Summit meeting with Vajpayee had broken down over the Kashmir issue. After the Ferozeshah Kotla cricket match, Dr Singh and Musharraf retreated to Hyderabad House to set up a framework for the peaceful settlement of the

Kashmir dispute, one that came to be known as the Musharraf four-point formula. The four-step solution included: first, making the LoC between the two countries a soft border that would enable the people of the two regions to visit and trade with each other, as they had done before Partition. Second, to establish and strengthen freely and impartially elected democratic governments on both sides of Jammu and Kashmir. Third, to set up a political mechanism to be established by Jammu and Kashmir leaders for the joint governance of the two regions, except defence and foreign affairs, which would be the responsibility of Pakistan and India for the regions under their control. The fourth step contingent upon the restoration of the peace, would be a mutually agreed withdrawal of troops from Jammu and Kashmir by both India and Pakistan.[76]

What the four-step formula implied was that Pakistan would give up its claim upon 'Indian Kashmir' if India guaranteed complete internal autonomy to Jammu and Kashmir, along with the gradual withdrawal of troops, with the proviso that Islamabad and New Delhi would jointly oversee the region. It was a proposal for a kind of political condominium over which India and Pakistan would exercise joint sovereignty while ensuring local autonomy over the two regions and maintaining the existing borders. The proposal did not take into account that Jammu and Kashmir, under Article 370 of the Constitution, already had a special status that no other Indian state had been given. On the contrary, the so-called Azad Kashmir, part of the state under Pakistan's control, did not have the same status under Pakistan's Constitution. The idea that borders could be made irrelevant, 'just lines on a map,' was a pipe dream of two refugee politicians, Dr Singh and Musharraf, whom fate had catapulted into positions of power, and who failed to realize, as poet Robert Frost said, that 'Good fences make good neighbours'.

Musharraf had come a long way from the 1999 Kargil War that he, as the army general had masterminded, even keeping his prime minister Sharif in the dark. Now he was in his Second Act, a self-confident jolly good statesman seeking peace with his most important neighbour, as Zulfikar Bhutto had tried to do after the 1971 Bangladesh Liberation War. In Pakistan, the deep state consisting of army generals, the ISI, and the non-state terrorist groups had a different view of India. Their response to Musharraf's Four-Step Solution was a string of deadly attacks on major cities in India. By 2007, Musharraf had begun the Third Act of his remarkable military-political career when he began the downhill slide, the denouement, as he came into conflict with the judiciary and the civic society. The assassination of former Pakistan prime minister, Benazir Bhutto, on 27 December 2007, who had returned from an eight-year exile to fight the general election in 2008 and restore democracy, added to Musharraf's political woes. But after elections in Pakistan, Musharraf was forced to step down; and when threatened with impeachment, he left for London. With that self-imposed exile, the Musharraf Four-Step Solution for Kashmir went into limbo, leaving Prime Minister Singh with one hand clapping in the dark.

Taking advantage of the political turmoil, Pakistan's alternative state, the terrorist–ISI nexus, launched its well-planned strategy of an asymmetrical war against India.

THE WORLD WATCHES INDIA BLEED HELPLESSLY

In a daring, audacious, meticulously planned and well-executed military mission, call it a terrorist attack if you will, carried out by Pakistan's ISI under the leadership of General Ahmed Shuja Pasha and its non-state affiliate Lashkar-e-Taiba led by Hafiz Muhammad Saeed, ten do-and-die terrorists, sailing 589 nautical miles from Karachi port in their inflatable speedboats, landed at dusk on the coast of Colaba, Mumbai, on 26 November 2008.[77] The United States had just elected a new president, a young African–American man named Barack Obama. Americans were taking to the skies and jamming highways and roads bumper-to-bumper on their way to their grandmas and friends to celebrate their Thanksgiving. Indians were enjoying the historical romance in *Jodhaa Akbar* and humming and swaying with A.R. Rahman's soul-spiritual, 'Khwaja Mere Khwaja'. England's cricket team had been touring India since

9 November for seven One-Day Internationals (ODIs) and two Test matches.

By the time the terrorists struck Mumbai, the Indian cricket team was celebrating its five ODI victories, with Yuvraj Singh the player of the series, who had hit two centuries on his journey to a grand total of 325 runs.[78] Indians were looking forward to enjoying the remaining two ODIs and the Test matches against the visiting England team when their faces, eyes and ears were plucked away from Barabati Stadium in Cuttack in eastern India to the killing fields of Mumbai. A bloody bull had rammed through a wedding party with guests enjoying their sumptuous feast. NDTV blared, 'Mumbai, the city which never sleeps, was brought to its knees on Wednesday night as it came under unprecedented multiple terror attacks. Even as heavily armed police stormed into Taj Hotel, just opposite the Gateway of India, where suspected terrorists were still holed up, blood-soaked guests could be seen carried out into the waiting ambulances.'[79] The *Sunday Times of India* banner headlined on the front page, 'There's No One Alive Here,' editorializing, 'Our Politicians Fiddle as Innocents Die.'[80]

Pakistan was passing through another periodic military-sanctioned democratic phase with Asif Ali Zardari, the widower husband of the assassinated prime minister, Benazir Bhutto, as its president; and Yousaf Raza Gillani as the prime minister, both of the Pakistan People's Party (PPP). The real power lay in the hands of the Chief of Army Staff, General Ashfaq Parvez Kayani, to whom General Ahmed Shuja Pasha of the ISI reported. Lashkar-e-Taiba, an Islamic militant organization, was a highly valued asset of the Pakistan military's unconventional warfare against India.[81] In sharp contrast to the security state mentality of Pakistan, Indian leaders, including Prime Minister Singh and Home Minister Palaniappan Chidambaram, were more interested in economic development than in homeland security. Nor did Chief Minister Vilasrao Deshmukh of Maharashtra anticipate any trouble in spite of the fact that Mumbai, the financial capital of India, the maximum city that contributes 10 per cent to India's GDP and attracts the most talented people, had been the target of several terrorist attacks during the past decade.

In fact, Mumbai had been a terrorists' paradise. On 12 March 1993, it was hit by a series of coordinated bomb attacks, including at the Bombay Stock Exchange, that killed 257 people and injured 713. It was presumably a revenge attack against the demolition of the Babri Masjid. In 2002–2003 there were five terrorist attacks in various parts of Mumbai, killing and injuring hundreds of people. The worst terrorist acts were carried out simultaneously on seven commuter trains on 11 July 2006, which killed 181 people and injured 890, according to reports.[82] The local police blamed the LeT along with an Indian Jihadist outfit, the Students' Islamic Movement of India, for the attacks. The politico establishment called the attacks an international conspiracy.

But the 2008 attacks were different. They were a non-traditional foreign invasion directed from abroad and carried out by indoctrinated, knowledgeable, well-trained robotized humans who knew what they had come to do and also knew that there was no retreat or exit except death for a 'noble' cause. The closest parallel to this kind of remote terrorist operation is, ironically, the US military working its drones from its Colorado base via satellite to control, execute and eliminate its targets in the badlands of Pakistan. It was remarkable that the ISI and its affiliate could carry out such a daring enterprise about which *Indian authorities did have some information but did not take any preemptive measures.*[83] The terrorists had the blueprints of the major targets, including the Taj Mahal Palace Hotel, the Oberoi Trident Hotel, the Nariman/Chabad House, and the Chhatrapati Shivaji Maharaj Terminus. In order to avoid being targeted as a group, they tactically divided themselves into smaller teams of two to four.[84]

The Chhatrapati Shivaji Maharaj Terminus, formerly known as the Victoria Terminus, was built in 1887 to celebrate the golden jubilee of Queen Victoria. Known for its unique Gothic architecture, the railroad terminus, the headquarters of the Central Railways is a landmark legacy of the British Raj and is a UNESCO World Heritage site. Spread over thirty thousand square metres, with eighteen platforms and multiple tracks that serve commuter trains and connect Mumbai with the rest of India, the terminus is the busiest railroad station in the world. Like the cardiovascular system, it maintains Mumbai's ebb and flow of daily life, commerce and culture. On any given day, it carries more than three million passengers, local and long distance. A month before the attack, the terminus was the background for the song-and-dance 'Jai Ho' of the Indian–British film *Slumdog Millionaire.* The terminus had minimum security, and any time, a couple of well-armed terrorists with automatic guns could have created havoc; which they did in 2008. Beginning around 9:30 p.m., for about an hour and a half, the first team of two armed men with AK-47s turned the terminus into a killing field, shooting at commuters indiscriminately from platform to platform until the security forces arrived and the gunmen escaped into the streets, shooting randomly at pedestrians and the cops as they went along. The two-man killer team continued towards the Cama and Albless Hospital, but having been alerted, the hospital locked all its patient wards. After a shootout with the police on the street, the duo tried to escape in a hijacked car but ran into a police roadblock where one of the gunmen, Ismail Khan, was killed and the other, Mohammad Ajmal Amir Kasab, was wounded and arrested. Eventually, Kasab would tell the remarkable story of how the Pakistan ISI–LeT planned and executed the attack.[85]

The second carnage took place at the Leopold Café, a popular haunt of foreigners and trendy uppity Indians, where another team of two killers went in at about 9:40 p.m., lobbed a grenade and began shooting with AK-47 assault rifles, killing ten and injuring many in a short spell of five minutes. They then left for their third target, the Taj Mahal Palace hotel and the Oberoi's Trident, located not far from Leopold. The attacks, which were carried out by a team of four, were the most shocking live events watched by millions in India and abroad. In the first few minutes, the first pair killed 20 people in the main lobby of the Taj. The second pair of attackers entered from the North Court, lobbing grenades and firing all around indiscriminately. The team then set fire to a portion of the hotel, which spread and gutted the first, fifth and sixth floors.

Even after the police cordoned off the area and the Indian Naval commandos arrived, the situation remained out of control until the next morning, when the National Security Guard flew from Delhi and the rescue operation continued until the morning of 29 November 2008. By then, the terrorists had killed 32 people, including guests and hotel staff. All four terrorists were killed; a major of the National Security Guards was also martyred. According to the official dossier, the police recovered Kalashnikov assault rifles, magazines, pistols and unexploded grenades, apart from several cases of ammunition, mobile phones and a GPS device.[86]

Throughout the assault on the Taj Palace, the terrorists and their Pakistani handlers were in constant communication via cell phones receiving instructions on how to go about it and were being urged to take high-value people as hostages. In their attack on the fourth target, the Oberoi Trident Hotel, another team of two terrorists followed the same set of preplanned blueprints as they entered the hotel, spraying bullets and firing haphazardly, exploding IEDs, moving from floor to floor, killing guests and staff, and finally holing up and taking hostages on the sixteenth and seventeenth floors. Consider the remarkable endurance, stamina and stubbornness of the terrorists! It took the NSG Commandos 42 hours before the situation was brought under control. The terrorists had killed 33 people before they were killed. The Taj Palace is a prominent landmark for foreign and Indian dignitaries visiting Mumbai. During the attack, several trade delegations and diplomats were in the city, including Germany's Social Democrat Erika Mann, Spanish politician Ignasi Guardians, British politicians Sajjad Karim and Syed Kamall, and Polish politician Jan Masiel—all members of the European Parliament. Another Spanish politician, Esperanza Aguirre, had just checked in at the Oberoi's Trident. Several Indian businessmen and politicians were having dinner at the Taj Palace when the terrorists barged into the hotels. The Pakistani attack planners, the ISI–LeT, had selected their targets for maximum international and emotional impact, and they knew what they were doing in selecting their targets, including Chabad House, the Jewish centre.

In 2006 an orthodox Jewish organization, the Chabad Liberation Movement of Hasidic Jews, purchased a five-storied building named Nariman House, located in Colaba, South Mumbai, not far from where the terrorists had landed in their inflatable boats the night of 26 November 2008. It was renamed the Chabad House, a Jewish home away from home for the visiting Jewish, run by American Rabbi Gavriel Noach Holtzberg and his wife, Rivka Holtzberg. The Chabad House had a synagogue and educational centre and offered drug rehabilitation services. It was the terrorists' fifth target. Around 11:30 p.m., the terrorists entered the House and took hostages. They killed five hostages, including Rabbi Holtzberg and his five-month pregnant wife, Rivka. Thanks to their Indian nanny Sandra Samuel, the Holtzbergs' two-year-old son Moshe survived the attack. Moreover, the police rescued 14 persons after the operation. During the Chabad House attack, the terrorists kept receiving instructions and alerts from their Pakistani controllers before they were killed.[87]

According to a RAND Corporation research report, 'Lessons of Mumbai,' the megacity was picked because:

> From the terrorist perspective, the Taj Mahal Palace and Trident-Oberoi Hotels provided ideal venues for killing fields and final bastions. …They were filled with people—foreigners and the local elite. The attacks on foreigners guaranteed international media coverage. The message to India was, 'Your government cannot protect you. No place is safe.'[88]

Due to a deeply ingrained lack of historical sense and sensibility, a form of collective historical dementia, Indians have seldom learnt the lessons of the past. In a most perceptive analytical article, 'The Uneducable Indian,' published in *Outlook* after the Mumbai attacks, Ajai Sahni, the executive director of the Institute for Conflict Management, wrote that Indians prefer to fight national crises such as terrorism with 'imitative mantras,' what they call 'strong laws,' which are not enforced, rather than any executable strategic plan. 'Many journalists,' Sahni added, 'ask the routine question after each of the increasingly major terrorist strikes across India: why did this happen again? The more rational question, given India's capacities for intelligence, enforcement, and CT [counter-terrorism] response, is: why does this not happen more often?'[89]

INDIA CAUGHT NAPPING, AS ALWAYS

In response to *The Washington Post* editors' question about India's relations with Pakistan, Prime Minister Singh said that in spite of his desire to work with General Musharraf, 'I have to be realistic enough to recognize the role that terrorist elements have played in the last few years in the history of Pakistan,' keeping in mind that 'Taliban was the creation of Pakistan extremists, the Wahhabi Islam which has flourished, thousands and thousands of schools, the madrassas, were set up to preach this jihad based on hatred of other religions.' [90] But in spite of the assessment of the high probability of terrorist threats from Pakistan, the Indian government did not take any preventive measures.

It has been said, 'Coming events cast their shadows before them'. In this case, Indian intelligence had received some credible information, which was corroborated by the United States' sources, that a serious seaborne terrorist attack in Mumbai was highly probable. But the lead was not pursued.[91] According to the US Office of National Intelligence, 'The US intelligence community—on multiple occasions between June and November 2008—warned the Indian government about Lashkar threats in Mumbai,' identifying 'several potential targets in the city, but we did not have specific information about the timing or the method of attack.'[92] But in India, there wasn't any well-established coordinating mechanism. If the Research and Analysis Wing (R&AW) or the Intelligence Bureau (IB) received any threat information, the challenge was how they were to activate the local police and the law enforcement to take preventive measures, especially when the information was rather unspecific.

The attacks also showed that the Indian Coast Guard lacked the manpower, equipment, surveillance and intelligence capabilities to guard the Mumbai shoreline. When only a two-person team armed with automatic weapons could terrorize a vast sea of bustling humanity at the Chhatrapati Railway Terminus, it left no doubt that the Railway Protection Force, poorly trained and inadequately equipped, was no match for the terrorists. The same was true of the first responders, the city Fire and Emergency Services, the local police and the Anti-Terrorism Squad (ATS), who, in spite of their best efforts, did not know how to handle and contain multi-locational attacks. The slow response of Marine Commandos and especially of the National Security Guard, India's topmost rapid response force, was inexcusable albeit unsurprising due to the fact that at that time, the National Security Guard was located only in one location, Delhi, without any other base elsewhere in the vast country. Nor did the National Security Guard have its own dedicated aircraft to fly out in prompt rapid response. The 200 commandos of the National Security Guard took about ten hours to reach Mumbai because the transport plane was not available, and by the time they reached Mumbai, the terrorists had done most of the killings.

It took 62 hours for the ordeal to be over because the Indian commandos, unlike the omniscient terrorists, 'went into the locations, blind' without any brief or map of the Taj Mahal Hotel and the Oberoi Trident complex and were unsure how to engage with and eliminate the terrorists without harming civilians and guests trapped in the locations.[93] Aggravating the situation was a total lack of strategic communications and an effective public information system that the security forces and the government could have used, assuring and informing the people about what was being done and what they should do to protect themselves. It seemed that the government was not in control of the situation.

Just as Indians watched the bloody terrorism drama unfolding in Mumbai, so did Zarrar Shah, the technology and communications chief of LeT, who had given eyes and ears to the LeT operatives via Google Earth, mapsofindia.com and GPS, from his Karachi control room and guided them to the chosen targets. So did a Pakistani–American citizen David Coleman Headley, born Daood Sayed Gilani, to a Pakistani father and an American mother, who had changed his Muslim name to hide his identity; a man with three wives and several drug convictions, who, once upon a time was an informant of the US Drug Enforcement Administration. He was watching the carnage on television from Lahore. His Moroccan wife Faiza Outalha knew that he was a terrorist and had informed the US embassy in Islamabad.

Celebrating the carnage was his former wife living in Chicago, who watched the Mumbai carnage—'I watched the movie the whole day'—and congratulated him on his 'graduation.' Headley had conducted several surveillance missions in Mumbai, the information that he supplied to Zarrar Shah for planning the Mumbai attacks.[94] The unknown was knowable and known to many intelligence agencies in the UK and the US, which Indian intelligence too knew but did not comprehend its full implication.

It's in the realm of probability that the next ISI terrorist mission would be equipped with a suitcase of the so-called 'dirty bomb,' a device that combines dynamite with radioactive material.[95] Protected by its nuclear umbrella, the ISI-supported terrorist groups under different nomenclature had carried out attacks on the Red Fort, the Indian Parliament, and the Mumbai Stock Exchange and railroad system, as previously mentioned. In the absence of India's strategic capabilities and willingness to strike, Pakistan had no incentive in dismantling its terrorist training camps and infrastructure. Nor had the Indian domestic intelligence network and the state police the capabilities to locate and eliminate Islamic terrorist sleeper cells in India, without whose cooperation the LeT and other organizations would not have succeeded in carrying out the Mumbai 26/11 attacks. As Sahni argued, because of 'the country's turgid and obstructive bureaucracy,' the prospects of India 'responding on a war footing, cutting through red tape and existing institutional limitations, does not appear to exist in any aspect of the country's counter-terrorism responses.'[96]

Unsurprisingly, the Pakistan government initially denied the involvement of Pakistanis in spite of the fact that Ajmal Kasab, the sole survivor of the ten attackers, claimed that he was born in Faridkot, Pakistan, and was trained by the LeT. In the course of time, as more and more evidence piled up from Indian and international sources, Pakistan's National Security Adviser Mahmud Ali Durrani, a former army general and ambassador to the US, acknowledged that the surviving gunman was a Pakistani. Soon after the announcement, Prime Minister Gillani fired Durrani for his 'irresponsible behaviour,' showing, as *The New York Times* reported, 'how deeply the aftermath of the Mumbai siege has riven the country's fragile government as it struggles to come to grips with what American officials have said is clear evidence that Pakistani nationals plotted the attack'.[97]

Despite the fact that the ISI had denied its ties with Islamic militants, 'evidence continued to grow that it was a militant group established by the agency two decades ago that carried out the Mumbai attacks...until Mr Durrani spoke publicly on Wednesday, the Pakistani government had not admitted that Mr Kasab was a citizen'.[98] In an interview with Cyril Almeida of *Dawn*, Nawaz Sharif, former prime minister, said, 'Militant organizations are active. Call them non-state actors; should we allow them to cross the border and kill 150 people in Mumbai? Explain it to me. Why can't we complete the trial?'[99]

Prime Minister Singh, unable to muster any strategic military response to the ISI–LeT attacks, took the road of least resistance—what the counter-terrorism and conflict management expert Ajay Sahni called the Indian habit of chanting 'mantras,' whenever India was hit with a crisis. The UPA government put another layer of legal framework to fight terrorism by enacting the Unlawful Activities (Prevention) Amendment Act, 2008, and the establishment of the National Investigating Agency (NIA), a counter-terrorism agency with wide powers, modelled on the US Federal Bureau of Investigation. The NIA's mission or 'mantra' was to 'be a thoroughly professional investigative agency matching the best international standards... to set the standards of excellence in counterterrorism and other national security-related investigations at the national level by developing into a highly trained, partnership-oriented workforce... at creating deterrence for existing and potential terrorist groups/individuals... to develop as a storehouse of all terrorist-related information'.[100] From Quaid-e-Azam Mohammed Ali Jinnah's ferocious and lusty tribal hordes that ravaged and raped the Muslim dominated Kashmir Valley in 1947 to the ISI–LeT's most sophisticated remote controlled Mumbai 2008 military operation, Pakistan had come a long way. Like nuclear-armed North Korea,

Pakistan, bonded with China through the Belt and Road Initiative, couldn't be ignored or managed—until India took a political turn in 2014 and its leadership began to think outside the box with bold new initiatives.

UPA'S SECOND INNING

In 2009, the Indian electorate, 714 million eligible voters—of whom about 60 per cent voted—did not penalize the Singh-led UPA government under whose watch a handful of Pakistani ISI–LeT militants carried out that most horrendous attack on Mumbai.

The general election for the 15th Lok Sabha was carried out in five phases, 16 April 2009 through 13 May 2009—until then the largest democratic game ever played. A total of 8,070 high-stake political seekers, mostly men, from the UPA and the NDA political alliances and other regional parties and fronts and many independent candidates fought for 543 Lok Sabha seats. But Dr Singh was not one of them. He had always been protected from the hazards of competitive politics by representing a Rajya Sabha constituency from Assam.

As a Rajya Sabha member from the restive and conflict-ridden Assam, Dr Singh was elected to become the prime minister of India, for the second time, on 22 May 2009, just about four months after he had undergone cardiac bypass surgery. Only Nehru had done so, in 1957, for a full second term. However, Nehru was a man of the masses. The people adored him. They emulated his speech, manners and dress sense. Dr Singh, on the other hand, had no such claims. In the Indian game of democracy, Dr Singh would show that there's always room at the top and there are many paths to get there.

Only once in his long and distinguished political career did he have the audacity to contest a Lok Sabha election from the South Delhi seat in 1999; he lost by a margin of 30,000 votes. He never tried again. He neither knew how to raise money for the election nor how to emotionalize and capture the imagination of his constituents. He was an atypical politician, in a class by himself, for whom the Constitution and the political system had created space.

There were some new features in the 2009 general election. It was conducted on delimited constituencies based on the 2001 Census, which necessitated the upending of the electoral rolls with an increase of 43 million voters from the 2004 election. This was the first time that, except in Jammu and Kashmir and Assam, photo electoral rolls were used to prevent voter fraud. An overwhelming majority of the voters—82 per cent, according to the Election Commission of India (ECI)—used Electors' Photo Identity Cards (EPIC), a massive undertaking for which the ECI had already carried out successful pilot projects in some state elections, including Kerala, Haryana and Punjab in 2005.[101] The Election Commission of India is a statutory autonomous body that has conducted impartial elections since its inception. It is among the most trusted institutions in India, on whose honest and efficient functioning depends the Indians' faith in electoral democracy.

Keeping up with its motto, 'No Voter to be left behind,' the ECI saw to it that even a lone voter, Guru Shree Bharatdas Darshandas, who resided in the midst of the Gir Forest known for its Asiatic lion sanctuary and performed priestly duties for the Shiva Temple, too had the opportunity to vote. A team of five election officials slogged through the dense forest in Junagadh in Gujarat to reach the temple and enable the priest 'to exercise his franchise!'[102] But in 2009, the ECI was also going through internal turmoil. Chief Election Commissioner N. Gopalaswami alleged that the Election Commissioner Navin Chawla, who was expected to succeed him after his forthcoming retirement, showed biased partisan conduct in favour of the Congress party and recommended to President Pratibha Patil that he be fired. But President Patil, under the advice of the UPA government, rejected the report, and the ECI continued with its plan to schedule the general election. Chawla took over as the 16th Chief Election Commissioner on 21 April 2009, in the middle of the general election, assuring other commissioners that he was '*primus inter pares*—first among the equal... All our decisions will be taken jointly.'[103] After the election, no one complained of any bias or partisanship. The ECI retained its reputation as a trusted institution, a pillar of Indian democracy.

The UPA helmed by Congress party leader Sonia Gandhi won 322 seats, 13 short of the figure it had in the last election; nonetheless, a comfortable majority with the support of the Bahujan Samaj Party, the Samajwadi Party, the Janata Dal, the Rashtriya Janata Dal, and others. Sonia Gandhi as the alliance leader, could have become the prime minister, but she once again chose not to. The Sikh gentleman-politician, utterly civil and humane and personally incorruptible, would continue as the prime minister. The political arrangement was not dissimilar to the Soviet system, where the Communist Party secretary wielded political power and authority and the prime minister carried out the party mandate. For Indian democracy, it was a bold political experiment, and the system of shared power and responsibilities had worked well in the UPA-1 government.

With the 'Jai Ho' slogan borrowed from the film *Slumdog Millionaire*, the Congress unleashed its election platform, highlighting its past five years' achievements and promising more of the welfare-based economic growth aimed at the rural population and the poor: '*Aam admi ke badhte kadam har kadam par bharat buland*' (Hindi: The common man marches ahead, and India grows strong with every step taken). Embracing the country's achievements since independence as its own accomplishments, the party's election manifesto had claimed, 'It has been the privilege of the INC to have provided the political leadership that heralded these accomplishments under the prime ministerships of Jawaharlal Nehru, Lal Bahadur Shastri, Indira Gandhi, Rajiv Gandhi, Narasimha Rao and Dr Manmohan Singh.'[104]

The platform promised, among other things, the highest level of defence preparedness, police reforms, national food security, health security for all, comprehensive social security to those at special risk, quality education affordable to everyone, nationwide skill development programme, the well-being of farmers and their families, combating communalism of all kinds and caste atrocities, special needs of the girl child, connecting all villages to a broadband network in three years' time, introducing the Goods and Services Tax (GST) from 1 April 2010, carrying out a massive renewal of science and technology infrastructure, ensuring energy security, continuing to pursue an independent, pro-India foreign policy, and intensifying the involvement of overseas Indians in development.[105] All that the Congress party asked was a mandate for another five years.

The BJP-led NDA highlighted in its election platform the need for good governance, development and security. While the Congress–UPA manifesto began with the times of Jawaharlal Nehru, the BJP–NDA manifesto was evocative and harked back to India's ageless glory. Parts of the manifesto read like gems of ancient philosophy and history, for example, *vasudhaiva kutumbukam*—the world is a family, and *Ekam Sad Viprah Bahudha Vadanti*—truth or reality is one but wise men describe it in different ways. The manifesto said, 'A quirk of fate brought the Congress to power at the Centre in the summer of 2004…a government totally divorced from the twin principles of collective responsibility and accountability,' and bemoaned that 'the nation was thus burdened with a prime minister who was in office but not in power; and, a government that was in power but not in authority'.[106] The manifesto accused the UPA government of four cardinal sins, including the government 'headed by the weakest prime minister the country has ever had…a mounting sense of insecurity fuelled by repeated terrorist attacks, Maoist insurgency and separatist violence which together have claimed hundreds of innocent lives…gross mismanagement of the economy (that) has caused inflation, job losses and lockouts… has shielded corruption at high places by misusing agencies of the state…'[107]

Declaring Lal Krishna Advani to be its leader and the candidate for prime ministership, the manifesto promised that the BJP 'immediately upon coming to power, will address the key issues of security and economy…will resume the employment-generating, prosperity-creating policies of the NDA Government headed by Shri Atal Bihari Vajpayee, through massive investments in infrastructure projects, by nursing agriculture back to health, and by making credit easily accessible to industry, while ensuring the safety and security of all people from the depredations of terrorists,'[108] re-emphasizing its three goals: good governance, development and security. The

BJP manifesto was much more security-focused than that of the Congress, especially when it emphasized that 'The BJP will launch an innovative programme to establish a countrywide system of multipurpose *national identity cards* [Italics added] so as to ensure national security, correct welfare delivery, accurate tax collection, financial inclusion and voter registration.'[109]

But it would be left to Narendra Modi to fulfil the promise after he won the power in 2014.

Imagine the abundance of democratic aspirations in the Lok Sabha elections! There were 372 political parties and Independents in the fray, but only 38 of them, including Independents were able to make it to the Lok Sabha, with the Congress garnering 206 seats with 28.55 per cent votes, and the BJP getting 116 seats with 18.80 per cent of votes. The Congress-led UPA won 262 seats but with the support of post-election allies and supporters, including the Samajwadi Party, the Bahujan Samaj Party, the Rashtriya Janata Dal, the Janata Dal (Secular) and some Independents, the alliance had a comfortable majority of 322 to form the government.[110] The BJP-led NDA sat on the opposition benches with 159 seats along with the Communist Party-led Third Front with 79 seats, the Samajwadi Party-led Fourth Front with 27 seats, and the remainder, including Independents, getting 16 seats.

After being re-elected as chairperson of the Congress party, Sonia Gandhi said, 'The verdict of the voter in 2009 is visibly and strongly different from the mandate in previous elections during a decade and a half. The people of India have given a mandate for secularism and inclusive growth... It has become a watershed verdict for the welfare of the *aam aadmi* (common man).' Re-nominating Singh as the Congress party Parliamentary leader and therefore the prime minister and reposing full faith in him, she said, 'His dignified, determined and effective leadership of the government has been an inspiration for us all and has received overwhelming approval from the people of the country... We look forward to his leadership in the coming years.'[111] Dr Singh was sworn in as the 13th prime minister for a second term on 22 May 2009 with 76 Council of Ministers, which also included Farooq Abdullah from the Jammu and Kashmir National Conference, Chaudhary Ajit Singh from the Rashtriya Lok Dal, and Sharad Pawar and Praful Patel from the National Congress party. But his second term was not a bed of roses. In spite of his personal integrity, corruption scandals and charges of incompetency stalked him until the end of his time in office.

THE WEALTH OF THE NATION AND POLITICAL CARPETBAGGERS

On 2 February 2012, the Supreme Court of India did what Singh and his UPA Cabinet could not do in 2008. In response to a petition filed by the Centre for PIL and the Janata Party leader Subramanian Swamy regarding spectrum allotment, the court ruled that the spectrum allocation was 'wholly arbitrary, capricious and contrary to public interest apart from being violative of the doctrine of equality,' which was carried out in order to 'favour some companies at the cost of public exchequer.' The court not only cancelled 122 licences held by eight telecom companies but also imposed a fine of ₹50 million for selling off their shares after getting the licences. The adversely affected companies were allowed to use the licences for another four months, during which the regulator, the Telecom Regulatory Authority of India (TRAI), was asked to develop a new market-based policy.[112]

The licences were issued by Andimuthu Raja of the DMK, who held the portfolio of Telecommunications and Internet Technology (2007–2009) and allotted second-generation (2G) radio frequency spectrum licences at the 2001 base price rather than auctioning them at the open market prices of 2008, costing the exchequer from about ₹175,000 crores to ₹300,000 crores ($25 billion to $43 billion). The Court said that Telecom Minister A. Raja gave away important national assets at much below the market price to some of the favoured companies, rejecting the argument of zero-loss theory. The zero-loss theory implied that since the radio frequency spectrum was a free natural public resource, it cost the government nothing to give it away to serve the larger public interest, which in this case meant increasing public access to mobile communication.[113] Not only did Telecom Minister A. Raja ignore the advice of Prime Minister Singh, who had asked him in a letter to be transparent, as well as the concerns of Finance Minister P. Chidambaram regarding procedural proprieties, but he also advanced the first-come-first-served cut-off date from 1 October to 5 September 2007 in order to exclude select telecom companies from competition.[114]

As the wheels of justice turn in India in a 'curiouser and curiouser' manner, on 21 December 2017, a special court in New Delhi, which was set up by the Supreme Court, acquitted Telecom Minister A. Raja, businesswoman Muthuvel Karunanidhi Kanimozhi, daughter of DMK boss M. Karunanidhi, bureaucrats and others accused in the 2G-spectrum case. The court based its verdict on the grounds, according to it, that the Central Bureau of Investigation (CBI) did not have enough evidence against the accused. Kanimozhi, who owned a substantial interest in the family-owned broadcast station Kalaignar TV was accused of conspiring with A. Raja to pressure Shahid Balwa, co-founder of DB Realty, to invest ₹2 billion in the TV station. Based on the prima facie evidence, she was charged with criminal conspiracy, cheating and forgery under the Prevention of Corruption Act. She was arrested on 20 May 2011 and held in custody for 188 days before being granted bail. A. Raja, too, was charged with criminal conspiracy, cheating, forgery and illegal gratification under the Prevention of Corruption Act. He was jailed on 2 February 2011 and after 15 months, was let go on bail on 15 May 2012.[115]

The special court judge O.P. Saini ruled that the 2G scam was created by 'artfully arranging a few selected facts and exaggerating things beyond recognition to astronomical levels,' adding that 'Nobody believed the version of DoT (Department of Telecommunications) and a huge scam was seen by everyone where there was none,' and held without hesitation that 'the prosecution miserably failed to prove any charge against any of the accused, made in its well-choreographed [sic] chargesheet.'[116] Earlier the same court had found the former UPA Telecom Minister Dayanidhi Maran and his sibling Kalanithi Maran, both grandnephews of the DMK party chief Karunanidhi, not guilty in the illegal television exchange case concerning the Sun TV Network.

The scandal shook the country as an exemplar of crony capitalism under the Congress-led UPA dispensations and was successfully used by the BJP during the 2014 general election campaign. For a historian, the issue raised some interesting legal and constitutional questions. In its 2 February 2012 decision, the Supreme Court of India not only ruled that the allotment of 2G spectrum violated the constitutional principle of equal opportunity and was therefore arbitrary, but it also took over the government's executive authority and cancelled the licences to the recipients, besides imposing fines on them. This was the function of the executive branch, Prime Minister Singh and his cabinet that held office at the pleasure of the president. The Supreme Court, under the Constitution, is the final interpreter of constitutional law, but it has no authority to execute the laws, which is the function of the executive branch answerable to Parliament. If the Supreme Court ruling was preliminary (equivalent to the Grand Jury findings in the US justice system) instructing the law enforcement authorities to investigate the crime and people involved in it, it should have suspended its judgement until the investigation was done. In this case, the special trial court under Judge O.P. Saini set up by the Supreme Court overturned its own decision that had already found people and businesses involved in the spectrum case guilty. Under what principle of the criminal justice system could a lower court in India overturn the decision of the Supreme Court?

In his ruling, Judge O.P. Saini said, 'For seven years… I religiously sat in open court…waiting for someone with some legally admissible evidence in his possession, but in vain.'[117] It seemed that between the hasty and rushed ruling of the Supreme Court of India and the much-delayed decision of the special court, the truth of the case fell through the cracks, a sad commentary on how justice is done in India.

The scandal shed light on the working of the coalition party political system and how it distorted the parliamentary cabinet system under which all decisions are taken collectively under the leadership of the prime minister, first among equals (primus inter pares). It seemed that in the UPA coalition cabinet of Dr Singh, some cabinet ministers appointed by their political parties, for example, A. Raja of DMK, had their own fiefdoms, acted incommunicado with their cabinet colleagues, and worked to serve their own regional and political interests rather than working for the national good.

AND THEN THERE WAS BLACK GOLD

The coal block allocation scandal, which in many ways was not too dissimilar to the 2G scam that had shaken up the government about a year and a half earlier, was also based on a faulty assessment of the market prices of the resources and non-transparent procedures for distribution of coal mining blocks to mining companies.[118]

India is one of the largest producers of coal with estimated reserves of about 267 billion metric tons, mostly concentrated in Odisha, Jharkhand, Chhattisgarh, as well as in West Bengal, Madhya Pradesh, Maharashtra, Telangana, Tamil Nadu and some other regions. It is a major source for producing electric energy and for manufacturing steel and cement. Coal India Limited (CIL), a public sector company, controlled the production and sale of coal since 1973. Beginning in 1976, however, private iron and steel producers and later power-generating companies were permitted to own some coal mines. In 2012, the year of the scandal, 435 million metric tons of coal was produced, not enough to meet the increasing demand. The Vajpayee BJP-led government with its policy goal of 'power to all by 2012' decided in 2003 to speed up the production of coal and allowed private and state-owned companies to mine their own allotted coalmines in order to add another 100,000 MW to the grid by 2012.

When the Congress-led UPA government took power, it faced the same dilemma as had the BJP, that is, CIL couldn't produce enough coal to feed the new thermal plants. From 2004 through 2009, the coal ministry, under the direct control of Prime Minister Singh, issued licences for 155 coal block acreages to 100 private companies as well as state-run companies. The issuing of coal mining licences was based on a selection process through a screening committee, the process that was established in 1992 when Narasimha Rao was the prime minister rather than through competitive bidding or open market auctioning. The independent government watchdog, the CAG, the same authority that had also raised questions about 2G spectrum allotments, said that the coal blocks allotment process was flawed, unfair and non-transparent; and had cost the exchequer a staggering amount of about ₹10.7 lakh crores (US$150 billion) at 2011 prices.[119] In the CAG's final report, however, the loss to the exchequer had come down to ₹1.9 lakh crores (US$26 billion), based on extractable coal rather than the estimated available coal in the allocated coal blocks.

The drastic reduction in the estimated loss did not reduce its main legal and moral argument that the selection process created an unequal playing field for coal users. A coal mining company that was allotted a coal block at a non-competitive price got cheaper coal than a company that bought coal from the CIL or open market, which was more expensive. The process of application evaluation and decision-making was not transparent, and the CAG argued that since coal is a natural resource, it 'ought to have been allocated to private players on competitive bidding as it brings in more transparency and objectivity in the system,' adding that 'audit observations have also been corroborated by the recent SC (Supreme Court) judgement on 2G spectrum which, inter alia, held that the State is deemed to have a propriety interest in natural resources and must act as a guardian and trustee in relation to the same.' The government argued that ultimately the country benefitted through a tariff on the power sector and the consumer benefitted through a competitive marketplace in steel and cement products, three sectors that gained from coal block allocations.[120] While the government talked of trickle-down benefits, the CAG flawed the government for not being open and transparent in dealing with natural resources, which belong to the public.

Chief ministers of the coal mining states of West Bengal, Chhattisgarh, Jharkhand, Orissa and Rajasthan that were ruled by opposition parties too had their commercial and political stakes in coal block allotments; they had their own favourite rent-seeking clients. There were complaints of some companies selling their coal in the open market rather than for their own consumption. While it's true that coal mining is not a quick switch-button instant process and the operation needs a gestation period apart from clearing procedural hurdles, it was alleged that some companies just sat on their allotted coal blocks rather than mining them, thereby defeating the goal of increasing coal production, according to the CAG report.

The political resistance to the open marketplace solution that came from the coal states' chief ministers could not have been ignored. They did not want to lose their political patronage. Power generating companies had an irrational fear of the marketplace, thinking that they might have to pay more for the coal.[121]

Thus scandalized and sensationalized by the irrational exuberance of the CAG's charge of 'windfall gain to the allocatees' of US$26 billion (a climbdown from the original guestimate amount of US$150 billion), the Opposition and the news media shut their eyes and ears to the point-by-point rational explanation of Dr Singh to the Lok Sabha, when he said that, 'even if we accept CAG's contention that benefits accrued to private companies...a part of the gains would in any case get appropriated by the government through taxation and under the MMDR Bill, presently being considered by the parliament, 26 per cent of the profits earned on coal mining operations would have to be made available for local area development.'[122]

Months before defending his government on the coal allotment policy, which was, in fact, nothing but the continuation of the BJP–NDA policy practices, Singh said in response to anti-corruption activists led by Anna Hazare:

> I will give up my public life even if there is an iota of truth in allegations levelled against me, and the country can give me my punishment. My long public career ...has been an open book... It is unfortunate that irresponsible allegations relating to irregularities in allocation of coal blocks are being made without confirming facts.[123]

The public discourse in India had begun to descend into the gutter when politicians and anticorruption activists called Singh 'Shikhandi', a girlie man who had allowed himself to be used as a shield for corruption, an extremely derogatory expression about one of the finest and most honest statesmen India had sprung forth since Independence.[124] Arnold Schwarzenegger, former California governor, used the pejorative term 'girlie men' during the United States 1988 presidential election while accompanying Vice President George H.W. Bush on an election campaign. Indian politicians were beginning to mimic the coarse language of American political campaigns.

But the scandal, fuelled by the media and public outrage, did not die down and played a big role in the 2014 general election, especially after the Supreme Court took up a PIL case in September 2012 and stood by the Comptroller and Auditor General's critical assessment. The Supreme Court bench stated that the issues raised regarding 'the distribution of state property' required explanation because while 'You may have well laid down policy but was it implemented? Is it a sheer coincidence that a large number of beneficiaries were either politicians or their relatives or associates?'[125]

The Parliamentary Standing Committee, too, in its 23 April 2013 report, echoed what the CAG and the Supreme Court bench had said that the coal blocks distributed between 1993 (when the BJP–NDA coalition under Vajpayee was in power) through the 2008 UPA administration were inappropriately done.[126] In its 24 September 2014 decision the Supreme Court cancelled 214 out of 218 blocks allocated since 1993, from the era of the BJP–NDA through the Congress-UPA administrations, apart from imposing fines on the beneficiaries of operational mines.[127]

Apart from a robust and unbridled free press and independent watchdogs such as the Comptroller and Auditor General, the Supreme Court of India began to play an active role in the governance of the country. Social activism, rising scandals and PILs were increasingly becoming strategic tools for playing the game of democracy in India.

COME ON INDIA, PLAY THE GAME

It was the era of the UPA-2 coalition government. During this era, the Commonwealth Games of 2010 were held from 3 October to 14 October at the Jawaharlal Nehru Stadium in New Delhi. Expected to be a game changer, it was a highly anticipated event. More than 7,000 athletes participated in 272 events in 21 athletic categories.[128] However, for some reason or other, it turned out to be passable by international standards. The Games exposed India's poor organizational capabilities for planning and executing a large multinational event that required imagination, anticipation, and multifactorial coordination and disciplined execution. The Games were, as J.K. Galbraith would have said, the result of 'functional anarchy', not systematic planning under resourceful and creative leadership. Once again, it illustrated that somehow things do happen or get done in India in chaotic conditions.

It seemed the Gandhi–Singh dual command-and-control centre of shared power and responsibility had begun to come unglued and become dysfunctional. Apart from poor management, the administration was once again embroiled in corruption. With a price tag of more than US$9 billion, it was by far the most expensive Commonwealth Games. Besides the exorbitant budget overruns, concerns were raised about poor infrastructure and dismal living conditions in the Commonwealth Games Village as well as delays in construction of the Games venues, which prompted John Coates, president of the Australian Olympic Committee, to say that 'India should not have been allowed to host the 2010 Commonwealth Games.'[129] And then there was the looming danger of terrorism. Only two years before the Games, Pakistani terrorists had struck Mumbai. Most of all, there was a charge of pervasive corruption against the Games organizer Suresh Kalmadi, president of the Indian Olympic Association and chairman of the 2010 Commonwealth Games, who was accused of conspiracy, forgery and misconduct under the provisions of the Prevention of Corruption Act for which he was arrested in April 2014 along with eight others.

A former Indian Youth Congress leader from Pune, air pilot,

veteran of 1965 and 1971 wars, and MP from 1996 through 2004, Kalmadi was minister of state for Indian Railways during the tenure of Prime Minister V.P. Narasimha Rao. But the Commonwealth Games was his undoing as 'skeleton after skeleton seemed to tumble out and investigations began into allegations of big financial irregularities.'[130] Soon after the conclusion of the Games, the central government set up a special committee under the leadership of V.K. Shunglu, former Comptroller and Auditor General of India. This was apart from other investigations that were being conducted by the Central Bureau of Investigation, Enforcement Directorate and Central Vigilance Committee.[131]

The opening ceremony, nonetheless, was spectacular. 'India has arrived,' wrote Jason Burke for *The Guardian*, and the 'Concerns of recent weeks forgotten as dazzling event launches games amid atmosphere of national pride and celebrations... the moment that 1.2 bn people—there are few in India who were still unaware of the event—had been waiting for.'[132] The President of India, Pratibha Patil, and Prince Charles representing Queen Elizabeth II as the head of the Commonwealth, accompanied by his wife Camilla, the Duchess of Cornwall, declared the Games open on Sunday 3 October at 7 p.m., with the melodious voice of A.R. Rahman singing the anthem 'Jio Utho Badho Jeeto'. The welcome song 'Swagatam' was performed by the playback singer and fusion music pioneer Hariharan with thousands of school children.

Directed by Tamil film producer-director Ganapathy Bharat, the ceremony, lasting for two and a half hours, showcased 8,000 performers from all over India in six tableaus representing India's diversity of cultures, including the arts, dance, music, painting and yoga. The main attraction at the opening ceremony was the giant circular tabular helium balloon, the aerostat that provided the audience with a 360-degree multidimensional view of the performances.[133] Of the 71 Commonwealth nations and territories, only three heads of state, including President Mohamed Nasheed of Maldives, President Marcus Stephen of Nauru and Governor-General of New Zealand Sir Anand Satyanand, were present, apart from Prince Albert II of Monaco representing the International

Olympic Committee, and several guests of honour.

The closing ceremony showcasing performers from India and Scotland, the 2014 host of the Commonwealth Games, was more like the closure of 'a big, fat Indian wedding,' as a media report said, 'a dampener after the spectacular opening 12 days ago.'[134] Rather, a more charitable view of the Games was that 'The most controversial Commonwealth Games in history—marked by oppressive security and low spectator turnout—came to a close without any major glitches as India celebrated the finale with an extravagant cultural show,' and despite the fact that Indian organizers were much criticized 'by local and international media and foreign sports delegations before the games for delays in getting the facilities ready but once the games started, all the venues were cleaned up and ready.'[135] In spite of India winning 101 medals, the next highest to Australia, the Commonwealth Games were not a transformative moment for India. The Games did not turn India into a sporting nation with a 'culture of winning.' India has mostly remained a nation of gullidanda, kabbadi and other backyard and street sports.[136] Except for cricket!

TIME TO GO AND LET HISTORY JUDGE THE SIKH GENTLEMAN

The BJP–NDA coalition government under Vajpayee had left a legacy of strong economic growth of 8.52 per cent GDP in 2003–2004 when the Congress–UPA-1 under Singh took over the government. The average annual growth of GDP for the ten-year tenure of Dr Singh's administration was 7.6 per cent albeit during the last two years when the administration was struck with a series of scandals, the growth had shrunk to 4.6 per cent, which according to an official account was 'due largely to domestic policy logjam, tax disputes and shaken investor confidence in the Indian economy with attendant lower gross domestic savings rate (GDSR) and gross fixed capital formation (GFCF).' [137] Apart from rising inflation, the fall of the rupee and worsened foreign trade, and the increasing current account deficit, scandals added to the public grief.

In the whirligigs of 24/7 news media and its adversarial relations with the government, a hallmark of how Indians play the game of democracy, people forgot that only a few years earlier, India never had it so good. For three years in a row, the GDP growth was spectacular: 9.48 per cent in 2004–2005, 9.57 per cent in 2006–2007, and 9.32 per cent in 2007–2008.[138] In 2004 India's total GDP was US$721 billion, and in 2014 when Manmohan Singh handed the power to BJP's Prime Minister Narendra Modi, the economy had grown to US$2.039 trillion, almost three times. Per capita GDP rose from US$621 in 2004 to US$1,576, which meant an average Indian had 2.5 times more money to spend than he had in 2004.[139] The poverty rate declined substantially during the decade of Dr Singh's administration from 45 per cent to less than 22 per cent in 2012; or simply put, 133 million Indians rose out of poverty.[140] Equally noteworthy was the fact that during the same period, 2004–12, the middle class doubled from 300 million to 600 million, whose demographics were not limited to white-collar professionals only but also included street vendors, food workers, carpenters, drivers and many others, which meant that Indians had found many paths to get to relative prosperity. By 2014 there were about 50 million Indians with a disposable income of US$10,000. As incomes increased, so did the household savings, which tripled during the period.[141]

In spite of all the economic growth and widespread prosperity, why did India pull a long face at Dr Singh? For eight years out of ten during his tenure, India showed unprecedented economic growth, lifting millions of people out of poverty and pushing millions into the middle-class status. With the Nuclear Deal with the United States, his most singular achievement, Dr Singh not only brought India out of the cold and made India an acknowledged global nuclear power, he also built bridges with the United States, the European Union and Japan for future collaboration in high technology fields. Most importantly and perhaps unselfconsciously, Dr Singh, by carrying out the Nuclear Deal, was breaking the backbone of the state capitalism and the leftist ideology that had shackled the spirit of India for decades. Just as in 1947, the INC, under the leadership of Nehru, Sardar Patel and other freedom stalwarts, had liberated India from the stranglehold of Jinnah and his Muslim League hordes so that India could play the game of democracy on its own terms, Dr Singh by defying the blackmail of Prakash Karat of the CPI(M) and other leftist and socialist gangs during the nuclear treaty negotiations, liberated India from the curse of the bureaucratic state-controlled economy that had stifled the country and the Indian spirit. By a great act of moral and political courage, he shut close into a box the Left and the leftist ideology that had ruled the Indian mind for decades.

Dr Singh set India free on the path of an open and competitive marketplace entrepreneurial economy *without giving up on the poor*. Like Nehru and Sardar Patel, Dr Singh was a great liberator: he liberated India from the shackles of socialism that had lost its political and economic purpose after the Nehru era, and he was a great integrator: he opened up the Indian economy and integrated it with the global economy.

For a historian who must see through the smog and dust storm of the passing moments that cloud the judgement of footloose media commentators and kitchen-maid telltale storytellers, Dr Singh stands tall and ranks with Nehru and Sardar Patel. Ironically, it would be the BJP's Narendra Modi who would build upon Dr Singh's 'enduring legacy in the foreign-policy trajectory that he launched,' as well as the definitive policy initiatives and measures he took for the open marketplace entrepreneurial economy to flourish by establishing strong strategic bonds with industrial democracies, including Japan, South Korea, the European Union and the United States.[142]

Manmohan Singh was born to Sikh parents Gurmukh Singh and Amrit Kaur on 26 September 1932 in Gah, a poor desolate village without electricity, telephone, tap water or any other modern amenities—not an unusual picture of a village in the West Punjab (Pakistan) or any other part of British India in 1947.[143] His father, a small-town cloth merchant, had, later on, moved his family to a nearby town Chakwal, perhaps a better place to educate the boy. Young Manmohan was a 15-year-old motherless boy when his family migrated after Partition to a bustling Indian city, Amritsar, a commercial and trading centre as well as the seat of the most famous and the holiest Sikh Golden Temple, Harmandir Sahib. He was one of the millions of kids who, along with their parents, were forced to migrate from Pakistan to India, the kids whom Independent India would offer unprecedented opportunities, including scholarships, free books and other amenities to help them rise and shine. The Government of India and state governments spared no effort to rehabilitate the refugees and mainstream them to their new homes in the newly independent India. Hundreds of new schools and colleges were opened to accommodate the youth. As they say, geography is destiny. Migrating to India opened many doors for young Manmohan Singh that would have remained shut had Partition not forced the family to quit the rural backwardness of Gah/Chakwal.

Once historians transcend the trauma of Partition, they see the rise of thousands and thousands of young people like Manmohan Singh and Inder Kumar Gujral, another prime minister whose family too had migrated from the backwaters of Chakwal area, creating new opportunities for themselves and India. Dr Manmohan Singh's story, however, is not a Horatio Alger tale of an impoverished boy who rose through sheer hard work, persistence, determination, and courage from a humble background to eminence. That honour goes to a Gujarati boy, Narendra Modi.

Nevertheless, the young Manmohan Singh displayed in abundance the Sikh community's work ethics, austerity and dedication. And as a student in India and later in Cambridge, to use an old English phrase, he 'burnt the midnight oil' to rise to unparalleled intellectual heights as an economist—someone who would see the necessity of using political tools to achieve economic ends. Most people associate the Sikh community with the virtues of the martial race, perhaps because of their overwhelming presence in the Indian Armed Forces and with their Bhangra-style flamboyance, ostentatiousness and exuberance for life. But behind the veil of grandeur and full-blooded colourfulness of the community, there's another abiding trait, a deep fount of meditative austerity and silent courage born of the suffering of their long line of gurus. It is this aspect of the virtuousness of the Sikh community, its taciturn austerity and deep thinking that Dr Singh embodied throughout his political career. And at the tail end of his long, illustrious, political career, when the economy was passing through a cyclical dip and his impatient critics howled at him like jackals, all he said was 'look at my lifelong work'.

Dr Singh traces his intellectual influences, as he told the BBC's former India correspondent Mark Tully, to his formative days in Cambridge where he studied with Keynesian-Left economist Joan Robinson and Keynesian-Right economist Nicholas Kaldor, both of whom later on, were associated with the Centre for Development Studies (CDS), Thiruvananthapuram, Kerala, India. Professor K.N. Raj (1924–2010), a Keynesian-Marxist economist, who was instrumental in the establishment of the Delhi School of Economics—academic home to such diverse economic thinkers as Amartya Sen, Jagdish Bhagwati and Manmohan Singh—played an enormous role in shaping and moulding the collective socialistic mind of India during the Nehru era. K.N. Raj established the Centre for Development Studies in 1971, which developed the 'Kerala Model' that emphasized education, healthcare, high life expectancy, egalitarianism, distributive justice, and political activism rather than establishing industrial and manufacturing infrastructure that create the wealth of a nation. As Dr Singh told journalist and author Mark Tully:

> At university, I first became conscious of the creative role of politics in shaping human affairs, (thanks) to my teachers, Joan Robinson and Nicholas Kaldor (both Keynesians, leftwing and rightwing respectively). *So I was exposed to two alternative schools of thought. I was very close to both teachers, so the clash of thinking sometimes got me into difficulties. But that made me think independently* [emphasis added].[144]

It was this independent mode of thinking and his preference for Nicholas Kaldor's pragmatic economic model that enabled Singh to quietly break away from the chains of the socialistic mode of thinking of K.N. Raj and others of the Nehru era. This empowered him during the 1970s financial crisis to take small steps to liberalize the economy and set it on an irreversible course to become a marketplace economy à la South Korea, Japan and the US. It was this independent mode of thinking that made the India–US Nuclear Deal possible and brought India and the US closer.

Dr Singh's whole political life was spent in doing politics; as Otto von Bismarck said, 'Politics is the art of the possible—the art of the next best.' In the 2004 United Progressive Alliance (UPA-1), there were 12 political parties, all of them regional except for the INC, and to form the government, Singh's UPA had to take the outside support of the Left Front, the Samajwadi Party and the Bahujan Samaj Party. Apart from the constraints of the multiparty coalition, he had to share power with Congress party president Sonia Gandhi. The 2009 elections also resulted in a similar pattern of power-sharing at the Centre between Dr Singh and Sonia Gandhi, on the one hand, and the UPA's regional political partners, including the communists (CPI and CPI-M), on the other hand. Since the members of his cabinet owed their positions and allegiance to different centres of power, Dr Singh's challenge during his decade-long administration was to seek the possible and attainable without rocking the boat. Besides, since different political parties ruled the states, they exercised their autonomy independent of the Centre and exerted political influence on the working of the Centre.

Dr Singh's India had come a long way since the times of Nehru, whose 14-year rule (1947–64) was characterized by the dominance of the INC both at the Centre and in the states. Nehru was the monarch of all he surveyed. There was very little challenge to his authority. Nehru created a massive political class of secular Left-leaning intellectuals spread over universities, think tanks, news media and the top echelon of his administration, the thinkers and the decision-makers who mimicked him every which way, who supported his every move, all his initiatives from the non-alignment to the centrally planned democratic socialism, which gave India a sense of unity that the nation had never experienced before.

Dr Singh inherited and worked for a different India: polarized and turbulent and self-confident; and hungry for economic growth; with a dynamic federal-parliamentary system in full sway as the nation's founders had intended it. India was passing through transformative changes from the socialistic mode of thinking to the marketplace economy, the transition that Dr Manmohan Singh managed admirably by practising politics as the art of the possible.

14

SECULAR NEHRU TO DIGITAL MODI

Can't we find some other God?

—Sundarar, Tamil Bhakti saint-poet

He must be checked. We want no Caesars.

—Jawaharlal Nehru

India is a geographical and economic entity, a cultural unity amidst diversity, a bundle of contradictions held together by strong but invisible threads.

—Jawaharlal Nehru

I draw pleasure in governance, in doing new things and bringing people together. That pleasure is all I need from life.

—Narendra Modi

I believe that a government has only one religion—India first. A government has only one holy book—our Constitution. A government has only one kind of devotion—towards nation.

—Narendra Modi

When Manmohan Singh resigned as prime minister on 17 May 2014 and announced that he would not seek another term, India had two choices: Rahul Gandhi, the personable and charming great-grandson of Jawaharlal Nehru, the Gandhian disciple who had set India on the path of secularism, socialism and democracy, and through non-alignment had given India the illusion of being a global power. Or Narendra Modi, an autodidact and hardscrabble son of a railroad tea vendor who had risen to political power by the sheer force of self-discipline and willpower of which there are few parallels in Indian history. India chose Narendra Modi, the man who promised to liberate the country from the shackles of deadened socialism and hasten the country on the path of the digital age and marketplace economy, making India aspirational as an emerging global power. Modi's extreme passion for economic development and social welfare based on entrepreneurialism and digital technology, as well as India's place and role on the global stage, would eventually clash with his Hindutva–Rashtriya Swayamsevak Sangh (RSS) upbringing. Global events had made Nehru's socialism and non-alignment a burdensome legacy that was discarded eventually. Now, the question was whether Modi and the BJP would cast off Hindutva or transform and neutralize it into a harmless shibboleth.

Just as the Christian Democratic Union of Germany, which had brought Angela Merkel to power, was hardly Christian, perhaps the BJP would become a truly progressive secular party drawing its support from a wider base than its unsustainable Hindutva base. The growing demand for state autonomy under India's federalism would be the greatest challenge to Modi–BJP's Hindutva ideology apart from the demands of the competition of the marketplace economy where merit matters more than religiosity or ideology. Prime Minister Modi would soon realize that digital inclusiveness and Hindutva exclusiveness couldn't co-exist.

THE 16TH PARLIAMENTARY ELECTION

The results of the 2014 general election for the 16th Lok Sabha were a shocker. The UPA led by the INC, under the leadership of Rahul Gandhi and his mother and Party President Sonia Gandhi, met its Waterloo, winning just 59 out of 543 seats. This was the fourth time in India's post-Independence history when the Lok Sabha had no official opposition party. The Congress won only forty-four seats, eleven short of being recognized as the opposition. According to the rules of Parliament, a party must have at least ten per cent of parliamentary seats for it to have a formal Leader of the Opposition. It happened earlier during the times of Nehru (1952 and 1957) and Rajiv Gandhi (1984) when the Congress had overwhelming majorities in the Lok Sabha, and there were no leaders of the opposition.[1] However, in the Rajya Sabha, the Upper House, Ghulam Nabi Azad of Jammu and Kashmir became the Leader of the House with the Congress party having sixty-seven members, while Arun Jaitley of the BJP became Leader of the Opposition. The next biggest winner in the Lok Sabha election was a regional party, the AIADMK under the leadership of J. Jayalalithaa of Tamil Nadu, with thirty-seven seats, followed by other regional parties such as the West Bengal left of centre Trinamool Congress led by Mamata Banerjee, with thirty-four seats; the Biju Janata Dal (BJD) of Odisha under Naveen Patnaik with twenty seats; the Shiv Sena in Maharashtra under Uddhav Thackeray with eighteen seats; the Telugu Desam Party (TDP) in Andhra Pradesh under Nara Chandrababu Naidu with sixteen seats; and in Telangana, the Telangana Rashtra Samithi (TRS) under Kalvakuntla Chandrashekar Rao with eleven seats. The worst electoral performer, apart from the Congress party, was the CPI(M), with only nine seats under the leadership of Prakash Karat, a hardened communist who had tried to sabotage the India–US nuclear deal by withdrawing support from Manmohan Singh's UPA government.[2] The other communist party, the CPI, got only one seat. This was a most dynamic picture of India's parliamentary federalism. The states were not only represented in the Rajya Sabha, as the constitution had provided, but they also had a significant presence in the Lok Sabha, where the BJP dominated.

The election results clearly showed not only the rout of the INC but also the near decimation of the socialist and communist ideology in India that had dominated the political class and academia since the era of Nehru. The business and entrepreneurial class that had been suppressed during the state capitalism-socialistic pattern of society era (1950–91) had begun to re-emerge during the liberalization of the economy-under-duress when in the early 1990s Prime Minister

Narasimha Rao and his finance minister Manmohan Singh, under compelling circumstances, broke the socialistic mould and let India footloose on the global marketplace. By 2014 the mode of consciousness, the zeitgeist, had changed in India, and, as they say in common parlance, India had learnt 'a thing or two' because India had experienced 'a thing or two' of economic growth and wealth creation.[3]

And in this sense, the BJP–NDA election victory under the dynamic leadership of Modi was the triumph of the business and entrepreneurial classes; perhaps, a rebirth of the spirit of the Swatantra Party (1959–74) founded by C. Rajagopalachari, Minoo Masani, K.M. Munshi, N.G. Ranga and T.P. Pantulu, who felt that Nehru's INC had become progressively and obsessively socialistic in outlook and needed an alternative.[4] It took India a generation or two to gradually rediscover and embrace the spirit of the Swatantra Party, albeit in the incarnation of Modi's India First and Digital India nationalism with a touch of Hindutva. But more importantly, as a scholar astutely observed:

> Narendra Modi…was the first Indian prime minister elected from a generation born after Independence; his election to high office despite humble beginnings illustrated the political mobility of a genuinely democratic system; and his elevation to national power from his previous perch as the chief minister of a state highlighted both the ferment and the possibilities inherent in Indian federalism.[5]

HOW DID BJP DO IT?

In preparation for the 2014 general election, the BJP built an efficient organizational structure and worked out a winning strategy. Modi, a shrewd political strategist, a great symbolic image builder and communicator with mass appeal, someone who had a successful run for a little more than fourteen years as the chief minister of Gujarat and built the state into a dynamic economic powerhouse, was the shining star of the party. He was appointed to the BJP Parliamentary Board, the top decision-making body, as well as the chairman of the Central Election Committee, to lead the election campaign. Modi, who had the wholehearted support of the Rashtriya Swayamsevak Sangh (RSS) as well as the highly regarded former Prime Minister Vajpayee, despite some opposition from senior party leaders including L.K. Advani and others, became the face of the BJP. The party announced his name as the prime ministerial candidate for the Lok Sabha election. In India, party brand names are built around party leaders, for example, Nehru and Indira Gandhi for the Congress party; Vajpayee for the BJP; and now again in 2014, Modi for the BJP.[6] Once chosen by the party to lead, Modi rose like a primal force in Indian politics.

In India, voters can be ungrateful. They tossed Indira Gandhi out after the post-Emergency general election in spite of the fact that she had enabled the creation of Bangladesh, incorporated Sikkim into India and changed the geopolitics of the subcontinent. They dumped Vajpayee and the BJP in the 2004 general election despite high economic growth, the bus to Lahore for peace and the Pokhran nuclear tests. And in 2014, voters threw into the dustbin the Congress party, disregarding Manmohan Singh's achievements as a persistent and enduring political coalition builder in extremely challenging circumstances; and in spite of the overall spectacular economic performance during his decade-long administration and his legacy of the India–US nuclear deal that opened up many doors of opportunities for India. The voters in 2014 did not forgive the Congress party for the myriad corruption scandals and the economic setback during the last two years of the administration that had led to high inflation, falling rupee value, current account deficit and slower economic growth.[7] There was a diffused impression of governmental inefficiency, lack of control and a sense of drift at the tail end of the UPA–Congress administration, the public perception of a political party with a dual centre of power, Singh and Sonia, as it were, a house divided against itself. Democracy tolerates few heroes. Remember what happened to Winston Churchill?

The BJP manifesto exploited the social and economic anxieties of voters who had taken economic growth as a never-ending phenomenon. The manifesto promised a better India through forward-looking, dynamic policies, improved economy and infrastructure while curbing pervasive corruption.[8] With the slogan '*Ek Bharat, Shreshtha Bharat*' (Hindi: One India, Absolute India), the manifesto promised to use digital technology to ensure maximum governance with minimal government, to empower people through broadband access, mobile and e-banking for financial inclusiveness, digitalization of government records for transparency and time-bound delivery of services to people. It proposed to establish the National Agriculture Market supported by the Price Stabilization Fund and by leveraging digital technology 'to disseminate real-time data, especially to farmers on production, prices, imports, stocks and overall availability'. Throughout the BJP manifesto, there's a repeated emphasis on information technology (IT) as the panacea for solving India's myriad problems from economic growth to social justice. Believing that 'IT is a great enabler for empowerment, equity and efficiency', the BJP promised that 'e-Governance will become the backbone for good Governance' in order 'to nurture a Digital India—making every household and every individual digitally empowered... to make every household digitally literate with a goal to make India the Global Knowledge hub, with IT being a major driver and engine of growth.'[9] This was a new sound and the beginning of a new political conversation in India.

The manifesto promised much more, for example, including a more productive Centre–state partnership, stating, 'Team India shall not be limited to the prime minister led team sitting in Delhi, but will also include chief ministers and other functionaries as equal partners'. The BJP would focus on rural and urban development since 'agriculture, rural development and poverty alleviation go hand in hand...(And the emphasis) for rural development would be to improve village level infrastructure in terms of roads, potable water, education, health, supply chain, electricity, broadband, job creation, security in rural areas and linkage to markets'. It promised to build 100 new cities and launch the Diamond Quadrilateral project of a high-speed train network including the development of freight and industrial corridors and enhance the development of coastal regions through a massive programme called the Sagar

Mala project setting up new ports and Coastal Employment Zones. It promised to open up the Indian market, stating that barring 'the multi-brand retail sector, FDI will be allowed in sectors wherever needed for job and asset creation, infrastructure and acquisition of niche technology and specialized expertise.'[10]

Buried in the manifesto were references, albeit within the constitutional framework, for the enactment of the Uniform Civil Code and bringing the status of Jammu and Kashmir at par with other states by abrogating Article 370. And building the Ram Temple in Ayodhya, which, however, did not appear in the day-to-day election campaign—one of the most sophisticated American-style marketing campaigns ever held to build up the Modi brand.[11] Some of the most renowned global marketing, advertising and public relations companies including Ogilvy & Mather, McCann Worldgroup, Madison World and Soho Square of WPP Group, conducted a well-coordinated multimedia election campaign with a memorable catchphrase, '*Ab Ki Baar Modi Sarkar*' (Hindi: Now is the time for the Modi government).[12]

The media campaign lifted Modi from a regional leader to a prominent national leader, the man who is not only a great orator in Hindi, the most widely understood Indian language, and spoken by 600 million, but also someone who could take quick decisions and implement them as he had done in 2008 when he helped Tata Motors to move the Nano, the people's inexpensive little car, from West Bengal to Gujarat at lightning speed. India's zeitgeist, the network of assumptions, had changed. India's long bottled-up entrepreneurial spirit had begun to rise again. The socialism of the Southern and Eastern intellectuals and think-tankers who had dominated the Nehru–Indira Gandhi era was dissipating. The middle classes and the youth of India had begun to admire corporate and business India.

DIGITAL INDIA

The BJP's Digital India would leave no Indian untouched. Keeping this comprehensive goal in mind to make India digitally connected and integrated, the manifesto promised to increase the usage of broadband across the country including in every village; leverage technology for mobile and e-Banking to ensure financial inclusion; e-Governance for effective public grievance redressal mechanism; digital learning and training for IT-based jobs in rural and semi-urban areas; the use of telemedicine and mobile healthcare for rural healthcare delivery; real-time information for agriculture, retail trade and small and medium enterprises (SMEs) and rural entrepreneurs; to bring SC/ST, OBCs and other weaker sections of society within the scope of IT-enabled development; digitization of all government work to reduce corruption and delays; high-speed digital highways to unite the nation; technology to reduce transmission and distribution losses; and to protect India's priceless cultural and artistic heritage, including digitization of all archives and museology.[13] Would Modi's digital India enhance Nehru's secularism or selectively exclude Muslims because of the BJP's Hindutva ideology? That's a question for future historians.

When the 2014 general election knocked off the UPA government from power at the Centre, India's IT industry was a global player and a significant contributor to India's GDP. The fifth-largest industry in India, the IT industry contributed about US$118 billion in 2014–15 to the GDP, twice the amount than when Dr Manmohan Singh had begun his second term in 2009.[14] The foundation of Digital India had already been laid when Modi took over as the prime minister. Nandan Nilekani, the legendary chairman of the UIDAI-Aadhaar, in spite of his national influence, global reputation and wealth, lost the election for a parliamentary seat from Bengaluru to an unknown BJP rival. He was nonetheless savvy enough to persuade Prime Minister Modi that the continuation of the Aadhaar was in the national interest.

In a personal meeting with Modi on 1 July 2014, Nilekani delineated the promises and future possibilities of 'the platform, its expansion across many states, the applications that had been developed, the possibilities recommended by task forces and committees'.[15] Prior to the meeting, according to Shankkar Aiyar's account, *Aadhaar: A Biometric History of India's 12-Digit*

Revolution, Ram Sewak Sharma of the Department of Electronics and Information Technology, formerly the chief secretary of Jharkhand, had made a presentation to Modi as to how the Aadhaar-based biometric dashboard attendance system in the state had helped the Jharkhand government and state institutions such as hospitals, cooperative banks, schools and district offices to improve their efficiencies by targeting employee absenteeism. 'Sharma's presentation,' wrote Aiyar, 'included the subject of e-governance, the entire architecture of UIDAI, the promise of Aadhaar and its potential to save billions of rupees for the government.' He mentioned, 'Even if the government could reduce leakage and theft by 10 per cent it would be a big sum.'[16]

Modi, who 'is constantly looking for technology solutions, not just for processes but also to engender a change in work culture,' was easily persuaded and asked Sharma to implement the Jharkhand Aadhaar-based e-governance scheme for the central government.[17] It was on the advice and encouragement of Sharma that Nilekani had met with Modi. As Gujarat's chief minister, Modi had expressed serious doubts about Aadhaar, calling it a programme with 'no vision, only political gimmick.'[18] But his techno-cultural mind made a quantum leap, and he took to Aadhaar as naturally and smoothly as a duck takes to water. He began to see the future of the nation beyond UIDAI-Aadhaar, the future as Digital India. Nandan Nilekani and Narendra Modi were made for each other, and if Nilekani had curbed his enthusiasm for a political future and remained an apolitical entrepreneurial technocrat, as the nuclear scientist Homi Bhabha had done during the times of Jawaharlal Nehru, he would have remained the guiding light for Prime Minister Narendra Modi's grand vision of Digital India.

But Nilekani did light the holy fire in Modi's saffron imagination, and there was no going back. Modi began to see the promises of the election campaign *'Achhe Din'* (Hindi: Good Days) for India being materialized through the convergence of the seemingly incompatible diversity of the nation on a virtual platform, Aadhaar. No doubt, Nilekani and his team in a matter of a few years, through their missionary zeal and speed, had done a yeoman's job, conceptualizing and operationalizing the idea of digital identity of individuals in a country where people by and large tend to metamorphose every abstract concept into colourful visual forms, motifs and symbols. It's also important to remember, on the other hand, that few other cultures are as numerically and mathematically oriented as India, where early home education begins with numbers, numerology, and mental calculations as well as chants and mantras. Indians, for example, had no difficulty in adopting the metric system in 1956, albeit in stages.

DIGITAL IDENTITY AND ITS PROMISES

One, however, has to be careful about the claim that Aadhaar gives a person their identity. The identity of a person in India is associated with their name, caste/class, language, religion, profession and associations. Ranjana Sonawane, the tribal woman who was the first to get her Aadhaar number (29 September 2010) had an identity in her own community, as had Nilekani who co-founded the Infosys that shook up India. From the year of the Millennium Bug, Y2K, when Indian IT companies saved the world from digital doom through 2009, when Dr Manmohan Singh's UPA government issued an announcement to constitute the UIDAI, India had already built up the digital infrastructure, capabilities and talents to build Aadhaar.[19] No wonder in the very first year of its launch, Aadhaar enrolled 100 million people. If India had done the same with its manufacturing base, it would have been the factory floor of the world. But that's another story.

It is important to see the parallel between the Aadhaar and the Internet architectures. The Internet was designed by the U.S Pentagon information technology experts to overcome computer systems' incompatibilities through Transmission Control Protocol/ Internet Protocol protocols so that a computer system running on one protocol could connect and communicate with other computer systems running on different protocols without disruption even if a computer system in the network went down. Interoperability, connectivity and autonomy of the networked systems are at the heart of the Internet, which makes information indestructible. Similarly, the Aadhaar system overcomes and transcends the diversity of India through the convergent digital platform, Aadhaar, which communicates and connects services and people whether living in Kerala or Kashmir, Hindu or Muslim.

Aadhaar is communal-blind. Like the Internet, Aadhaar is simultaneously centralized and decentralized: the central government could use it for its all-India programmes, and each state could use it for its own programmes. Like the Internet, it is theoretically indestructible; it's also potentially corruptible, raising concerns similar to what the Internet does, including privacy and security.

Modi, having seen what had been done and accomplished with the UIDAI-Aadhaar enterprise and what were the evolutionary possibilities of the multidimensional digital platform, was quick to grasp its importance and put it to use. The UIDAI had already issued Aadhaar cards to 650 million people when the BJP administration took political charge in 2014. Five days after the meeting with Nilekani, Prime Minister Modi increased the Aadhaar budget for the fiscal year 2014–15 by about 32 per cent to $300 million, targeting to expand the programme to link it with the direct benefit transfer (DBT) scheme and passports. By 2017 the programme had enrolled a billion people and was enabling the central government to save a substantial amount of money by linking it with the DBT scheme and plugging the leakage.[20]

To meet the long-standing public criticism that UIDAI-Aadhaar was being run as a government programme and lacked parliamentary authorization, Finance Minister Arun Jaitley introduced the Aadhaar (Targeted Delivery of Financial and Other Subsidies, Benefits and Services) Bill, 2016, in the Lok Sabha. Since the BJP-led government did not have a majority in the Rajya Sabha (the Upper House), the Bill was introduced as a Money Bill in the Lok Sabha. Under the Constitution, a Money Bill does not require the approval of the Rajya Sabha, though the Upper House may debate it and make recommendations for amendments. Returning (rejecting) the Rajya Sabha amendments, the Lok Sabha passed the Aadhaar Bill on 11 March 2016, despite the fact that the privacy concerns regarding the data collection under the UIDAI-Aadhaar scheme were under review of the Supreme Court. The Aadhaar Act made the use of Aadhaar mandatory for availing of government subsidies.[21]

The Aadhaar Act grandfathered the benefit programmes originally initiated by the UPA government of Dr Manmohan Singh. The change of the government at the Centre in 2014 led to enhancement and improvement, not disruption, of the benefit programmes, ensuring democratic continuity and thereby sustaining people's faith in the system. The Direct Benefit Transfer of Liquid Petroleum Gas (LPG), the subsidized programme introduced in 2013 by the UPA government, required the recipient to purchase the cooking gas at full price from the market and thereafter, the government subsidy would be credited to their Aadhaar-connected bank accounts. But the Supreme Court asked the government not to make the LPG conditional upon a beneficiary having an Aadhaar account. Modified as the nationwide PaHaL (Pratyaksha Hastaantarit Laabh) programme, the direct benefit subsidy began to be credited to the beneficiary's bank account regardless of the Aadhaar account. The government claimed, according to media reports, substantial saving in energy consumption due to the plugging of illegal duplicate gas connections.

What was earlier sold fraudulently under the guise of subsidized rate, after the implementation of the PaHaL, nonetheless, it began to be sold in the open marketplace. Aadhaar eliminated the pilferer, and in the first year alone, the government claimed to have saved ₹12,700 crores. Arvind Subramanian, Chief Economic Adviser (2014–18) to the Modi government, cautioned that 'It's necessary that we don't overestimate the gain and under-recognise possible cost of doing this and in the case of DBT and PAHAL, we have some preliminary evidence to suggest that a lot of it is the elimination of ghost beneficiaries, but we can't rule out that there could be an exclusion of genuine beneficiaries.' [22] Nilekani, the former chairman of UIDAI, was more enthusiastic about the programme's achievements. At a World Bank–IMF meeting on 12 October 2017, he said that the programme had 'saved the government about USD 9 billion in fraud and wastage because by having that unique number, you eliminate fakes and duplicates from your beneficiary and employee list...We have about half a billion people who have connected their ID directly to a bank account.' Because of the fin-tech connectivity, the government 'transferred about US$12 billion into bank accounts electronically in real time to the world's largest cash transfer system.'

Projecting the future of Aadhaar as a socioeconomic platform, Nilekani said, 'In a society where per capita income is US$1,500, and you are data-rich, the business model is how do we create an architecture where individuals and businesses are able to trade in their data to improve their lives... If I as a consumer can use my data to get better loans, better education, better jobs and better skills, and if we can get a billion people to get access to that they will use data as the ladder to improve their lives.'[23]

As the governmental authorities became increasingly familiar with the working and the potential economic and political power of Aadhaar, they began to integrate more and more government functions into the system. For the government crop insurance programme, the Pradhan Mantri Fasal Bima Yojana, it was necessary to integrate land records with Aadhaar. In order to mitigate the national scourge of workplace absenteeism, the government introduced in July 2014 an Aadhaar-based biometric attendance system for central government employees, a system that had been successfully implemented in the Jharkhand State. The issuing of the passport began to be linked with Aadhaar for security reasons as well as for speedy delivery.[24] The massive government retirement pension scheme, the Employees' Provident Fund Organization of India, with a subscriber base of more than 42 million (2014–15), started linking its subscribers with their Aadhaar accounts though under the Supreme Court directive having an Aadhaar account was not mandatory for the Provident Fund transactions.

Since a trusted electoral system is at the heart of democracy, on 3 March 2015 the Election Commission of India began the National Electoral Roll Purification and Authentication Programme (NERPAP) to link the registered voters' Aadhaar numbers with their photo ID cards in order to eliminate duplications and voter fraud, though the Aadhaar card was not mandatory for voting, vide the Supreme Court directive.[25] Authorities began to explore other uses of Aadhaar. For example, cows, regarded by most Indians as sacred, were proposed to get an Aadhaar-like-identity number for a massive artificial insemination drive to improve India's cattle population of 45 million milk cows. Matrimonial websites widely used by Indians for matchmaking were asked to consider including users' Aadhaar number for identity verification and authentication.[26] To implement the Right to Education, Maharashtra State started enrolling all school students in the Aadhaar scheme.

It's worthwhile reviewing the timeline of how the national security needs of checking the identity of illegal aliens post-Kargil War evolved into creating UID for the below poverty line (BPL) population database, which further led to the development of a national identity programme and the establishment of the UIDAI, and finally, the 12-digit biometric Aadhaar system that has had a transformative impact on India. But every new technology tests the boundaries of freedom and raises questions about the sanctity of individual autonomy. In a landmark case in 2017, the Supreme Court of India ruled that the right to privacy was an intrinsic component of Part III Article 21 of the Constitution that protects life and liberty.[27] In spite of serious questions raised by civil society activists regarding privacy and security concerns; data leaks and hacking by a foreign state and non-state actors; fraudsters gaming the system; and the legality of sharing UIDAI data with law enforcement authorities as well as legal challenges in the Supreme Court, the Modi government, as of March 2017, went ahead and connected 92 central government-sponsored schemes with the Aadhaar system in the pursuit of its grand vision of Digital India.[28]

The Digital India initiative targeted 'to provide the much-needed thrust to the nine pillars of growth areas, namely Broadband Highways, Universal Access to Mobile Connectivity, Public Internet Access Programme, e-Governance: Reforming Government through Technology, e-Kranti-Electronic Delivery of Services, Information for All, Electronics Manufacturing, IT for Jobs and Early Harvest Programmes.'[29] The nine pillars of Digital India stand on a massive digital foundation, Aadhaar, established as mentioned earlier in January 2009 by the UIDAI to collect and secure in a central database biometric (photograph, iris-scan and fingerprints) and demographic data of *Indian residents* [emphasis added] and issue to each individual resident a 12-digit UID. Although it is not mandatory to have a UID number, with more than 1.295 billion UID holders (June 2021), Aadhaar is the world's largest database.[30] Originally it was designed to strengthen the social safety net and help people at the bottom of the socioeconomic pyramid to receive direct benefits from the government as well as to eliminate pilferage, fraud and corruption.

But in the course of time, the programme became increasingly ambitious and popular. Most of the essential activities in India, public as well as private, began to be linked with and channelled through Aadhaar, making India an evolving digitally-gated nation that requires an ID number. Aiming to provide universal broadband access for mobile connectivity so that people can use their ID numbers to access electronic delivery of services, education, e-commerce, search for jobs, participate in government activities and start or enhance their businesses, Aadhaar combined with Digital India was meant to empower people.

DIGITAL ENTERPRISES

Sooner than later, Aadhaar began to capture the imagination of the people of India. Apart from the government, many private enterprises, including some places of worship, began to use Aadhaar to prevent fraud and facilitate transactions. A Hindu temple in Almora, a town in Uttarakhand State in northern India, for example, made Aadhaar cards mandatory for getting married because, according to the temple priest, 'There have been instances when couples who came to the temple were found to be underage, and it turned out they had eloped to get married. There have also been cases of Nepalese underage girls coming here to get married. So the temple committee took the decision of checking Aadhaar cards before agreeing to conduct the wedding.'[31] The Indian Railways, one of the world's largest railroad networks, the transport system that carries more than 22 million passengers a day, linked subsidized concessional tickets for senior citizens and other disadvantaged people with Aadhaar in order to prevent fraud.[32] In a major reshaping of the public health system, Aadhaar numbers began to be used as unique patient identifiers in the electronic health records system. National identification numbers were generated and assigned to all health facilities, beginning with public health facilities.[33] To encourage the use of Aadhaar, the Reserve Bank of India (RBI) asked all banks to ensure that all new transactional cards, effective 1 January 2017, were also enabled to process payment using Aadhaar-based biometric authentication. Under the financial inclusion scheme called Jan Dhan, any Indian older than 10 years who did not have a bank account could open one in their name with an initial deposit of Rs zero in any registered bank specially designated to facilitate account opening under the Jan Dhan Scheme.[34]

There have been concerns about privacy and misuse of biometric data. Sociologist S.L. Rao, the former director-general of the National Council of Applied Economic Research, for example, said, 'I think it is a good move if Aadhaar is being made compulsory, but people need to be assured about Aadhaar being an authentic form of identification, as biometrics can be misused.'[35] Aadhaar uses the highest available public key cryptography encryption (PKI-2048 and AES-256), with each data record having a built-in mechanism to detect tampering. The system uses layers of firewalls, just as the US Military uses them for data protection. Besides, Aadhaar databases are segregated from other databases. Segregation adds to security. Security, nonetheless, is a tough question.

However, since Aadhaar is based on photographic, iris-scan and fingerprints information of an individual, it is unique to the person and cannot be used by anyone else. It is also password protected. The Aadhaar Act 2016 contained a regulatory framework to ensure that the biometric details of a person the system collected were kept confidential and used only to generate Aadhaar numbers or authenticate them. In cases of national security, an officer not below the rank of a joint secretary was empowered to call for disclosure of such information. There had been some cases of individual Aadhaar card users who had become victims of fraudsters. Penalties for fraud vary from a three-year to ten-year imprisonment and a fine from ₹10,000 to ₹10 million.[36] Lost cards could be replaced by calling a toll-free number to reset the password. Data centre hacking could not be ruled out, nonetheless.

While not ignoring these concerns, there are entrepreneurs in India and the United States who regard the Digital India venture as an extremely bold initiative. Jack Hidary, a senior adviser at Google X Labs, speaking at EmTech 2016: The Digital Future, organized by *Mint* and *MIT Technology Review*, called India a moonshot nation that is 'going through a radical transformation—the like of that we have never seen.'[37] A moonshot, he said, is an initiative that aims to achieve a goal that was previously thought to be impossible because it attracts the best human capital and finance from long-term investors.[38] Sharad Sharma, the co-founder of iSPIRT, a think-tank for tech startups, said at the conference, 'India is entering a phase of innovation that is substantially different from what we have seen until now.'[39] Aadhaar, he stated, would create other digital possibilities such as 'the presence-less layer, which means I can open a bank account and establish who I am without doing in-person verification.'[40]

Aadhaar would enable millions of people to use their e-signs for paperless transactions. Aadhaar made possible the Unified Payments Interface (UPI), a debit card system that's a less expensive alternative to MasterCard and Visa. UPI makes this facility available on mobile phones. With 775 million mobile phone users and rising, it is expected that mobile cash would become all-pervasive in India, especially when the 'digital consent' becomes an operational and integral part of the cashless payment system. As Sharma said, 'We are data-poor right now, but we are putting in place a new system to managing digital consent, so nobody can aggregate data about you without a digital permission token from you. This is going to be the largest country-scale system in the world—a techno-legal solution... a very modern approach...to manage privacy.'[41] Digital consent is similar to 'opt-in' option in the United States, under which a customer has to give permission for using their data. 'Opt-out' option gives automatic permission for a user's data.

While the federal, state and local governments use Aadhaar to ensure delivery of benefits and services to all Indians, albeit with a special focus on the poor and the underprivileged, technical and business enterprises are developing Aadhaar-based apps for the nation's burgeoning e-commerce. That's drawing Amazon, Google, Microsoft, Facebook, Alibaba and others to collaborate with Indian enterprises to reach rural India.[42] Google and Tata Trusts, for example, have trained thousands of female trainers and sent them to rural India on motorbikes to help rural women to learn the use of smartphones and tablets for accessing information and building their small home-based businesses.[43]

ONE AND ABSOLUTE INDIA VIA GST

It is only Modi whose sweeping rhetoric and fiery imagination could have turned the dullest tax reform legislation, the GST, into a momentous event for edification—speaking in a manner that appropriated the most poetic moment of Jawaharlal Nehru's immortal words, 'Tryst with Destiny.'[44] Quoting in Sanskrit from Chanakya and the Rig Veda and Lokmanya Tilak's *Gita Rahasya*, he talked about the GST as a moment of arrival:

> At the stroke of the midnight hour today, together we shall ensure a pioneering future of the nation... in this Central Hall... The same House which once on 14 August, 1947, at the stroke of the midnight hour, witnessed the most pious moment of the nation attaining freedom! ...this House shall once again go down in the annals of history as there couldn't have been a more anointed venue than this for the launch of one of the biggest strengths of Federal structure, the GST Reform...When the Constitution was framed, it introduced a framework of equal opportunity and rights for all. Very importantly, GST also intends to bring in economic reforms...a great example of Co-operative Federalism which shall facilitate inclusive growth

of the nation. ...one nation, one tax...from Ganganagar to Itanagar and from Leh to Lakshadweep....*Ek Bharat Sreshtha Bharat.* Its impact will be appreciated by the forthcoming generations with great pride.[45]

The GST was implemented on 1 July 2017, after a constitutional amendment. It replaced the hitherto complicated multiple tax regimes levied by the central and state governments with a simple concept that the consumer at the final destination must pay the tax. In other words, the GST is a destination-based tax system under which taxes are paid to the state where the goods or services are disbursed and consumed and not the state in which they are produced. By integrating and subsuming the existing central excise and customs duties, service taxes, surcharges, value-added taxes and local octroi duties into one system, the GST has converted India into one common market. Under the GST model, both the central and state governments levy taxes on the supply of goods and services simultaneously based on common taxable standards. However, for inter-state transactions and imported goods or services, an integrated GST (IGST) is levied only by the central government.

The central and the state governments share the earnings from the IGST transactions equally. The GST Council comprising the Union Government finance minister and state finance ministers is the governing body that regulates the functioning of the GST, whose mission is 'To establish highest standards of cooperative federalism in the functioning of GST Council, which is the first constitutional federal body vested with powers to take all major decisions relating to GST.'[46]

Indirect Tax reform began in 1985 with finance minister V.P. Singh in Prime Minister Rajiv Gandhi's administration. But the idea of a single unified tax regime, Goods and Services Tax, began in earnest in 1999 with Prime Minister Vajpayee, when he set up an economic advisory panel tasking it to formulate a GST regime.[47] Later on, based on the recommendation of the 12th Finance Commission, the proposal to roll out GST was taken up seriously, but the Vajpayee BJP–NDA lost the 2004 general election. It was left to Finance Minister P. Chidambaram in Dr Manmohan Singh's administration to pursue the GST project, which he proposed to roll out in April 2010. But once again, in the whirligig of democratic politics and ensuing general election, the GST Bill was put on the backburner. It would be to Modi's credit that he took it up where his predecessor had left off and saw to it that Parliament passed the constitutional amendment to enable the GST Bill to become the law, including the ratification by the states.

On 1 July 2017, President Pranab Mukherjee launched the GST in a historic midnight session in the Central Hall of Parliament, where on 15 August 1947, the first prime minister of India, Jawaharlal Nehru, had asked his people to wake up to the call of destiny. How ironic that the Congress party that had initiated the idea of the GST boycotted the historic launch. It's also worth noting that Modi when he was the chief minister of Gujarat, had warned that the GST would never be successful without IT infrastructure in place, but after becoming the prime minister, he not only fully embraced it but vowed to make it successful by making it part of his larger vision of Digital India.[48] Times change, politicians change too. As Ralph Waldo Emerson said, 'A foolish consistency is the hobgoblin of little minds, adored by little statesmen and philosophers and divines.'

DEMONETIZATION: POLITICS AND ECONOMICS

'Brothers and sisters, to break the grip of corruption and black money,' thus said Modi in a messianic tone on the national television Doordarshan the night of 8 November 2016, 'we have decided that the five hundred rupee and thousand rupee currency notes presently in use will no longer be legal tender from midnight tonight. The five hundred rupee and thousand rupee notes hoarded by anti-national and anti-social elements will become just worthless pieces of paper.'[49]

For the Indian economy, of which 90 per cent was dependent upon cash, the demonetized notes constituted 86 per cent of the total currency in circulation. The informal sector of the economy—

housemaids, day labourers, storekeepers, petty clerks and delivery people—which employed 90 per cent of the workforce had to be paid in cash. The government announced that new ₹500 and ₹2,000 notes would replace the demonetized notes, which could be deposited with banks by 30 December 2016. For a short window of time and for a limited amount per person, the demonetized notes could also be exchanged with new notes at the banks' counters. Certain facilities such as fuel pumps, government hospitals, railway and airline booking counters, and ration shops too were allowed to accept the demonetized banknotes for a limited amount of time.

Cash withdrawals from bank accounts initially limited to ₹10,000 were subsequently raised to ₹50,000 and finally, by March 2017, all restrictions for bank account withdrawal were removed. Similarly, restrictions were also imposed on ATM withdrawals. On 28 December 2016, under the Specified Bank Notes Ordinance, the Government of India ceased its liability for the demonetized currency notes and, moreover, criminalized transactions carried out in the banned currency notes.[50]

Unfortunately, what added to the confusion, uncertainty and public panic were frequent official announcements regarding how much money could be withdrawn or deposited at what public facilities. Even those who did not have much of unaccounted or 'black money' suffered a sense of diffused anxiety and depression.[51] Apart from targeting unaccounted and untaxed money as well as wealth gained through corruption, money laundering and other illegal means, the government aimed to hit terrorists such as Maoists, Naxalites, and Kashmiri militants who supposedly used counterfeit currencies to support their terrorist activities. Later on, the government added other goals such as integration of formal and informal economies, increasing the tax base by adding more taxpayers and moving India to a digital cashless society.[52]

But Indians, who had large amounts of money in demonetized notes, proved smarter than the government. They tasked their employees and hired trusted people to exchange notes through multiple transactions carried out at different bank branches. According to a 2018 Reserve Bank of India report, 99.3 per cent of the demonetized notes had been returned into the banking system.[53] This was wide of the mark because the government expected that approximately 20 per cent of the demonetized banknotes would be permanently eliminated from circulation, which did not happen. In other words, the demonetization turned out to be a legal money-laundering scheme. To conceal the black money, rich people rushed to buy gold and jewellery. Temples were some of the biggest beneficiaries of demonetization. The gods of India have always protected Indians from their rapacious governments. According to a media research report:

> ...The amount of cash in India has reached pre-demonetisation levels...Even on digital payments, demonetisation does not seem to have provided a significant and sustained push. Mobile payments and card payments through PoS have increased significantly since November 2016 but they were also increasing in the months preceding demonetization.... The costs of demonetisation seem to outweigh the benefits. [54]

The report suggested that digital payments increased initially, but with the return of cash, digital payments became more modest.

Regarding the goal of increasing the taxpayer base, the report said, 'The 2018 Economic Survey suggests that demonetisation has helped increase India's tax base, in terms of taxpayers, and this may have played some role in the increase in the tax-to-GDP ratio over the last two years.'[55] The negative impact of demonetization was significant on rural areas due to the paucity of banking facilities and overwhelming informal workforce, and consequently, the rural economy 'grew at a significantly slower rate in the quarter after demonetisation and, while the shock was only temporary, the short-term local impact was sizeable.'[56] The stock market, which captured only a slice of Indian economic life, swooned initially but eventually adjusted to the emerging domestic and global realities, which also included the new political scene in the United States, the election of Donald Trump as president and consequently the strengthening of the dollar and outward flow of funds from emerging markets including India.

It looked as though demonetization would not affect the overall market significantly because investors believed the impact would be temporary especially with lower interest rates and increased government spending to offset any adverse effects. [57]

Three weeks after the demonetization, *The Indian Express* aggregated the views of some of the most prominent economists and politicians regarding demonetization. The strongest reaction came from Harvard economist Amartya Sen, who said, 'At one stroke the move declares all Indians—indeed all holders of Indian currency—as possible crooks, unless they can establish they are not... It is hard to see how.'

Manmohan Singh called demonetization 'organised loot' and 'legalized plunder.' Arun Shourie, a former economist at the World Bank and former Union government minister, said that demonetization would not eliminate black money because 'those who hold this black money or who have black assets, they don't hold them in cash...'

Surjit Bhalla, an economist, said that the 'BJP policy is bold and courageous...If successful, this will go down as the biggest reform in India, bigger than the GST (though the two are related) and bigger than the industrial policy reform of 1991.'[58] A year after the demonetization, the GDP data seemed to confirm the pessimistic views of the critics. Writing in the *Harvard Business Review*, economist Bhaskar Chakravorti observed 'the policy was poorly thought out and executed and that its net impact would be negative and particularly bad for the poor. Indeed, India subsequently suffered a dramatic drop in its GDP growth rate... Its most recent GDP growth figure has fallen to 5.7 per cent, and part of that, too, can be attributed to the policy move from last November.'[59] Researchers at Harvard University, IMF, Goldman Sachs Group, and the Reserve Bank of India came to similar conclusions that demonetization was tantamount to 2 percentage point tightening of bank credit that adversely affected employment and output, and determined that 'in modern India, cash serves an essential role in facilitating economic activity.'[60]

VOTERS' PARADOX

It was expected that the 2017 state assembly elections held in Uttar Pradesh, Uttarakhand, Himachal Pradesh, Punjab, Goa and Manipur would reflect the voters' wrath with Modi and the BJP over demonetization, as they had done with Indira Gandhi in the post-Emergency election. While in Gujarat, the BJP maintained its power, it won absolute majorities in Uttar Pradesh, 312 of 403 seats, Uttarakhand, 57 of 70 and Himachal Pradesh, 44 of 68. In Goa, the BJP won 13 out of 40 seats, but by winning over defectors from the Congress party, it was able to form a stable government. In Manipur, too, in spite of winning only 21 out of 60 seats, it was able to form the government with the help of others. It was only in Punjab that the Congress party succeeded in forming the government.[61]

By all accounts, media and scholarly research, demonetization, inadequately planned and poorly executed, was socially and economically a disaster. But why did not the Indian voter punish the BJP in the 2017 state assembly elections? Some researchers concluded that the 'negative impact was unevenly distributed across the country...the economic impact of demonetization was felt most acutely in relatively 'unbanked' rural areas, where households and businesses are most dependent on cash and were least able to use the formal financial system to smooth their economic activities.' Why was the BJP not punished in 'underbanked' districts or districts with few bank branches? Why did not voters 'who bore most heavily the brunt of the negative economic impact of demonetization' reduce their support for the BJP in the 2017 state elections? The research suggested that other factors drove a large percentage of the voting population. In spite of economic dislocation, most people in the state assembly elections, for example, 63.5 per cent in Uttar Pradesh, 72 per cent in Uttarakhand, 49 per cent in the Punjab, 59 per cent in Goa, responded that demonetization 'will benefit the nation and the people in the coming years.' Modi had framed the demonetization message as a campaign against 'fighting corruption, tax evasion, terrorism' as well as 'moving the country toward a more modern, formal economy,' which might have 'resonated strongly with rural voters.'[62]

But a year is a long time in politically volatile India, and voters were not deferential to the BJP in the 2018 assembly elections held in nine states, including Karnataka, Madhya Pradesh, Telangana, Chhattisgarh and Rajasthan. These state elections were deemed to be an indicator of the preferences of the public for the 2019 general election. The BJP, in alliance with the People's Front of Tripura, took political control of Tripura from the CPI(M), which had ruled over the state for 25 years. The Congress was completely routed from the state. In Nagaland, the BJP formed a coalition government with the Nationalist Democratic Progressive Party. In Meghalaya, neither the Congress nor the BJP held any sway, yielding control to two state parties, the National People's Party and the United Democratic Party. In Telangana, the Telangana Rashtra Samithi (TRS) retained its political control. While the Congress party lost in Mizoram to the Mizo National Front, it captured power in Karnataka (in alliance with the Janata Dal-S). Most shockingly, the BJP lost in Rajasthan, Madhya Pradesh and Chhattisgarh, parts of the vast Hindi heartland that the party had controlled earlier. In Rajasthan, Madhya Pradesh and Chhattisgarh, the Congress party captured outright power, which came as a big surprise to some political observers, keeping in mind that collectively the three states in the Hindi heartland account for 14 per cent of the Indian population represented by about 12 per cent of Lok Sabha seats. It seemed that the Congress party under the leadership of Rahul Gandhi was showing resurgence, raising the possibility of forming a winning alliance for the 2019 general election. In the 2014 general election, the Congress party was beaten so badly by the BJP, shrinking from 206 seats to 44, that it couldn't claim its place as the official opposition party in the Lok Sabha. In one state after another, the Congress had yielded power to the BJP, which controlled 20 out of 29 states. The Congress and its allies controlled only three states before the mid-term 2018 elections.[63] The BJP state assembly election debacle in 2018 was, to some extent, perhaps due to the delayed effect of the demonetization and the

GST. But primarily, the electoral setback was due to the farm crisis aggravated by low commodity prices, sluggish rural incomes and farmers' indebtedness.

The question was: whether the distressed rural voters would decide the future of the BJP in the 2019 general election, disregarding Modi's successful push for rural public works, roads, electricity, Internet connectivity, LPG and toilets.[64] Besides the disenchantment of rural voters towards the BJP, the party was in danger of losing the support of Dalits and tribal people, a crucial demographic for the party. [65] The promises of fighting rural indebtedness through farm loan waivers might turn out to be palliative care unless the two major national parties, the Congress and the BJP, developed a comprehensive rural development plan that ensured well-paying jobs and assured farm incomes. The farmer needed empowerment through sustained earned income that could provide him with cash in hand, which wasn't available due to falling crop prices in comparison with overall inflation. According to a media report, since the BJP took power in 2014, 'the average annual increase in the wholesale price index' had been only 2.75 per cent for food articles and 0.76 per cent for non-food agricultural articles compared to 12.26 per cent and 11.04 per cent respectively in the preceding five years when the UPA government under Manmohan Singh was in power. Added to the misery was 'a marked decline in rural wage growth for agricultural and non-agricultural occupations after 2014–15... The reason here has partly to do with low crop prices, reducing the demand for farm labour...a sluggish economy has led to a drying up of job opportunities for rural migrant workers, especially in sectors such as construction, real estate and manufacturing. This is in contrast to the UPA period, which witnessed double-digit rural wage growth on the back of a booming farm as well as non-farm economy.'[66]

It seemed that Prime Minister Modi's Make in India programme had yet to develop a rural counterpart, especially for agricultural workers (farmers and labourers). Similarly, the 'Digital India' plan had yet to find its way to connect rural India to the expanding digital marketplace in order to turn the farmer from cultivator-producer to agri-entrepreneur. Early in 2016, Modi had set a goal of doubling the income of farmers by 2022, the seventy-fifth year of India's independence.[67]

ONIONS, POTATOES AND HINDUTVA

On 29 November 2018, only weeks before the crucial state legislative assembly elections, more than a hundred thousand farmers from all over India, under the banner of the All India Kisan Sangharsh Coordination Committee, supported by opposition parties including the Congress and the CPI(M), among others, led a march—Mukti (Freedom) March—to the Parliament House in New Delhi. They wanted freedom from debt, which in the past two decades had driven at least three hundred thousand farmers to suicide. They wanted a sustainable farm price structure that wouldn't drive them to perpetual indebtedness. The Modi government, following the Swaminathan Commission's recommendations, raised the minimum support price (MSP) in order to enable the farmers to get 50 per cent over and above the total cost, the cost of planting and tending the crop.[68] The protesting farmers asked that while consumers, for example, paid ₹30 per kilogram for tomatoes in the marketplace, the farmers got only ₹5. So, the question was, where did the rest of the money go? Apparently, the middleman was making more money than the farmer. In June 2018, farmers in seven states, including Haryana, Rajasthan, Jammu and Kashmir, Madhya Pradesh, Maharashtra, Karnataka and Kerala, went on a 10-day protest suspending supplies of vegetables and dairy produce to several cities. The protests were also for the observation of the first anniversary of the police firing on farmers in Mandsaur, Madhya Pradesh, where five people were killed. In March 2018, tens of thousands of farmers from Maharashtra led a hundred-mile march to Mumbai, India's financial hub in support of similar demands. A year before, 'drought-hit farmers from the southern state of Tamil Nadu brandished human skulls and held live mice in their mouths to draw attention to their plight.'[69]

In 2004, Prime Minister Manmohan Singh had set up the National Commission on Farmers under the chairmanship of the Swaminathan Commission, tasking it to recommend solutions to farmers' problems. The commission submitted five reports between 2004 and 2006 recommending that farmers 'needed to have assured access and control over basic resources including land, water, bio-resources, credit and insurance, technology and knowledge management, and markets.' One of the most important recommendations was to 'give farmers a minimum support price at 50 per cent profit above the cost of production classified as C2 by the Commission for Agricultural Costs and Prices.' C2 was deemed as the most inclusive definition of production cost of crops since it also took into account the rentals, interest loans, owned land, and fixed capital assets over and above other costs. The Swaminathan Commission recommended it to be the basic cost and prescribed MSP 50 per cent above C2.[70]

Why did the system not work? Partly, the state governments who set the MSPs were not doing due diligence in their calculations. Some of them were tardy in making payments to their farmers, increasing their distress in spite of bumper crops. But more serious than shortchanging the farmers was the issue of surpluses of farm products, which were perishable and needed cold storage and food processing units. According to Dr Ashok Gulati, an agriculture specialist at the Indian Council for Research on International Economic Relations, 'If the rains are good, you end up with a glut of crops and prices crash. The glut only highlights the inefficiencies of the farming value chain and hits farmers,' to avoid which the cold storage chain system from the farm to the marketplace needed to be 'so efficient that the customer, farmer and the storage owner are happy. Unfortunately, India hasn't been able to make that happen.'[71] In 2018 farming became an albatross around Modi's neck. The skyrocketing prices of onions were one of the reasons that had pulled down the Janata coalition and brought Indira Gandhi back to power in 1980.[72] Would the humble onion and potato determine the future of the Modi government as they had done in the past? Modi was determined not to let history repeat itself, for which he took serious steps to mitigate the plight of the farmers.

It seemed that the 2018 farm agitations had dulled the Hindutva fervour as the BJP's political and electoral strategy. In November

2018, RSS Chief Mohan Bhagwat, speaking at a rally organized by the VHP in Nagpur, warned of a mass agitation since the Supreme Court had deferred its decision about the Ram Temple dispute. He said the time for patience was over, and it was time 'to mobilise people. Now we should demand a law... If, for whatever reasons, because the court has a busy schedule or maybe it does not understand the sensibilities of the society, the Ram temple case is not a priority for them, then the government should think how to bring a law for the construction of the temple...the law should be introduced at the earliest.'[73] On 25 November, the city and surrounding areas of Ayodhya, the religious and political centre of the Ram Temple vs Babri Masjid dispute that had turned deadly in 1992, wore saffron colour with the slogan 'Chalo [Let's go to] Ayodhya'. Posters called for 'Shankhnaa' (war cry) for building the temple. Mobile vans showed Ramanand Sagar's 1986 TV series *Ramayan*. The Hindutva groups, including VHP, RSS, Bajrang Dal and Shiv Sena, launched the campaign.[74] A month later, the VHP leaders claimed that the BJP must fulfil its 2014 electoral promise of building the Ram Temple, adding that those who did not support the passage of the law in Parliament would face defeat in the 2019 elections. But suddenly, the political atmospherics changed. The 2018 state assembly elections, especially the BJP's defeat in Chhattisgarh, Madhya Pradesh and Rajasthan convinced the party leadership and the Sangh Parivar (the family of Hindu organizations) that economic issues were voters' major concerns and the cry for building the temple might not work in the 2019 general election. Onions and potatoes, bread and butter issues, dumbed down Hindutva.

MODI GOES GLOBAL TO MAKE IN INDIA

Nehru had created a unique and innovative platform of nonalignment to project and achieve the geopolitical and socialistic developmental goals, which, however, tended to lean India towards the Soviet Union. Modi chose the route of multiple strategic partnerships in the quest for the Make in India industrial objectives as well as to pursue India's security and geopolitical goals, which necessitated moving India towards the economic and technological powers in East Asia, the United States and European Union without however giving up its bonds with its old reliable ally Russia. In some sense, it's the continuation of Nehru's nonalignment independent policy but set in a distinctive new key, like a fresh new song sung on an old familiar tune, rhythm and beat.

In an op-ed piece Modi wrote for the *The Wall Street Journal* on the occasion of his official visit to the United States at the invitation of President Barack Obama, he reminded his American audience:

> India and the U.S. have a fundamental stake in each other's success ...in securing our seas, cyber space and outer space, all of which now have a profound influence on our daily lives... in the destiny of our two nations...democracy is the greatest source of renewal and, with the right conditions, offers the best opportunity for the human spirit to flourish.[75]

Having laid the public diplomacy tractions for the 27–30 September 2014 visit in a most media sophisticated democratic nation, Modi went to New York's famed Madison Square Garden 'filled with dancers in traditional dress, while a laser show and holograms of historical Indian figures lit up the backdrop...rising skyscrapers, microchip factories and Asia's largest solar-energy plant...framed by balloons in the colours of the Indian and US flags.' Speaking in fluent Hindi, which he speaks as naturally as his mother tongue Gujarati, he told a crowd of 20,000 that India 'has something that other countries in the world don't.' Although he did not specify what's unique and exceptional about India, addressing the Global Citizen Festival in New York's Central Park, he said that on the back of the youth of India his government aimed 'To put the light of hope in every eye. And the joy of belief in every heart. Lift people out of poverty. Put clean water and sanitation within reach of all. Make healthcare available to all. A roof over every head.'[76] If this were the essence of Hindutva, Mahatma Gandhi and Jawaharlal Nehru, too, would have embraced it.

The Indian-American Community Foundation representing

roughly 3 million Indian-Americans, one of the wealthiest (with a median household income of US$122,000 in 2016) and the most highly educated and influential ethnic community in the United States, organized the spectacular mega event. Indian-Americans occupy top echelons in every field, including Ivy League universities, medical professions, businesses, mass media, Silicon Valley, diplomacy as well as the political establishment. Consider, for example, Nikki Haley, the governor of South Carolina (2011–17) and US ambassador to the UN (2017–18), Bobby Jindal, Louisiana governor (2008–16), and Richard Rahul Verma, US Ambassador to India (2015–17), among others. The Indian-American diaspora was Modi's ardent supporter during the 2014 general election. Present at the Madison Square Garden were scores of US Congressmen who had come to see the real-life incarnation of Horatio Alger's small man, a tea stall boy, rising to become the prime minister of India, the stuff American dreams are made of.

On his way to have an Oval Office meeting and private dinner with President Barack Obama, he met several CEOs of some of the topmost multinationals, including Google, Boeing, IBM, PepsiCo and MasterCard, to welcome them to India. After the Oval Office meeting, President Obama remarked:

> I think that the entire world has watched the historic election and mandate that the people of India delivered in the recent election...everyone has been impressed with the energy and the determination with which the Prime Minister has looked to address not only India's significant challenges but more importantly, India's enormous opportunities for success in the twenty-first century.[77]

Keeping the focus on India's economic development for which the United States had to be a big player, Modi invited Obama to be the chief guest for India's sixty-sixth Republic Day, the first US president ever to be invited on such an occasion. It was an attempt at forging a strategic partnership—foreign policy in a new key—without formal alignment. In the spirit and echo of the movie *Guess Who's Coming to Dinner?* Modi tweeted, "This Republic Day, we hope to have a friend over... invited President Obama to be the first US president to grace the occasion as chief guest.'[78]

Even before becoming the prime minister, Modi as the Gujarat state chief minister had begun to build diplomatic relations in order to attract foreign direct investment for his state's industrial development project: Vibrant Gujarat; for example, with Japanese Prime Minister Shinzo Abe of Japan, whom he met in 2007 and 2012; Israel, which he visited in 2006; and China too in spite of his strong views regarding its avowedly aggressive claims in Arunachal Pradesh. Development agenda and trade deals seemed more important to him than geopolitical initiatives, though in the course of time he would realize that they reinforce each other.

But economic development necessitated keeping peace in the neighbourhood. The inaugural swearing-in ceremony presented him with a unique diplomatic opportunity to build bridges with South Asian and Indian Ocean neighbours. His foreign guests included Navin Ramgoolam of Mauritius, the island nation in the Indian Ocean; Afghanistan's President Hamid Karzai; Bhutan's Prime Minister Tshering Tobgay; Maldives', another island nation, President Abdulla Yameen; Nepal's Prime Minister Sushil Koirala; Sri Lanka's President Mahinda Rajapaksa; Parliamentary Speaker Shirin Sharmin Chaudhury representing the Bangladeshi Prime Minister Sheikh Hasina; and Pakistan's Prime Minister Nawaz Sharif. Much to the chagrin of China, Lobsang Sangay, the Prime Minister of Tibetan Government-in-Exile, too was present.

The US media took a special note of Modi's grand gestures to India's neighbours, especially the coming of Pakistan Prime Minister Sharif, 'who was said to have made the trip' said the *Chicago Tribune*, 'despite the opposition of his country's powerful Inter-Services Intelligence (ISI) agency...'[79] *The Washington Post* remarked, 'Sharif's attendance was seen as a gesture of goodwill between the rival nations...Modi, a lover of technology, had run the most costly, tech-savvy and ambitious political campaign in India's history, travelling more than 180,000 miles and appearing at more than 5,000 events after he was officially named the party's choice for prime minister in September.'[80] A BBC correspondent reported from Islamabad, 'People close to Pakistan's prime minister say he was keen to accept the invitation, but it was still a tough decision to make. Turning down Mr Modi's gesture of friendship could have caused renewed tensions between the two countries. …His decision to travel to Delhi will add to the already growing tension between Pakistan's civilian leadership and the powerful army.'[81]

The rise of Modi as a shining star on the political horizon of India, especially after the last few turbulent years of the Congress–UPA dithering government, drew the interest of major global powers. China was the first to reach out to Modi's India. On 8 June 2014, Chinese Foreign Minister Wang Yi visited New Delhi and held a dialogue with Foreign Minister Sushma Swaraj. At the end of his visit he said, 'China–India cooperation is like a massive buried treasure waiting to be discovered.'[82] China had a trade surplus of $48.48 billion with India in 2014–15, which increased to $63 billion (including Hong Kong) in 2019. If the trade imbalance kept growing, its 'geostrategic dimension' and threat to India would be much greater than it was from across the Himalayas in the times of Mao Zedong and Jawaharlal Nehru.[83]

The Russian deputy prime minister, in charge of defence industry, Dmitri Rogozin's two-day June 2014 visit to India, during which he met the prime minister, was primarily aimed at collaboration in joint defence production. According to the official account, 'Prime Minister described Russia as a time-tested and reliable friend that had stood with India in difficult times and a major partner in building India's defence capabilities, for which Russia enjoys enormous goodwill in India…expressed his intention to take the relationship to a higher level…thanked Deputy Prime Minister Rogozin for Russian contribution to the realisation of a major milestone in India's naval capabilities (INS Vikramaditya).'[84] The 29 June–2 July 2014 visit of French Foreign Minister Laurent Fabius and British Foreign Secretary William Hague's 7–8 July visit to India were both meant to sell defence weapons to India. The French lobbied to sell Dassault Rafale fighter aircraft jets to India that later on would create charges of irregularity against the Modi government.[85] The British lobbied for the Eurofighter Typhoon manufactured by a consortium of Airbus and BAE Systems.

While China coveted increasing its penetration into India's expanding commercial marketplace, Russia, France and the UK wanted to maintain their footholds in India's increasing security and defence space. The United States, on the other hand, held the prospects of offering India much more than any other global power could provide, including nuclear technology, defence production, trade and commerce, information technology, and most importantly, geopolitical strategic opportunities, especially in the Indo–Pacific region.

Economic developmental goals, national security from the Himalayas to the Indian Ocean, and India's place at international forums became major determining factors for India's well-integrated and comprehensive foreign policy under Prime Minister Modi. These foreign policy goals could be achieved through a delicate balance between strategic autonomy and multiple strategic partnerships because 'the unprecedented level of economic interdependence produced by globalization and the high degree of strategic interdependence produced by nuclear weapons have together sharply circumscribed the choices available to national leaderships,' thus limiting any attempt at excessive muscular nationalistic foreign policy.[86] Keeping strategic flexibility and manoeuvrability in view, a scholar observed:

> The India–US partnership tops the list, raising fears among some Indians about undue American influence. To underline that it will not be a camp follower, India has cultivated a 'special and privileged partnership' with Russia and a 'strategic and global partnership' with Japan...Multilateral strategic relationships ... provide additional leverage, strengthening links with friends and further circumscribing an adversary's options...'[87]

MODI AND THE MUSLIM WORLD

India's foreign policy accomplishments under Prime Minister Modi during his first five-year term, apart from maintaining a close strategic relationship with the United States, the European Union and Japan without giving up on Russia and China, included India's successful engagement with its Muslim neighbours, especially Bangladesh and Afghanistan as well as the Persian Gulf and Middle East Arab countries. On 6 June 2015, Modi signed the Land Boundary Agreement with Bangladesh Prime Minister Sheikh Hasina, swapping 106 Indian enclaves with 92 Bangladeshi enclaves giving the residents of the enclaves the right to stay where they were or move to the other side of the border. The original land accord that was agreed upon in 1974 between Indira Gandhi and Bangladesh leader Mujibur Rahman could not be carried out because of the assassination of Mujibur Rahman, and since then, it had remained in suspended animation. Besides the enclave exchange agreement, the two countries also strengthened their trade relations with India's announcement of a US$2 billion new credit line, apart from a $4.5 billion investment by Adani Power Ltd. and Reliance Power Ltd. for the development of the Bangladesh power sector. India also conferred upon Bangladesh zero-tariff on all but twenty-five import tariff lines.[88]

A year before the boundary agreement, India and Bangladesh had resolved their maritime dispute through arbitration when the UN tribunal, the Permanent Court of Arbitration, awarded Bangladesh 19,467 sq. kilometres of the 25,602 sq. kilometres area of the Bay of Bengal, which India accepted gracefully. For Bangladesh, the award had huge economic implications since it 'cleared the obstacles for Dhaka to open up its waters for foreign firms to explore and exploit hydrocarbons in the Bay.' Until then, Bangladesh's maritime dispute with India had 'deterred many international petroleum companies to invest in the sea-blocks previously offered by it. The ruling has confirmed Bangladesh's right to exploit the potentially rich waters in the Bay region...The economic prospects of the Bay region have increased enormously after Myanmar and India discovered huge natural gas deposits beneath the sea.'[89] The Bay of Bengal maritime dispute settlement with Bangladesh was as significant as the 1960 Indus Water Treaty with Pakistan. But its significance goes beyond good neighbourly relations because the 'Asian maritime landscape is undergoing significant changes marked by great power rivalry, geopolitical competition, and increased hostilities. In this changing Asian security dynamic, the Bay of Bengal is emerging as a critical theatre for economic and strategic competition in the region. A historical bridge between South and East Asia, the bay today appears to be the fulcrum of a wider Indo-Pacific strategy. A quest for new connectivity corridors across the bay has renewed its geoeconomic significance while highlighting its strategic undertones.'[90]

Under Modi, India continued strengthening its ties with Afghanistan, which in 2007 became a geopolitical part of the Indian subcontinent through its newly acquired membership of the South Asia Association of Regional Cooperation (SAARC). In 2011, India and Afghanistan established a wide-ranging strategic partnership, which, besides providing training and military equipment for Afghanistan's armed forces also included assistance for trade as well as for economic, educational, social, cultural and civil society programmes. Modi, on his visit to Afghanistan in 2015, inaugurated the India-financed-and-built Afghanistan Parliament building and Afghanistan–India Friendship (Salma) Dam. In May 2016, India signed a deal with Afghanistan and Iran to develop the strategic Chabahar Port and build a transport-and-trade corridor to bypass Pakistan in order to trade with Afghanistan and resource-rich Central Asia, the original home of the Mughals. The US State Department exempted the Chabahar Port project from President Trump's sanctions against Iran because the US did not demur to India's strategic goal of helping landlocked Afghanistan. In December 2018, the state-owned corporation India Ports Global Limited (IPGL) formally took over the operation of the Chabahar Port based on a lease for a ten-year period.[91] The Chabahar Port is only 70 kilometres from Pakistan's Gwadar Port, which is being developed by China as part of its ambitious China–Pakistan Economic Corridor (CPEC) to access the Arabian Sea and the Middle East and expand its Belt and Road Initiative (BRI) for global trade and international dominance. But the Middle East region is also crucially important to India for economic and cultural reasons.

WEST ASIA WELCOMES MODI

Inviting India to the Organization of Islamic Conference 1–2 March 2019, the United Arab Republic (UAE), the conference host, said, 'The friendly country of India has been named as the guest of honour in view of its great global political stature as well as its time-honoured and deeply rooted cultural and historical legacy, and its important Islamic component.'

The move to invite India had broad backing from its members; however, the most vociferous support came from Bangladesh and Turkey. Considering reforms necessary for the Islamic group, Conference members said, 'There is a need to build bridges with those non-OIC countries so that a large number of Muslim populations do not remain untouched by the good work of OIC.'[92] The question of Kashmir and Pakistan's opposition to India's presence at the OIC did not deter the organization from reaching out to India. Because of India's sustained and rapid economic growth, many Muslim countries had been increasing their trade and investment relations with India. Despite the United States sanctions against Iran, an OIC member, India maintained steady commercial and cultural relations with Iran, which with the development of Chabahar Port became extremely significant. It's noteworthy that India's participation at the OIC gathering took place in the aftermath of the Pakistan-supported Jaish-e-Mohammed militant Pulwama terrorists' attack in Jammu and Kashmir that had killed 40 Central Reserve Police and provoked India to launch surgical strikes at Balakot, deep into Pakistan, raising the spectre of another all-out war between the two countries.

The bonds between India and the UAE, too, had been strengthening since Modi visited the country in August 2015, and the OIC invitation further enhanced the ties. Accepting the UAE invitation, India's MEA said in a statement, 'We see this invitation as a milestone in our comprehensive strategic partnership with the UAE. *We also see this invitation as a welcome recognition of the presence of 185 million Muslims in India and of their contribution to its pluralistic ethos, and of India's contribution to the Islamic world* [emphasis added].'[93] Diplomatically, the OIC invite was also important for the BJP government because it came after the visit of the powerful Saudi Crown Prince Mohammed bin Salman to New Delhi, who had been seeking to expand relations with India, and especially looking for investment opportunities for Saudi Aramco with Reliance Industries.

The West Asia region was home to about 10 million Indian expatriates who, in 2018, sent $35 billion out of a total amount of $80 billion overseas remittance to India, according to World Bank data.[94] It is of great historical importance as to how BJP's Hindutva nationalism would get modified by India's deep economic and diplomatic engagements with the OIC and Middle East countries. And added to this geopolitical and economic complexity was India's strengthening relations with Israel.

INDIA-ISRAEL SONG AND DANCE

Although India–Israel relations had been developing since January 1992 when India opened its embassy in Tel Aviv, Prime Minister Modi's 2017 visit to Israel was of great significance. By that time, India had overcome its apprehension about any diplomatic backlash from Arab–Muslim countries and from its own substantial Muslim population who were wary of India developing close relations with the Jewish nation fearing that it might diminish the Palestinian cause. In fact, Modi did not visit Palestine during the Israeli visit, breaking the established tradition under which Indian ministers visited both Israel and Palestine. By de-hyphenating Israel from Palestine, India increased its diplomatic space in the Middle East region and raised its relations with Israel to a new platform for collaboration in high-tech industries, including agriculture, pharmaceuticals, information technology, and defence, as well as trade and tourism. In spite of its fanatical policy of self-reliance since Independence and the development of nuclear weapons, India had not succeeded in building a modern defence industry and remained dependent upon the Soviet Union/Russia, France, Switzerland, the United Kingdom, and more recently, Israel and the United States.

At the time of Modi's visit, Israel's defence exports to India had risen to US$600 million. India was slated to buy from Israel anti-tank guided missiles, Phalcon airborne surveillance radars, drones, launchers and other weapon subsystems worth billions of dollars, not a pretty picture of a nation that aspired to become a global power. No doubt trade too had been increasing between the two nations, amounting to US$4.167 billion in 2016, hoping that closer diplomatic relations would go beyond defence and security and lead to enhanced growth in exchange of goods and services and the development of technology, innovation and entrepreneurship.

During the visit, India and Israel upgraded their relations to a strategic partnership with Israeli Prime Minister Benjamin Netanyahu, saying that, 'This is a marriage made in heaven, but we are implementing it here on earth.' Modi responded by saying, 'India admires the success of your people in overcoming adversity to advance, innovate and flourish against all odds...India has suffered first-hand the violence and hatred spread by terror, so has Israel. PM Netanyahu and I have agreed to do much more together to protect our strategic interests and also cooperate to fight growing radicalization.' They signed several Memorandums of Agreement, including three on space collaboration: Atomic Clocks, GEO-LEO optical link and Electric Propulsion for Small Satellites. The agreements also included setting up the Israel–India Industrial R&D Development and Technological Innovation Fund; Water Conservation and Water Utility Reform programme; India–Israel Development Cooperation work for Agriculture.[95] Netanyahu reciprocated the visit the following year, leading a delegation of 130 members to increase trade and defence relations with India.

It was 25 years earlier, in 1992 when Israeli–India diplomatic relations had cautiously opened up and since then, they had been steadily growing. In 2003, Prime Minister Vajpayee welcomed Israeli Prime Minister Ariel Sharon in India, much to the chagrin of pro-Islamic and leftist organizations that had strongly protested his visit. But the milieu had changed in January 2018 when Netanyahu was welcomed to India as a most valued friend. As a guest of honour to inaugurate the geopolitical conference, Raisina Dialogue, in New

Delhi, Netanyahu said, 'The weak do not survive, the strong survive, you make alliances with the strong, you are able to maintain peace by being strong.'[96] The six-day visit was concluded with a wide-ranging memorandum of understanding for cooperation in several areas, including cyber security cooperation, oil and gas sector cooperation, air transport and cooperation regarding metal-air batteries.[97]

Israel was founded as a nation on 14 May 1948, only nine months after India became independent. Nonetheless, in seven decades since its *re-birth* as a nation, Israel, in spite of a myriad of problems with Arab neighbours and terrorism as well as domestic political uncertainty due to coalition politics, has been relentlessly leaping forward; it has become an economic and technological powerhouse. That India, a nation of 1.3 billion people aspiring to be a global power, would depend upon a small, beleaguered country for critical military weapons and technology was a sad and silent commentary upon India's inability to make weapons of self-defence. India could launch satellites and kill satellites in space, but it could not defend its borders, whether with Pakistan or China. Personal diplomacy and bonhomie with global leaders, for which Modi has a penchant, is no substitute for economic and military power. Soft power must rest on muscle power, a lesson Nehru learned too late in his life.

CHINA CHALLENGES MODI

When China's President Xi Jinping visited India on 17–19 September 2014, Modi, bypassing diplomatic protocols, received him at Ahmedabad in his home state, Gujarat, where they visited the Gandhi Ashram, promenaded on the Sabarmati riverfront and in the Gujarati tradition of welcoming guests, they sat side-by-side on a swing (jhoola). In Delhi, President Xi offered to invest $20 billion in India's infrastructure for the next five years, part of a slate of 12 agreements that both sides signed during the visit. Curiously enough, when they were building rapport and bonding with each other in Ahmedabad, the Chinese troops were sneaking into Ladakh to build a road that led to a confrontation, and after a five-day standoff, the Chinese troops retreated from Ladakh. What

China said was different from what China might do, it seemed.

China's frequent transgressions into India across the 2,520-mile-long Himalayan border (411 incursions in 2013, for example) normally go unreported in the media; but when the Chinese troops tried road building in the Indian territory as happened in Ladakh during President's Xi visit, it could not be ignored. According to a South Asian expert, this wasn't 'the first example of incursions preceding major bilateral meetings. Last year (2013), a significant mid-April incursion led to Chinese troops setting up camp in tents, also in the Ladakh area (Depsang). This extended over a two-week period into early May, and Indian media reported that the Chinese troops had extended nineteen kilometres into Indian territory. Premier Li Keqiang visited Delhi May 19 to 21 of last year (2013).'[98]

Reciprocating the visit to Modi's home state, President Xi hosted Prime Minister Modi in his home town Xian, 14–15 May 2015, where they talked and walked like friends discussing matters of mutual concerns including the boundary dispute and terrorism and establishing confidence-building measures. But underneath the bonhomie, there was tension. Less than a month before Modi's visit, Xi had paid a highly acclaimed visit to Pakistan, its all-weather friend, where he signed an agreement to invest $46 billion for projects under the CPEC that would pass through Kashmir (Pakistan occupied territory). But during the G20 summit in Hangzhou, China, on 4 September 2016, when Modi told Xi 'to ensure durable ties and their steady development, it is of paramount importance that we respect each other's aspirations, concerns and strategic interests,'[99] the Indian concerns were ignored.

Again, when during a meeting on the sidelines of the BRICS and Shanghai Cooperation Organization (SCO) summits in Ufa, Russia, Modi raised serious issues about China blocking US Security Council action against Pakistan for setting free the 26/11 Mumbai terror attacks' mastermind Zaki-ur-Rehman Lakhvi, Xi was not persuaded. Nor did China agree to support India's membership in the NSG that controlled access to sensitive nuclear technology in spite of the India–United States Nuclear Agreement. China refused to accept India as a legitimate nuclear-weapons power state as the rest of the world had done. Apart from blocking India's entry to NSG, China vetoed the UN Security Council proposal to ban Pakistan's terrorist organization Jaish-e-Mohammed and its leader Masood Azhar. Similar fruitless exchanges continued in 2017 between the two leaders on the sidelines of the summits at BRICS, Goa, India, SCO, Astana, Kazakhstan and G20, Hamburg, Germany.

India not only strongly protested against the CPEC passing through its sovereign Kashmir territory but much to China's chagrin, India also declined the invitation to join its Belt and Road Initiative summit held in Beijing, 14–15 May 2017. India also found that China had begun to make creeping advances in its Himalayan backyard, which led to the eruption of hostilities at Doklam, a crucial strategic plateau located between Bhutan's Ha Valley to the east, India's Sikkim state to the west and Tibet's Chumbi Valley to the north. India discovered that the Chinese army had begun to extend an existing road from Chumbi Valley into Doklam, the region that is part of Bhutan but claimed by China. On 18 June 2017, India, under the aegis of the Bhutan–India Friendship Treaty (2007), moved its troops from Sikkim into Doklam to stop the Chinese troops from constructing the road. The road would have threatened India's strategic Siliguri Corridor, the so-called Chicken Neck, a narrow 17-mile-wide stretch of land located in West Bengal, between Nepal and Bangladesh, that connects India's entire northeast region with the rest of India. Much was at stake because Siliguri city is the strategic nodule that links Bhutan, Nepal, Bangladesh, Sikkim, Darjeeling Hills and Northeast India, including Arunachal Pradesh, upon which China has laid fictitious claims. The Chinese control of the Doklam plateau would have made the entire region defenceless. After a long military and diplomatic standoff, India and China withdrew their troops from Doklam on 28 August 2017 without however reaching a conclusive resolution to the dispute, although both countries promised to find fresh modes of engagement and instructed their border forces to build trust and understanding in order to maintain the peace at the borders.

When the two leaders met for a one-to-one informal summit in Wuhan, China, 26–28 April 2018, to reassess their strategic positions and strengthen bilateral trade relations, there was a palpable thaw between the two leaders, though Doklam, China's resistance to Indian membership of the Nuclear Supplier Group and China's puzzling ambivalence about Pakistan's terrorist organization Jaish-e-Mohammed had not been forgotten.

India–China experts at Brookings observed that the changing international situation, especially China's deteriorating trade relations with the US and 'the unpredictability of the U.S. administration have made the Chinese leadership nervous...With the U.S. following a more confrontational policy, China has been making outreach efforts to countries in its periphery...An attempt to thaw relations with India should also be seen in this context... [Nonetheless] assessments of Chinese behaviour...will be a challenge for India over the next year...'[100]

China's two-track relations, on the one hand growing trade and commerce relations and on the other hand frequent transgressions on the Himalayan border along with denial of support for the NSG membership and the inexplicable reluctance to denounce Pakistan-based terrorist groups, were the biggest challenges for Modi in his first term. The resilience and strength of India have always existed in its unfathomable capacity to live and thrive amidst confusion, doubts and uncertainties. Not only China but the United States too would be continuously challenging India.

MODI AND UNCLE SAM

For about a decade, Modi as the chief minister of Gujarat, had been declared persona non grata in the United States for 'a comprehensive failure on the part of the state government to control the persistent violation of rights of life, liberty, equality, and dignity of the people of the state,' arising out of the 2002 Ayodhya–Gujarat pilgrim train-bombing that had triggered horrendous communal riots, which according to official reports killed 790 Muslims and 254 Hindus, and left thousands and thousands of people homeless and destitute.[101] The Hindu–Muslim riots had taken place in the background of a most serious threatened war between India and Pakistan, which was precipitated by Lashkar-e-Taiba and Jaish-e-Mohammed, Pakistan-based terrorist organizations' attack on the Indian Parliament on 13 December 2001. Prime Minister Vajpayee had just managed to pull India back from the brink of war with Pakistan. The BJP that ruled at the Centre appointed Modi as the state chief minister in October 2001; and he was just five months into his new job when the communal inferno erupted which the state failed to control. But the BJP's resounding electoral victory, spearheaded by Modi, for the 16th Lok Sabha dimmed the memories of the bloody past, as had also happened with the massacre of the Sikhs in 1984 when Rajiv Gandhi became the prime minister after his mother's assassination.

On 16 May 2014, President Barack Obama called Modi 'to congratulate him on the Bharatiya Janata Party's success in India's historic election' adding that he looked forward 'to working closely with Mr Modi to fulfil the extraordinary promise of the U.S.-India strategic partnership, and they agreed to continue expanding and deepening the wide-ranging cooperation between our two democracies.'[102] President Obama invited Prime Minister Modi to visit Washington DC to further strengthen the US–India bilateral relationship. Americans being pragmatists, were looking to the future rather than what had happened more than a decade ago. While campaigning as a prime ministerial candidate for the BJP, Modi 'promised to revive the growth rate by attracting foreign investment, reducing red tape, making hiring and firing easier, and improving the nation's infrastructure,' which attracted the support of the business community. As Gujarat state chief minister (2002–14), 'he courted foreign companies, oversaw GDP growth that exceeded the national average, and helped start irrigation projects that have boosted agricultural yields. Capitalizing on this success, he organized a series of conferences for international investors that he called Vibrant Gujarat.'[103] Observers wondered whether Modi would be able to scale up the Gujarat success story at the national platform, which is predicated upon the dynamics of the federal system, a robust free press and India's street democracy.

When Prime Minister Modi visited the United States from 27 to 30 September 2014 for addressing the UNGA, the gala public reception hosted by the most affluent immigrant group, the Indian–American community, and corporate America, all that was on his mind was the Make in India theme for transforming India into a global manufacturing hub. He found in President Obama a willing and sympathetic partner. The Vision Statement for the Strategic Partnership under the rubric of *'Chalein Saath Saath':* Forward Together We Go, pledged both countries to work together for economic growth; energy and climate change; defence and homeland security; high technology; space and health cooperation; and mutual consultation on global and regional issues. There was a particular mention of increasing two-way trade by five-fold to $500 billion; enhanced participation of US companies in infrastructure projects; US industry participation in the development of smart cities in Ajmer, Vishakhapatnam and Allahabad (now Prayagraj); contribution to Prime Minister's 500 Cities National Urban Development Mission and Clean India Campaign; steps towards the full implementation of the US–India civil nuclear cooperation agreement 'including but not limited to administrative issues, liability, technical issues, and licensing to facilitate the establishment of nuclear parks, including power plants with Westinghouse and GE-Hitachi technology'; renewal of the 2005 Framework for the US–India Defence Relationship for another ten years; and strengthening 'cooperation in maritime security to ensure freedom of navigation and unimpeded movement of lawful shipping and commercial activity, in accordance with accepted principles of international law.' Most significant from India's national interest was the US commitment 'to continue work towards India's phased entry into the NSG, the Missile Technology Control Regime (MTCR), the Wassenaar Arrangement and the Australia Group... [Affirming] that India meets MTCR requirements and is ready for membership... in all four regimes.'[104]

The chief guest of the 26 January 2015 Republic Day of India was Barack Obama, the first US president to be honoured on a most celebrated national day when India showcases its cultural diversity and military might through a spectacular parade. During Obama's three-day visit, although both leaders had much to discuss especially about trade and energy and other topics of mutual interest, the main focus was China's rise and its aggressive efforts to exert its influence in the region, including the militarization of islands in the South China Sea. Modi was open to security cooperation, including the United States, India, Japan and Australia, along the lines of the 2007 Quadrilateral Security Dialogue that was abandoned. He also showed his willingness to play a greater role in the Asia–Pacific Economic Cooperation forum. This was a sea change in India's international outlook. Modi seemed 'not only willing but eager to redefine India's relationship with the United States at a time China is on the rise economically, militarily and politically.' The strategic cooperation with the United States was India's foreign policy in a new key, keeping in mind that for a long time:

> American presidents have tried to enlist India, the world's largest democracy, in a more robust partnership, partly to offset China's rising power...In effect, American officials hope the two powers can do much more together than the United States could do alone to restrain China's ambitions and preserve the postwar (rule-based) order in the region.[105]

Modi's 'Act East' economic policy necessitated diplomatic and security alliances in the region that wouldn't be possible without the United States' cooperation. China's threat is not only in the South China Sea but also in the Indian Ocean where Chinese nuclear submarines have been spotted patrolling in the Bay of Bengal; in Sri Lanka where China controls a strategic maritime port at Hambantota; and in the Maldives, groaning under the debt-ridden two-kilometre-long China–Maldives Friendship Bridge. In the Himalayas, China keeps India on constant tenterhooks through its sporadic transgressions, road-building activities and confrontation with Indian troops. As Obama realized during his myriad dealings with the Chinese leaders, Modi too 'discovered that the more charming and hospitable you are to the Chinese, the tougher they decide to be with you...Obama's visit shows that Mr Modi has concluded that the U.S. is not just a strategic partner but is India's principal strategic partner in the world...It's a clear upgradation in the relationship, and it signals a new direction of Indian foreign policy.'[106] Although a nation's deep state, especially in regard to its international relations, remains stable over a long period of time, in the case of the United States however there are continuities and discontinuities and sometimes, disruptions when a new president occupies the White House, as happened in the case of Donald J. Trump who threatened to upend the international order with his campaign slogan 'America First,' which after the election victory became his governing policy. Modi's Make in India policy incentivizing foreign companies to set up production in India confronted with Donald Trump's 'America First' policy threatening to punish American companies who shipped jobs and production overseas.

When Modi and Trump met face to face with a bear hug on 26 June 2017, America was a different country from when Obama entered the White House as its chief occupant. In the Rose Garden at the White House, President Trump said that India and the United States' relations have 'never been stronger, has never been better.' With millions of Twitter followers, both were world leaders on social media. But the ground reality was different.

In April, Trump's 'Buy American, Hire American' executive order overhauling the H-1B visa programme hit Indians the most. While withdrawing from the Paris Agreement on Climate Change, Trump criticized India for financially benefitting from the agreement (through the provision of the Green Climate Fund). Modi, unperturbed by these disruptive policy outbursts, said in a press briefing, 'India's interests lie in a strong, and prosperous, and successful America. In the same way, India's development and its growing role at the international level are in the USA's interest.'[107] This was Modi's fifth visit to the United States, and it was different from the intense engagement he had with Obama. The challenge for Modi has been how to continue the mutual understanding, achievements and strategic goals established during the Obama administration with the unsettling and uncertain era of the Trump administration. There was an overhanging threat of imposing tariffs on Indian exports to the United States, constraints on outsourcing of work and jobs, and restrictions on visas for high-end professionals.

In spite of the transactional nature of Trump's diplomacy and international relations anchored on the 'America First' principle, Ashley Tellis observed optimistically:

> Given the steady expansion of the bilateral partnership over the last two decades, the range of joint activities today is breathtaking: …the US and India today engage in numerous strategic consultations, wide-ranging defence, counterterrorism, homeland security, cybersecurity and intelligence cooperation, as well as myriad activities in energy, education, science and technology, public health and culture.[108]

International relations have long-term objectives and knowing the value of strategic relations with the United States and other democratic nations for India's economic growth and national security—keeping in mind China's looming shadow over the Himalayas and the grand global strategy of the Belt and Road Initiative—Modi had a huge task cut out for him in his second term for resetting and strengthening relations with Trump's America and beyond.[109]

MODI'S FIRST TERM: ACCOMPLISHMENTS AND FAILURES

Does time run faster in the digital age? Maybe, maybe not, but there's certainly a sense of acceleration of time. The digital age created for Indians greater opportunities for participation in local, national and global conversations than ever before. Because of the digital connectivity, Indians began to have rising expectations about economic progress, jobs and betterment of life. No one wanted to be left behind. In the emerging and evolving digital ecosystem that Modi augmented through his policies and rhetoric in his first five years—the equivalent of a generational time span in the cyber age—he aroused greater aspirations than in the same period of time when Nehru was the prime minister.

With so much political power in his hands, perhaps as much as Nehru and Indira Gandhi had during their times, Modi promised much and ventured much. But how much did he accomplish? And where did he go wrong? The pace of activities in the first five years—Jan Dhan, Swachh Bharat, Start-Up India, Stand-Up India, Micro Units Development and Refinance Agency (MUDRA) micro-loans, Smart Cities, Digital India, Pradhan Mantri Ujjwala Yojana, Saubhagya, 100 per cent last-mile electrification, Prime Minister Fasal Bima Yojana and Kisan Samman Nidhi, and Beti Bachao, Beti Padhao—was breathtaking, even though some of the programmes were rhetorically repackaged or built on the foundations laid by his predecessors. One wonders whether Modi's fierce economic ambitions and grandiloquent rhetoric outpaced and outmatched India's abilities and capabilities, thus creating a cultural and political drag on the nation that walks like an elephant.

To transform India into a globally competitive technology and manufacturing hub through foreign direct investment and knowledge transfer, the Modi government launched, on 25 September 2014, with much fanfare the Make in India programme, opening up twenty-five economic sectors of the economy by relaxing foreign equity caps and streamlining norms and procedures for online applications. The sectors included the whole gamut of manufacturing industries such as automobiles, biotechnology, defence manufacturing, electronic systems, electrical machinery, food processing, information technology, media and entertainment, oil and gas, pharmaceuticals, ports and shipping, railways, roads and highways, space and astronomy, renewable energy and thermal power, textiles and garments, tourism and hospitality, and healthcare. Borrowing an American supply-chain quality management concept, Modi propounded in his 15 August 2014 address to the nation the 'Zero Defect, Zero Effect' model of manufacturing that would enable India to make high-quality products without adverse environmental effects, adding that 'India used to be called a land of snake charmers...[but today] our youth has surprised the world with its IT skills. Our dream is to build a "Digital India".'[110]

The Make in India initiative generated lots of enthusiasm from the international investment community. From the launch of the programme in September 2014 through February 2016, foreign direct investment (FDI) commitments worth US$240 billion were received. In 2015 India received more than US$63 billion in FDI surpassing China, and according to *The Financial Times* intelligence report 'the Make in India campaign and the resultant boost in FDI has resulted in a whopping increase in FDI job creation from 1.16 lakh new jobs in 2013 to 2.25 lakh in 2015—the highest number in the world.'[111] The Make in India programme allows 100 per cent FDI in most of the 25 open sectors, except in space, defence and media industries. The cumulative impact of the schemes such as Bharatmala, Sagarmala, Dedicated Freight Corridors, Industrial Corridors, UDAN (air travel Regional Connectivity Scheme), and Bharat Broadband Network and Digital India in conjunction with the Make in India programme was quite significant.

By the end of 2017, India had improved its standing in the Ease of Doing Business Index, the World Forum's Global Competitive Index and the Logistics Performance Index. In 2020 India ranked sixty-third among 190 countries on the ease of doing business index.[112] Although periodic assessment and course correction are necessary, there cannot be any closure to the Make in India project because it's essentially a long-term rolling development plan to make India competitive in the global marketplace. The plan's continuous success is predicated upon India's domestic peace, banking and economic reforms, and most importantly, foreign policy initiatives especially building strategic relations with countries from where technology and FDI could be resourced.

Although demonetization—the shock-and-awe dramatic move to end corruption and black money, which is a constant problem in many developing countries—was not an imaginative and well-planned scheme and caused tremendous suffering to some sections of society and damaged the economy to some extent, Modi in his first five years took some very brave steps that would have long-term effects upon the country. Apart from the GST that has turned India into one uninterrupted unified common market, the government enacted the Insolvency and Bankruptcy Code (IBC), an essential creative destruction process for rejuvenating the free enterprise capitalist system. The IB Code allows domestic and international businesses to acquire bankrupt companies burdened with large nonperforming bank assets but whose underlying fundamentals are strong. Freed from unproductive loans, banks too could be reinvigorated to lend money to new viable projects. The Fugitive Economic Offenders Act (2018) that further strengthened banks' position to confiscate the properties of fraudsters and absconders was necessary. But equally important was the governmental proposal in October 2017 for a massive capital infusion (₹2.11 lakh crore) to re-capitalize the public sector banking system, albeit a palliative in the absence of genuine bank reforms. Summing up the banking problem, *The Economic Times* observed, 'India's economic growth plunged to a three-year low in the June quarter to 5.6 per cent as over-leveraged companies struggled to borrow more and invest. At the same time, banks were reluctant to lend as they feared more bad loans. Furthermore, the sins of the past were squeezing the banks.'[113] The government privatization and disinvestment policy did not make much headway either.

LANDMARK ACHIEVEMENTS OF MODI SARKAR

However, some of the successful landmark programmes are noteworthy. Under the Swachh Bharat programme, over 90 million toilets were built to make India free from open defecation by 2019. The programme that impacts the health and dignity of all, especially the people in rural areas, entered into the national conversation and popular culture. The 2017 Bollywood film, *Toilet: Ek Prem Katha*, a popular satirical drama, told the story of a newly married woman who left her husband and filed for divorce because he had no toilet at his home in the village. The husband, however, won her back only when the construction of toilets had begun to take place not just for her but for the entire village. In the northern state of Haryana, a government minister directed all village heads to watch the movie.[114]

To improve the quality of life and health of the rural population, the Modi government, under the Pradhan Mantri Ujjwala Yojana scheme, gave 80 million households free gas connections, including the first cylinder, which cost about ₹600, though most villagers still prefer to use cow-dung patties as fuel for cooking while some others use both. More ambitious is the National Health Protection Mission—Ayushman Bharat—said to be the world's largest government-funded healthcare programme. Launched in 2018, it aims to deliver comprehensive care to more than 100 million 'poor, deprived rural families and identified the occupational category of urban workers' families as per the latest Socio-Economic Caste Census (SECC) data covering both rural and urban. The scheme is designed to be dynamic and aspirational, and it would take into account any future changes in the exclusion/ inclusion/ deprivation/ occupational criteria in the SECC data.' The healthcare scheme, covering 40 per cent of the population, provides coverage up to five lakh rupees per family per year for secondary and tertiary care hospitalization, subsuming the already existing centrally sponsored healthcare schemes. The national healthcare protection scheme also includes 150,000 health and wellness centres that 'provide pregnancy care and maternal health services, neonatal and infant health services, child health, chronic communicable diseases, non-communicable diseases, management of mental illness, dental care, and geriatric care emergency medicine.' [115]

On 8 April 2015, the Modi government launched a renewed version of loans for small- and micro-businesses that was already in existence and called it MUDRA bank to provide affordable financial services and loans from ₹50,000 to ₹1 million to small entrepreneurs, including small shopkeepers, fruit and vegetable vendors, and artisans and manufacturing units. As of March 2019, total disbursement under the MUDRA scheme since the beginning of the programme was ₹6.70 lakh crores though the data as to how many new ventures were started and how many new jobs were created is yet to be available.[116]

When Modi came to power in 2014, he promised India '*achhe din*' (good days), so much so that even British Prime Minister David Cameron, while introducing him to an audience in Wembley Stadium, London, on 13 November 2015, babbled enthusiastically, 'They said a "chai wala" would never govern the largest democracy, but he proved them wrong. He rightly said "acche din aane wale hain". But with his energy, with his vision, with his ambition, I will go on further and say "achhe din zaroor aayega" (Good days will certainly come)." In fact, Cameron seemed to be echoing Modi's national agenda about building smart cities, Digital India, and India with a permanent seat of the UNSC.[117]

BUT DATA DON'T LIE

Modi's 'Achhe Din' promise included rapid economic growth, more jobs, a better business environment, elimination of corruption and better national security. During the first five years of the Modi government (2014–18), the economy was reported to have grown about 7.5 per cent on average, making India the world's fastest-growing economy for the first time.[118] But keeping in mind the controversial GDP re-calculation methodology, some experts raised serious questions about the accuracy of the data.[119] In a working paper, 'India's Mis-estimation: Likelihood, Mechanisms, and Implications,' published at Harvard University's Centre for International Development, economist Arvind Subramanian threw a spanner at the veracity of the GDP data. According to the research findings, 'A variety of evidence—within India and across countries—suggests that India's GDP growth has been overstated by about 2.5 percentage points per year in the post-2011 period... The Indian policy automobile has been navigated with a faulty, possibly broken, speedometer.' In conclusion, Subramanian said,

> These findings alter our understanding of India's growth performance after the Global Financial Crisis, from spectacular to solid. Two important policy implications follow: the entire national income accounts estimation should be revisited, harnessing new opportunities created by the Goods and Services Tax to significantly improve it; and restoring growth should be the urgent priority for the new government.[120]

Surprisingly these doubts never arose in Subramanian's mind when he was the chief economic adviser to the Government of India (16 October 2014 to 20 June 2018). But it is never too late to discover and speak up the truth about India because, as he said, 'Nothing less than the future of the Indian economy and the lives of 1.4 billion citizens rides on getting numbers and measurement right. As we measure, so India will go.'[121]

Regardless of the GDP data accuracy, India is soon poised to become the fifth-largest global economy. Nevertheless, India lags far behind China not only in GDP but also in military power and global influence. It also trails behind other emerging economies in Asia, including South Korea, Indonesia, Thailand and Malaysia in terms of per capita GDP. Despite notching up in the World Bank's ranking of ease of doing business, increased foreign direct investment amounting to US$268.53 billion (compared with US$189. 5 billion during the UPA government) and the industrial production going up, exports did not increase significantly during the Modi administration indicating that the Make in India programme needed revamping.

In spite of the overall impressive economic growth of more than 7 per cent, according to Statista and the Centre for Monitoring Indian Economy (compare: Subramanian), the job growth has not kept pace with the rising labour market; and in fact, in 2018, the unemployment rate shot up to 7.4 per cent with a total job loss of 11 million jobs.[122] The seriousness of the job crisis could be gauged from the fact that in 2018 when the Indian Railways advertised 90,000 jobs for its massive modernization programme, it drew 28 million applicants. International Labour Organization's India Wage Report based on the 2011–12 data characterized the Indian labour market 'by high levels of segmentation and informality... more than half were self-employed (51.4 per cent, or 206 million people), and (of the 195 million wage earners), 62 per cent... were employed as casual workers. Employment in the organized sector has grown, but even in this sector, many jobs have been casual or informal'. The report showed that 'low pay and wage inequality remain a serious challenge to India's path to achieving decent working conditions and inclusive growth.'[123]

PEOPLE'S VOICE

According to a survey conducted by the Association for Democratic Reforms in October–December 2018, covering 534 out of 543 election constituencies and a sample of 273,487 rural and urban voters, about 47 per cent respondents selected employment opportunities as one of the top five issues, followed by healthcare, drinking water, better roads and public transportation. Surprisingly, 'Terrorism or the need for a strong military did not figure in this list. The only security concern that voters had in the top ten issues was of the need for better law and order and policing. Voters' worry about the threat to their own security locally more than the problems from across our national borders. Even this local law and order problem ranked tenth.' [124]

Two weeks before the declaration of the 2019 Indian general election (11 April through 19 May) results, economist and journalist Surjit S. Bhalla, travelling through Uttar Pradesh for an on-the-spot experiential assessment, wondered whether the 'silent voter' would punish the Modi government for its acts of omission and commission. He observed that with 'broadly defined' income levels going up, road constructions, toilets, LPG, bank accounts, national health insurance, scooters, there was a sense of satisfaction in UP.

But Bhalla's conclusion regarding the 'Farmer distress and cow politics' read in conjunction with the Association for Democratic Reforms survey results gave a fairly good idea of what was happening—a mixed picture of the Modi government's achievements and failures at the end of its first five-year term. Bhalla reported:

> If there is one unanimous view emanating from UP travel, it is that farmer distress is real and that cow politics has deepened the distress among all, farmers and non-farmers...The poor Hindu farmer is hurt; Muslims have lost jobs, and in some instances, life; the rural economy is hurt. *Yet, Hindu India continues to support this madness* [emphasis added].[125]

On the brighter side, one might say, in spite of Hindu nationalism, sporadic religious intolerance, citizenship issues, human rights concerns and sluggish-to-solid economic performance, India, a robust dynamic democratic system, has continued to play the game of democracy by and large, under the rule of law.

THE 17TH LOK SABHA ELECTION

This was the biggest democratic exercise ever carried out in the world. Of the more than 900 million eligible voters to elect the seventeenth Lok Sabha in the general election that was held in seven phases from 11 April through 19 May 2019, there were 432 million women, 38,325 transgender people and 15 million first-time voters in the18–19 age group who voted for 8,000 candidates to fill up 543 parliamentary seats. Seven national parties, more than 300 state parties and independent candidates spent US$14 billion to win the election, twice the amount that was spent in the 2014 general election. Every vote mattered because in the first-past-the-post electoral system, a small group of voters could have a disproportionate impact on the outcome. In the 2014 general election, the BJP, with 31.34 per cent of votes, had won more than 50 per cent of parliamentary seats, 282 out of 543. On the other hand, the Congress party, with 19.52 per cent votes, won 8 per cent of the seats, only 44 out of 543. In other words, about a 12 per cent vote difference gave the BJP 238 more seats than the Congress party. Or one might say, about 69 per cent of people of India did not vote for Narendra Modi's BJP in 2014.

In 2019, four states, including Andhra Pradesh, Arunachal Pradesh, Odisha and Sikkim held their Legislative Assembly elections along with the national election. But before the Election Commission of India announced the election schedule on 10 March along with the Model Code of Conduct, two major political parties—the BJP leading the NDA and the INC leading the UPA, had already launched their campaigns. The BJP election manifesto, 'Sankalp Patra' (Document of Intent and Resolve), promised a comprehensive socio-economic development of the nation, including farm economy, education, infrastructure, railways, health, economic development, governance and development, and social justice. The manifesto included making India the third-largest global economy in a decade, *the abrogation of Jammu and Kashmir's special status vide Articles 370 and 35A* [emphasis added], building the controversial Ram Temple at Ayodhya, and absolutely no tolerance for terrorism.[126]

Most importantly, the manifesto promised to double farmers' income by 2022 by opening more markets and farm produce storage centres, implementing minimum price supports for agricultural produce, providing farmers with loans, building all-weather rural roads, and providing social security for small and marginal farmers after 60 years of age.

Regarding education, the BJP platform proposed to bring all secondary schools under the national board quality purview, though education is a state subject; invest one lakh crores (US$14 billion) in higher education, increase and open new seats at existing engineering, management and law schools; establish skills and innovations centre; and augment higher education opportunities for women by introducing financial support and subsidies programmes.

Other manifesto provisions included: providing good housing, potable water, toilet, LPG cylinder, electricity and banking account for every family; doubling the length of national highways; improving renewable energy capacity to 175 gigawatts; electrifying and converting all Indian railway tracks to broad gauge; establishing 150,000 health and wellness centres across India; starting 75 new medical colleges; and achieving 100 per cent immunization of all babies in India. The manifesto promised to raise India's global business ranking further in 'ease of doing business;' doubling India's exports and introducing single-window compliance procedures for all businesses; digitizing paperwork and proceedings; modernizing the courts in India; and launching and promoting National Digital Library with e-books and leading journals to provide free knowledge access to all students.

Under the rubric of social justice and inclusive development, the manifesto promised to provide all unorganized labourers comprehensive social security coverage, including insurance and pension; greater female workforce participation rate; and most interestingly, justice for Muslim women by enacting a law against triple talaq. The BJP manifesto promised to clean up the sacred Ganges by 2022.[127]

The INC released its manifesto on 3 April and called it 'Congress Will Deliver,' which promised wealth distribution and welfare through jobs and direct transfer of ₹72,000 annually to the 20 per cent poorest families in India. The Congress party president Rahul Gandhi coined the slogan *'Garibi Pe Waar'* (War on Poverty), which was a reinvention of his grandmother Prime Minister Indira Gandhi's 1971 slogan *'Garibi Hatao'* (Eradicate Poverty). While Indira Gandhi had tried to do it through nationalization and state capitalism, calling it 'socialistic pattern of society,' Rahul Gandhi, chary of socialism, as are most of the Indian political parties, retreated into the safer haven of welfare economics, eschewing tougher challenges of entrepreneurialism, open marketplace and making India globally competitive. Party spokesman P. Chidambaram, a Harvard graduate and former minister of finance with vast political experience, listed unemployment, farm distress, security of women and social divisiveness and hyper-nationalism as the top political issues.[128]

The Congress manifesto, apart from its welfare programme Nyuntam Aay Yojana of direct fund transfer of ₹72,000 annually to a woman-member of the bottom 20 per cent of families, promised to create 1 million jobs in rural, local and urban government bodies, fill up 400,000 central government vacancies, and encourage state governments to do the same; enact a law requiring private employers with over 100 employees to implement an apprenticeship programme; introduce Kisan Budget in Parliament every year and waive all farmer loans in all states with any amount outstanding; authorize Right to Homestead Act that will provide free land to every household that does not own a home; enact Right to Healthcare Act that guarantees every Indian citizen free diagnostics, free medicines, free hospitalization and free outpatient care; double India's healthcare spending to 3 per cent of GDP by 2024; double India's education expenditure to 6 per cent of GDP by 2024; revise and rationalize GST; and increase the total length of national highways, and massively modernize Indian railway infrastructure.

The manifesto promised to make India one of the top manufacturing hubs in the world and increase defence spending to muscle up the Indian Armed Forces. In contrast to the BJP's manifesto, the Congress party's platform was committed to the preservation of the special status of Jammu and Kashmir under Articles 370 and 35A of the Indian Constitution. It also promised to amend the Armed Forces (Special Powers) Act of 1958 to remove immunity for 'enforced disappearance, sexual violence and torture' and also end the Sedition law.[129]

While the BJP became a dominant political force in India and the Congress party showed no signs, not yet, of terminal illness, the performance of the regional parties was crucial for their own survival because the BJP had been making inroads and encroachments into their political citadels. To limit the appeal of Hindutva and the penetration of the BJP into their states, some regional parties and their leaders set aside their political and personal differences and formed opportunistic alliances to shut the enemy out. In the 2019 general election, there were more than 50 regional and state parties in the fray, but most of them had little appeal outside of their regions or states; nonetheless, they could upset the apple cart and create uncertainties. For a quarter of a century—1989 through 2014—Indians played the game of democracy through political alliances with national and regional parties, although the first experiment with a coalition government was attempted in 1977 and lasted for a couple of years before Indira Gandhi roared back into power. It was only in 2014 that a single party, the BJP, swept the polls with 282 seats (for a total of 336 seats for the BJP-led NDA) out of 543 parliamentary seats. Political alliances have become the norm as well as a most important political necessity in India because adequate regional representations and aspirations could be fulfilled only through alliances, even when a single party dominates the country.

In the 2019 general election, apart from the BJP-led NDA and the Congress-led UPA, there was the Left Front alliance of pro-communist parties; and the grand alliance of some regional parties, for example, the Bahujan Samaj Party and Samajwadi Party in Uttar Pradesh, the state with 80 parliamentary seats. Unlike the two-party political system in the United States, India has developed a more fluid, Lego-type, two-party alliance system, each alliance with a dominant party. But alliances by their nature are based on ideological compromises and, therefore, how far the BJP would push its Hindutva agenda on its allies in the states has yet to be seen. In the federal-parliamentary system of India, states play a crucial role in the general election electoral calculus because no major national party has a controlling or decisive presence in all 29 states, thereby, leaving political space to smaller regional parties who, by championing local issues, play crucial roles in their states and some time at the Centre. Thus regional political parties, with their diversity of interests and ideologies, present an immense challenge to a national party or a coalition in order 'to bridge India's enormous federal plurality.'[130] But the 2019 general election was different.

BJP'S ELECTORAL SWEEP

The election results once again bamboozled most of the Indian liberal thinking classes who hoped that the 2019 election would correct the previous election's aberration, a black swan outlier event, and India would revert to some form of a coalition government, which even if it were under the BJP would not threaten the 'Idea of India' as they had imagined.[131] On the contrary, the 2019 election catapulted Modi to greater heights of popularity and mass adulation than ever before, placing him on the same pedestal as Jawaharlal Nehru and Indira Gandhi, the two most admired leaders since India began to experiment with freedom and play the game of democracy. Rahul Gandhi, the leader of the INC, Nehru's great-grandson, suffered the most humiliating defeat. He lost his parliamentary seat from Amethi, the Nehru–Gandhi family pocket borough—the seat that he had held for the past 15 years—to a BJP candidate, Smriti Irani. But Parliament won't miss Rahul Gandhi's absence because he won a parliamentary seat from Wayanad, a rural constituency in Kerala, 1,300 miles away from his home constituency. The Congress won only 52 seats, once again losing its status as the official opposition in the Parliament, though the Congress-led UPA won 91 seats, and regional and state parties bagged 96 parliamentary seats.

The BJP, defying all pre-poll projections and political experts' analyses and opinions, won 303 seats, 21 more than in the 2014 parliamentary election, giving the BJP-led NDA 335 seats—a sweeping mandate for a second five-year term. More important than winning the landslide victory was the BJP's expansion into non-Hindi-speaking regions of the country, the regions other than Prime Minister Modi's home state Gujarat where he was the state chief minister for 12 years and Maharashtra, where the BJP had been in power with its ally Shiv Sena. In the four state assembly elections that were held along with the 2019 parliamentary election, the results showed the power of federal plurality. In Andhra Pradesh, the Yuvajana Shramika Rythu (YSR) Congress party led by Y.S. Jaganmohan Reddy won a thumping majority beating the incumbent Telugu Desam Party (TDP), headed by Chief Minister N. Chandrababu Naidu, by 151 seats out of 175 seats. The BJP made no dent in state politics. In Odisha, the Biju Janata Dal (BJD), under the leadership of Naveen Patnaik, the state chief minister, held its sway in the assembly election though the BJP won 23 assembly seats. While in Arunachal Pradesh, the BJP won 41 seats out of 60 to form the government, in Sikkim, it did not win a single assembly seat. In the 2019 general election, the BJP won 135 parliamentary seats from non-Hindi regions out of a total of 393. In the South, the BJP's best showing was in Karnataka, where it won 25 seats out of 28. The party bagged 4 seats in Telangana but was absolutely no show in Andhra Pradesh, Kerala and Tamil Nadu. By winning 18 parliamentary seats in West Bengal, the BJP presented a most serious challenge to the Trinamool Congress and Chief Minister Mamata Banerjee's hold on power. The election also saw the total elimination of the CPM, the party that had earned the notoriety of ruling West Bengal, one of the most intellectualized and articulate states in India that had given birth to Naxalism–Maoism, for more than three decades. The lone communist voice in the 17th Lok Sabha would be one from the Kerala CPM.[132]

MODI'S ENDLESS CHARM

Narendra Modi won in spite of increased joblessness, distressed farm incomes, slumping industrial production, the unforeseen damage of demonetization that was rushed upon to unearth black money and stop terrorists' funding, and the complexities of the GST. Nothing seemed to have hurt his popularity as a powerful leader because people also saw the benefits of his welfare schemes, including the distribution of cooking gas, building toilets, providing credit for small businesses and building homes for the poor. Born poor, Modi is for the poor, first and foremost. After the Pakistan-based militant attack on 14 February 2019 in Pulwama in Kashmir that killed 40 Central Reserve Police Force (CRPF) personnel and Modi's lightning response attacking deep into Pakistan's territory created the impression that Pakistan could not mess with India by hiding behind its militant organizations. During his nonstop campaign speeches, he reminded the voters that India needed a strong and decisive leader, and there was no one else. 'I'm the one, the only one'—he seemed to be saying from campaign stop to campaign stop, Twitter feed to Twitter feed. The convergence of the welfare state with the security state proved a winsome political game for the BJP. More importantly, Modi is a great communicator. Apart from his soaring and inspiring public oratory, he understands the power of symbols in mobilizing people.

A year before 900 million eligible Indians were to cast their vote in the 2019 general election that brought back the BJP to the Lok Sabha with a thundering majority, the Pew Research Centre conducted a survey among 2,521 respondents from 23 May through 23 July 2018 about the state of the nation. The survey found that a substantial majority of the people (65 per cent) was optimistic about the direction of the country, economic gains, their financial situation and the future of their children.[133] Unemployment was, however, a serious concern, according to three-quarters of the respondents. Corruption, terrorism and crime were big problems, according to two-thirds of the people surveyed, and about the same percentage also held that most politicians were corrupt. In various degrees, both the BJP and the Congress party supporters believed that democracy worked and delivered economic opportunity.

By far the most important finding of the survey was the respondents' attitude towards trade and globalization. An overwhelming majority of Indians surveyed opined that trade was good for the country and many felt that trade and business ties with other countries were very good. In sharp contrast to other countries, especially Japan, Europe and the United States, the majority of respondents said that trade created jobs and raised wages. Another significant survey finding was:

> Throughout Prime Minister Narendra Modi's term in office, international perceptions of India have been mostly positive. Majorities in all five Asia-Pacific countries surveyed have a favourable view of India, with such positive judgement ranging from 64 per cent in South Korea to 57 per cent in Indonesia and Australia. Half the American public also shares this upbeat opinion of the world's largest democracy...Across the Asia-Pacific region, as well as in the U.S., the share of the public who express confidence in Indian Prime Minister Narendra Modi exceeds the share who lack confidence in him.[134]

With so much political capital, Modi began his second term with a 1000-day plan, the Strategy for New India @75, when India would celebrate its platinum jubilee in 2022. In order to achieve India's full potential, different areas would require 'either a sharper focus on implementing the flagship schemes already in place or a new design and initiative.'[135] In other words, the state-directed economy, more or less, would continue.

Although the Modi government dissolved the Planning Commission that was established in 1950 to carry out economic growth through Five-Year Plans, the idea of welfare-based planning for political reasons became so ingrained that Indian politicians could not think without it. Instead of carrying out structural reforms, India was to continue economic development through projects and schemes, as previous governments had done. The plan enjoined that the 'development must become a mass movement...

Collective effort and resolve will ensure that we achieve a New India by 2022 just like independence was achieved within five years of Mahatma Gandhi giving his call of Quit India in 1942.'[136] Some of the highlights of New India @75 included doubling farmers' income, financial inclusion, housing for all, water resources and sustainable environment, health management and universal healthcare, education and skill development, modernizing city governance for urban transformation, and most importantly, digital connectivity, smart cities and data-led governance and policymaking. There was no mention of greater economic freedom and entrepreneurialism.

MODI: VICTORIOUS AND ASPIRATIONAL

In his victory speech, Modi said, *'Aapne fakir ki jhholi bhar di.* [Your generosity has made my dreams come true]'. I bow my head to the 130 crore Indians. The election in India was the biggest episode in the democratic world. People came out to vote in 40–45° Celsius heat. What happened in these elections will continue to inspire generations to come.' Referring to the battle of Kurukshetra, he said the victory was for the people of India. 'When Mahabharat ended,' he said, 'Krishna was asked, "Whose side are you on?" Krishna replied, "I'm not on anyone's side. I'm only on the side of Hastinapur" (India).'

Denouncing caste-based identity politics, Modi said:

> There are just two castes in the country now. ... those who are poor and want to get out of poverty and those who want to help poor out of their poverty...Though governments are formed with a majority but country runs with the consensus... We need to take everyone together. We have to work together for the interests of the country.[137]

Although Modi has been perceived as a polarizing figure, his unstoppable Hindu nationalistic juggernaut is as much against casteism and regionalism as it is a force to integrate India as a strong nation, a vision that he shares with Sardar Vallabhbhai Patel and Swami Vivekananda; and one might venture to say, no less with Jawaharlal Nehru who envisioned the unity of India through secularism and a socialistic pattern of society.

At the same time, although he has been talking about '*Sab ka saath, sab ka vikas, sab ka vishwas*' (Collective efforts, inclusive growth, everyone's trust) as his guiding political philosophy, Modi has yet to operationalize the dictum into tangible and credible actionable terms so that every Indian has a sense of inclusiveness in his grand vision of the New India by 2022 when India would celebrate its seventy-fifth freedom anniversary. The Indians of the freedom movement, modern India's greatest generation, transcended their limitations and created something greater than themselves: the Constitution, a freedom document that binds and bonds Indians together. It's important to revisit the fundamental human rights enshrined in the Constitution, the noblest document the Indian mind has created since the Vedas. We might pooh-pooh the Indian intellectual class for its fake secularism, but we cannot ignore other voices, the global public opinion on whose goodwill India's grand plans such as Make in India, Digital India, and FDI and Technology Transfer, and not least, international trade, depend. It is through trade that India can export its ideas. The ultimate test of Narendra Modi's nationalism is the competition of the marketplace, the global marketplace of goods, as well as ideas, where the Darwinian rule of 'survival of the fittest' prevails.

The fate of BJP's Hindutva, like that of Nehru's socialism, would be determined to a great extent by the marketplace, which values competition and innovation rather than sloganeering and mythologizing. Nehru's socialism, instead of transforming India into a manufacturing and industrial nation, turned India into a nation of babus and coffee house intellectuals, argumentative Indians with their endless arguments and no sense of closure. Hindu nationalists would soon discover that peddling myths, to paraphrase historian Romila Thapar, as historical truths would destroy creativity and innovation; and would turn India into a nation of fakirs and fakers and daydreamers.[138]

As has been said earlier, the digital age gives us a sense of an accelerated future. Five years is too long a period in the digital age, the time period of a generation past, for the young and the restless, multitasking and globalized, to keep waiting for their first jobs. Can Modi reinvent and reshape Hindutva nationalism to create a unified Indian consciousness, to make it so inclusive that no Indian is left behind, in order to meet the challenges of the digital age, the age of artificial intelligence and the Internet of Everything, the age of ruthless networked competition, the ecosystem that's being increasingly dominated by the United States, China, Russia, Europe and Japan?

Narendra Modi needs to remember the words of Sundarar, Tamil bhakti saint-poet, who said, 'Can't we find some other god?'

15

HOW INDIANS THINK

*...He could not open his lips without provoking admiration.
This was a dangerous state of affairs.*

—R.K. Narayan, *The Guide*

*We have to build the noble mansion of free India
where all her children may dwell.*

—Jawaharlal Nehru

*India does not need to become anything else. India must
become only India. This is a country that once upon a time was
called the golden bird.*

—Narendra Modi

The Indian mode of thinking is driven by an overwhelming sense and sensibility of exceptionalism and loss, based on a claim to moral superiority, intellectual achievements, and historical uniqueness that must be revived and preserved, or whose loss must be recovered through salvage of the mythical past. Fearing the loss of democracy, Ambedkar had, in his final speech to the Constituent Assembly, asked, 'What would happen to her democratic Constitution? Will she be able to maintain it or will she lose it again?' The operative word is 'again,' but when was India ever democratic? According to Ambedkar, India once upon a time was 'studded with republics, and even where there were monarchies, they were either elected or limited. They were never absolute. It is not that India did not know Parliaments or parliamentary procedure.' He was referring to the 'Buddhist Bhikshu Sanghas,' who,

Ambedkar surmised, must have borrowed their procedures from 'the rules of the Political Assemblies functioning in the country in his (the Buddha) time.' And that was the democratic system that India had lost. Then he asked, 'Will she lose it a second time?... But it is quite possible in a country like India—where *democracy from its long disuse* [emphasis added] must be regarded as something quite new—there is a danger of democracy giving place to dictatorship. It is quite possible for this newborn democracy to retain its form but give place to dictatorship, in fact. If there is a landslide, the danger of the second possibility becoming actuality is much greater.'[1] The fascination and obsessiveness about the intellectual, political, spiritual and cultural treasures of ancient India and their recovery were not limited to Ambedkar. Many other members of the Constituent Assembly expressed similar sentiments, some referring to the village Panchayat system as grassroots village democracies.

The sense and sensibility of exceptionalism and loss come from a unique interpretation and re-imagination of history and mythology. In 1904 Urdu poet Muhammad Iqbal (1877–1938) wrote a stirringly beautiful patriotic poem, *Sare Jahan Se Accha*, in which he sang about the Indian civilizational exceptionalism and sense of loss and pain. The Urdu ghazal (ode) intoned, 'Better than the whole world, our Hindustan... we are Indian, our homeland is Hindustan... Greece and Egypt and Byzantium all became erased from the world but until now our identity lives on...there's something, that our existence does not become erased...[for] centuries the cycle of time has remained our enemy... what does anyone know of our hidden pain?'[2]

From the great Indian awakening, beginning with the Bengali Renaissance and nationalism epitomized in Bankim Chandra Chatterjee's *Vande Mataram* and Rabindranath Tagore's soulful 'Freedom from fear is the freedom I claim for you my motherland'; through Mahatma Gandhi's non-violence and Satyagraha to Jawaharlal Nehru's call of destiny at the dawn of Independence, the Indian mind has been infused with this overpowering sense and sensibility of exceptionalism and loss. To a great extent, Nehru's non-alignment foreign policy was driven by the sensibility of exceptionalism that India was a unique site for *alternative universality*. Although Nehru had an Indo-European assimilative mind, he drew his strength from India's great historical and spiritual heritage from the Indus Valley Civilization, the Buddha and Ashoka.

Not only has the foreign policy of India from non-alignment and assertive nationalism to strategic autonomy been driven by this unique sense and sensibility of exceptionalism, but in many ways, it also informs and strengthens federalism; and defines relations between the states and various cultural communities. It pervades the national discourse and the popular media, and sometimes it also becomes a site for domestic conflicts. Consider this: Speaking at Jadavpur University in Kolkata on 5 July 2019, economist Amartya Sen said that 'Jai Sri Ram' was not associated with Bengali culture, where 'Maa Durga' is ubiquitous, saying, 'I asked my four-year-old grandchild who is your favourite deity? She replied that it is Maa Durga. Maa Durga is so much omnipresent *in our lives* [emphasis added]'. [3] Don't mess with Bengali culture, which is unique and exceptional; he seemed to be admonishing the Hindutva followers who were chanting 'Jai Sri Ram', a common greeting in northern India but which he thought was being used as a political slogan. Dr Sen's spur of the moment reaction to a local political situation was very different from the views of Tagore when he sang Bhuban Jora Asankani invoking the Almighty, as historian Sugata Bose said, 'to spread his seat of universality in the individual's heart':

> Your universe-encompassing prayer mat
> Spread it out in the core of my heart.
> The night's stars, the day's sun, all the shades of darkness
> and light,
> All your messages that fill the sky–
> Let them find their abode in my heart.
> May the lute of the universe
> Fill the depths of my soul with all its tunes.
> All the intensity of grief and joy, the flower's touch, the
> storm's touch—
> Let your compassionate, auspicious, generous hands
> Bring into the core of my heart. [4]

Sen was perhaps unselfconsciously describing India as a congeries of unique cultures of which Bengal is an epitome. The Bengali sensibility of exceptionalism and sense of loss is rooted in an accident of history because:

> ...Bengal was at the forefront of modern subcontinental aspiration in colonial India. The British had their capital in Kolkata (then Calcutta) and Bengalis were among the first to receive the benefits of Western education and enlightenment—a process that contributed to the so-called Bengal Renaissance. For about 100 years from the late 18th century onwards, Bengal witnessed a remarkable cultural efflorescence, spawning a number of writers, thinkers, social reformers, educationists... [5]

There is no field of human endeavour in which Bengalis have not distinguished themselves. They're proud of their Nobel laureates, renowned scientists, political leaders and revolutionaries, great movie stars and directors, and writers, thinkers, philosophers, painters, poets and musicians. But the sense of loss has been equally deep because of the fact that Bengal was broken up twice, once in 1905 by Lord Curzon, Viceroy of India, which was undone in 1911, and the other when Bengal was partitioned in 1947; and the memories of the terrible famine of 1943. It seemed as if an exceptional people had no control over their destiny. But the sense of superiority to non-Bengalis, 'Obangalis', people from other parts of India, never goes away.[6]

And again, Dr Sen's treatise *The Argumentative Indian* is a paean to the Indian sense of exceptionalism and the fear of loss of its culture of heterogeneity, heterodoxy and pluralism; nonetheless, forgetting that no other society had ever reduced humans to a *state of nothingness* (Sanskrit: Shunya) as the Indian caste system had done to the untouchables. Exceptionalism comes in many incarnations.

The overwhelming sense and sensibility of exceptionalism and fear of loss are not limited to the Bengali culture; it's an Indian phenomenon. The Tamils, the Andhras, the Marathas, the Rajputs, the Sikhs and the Kashmiris, for example, have the same self-consciousness of exceptionalism and fear of its dilution, dissipation and loss, as Nobel laureate Sen has about the Bengali culture. The Sikh sense and sensibility of exceptionalism and fear of loss come from the historical fact that they created a new unique syncretic religion, which historian and writer Khushwant Singh, in his lighter moments, called a heady religious cocktail. Under Maharaja Ranjit Singh, they established the great Sikh empire that extended from Afghanistan and Punjab to Kashmir and was lost. Consider their pre-eminence in the military today; and their prodigious confidence that a Sikh can do anything.[7]

Few other people in India pose 'a challenge to common sense,' wrote historian and author A.R. Venkatachalapathy, as the Tamils with their 'long claims to Tamil distinctiveness and exceptionalism. The "South", especially Tamil Nadu, has posed problems to the Indian nation…(because) Tamil Nadu has been part of the Indian mainstream, yet maintains its distinctiveness.' In many ways, Tamil Nadu has been more progressive than any other state, including the central government, especially considering that 'Systematic caste-based reservations in employment and education were introduced in Tamil Nadu nearly a century ago, while most of India is still struggling to reconcile itself to such positive discrimination and affirmative action.' The Tamils not only take great pride in their icon Chinnaswami Subramania Bharati, freedom fighter and social reformer, regarded as one of the greatest Tamil literary figures, but also in their native bullfight, jallikattu, held during Pongal, something unique to Tamil Nadu, for which they defied the Supreme Court ban in 2017. 'The intertwining of film songs and politics,' wrote Venkatachalapathy, 'is most apparent in the fact that the state has been ruled for nearly fifty years by four chief ministers whose popularity was derived in large measures from their film career.'[8] The Tamils' great pride and love of the Tamil language and intense opposition to the imposition of Hindi as the sole national and official language of India led to the acceptance of English as the co-official language, making Hindi-English the lingua franca of India. Hindi threatened the Tamil sense of exceptionalism and they fought against it. Ironically, one of the most popular Bollywood Hindi film singers is a Tamilian, A.R. Rahman, whose 'Jai Ho' reverberated across India for a long time.

The Andhras, who asserted that they weren't Tamils or Madrasis, instigated the linguistic reorganization of India. And tracing their cultural lineage to the epic Mahabharata and heritage to the great Vijayanagara Empire, they said their language (Telugu) and culture were unique. The linguistic reorganization of India was based partly upon the fact that each region with its own language, literature, historical icons, legends and *ruling deities* had a sense of exceptionalism and feared obliteration if not allowed to be politically separate. It's a great tribute to the wisdom and farsightedness of the founders of the Indian Republic, Nehru, Sardar Patel, Ambedkar, Rajagopalachari, Rajendra Prasad, Maulana Azad and others that they structured this sense and sensibility of exceptionalism into constitutional federalism, which makes Indians uniquely separate but nonetheless together.

The sense of exceptionalism, and the fear of its loss, is not limited to linguistic and regional cultures. It encompasses the caste system because, in spite of its widespread condemnation as an evil system, no one in India wants to give up their caste. Throughout his public life, Nehru was referred to as *Pandit* Nehru, a Kashmiri Brahmin, but he never objected to it, though he was formally agnostic and secular. As has been said elsewhere, 'At the heart of a self-organizing social system is a nucleus of core values that shapes the emergent culture and behaviour of the people. It is "a preferred position of the system" to which the system returns from any state, repositioning itself in a state of equilibrium.'[9] In the Indian parliamentary federal system, the nucleus of core values is ensconced in caste-language-regionalism, the framework that determines the mode of thinking and behaviour of the people and their identities in spite of the fact that the Indian Constitution is based on freedom and equality. Subliminally and subconsciously, even the most secular, agnostic and atheist Indian elites think in the caste-language-regionalism mental framework, as happened in the case of Amartya Sen when his Bengali sensibility was pricked by the Hindutva catfish.

At the most unguarded moment, like the proverbial Freudian slip of the tongue, the culturally suppressed feeling sometimes erupts like a spring of fresh water and sometimes like a poisonous volcano. P.V. Narasimha Rao, the ninth prime minister of India, was an unabashedly self-conscious Telugu Brahmin, and he let it be known. Nehru never demurred being called 'Pandit,' just as M.K. Stalin, a Tamil political leader of the supposedly atheist political party, in spite of his un-Indian name, doesn't object to being called a Dravidian; Mayawati, twice the chief minister of the most politically significant state, Uttar Pradesh, feels proud to be a Dalit; and Mamata Banerjee, the great destroyer of Bengali communists, professes to be a Maa Durga devotee, for example. Sheikh Abdullah, who, like most Indians, lived comfortably with a sense of cognitive dissonance, always thought he was above all a patriotic Kashmiri Muslim. *An Indian becomes an Indian only when he steps out of India.*

A.K. Ramanujan, poet, scholar and philologist, gave a fascinating thumbnail portrait of his father that embodies the Indians' capacity to live in contradictions, with a high sense of exceptionalism and fear of loss:

> My father's clothes represented his inner life very well. He was a South Indian Brahmin gentleman. He wore neat white turban, a Sri Vaisnava caste mark (in his earlier pictures, a diamond ring), yet wore Tootal ties, Kromentz buttons and collar studs, and donned English surge jackets over his muslin *dhotis* which he wore draped in traditional Brahmin style... He was a mathematician, an astronomer. But he was also a Sanskrit scholar, an expert astrologer. He had two kinds of exotic visitors: American and English mathematicians...and local astrologers, orthodox pundits who wore splendid gold-embroidered shawls dowered by the Maharaja... I looked for consistency in him, a consistency he did not seem to care about or think about. When I asked him what the discovery of Pluto and Neptune did to his archaic nine-planet astrology, he said, 'You make the necessary corrections, that's all.[10]

Unlike Americans, Indians don't want to be assimilated into one unified homogenized culture because assimilation means loss of exceptionalism. It is the non-assimilative yet distinctively integrating feature of the Indian parliamentary federal system that has made democracy an operational success in India. Democracy functions well in India because it makes people, various caste-linguistic-cultural groups, feel free and autonomous with their sense of exceptionalism (like Ramanujan's father); and yet it brings them together for dialogue and shared governance. The democratic parliamentary federalism in India acts as a shock-absorbing mechanism, which keeps the system stable, adaptable and dynamic by channelling and redistributing excessive energy generated by the social and political conflicts that are spawned by the claims of egalitarianism and exceptionalism.

But sometimes, the claims of exceptionalism have led not only to the misinterpretation of history but also the appropriation of folklore, mythology and religious fantasies as historical truths. What used to be street and backyard folklore surfaced in recent times as historical achievements proudly proclaimed by prominent Hindutva politicians on public platforms. Consider, for example, some of the following inexplicable claims of exceptionalism by some of our leaders:

> *Mahabharata says Karna was not born out of his mother's womb. This means people then were aware of genetic science. There must have been a plastic surgeon who fixed an elephant's head on Ganesha.*
>
> —Narendra Modi

> *Today we are talking about nuclear tests. Lakhs of years ago, Sage Kanad had conducted a nuclear test. Our knowledge and science do not lack anything.*
>
> —Ramesh Pokhriyal, BJP MP

> *India has been using [the] internet for ages.*
> *In Mahabharata, Sanjay was blind but he narrated what was*

happening on the battlefield to Dhritarashtra anyway.
This was due to [the] internet and technology.
The satellite also existed during that period.

—Biplab Deb, Tripura CM[11]

But the idea of Indian exceptionalism is not limited to Indians. Even some foreigners have accepted it wholeheartedly. Sir William Jones, the English philologist, said, 'From the vedas (ancient Indian Scriptures), we learn a practical art of surgery, medicine, music, house building under which ... They are encyclopedia of every aspect of life, culture, religion, science, ethics, law, cosmology and meteorology.'[12] The ancient Indian surgeon, Sushruta is credited with being the father of the nose job, whose treatise, Sushruta Samhita, 'describes more than a thousand diseases (including a very early awareness of diabetes), and about 650 types of drugs...includes a special focus on surgery, which it considers the apex of the healing art. The roughly 300 surgical procedures it describes include cataract surgery, the removal of bladder stones, hernia repair, eye surgery, and caesarean sections... The text also stresses the importance of cleanliness in both surgeons and their instruments—safeguards Europe wouldn't adopt for the better part of two millennia.'[13]

American historian and philosopher Will Durant called India:

> ...[T]he motherland of our race, and Sanskrit the mother of Europe's languages: she was the mother of our philosophy; mother, through the Arabs, of much of our mathematics; mother, through the Buddha, of the ideals embodied in Christianity; mother, through the village community, of self-government and democracy. Mother India is in many ways the mother of us all.[14]

The foreigners' assessment of the glory of ancient Indian science, medicine, philosophy, mathematics and technology feeds into the Indian mind, looking for recovery and redemption of the glorious past. The sense and sensibility of exceptionalism as to how unique Indians were once upon a time and must salvage the past glory through rediscovery and recovery found expression not only in the rebuilding of the Somnath Temple, the Nalanda University and the Ram Janmabhoomi resurrection but also in India's foreign policy. It was through its foreign policy that India presented itself to the world as a 'unique and universal' civilization founded on a higher spiritual order. Discussing the concept of exceptionalism, Nicola Nymalm and Johannes Plagemann say:

> This link (unique and universal) is peculiar because it establishes uniqueness as a foundation for, first, a conviction of moral superiority over virtually every other society, based on which the self-ascribed exceptionalist state pursues an allegedly universal common good in its foreign policy conduct. Second, exceptionalism based on uniqueness implies the belief in an exceptional state's disposition as impossible to be replicated by others. This interplay between uniqueness (or particularity) and universality is what constitutes the paradox of exceptionalism: A unique insight into supposedly universal values and their foreign policy implications is derived from a particular civilizational or spiritual heritage, political history, and/or geographical location.[15]

Iqbal beautifully captured the concept of Indian exceptionalism when he said; there's something about India that had made it an indestructible civilization (Urdu: Kuch bāt hai kih hastī, mi̱ttī nahīn hamārī).[16] For India, the struggle for freedom was essentially a spiritual and moral struggle under the leadership of Gandhi, who based his peaceful activism on Ahimsa (non-violence) and Satyagrah (commitment to truth). After Independence, the non-alignment foreign policy of Prime Minister Nehru, drawing inspiration from its unique form of freedom struggle, was based on India's capacity to offer moral leadership to the world. Fighting economic and political imperialism by bringing newly independent third world countries together, without entanglement with or antagonism against the Cold War blocs led by the Soviet Union and the US, was the main plank of foreign policy. The idea that India was a unique cradle of religion and spirituality 'supported a *missionary* claim that India had the capacity and obligation to provide moral leadership in world affairs.'[17]

Although India failed to resolve the Kashmir issue and the chronic communal and caste conflicts, there was an overwhelming feeling among the political elites that India had the unique 'capacity to synthesize different and conflicting perspectives and merge with other modes of thought and belief... implicit in this discourse of synthesis and universalism was, of course, a sense of superiority: the idea that Indians—or a certain type of Indians—were innately predisposed to engage in the task of conflict resolution and, therefore, morally above those who were repeatedly drawn to violence.'[18]

The sense of exceptionalism also arose from the fact that India had established a constitutional secular democracy with fundamental rights, which encompassed diversity through federalism, and had held fair and peaceful general elections based on universal franchise, no mean achievements for a newly independent country. India's five-year time-based planned socialistic economy to fight colonial-era massive poverty and economic backwardness added to its sense of an exceptional nation. With his democratic sway at home and diplomatic activism in pursuit of peaceful resolution of international conflicts, for example, Korea and Suez Canal, Nehru conducted his foreign policy based on the 'belief in India's unquestioned civilizational moral pre-eminence' with 'a sense of mission that encouraged the projection of "moral conduct" into the international sphere.'[19]

Although Nehru pursued with missionary zeal global issues such as the apartheid in South Africa, decolonization, the Palestinian cause, developmental aid for the poor countries, and gave voice to the voiceless in Asia and Africa, he did not know what to do when China invaded and occupied Tibet, which was no different from the Soviet Union occupying Poland. India's moral exceptionalism in international affairs became subdued and lustreless after China's 1962 massive aggression across the Himalayas when Nehru had to make frantic SOS calls to President John F. Kennedy for arms and ammunition. India learned that a sense of moral exceptionalism and its practice in international affairs did not give the nation immunity from aggrandizement and predatory behaviour of a neighbour who had deceptively vouched for the Panchsheel.

Although India still believes in its ethical exceptionalism, its special destiny and place in the world, and whatever form it takes in the future, whether universal or conflated with the Hindutva, the sense of loss has been profound since the endgame of the Nehru era. And the necessity for its redemption could be seen in a document *NonAlignment 2.0* generated by a group of intellectuals led by King's College academic Sunil Khilnani (the author of the celebrated treatise *The Idea of India*) and other analysts and policymakers, including economist Rajiv Kumar, academic Pratap Bhanu Mehta, Lt. Gen. (Retd) Prakash Menon, Nandan Nilekani (digital revolutionary and the developer of Aadhaar), strategist Srinath Raghavan, diplomat Shyam Saran and journalist Siddharth Varadarajan, who held a periodic conclave November 2010 through January 2012, as it were, to recover the sunken Titanic. Taking stock of the achievements and unfulfilled promises and challenges, the group concluded, 'India has done all this while maintaining a commitment to a liberal, secular, constitutional democracy. India has held together as a nation because of a commitment to these values.'

The foreign policy conclave was held during the second term of Manmohan Singh's UPA coalition government. And it was during this time that the United States, under President George W. Bush, treated India, not as a nonaligned nation of the Nehru era, but as an *exceptional,* therefore, *exemptional* nation for America's own national interests by signing the US–India Civil Nuclear Agreement, in spite of the fact that India was a nuclear weapon state and had not signed the Treaty of the Non-Proliferation of Nuclear Weapons (NPT).

But the *NonAlignment 2.0* group of scholars, eschewing the reality of how India had been transformed during the last several decades, harked back wistfully, urging that India must redeem its moral exceptionalism. This is because:

India has had a special history in one respect. Its nationalist movement was unique. It was unique in the techniques it deployed. It was unique in its intellectual ambition. All of India's great leaders—Gandhi, Tagore, Nehru, Ambedkar—had one aspiration: *that India should be a site for an alternative universality* (emphasis added). India's legitimacy today will come from its ability to stand for the highest human and universal values. These values gave India enormous moral and ideological capital.[20]

The document claimed that 'the rest of the world has looked upon India with a certain admiration for holding onto these values,' for which the scholars presented no evidentiary examples. As India becomes a global power, the document admonished, 'India must remain true to its aspiration of creating a new and alternative universality... India's adherence to values will be a great source of legitimacy in the international system.' It should, as it rises, 'be clear about what values it stands for.'[21] The secularists' search and recovery for 'alternative universality,' on which India's moral exceptionalism was based, is no different from the Hindutva nationalists who seek inspiration from India's imagined glorious mythological past when there was 'instant communication, plastic surgery for an organ transplant, satellites, space travel and much more.'

HOW INDIANS OUGHT TO THINK

Although the Indian mode of thinking is framed by particularism (caste, language and regionalism) and universalism (Vasudhaiva Kutumbakam, Vishwa Guru), the common man, or the *aam aadmi,* is a practical thinker, innovator and a problem solver. India is an ordinary nation filled with remarkably smart people, as historian Patrick French narrates in his book, *India: A Portrait.*[22] Whenever struck with harsh reality and existential challenges, Indians break out of the particularism–universalism and mundane–sublime syndrome and think most rationally and realistically; as it happened, for example, when millions of refugees had to be resettled; national resources had to be assessed and enhanced through scientific planning; the subcontinent had to be politically reconfigured with marching boots on the ground; insurgencies and anarchies had to be crushed through brute force and the emergency; financial health had to be restored by opening up the shuttered socialistic windows and moral *exceptionalism* had to be transformed into *exemptionalism* for nuclear technology transfer.

It's difficult to say whether the Indian mythopoeic imagination, similar to the American sci-fi imagination, stimulates and inspires creativity and innovation, but Chandrayaan lunar missions II and I were a response to the challenges of space and the test of Indian exceptionalism. From Jawaharlal Nehru's moral exceptionalism to Narendra Modi's techno-economic exceptionalism, it has been quite a journey for India since its independence.

Under Modi, the mode of thinking has begun to change. India is not looking for 'a site for an alternative universality,' a platform from where it could tutor and teach morality to the world. Beyond the sound and fury of Hindutva sloganeering for political proselytizing to expanding its base into the lands of unbelievers in the east and the south, Indians have begun to think in terms of US$5 trillion GDP, becoming the third biggest global economy, moon landing and space travel, and building strategic alliances for national security, economic growth and technology transfer to serve the needs of 1.35 billion people. This is the first time that Indians have begun to think that they can compete with the best in the world—a quiet and discreet form of refurbished Indian exceptionalism based on science and technology and the growing wealth of the nation.

Modi's digital India might become the driving engine for India's global competitiveness in trade, commerce and manufacturing. Nonetheless, the question is whether aspirational India can do without fundamental economic reforms and feed itself only on mantras and magical thinking. As Harvard and IMF economist Gita Gopinath said, 'To keep that pace of progress would entail further structural and institutional reforms. But if that is done, then it will be mind-blowing for India.'[23] The race for 8–10 per cent economic growth and global competitiveness for trade, no doubt, would require structural and institutional reforms as well as technological innovations. More importantly, however, it would require transparency, respect for data, objective assessment of goals and openness to public criticism, thereby necessitating a fundamental change in how Indians think, especially if India wants to be a manufacturing and innovative nation. Manufacturing and innovation breed each other in a virtual upward spiral. A software nation without being a hardware nation cannot be a great nation. And without being a topnotch hardware manufacturing nation, India would always beg and buy arms for national defence from Russia, the United States, Israel, and who knows, even from China—the ultimate shame and humiliation. Indians have the unique ability to live in contradictions; and immense tolerance for cognitive dissonance. And perhaps the Hindutva culture based upon the power of sacred words (mantras) to change physical reality and the manufacturing culture based upon empiricism would coexist. But can India handle the truth?

In the digital age, the national motto: Satyameva Jayate (Truth Shall Win), assumes a new significance because 'data is king.' As Justice Oliver Wendell Holmes said, 'The best test of truth is the power of the thought to get itself accepted in the competition of the market.'[24] In the marketplace, measurement—not mantra—is all. Facts, facts, facts, whether about the accuracy of gross domestic product (GDP), the enforcement of contracts, the quality of the environment and the parameters for inter-communal peace, for example, must be precisely established, objectively assessed and respected. Hindutva's mythical thinking and the sense of exceptionalism must meet the test of the marketplace of ideas, what the ancient Greeks called 'agora': the ultimate abode of Satyamev Jayate.

ACKNOWLEDGEMENTS

In a larger sense, *India in a New Key* is a manifestation of the Buddhist doctrine, Pratītyasamutpāda, the principle of dependent origination, an event arising from multiple interdependent processes—human, intellectual, emotional, psychological and geographical. Nonetheless, in this massive sweep of modern Indian history, from Jawaharlal Nehru to Narendra Modi, some individuals have made distinctive contributions to my work, for which I'm grateful. Senior Commissioning Editor Yamini Chowdhury, a person with a beautiful mind and calm temperament, quickly grasped the value of the project and, in spite of its massive length, felt persuaded that the book would do well and was worth the risk. During the COVID-19 epidemic, when I developed doubts about its publication, she assured me, through a virtual meeting and frequent exchanges, that it was going to be all right. At this moment, Deputy Managing Editor, Nishtha Kapil, a problem-solver and a person of last resort, stepped in with a firm commitment to the book's publication, which restored my faith in Rupa Publications and its visionary and ambitious Managing Director, Kapish Mehra.

It's a most ardent desire of a writer that the reader would find the book flawless. At Rupa Publications, there are many capable editors who have done their best to make the book impeccable. I'm particularly thankful to C. Sandhya, development editor, whose keen eyes for details, passion for fact-checking, attention to copyright issues, and editorial insights helped to improve the manuscript. Equally important has been the contribution of Rajesh Singh, consultant editor, whose comments and suggestions proved very valuable. Soumya Rampal, the copy editor, saw to it that the manuscript is as faultless as humanly possible. In this visual age, the importance of the cover design cannot be underestimated because that's what attracts the reader in the first place, which has been the forte of cover designer, Rachita Rakyan.

Unlike other fortunate professors in major research universities, I did not have the luxury of having research assistants to help me with the book. However, I am grateful to Norwich University, a 200-year old institution that conceived the idea of citizen-soldier and gave me research release time, a sabbatical, and a Chase grant for research and international travel.

But, having been an academic and a journalist and given to working under the pressure of deadlines, and in the habit of doing my own research, including interviewing and listening to people, I did as well as I could depending, however, upon scholarly databases which I used judiciously as a launching pad to stimulate my thinking and pursue further research.

Varsha, my wife of many wonderful years, a woman of extraordinary intuitive intelligence and strength of character, has always been there for me; she is the rock that I lean on and rest when I feel shaken up. Not in the least, it is the presence of my two sprightly grandchildren, Nayan and Nirali, who make me feel that I must keep up with their exuberance.

Narain D. Batra
Hartford, Vermont
January 2022

NOTES

INTRODUCTION: BORN AGAIN INDIA

1. Sunil Khilnani, *The Idea of India*, Penguin Books, New Delhi, 1998, p. 5.

2. Subrata Dasgupta, *Awakening: The Story of the Bengal Renaissance*, Random House India, New Delhi, 2010; Dermot Killingley, 'Rammohun Roy and the Bengal Renaissance' in Torkel Brekke ed., *The Oxford History of Hinduism: Modern Hinduism*, Oxford University Press, August 2019.

3. Poetry Foundation, 'On Negative Capability: Letter to George and Tom Keats', Selections from Keats's Letters, Poetry Foundation, https://www.poetryfoundation.org/articles/69384/selections-from-keatss-letters. Accessed 27 September 2021.

4. In conversation with a Muslim storekeeper of Ballimaran, Jama Masjid, Delhi, in the 1950s, who used very colourful language to refer to the creation of Pakistan: *Sar dhakne ko to mila laiken gaand nangi rehe gai.*

5. Prabhash K. Dutta, 'The other side of Atal Bihari Vajpayee, 3 instances', *India Today*, 24 August 2018, https://www.indiatoday.in/amp/india/story/the-other-side-of-atal-bihari-vajpayee-3-instances-1322548-2018-08-24. Accessed on 27 September 2021.

6. Siddharth Varadarajan, ed., *Gujarat, the Making of a Tragedy*, Penguin Books India, New Delhi, 2002; 'Speech delivered by Atal Bihari Vajpayee, Goa, April 12, 2002', *The Wire*, https://thewire.in/communalism/vajpayees-goa-speech-april-2002. Accessed on 27 September 2021.

7. 'Presidential address by Muhammad Ali Jinnah to the Muslim League Lahore, 1940', Columbia University: Islam in South Asia: Some Useful Study Materials, http://www.columbia.edu/itc/mealac/pritchett/00islamlinks/txt_jinnah_lahore_1940.html; 'Speeches and statements by Jinnah 1938–1940', *India's Constitutional Question - The Cabinet Mission Plan 1946* https://sites.google.com/site/cabinetmissionplan/speeches-and-statements-by-jinnah-1938–1940. Accessed on 27 September 2021.

8. Meghna Guhathakurta and Willem van Schendel, eds., *The Bangladesh Reader: History, Culture, Politics*, Duke University Press, Durham, North Carolina, 2013, p. 214; Muhammad Nurul Huda, 'Bangabandhu's galvanising speech of March 7', The Daily Star, 7 March 2020, https://www.thedailystar.net/opinion/straight-line/news/bangabandhus-galvanising-speech-march-7-1877350. Accessed on 22 December 2021.

CHAPTER 1: IN THE BEGINNING, THERE WAS JAWAHARLAL

1. Jawaharlal Nehru, *Jawaharlal Nehru's Speeches*, Vol. 1, Publications Division: Ministry of Information and Broadcasting, Govt. of India, New Delhi, 1983, p. 25.

2. Ibid.

3. Jawaharlal Nehru, G. Parthasarthi ed., *Letters to Chief Ministers 1947–1964*, Vol. 4, Oxford University Press, 1985–9, New Delhi, p. 366.

4. V.P. Menon, *The Transfer of Power in India*, Princeton University Press, 1957, p. 423.

5. Ibid.

6. Ibid. 427.

7. Ibid. 434.

8. Jawaharlal Nehru, *Jawaharlal Nehru's Speeches*, Vol. 1, Publications Division: Ministry of Information and Broadcasting, Govt. of India, New Delhi, 1983, p. 42.

9. Jawaharlal Nehru, G. Parthasarthi ed., *Letters to Chief Ministers 1947-1964*, Vol. 1, Oxford University Press, 1985–9, New Delhi, p. 33.

10. S. Gopal ed., *Jawaharlal Nehru, Selected Works*, Vol. 4, Jawaharlal Nehru Memorial Fund, New Delhi, 1984, p. 118.

11. Bipan Chandra, *India Since Independence*, Penguin Random House, New Delhi, 2017, p. 84.

12. Rajmohan Gandhi, 'Vallabhbhai Patel: "I say bitter things to Hindus and Muslims alike. But I am a friend of Muslims"', *Scroll.in*, 31 October 2018, https://scroll.in/article/900187/i-say-bitter-things-to-hindus-and-muslims-alike-but-i-am-a-friend-of-muslims-vallabhbhai-patel. Accessed on 23 December 2021.

13. Dr Hari Desai, 'Vallabhbhai Patel and the Indian Muslims', *Asian Voice*, 12 June 2018, https://www.asian-voice.com/Opinion/Columnists/Vallabhbhai-Patel-and-the-Indian-Muslims. Accessed on 23 December 2021.

14. Christophe Jaffrelot, *The Hindu Nationalist Movement and Indian Politics*, C. Hurst & Co Publishers Ltd, 1996, pp. 33–40.

15. Jean A. Curran, 'The RSS: Militant Hinduism', *Far Eastern Survey*, Vol. 19, No. 10, 1950, pp. 93–98, https://doi.org/10.2307/3023941. Accessed on 23 December 2021.

16. Gene D. Overstreet and Marshall Windmiller, *Communism in India*, University of California Press, Berkeley, 1959, pp. 229–233, 270–274.

17. 'Statistical Report on General Elections, 1951 to the First Lok Sabha, Vol. I., Election Commission of India, New Delhi, https://eci.gov.in/files/file/11891-report-on-the-first-general-elections-in-india-1951-52-volume-1-general/. Accessed on 23 December 2021.

18. R.K. Karanjia, *The Philosophy of Mr Nehru*, George Allen & Unwin, London, 1966, pp. 159–60.

19. Ananya Jahanara Kabir in Sorcha Gunne and Zoe Brigley Thompson, ed.,

Feminism, Literature and Rape Narratives: Violence and Violation, Routledge, New York, 2010, p. 149; Geeta Chowdhry in Sita Ranchod-Nilsson and Mary Ann Tétreault, ed., *Women, States, and Nationalism: At Home in the Nation?*, Routledge, New York, 2000, pp. 107–110.

20. Barbara D. Metcalf and Thomas R. Metcalf, *A Concise History of Modern India*, 3rd edn., Cambridge University Press, Cambridge, 2012, p. 226.

21. V.N. Datta, 'Punjabi Refugees and the Urban Development of Greater Delhi,' in R. Frykenberg ed., *Delhi Through the Ages: Selected Essays in Urban History, Culture and Society*, Oxford University Press, New Delhi, 2002, pp. 442–60.

22. P. Bharadwaj and R.A. Mirza, 'Displacement and Development: Long Term Impacts of the Partition of India,' Working Paper, UC San Diego, 2017, quoted in Prashant Bharadwaj and Saumitra Jha, 'Drawing the line: The short-and long-term consequences of partitioning India,' 8 September 2017, *Ideas for India*, https://www.ideasforindia.in/topics/governance/drawing-the-line-the-short-and-long-term-consequences-of-partitioning-india.html. Accessed on 29 December 2021.

23. P. Bharadwaj and J. Fenske, 'Partition, Migration, and Jute Cultivation in India,' *Journal of Development Studies* 48(8), 2012, quoted in Prashant Bharadwaj and Saumitra Jha, 'Drawing the line: The short- and long-term consequences of partitioning India,' 8 September 2017, *Ideas for India*, https://www.ideasforindia.in/topics/governance/drawing-the-line-the-short-and-long-term-consequences-of-partitioning-india.html. Accessed on 29 December 2021.

24. 'Evacuee Property,' *The Economic Weekly*, vol. 4, no. 20, 15 May 1954, https://www.epw.in/system/files/pdf/1954_6/20/evacuee_property.pdf. Accessed on 29 December 2021.

25. Ibid.

26. 'Dandakaranya,' *The Hindu*, 10 April 1960, http://www.thehindu.com/todays-paper/tp-miscellaneous/dated-April-10-1960-From-an-editorial-Dandakaranya/article16017819.ece. Accessed 29 December 2021.

27. Ibid.

28. 'Chapter 38: Rehabilitation Of Displaced Persons,' Government of India, Planning Commission, NITI Aayog, https://www.niti.gov.in/planningcommission.gov.in/docs/plans/planrel/fiveyr/1st/1planch38.html. Accessed on 29 December 2021.

29. Ibid.

30. Madhusree Mukerjee, *Churchill's Secret War: The British Empire and the Ravaging of India during World War II*, Basic Books, New York, 2011; Soutik Biswas, 'How Churchill "starved" India,' BBC, 28 October 2010, http://www.bbc.co.uk/blogs/thereporters/soutikbiswas/2010/10/how_churchill_starved_india.html. Accessed 29 December 2021.

31. Taylor C. Sherman, 'From 'grow more food' to 'miss a meal': hunger, development and the limits of post-colonial nationalism in India, 1947–1957,' *South Asia: Journal of South Asian Studies*, 2013, vol. 36, no. 4, pp. 571–588,

https://doi.org/10.1080/00856401.2013.833071. Accessed 29 December 2021.

32. Ibid.

33. Ibid.

34. *Pioneer*, 14 June 1950, NMML, Munshi Papers, reel 124, f.406, quoted in Taylor C. Sherman, 'From 'grow more food' to 'miss a meal': hunger, development and the limits of post-colonial nationalism in India, 1947–1957', *South Asia: Journal of South Asian Studies*, 2013, vol. 36, no. 4, pp. 571–588, https://doi.org/10.1080/00856401.2013.833071. Accessed 29 December 2021.

35. Taylor C. Sherman, 'From 'grow more food' to 'miss a meal': hunger, development and the limits of post-colonial nationalism in India, 1947–1957', *South Asia: Journal of South Asian Studies*, 2013, vol. 36, no. 4, pp. 571–588, https://doi.org/10.1080/00856401.2013.833071. Accessed 29 December 2021.

36. Ibid.

37. *The Bombay Chronicle*, 4 June 1951, p. 3; *The Bombay Chronicle*, 25 April 1951, p. 5, quoted in Taylor C. Sherman, 'From 'grow more food' to 'miss a meal': hunger, development and the limits of post-colonial nationalism in India, 1947–1957', *South Asia: Journal of South Asian Studies*, 2013, vol. 36, no. 4, pp. 571–588, https://doi.org/10.1080/00856401.2013.833071. Accessed 29 December 2021.

38. Dennis Merrill, *Bread and the Ballot: the United States and India's Economic Development, 1947–1963*, University of North Carolina Press, Chapel Hill, 1990.

39. 'Theosophical Society, Objects of the', Theosophy World, https://www.theosophy.world/encyclopedia/theosophical-society-objects. Accessed on 29 December 2021.

40. Frank Moraes, *Jawaharlal Nehru*, Jaico Publishing House, Mumbai, 2007.

41. Quoted in Om Prakash Misra, *Economic Thought of Gandhi and Nehru: A Comparative Analysis*, M.D. Publications, Delhi, 1995, pp. 49–65.

42. Anne Bostanci, 'How was India involved in the First World War?', British Council, 30 October 2014, https://www.britishcouncil.org/voices-magazine/how-was-india-involved-first-world-war. Accessed on 29 December 2021.

43. Ibid.

44. Barbara D. Metcalf and Thomas R. Metcalf, *A Concise History of Modern India*, 3rd edn., Cambridge University Press, 2012, p. 169.

45. Frank R. Moraes, Jawaharlal Nehru, Encyclopedia Britannica, https://www.britannica.com/biography/Jawaharlal-Nehru. Accessed on 29 December 2021.

46. Indian National Congress, 'Declaration of Purna Swaraj', Constitution of India, 26 January 1930, https://www.constitutionofindia.net/historical_constitutions/declaration_of_purna_swaraj__indian_national_congress__1930__26th%20January%201930. Accessed on 29 December 2021.

CHAPTER 2: INDIA BEGINS THE GAME OF DEMOCRACY

1. 'Constituent Assembly Of India Debates (Proceedings)—Volume I', 9 December 1946, Constitution of India, https://www.constitutionofindia.net/constitution_assembly_debates/volume/1/1946-12-09. Accessed on 29 December 2021.

2. Malvika Singh, *New Delhi: Making of a Capital*, Roli Books, New Delhi, 2012; Shashank Shekhar Sinha, 'Lutyens and Baker: A Friendship That Faltered on Raisina Hill', *The Wire*, 6 August 2017, https://thewire.in/history/friendship-faltered-raisina-hill. Accessed on 30 December 2021; Sidhartha Roy, 'Parliament House: 144 pillars of pride', *Hindustan Times*, 1 September 2011, https://www.hindustantimes.com/delhi-news/parliament-house-144-pillars-of-pride/story-UBRQJ3tqmspQR34gkx1O2K.html. Accessed on 30 December 2021.

3. Ramachandra Guha, *India After Gandhi: The History of the World's Largest Democracy*, Picador India, 2017, pp. 113–134; S.K. Chaube, *Constituent Assembly of India: Springboard of Revolution*, Manohar Books, New Delhi, 2000.

4. '"Objective Resolution" moved by Jawaharlal Nehru', The Nehru Blog, https://www.thenehru.org/2020/12/objective-resolution-moved-by.html. Accessed on 30 December 2021.

5. Subhash C. Kashyap, *Indian Constitution: Conflicts and Controversies*, Vitasta Publishing, 2010, New Delhi, pp. 131–199; Ramachandra Guha, *India After Gandhi: The History of the World's Largest Democracy*, Picador India, 2017, p. 118.

6. Granville Austin, *The Indian Constitution: Cornerstone of A Nation*, 2nd edn., Oxford University Press, New York, 2003, pp. 8–9.

7. 'Constituent Assembly Of India Debates (Proceedings)—Volume VII', Constitution of India, 5 November 1948, https://www.constitutionofindia.net/constitution_assembly_debates/volume/7/1948-11-05. Accessed on 30 December 2021.

8. Granville Austin, *The Indian Constitution: Cornerstone of A Nation*, 2nd edn., Oxford University Press, New York, 2003, pp. 5–52.

9. 'Constitution of India, 1950', Constitution of India, https://www.constitutionofindia.net/constitution_of_india. Accessed on 30 December 2021.

10. Ibid.

11. Zoya Hasan, Eswaran Sridharan, and R. Sudarshan, *India's Living Constitution: Ideas, Practices, Controversies*, Permanent Black, Delhi, 2004; 'Quasi Federal Law', Uslegal.com, https://definitions.uslegal.com/q/quasi-federal. Accessed on 30 December 2021.

12. Ayesha Jalal, *The Sole Spokesman: Jinnah, The Muslim League and the Demand for Pakistan*, Cambridge University Press, Cambridge, 1994.

13. S.R. Bommai v. Union of India ([1994] 2 SCR 644: AIR 1994 SC 1918: (1994)3

SCC 1); Sukumar Muralidharan, 'Who's afraid of Article 356', *Frontline*, Vol. 15, No. 14, July 04–July 17, 1998, https://frontline.thehindu.com/static/html/fl1514/15140040.htm. Accessed on 30 December 2021.

14. Zoya Hasan, Eswaran Sridharan, and R. Sudarshan, *India's Living Constitution: Ideas, Practices, Controversies*, Permanent Black, Delhi, 2004.

15. H.M. Seervai, *Constitutional Law of India*, 3rd edn., vol. 1, N.M. Tripathi, Bombay, 1983, p. 237.

16. Granville Austin, *Working a Democratic Constitution : A History of the Indian Experience*, Oxford University Press, New Delhi, 1999, p. 319; Gary Jacobsohn, *Constitutional Identity*, Harvard University Press, Massachusetts, 2010, p. 57.

17. Minerva Mills v. Union of India, AIR 1980 SC 1789, 31 July 1980, https://indiankanoon.org/doc/1939993/. Accessed on 30 December 2021.

18. Ibid.

19. Ibid.

20. 'Constituent Assembly Of India Debates (Proceedings) - Volume XI', Constitution of India, 25 November 1949, https://www.constitutionofindia.net/constitution_assembly_debates/volume/11/1949-11-25#11.165.322. Accessed on 30 December 2021.

21. Ibid.

22. Ibid.

23. 'Constituent Assembly Of India Debates (Proceedings) - Volume V', Constitution of India, 27 August 1947, https://www.constitutionofindia.net/constitution_assembly_debates/volume/5/1947-08-27#5.43.102. Accessed on 31 December 2021.

24. Ibid.

25. 'Constituent Assembly Debates (Proceedings) - Volume VIII', Constitution of India, 26 May 1949, 'https://www.constitutionofindia.net/constitution_assembly_debates/volume/8/1949-05-26#8.92.50. Accessed on 7 January 2022.

26. 'Constituent Assembly Of India Debates (Proceedings) - Volume V', Constitution of India, 27 August 1947, https://www.constitutionofindia.net/constitution_assembly_debates/volume/5/1947-08-27#5.43.102. Accessed on 31 December 2021; 'Constituent Assembly Debates (Proceedings) - Volume VIII', 26 May 1949, https://www.constitutionofindia.net/constitution_assembly_debates/volume/8/1949-05-26#8.92.39. Accessed on 31 December 2021

27. 'Section II: Extracts From Letters from Selected Works of Mahatma Gandhi: Vol – 4', Gandhi Sevagram Ashram, http://www.gandhiashramsevagram.org/selected-letters-of-mahatma/gandhi-letter-extracts-caste-system-and-untouchability.php. Accessed on 31 December 2021.

28. Stanley Wolpert, *Gandhi's Passion: The Life and Legacy of Mahatma Gandhi*, Oxford University Press, New York, 2001, p. 168; S. Ramanathan, 'Labelling Dalits 'Harijans': How we remain ignorant and insensitive to Dalit identity', *TheNewsMinute*, 27 October 2015, https://www.thenewsminute.com/article/

labelling-dalits-harijans-how-we-remain-ignorant-and-insensitive-dalit-identity-35486. Accessed on 31 December 2021.

29. 'Ambedkar's last words of wisdom', *The Indian Panorama*, 14 April 2017, https://www.theindianpanorama.news/featured/ambedkars-last-words-wisdom/. Accessed on 31 December 2021.

30. 'Constituent Assembly Of India Debates (Proceedings) - Volume VII', Constitution of India, 30 November 1948, https://www.constitutionofindia. net/constitution_assembly_debates/volume/7/1948-11-30#7.63.138. Accessed on 5 January 2021.

31. 'Constituent Assembly Of India Debates (Proceedings) - Volume VII', Constitution of India, 30 November 1948, https://www.constitutionofindia. net/constitution_assembly_debates/volume/7/1948-11-30#7.63.134. Accessed on 5 January 2021.

32. Richard Leonard Park, 'Indian Democracy and the General Election', *Pacific Affairs*, Vol. 25, No. 2, June 1952, pp. 130–139, https://doi. org/10.2307/2753531. Accessed on 5 January 2021.

33. '"We have met the enemy and he is us"', This Day in Quotes, 22 April 2015, http://www.thisdayinquotes.com/2011/04/we-have-met-enemy-and-he-is-us.html. Accessed on 5 January 2022.

34. Ramachandra Guha, *India After Gandhi: The History of the World's Largest Democracy*, Picador India, 2017, pp. 143–159.

35. Walter Jackson Ong, *Orality and Literacy: The Technologizing of the Word*, 2nd edn., Routledge, New York, 2002.

36. Government of India, 'Part XV, Elections', Ministry of Law and Justice, http:// dtf.in/wp-content/files/Constitution_of_India_-_Part_XV_Articles_324_ to_329A_As_on_MOL_website_-_15.05.2013.pdf. Accessed on 5 January 2022.

37. Government of India, 'The Representation of the People Act, 1951', Ministry of Law and Justice, https://legislative.gov.in/sites/default/files/04_ representation%20of%20the%20people%20act%2C%201951.pdf. Accessed on 5 January 2022.

38. Election Commission of India, 'Report on the First General Elections in India, 1951–52', Election Commission of India, Government of India Press, New Delhi, 1952, https://eci.gov.in/files/file/4111-general-election-1951-vol-i-ii/. Accessed on 5 January 2022.

39. Election Commission of India, 'Key Highlights Of General Elections, 1951 To The First Lok Sabha', Election Commission of India.

40. Indian Saga, 'The First General Elections', Indian Saga, http://indiansaga.com/ history/postindependence/elections.html. Accessed on 5 January 2022.

41. Election Commission of India, 'Report on the First General Elections in India, 1951–52', Election Commission of India, Government of India Press, New Delhi, 1952, p. 192, https://eci.gov.in/files/file/4111-general-election-1951-vol-i-ii/. Accessed on 5 January 2022.

42. Ibid. 193–195.

43. John Milton, *Areopagitica*, Oxford University Press, New York, 20 September 1973.

44. Jawaharlal Nehru, 'We Want No Caesars', *Outlook*, 14 November 2014, https://www.outlookindia.com/website/story/we-want-no-caesars/292586. Accessed on 5 January 2022.

45. Ramachandra Guha, *India After Gandhi: The History of the World's Largest Democracy*, Picador India, 2017, p. 155.

46.   India is merely a geographical expression...To leave India to the rule of the Brahmins would be an act of cruel and wicked negligence...the judicial, medical, railway and public works departments would perish and India will fall back quite rapidly through the centuries into the barbarism.

                              —Winston Churchill, British prime minister,
                                      at Albert Hall, December 1930;

    Richard M. Longworth ed., *Churchill: In His Own Words*, Ebury Press, London, 2008, p. 163; 'Our Duty in India', The International Churchill Society, Winstonchurchil.org, https://www.winstonchurchill.org/resources/speeches/1930-1938-the-wilderness/our-duty-in-india./. Accessed on 5 January 2022.

47. Ramachandra Guha, *India After Gandhi: The History of the World's Largest Democracy*, Picador India, 2017, p. 157.

48. Richard Leonard Park, 'Indian Democracy and the General Election', Pacific Affairs, Vol. 25, No. 2, June 1952, pp. 130–139, https://doi.org/10.2307/2753531. Accessed on 5 January 2021

49. Quoted in 'dated February 13, 1952: British Tribute to Conduct of Elections in India', *The Hindu*, 13 February 2002, https://www.thehindu.com/todays-paper/tp-national/tp-tamilnadu/dated-february-13-1952-british-tribute-to-conduct-of-elections-in-india/article27830987.ece. Accessed on 5 January 2021.

50. Jawaharlal Nehru, 'We Want No Caesars: Nehru Warning to Himself', *The Caravan*, 14 November 2016, https://caravanmagazine.in/vantage/want-no-caesars-nehrus-warning. Accessed on 6 January 2022.

51. Bipan Chandra, Aditya Mukherjee, Mridula Mukherjee, *India Since Independence*, Penguin Random House, New Delhi, 2017, p. 84.

52. Robert Trumbull, 'Nehru Withdraws Anti-Strike Bill', *The New York Times*, 6 March 1949, https://www.nytimes.com/1949/03/06/archives/nehru-withdraws-antistrike-bill-says-india-is-now-fully-able-to.html. Accessed on 30 January 2022; Ramachandra Guha, *India After Gandhi: The History of the World's Largest Democracy*, Picador India, 2017, pp. 13–14.

53. All India Congress Committee, *Resolutions on Economic Policy and Programme 1955–56*, New Delhi, 1956, 1; Quoted in Bipan Chandra, Aditya Mukherjee, Mridula Mukherjee, *India Since Independence*, Penguin Random House, New Delhi, 2017, p. 187; K. V. Viswanathaiah, 'Jawaharlal Nehru's Concept Of Democratic Socialism', *The Indian Journal of Political Science*,

Vol. 26, No. 4, October–December 1965, pp. 91–99, https://www.jstor.org/stable/41854092.

54. Shantanu Bhagwat, 'The nonsense about the "Hindu Rate of Growth"', *The Times of India*, 8 February 2013, https://timesofindia.indiatimes.com/blogs/reclaiming-india/the-nonsense-about-the-hindu-rate-of-growth/. Accessed on 5 January 2022; 'India Redefines its Role', The Adelphi Papers, 2 May 2008, Vol. 35, No. 293, https://doi.org/10.1080/05679329508449290. Accessed on 5 January 2022.

55. The Hindu rate of growth refers to low growth of rate around 3.5 per cent before the 1991 reforms.

56. Sanjeev Sanyal, 'The left paralysis', *The Week*, 21 February 2016, https://www.theweek.in/columns/guest-columns/the-left-paralysis.html. Accessed on 5 January 2022.

57. Inder Malhotra, 'Nehru's mantle on Shastri's shoulders', *The Indian Express*, 28 May 2012, https://indianexpress.com/article/opinion/columns/nehrus-mantle-on-shastris-shoulders/lite. Accessed on 5 January 2022.

CHAPTER 3: FREEDOM TRAIL RUNS THROUGH PRINCELY STATES

1. William Dalrymple, 'The East India Company: The original corporate raiders', *The Guardian*, 4 March 2015, https://www.theguardian.com/world/2015/mar/04/east-india-company-original-corporate-raiders. Accessed 3 January 2022.

2. John Keay, *India: A History*, Grove Press (Books, New York, 2000, p. 433; Stanley Wolpert, *A New History of India*; 3rd edn., Oxford University Press, New York, 1989, pp. 226–228.

3. Sunil Khilnani, *The Idea Of India*, Farrar, Straus and Giroux, New York, 1997.

4. V.P. Menon, *The Story of the Integration of the Indian States*, Macmillan, New York, 1956, p. 13.

5. R.P. Bhargava, *The Chamber of Princes*, Northern Book Centre, New Delhi, 1991.

6. John Keay, *India: A History*, Grove Press Books, New York, 2000.

7. John Wood, Penderel Moon, David M. Blake, and Steven R. Ashton, 'Dividing the Jewel: Mountbatten and the Transfer of Power to India and Pakistan', *Pacific Affairs*, Vol. 58, No. 4, 1985, pp. 653–662, https://doi.org/10.2307/2758474.

8. Ian Copland, 'Lord Mountbatten and the Integration of the Indian States: A Reappraisal', *The Journal of Imperial and Commonwealth History*, Vol. 21, No. 2, 1993, pp. 385–408, https://doi.org/10.1080/03086539308582896; E.W.R Lumby, *The Transfer of Power in India, 1945–7*, George Allen & Unwin, London, 1954, pp. 215–227.

9. Rajmohan Gandhi, *Patel: A Life*, Navajivan Publishing House, 1991,

Ahmedabad, pp. 413–414.

10. Ian Copland, *The Princes of India in the Endgame of Empire, 1917–1947*, Cambridge University Press, Cambridge, 1997, p. 256.

11. V.P. Menon, *The Story of the Integration of the Indian States*, Macmillan, New York, 1956, pp. 116–117.

12. Ramachandra Guha, *India After Gandhi: The History of the World's Largest Democracy*, Picador India, 2017, pp. 60-61; Binu Johnson, 'The Dewan's ordeal', *The Hindu*, 7 April 2003, http://www.thehindu.com/thehindu/mp/2003/04/07/stories/2003040701550300.htm; A.G. Noorani, 'C.P. and independent Travancore', *Frontline*, July 04 2003, http://www.frontline.in/static/html/fl2013/stories/20030704000807800.htm.

13. V.P. Menon, *The Story of the Integration of the Indian States*, Macmillan, New York, 1956, p. 92.

14. Ibid. 97.

15. Ibid.

16. Ibid. 98.

17. R. Ankit, 'The accession of Junagadh, 1947-48: Colonial sovereignty, state violence and post-independence India', *Indian Economic & Social History Review* Vol. 53, No. 3, 2016, pp. 371–404, https://doi.org/10.1177/0019464616651167.

18. V.P. Menon, *The Story of the Integration of the Indian States*, Macmillan, New York, 1956, p. 100.

19. Ibid. 85 102.

20. Various sources including: William Dalrymple, 'The Lost World', *The Guardian*, 8 December 2007, https://www.theguardian.com/lifeandstyle/2007/dec/08/weekend.williamdalrymple; Julie McCaffrey, 'The last Nizam of Hyderabad was so rich he had a £50m diamond paperweight', *Mirror*, 3 February 2012, https://www.mirror.co.uk/news/uk-news/exclusive-the-last-nizam-of-hyderabad-was-so-rich-302814; Yunus Y. Lasania, '"The last Nizam of Hyderabad was not a miser"', *The Hindu*, 25 February 2017, http://www.thehindu.com/news/cities/Hyderabad/the-last-nizam-of-hyderabad-was-not-a-miser/article17367987.ece.

21. Mark Curtis, 'Partition: "Keep a bit of India"', Mark Curtis British foreign policy declassified, 8 November 2016, http://markcurtis.info/2016/11/08/partition-keep-a-bit-of-india/. Accessed on 10 January 2022.

22. Carolyn M. Elliot, 'Decline of a Patrimonial Regime: The Telengana Rebellion in India, 1946-51', *Journal of Asian Studies*, Vol. 34, No. 1, November 1974, pp. 24–47, https://doi.org/10.2307/2052408. Accessed on 10 January 2022.

23. Gollapudi Srinivasa Rao, 'Razakar carnage survivor reminisces horror', *The Hindu*, 12 September 2016, http://www.thehindu.com/news/national/telangana/Razakar-carnage-survivor-reminisces-horror/article14633387.ece. Accessed on 10 January 2022.

24. Ramachandra Guha, *India After Gandhi: The History of the World's Largest Democracy*, Picador India, 2017, pp. 793; O. V. Ranga Rao, 'Exodus of C.

P. Muslims to Hyderabad', *Swatantra*, 11 October 1947; Lanka Sundaram, 'Nizam's Acts of War and India's Duty', *Swatantra*, 1 November 1947.

25. Nisid Hajari, *Midnight's Furies: The Deadly Legacy of India's Partition*, Houghton Mifflin Harcourt, New York, 2015, pp. 235–243.

26. Ibid.

27. Ibid.

28. K.M. Munshi, *Pilgrimage to Freedom*, 2nd edn., Bharatiya Vidya Bhavan, Bombay, 2012.

29. Mike Thomson, 'Hyderabad 1948: India's hidden massacre', BBC, 24 September 2013, http://www.bbc.com/news/magazine-24159594. Accessed on 10 January 2022; A.G. Noorani, 'Of a massacre untold', *Frontline*, Vol. 18, No. 5, 3 March 2001, https://frontline.thehindu.com/other/article30159646.ece. Accessed on 10 January 2022.

30. 'From the Sundarlal Report', *Frontline*, Vol. 18, No. 5, 3 March 2001, https://frontline.thehindu.com/other/article30159647.ece. Accessed on 10 January 2022.

31. PTI, 'Owaisi rejects UN Kashmir report, backs Centre', *The Times of India*, 16 June 2018, https://timesofindia.indiatimes.com/india/owaisi-rejects-un-kashmir-report-backs-centre/articleshow/64616811.cms. Accessed on 10 January 2022.

32. Ministry of Law and Justice, 'The Jammu and Kashmir Reorganization Act, 2019', *The Gazette of India*, 9 August 2019, https://egazette.nic.in/WriteReadData/2019/210407.pdf. Accessed on 10 January 2022.

33. Venkatesh Nayak, 'The Backstory of Article 370: A True Copy of J&K's Instrument of Accession', *The Wire*, 26 October 2016, https://thewire.in/history/public-first-time-jammu-kashmirs-instrument-accession-india/. Accessed on 10 January 2022.

34. 'The Constitution of Jammu and Kashmir', J&K Legislative Assembly, 12 March 2003, *NIC*, https://jkdat.nic.in/pdf/Rules-Costitution-of-J&K.pdf. Accessed on 10 January 2022.

35. 'Kashmir and Jammu', *Imperial Gazetteer of India*, Vol. 15, pp. 72–89, http://dsal.uchicago.edu/reference/gazetteer/pager.html?objectid=DS405.1.I34_V15_085.gif. Accessed on 10 January 2022.

36. Navnita Chadha Behera, *Demystifying Kashmir*, Pearson, Noida, 2007.

37. Victoria Schofield, *Kashmir in Conflict*, I.B. Tauris & Co, London, 2003.

38. Onkar S. Kalkat, *The Far-flung Frontiers*, Allied Publishers, New Delhi, 1983, pp. 40–42.

39. Manoj Joshi, *Kashmir, 1947–1965: A Story Retold*, India Research Press, New Delhi, 2008, p. 59; Samir Bhattacharya, *Nothing But! What Price Freedom*, Partridge New Delhi, 2013, pp 39–42.

40. Lt. Gen. S.K Sinha, *Operation Rescue: Military Operations in Jammu & Kashmir 1947–49*, Vision Books, New Delhi, 1977, pp. 80–102.

41. Victoria Schofield, *Kashmir in Conflict*, I.B. Tauris & Co, London, 2003, p. 41; Parmanand Parashar, *Kashmir and the Freedom Movement*, Sarup & Sons,

New Delhi, 2004, pp. 178–179.

42. Christopher Snedden, *Kashmir: The Unwritten History*, HarperCollins, New Delhi, 2013, p. 42.

43. Srinath Raghavan, *War and Peace in Modern India*, Palgrave Macmillan, London, 2010, p. 103.

44. Ibid. 106.

45. Ibid. 49–51.

46. Sumit Ganguly, 'Wars without End: The Indo-Pakistani Conflict', *The Annals of the American Academy of Political and Social Science*, Vol. 541, September 1995, pp. 167–178, https://doi.org/10.1177/0002716295541001012. Accessed on 10 December 2022.

47. Sumantra Bose, *Kashmir: Roots of Conflict, Paths to Peace*, Harvard University Press, Cambridge, MA, 2003, p. 100.

48. Praveen Swami, *India, Pakistan and the Secret Jihad: The covert war in Kashmir, 1947-2004, Asian Security Studies*, Routledge, London, 2007, p. 19.

49. V.P. Menon, *The Story of the Integration of the Indian States*, Macmillan, New York, 1954, p. 273.

50. Brigadier Samir Bhattacharya, *Nothing But! What Price Freedom*, Partridge, New Delhi, 2013, pp. 43–55.

51. Ibid. 48.

52. Ibid. 53.

53. Ibid. 54.

54. Ibid.

55. The account is from Brig. Amar Cheema, *The Crimson Chinar: The Kashmir Conflict: A Politico-Military Perspective*, Lancer, New Delhi, 2014, pp. 58–65.

56. Ibid. 60.

57. Quoted in *The Crimson Chinar: The Kashmir Conflict: A Politico-Military Perspective*, Lancer, New Delhi, 2014, p. 60.

58. Kuldip Singh Bajwa, *Jammu and Kashmir War, 1947–1948: Political and Military Perspective*, Har-Anand Publications, Delhi, 2003, p. 117.

59. Ibid. 118.

60. Ibid. 117.

61. Victoria Schofield, *Kashmir in Conflict*, I.B. Tauris & Co, London, 2003, p. 61.

62. George Cunningham, NWF Governor quoted in Srinath Raghavan, *War and Peace in Modern India*, Palgrave Macmillan, London, 2010, p. 111; A. G. Noorani, *The Kashmir Dispute*, Oxford University Press, Delhi, 2014, pp. 13–14.

63. V.P. Menon, *The Story of the Integration of the Indian States*, Macmillan, New York, 1956, p. 279.

64. Ishaan Tharoor, 'Pakistan may be the next victim of China's new 'imperialism', *Washington Post*, 10 August 2018, https://www.washingtonpost.com/world/2018/08/10/pakistan-may-be-next-victim-chinas-new-imperialism/. Accessed on 10 January 2022.

65. Victoria Schofield, *Kashmir in Conflict*, I.B. Tauris & Co, London, 2003, pp. 68–69.

66. Josef Korbel, 'The Kashmir Dispute After Six Years', *International Organization*, Vol. 7, No. 4, November 1953, pp. 498–510, https://doi.org/10.1017/S0020818300007256. Accessed on 10 January 2022.

67. Rakesh Ankit, 'Britain and Kashmir, 1948: "The Arena of the UN"', *Diplomacy & Statecraft*, Vol. 24, No. 2, 2013, pp. 273–290, https://doi.org/10.1080/09592296.2013.789771. Accessed on 10 January 2022.

68. Jyoti Bhusan Das Gupta, *Jammu and Kashmir*, Martinus Nijhoff, The Hague 1968, pp. 152–162.

69. Robert W. Bradnock, 'Regional geopolitics in a globalising world: Kashmir in geopolitical perspective', *Geopolitics*, Vol. 3 No. 2, 19 October 2007, pp. 1–29, https://doi.org/10.1080/14650049808407617. Accessed on 10 January 2022.

70. Victoria Schofield, *Kashmir in Conflict*, I.B. Tauris & Co, London, 2003, pp 83–86.

71. Jawaharlal Nehru Correspondence, Vijayalakshmi Pandit Papers, NMML quoted in Ramachandra Guha, *India After Gandhi: The History of the World's Largest Democracy*, Picador India, 2017.

72. Sandeep Bamzai, 'America's Great Fishing Expedition in Kashmir', *Observer Research Foundation*, 26 August 2016, https://www.orfonline.org/research/americas-great-fishing-expedition-in-kashmir/. Accessed on 10 January 2022.

73. Ibid.

74. '"Truthiness": Can Something "Seem" Without Being, True?' Merriam-Webster, https://www.merriam-webster.com/words-at-play/truthiness-meaning-word-origin. Accessed on 10 January 2022.

75. *Current*, 26 August 1953, quoted in Ramachandra Guha, *India After Gandhi: The History of the World's Largest Democracy*, Picador India, 2017, p. 259.

76. 'Speech Of the Hon'ble Sheikh Mohammed Abdullah in the Constituent Assembly: Kashmir Historical Documents', *JKashmir.net*, http://ikashmir.net/historicaldocuments/122.html. Accessed on 10 January 2022.

77. Jyoti Bhusan Das Gupta, *Jammu and Kashmir*, Martinus Nijhoff, The Hague 1968, pp. 184–207.

78. 'The Delhi Agreement', Institute for Conflict Management, http://www.satp.org/satporgtp/countries/india/states/jandk/documents/papers/delhi_agreement_1952.htm. Accessed on 10 January 2022.

79. David Devadas, 'Controversy over separate state flag for Jammu and Kashmir goes to the root of its autonomous status', *FirstPost*, 2 January 2016, https://www.firstpost.com/politics/controversy-over-separate-state-flag-for-jammu-and-kashmir-goes-to-the-root-of-its-autonomous-status-2568588.html. Accessed on 10 January 2022.

80. Ramachandra Guha, *India After Gandhi: The History of the World's Largest Democracy*, Picador India, 2017, pp. 254.

81. M.J. Akbar, '1953, a lesson in Krisis management', *The Times of India*, 17

August 2008, https://timesofindia.indiatimes.com/home/sunday-times/deep-focus/1953-a-lesson-in-Krisis-management/articleshow/3371857.cms. Accessed on 10 January 2022.

82. Rafiq Dossani and Henry S. Rowen, eds., *Prospects for Peace in South Asia*, Stanford University Press, 2005.

83. Shiri Ram Bakshi, *Struggle for Independence: Syama Prasad Mookerjee*, Anmol Publications, Delhi, 1991, pp. 278–306.

84. Jagmohan, 'The Politics of Maximum Autonomy', *India International Centre Quarterly*, Vol. 37, No. 3, 2010, pp. 126–41, https://www.jstor.org/stable/i40084997. Accessed on 10 January 2022.

85. A.G. Noorani, 'Kashmir: blunders of the past', *Frontline*, 29 December 2006, https://frontline.thehindu.com/other/article30211954.ece. Accessed on 10 January 2022.

86. Jyoti Bhusan Das Gupta, *Jammu and Kashmir*, Martinus Nijhoff, The Hague 1968, pp. 210-211; Josef Korbel, 'The National Conference Administration of Kashmir 1949-1954', *Middle East Journal*, Summer, 1954, Vol. 8, No. 3, 1954, https://www.jstor.org/stable/4322613, pp. 283-294. Accessed on 10 January 2022.

87. Arvind Lavakare, 'Forgotten Day in Kashmir's history', *rediff.com*, 8 March 2004, http://www.rediff.com/news/2004/mar/08arvind.htm. Accessed on 10 January 2022.

88. 'Kashmir's accession', *The Hindu*, 17 February 1954, http://www.thehindu.com/2004/02/17/stories/2004021700320900.htm. Accessed on 10 January 2022.

89. 'Achievements of the Bakshi Regime from 1953–1964', Kashmirnetwork.com, http://www.kashmirnetwork.com/bgm/achievefull.htm. Accessed on 10 January 2022.

90. B.N. Mullik, *My Years with Nehru*, Allied Publishers, New Delhi, p. 142.

91. '3 Kashmiri Moslems Held in Theft of Prophet's Hair', *The New York Times*, 18 February 1964, https://www.nytimes.com/1964/02/18/3-kashmiri-moslems-held-in-theft-of-prophets-hair.html?src=DigitizedArticle. Accessed on 10 January 2022.

92. Raju G.C. Thomas, ed., *Perspectives on Kashmir: The Roots of Conflict in South Asia*, Westview Press, Boulder, Colorado, 1992, p. 239.

93. Ramachandra Guha, *India After Gandhi: The History of the World's Largest Democracy*, Picador India, 2017, p. 362.

94. *The Statesman*, 31 January 1948, quoted in Ramachandra Guha, *India After Gandhi: The History of the World's Largest Democracy*, Picador India, 2017, pp. 38–39.

95. Quoted in Gopalkrishna Gandhi, 'Sardar Patel, a shared inheritance', *The Hindu*, 31 October 2017, http://www.thehindu.com/todays-paper/tp-opinion/sardar-patel-a-shared-inheritance/article19952875.ece. Accessed on 10 January 2022; Ramachandra Guha, *India After Gandhi: The History of the World's Largest Democracy*, Picador India, 2017, p. 768.

96. Quoted in Kapil Dave, 'Sardar opposed memorials, statues', *The Times of India*, 2 November 2015, https://timesofindia.indiatimes.com/india/Sardar-opposed-memorials-statues/articleshow/49603778.cms. Accessed on 10 January 2022.

97. Rajmohan Gandhi, *Patel: A Life*, Navajivan Publishing House, 1991, Ahmedabad.

98. Ayesha Jalal, *The Sole Spokesman: Jinnah, the Muslim League and the Demand for Pakistan*, Cambridge University Press, UK, 1985.

99. Rajmohan Gandhi, *Patel: A Life*, Navajivan Publishing House, 1991, Ahmedabad, pp. 395–397.

100. V.P. Menon, *The Transfer of Power in India*, Orient Longman, Delhi, 1970, p. 385.

101. Madhav Khosla, ed., *Letters for a Nation From Jawaharlal Nehru to His Chief Ministers 1947–1963*, Penguin Books, New Delhi, 2014.

CHAPTER 4: INDIA MARCHES WITH NEHRU

1. Dinesh Raheja, 'Do Bigha Zamin: Poignant, stark, human', *rediff.com*. http://m.rediff.com/movies/2002/may/09dinesh.htm. Accessed on 10 January 2022.

2. Telegraph India Special Correspondent, 'CPM supports CM and Sen on Singur', *The Telegraph*, 13 October 2006, https://www.telegraphindia.com/states/west-bengal/cpm-supports-cm-and-sen-on-singur/cid/767769; Kenneth Bo Nielsen, 'Farmers' Use Of The Courts In An Anti-Land Acquisition Movement In India's West Bengal', *Journal of Legal Pluralism*, 2009, https://doi.org/10.1080/073291 13.2009.10756632. Accessed 10 January 2022.

3. Jawaharlal Nehru, G. Parthasarathi ed., *Letters to Chief Ministers 1947-1964*, Vol. 4, Oxford University Press, 1985–9, New Delhi, p. 346.

4. Government Of India, Cabinet Secretariat Resolution, 'Government of India's Resolution setting up the Planning Commission', NITI Aayog, https://niti.gov.in/planningcommission.gov.in/docs/aboutus/history/PCresolution1950.pdf. Accessed on 10 January 2022.

5. Ibid.

6. L.N. Dash, *World Bank and Economic Development of India*, APH Publishing, New Delhi, 2000, pp. 114–115.

7. '5 Year Plans', Government of India, Planning Commission, NITI Aayog, https://niti.gov.in/planningcommission.gov.in/docs/plans/planrel/fiveyr/welcome.html. Accessed on 29 December 2021.

8. Vibhor Mohan, 'Bhakra dam project was first mooted by British', *The Times of India*, 23 October 2013, https://timesofindia.indiatimes.com/india/Bhakra-dam-project-was-first-mooted-by-British/articleshow/24563132.cms. Accessed 27 September 2021.

9. 'Developmental History of Bhakra–Nangal Dam Project', Bhakra Beas Management Board, http://bbmb.gov.in/bhakra-project.htm. Accessed on 10 January 2022.

10. Ramachandra Guha, *India After Gandhi: The History of the World's Largest Democracy*, Picador India, 2017, pp. 217-218.

11. Gavin Karunaratne, 'The Failure of the Community Development Programme in India', *Community Development Journal*, 1 April 1976, pp. 95–118, https://doi.org/10.1093/cdj/11.2.95. Accessed on 10 January 2022.

12. Baldev Raj Nayar, 'Community Development Programme: Its Political Impact', *The Economic Weekly*, 17 September 1960, http://www.epw.in/system/files/pdf/1960_12/38/community_development_programme_its_political_impact.pdf. Accessed on 10 January 2022.

13. Naoyuki Yoshino, Saumik Paul, eds., *Land Acquisition in Asia: Towards a Sustainable Policy Framework*, Springer, Singapore, 2019.

14. Maitreesh Ghatak and Sanchari Roy, 'Land reform and agricultural productivity in India: a review of the evidence', *Oxford Review of Economic Policy*, Vol. 23, No. 2, 2007, pp. 251–269, http://personal.lse.ac.uk/ghatak/oxrep2.pdf. Accessed on 10 January 2022; Kaushik Basu, ed., *Oxford Companion to Economics in India*, Oxford University Press, New Delhi, 2007.

15. K.S. Gill, 'The Nagpur Resolution: Agrarian Organisation Pattern', *The Economic and Political Weekly*, Vol. 11, Issue 4–5, January 1959, http://www.epw.in/system/files/pdf/1959_11/4-5-6/the_nagpur_resolution_agrarian_organisation_pattern.pdf. Accessed on 10 January 2022.

16. Howard L. Erdman, 'India's Swatantra Party', *Pacific Affairs*, Vol. 36, No. 4, Winter 1963–64, pp. 394–410; EPW, 'The Swatantra Party', *The Economic and Political Weekly*, July 1959, pp. 893–894, https://www.epw.in/system/files/pdf/1959_11/28-29-30/the_swatantra_party.pdf. Accessed on 10 January 2022.

17. Bipan Chandra, Aditya Mukherjee, Mridula Mukherjee, *India Since Independence*, Penguin Random House, New Delhi, 2017, p. 554.

18. Ludwig von Bertalanffy, *General Systems Theory, Foundations, Development, Applications*, George Braziller, New York, 1968.

19. Bipan Chandra, Aditya Mukherjee, Mridula Mukherjee, *India Since Independence*, Penguin Random House, New Delhi, 2017, p. 570.

20. Indian Science Congress Association, *The Shaping of Indian Science: Presidential Addresses*, Vol. 1, Universities Press, Hyderabad, 2003, pp. 574–575.

21. Government of India, 'Scientific Policy Resolution', UNESCO, March 4 1958, https://unesdoc.unesco.org/ark:/48223/pf0000154344; Nasir Tyabji, 'Jawaharlal Nehru and Science and Technology', *History and Sociology of South Asia, Sage Journals*, Vol.1, No.1, June 1, 2007, pp. 130–136, https://doi.org/10.1177/223080750700100109. Accessed on 10 January 2022.

22. Ibid.

23. David Arnold, 'Nehruvian Science and Postcolonial India', *Isis—The University of Chicago Press Journals*, June 2013, Vol. 104, No. 2, pp. 360–370, https://doi.org/10.1086/670954. Accessed on 10 January 2022.

24. Soma S. Marla, 'Jawaharlal Nehru—Builder of Modern Science and Promoter of Scientific Temper', *Mainstream*, Vol. 501, No. 48, 16 November 2013, http://

www.mainstreamweekly.net/article4588.html. Accessed on 10 January 2022.

25.   David Arnold, 'Nehruvian Science and Postcolonial India', *Isis—The University of Chicago Press Journals*, June 2013, Vol. 104, No. 2, pp. 360–370, https://doi.org/10.1086/670954. Accessed on 10 January 2022.

26.   Bipan Chandra, Aditya Mukherjee, Mridula Mukherjee, *India Since Independence*, Penguin Random House, New Delhi, 2017, pp. 179–181.

27.   Ibid.

28.   'Education: 1st Five Year Plan', Government of India, Planning Commission, NITI Aayog, https://www.niti.gov.in/planningcommission.gov.in/docs/plans/planrel/fiveyr/1st/1planch33.html. Accessed on 10 January 2022.

29.   'Education: 2nd Five Year Plan', Government of India, Planning Commission, NITI Aayog https://www.niti.gov.in/planningcommission.gov.in/docs/plans/planrel/fiveyr/2nd/2planch23.html. Accessed on 10 January 2022; Bipan Chandra, Aditya Mukherjee, Mridula Mukherjee, *India Since Independence*, Penguin Random House, New Delhi, 2017, pp. 143–44.

30.   'Education: 3rd Five Year Plan', Government of India, Planning Commission, NITI Aayog, https://www.niti.gov.in/planningcommission.gov.in/docs/plans/planrel/fiveyr/3rd/3planch29.html. Accessed on 10 January 2022.

31.   FE Online, 'While 'India' detested demonetisation, 'Bharat' welcomed it, says Narayana Murthy', *The Financial Express*, 22 March 2018, http://www.financialexpress.com/economy/while-india-detested-demonetisation-bharat-welcomed-it-says-narayana-murthy/1107296. Accessed on 10 January 2022.

32.   Kishalay Bhattacharjee, 'Not Temples, But Toilets: A Look at India's Elections', *Vice News*, 11 April 2014, https://www.vice.com/en/article/qvaexv/not-temples-but-toilets-a-look-at-indias-elections. Accessed on 10 January 2022.

33.   Sabyasachi Bhattacharya, 'Jawaharlal Nehru and the Indian Working Class: A Historical Review', *The Economic and Political Weekly*, Vol. 50, No. 16, 18 April 2015, http://www.epw.in/journal/2015/16/perspectives/jawaharlal-nehru-and-indian-working-class.html. Accessed on 10 January 2022.

34.   Mulk Raj Anand, *Untouchable*, The Penguin Classics, London, 2014.

35.   Prem Kumar Chumber, 'Freedom, Caste and Nation', *Ambedkar Times*, 27 January 2021, http://www.ambedkartimes.com/AT-4-January%2027,%202021.pdf. Accessed on 10 January 2022.

36.   Rakesh Chandra, 'Social justice and untouchability in India: A constitutional perspective', *International Journal of Law*, vol. 3, No. 4, July 2017, pp. 107–111, https://www.lawjournals.org/archives/2017/vol3/issue4/3-4-28. Accessed on 10 January 2022.

37.   Shiv Prem, 'Abolition of Untouchability and Titles in Indian Constitution', *LexCliq*, 27 August 2021, https://lexcliq.com/abolition-of-untouchability-and-titles-in-indian-constitution-by-shiv-prem-at-lexcliq/. Accessed on 10 January 2022.

38.   David Arnold, *Everyday Technology: Machines and the Making of India's Modernity*, The Chicago University Press, Chicago, 2013.

39.   J.D.M. Derrett, *Hindu Law Past and Present*, A. Mukherjee and Company,

Calcutta, 1957, pp. 1–80.

40. Rina Williams. *Postcolonial Politics and Personal Laws*, Oxford University Press, New Delhi, 2006, p. 96

41. Ibid. 107.

42. Poonam Chaudhary, 'Hindu Code Bill: Towards Liberation of Women', *Contemporary Voice of Dalit, Sage Journals*, Vol. 8, No. 2, 24 October 2016, https://doi.org/10.1177/2455328X16661083. Accessed on 10 January 2022.

43. Quoted in Smita Nayak edited, *Whither Women: A Shift from Endowment to Empowerment*, Edupedia Publications, New Delhi, 2016, p. 48.

44. K.V. Narayana Rao, *The Emergence of Andhra Pradesh*, Popular Prakashan, Bombay, 1973.

45. Quoted in Ramachandra Guha, *India After Gandhi: The History of the World's Largest Democracy*, Picador India, 2017, p. 195.

46. A. Srivathsan, 'The fight for Madras', *The Hindu*, 18 August 2013, http://www.thehindu.com/news/cities/chennai/the-fight-for-madras/article5033034.ece. Accessed on 10 January 2022.

47. G.S.V. Prasad, 'Nehru and linguistic states: The merger and the bifurcation of Telugu state', *International Journal of Applied Research*, 2016, Vol. 2, No.11, pp. 295–299, http://www.allresearchjournal.com/archives/2016/vol2issue11/PartE/2-11-25-678.pdf. Accessed on 10 January 2022.

48. Suketu Mehta, *Maximum City: Bombay Lost and Found*, Vintage Books, New York, 2004.

49. EPW, 'Reorganisation of States', *Economic and Political Weekly*, Vol. 7, No. 42, 15 October 1955, http://www.epw.in/system/files/pdf/1955_7/42/reorganisation_of_statesthe_approach_and_arrangements.pdf. Accessed on 10 January 2022.

50. 'Report of the States Reorganisation Commission', Ministry of Home Affairs, 1955), https://www.mha.gov.in/sites/default/files/State%20Reorganisation%20Commisison%20Report%20of%201955_270614.pdf. Accessed 27 September 2021.

51. Ibid.

52. Marshall Windmiller, 'The Politics of States Reorganization in India: The Case of Bombay', *Far Eastern Survey*, 1956, Vol. 25, No. 9, pp. 129–143, https://doi.org/10.2307/3024387. Accessed on 10 January 2022.

53. Ramachandra Guha, *India After Gandhi: The History of the World's Largest Democracy*, Picador India, 2017, p. 203.

54. Thomas Blom Hansen, *Wages of Violence: Naming and Identity in Postcolonial Bombay*, Princeton University Press, 2001, p. 42.

55. Sadhna Sharma, *States Politics in India*, Mittal Publications, New Delhi, 1995, pp. 183–191.

56. Ibid.

57. Niranjan Rajadhyaksha, 'The anxiety that lingers', *Mint*, 7 December 2012, https://www.livemint.com/Leisure/vSENKsR3LEwbCgaG4zMw8K/The-anxiety-that-lingers.html. Accessed 27 September 2021.

58. Bipan Chandra, Aditya Mukherjee, Mridula Mukherjee, *India Since Independence*, Penguin Random House, New Delhi, 2017, pp. 102–108.

59. M.K. Gandhi, *Hind Swaraj*, Navajivan Publishing House, Ahmedabad, India, 1938 and 1962, p. 62.

60. Sankar Ghose, *Jawaharlal Nehru, a Biography*, Allied Publishers, Bombay, 1993, p. 234.

61. B.R. Ambedkar quoted in E. Venkatesu ed., *Democratic Decentralization in India: Experiences, Issues and Challenges*, Routledge, London, 2016, p. 12.

62. G.N. Devy, *The Oxford India Elwin: Selected Writings*, Oxford University Press, New Delhi, 2009, quoted on the cover.

63. Verrier Elwin quoted in Bipan Chandra, Aditya Mukherjee, Mridula Mukherjee, *India Since Independence*, Penguin Random House, New Delhi, 2017, pp. 109; Verrier Elwin, *The Tribal World of Verrier Elwin*, Oxford University Press, London, 1964.

64. David Meren Jamir, *A Study on Nagaland, A Theology of Justice in Cross-Cultural Mission*, Bethany Theological Seminary, Lombard, 1986.

65. Dinesh Kotwal, 'The Naga insurgency: The past and the future', *Strategic Analysis*, 2008, Vol. 24, No. 4, pp. 751–772, https://doi.org/10.1080/09700160008455245; Nirmal Nibedon, *Nagaland: The Night of the Guerrillas*, Lancer, Atlanta, Georgia, 2003; Wasbir Hussain, 'Ethno-Nationalism and the Politics of Terror in India's Northeast', *South Asia: Journal of South Asian Studies*, 2007, Vol. 30, No.1, pp. 93–110, https://doi.org/10.1080/00856400701264043. Accessed on 10 January 2022.

66. Ramachandra Guha, *India After Gandhi: The History of the World's Largest Democracy*, Picador India, 2017, pp. 276.

67. Khrietuonyü Noudi, 'Jawaharlal Nehru in Kohima', *The Morung Express*, 13 September 2011, https://morungexpress.com/jawaharlal-nehru-kohima. Accessed on 19 October 2021.

68. Shibani Kinkar Chaube, *Hill Politics in Northeast India*, 3rd edn., Orient Blackswan, New Delhi, 2012, pp. 153–161.

69. 'The 16 Point Agreement between the Government of India and the Naga People's Convention', United Nations Peacemaker, 26 July 1960, https://peacemaker.un.org/sites/peacemaker.un.org/files/IN_600726_The%20sixteen%20point%20Agreement_0.pdf. Accessed on 10 January 2022.

CHAPTER 5: INDIA DANCES WITH NEHRU ON THE WORLD STAGE

1. The World Bank, 'The Indus Waters Treaty', The World Bank, https://siteresources.worldbank.org/INTSOUTHASIA/Resources/223497-1105737253588/IndusWatersTreaty1960.pdf.

2. Niranjan D. Gulhati, *The Indus Waters Treaty: An Exercise in International Mediation*, Allied Publishers, Bombay, 1973; Aloys Arthur Michel, *The Indus*

Rivers: A Study of the Effects of Partition, Yale University Press, New Haven, 1967.

3. Jawaharlal Nehru quoted in Bipan Chandra, Aditya Mukherjee, Mridula Mukherjee, *India Since Independence*, Penguin Random House, New Delhi, 2017, p. 190.

4. GOI, 'Panchsheel', Ministry of External Affairs, http://www.mea.gov.in/Uploads/PublicationDocs/191_panchsheel.pdf.

5. Edward L. Katzenbach, Jr. and Gene Z. Hanrahan, 'The Revolutionary Strategy of Mao Tse-Tung', *Political Science Quarterly*, September 1955, Vol. 70, No. 3, pp. 321–340, https://www.jstor.org/stable/2145469.

6. Ed. George Harris, ed., *50 Greatest Speeches of the World*, Ocean Books, New Delhi, 2014, p. 121.

7. Ibid.

8. T. Friend, *Indonesian Destinies*, Harvard University Press, Cambridge, 2003.

9. G. M. Kahin, *The Asian-African Conference*, Cornell University Press, Ithaca, New York, 1956, pp. 64–72.

10. Ibid.

11. Swapna Kona Nayudu, 'Nehru's India & the Suez Canal Crisis', Center for the Advanced Study of India, University of Pennsylvania, 7 November 2016, https://casi.sas.upenn.edu/iit/swapnakonanayudu2016. Accessed on 24 September 2021.

12. Gordon L. Rottman, *Korean War Order of Battle*, Greenwood Publishing Group, Westport, 2002, p. 191.

13. Charles S. Kennedy, 'Nixon Goes to China', *The Association for Diplomatic Studies and Training: Foreign Affairs Oral History Project*, 28 April 1998, https://adst.org/2013/02/nixon-goes-to-china/. Accessed on 24 September 2021.

14. B.R. Nanda, ed., *Indian Foreign Policy: The Nehru Years*, Vikas Publishing House, New Delhi, 1975, p. 135.

15. Inder Malhotra, 'A peep into the past', *The Hindu*, 7 September 2003, https://www.thehindu.com/todays-paper/tp-features/tp-literaryreview/a-peep-into-the-past/article28498852.ece. Accessed on 24 September 2021.

16. Ibid.

17. Quoted in Surjit Mansingh, 'Indo-Soviet Relations in the Nehru years: the view from New Delhi', Parallel History Project, 28 October 2016, http://www.php.isn.ethz.ch/lory1.ethz.ch/collections/coll_india/NehruYears-Introduction3593.html?navinfo=96318.

18. O.T.P, 'Three Conversations of J.V. Stalin and Indian Ambassadors 1950-1953: Record of the Conversation of J.V. Stalin and Sarvepalli Radhakrishnan, January 15th, 1950', CCB No. 397, http://www.revolutionarydemocracy.org/rdv12n1/3convers.html

19. Ibid. 'Record of the Conversation of J.V. Stalin and Sarvepalli Radhakrishnan, April 5th, 1952

20. Ibid. 'Record of the Conversation of J.V. Stalin and Sarvepalli Radhakrishnan, April 5th, 1952.

21. Ibid. 'Record of the Conversation of J.V. Stalin and Sarvepalli Radhakrishnan, April 5th, 1952

22. Ibid. 'Record of the Conversation of J.V. Stalin and Sarvepalli Radhakrishnan, April 5th, 1952

23. CLII, 'Trade Agreement Between The Government Of India And The Government Of The Union Of Soviet Socialist Republics', LII of India, 2 December 1953, http://www.commonlii.org/in/other/treaties/INTSer/1953/16.html. Accessed on 24 September 2021.

24. Vladislav Zubok, *A Failed Empire: The Soviet Union in the Cold War from Stalin to Gorbachev*, University of North Carolina Press, Chapel Hill, NC, 2007.

25. Surjit Mansingh, 'Indo-Soviet Relations in the Nehru years: the view from New Delhi', Parallel History Project, 28 October 2016, n.11, http://www.php.isn.ethz.ch/lory1.ethz.ch/collections/coll_india/NehruYears-Introduction3593.html?navinfo=96318; 'Letter from Ambassador K.P.S. Menon to Foreign Secretary R.K. Nehru', 30 April 1954 and Report on Trade Relations, 1954, National Archives of India, Ministry of External Affairs, D/3042/Europe, New Delhi, http://www.php.isn.ethz.ch/kms2.isn.ethz.ch/serviceengine/Files/PHP/95025/ipublicationdocument_singledocument/0ce7cc48-ea6d-4b6b-8e20-e9e4e985a8a1/en/Letter_Menon_1954_04.pdf

26. Ramachandra Guha, *India After Gandhi: The History of the World's Largest Democracy*, Picador India, 2017, pp. 42, 784; Mikhail Gorbachev, *Memoirs*, Doubleday, London, 1996, pp. 52–53

27. Surjit Mansingh, 'Indo-Soviet Relations in the Nehru years: the view from New Delhi', Parallel History Project, 28 October 2016, n.11, http://www.php.isn.ethz.ch/lory1.ethz.ch/collections/coll_india/NehruYears-Introduction3593.html?navinfo=96318

28. Rone Tempest, 'Old India Mood, New Ideas Await Gorbachev Visit', *Los Angeles Times*, 23 November 1986, http://articles.latimes.com/1986-11-23/news/mn-12608_1_soviet-union. Accessed on 10 January 2022.

29. Inder Malhotra, 'A peep into the past', *The Hindu*, 7 September 2003, https://www.thehindu.com/todays-paper/tp-features/tp-literaryreview/a-peep-into-the-past/article28498852.ece. Accessed on 24 September 2021.

30. Moni Chadha, '1956-a real life story', *Hindustan Times*, 21 April 2007, https://www.hindustantimes.com/india/1956-a-real-life-story/story-A9kcd8xGP6IKbNEgJ3BjuI.html. Accessed on 24 September 2021.

31. Swapna Kona Nayudu, 'Responses to Russian Interventionism: India and the Questions of Hungary, 1956 and Crimea, 2014', Center For The Advanced Study of India, 12 January 2015, https://casi.sas.upenn.edu/iit/swapnakonanayudu.

32. Charles H. Heimsath and Surjit Mansingh, *A Diplomatic History of Modern India* (Bombay: Allied Publishers, 1971), p. 427

33. Quoted in Vojtech Mastny, 'The Soviet Union's Partnership with India', *MIT Press Journal*, Vol. 12, No. 3, https://doi.org/10.1162/JCWS_a_00006;

'Document No. 3 Memorandum of Conversation of N.S. Khrushchev with Mao Zedong, Beijing, 2 October 1959', *Cold War International History Project Bulletin*, No. 12–13, Fall 2001, p. 266, https://www.wilsoncenter.org/sites/default/files/media/documents/publication/CWIHP_Bulletin_12-13.pdf. Accessed 10 January 2022.

34.   David Geary, 'Rebuilding the Navel of the Earth: Buddhist pilgrimage and transnational religious networks', *Modern Asian Studies*, Vol. 48, No. 3, May 2014, note. 22, https://doi.org/10.1017/S0026749X12000881. Accessed 10 January 2022.

35.   Ibid. 645–692.

36.   Alex McKay, *History of Tibet*, Routledge, London, 2003.

37.   'Proclamation Issued By H.H. The Dalai Lama XIII, On The Eighth Day Of The First Month of The Water-Ox Year (1913)' Tibet Justice, http://www.tibetjustice.org/materials/tibet/tibet1.html. Accessed 24 September 2021; Tsepon W.D. Shakabpa, *Tibet: A Political History*, Yale University Press, New Haven, 1967, pp. 246–248.

38.   Quoted in A. Tom Grunfeld, *The Making of Modern Tibet*, Routledge, New York, 2015, p. 65.

39.   Ibid; Dalai Lama, *My Land and My People*, Warner Books, New York, 1962.

40.   Melvyn C. Goldstein, *A History of Modern Tibet, 1913–1951: The Demise of the Lamaist State*, University of California Press, Berkeley, CA, 1989.

41.   Melvyn C. Goldstein, *A History of Modern Tibet: The Calm before the Storm: 1951–1955*, Vol.2, University of California Press, Berkeley, CA, 2009, p. 5.

42.   Goldstein, *The Snow Lion and the Dragon: China, Tibet, and the Dalai Lama*, University of California Press, Berkeley, CA, 1997.

43.   Fan Ming quoted in Melvyn C. Goldstein, *A History of Modern Tibet: The Calm before the Storm: 1951–1955*, Vol.2, University of California Press, Berkeley, CA, 2009, p. 276.

44.   Melvyn C. Goldstein, *A History of Modern Tibet: The Calm before the Storm: 1951–1955*, Vol.2, University of California Press, Berkeley, CA, 2009, p. 276.

45.   Ibid.

46.   'Sino-Indian Border War, 1962', Digital Archives: Wilson Center, http://digitalarchive.wilsoncenter.org/collection/71/sino-indian-border-war-1962.

47.   Alfred P. Rubin, 'The Sino-Indian Border Disputes', *The International and Comparative Law Quarterly*, Vol. 9, No. 1. January 1960, pp. 96–125, https://www.jstor.org/stable/756256; Parshotam Mehra, *An 'agreed' frontier: Ladakh and India's northernmost borders, 1846-1947*, Oxford University Press, 1992, pp. 57, 243.

48.   Dorothy Woodman, *Himalayan Frontiers: A Political Review of British, Chinese, Indian, and Russian Rivalries*, Praeger, Santa Barbara, CA 1970, pp. 73–78.

49.   Margaret W. Fisher, Leo E. Rose, and Robert A. Huttenback, *Himalayan Battleground: Sino-Indian Rivalry in Ladakh*, Praeger, Santa Barbara, CA, 1963, p. 101; Neville Maxwell, *India's China War*, Anchor Books, New York, 1972.

50. Melvyn C. Goldstein, *A History of Modern Tibet: The Calm before the Storm: 1951–1955*, Vol.2, University of California Press, Berkeley, CA, 2009.

51. P.B. Sinha, A.A. Athale, S.N. Prasad, eds., *History of the Conflict with China, 1962*, History Division, Ministry of Defence, New Delhi, 1992.

52. A.G. Noorani, 'Facts of History', *Frontline*, 12 September 2003, https://frontline.thehindu.com/world-affairs/article30218740.ece#. Accessed on 4 October 2021.

53. Ramachandra Guha, *India After Gandhi: The History of the World's Largest Democracy*, Picador India, 2017, pp. 307–24.

54. Johan Skog Jensen, 'A Game of Chess and a Battle of Wits: India's Forward Policy Decision in Late 1961', *Journal of Defence* Studies, Vol. 6, No. 4, pp. 55–70, https://www.idsa.in/system/files/jds_6_4_JohanSkogJesen.pdf. Accessed 10 January 2022.

55. John J. Mearsheimer, *The Tragedy of Great Power Politics*, W.W. Norton, New York, 2001.

56. Anil Athale, 'Remembering a War', *rediff.com*, 7 November 2002, http://www.rediff.com/news/2002/nov/07china.htm. Accessed on 24 September 2021.

57. Alexander Pope, 'Portrait of Addison', Bartleby, https://www.bartleby.com/371/431.html. Accessed on 10 January 2022.

58. Robert Farley, 'How Mao Zedong Benefited From the Cuban Missile Crisis', *The Diplomat*, 8 April 2016, https://thediplomat.com/2016/04/how-mao-zedong-benefited-from-the-cuban-missile-crisis/. Accessed on 10 January 2022.

59. John P. Dalvi, *Himalayan Blunder: The Curtain-Raiser to the Sino-Indian War of 1962*, Thacker & Co., Bombay, 1968.

60. KCA, 'The Himalayan Border Crisis', *Keesing's Record of World Events*, Vol.8, December 1962, http://web.stanford.edu/group/tomzgroup/pmwiki/uploads/2094-1962-12-KS-a-JHS.pdf. Accessed on 24 September 2021.

61. Government of India, *Prime Minister on Sino-Indian Relations*, vol.1, External Publicity Division, Ministry of External Affairs, New Delhi, 1961, p. 189.

62. Anil Athale, 'Remembering a War', *rediff.com*, 7 November 2002, http://www.rediff.com/news/2002/nov/07china.htm. Accessed on 24 September 2021.

63. Rup Narayan Das, 'India-China Relations: A New Paradigm', *IDSA Monograph Series*, No. 19, Institute for Defence Studies and Analyses, May 2013, p. 25, https://idsa.in/system/files/Monograph19.pdf. Accessed 24 September 2021.

64. L.N. Subramanian, The Battle of Chushul', *Bharat Rakshak Monitor*, Vol. 3, No. 3, November–December 2000, https://www.bharat-rakshak.com/ARMY/history/1962war/264-chushul.html. Accessed 24 September 2021; Anil Athale, 'Remembering a War', *rediff.com*, 7 November 2002, http://www.rediff.com/news/2002/nov/07china.htm. Accessed on 24 September 2021.

65. S.K. Shah, *India and China: The Battle between Soft and Hard Power*, Vij Books, Alpha Editions, Delhi, 2015, p. 109.

66. Quoted in KCA, 'The Himalayan Border Crisis', *Keesing's Record of World Events*, Vol.8, December 1962, http://web.stanford.edu/group/tomzgroup/

pmwiki/uploads/2094-1962-12-KS-a-JHS.pdf. Accessed on 24 September 2021.

67.   Inder Malhotra, 'The Colombo "compromise"', *The Indian Express*, 17 October 2011, http://archive.indianexpress.com/news/the-colombo-compromise/860792/0; Steven A. Hoffman, *India and the China Crisis*, University of California Press, Berkeley, California, 1990, pp. 227–228.

68.   Anil Athale, 'The Untold Story: How Kennedy came to India's aid in 1962', *rediff.com*, http://www.rediff.com/news/special/the-untold-story-how-the-us-came-to-indias-aid-in-1962/20121204.htm. Accessed 24 September 2021.

69.   Andrew Buncombe, 'JFK was ready to use nuclear bomb on China, tapes reveal', *Independent*, 12 July 2013, https://www.independent.co.uk/news/world/americas/jfk-was-ready-to-use-nuclear-bomb-on-china-tapes-reveal-308341.html. Accessed 24 September 2021.

70.   Vojtech Mastny, 'The Soviet Union's Partnership with India', *MIT Press Journal*, Vol. 12, No. 3, https://doi.org/10.1162/JCWS_a_00006. Accessed 24 September 2021.

71.   Ibid. 62, note 34, Prozumenshchikov, 'The Sino-Indian Conflict', 253; Records of Jaipal–Benediktov and Kaul–Benediktov Conversations, 24 October 1962, in NSArchive.

72.   Bertil Lintner, *China's India War: Collision Course on the Roof of the World*, Oxford University Press, New Delhi, 2018, pp. 135–36.

73.   Ibid.

74.   Steven A. Hoffman, *India and the China Crisis*, University of California Press, Berkeley, California, 1990, pp. 229–30.

75.   Sunil Khilnani, *Incarnations: India in Fifty Lives*, Farrar, Straus and Giroux, New York, 2016, pp. 342–349.

76.   D. R. Mankekar, *The Guilty Men of 1962*, quoted in Bertil Lintner, *China's India War: Collision Course on the Roof of the World*, Oxford University Press, New Delhi, 2018, p. 122.

77.   Bertil Lintner, *China's India War: Collision Course on the Roof of the World*, Oxford University Press, New Delhi, 2018, p. 122.

78.   Ramachandra Guha, *India After Gandhi: The History of the World's Largest Democracy*, Picador India, 2017, pp. 305–307.

79.   V.K. Madhvan Kutty, *V.K. Krishna Menon*, Ministry of Information and Broadcasting, New Delhi, 1988.

80.   Bertil Lintner, *China's India War: Collision Course on the Roof of the World*, Oxford University Press, New Delhi, 2018, pp. 126–127; James Griffiths, 'India's Forgotten Chinese Internment Camp', *The Atlantic*, 9 August 2013, https://www.theatlantic.com/china/archive/2013/08/indias-forgotten-chinese-internment-camp/278519/. Accessed 24 September 2021.

81.   S. Gopal, *Jawaharlal Nehru: A Biography*, Vol. 3, Oxford University Press, New Delhi, 2011, p. 223.

82.   Quoted in Ramachandra Guha, *India After Gandhi: The History of the World's Largest Democracy*, Picador India, 2017, pp. 165–166.

83.   B.G. Verghese, 'Fifty Years After 1962', *Asian Conversations*, January 2013, http://www.asianconversations.com/IndiaChinaWar.php.   Accessed   24 September 2021.

84.   Dennis Kux, *India and the United States: Estranged Democracies 1941–1991*, National Defense Press, Washington, DC, 1992, pp. 193–195.

85.   Ibid 195.

86.   Ibid.

87.   Geoffrey Tyson, *Nehru: The Years of Power*, Praeger, London, 1966, p. 173.

88.   Jawaharlal Nehru, *An Autobiography*, Oxford University Press, 1980, p. 228–231.

89.   Narain D. Batra, *The First Freedoms and America's Culture of Innovation: The Constitutional Foundations of the Aspirational Society*, Rowman & Littlefield, Lanham, Maryland, 2013.

CHAPTER 6: THE LITTLE MAN SHASTRI, WHO COULD

1.   Selig S. Harrison, *India: The Most Dangerous Decades*, Princeton University, Princeton, NJ, 1960.

2.   Promilla Kalhan, *Gulzarilal Nanda: A Life in the Service of the People*, Allied Publishers, New Delhi, 1997; R.K. Murthi, *Encyclopedia of Bharat Ratnas*, Pitambar Publishing Company, Delhi, 2005.

3.   P. Kandaswamy, *The Political Career of K. Kamaraj*, Concept Publishing Company. New Delhi, 2001; R.K. Murthi, *Encyclopedia of Bharat Ratnas*, Pitambar Publishing Company, Delhi, 2005, p. 89.

4.   Ramachandra Guha, *India After Gandhi: The History of the World's Largest Democracy*, Picador India, 2017, p. 190.

5.   C.R. Kesavan, *Unfolding Rajaji*, East West Books, Madras, 2003.

6.   R. Kannan, *Anna: The life and Times of C.N. Annadurai*, Penguin, New Delhi, 2010.

7.   Swarna Rajagopalan, *State and Nation in South Asia*, Lynne Rienner Publishers, Boulder, Colorado, 2001, p. 154.

8.   B.C. Chakravorty, *The History of Indo-Pak War, 1965*, History Division, Ministry of Defence, New Delhi, 1992.

9.   Farooq Bajwa, *From Kutch to Tashkent: The Indo-Pakistan War of 1965*, C. Hurst & Company, London, 2013.

10.   Bruce Riedel, *Avoiding Armageddon: America, India, and Pakistan to the Brink and Back*, Brookings Institution Press, New York, 2013.

11.   Owen Bennett Jones, *Pakistan: Eye of the Storm*, Yale University Press, New Haven, 2002, p. 78.

12.   Stanley Wolpert, *An Introduction to India*, University of California Press, 1991, Berkeley, 234–5; Virginia Fortna, *Peace Time: Cease-Fire Agreements and the Durability of Peace*, Princeton University Press, Princeton, New Jersey, 2004.

13. Paul McGarr, *The Cold War in South Asia: Britain, the US and the Indian Subcontinent, 1945–1965*, Cambridge University Press, Cambridge, UK, 2013, pp. 330–331.

14. Jeremy Black, *War in the Modern World Since 1815*, Rowman & Littlefield, Lanham, Maryland, 2005, p. 65.

15. B.C. Chakravorty, *The History of Indo-Pak War, 1965*, History Division, Ministry of Defence, New Delhi, 1992.

16. Jeremy Black, *War in the Modern World Since 1815*, Rowman & Littlefield, Lanham, Maryland, 2005, p. 65.

17. Rahul Mukherji, 'The State, Economic Growth, and Development in India', *India Review*, Vol. 8, No. 1, 2009, https://doi.org/10.1080/14736480802665238. Accessed on 10 January 2022.

18. Michael Brecher, 'India's Devaluation of 1966: Linkage Politics and Crisis Decision-Making', *Review of International Studies*, Vol. 3, No. 1, 1977, pp. 1–25, https://doi.org/10.1017/S0260210500116857. Accessed on 10 January 2022.

CHAPTER 7: THE WOMAN WHO RESHAPED THE SUBCONTINENT

1. 'Who was your choice as The Greatest Woman for the last 1000 years: Indira Gandhi', BBC Online, December 1, 1999, http://news.bbc.co.uk/hi/english/static/events/millennium/nov/winner.stm. Accessed on 30 September 2021.

2. Sunil Khilnani, *Indira Gandhi: The Centre of Everything*, BBC Radio 4, 21 March 2016, https://www.bbc.co.uk/programmes/b0741lv7. Accessed on 13 January 2022; *Incarnations: A History of India in Fifty Lives*, Farrar, Straus and Giroux, New York, 2016.

3. Chhotu Karadia, 'We were never a part of India: MNF chief Laldenga', *India Today*, 31 December 1979, https://www.indiatoday.in/magazine/special-report/story/19791231-we-were-never-a-part-of-india-mnf-chief-laldenga-822328-2014-02-18. Accessed on 13 January 2022.

4. Suhas Chatterjee, *Making of Mizoram: Role of Laldenga*, M.D. Publications, New Delhi, 1994.

5. Indranil Banerjie, 'The Rebels Rule', *India Today*, 15 March 1987. https://www.indiatoday.in/magazine/indiascope/story/19870315-former-insurgent-and-mnf-strongman-laldenga-becomes-fourth-chief-minister-of-mizoram-798662-1987-03-15. Accessed on 30 September 2021.

6. Prabin Kalita, 'Nagaland: Nienu urges NPF members to stay united', *The Times of India*, 16 July 2017, http://timesofindia.indiatimes.com/india/nagaland-nienu-urges-npf-members-to-stay-united/articleshow/59620751.cms. Accessed on 30 September 2021.

7. Jonathan Glancey, *Nagaland: a Journey to India's Forgotten Frontier*, Faber & Faber London, 2011; Jonathan Glancey, 'Nagaland: India's Final Frontier', *The*

Guardian, 10 December 2010, https://www.theguardian.com/travel/2010/dec/11/india-nagaland-jonathan-glancey. Accessed on 30 September 2021.

8.   Paul Hattaway, *From Head Hunters to Church Planters*, InterVarsity Press, Westmont, 2006.

9.   Max Martin, 'For India's Farmers, Harder Life Ahead: Latest Studies', *IndiaSpend*, 28 April 2015, http://www.indiaspend.com/cover-story/for-indias-farmers-harder-life-ahead-latest-studies-77368. Accessed on 30 September 2021.

10. KumKum Dasgupta, 'Farmer protests: India's acute groundwater crisis is fuelling distress', *Hindustan Times*, 13 June 2017, http://www.hindustantimes.com/opinion/farmer-protests-india-s-acute-groundwater-crisis-is-fuelling-distress/story-MeC6O3Stc7eaVAm3mquonL.html. Accessed on 30 September 2021.

11. Ibid.

12. WaterAid, India, http://www.wateraid.org/where-we-work/page/india. Accessed on 30 September 2021.

13. C. Subramaniam, *Hand of Destiny: The Green Revolution*, Vol. 2, Bharatiya Vidya Bhavan, Bombay, 1995.

14. Inder Malhotra, 'Swallowing the humiliation', *The Indian Express*, 12 July 2010, http://archive.indianexpress.com/news/swallowing-the-humiliation/645168/0. Accessed on 30 September 2021.

15. Devika Johri and Mark Miller, 'Devaluation of the Rupee: Tale of Two Years, 1966 and 1991', CCS, https://ccs.in/internship_papers/2002/28.pdf. Accessed on 30 September 2021.

16. Rahul Mukherji, 'India's aborted liberalization – 1966', *Pacific Affairs*, Vol. 73, No. 3, Fall 2000, pp. 375–392, https://doi.org/10.2307/2672025. Accessed on 13 January 2022.

17. Jagdish Bhagwati, K. Sundaram and T. N. Srinivasan, 'Political Response to the 1966 Devaluation-I', *Economic and Political Weekly*, Vol. 7, No. 36, 2 September 1972, pp. 1835–1836, http://www.jstor.org/stable/4361764; K. Sundaram, 'Political Response to the 1966 Devaluation-II: Politicians and Parties', *Economic and Political Weekly*, Vol. 7, No. 37, 9 September 1972, pp. 1883–1892, http://www.jstor.org/stable/4361795. Accessed on 13 January 2022.

18. Jason A. Kirk, *India and the World Bank*, Anthem Press, New York, 2011, pp. 15–21.

19. IEO, 'The Bank and 1966 Forex Crisis', *Indian Economy Review*, https://rbidocs.rbi.org.in/rdocs/content/PDFs/90039.pdf. Accessed on 30 September 2021.

20. Jason A. Kirk, *India and the World Bank*, Anthem Press, New York, 2011, p. 17.

21. Stephen P. Cohen, *India: Emerging Power*, The Brookings Institution Press, Washington, DC, p. 279.

22. K. Sundaram, 'Political Response to the 1966 Devaluation-II: Politicians and Parties', *Economic and Political Weekly*, Vol. 7, No. 37, 9 September 1972,

pp. 1883–1892, http://www.jstor.org/stable/4361795. Accessed on 13 January 2022.

23. Francine Frankel, *India's Political Economy*, Oxford University Press, New York, 2005.

24. Rahul Mukherji, 'India's aborted liberalization – 1966', *Pacific Affairs*, Vol. 73, No. 3, Fall 2000, pp. 375–392, https://doi.org/10.2307/2672025. Accessed on 13 January 2022.

25. 'Why Devaluation: Some Questions Answered', Finance Ministry, June 1966; Note circulated among members of the Lok Sabha' quoted in K. Sundaram, 'Political Response to the 1966 Devaluation-II: Politicians and Parties', *Economic and Political Weekly*, Vol. 7, No. 37, 9 September 1972, pp. 1883–1892, http://www.jstor.org/stable/4361795. Accessed on 13 January 2022.

26. Kuldip Nayar, *Between the Lines*, Allied Publishers, New Delhi, 1969, pp. 103–104.

27. Election Commission of India 'Statistical Report On General Elections, 1967 To The Fourth Lok Sabha', Election Commission of India, New Delhi, 1968, https://ceomadhyapradesh.nic.in/Links/Books/67_Vol_I.pdf. Accessed on 30 September 2021.

28. Dwaipayan Bhattacharyya, *Government as Practice: Democratic Left in a Transforming India*, Cambridge University Press, Delhi, 2016, p. 6.

29. J.C. Johari, 'Young Turks And The Radicalization Of Congress Leadership', *The Indian Journal of Political Science*, Vol. 34, No. 2, April –June 1973, pp. 173 –198, https://www.jstor.org/stable/41854568?seq=1#page_scan_tab_contents. Accessed on 13 January 2022.

30. Robert L. Hardgrave, Jr., 'The Congress in India—Crisis and Split', *Asian Survey*, Vol. 10, No. 3, March 1970, pp. 256 –262, https://doi.org/10.2307/2642578. Accessed on 13 January 2022.

31. Election Commission of India, 'Statistical Report On General Elections, 1971 To The Fifth Lok Sabha', Election Commission of India, 1973, https://ceomadhyapradesh.nic.in/Links/Books/71_Vol_II.pdf. Accessed on 13 January 2022.

32. Abu Md. Delwar Hossain, 'Operation Searchlight', quoted in Sirajul Islam and Ahmed A. Jamal, *Banglapedia: National Encyclopedia of Bangladesh*, Asiatic Society of Bangladesh, Dhaka, 2012.

33. Mark Dummett, 'Bangladesh war: The article that changed history', BBC News, 16 December 2011, http://www.bbc.com/news/world-asia-16207201. Accessed on 13 January 2022.

34. Amita Malik, *The Year of the Vulture*, Orient Longman, New Delhi, 1972.

35. Sezan Mehmud, *Operation Jackpot*, Banglaprakash, Dhaka, 2009; Amitava Kar, 'Naval Commandos in Operation Jackpot', *The Daily Star*, 26 March 2015, http://www.thedailystar.net/supplements/independence-day-special-2015/submariners-heroism-and-the-first-military-response-france. Accessed on 30 September 2021.

36. Clyde Haberman, 'Decades Later, Kissinger's Words Stir Fresh Outrage Among Jews', *The New York Times*, 17 December 2010, http://www.nytimes.com/2010/12/17/nyregion/17nyc.html. Accessed on 30 September 2021.

37. 'Crisis in South Asia: A Report by Senator Edward M. Kennedy to the Subcommittee to Investigate Problems Connected with Refugees', US Government Publishing Office, 1 November 1971; Gary J. Bass, *Nixon, Kissinger, and a Forgotten Genocide*, Knopf, New York, 2013; Gary J. Bass, 'What a senator can do', *The Boston Globe*, 29 November 2013, https://www.bostonglobe.com/opinion/2013/11/29/what-senator-can/dehi8mBCmm0iu4lGmxzKAL/story.html. Accessed on 30 September 2021.

38. Banglapedia 'Language Movement', *Banglapedia*, http://en.banglapedia.org/index.php?title=Language_Movement. Accessed on 13 January 2022.

39. Anwar S. Dil, *Bengali language movement to Bangladesh*, Ferozsons, Lahore, 2000.

40. Sashanka S. Banerjee, 'The True Story of India's Decision to Release 93,000 Pakistani POWs After 1971 War', *The Wire*, 26 March 2017 https://thewire.in/118134/the-untold-story-behind-indira-gandhis-decision-to-release-93000-pakistani-pows-after-the-bangladesh-war/. Accessed on 30 September 2021.

41. 'India's Nuclear Weapons Program: The Beginning: 1944–1960', http://nuclearweaponarchive.org/India/IndiaOrigin.html. Accessed on 30 September 2021.

42. Raj Chengappa, *Weapons of Peace: The Secret Story of India's Quest to Be a Nuclear Power*, HarperCollins Publishers, New Delhi, 2000; George Perkovich, *India's Nuclear Bomb: The Impact on Global Proliferation*, University of California Press, Berkeley, 1999.

43. TNN, 'WikiLeaks: Indira had offered to share N-tech with Pakistan in 1974', *The Times of India*, 9 April 2013, https://timesofindia.indiatimes.com/india/WikiLeaks-Indira-had-offered-to-share-N-tech-with-Pakistan-in-1974/articleshow/19467959.cms. Accessed on 30 September 2021.

44. NSG, 'Nuclear Suppliers Group', http://nti.org/e_research/official_docs/inventory/pdfs/nsg.pdf.

45. Sumantra Bose, *Kashmir: Roots of Conflict, Paths to Peace*, Harvard University Press, Cambridge, 2019, pp. 88.

46. Victoria Schofield, *Kashmir in Conflict: India, Pakistan and the Unending War*, I.B. Tauris, New York, 2010, p. 123.

47. Ramachandra Guha, *India After Gandhi: The History of the World's Largest Democracy*, Picador India, 2017, p. 467. The statement was made in the annual Congress national executive meeting at Guwahati in 1976 by then Congress President Devakanta Barooah.

48. Malavika Sanghvi, 'Of grace and intellect', *DNA*, 3 November 2017, https://www.dnaindia.com/mumbai/column-of-grace-and-intellect-1131381. Accessed on 30 September 2021.

49. H. R. Khanna. *Making of India's Constitution*, Eastern Book Co., Lucknow,

1981; Pratap Bhanu Mehta, 'The Rise of Judicial Sovereignty', *Journal of Democracy* (2007) Vol. 18, No. 2, pp. 70–83, https://doi.org/10.1353/jod.2007.0030. Accessed on 13 January 2022.

50. Austin Granville, *Working a Democratic Constitution – A History of the Indian Experience*, Oxford University Press, New Delhi, 1999, pp. 290.

51. Inder Malhotra, 'The abrupt end of Emergency', 4 August 2014, https://indianexpress.com/article/opinion/columns/the-abrupt-end-of-emergency/. Accessed on 30 September 2021.

52. *Mail Today Reporter*, 'Congress slams WikiLeaks revelations linking Rajiv Gandhi to Swedish fighter-jet deal', 8 April 2013, http://www.dailymail.co.uk/indiahome/article-2306057/Congress-slams-WikiLeaks-revelations-linking-Rajiv-Gandhi-Swedish-fighter-jet-deal.html. Accessed on 30 September 2021.

53. I was a college teacher in Jamnagar when he addressed the student audience.

54. P.N. Dhar, *Indira Gandhi, the 'Emergency' and Indian Democracy*, Oxford University Press, New Delhi, 2008; Ravi Visvesvaraya Prasad, '14 Days to the Darkest Phase of Indian Democracy', *Open*, 15 June 2021, https://openthemagazine.com/columns/14-days-darkest-phase-indian-democracy/. Accessed on 30 September 2021.

55. Ravi Visvesvaraya Prasad, '40th anniversary of Emergency: My memories of the Emergency days (Part 1)', News18, 24 June 2015, http://www.news18.com/news/india/40th-anniversary-of-emergency-my-memories-of-the-emergency-days-1010106.html. Accessed on 30 September 2021.

56. Manoj C.G., 'SS Ray to Indira Gandhi six months before Emergency. Crack down, get law ready', *The Indian Express*, 13 June 2015, http://indianexpress.com/article/india/india-others/six-months-before-emergency-s-s-ray-to-indira-gandhi-crack-down-get-law-ready/. Accessed on 30 September 2021.

57. Granville Austin, *Working a Democratic Constitution - A History of the Indian Experience*, Oxford University Press, New Delhi, 1999, pp. 320.

58. P.N. Dhar, *Indira Gandhi, the 'Emergency' and Indian Democracy*, Oxford University Press, New Delhi, 2008.

59. Quoted in 'A Once and Future Tragedy: India's sterilization campaign 39 years later', Population Research Institute, 24 June 2014, https://www.pop.org/a-once-and-future-tragedy-indias-sterilization-campaign-39-years-later/. Accessed on 13 January 2022.

60. Ibid.

61. Excerpt taken from *For Reasons of State: Delhi under Emergency* (Delhi: Penguin Random House, 1977), John Dayal and Ajay Bose, 'The Khooni Kissa of Turkman Gate', The Wire, 25 June 2015, https://thewire.in/4761/the-khooni-kissa-of-turkman-gate. Accessed on 30 September 2021.

CHAPTER 8: INDIA REVERTS TO FREEDOM AND TURMOIL

1. G.G. Mirchandani, *320 Million Judges*, Abhinav Publications, New Delhi, 2003, p. 101.
2. Election Commission of India, 'Statistical Report On General Elections, 1977 To The Sixth Lok Sabha, Volume I', Election Commission of India, 26 September 2018, https://eci.gov.in/files/file/7453-sixth-general-elections-vol-i-1977/. Accessed on 14 January 2022.
3. G.G. Mirchandani, *320 Million Judges*, Abhinav Publications, New Delhi, 2003, pp. 176–191.
4. Jnanadhir Sarma Sarkar, *Commissions of Inquiry: Practice and Principle With Up to Date Case Laws and Commentaries*, APH Publishing, New Delhi, 1990.
5. Jussi M. Hanhimaki, *The Flawed Architect: Henry Kissinger and American Foreign Policy*, Oxford University Press, New York, 2004.
6. A.G. Noorani, 'Foreign Policy of the Janata Party Government', *Asian Affairs: An American Review*, Vol. 5, No. 4, March–April 1978, pp. 216–228, https://doi.org/10.1080/00927678.1978.10554044. Accessed on 14 January 2022.
7. 'India's Visit to China Cut Off in Protest', *The New York Times*, 19 February 1979, http://www.nytimes.com/1979/02/19/archives/indians-visit-to-china-cut-off-in-protest-demonstrations-planned.html. Accessed on 14 January 2022.
8. Rama Lakshmi, 'A U.S. President's Second Birthplace', *The Washington Post*, 21 March 2000, http://www.washingtonpost.com/wp-srv/WPcap/2000-03/21/037r-032100-idx.html. Accessed on 14 January 2022.
9. PTI, 'Atal Bihari Vajpayee, The 1st Indian Leader To Address UNGA In Hindi', NDTV, 16 August 2018, https://www.ndtv.com/india-news/atal-bihari-vajpayee-the-1st-indian-leader-to-address-unga-in-hindi-1901549. Accessed on 14 January 2022.
10. *India Today*, 'Govt's 'rolling plan' as a substitute for Five Year Plans elicits mixed reaction', *India Today*, 15 October 1977, http://indiatoday.intoday.in/story/govts-rolling-plan-as-a-substitute-for-five-year-plans-elicits-mixed-reaction/1/435719.html. Accessed on 14 January 2022.
11. Shashi Tharoor, *India: From Midnight To The Millennium and Beyond*, Arcade Publishing, New York 2006, pp. 164–66.
12. Steven, 'The cycle of struggle 1973 to 1979 in India', *Libcom.org*, 31 October 2015, https://libcom.org/history/cycle-struggle-1973-1979-india Accessed on 14 January 2022.
13. Richard M. Weintraub, 'Parliament Expels Gandhi, Orders Her to Delhi Jail Cell', *Washington Post*, 20 December 1978, https://www.washingtonpost.com/archive/politics/1978/12/20/parliament-expels-grandhi-orders-her-to-delhi-jail-cell/2564b899-f0bc-473c-950e-4c29f1767e49/?utm_term=.8f99d63f4fcb Accessed on 14 January 2022.
14. Bipan Chandra, Aditya Mukherjee, Mridula Mukherjee, *India Since Independence*, Penguin Random House, New Delhi, 2017, p. 248.

15. Chandan Mitra, 'Revolving door politics became the hallmark of Indian democracy', *India Today*, 26 December 2005, https://www.indiatoday.in/magazine/cover-story/story/20051226-revolving-door-politics-became-the-hallmark-of-indian-democracy-786334-2005-12-26. Accessed on 14 January 2022; Also see, 'Charan Singh' in Sunil Khilnani *Incarnations: A History of India in Fifty Lives*, Farrar, Straus and Giroux, New York, 2016, pp. 375–382.

CHAPTER 9: WHEN INDIRA GANDHI RETURNED

1. Ramachandra Guha, *India After Gandhi: The History of the World's Largest Democracy*, Picador India, 2017, p. 542.

2. Arul B. Louis, Sunil Sethi, Anil Saari and Dilip Bobb, 'Janata Party collapses, Charan Singh emerges victorious as new PM in battle for succession', *India Today*, 15 August 1979, https//www.indiatoday.in/magazine/cover-story/story/19790815-janata-party-collapses-charan-singh-emerges-victorious-as-new-pm-in-battle-for-succession-822657-2014-02-26#ssologin=1#source=magazine. Accessed on 14 January 2022.

3. Arul B. Louis and Prabhu Chawla, 'PM Indira Gandhi dismisses governments in nine states, looks to put Congress in power', *India Today*, 15 March 1980, http//indiatoday.intoday.in/story/pm-indira-gandhi-dismisses-governments-in-nine-states-looks-to-put-congress-in-power/1/409511.html. Accessed on 14 January 2022.

4. Steven R. Weisman, 'Assassination in India; Rajiv Gandhi: A Son Who Won, Lost and Tried a Comeback', *The New York Times*, 22 May 1991, https//www.nytimes.com/1991/05/22/obituaries/assassination-in-india-rajiv-gandhi-a-son-who-won-lost-and-tried-a-comeback.html. Accessed on 14 January 2022.

5. Chander Uday Singh, 'Bombay textile industry owners rejoice as strike called by Datta Samant ends', *India Today*, 31 July 1983, http//indiatoday.intoday.in/story/bombay-textile-industry-owners-rejoice-as-strike-called-by-datta-samant-ends/1/371785.htm. Accessed on 14 January 2022.

6. Michael T. Kaufman, '3 Months Into Strike, Bombay's Workers Bear Up', *The New York Times*, 4 May 1982, http//www.nytimes.com/1982/05/04/world/3-months-into-strike-bombay-s-workers-bear-up.html. Accessed on 14 January 2022.

7. AP, 'Four Are Killed in Bombay Riots Set off by Rebellion of Policemen', *The New York Times*, 19 August 1982, http//www.nytimes.com/1982/08/19/world/four-are-killed-in-bombay-riots-set-off-by-rebellion-of-policemen.html. Accessed on 14 January 2022.

8. Sandip Pendse, 'The Datta Samant Phenomenon', *Economic and Political Weekly*, Vol. 16, No. 16–17, April 18–25, 1981, pp. 695–697, pp. 745–749, https//www.jstor.org/stable/4369716.

9. Gautam Kumar Bera, *The Unrest Axle: Ethno-Social Movements in Eastern India*, Delhi Mittal Publications, New Delhi, 2008, pp. 32–35.

10. Yambem Laba, 'A tale of two ambushes', *The Statesman*, 22 June 2015, http//www.thestatesman.com/supplements/north/a-tale-of-two-ambushes-70817.html. Accessed on 14 January 2022.

11. 'Shillong Agreement between the Government of India and the Underground Nagas', 11 November 1975, United Nations Peacemaker, https//peacemaker.un.org/sites/peacemaker.un.org/files/IN_751111_Shillong%20Agreement_0.pdf. Accessed on 14 January 2022.

12. Pradip R. Sagar, 'Centre Inks Landmark Peace Pact With Nagaland Insurgents', *The New Indian Express*, 4 August 2015, http//www.newindianexpress.com/nation/2015/aug/04/Centre-Inks-Landmark-Peace-Pact-With-Nagaland-Insurgents-794232.html. Accessed on 14 January 2022.

13. Meeta Deka, *Student Movements in Assam*, Vikas Publication House, New Delhi, 1996; Subir Bhaumik, *Troubled Periphery: Crisis of India's North East*, Sage Publications, New Delhi, 2009, pp. 29–31; Makiko Kimura, *The Nellie Massacre of 1983: Agency of Rioters*, Sage Publications, New Delhi, 2013.

14. '83 polls were a mistake: KPS Gill', *Assam Tribune*, 18 February 2008, https://web.archive.org/web/20120207000801/http://www.assamtribune.com/scripts/details.asp?id=feb1908%2Fat02; ACHR, 'Assam Riots Preventable but not Prevented', Asian Centre For Human Rights, 11 September 2012, http//www.achrweb.org/info-by-country/india/assam-riots-preventable-but-not-prevented/. Accessed on 14 January 2022.

15. 'IMDT Act is the biggest barrier to deportation, says Supreme Court', *The Hindu*, 14 July 2005, https//www.thehindu.com/todays-paper/tp-national/imdt-act-is-the-biggest-barrier-to-deportation-says-supreme-court/article27422912.ece. Accessed on 14 January 2022.

16. 'Sarbananda Sonowal vs Union of India on 5 December 2006', ikanoon, http//indiankanoon.org/doc/1436100/. Accessed on 14 January 2022.

17. Tavleen Singh, 'Builders & Breakers—Prophet of Hate J.S. Bhindranwale', *India Today*, 20 June 2000; Mark Tully and Satish Jacob, *Amritsar – Mrs Gandhi's Last Battle*, Calcutta Rupa Publications, 1985; Kuldip Nayar and Khushwant Singh, *Tragedy of Punjab: Operation Bluestar & After*, Vision Books, New Delhi, 1984.

18. K. S. Brar, *Operation Blue Star: The True Story*, South Asia Books, New Delhi, 1993.

19. Ibid.

20. Sir Mark Tully, 'Operation Blue Star: How an Indian army raid on the Golden Temple ended in disaster', *The Telegraph*, 6 June 2014, http//www.telegraph.co.uk/news/worldnews/asia/india/10881115/Operation-Blue-Star-How-an-Indian-army-raid-on-the-Golden-Temple-ended-in-disaster.html. Accessed on 14 January 2022.

21. Rahul Bedi, 'Indira Gandhi's death remembered', BBC, 1 November 2009, http//news.bbc.co.uk/2/hi/south_asia/8306420.stm. Accessed on 14 January 2022.

22. G.T. Nanavati, 'Justice Nanavati Commission of Inquiry (1984 Anti-Sikh

Riots)', 2 September 2005, https//www.mha.gov.in/sites/default/files/Nanavati-I_eng_0.pdf

23. Ibid., Nanavati, 179.

24. Manoj Mitta and H.S. Phoolka, *When a Tree Shook Delhi: The 1984 Carnage and its Aftermath*, Lotus Roli Books, Delhi, 31 December 2008; 'When a big tree falls, earth shakes Former PM Rajiv Gandhi' [video], YouTube (broadcast by ABPNews), https//www.youtube.com/watch?v=4l-FoRDuunI. Accessed on 14 January 2022.

25. BBC, 'Leaders "incited" anti-Sikh riots', BBC *News*, 8 August 2005, http//news.bbc.co.uk/2/hi/south_asia/4130962.stm. Accessed on 14 January 2022.

26. Pupul Jayakar, *Indira Gandhi: A Biography*, Penguin Books, New Delhi, 1995, p. 474.

27. Balraj Puri, 'Era of Indira Gandhi', *Economic and Political Weekly*, Vol. 20, No. 4, 26 January 1985, pp. 148–150, https//www.jstor.org/stable/4374003. Accessed on 14 January 2022.

CHAPTER 10: THE ASCENT OF PRINCE CHARMING, RAJIV GANDHI

1. Sanjoy Hazarika, 'A Poignant Memorial To Indira Gandhi Opens', *The New York Times*, 2 June 1985, https://www.nytimes.com/1985/06/02/world/a-poignant-memorial-to-indira-gandhi-opens.html. Accessed on 14 January 2022.

2. G. Palanithurai, *Memorable Quotes from Rajiv Gandhi and on Rajiv Gandhi*, Concept Publishing Company, New Delhi, 2009, p. 39.

3. Vera Schiavazzi, 'Sonia Gandhi: The Maino girl who kept her tryst with destiny in India', *India Today*, 17 January 2005, https://www.indiatoday.in/magazine/cover-story/story/20050117-sonia-gandhi-the-maino-girl-who-kept-her-tryst-with-destiny-in-india-788413-2005-01-17. Accessed on 14 January 2022.

4. Inder Malhotra, 'How "Mr Clean" lost his shine', *The Indian Express*, 22 December 2014, http://indianexpress.com/article/opinion/columns/how-mr-clean-lost-his-shine/. Accessed on 14 January 2022.

5. Jugdep S. Chima, 'The Punjab Crisis: Governmental Centralization and Akali–Centre Relations', *Asian Survey*, Vol. 34, No. 10, October 1994, pp. 847–862, https://doi.org/10.2307/2644965. Accessed on 14 January 2022.

6. Kent Roach, 'The Air India Report And The Regulation Of Charities And Terrorism Financing', *The University of Toronto Law Journal*, Vol. 61, No. 1, Winter 2011, pp. 45–57, https://www.jstor.org/stable/23018688?seq=1. Accessed on 14 January 2022.

7. SATP, 'Memorandum of Settlement between Rajiv Gandhi and Sant Harchand Singh Longowal', Institute for Conflict Management, https://www.satp.org/satpurgtp/countries/india/states/punjab/document/papers/memorandum_

of_settlement.htm. Accessed on 1 October 2021; J.C. Aggarwal and S.P. Agrawal, *Modern History of Punjab: A Look Back Into Ancient Peaceful Punjab Focusing Confrontation and Failures Leading to Present Punjab Problem, and a Peep Ahead: Relevant Select Documents*, Concept Publishing Company, Delhi, 1992.

8. Darshan Singh Tatla, *The Sikh Diaspora: The Search For Statehood*, Routledge, London, 1998, p. 277.

9. Sanjoy Hazarika, 'Sikhs Surrender to Troops at Temple', *The New York Times*, 19 May 1988, http://www.nytimes.com/1988/05/19/world/sikhs-surrender-to-troops-at-temple.html. Accessed on 14 January 2022.

10. Harinder Baweja, 'The cops who could recite Shakespeare, wield torture implements: The K.P.S. Gill I knew', *Hindustan Times*, 27 May 2017, http://www.hindustantimes.com/opinion/the-cop-who-could-recite-shakespeare-wield-torture-implements-the-kps-gill-i-knew/story-IL9C7yZ3LsU5s3WYGi8oaJ.html. Accessed on 14 January 2022.

11. Sarabjit Singh, *Operation Black Thunder: An Eyewitness Account of Terrorism in Punjab*, SAGE Publications, Delhi, 2002.

12. Sanjoy Hazarika, 'India Bans The Political and Military Use Of Shrines', The New York Times, 29 May 1988, https://www.nytimes.com/1988/05/29/world/india-bans-the-political-and-military-use-of-shrines.html. Accessed on 14 January 2022.

13. 'Maintenance under Section 125 of The Code of Criminal Procedure', Helpline Law, http://www.helplinelaw.com/family-law/MCCP/maintenance-under-section-125-of-the-code-of-criminal-procedure.html. Accessed on 14 January 2022.

14. Mohd. Ahmed Khan vs. Shah Bano Begum and Others, 23 April 1985; 1985 AIR 945, 1985 SCR, 3 844.

15. Samanwaya Routray, 'SC: Right to maintenance of a wife absolute, Section 125 of CrPC applicable on divorced women', *The Times of India*, 7 April 2015, https://timesofindia.indiatimes.com/india/SC-Right-to-maintenance-of-a-wife-absolute-Section-125-of-CrPC-applicable-on-divorced-women/articleshow/46833908.cms. Accessed on 14 January 2022.

16. Asghar Ali Engineer, 'Maintenance for Muslim women', *The Hindu*, 7 August 2000, https://www.thehindu.com/todays-paper/tp-miscellaneous/tp-others/maintenance-for-muslim-women/article28036671.ece. Accessed on 1 October 2021.

17. Ajaz Ashraf, 'Arif Mohammad Khan on Shah Bano case, "Najma Heptullah was key influence on Rajiv Gandhi"', *Scroll.in*, 30 May 2015, https://scroll.in/article/730642/arif-mohammad-khan-on-shah-bano-case-najma-heptullah-was-key-influence-on-rajiv-gandhi. Accessed on 14 January 2022.

18. Stuart Diamond, 'The Bhopal Disaster: How It Happened', *The New York Times*, 28 January 1985, http://www.nytimes.com/1985/01/28/world/the-bhopal-disaster-how-it-happened.html?pagewanted=all. Accessed on 14 January 2022.

19. Indra Sinha, 'Bhopal: 25 Years of Poison', *The Guardian*, 3 December 2009, https://www.theguardian.com/environment/2009/dec/04/bhopal-25-years-indra-sinha. Accessed on 14 January 2022.

20. UCC, 'Bhopal Gas Tragedy Information', Union Carbide Corporation, http://www.bhopal.com/. Accessed on 14 January 2022.

21. Edward Broughton, 'The Bhopal disaster and its aftermath: a review', National Center for Biotechnology Information, 10 May 2005, Vol. 4, No. 6, https://www.ncbi.nlm.nih.gov/pmc/articles/PMC1142333/. Accessed on 14 January 2022.

22. ET Bureau, 'India tops the world in pollution-related deaths', *The Economic Times*, 21 October 2017, http://economictimes.indiatimes.com/articleshow/61158263.cms?utm_source=contentofinterest&utm_medium=text&utm_campaign=cppst; Prof. Philip J Landrigan, Richard Fuller, Nereus J.R. Acosta, Dr Olusoji Adeyi, et al., 'The Lancet Commission on pollution and health', *The Lancet Commissions*, 19 October 2017 Vol. 391, No. 10119, pp. 462–512, https://doi.org/10.1016/S0140-6736(17)32345-0. Accessed on 14 January 2022.

23. Chitra Subramaniam-Duella, 'The Bofors story, 25 years after', The Hoot, 24 April 2012, https://web.archive.org/web/20140304093344/http://thehoot.org/web/home/story.php?storyid=5884. Accessed on 14 January 2022.

24. N. Ram, 'How Bofors scam was busted—and then buried', Daily O, 11 July 2017, https://www.dailyo.in/arts/bofors-scandal-congress-scam-ottavio-quattrocchi/story/1/18303.html. Accessed on 14 January 2022.

25. Zee News Bureau, 'Three decades of Bofors case – A timeline', Zee News, 18 October 2017, http://zeenews.india.com/india/three-decades-of-bofors-case-a-timeline-2050864.html. Accessed on 14 January 2022.

26. UNI, 'Bofors: CBI to study claims made by Michael Hershman', United News of India, 18 October 2017, http://www.uniindia.com/news/india/bofors-cbi-to-study-claims-made-by-michael-hershman/1021834.html#iLUz7GGimKkzY0M3.99; Saniya Rao, 'Republic Super Exclusive: Michael Hershman, The Man Who Stumbled Upon Bofors scandal, Exposes The Then Congress Government', Republic TV, 17 October 2017, https://www.republicworld.com/india-news/politics/republic-super-exclusive-michael-hershman-the-man-who-stumbled-upon-bofors-scandal-exposes-the-then-congress-government.html. Accessed on 14 January 2022.

27. James M. Markham, 'Rajiv Gandhi, In Speech To Nation, Pledges a Continuity of Policies', *The New York Times*, 13 November 1984, https://www.nytimes.com/1984/11/13/world/rajiv-gandhi-in-speech-to-nation-pledges-a-continuity-of-policies.html. Accessed on 14 January 2022.

28. Ibid.

29. Antony Clement, 'Rajiv Gandhi's Foreign Policy: Diplomacy in Tough Times' [Blog], *South Asia Journal*, 13 August 2018, http://southasiajournal.net/rajiv-gandhis-foreign-policy-diplomacy-in-tough-times/. Accessed on 14 January 2022.

30. NYT Archives, 'Excerpts from Gandhi Speech to Joint Meeting of Congress', *The New York Times*, 14 June 1985, https://www.nytimes.com/1985/06/14/world/excerpts-from-gandhi-speech-to-joint-meeting-of-congress.html. Accessed on 14 January 2022.

31. Jim Anderson, 'President Reagan and Indian Prime Minister Rajiv Gandhi engaged...' *UPI*, 12 June 1985, https://www.upi.com/Archives/1985/06/12/President-Reagan-and-Indian-Prime-Minister-Rajiv-Gandhi-engaged/5048487396800/. Accessed on 14 January 2022.

32. Ibid.

33. Inderjit Badhwar and Madhu Trehan, 'Rajiv Gandhi's visit proves 'a turning point' in Indo–US ties', *India Today*, 15 July 1985, https://www.indiatoday.in/magazine/special-report/story/19850715-rajiv-gandhis-visit-proves-a-turning-point-in-indo-us-ties-770198-2013-12-23. Accessed on 14 January 2022.

34. John P. Rafferty, '"Mr. Gorbachev, Tear Down This Wall!": Reagan's Berlin Speech', Britannica, https://www.britannica.com/story/mr-gorbachev-tear-down-this-wall-reagans-berlin-speech. Accessed on 14 January 2022.

35. Inderjit Badhwar, Dilip Bobb and Dev Murarka, 'India pulls out all stops for highly publicised visit by Soviet leader Mikhail Gorbachev', *India Today*, 15 December 1986, https://www.indiatoday.in/magazine/cover-story/story/19861215-india-pulls-out-all-stops-for-highly-publicised-visit-by-soviet-leader-mikhail-gorbachev-801642-1986-12-15. Accessed on 14 January 2022.

36. Ibid.

37. Ibid.

38. Dilip Bobb, 'Prime Minister Rajiv Gandhi's visit to China marks a new beginning in bilateral relations', *India Today*, 15 January 1989, https://www.indiatoday.in/magazine/cover-story/story/19890115-prime-minister-rajiv-gandhi-visit-to-china-marks-a-new-beginning-in-bilateral-relations-815628-1989-01-15. Accessed on 14 January 2022.

39. Ezra F. Vogel, *Deng Xiaoping and the Transformation of China*, Belknap Press of Harvard University Press, 2011.

40. N. Ram, 'Defining Moments', *Frontline*, 12 September 1998, https://frontline.thehindu.com/cover-story/article30248071.ece#. Accessed on 14 January 2022.

41. Bharat Rakshak, 'General Krishnaswamy Sundarji', Bharat Rakshak, 12 October 2006, http://www.bharat-rakshak.com/ARMY/personnel/chiefs/156-k-sundarji.html. Accessed on 14 January 2022.

42. Global Security, 'Brass Tacks', Global Security Organization, 7 November 2011, https://www.globalsecurity.org/military/world/war/brass-tacks.htm. Accessed on 14 January 2022.

43. P.R. Chari, 'Nuclear Signaling in South Asia: Revisiting A.Q. Khan's 1987 Threat', Carnegie Endowment for International Peace, 14 November 2013, https://carnegieendowment.org/2013/11/14/nuclear-signaling-in-south-asia-

revisiting-a.-q.-khan-s-1987-threat-pub-53328. Accessed on 14 January 2022.

44. Shaikh Aziz, 'A leaf from history: Cricket diplomacy checks war pitch', *Dawn*, 15 November 2015, https://www.dawn.com/news/1219397/a-leaf-from-history-cricket-diplomacy-checks-war-pitch. Accessed on 14 January 2022.

45. Sushant Singh, 'US had warned Zia of Indian strike on Pakistan n-sites', *The Indian Express*, 16 October 2015, https://indianexpress.com/article/india/india-news-india/us-had-warned-zia-of-indian-strike-on-pakistan-n-sites/. Accessed on 14 January 2022.

46. Shaikh Aziz, 'A leaf from history: Cricket diplomacy checks war pitch', *Dawn*, 15 November 2015, https://www.dawn.com/news/1219397/a-leaf-from-history-cricket-diplomacy-checks-war-pitch. Accessed on 14 January 2022.

47. Steven R. Weisman, 'Gandhi–Zia Talks Said To Bear Fruit', *The New York Times*, 18 December 1985, https://www.nytimes.com/1985/12/18/world/gandhi-zia-talks-said-to-bear-fruit.html. Accessed on 14 January 2022.

48. Steve Coll, 'India, Pakistan Agree on Treaty', *The Washington Post*, 21 December 1990, https://www.washingtonpost.com/archive/politics/1990/12/21/india-pakistan-agree-on-treaty/a2c8cadf-9270-464e-9008-2e88571ed58c/. Accessed on 14 January 2022.

49. Ralph R. Premdas and S.W.R. de A. Samarasinghe, 'Sri Lanka's Ethnic Conflict: The Indo-Lanka Peace Accord', *Asian Survey*, Vol. 28, No. 6, June 1988, pp. 676-690, https://doi.org/10.2307/2644660. Accessed on 14 January 2022.

50. Surjit Mansingh, *India's Search for Power: Indira Gandhi's Foreign Policy 1966–1982*, SAGE Publications, New Delhi, 1984.

51. 'Operation Liberation One', *Sunday Times*, 28 June 2009, http://www.sundaytimes.lk/090628/Plus/sundaytimesplus_08.html. Accessed on 14 January 2022.

52. Steven Weisman, 'India Airlifts Aid To Tamil Rebels', *The New York Times*, 5 June 1987, http://www.nytimes.com/1987/06/05/world/india-airlifts-aid-to-tamil-rebels.html. Accessed on 14 January 2022.

53. Amit Baruah, 'I was forced into a deal with India, Jayewardene told US envoy', *The Hindu*, 5 February 2017, https://www.thehindu.com/news/international/I-was-forced-into-a-deal-with-India-Jayewardene-told-US-envoy/article17195748.ece. Accessed on 14 January 2022.

54. Ibid.

55. Cyril Ranatunga, *Adventurous Journey: From Peace to War, Insurgency to Terrorism*, Vijitha Yapa Publications, Colombo, 2009.

56. 'Operation Liberation One', *Sunday Times*, 28 June 2009, http://www.sundaytimes.lk/090628/Plus/sundaytimesplus_08.html. Accessed on 14 January 2022.

57. MR Narayan Swamy, 'India–Sri Lanka Accord', *Institute of Peace and Conflict Studies*, No. 50, August 2007, https://www.files.ethz.ch/isn/44688/IPCS-IssueBrief-No50.pdf. Accessed on 14 January 2022.

58. Mark Fineman, 'Last Indian Troops Leave Sri Lanka: Peacekeeping: Nearly three years of fighting failed to crush Tamil separatists. It was a hard lesson for New Delhi', *LA Times*, 25 March 1990, https://www.latimes.com/archives/la-xpm-1990-03-25-mn-200-story.html. Accessed on 14 January 2022.

59. Sushant Singh, 'In fact: Happy Birthday peace: The Mizo Accord turns 30', *The Indian Express*, 30 June 2016, http://indianexpress.com/article/explained/mizo-accord-congres-mizoram-insurgents-mizo-accord-anniversary-2884305/. Accessed on 14 January 2022.

60. Romit Bagchi, *Gorkhaland: Crisis of Statehood*, SAGE Publications India, New Delhi, 2012; Shoaib Daniyal, 'Darjeeling 2017 is eerily similar to Subhash Ghising's violent Gorkhaland movement in 1986', *Scroll.in*, 23 July 2017, https://scroll.in/article/844660/darjeeling-2017-is-eerily-similar-to-subhash-ghisings-violent-gorkhaland-movement-in-1986. Accessed on 14 January 2022.

61. Sudhir Jacob George, 'The Bodo Movement in Assam: Unrest to Accord', *Asian Survey*, Vol. 34, No. 10, October 1994, pp. 878–892, https://doi.org/10.2307/2644967. Accessed on 14 January 2022.

62. Subir Bhaumik, *Tripura, Ethnic Conflict, Militancy and Counterinsurgency*, Mahanirban Publishing, Kolkata, 2012.

63. Ramachandra Guha, *India After Gandhi: The History of the World's Largest Democracy*, Picador India, 2017, pp. 588–89; Koenraad Elst, 'What If Rajiv Hadn't Unlocked Babri Masjid?' *Outlook*, 23 August 2004, https://www.outlookindia.com/magazine/story/what-if-rajiv-hadnt-unlocked-babri-masjid/224878. Accessed on 14 January 2022.

64. Krishna Pokharel and Paul Beckett, 'Ayodhya, the Battle for India's Soul', *The Wall Street Journal*, http://online.wsj.com/public/resources/documents/AyodhyaFinalSeries.pdf; Congressman, 'The Great Suicide', *Mainstream*, Vol. 53, No. 6, 31 January 2015, http://www.mainstreamweekly.net/article5438.html. Accessed on 14 January 2022.

65. Ajay Singh, 'How Rajiv Gandhi blundered on Ayodhya: Baba said 'bachcha' let it happen, and 'bachcha' did', *FirstPost*, 29 January 2016, http://www.firstpost.com/politics/the-errors-that-rajiv-gandhi-made-by-unlocking-doors-to-the-ram-janmabhoomi-temple-in-ayodhya-2603582.html. Accessed on 14 January 2022.

66. Madan Gaur, *V.P. Singh: Portrait of a Leader*, Press and Publicity Syndicate of India, New Delhi, 1990; G.S. Bhargava, *Perestroika in India: V.P. Singh's Prime Ministership*, Gyan Publishing House, New Delhi, 1990.

67. Pankaj Pachauri, 'Rubaiya Sayeed: Abduction anguish', *India Today*, 31 December 1989, http://indiatoday.intoday.in/story/kashmiri-militants-releases-rubaiya-daughter-of-union-home-minister-mufti-mohammed-sayeed/1/324242.html. Accessed on 14 January 2022.

68. Rahul Pandita, *Our Moon Has Blood Clots: A Memoir of a Lost Home in Kashmir*, New Delhi, Penguin Random House, 2017; Rahul Pandita, 'Left with No Choice', *Open*, 16 January 2013, https://openthemagazine.com/features/

india/left-with-no-choice. Accessed on 14 January 2022. Vivek Gumaste, 'Why we need to remember 19 January 1990', *The Sunday Guardian*, 18 January 2020, https://www.sundayguardianlive.com/opinion/need-remember-19-january-1990.

69. EFSAS, 'The Exodus of Kashmiri Pandits', European Foundation for South Asian Studies, https://www.efsas.org/publications/study-papers/the-exodus-of-kashmiri-pandits. Accessed on 14 January 2022.

70. Rekha Chowdhary, *Jammu and Kashmir: Politics of Identity and Separatism*, Routledge, New York, 2016.

71. Chaitanya Kalbag, 'Sheikh Abdullah's Hindu communalists speech in Hazratbal sets nerves jangling', *India Today*, 30 June 1982, https://www.indiatoday.in/magazine/indiascope/story/19820630-sheikh-abdullahs-hindu-communalists-speech-in-hazratbal-sets-nerves-jangling-771905-2013-10-09. Accessed on 14 January 2022.

72. Ibid.

73. Yoginder Sikand, 'The Emergence and Development of the Jama'at-i-Islami of Jammu and Kashmir, 1940s–1990', *Modern Asian Studies*, Vol. 36, No. 3, pp. 705–751, 1 July 2002, Cambridge University Press.

74. Naseer Ganai, 'JKLF Calls For Strike On Feb 9, 11 To Observe Death Anniversaries Of Afzal Guru, Maqbool Bhat', Outlook, 6 February 2020, https://www.outlookindia.com/website/story/india-news-jklf-calls-for-strike-on-feb-9-11-to-observe-death-anniversaries-of-afzal-guru-maqbool-bhat/346873. Accessed on 14 January 2022.

75. Colonel Tej K Tikoo, *Kashmir: Its Aborigines and Their Exodus*, Lancer Publishers, Atlanta, 2012, p. 397.

76. P.S. Verma, *Jammu and Kashmir at the Political Crossroads*, Vikas Publishing House, New Delhi, 1994, p. 214.

77. Paul R. Brass, *The Politics of India Since Independence*, 2nd edn. Cambridge University Press, Cambridge, 1994, pp. 221–222.

78. Sameer Arshad, 'History of electoral fraud has lessons for BJP in J&K', *The Times of India*, 22 November 2014, https://timesofindia.indiatimes.com/blogs/gray-areas/history-of-electoral-fraud-has-lessons-for-bjp-in-jk; Sten Widmalm, 'The Rise and Fall of Democracy in Jammu and Kashmir', *Asian Survey*, Vol. 37, No. 11, pp. 1005–1030, November 1997, https://doi.org/10.2307/2645738. Accessed on 14 January 2022.

79. Tej Kumar Tikoo, 'Kashmiri Pandits offered three choices by Radical Islamists', *Indian Defence Review*, 19 January 2021, http://www.indiandefencereview.com/news/kashmiri-pandits-offered-three-choices-by-radical-islamists/. Accessed on 14 January 2022.

80. J.N. Mohanty and S.K. Mohanty, 'Pakistan's Kashmir Policy, The Smoke-Screen of Fundamentalist Agenda', *The Indian Journal of Political Science*, Vol. 68, No. 1, January–March 2007, pp. 137–144, https://www.jstor.org/stable/41858826. Accessed on 14 January 2022.

81. Sumantra Bose, *Transforming India: Challenges to the World's Largest*

Democracy, Harvard University Press, Cambridge, 2013, pp. 225–286.

82. Vivek Gumaste, 'Why we need to remember 19 January 1990', *The Sunday Guardian*, 18 January 2020, https://www.sundayguardianlive.com/opinion/need-remember-19-january-1990. Accessed on 4 October 2021.

83. Rahul Pandita, *Our Moon Has Blood Clots: A Memoir of a Lost Home in Kashmir*, New Delhi, Penguin Random House, 2017.

84. Ibid.

85. Inder Malhotra, 'Mandal vs Mandir', *The Indian Express*, 23 March 2015, http://indianexpress.com/article/opinion/columns/mandal-vs-mandir/. Accessed on 14 January 2022.

CHAPTER 11: NARASIMHA RAO TURNS THE SHIP AROUND

1. P. Radhakrishnan, *India, The Perfidies of Power*, PRK Publications, Chennai, 2006, pp. 35–41.

2. Shekhar Gupta, 'The mole and the fox', *The Indian Express*, 29 July 2006 http://archive.indianexpress.com/news/the-mole-and-the-fox/9501/0. Accessed on 14 January 2022.

3. BBC, 'Alleged gun runner's conspiracy claims', BBC News, 23 July 1998, http://news.bbc.co.uk/2/hi/uk_news/138009.stm. Accessed on 14 January 2022.

4. Walter K. Andersen, 'India's 1991 Elections: The Uncertain Verdict', *Asian Survey*, Vol. 31, No. 10, October 1991, pp. 976–989, https://doi.org/10.2307/2645067. Accessed on 14 January 2022.

5. Inder Malhotra, 'Rear View: How Narasimha Rao became PM', *The Indian Express*, 6 April 2015, http://indianexpress.com/article/opinion/columns/rear-view-how-narasimha-rao-became-pm. Accessed on 14 January 2022.

6. Valerie Cerra and Sweta Chaman Saxena, 'What Caused the 1991 Currency Crisis in India?', *IMF Working Papers*, 2002, Vol. 49, No. 3, https://doi.org/10.5089/9781451857481.001. Accessed on 14 January 2022.

7. Arunabha Ghosh, 'Pathways through Financial Crisis: India', *University of Oxford, Global Economic Governance Programme*, Vol. 12, No. 4, October–December 2006, pp. 413–429, http://hdl.handle.net/10419/196269. Accessed on 14 January 2022.

8. Ibid.

9. 'Budget Speech of Shri Manmohan Singh Minister of Finance', Union Budget: Ministry of Finance, 24 July 1991, https://www.indiabudget.gov.in/doc/bspeech/bs199192.pdf. Accessed on 14 January 2022.

10. 'Celebrating 25 years of the ASEAN–India Dialogue Partnership', Ministry of External Affairs, Government of India, 28 January 2017, http://mea.gov.in/press-releases.htm?dtl/27970/Celebrating_25_years_of_the_ASEANIndia_Dialogue_Partnership. Accessed on 14 January 2022.

11. Harsh V. Pant, 'India–ASEAN partnership at 25', Observer Research Foundation, 4 July 2017, http://www.orfonline.org/research/india-asean-

partnership-at-25/. Accessed on 14 January 2022.

12. Ibid.

13. Arun Chacko, 'Chinese Premier Li Peng's India trip renews ties', *India Today*, 31 December 1991, https://www.indiatoday.in/magazine/diplomacy/story/19911231-chinese-premier-li-pengs-india-trip-renews-ties-815250-1991-12-31. Accessed on 14 January 2022.

14. Sudeep Chakravarti and Pranjal Sharma 'India–China business war hots up, Beijing ahead in investment sweepstakes', *India Today*, 30 September 1993, https://www.indiatoday.in/magazine/cover-story/story/19930930-india-china-business-war-hots-up-beijing-ahead-in-investment-sweepstakes-811579-1993-09-30. Accessed on 14 January 2022.

15. Pravin Sawhney and Ghazala Wahab, 'When Narasimha Rao visited China', *The Pioneer*, edited excerpts from *Dragon On Our Doorstep*, Aleph Book Company, New Delhi, 12 February 2017.

16. Hari Bansh Jha, 'Mahakali Treaty Outcome of Economic Nationalism', *The Himalayan Times*, 21 December 2009, https://thehimalayantimes.com/opinion/mahakali-treaty-outcome-of-economic-nationalism/. Accessed on 14 January 2022.

17. Dilip K. Das, 'The South Asian Free Trade Agreement: Evolution and Challenges', *MIT International Review*, Spring 2008, http://web.mit.edu/mitir/2008/spring/south.pdf. Accessed on 14 January 2022.

18. Aneek Chaterjee, *International Relations Today: Concepts and Applications*, Dorling Kindersley, New Delhi, 2010, pp. 217–218.

19. Albert Einstein, 'Letter From Einstein To Jawaharlal Nehru, June 13 1947', Worldpeace365, 20 April 2016, https://worldpeace365.wordpress.com/2016/04/20/letter-from-einstein-to-jawaharal-nehru/. Accessed on 14 January 2022.

20. Pinak Ranjan Chakravarty, 'When Einstein tried to convince Nehru to support Israel…but failed', Observer Research Foundation, 13 February 2017, http://www.orfonline.org/research/30081/. Accessed on 14 January 2022.

21. David Alexander, 'Arafat appeals for pressure to uphold land-for-peace principle', *UPI*, 21 January 1992, https://www.upi.com/Archives/1992/01/21/Arafat-appeals-for-pressure-to-uphold-land-for-peace-principle/7883695970000/?spt=su. Accessed on 14 January 2022.

22. Dilip Bobb, 'PM Narasimha Rao meets President Bill Clinton, talks business, plays down Kashmir', *India Today*, 15 June 1994, https://www.indiatoday.in/magazine/cover-story/story/19940615-pm-narasimha-rao-meets-president-bill-clinton-talks-business-plays-down-kashmir-809248-1994-06-15. Accessed on 14 January 2022.

23. Narain D. Batra, *The First Freedoms and America's Culture of Innovation*, Rowman & Littlefield, Lanham, Maryland, 2013.

24. Martin Luther King, Jr, *Stride Toward Freedom: The Montgomery Story*, Beacon Press, Boston, 1958, p. 84.

25. C-Span, 'India Prime Minister Address', C-Span, 18 May 1994, https://

www.c-span.org/video/?56890-1/india-prime-minister-address. Accessed on 14 January 2022.

26. Ibid.

27. Ibid.

28. Ibid.

29. Ibid.

30. Dilip Bobb, 'PM Narasimha Rao meets President Bill Clinton, talks business, plays down Kashmir', *India Today*, 15 June 1994, https://www.indiatoday.in/magazine/cover-story/story/19940615-pm-narasimha-rao-meets-president-bill-clinton-talks-business-plays-down-kashmir-809248-1994-06-15. Accessed on 14 January 2022.

31. Suma Athreye and Sandeep Kapur, 'Private Foreign Investment in India', *The World Economy*, Vol. 24, No. 3, March 2001, pp. 394–424, https://doi.org/10.1111/1467-9701.00362. Accessed on 14 January 2022.

32. AP, 'Guerrillas in Kashmir Kidnap Israelis: 3 killed in Gun Battle', *Los Angeles Times*, 28 June 1991, https://www.latimes.com/archives/la-xpm-1991-06-28-mn-1452-story.htm. Accessed on 14 January 2022.

33. Ajay Bharadwaj and Ravi Sharma, 'Indian Commandos kill hijacker, free hostages', *UPI*, 24 April 1993, https://www.upi.com/Archives/1993/04/24/Indian-commandos-kill-hijacker-free-hostages/1920735624000/. Accessed on 14 January 2022.

34. Harinder Baweja, 'Hazratbal siege raises anti-India tempo in Kashmir Valley, gives militants avoidable boost', *India Today*, 15 November 1993, https://www.indiatoday.in/magazine/cover-story/story/19931115-hazratbal-siege-raises-anti-india-tempo-in-kashmir-valley-gives-militants-avoidable-boost-811811-1993-11-15. Accessed on 14 January 2022.

35. John F. Burns, 'India Extends Emergency Powers in Kashmir', *The New York Times*, 9 August 1994, http://www.nytimes.com/1994/08/09/world/india-extends-emergency-powers-in-kashmir.html. Accessed on 14 January 2022.

36. Mark Tully, 'Tearing down the Babri Masjid', BBC, 5 December 2002, http://news.bbc.co.uk/2/hi/south_asia/2528025.stm. Accessed on 14 January 2022.

37. P.K. Gautam, 'The Upcoming Nalanda University', Institute for Defense Studies and Analyses, 31 August 2010, https://idsa.in/idsacomments/TheUpcomingNalandaUniversity_pkgautam_310810; Shashi Tharoor, 'Reconstructing Nalanda', *The Hindu*, 24 December 2006, http://www.thehindu.com/todays-paper/tp-features/tp-sundaymagazine/reconstructing-nalanda/article3232886.ece. Accessed on 27 September 2021; Amalananda Ghosh, *A Guide to Nalanda*, 5th edn., Archaeological Survey of India, New Delhi, 1965.

38. Romila Thapar, *Somanatha: The Many Voices of a History*, Penguin Books, New Delhi, 2004.

39. Legislative Department, 'The Nalanda University Act of 2010', The Ministry of Law and Justice, 22 September, 2010, http://lawmin.nic.in/ld/regionallanguages/THE%20NALANDA%20UNIVERSITY%20ACT,%20

2010%20,39%20OF%202010.pdf; Amartya Sen, 'Dr Amartya Sen's letter to Board members of Nalanda University', *The Hindu*, 19 February 2015, http://www.thehindu.com/news/resources/nalanda-university-letter-to-board-members/article6913582.ece. Accessed on 14 January 2022.

40. Vinay Sitapati, *Half-Lion: How P.V Narasimha Rao Transformed India*, Penguin Books, New Delhi, 2015, pp. 225–256.

41. Ibid.

42. Ibid.

43. Ibid. 237.

44. Sajeda Momin, 'When the last dome fell: a first-person account of the Babri Masjid demolition', *The Hindu*, 6 December 2017, http://www.thehindu.com/opinion/op-ed/when-the-last-dome-fell-a-first-person-account-of-the-babri-masjid-demolition/article21273367.ece. Accessed on 14 January 2022.

45. Chris Ogden, 'A Lasting Legacy: The BJP-led National Democratic Alliance and India's Politics', *Journal of Contemporary Asia*, Vol. 42, No. 1, February 2012, pp. 22–38, https://doi.org/10.1080/00472336.2012.634639. Accessed on 14 January 2022.

46. Suketu Mehta, *Maximum City: Bombay Lost and Found*, Alfred A. Knopf, New York, 2004, p. 81.

47. Asghar Ali Engineer, 'The Mumbai riots in historic context', *The Hindu*, 8 May 2012, http://www.thehindu.com/todays-paper/tp-features/tp-bookreview/the-mumbai-riots-in-historic-context/article3395359.ece. Accessed on 14 January 2022.

48. Meena Menon, *Riots and After in Mumbai: Chronicles of Truth and Reconciliation*, SAGE Publications, New Delhi, 2012.

49. TOI, 'Ruling on the 1993 Mumbai bomb blasts, Supreme Court sends a strong anti-terror message', *The Times of India*, 22 May 2013, https://timesofindia.indiatimes.com/home/opinion/edit-page/Ruling-on-the-1993-Mumbai-bomb-blasts-Supreme-Court-sends-a-strong-anti-terror-message/articleshow/19113142.cms?referral=PM. Accessed on 14 January 2022.

50. Edward A. Gargan, 'Indian Government Survives Parliament Vote', *The New York Times*, 29 July 1993, http://www.nytimes.com/1993/07/29/world/indian-government-survives-parliament-vote.html. Accessed on 14 January 2022.

51. N.K. Singh, 'Opposition parties accuse Narasimha Rao of bribing JMM MPs to vote in favour of govt', *India Today*, 15 March 1996, https://www.indiatoday.in/magazine/special-report/story/19960315-opposition-parties-accuse-narasimha-rao-of-bribing-jmm-mps-to-vote-in-favour-of-govt-834768-1996-03-15. Accessed on 14 January 2022.

52. S.C. Agrawal, 'Supreme Court of India: P.V. Narasimha Rao vs State (Cbi/Spe) on 17 April, 1998', iKanoon, 17 April 1998, https://indiankanoon.org/doc/1301360/. Accessed on 14 January 2022.

53. P. Radhakrishnan, *India, The Perfidies of Power*, PRK Publications, Chennai, 2006, pp. 35–41.

54. PTI, 'St Kitts case: Chronology of events', *The Times of India*, 25 October

2004, https://timesofindia.indiatimes.com/india/St-Kitts-case-Chronology-of-events/articleshow/898172.cms?referral=PM; Nirnimesh Kumar, 'Rao acquitted in Lakhubhai Pathak case', *The Hindu*, 23 December 2003 https://www.thehindu.com/todays-paper/narasimha-rao-acquitted-in-lakhubhai-pathak-case/article27817272.ece. Accessed on 14 January 2022.

55. K. Natwar Singh, 'How PV became PM', *The Hindu*, 2 July 2012, http://www.thehindu.com/opinion/op-ed/how-pv-became-pm/article3592050.ece. Accessed on 14 January 2022.

56. Vinay Sitapati, *Half-Lion: How P.V Narasimha Rao Transformed India*, Penguin Books, New Delhi, 2015, p. 2.

CHAPTER 12: ATAL BIHARI VAJPAYEE TAKES THE BULL BY THE HORNS

1. C-Span, 'Atal Bihari Vajpayee Speech in Hindi at UNGA', C-Span, 13 September 2002, https://www.c-span.org/video/?c4245212/user-clip-atal-bihari-vajpatee-speech-hindi-unga. Accessed on 14 January 2022.

2. Kingshuk Nag, *Atal Bihari Vajpayee: A Man for All Seasons*, Rupa Publications, New Delhi, 2015.

3. Election Commission of India, 'Statistical Report on General Elections, 1996 to the Eleventh Lok Sabha: Volume I', Chief Electoral Officer Madhya Pradesh, 1996, https://ceomadhyapradesh.nic.in/Links/Books/96_Vol_I.pdf. Accessed on 14 January 2022.

4. Sudha Pai, 'Transformation of the Indian Party System: The 1996 Lok Sabha Elections', *Asian Survey*, Vol. 36, No. 12, pp. 1177–1179, https://doi.org/10.2307/2645573. Accessed on 14 January 2022.

5. Ibid.

6. Anil Sharma, 'Gujral, the man behind the raw doctrine that set India behind', DNA, 1 December 2012, http://www.dnaindia.com/india/report-gujral-the-man-behind-the-raw-doctrine-that-set-india-behind-1771985. Accessed on 14 January 2022.

7. John F. Burns, '"Fodder Scam" Could Bring Down a Shaky Indian Government', *The New York Times*, 2 July 1997, https://www.nytimes.com/1997/07/02/world/fodder-scam-could-bring-down-a-shaky-indian-government.html. Accessed on 14 January 2022.

8. George Iype, 'Go easy on politicians, sensitive investigations, govt tells new CBI chief', *rediff.com*, 1997, http://www.rediff.com/news/jul/01cbi2.htm. Accessed on 14 January 2022.

9. Tara Shankar Sahay for UNI, 'Allahabad high court declares President's rule in UP "unconstitutional"', *rediff.com*, https://archive.is/20130218004307/http://www.rediff.in/news/1996/1912up.htm#selection-71.0-71.71. Accessed on 14 January 2022.

10. John F. Burns, 'Premier of India Quits, deepening political bedlam', *The New*

York Times, 29 November 1997, https://www.nytimes.com/1997/11/29/world/premier-of-india-quits-deepening-political-bedlam.html?pagewanted=all. Accessed on 14 January 2022.

11. Quoted in, IANS, 'Kesri's aim to become PM led to I.K. Gujral govt's downfall in 1997: Pranab', *Business Standard*, 14 October 2017, https://www.business-standard.com/article/current-affairs/kesri-s-aim-to-become-pm-led-to-i-k-gujral-govt-s-downfall-in-1997-pranab-117101400367_1.html. Accessed on 14 January 2022.

12. John F. Burns, 'Premier of India Quits, deepening political bedlam', *The New York Times*, 29 November 1997, https://www.nytimes.com/1997/11/29/world/premier-of-india-quits-deepening-political-bedlam.html?pagewanted=all. Accessed on 14 January 2022.

13. Bhumitra Chakma, 'Toward Pokhran II: Explaining India's Nuclearisation Process', *Modern Asian Studies*, Vol. 39, No. 1, 2005, pp. 189–236; https://doi.org/10.1017/S0026749X04001416; Sumit Ganguly, 'India's Pathway to Pokhran II: The Prospects and Sources of New Delhi's Nuclear Weapons Program', *International Security*, Vol. 23, No. 4, Spring 1999, pp. 148–177, https://www.jstor.org/stable/2539297. Accessed on 14 January 2022.

14. Raj Chengappa, *Weapons of Peace: The Secret Story of India's Quest to be a Nuclear Power*, HarperCollins Publishers, New Delhi, 2000.

15. John F. Burns, 'India Sets 3 Nuclear Blasts, Defying a Worldwide Ban; Tests Bring a Sharp Outcry', *The New York Times*, 12 May 1998, https://www.nytimes.com/1998/05/12/world/india-sets-3-nuclear-blasts-defying-a-worldwide-ban-tests-bring-a-sharp-outcry.html. Accessed on 14 January 2022.

16. Tim Weiner, 'Nuclear Anxiety: The Blunders; U.S. Blundered On Intelligence, Officials Admit', *The New York Times*, 13 May 1998, https://www.nytimes.com/1998/05/13/world/nuclear-anxiety-the-blunders-us-blundered-on-intelligence-officials-admit.html. Accessed on 14 January 2022.

17. Ibid.

18. Charan D. Wadhva, 'Costs of Economic Sanctions: Aftermath of Pokhran II', *Economic and Political Weekly*, Vol. 33, No. 26, 27 June–3 July 1998, pp. 1604–1607, https://www.jstor.org/stable/4406922?seq=1#page_scan_tab_contents. Accessed on 14 January 2022.

19. Manoj Joshi, 'China is the potential threat No. 1, says George Fernandes', *India Today*, 18 May 1998, https://www.indiatoday.in/magazine/cover-story/story/19980518-china-is-the-potential-threat-no.-1-says-george-fernandes-826430-1998-05-18. Accessed on 14 January 2022.

20. Ibid.

21. 'Nuclear Anxiety; Indian's Letter to Clinton On the Nuclear Testing', *The New York Times*, 13 May 1998, https://www.nytimes.com/1998/05/13/world/nuclear-anxiety-indian-s-letter-to-clinton-on-the-nuclear-testing.html. Accessed on 14 January 2022.

22. Carey Sublette, 'Pakistan's Nuclear Weapons Program,' The Nuclear Weapon Archive, 10 September 2001, http://nuclearweaponarchive.org/Pakistan/

PakTests.html; 'India's Nuclear Weapons Program', The Nuclear Weapon Archive, 30 March 2001, http://nuclearweaponarchive.org/India/IndiaShakti. html. Accessed on 14 January 2022.

23.   Thomas Graham Jr., 'Avoiding the Tipping Point', Arms Control Association, 1 November 2004, https://www.armscontrol.org/act/2004_11/BookReview. Accessed on 14 January 2022.

24.   Ibid.

25.   Quoted in Tishya Misra, 'John Abraham Wraps Parmanu - *The Story of Pokhran* Shoot. Here's When The Film Will Release', NDTV, 14 August 2017, https://www.ndtv.com/entertainment/john-abraham-wraps-parmanu-the-story-of-pokhran-shoot-heres-when-the-film-will-release-1737640. Accessed on 14 January 2022.

26.   George Iype, 'Vajpayee drives across the border into Pakistan and history', *rediff.com*, 20 February 1999, http://www.rediff.com/news/1999/feb/20bus1. htm. Accessed on 14 January 2022.

27.   Ibid.

28.   Ibid.

29.   USIP, 'The Lahore Declaration', United States Institute of Peace, 23 February 1999, https://www.usip.org/sites/default/files/file/resources/collections/peace_ agreements/ip_lahore19990221.pdf. Accessed on 14 January 2022.

30.   'Simla Agreement', Ministry of External Affairs, 2 July 1972, http://www.mea. gov.in/bilateral-documents.htm?dtl/5541/Simla+Agreement. Accessed on 14 January 2022.

31.   Quoted in Vikas Kapur and Vipin Narang, 'The Fate of Kashmir: International Law or Lawlessness', *Stanford Journal of International Relations*, 1 March 2006, https://web.archive.org/web/20170204135256/https://web.stanford. edu/group/sjir/3.1.06_kapur-narang.html. Accessed on 14 January 2022.

32.   Global Security, '1999 Kargil Conflict', GlobalSecurity.org, https://www. globalsecurity.org/military/world/war/kargil-99.htm. Accessed on 14 January 2022.

33.   UNI, 'Mujahideen will "not withdraw"', *rediff.com*, 5 July 1999, https://www. rediff.com/news/1999/jul/05kash5.htm. Accessed on 14 January 2022.

34.   PTI, 'India had deployed Agni during Kargil — Expert', *The Indian Express*, 19 June 2000, https://indianexpress.com/article/news-archive/india-had-deployed-agni-during-kargil-expert. Accessed on 14 January 2022.

35.   Vikas Kapur and Vipin Narang, 'The Fate of Kashmir: International Law or Lawlessness', *Stanford Journal of International Relations*, 1 March 2006, https://web.archive.org/web/20170204135256/https://web.stanford.edu/ group/sjir/3.1.06_kapur-narang.html. Accessed on 14 January 2022.

36.   Ibid.

37.   Ibid.

38.   Ibid; Jessica Stern 'Pakistan's Jihad Culture', *Foreign Affairs*, November–December 2000, https://www.foreignaffairs.com/articles/asia/2000-11-01/ pakistans-jihad-culture. Accessed on 14 January 2022.

39. 'Jayalalitha vs the BJP', *Frontline*, 25 April 1998, https://frontline.thehindu. com/politics/article30161298.ece. Accessed on 14 January 2022.

40. E. Sridharan, 'Coalition strategies and the BJP's expansion, 1989–2004', *Commonwealth and Comparative Politics*, Vol. 43, No. 2, 2005, https://doi. org/10.1080/14662040500151093. Accessed on 14 January 2022.

41. BJP, 'Elections to the 14th Lok Sabha', BJP Central Library, April–May 2004, http://library.bjp.org/jspui/bitstream/123456789/245/1/NDA%20 MANIFESTO%202004.pdf. Accessed on 14 January 2022.

42. Oliver Heath, 'Anatomy of the BJP's Rise to Power: Social, Regional and Political Expansion in 1990s', quoted in Zoya Hasan, *Parties and Party Politics in India*, Oxford India, New Delhi, 2004.

43. Election Commission of India, 'Statistical Report On General Elections, 1999 To The Thirteenth Lok Sabha: Volume I', Chief Electoral Officer Madhya Pradesh, https://ceomadhyapradesh.nic.in/Links/Books/99_Vol_I. pdf. Accessed on 14 January 2022.

44. Election Commission of India, 'Statistical Report On General Elections, 1967 To The Fourth Lok Sabha: Volume I', Chief Electoral Officer Madhya Pradesh, 1968, https://ceomadhyapradesh.nic.in/Links/Books/67_Vol_I.pdf. Accessed on 14 January 2022.

45. Bruce Riedel, *Deadly Embrace: Pakistan, America, and the Future of the Global Jihad*, The Brookings Institution, Washington DC, 2011, pp. 36–59; Celia W. Dugger, 'Hostages Land in India After Deal is Made With Hijackers, *The New York Times*, 1 January 2000, https://www.nytimes.com/2000/01/01/ world/hostages-land-in-india-after-deal-is-made-with-hijackers.html; Javed M. Ansari, 'IC-814 hijacking still haunts Jaswant Singh', *India Today*, 31 October 2013, https://www.indiatoday.in/india/story/ic-814-hijacking-still-haunts-jaswant-singh-216125-2013-10-31. Accessed on 14 January 2022.

46. BBC, 'How the 1999 Pakistan coup unfolded', BBC *News*, 23 August 2007, http://news.bbc.co.uk/2/hi/south_asia/6960670.stm. Accessed on 14 January 2022.

47. Ibid.

48. BBC, 'Musharraf wins huge backing', BBC News, 1 May 2002, http://news. bbc.co.uk/2/hi/south_asia/1961194.stm. Accessed on 14 January 2022.

49. Gaurav Kampani, 'Indo–Pakistani Military Standoff: Why It Isn't Over Yet', NTI, 31 May 2002, http://www.nti.org/analysis/articles/indo-pakistani-military-standoff/; Prof. Jayanta Kumar Ray, 'The Agra Summit', *India Quarterly: A Journal of International Affairs*, Vol. 57, No. 2, 1 April 2001, pp. 17–28, https://doi.org/10.1177/097492840105700203. Accessed on 14 January 2022.

50. Jaswant Singh, *A Call to Honour: In Service of Emergent India*, New Delhi, Rupa Publications, 2006.

51. Ibid.; also quoted in PTI, 'In Agra, there was only a draft, no agreement', *rediff.com*, 21 July 2006, https://m.rediff.com/news/2006/jul/21jaswant.htm. Accessed on 14 January 2022.

52. 'Advani admits he sabotaged Agra summit', *Dawn*, 18 March 2008, https://www.dawn.com/news/294167 quoted in L.K. Advani, *My Country, My Life*, Rupa Publications, Bombay, 2008. Accessed on 14 January 2022.

53. Bruce Riedel, 'Pakistan's Musharraf Accused of Knowing Osama bin Laden's Hideout', Brookings Institute, 14 February 2012, https://www.brookings.edu/opinions/pakistans-musharraf-accused-of-knowing-osama-bin-ladens-hideout/. Accessed on 14 January 2022.

54. J.T Vishnu, 'ISI supervised Parliament attack', *The Tribune*, 16 December 2001, http://www.tribuneindia.com/2001/20011217/main1.htm. Accessed on 14 January 2022.

55. BBC, '2001: Suicide attack on Indian parliament', BBC News, 13 December 2001, http://news.bbc.co.uk/onthisday/hi/dates/stories/december/13/newsid_3695000/3695057.stm; Harish Khare, 'Suicide squad storms Parliament; 5 militants killed; Army deployed', *The Hindu*, 14 December 2001, https://www.thehindu.com/todays-paper/suicide-squad-storms-parliament-5-militants-killed-army-deployed/article27991489.ece. Accessed on 14 January 2022.

56. PTI, 'Omar Abdullah slams Afzal Guru's hanging, says long-term implications "far more worrying"', *The Times of India*, 10 February 2013, http://timesofindia.indiatimes.com/articleshow/18432035.cms?utm_source=contentofinterest&utm_medium=text&utm_campaign=cppst. Accessed on 14 January 2022.

57. Arundhati Roy, '"And His Life Should Become Extinct": The Very Strange Story of the Attack on the Indian Parliament', *Revolutionary Democracy*, http://www.revolutionarydemocracy.org/afzal/afzal13.htm; 'India's shame', *The Guardian*, 15 December 2006, https://www.theguardian.com/world/2006/dec/15/india.kashmir. Accessed on 14 January 2022.

58. PTI, 'POT Bill passed by joint session of Parliament', *rediff.com*, 26 March 2002, http://www.rediff.com/news/2002/mar/26poto7.htm. Accessed on 14 January 2022.

59. 'Who will strike first?' *The Economist*, 20 December 2001, https://www.economist.com/asia/2001/12/20/who-will-strike-first. Accessed on 14 January 2022.

60. BBC, 'Musharraf declares war on extremism', BBC News, 12 January 2002, http://news.bbc.co.uk/2/hi/south_asia/1756965.stm. Accessed on 14 January 2022.

61. Steve Coll, 'The Standoff', *The New Yorker*, 5 February 2006, https://www.newyorker.com/magazine/2006/02/13/the-stand-off. Accessed on 14 January 2022.

62. Aditi Phadnis, 'Parakaram cost put at Rs 6,500 crore', *rediff.com*, 16 January 2003, http://www.rediff.com/money/2003/jan/16defence.htm. Accessed on 14 January 2022.

63. Joseph Conrad, *Great Short Works of Joseph Conrad*, Harper & Row, New York, 1966, p. 279.

64. 'Report of Forensic Science Labouratory, State of Gujarat', *Outlook*, 22 November 2002, https://www.outlookindia.com/website/story/report-of-forensic-science-labouratory-state-of-gujarat/218028. Accessed on 14 January 2022.

65. Uday Mahurkar, 'Godhra carnage a conspiracy: Nanavati report', *India Today*, 27 September 2008, https://www.indiatoday.in/latest-headlines/story/godhra-carnage-a-conspiracy-nanavati-report-30580-2008-09-27. Accessed on 14 January 2022.

66. 'Excerpt from the Justice U.C. Banerjee Committee report', *DNA*, 3 March 2006, http://www.dnaindia.com/india/report-excerpts-from-the-justice-u-c-banerjee-committee-report-1016092. Accessed on 14 January 2022.

67. M. Shah, 'Union of India (Uoi) vs Nilkanth Tulsidas Bhatia And 7... 20 March, 2006', https://indiankanoon.org/doc/892047/; Manas Dasgupta, 'Bannerjee Committee illegal: High Court', *The Hindu*, 14 October 2006, https://www.thehindu.com/todays-paper/bannerjee-committee-illegal-high-court/article3060882.ece. Accessed on 14 January 2022.

68. Christophe Jaffrelot, 'Gujarat 2002: What Justice for the Victims?', *Economic & Political Weekly*, 25 February 2012, Vol. 47, No. 8, pp. 77–80, https://www.epw.in/journal/2012/08/special-articles/gujarat-2002-what-justice-victims.html. Accessed on 14 January 2022.

69. Ashish Vashi, 'Gandhi-Jinnah, Hindu-Muslim: Godhra created many rifts', *DNA India*, 18 February 2012, https://www.dnaindia.com/india/report-gandhi-jinnah-hindu-muslim-godhra-created-many-rifts-1651743. Accessed on 4 February 2022.

70. Satish Jha, 'Court says of Gulberg massacre victim Jafri: His firing angered mob, made them kill', *The Indian Express*, 18 June 2016, https://indianexpress.com/article/india/india-news-india/11-get-life-for-gulberg-society-massacre-in-which-jafri-68-killed-2859387/. Accessed on 14 January 2022.

71. Smita Narula, 'Compounding Injustice: The Government's Failure to Redress Massacres in Gujarat', Human Rights Watch, 30 June 2003, https://www.hrw.org/report/2003/06/30/compounding-injustice/governments-failure-redress-massacres-gujarat. Accessed on 14 January 2022.

72. BBC, 'Gujarat riot death toll revealed', BBC News, 11 May 2005, http://news.bbc.co.uk/2/hi/south_asia/4536199.stm. Accessed on 14 January 2022.

73. CCT, 'Concerned Citizens Tribunal-Gujarat 2002: An inquiry into the carnage in Gujarat', Citizens for Justice and Peace, https://www.sabrang.com/tribunal/; Christophe Jaffrelot, 'Communal Riots in Gujarat: The State at Risk?', *Heidelberg Papers in South Asian and Comparative Politics*, July 2003, http://archiv.ub.uni-heidelberg.de/volltextserver/4127/1/hpsacp17.pdf. Accessed on 14 January 2022.

74. Sanjay Pandey, 'Riots hit all classes, people of all faith', *The Times of India*, 17 March 2002, https://timesofindia.indiatimes.com/city/ahmedabad/Riots-hit-all-classes-people-of-all-faith/articleshow/4007683.cms. Accessed on 14 January 2022.

75. Smita Narula, 'Compounding Injustice: The Government's Failure to Redress Massacres in Gujarat', Human Rights Watch, 30 June 2003, https://www.hrw.org/report/2003/06/30/compounding-injustice/governments-failure-redress-massacres-gujarat. Accessed on 14 January 2022.

76. Uday Mahurkar, 'Gujarat riots: As death toll rises, CM Narendra Modi's image hits a new low', *India Today*, 20 May 2002, https://www.indiatoday.in/magazine/states/story/20020520-gujarat-riots-as-death-toll-rises-cm-narendra-modi-image-hits-a-new-low-795273-2002-05-20. Accessed on 14 January 2022.

77. Laurent Gayer and Christophe Jaffrelot, *Muslims in Indian Cities: Trajectories of Marginalisation*, Columbia University Press, New York, 2012, pp. 53–60.

78. Ashutosh Varshney, 'Understanding Gujarat Violence', *Items & Issues,* Vol. 4, No. 1, winter 2002–3, https://items.ssrc.org/from-our-archives/understanding-gujarat-violence/. Accessed on 14 January 2022.

79. Christophe Jaffrelot, *India's Silent Revolution: The Rise of the Lower Castes in North India*, C Hurst & Co, London, 2003, pp. 325–326.

80. Ramachandra Guha, *India After Gandhi: The History of the World's Largest Democracy*, Picador India, 2017, pp. 624–650.

81. Andy Marino, *Narendra Modi: A Political Biography*, HarperCollins Publishers, New Delhi, 2014, pp. 103–146.

82. Manas Dasgupta, 'No evidence of Modi promoting enmity: SIT', *The Hindu*, 9 May 2012, https://www.thehindu.com/news/national/no-evidence-of-modi-promoting-enmsity-sit/article3398456.ece. Accessed on 14 January 2022.

83. Ibid.

84. Siddharth Varadarajan, 'Let Us Not Forget the Glimpse We Got of the Real Vajpayee When the Mask Slipped', *The Wire*, 18 August 2018, https://thewire.in/politics/let-us-not-forget-the-glimpse-we-got-of-the-real-vajpayee-when-the-mask-slipped. Accessed on 14 January 2022.

85. Jeffrey Tayler, 'India's Grand Trunk Road', *The Atlantic*, November 1999, https://www.theatlantic.com/magazine/archive/1999/11/indias-grand-trunk-road/377875; K.M. Sarkar, *The Grand Trunk Road in the Punjab: 1849–1886*, Atlantic Publishers & Distributors, 1927; Amrita Chaudhry, 'Cracks on a historic highway', *The Indian Express*, 27 May 2012, http://archive.indianexpress.com/news/cracks-on-a-historical-highway/954273/0. Accessed on 14 January 2022.

86. Republic of India, 'Rural Road Development in India: An assessment of distribution of PMGSY project benefits in three states by gender and ascribed social groups', *South Asia Sustainable Development Unit, World Bank*, 12 June 2014, https://documents1.worldbank.org/curated/en/970911468041343268/pdf/AUS54870ESW0wh085260B000PUBLIC00ACS.pdf. Accessed on 14 January 2022.

87. 'Pradhan Mantri Gram Sadak Yojana—(PMGSY)', Rural Works Department, Government of Bihar, https://rwdbihar.gov.in/SchemePMGSY.aspx. Accessed on 14 January 2022.

88. Ibid.

89. B.N. Puri, 'Private Sector Participation in the Transport Sector in India', Transport and Communications Bulletin for Asia and the Pacific, No. 73, 2003, https://www.unescap.org/sites/default/files/bulletin73_Article-3.pdf. Accessed on 14 January 2022.

90. Amy Waldman, 'Mile by Mile, India Paves a Smoother Road to Its Future', *The New York Times*, 4 December 2005, https://www.nytimes.com/2005/12/04/world/asia/mile-by-mile-india-paves-a-smoother-road-to-its-future.html. Accessed on 14 January 2022.

91. 'New Telecom Policy, 1999', Department of Telecommunications, http://www.dot.gov.in/new-telecom-policy-1999; Arvind Panagariya, *India: The Emerging Giant*, Oxford University Press, New York, 2008, pp. 370–395; Arvind Panagariya, 'India's Trade Reform', Brookings Institute, 2004, https://www.brookings.edu/wp-content/uploads/2016/07/2004_panagariya.pdf. Accessed on 14 January 2022; Rajeev Mantri and Harsh Gupta, 'The story of India's telecom revolution', *Mint*, 8 January 2013, https://www.livemint.com/Opinion/biNfQImaeobXxOPV6pFxqI/The-story-of-Indias-telecom-revolution.html. Accessed on 14 January 2022.

92. Steve Coll, *The Deal of the Century: The Breakup of AT&T*, Atheneum, New York, 1986.

93. Shobhaa De quoted in Celia W. Dugger, 'Clinton Fever: A Delighted India Has All the Symptoms', *The New York Times*. 23 March 2000, https://www.nytimes.com/2000/03/23/world/clinton-fever-a-delighted-india-has-all-the-symptoms.html. Accessed on 14 January 2022.

94. Media Reports, 'Make "new economy" useful for "infotech have-nots": Clinton', *rediff.com*, 24 March 2000, https://www.rediff.com/business/2000/mar/24usprez.htm. Accessed on 14 January 2022.

95. Office of the Press Secretary, 'The President's Trip to South Asia', The White House, 24 March 2000, https://clintonwhitehouse4.archives.gov/WH/New/SouthAsia/speeches/20000324_3.html. Accessed on 14 January 2022.

96. 'President Clinton's Visit to South Asia', Acronym Institute of Disarmament Diplomacy, 20–25 March 2000, http://www.acronym.org.uk/old/archive/spvisit.htm. Accessed on 14 January 2022.

97. 'US-China Competition in the Indo-Pacific', Rand Project Air Force, https://www.rand.org/paf/projects/us-china-competition.html. Accessed on 14 January 2022.

98. Ibid.

99. Ibid.

100. Peter Symonds, 'Clinton visit to the Indian subcontinent sets a new strategic orientation', The International Committee of the Fourth International, 23 March 2000, https://www.wsws.org/en/articles/2000/03/ind-m23.html. Accessed on 3 October 2021.

101. Sukumar Muralidharan, 'Clinton's Yatra', *Frontline*, 1 April 2000, https://frontline.thehindu.com/cover-story/article30253641.ece. Accessed on 14

January 2022.

102. ET, 'When Atal Bihari Vajpayee exposed China's designs with a flock of sheep', *The Economic Times*, 5 July 2017, https://economictimes.indiatimes. com/news/politics-and-nation/when-atal-behari-vajpayee-exposed-chinas-designs-with-a-flock-of-sheep/articleshow/59453326.cms; Claude Arpi, 'A World War over some sheep and a few Yaks?', Indian Defence Review, 3 July 2017, http://www.indiandefencereview.com/a-world-war-over-some-sheeps-and-a-few-yaks/. Accessed on 14 January 2022.

103. Brahma Chellaney, 'Vajpayee kowtows to China', *The Japan Times*, 8 July 2003, https://www.japantimes.co.jp/opinion/2003/07/08/commentary/vajpayee-kowtows-to-china/#.W1cilC2ZOCd. Accessed on 14 January 2022.

104. 'Indo-China Joint Declaration', *Outlook*, 1 January 1970, https://www. outlookindia.com/website/story/indo-china-joint-declaration/220531. Accessed on 14 January 2022.

105. G. Parthasarathy, 'Vajpayee visit—Foreign policy lessons from China', *The Hindu Business Line*, 18 July 2003, https://bit.ly/3J64lM3. Accessed on 14 January 2022.

106. Ibid.

107. Ibid.

108. Surjit Mansingh, 'India–China Relations in the Context of Vajpayee's 2003 Visit', The Elliot School of International Relations, https://www2.gwu. edu/~sigur/assets/docs/scap/SCAP21-Mansingh.pdf. Accessed on 14 January 2022.

109. Gary Kitchener, 'How will history remember Vajpayee?', BBC News, 30 December 2005, http://news.bbc.co.uk/2/hi/south_asia/3715315.stm. Accessed on 14 January 2022.

110. Ibid.

111. Staff Reporter, 'Sonia questions 'India shining' slogan', *The Hindu*, 25 January 2004, https://www.thehindu.com/todays-paper/tp-national/tp-newdelhi/sonia-questions-india-shining-slogan/article27555548.ece. Accessed on 14 January 2022.

112. Mark Tully, 'India's ruling party may rue poll slogan', BBC News, 25 February 2004, http://news.bbc.co.uk/2/hi/south_asia/3518029.stm. Accessed on 14 January 2022.

113. Roderick M. Hills Jr, 'The Political Economy of Cooperative Federalism: Why State Autonomy Makes Sense and "Dual Sovereignty" Doesn't', *Michigan Law Review*, 1998, Vol. 96, No. 4, https://repository.law.umich.edu/mlr/vol96/iss4/2. Accessed on 14 January 2022.

114. Election Commission of India, 'Statistical Report On General Elections, 1996 To The Fourteenth Lok Sabha Volume I', Chief Electoral Officer Madhya Pradesh, https://ceomadhyapradesh.nic.in/Links/Books/2004_Vol_I.pdf. Accessed on 14 January 2022.

115. '2004: Sensex on a roller coaster ride', *rediff.com*, 12 January 2005, https://www. rediff.com/money/2005/jan/12market.htm. Accessed on 14 January 2022.

116. Amy Waldman, 'Sikh Who Saved India's Economy Is Named Premier', *The New York Times*, 20 May 2004, https://www.nytimes.com/2004/05/20/world/sikh-who-saved-india-s-economy-is-named-premier.html. Accessed on 14 January 2022.

117. 'GDP Growth Rate of India (Constant Prices) during 2001–02 to 2013–14', community.data.gov.in, 4 February 2015, https://community.data.gov.in/gdp-growth-rate-of-india-constant-prices-during-2001-02-to-2013-14/. Accessed on 14 January 2022.

118. ET, 'Atal Bihari Vajpayee's five steps that changed India forever', *The Economic Times*, 25 December 2017, https://economictimes.indiatimes.com/news/politics-and-nation/atal-bihari-vajpayees-five-steps-that-changed-india-forever/articleshow/62240161.cms?from=mdr. Accessed on 14 January 2022.

CHAPTER 13: RISE OF THE SIKH GENTLEMAN AS PRIME MINISTER

1. Celia W. Dugger, 'Gandhi's Choices: Be Indian, and Lead Party', *The New York Times*, 25 May 1999, https://www.nytimes.com/1999/05/25/world/gandhi-s-choices-be-indian-and-lead-party.html. Accessed on 11 January 2022.

2. A.P.J. Abdul Kalam, *Turning Points: A Journey Through Challenges*, HarperCollins, New Delhi, 2012, p. 135; PTI, 'Abdul Kalam was ready to swear Sonia Gandhi in as PM in 2004', *The Times of India*, 30 June 2012, http://timesofindia.indiatimes.com/articleshow/14530068.cms?utm_source=contentofinterest&utm_medum=text&utm_campaign=cppst; Vembu, 'Sonia-as-PM in 2004: Has Kalam backtracked or is Swamy wrong?' *FirstPost*, 30 June 2012, https://www.firstpost.com/politics/sonia-as-pm-in-2004-has-kalam-backtracked-or-is-swamy-wrong-362466.html. Accessed on 11 January 2022.

3. Ibid.

4. Sanjaya Baru, *The Accidental Prime Minister: The Making and Unmaking of Manmohan Singh*, Penguin Random House, New Delhi, 2014.

5. Ibid. 3.

6. Ibid.

7. Amy Waldman, 'Sikh Who Saved India's Economy Is Named Premier', *The New York Times*, 20 May 2004, https://www.nytimes.com/2004/05/20/world/sikh-who-saved-india-s-economy-is-named-premier.html. Accessed on 11 January 2022.

8. 'UPA Government to adhere to six basic principles of governance', *The Hindu*, 28 May 2004, https://www.thehindu.com/todays-paper/tp-national/upa-government-to-adhere-to-six-basic-principles-of-governance/article27618381.ece. Accessed on 11 January 2022.

9. Ibid.

10. Ibid.

11. Saisuresh Sivaswamy, 'It's an attack on the prime ministership, no less', *rediff.*

com, 21 August 2007, https://www.rediff.com/news/2007/aug/21sai.htm. Accessed on 11 January 2022.

12. Mark Tully, 'Manmohan Singh: Architect of the New India', *The Sikh Times,* 14 November 2005, http://www.sikhtimes.com/bios_111405a.html. Accessed on 11 January 2022.

13. Statistics Times, 'GDP Growth of India,' Statistics Times, 8 March 2017, http://statisticstimes.com/economy/gdp-growth-of-india.php; 'India's GDP clocked 9% in 2008,' *rediff.com,* 16 February 2009, http://www.rediff.com/money/2009/feb/16bud-india-gdp-grows.htm; Deepak Lalwani, 'India Report,' Astaire Research, 21 May 2010, http://www.fullertreacymoney.com/system/data/images/archive/2010-05-24/21May2010IndiaReport.pdf. Accessed on 4 February 2022.

14. 'India joins trillion dollar club,' *The Hindu,* 27 April 2007, https://www.thehindu.com/todays-paper/tp-business/India-joins-trillion-dollar-club/article14755476.ece. Accessed on 11 January 2022.

15. 'Speech by Prime Minister Dr Manmohan Singh at India Today Conclave, New Delhi,' Ministry of External Affairs, 25 February 2005, https://www.mea.gov.in/Speeches-Statements.htm?dtl/2464/. Accessed on 29 September 2021.

16. Deoki Nandan, 'National Rural Health Mission: Turning into Reality,' *Indian Journal of Community Medicine,* October–December 2010, Vol. 35, No. 4, pp. 453–454, https://www.ncbi.nlm.nih.gov/pmc/articles/PMC3026119/. Accessed on 29 September 2021.

17. Government of India, 'Update on the ASHA Programme,' Ministry of Health & Family Welfare, January 2015, https://nhsrcindia.org/sites/default/files/2021-03/Update%20on%20ASHA%20Programme%20January%202015.pdf. Accessed on 14 January 2022.

18. Y. Balarajan, S. Selvaraj and S.V. Subramanian, 'Health care and equity in India,' *The Lancet,* 5 February 2011, Vol. 377, No. 9764, pp. 505–515. https://doi.org/10.1016/S0140-6736(10)61894-6. Accessed on 14 January 2022.

19. Jayakrishnan Thayyil and Mathummal Cherumanalil Jeeja, 'Issues of Creating a new Cadre of Doctors for Rural India,' *International Journal of Medicine and Public Health,* January 2013, Vol. 3, No. 1, http://ijmedph.org/article/50; Sabitri Dutta and Kaushik Lahiri, 'Is Provision of Healthcare Sufficient to Ensure Better Access? An Exploration of the Scope for Public-Private Partnership in India,' *International Journal of Health Policy and Management,* Vol. 4, No. 7, pp. 467–474, http://ijhpm.com/article_3006_616.html. Accessed on 14 January 2022.

20. N.S. Gehlot, *Current Trends in Indian Politics,* Deep & Deep Publications, Delhi, 1998, pp. 264–265.

21. Ramachandra Guha, *India After Gandhi: The History of the World's Largest Democracy,* Picador India, 2017, pp. 602–604; Shriram Maheshwari, *The Mandal Commission and Mandalisation: A Critique,* Concept Publishing Company, Delhi, 1991, pp. 18–26.

22. Aparna Ramamoorthy, 'Case Analysis: Indra Sawhney v. Union of India (1993),'

Legal Bites: Law and Beyond, 24 May 2020, https://www.legalbites.in/case-analysis-indra-sawhney-india-1993/. Accessed on 14 January 2022.

23. 'PA Inamdar & others Vs State of Maharashtra', Academics–India, http://www.academics-india.com/Inamdar%20case.htm. Accessed on 14 January 2022.

24. V. Venkatesan, 'Turning the clock back', *Frontline*, 9 September 2005, https://frontline.thehindu.com/the-nation/education/article30206219.ece. Accessed on 14 January 2022.

25. T.K. Viswanathan, 'The Constitution (Ninety-Third Amendment) Act, 2005', National Portal of India, Government of India, 20 January 2006, https://www.india.gov.in/my-government/constitution-india/amendments/constitution-india-ninety-third-amendment-act-2005. Accessed on 14 January 2022.

26. J. Venkatesan, 'Supreme Court upholds law for 27% OBC quota', *The Hindu*, 11 April 2008, https://www.thehindu.com/todays-paper/Supreme-Court-upholds-law-for-27-OBC-quota/article15201598.ece. Accessed on 14 January 2022.

27. Neena Vyas and Anita Joshua, 'Dual citizenship Bill passed', *The Hindu*, 23 December 2003, https://www.thehindu.com/todays-paper/dual-citizenship-bill-passed/article27817270.ece. Accessed on 29 September 2021.

28. 'The Citizenship (Amendment) Act, 2003', PRS Legislative Research, 7 January 2004, https://prsindia.org/files/bills_acts/acts_parliament/2003/the-citizenship-(amendment)-act-2003.pdf. Accessed on 14 January 2022.

29. Frances Zelazny, 'The Evolution of India's UID Program: Lessons Learned and Implications for Other Developing Countries', CGD Policy Paper 008, Centre for Global Development, August 2012, http://www.cgdev.org/content/publications/detail/1426371. Accessed on 14 January 2022.

30. Shankkar Aiyar, *Aadhaar: A Biometric History of India's 12-Digit Revolution*, Westland Publications Ltd, New Delhi, 2017.

31. K. Balchand, 'UID number gets brand name, logo', *The Hindu*, 26 April 2010, https://www.thehindu.com/news/national/UID-number-gets-brand-name-logo/article16372787.ece?ref=relatedNews. Accessed on 29 September 2021.

32. Amruta Byatnal, 'Tembhli becomes first Aadhar village in India', *The Hindu*, https://www.thehindu.com/news/national/Tembhli-becomes-first-Aadhar-village-in-India/article13673162.ece. Accessed 29 September 2021

33. Nandan Nilekani and Viral Shah, *Rebooting India: Realizing a Billion Aspirations*, Penguin Random House, New Delhi, 2015, p. 2.

34. Ibid.

35. Ibid.

36. TNS, 'Cash transfer of subsidies in 51 districts begins on Jan 1', *The Tribune*, 25 November 2012, https://www.tribuneindia.com/2012/20121125/main1.htm; Prasad Sanyal, 'PM launches Aadhar-based direct cash transfers in 51 districts of India', NDTV, 26 November 2012, https://www.ndtv.com/india-news/pm-launches-aadhar-based-direct-cash-transfers-in-51-districts-of-india-505663. Accessed on 14 January 2022.

37. Trisha Ray, '6 Years of Digital India: How successful has PM Modi's plan been?', Observer Research Foundation, 2 July 2021, https://www.orfonline.

org/research/6-years-of-digital-india-how-successful-has-pm-modis-plan-been/. Accessed on 14 January 2022.

38. Nandan Nilekani quoted in Rohin Dharmakumar, Seema Singh and N.S. Ramnath, 'How Nandan Nilekani Took Aadhaar Past The Tipping Point,' *Forbes*, 8 October 2013, http://www.forbesindia.com/article/big-bet/how-nandan-nilekani-took-aadhaar-past-the-tipping-point/36259/0. Accessed on 14 January 2022.

39. A. Sikri, 'Justice K.S. Puttaswamy (Retd) vs. Union of India on 26 September, 2018', iKanoon, https://indiankanoon.org/doc/127517806/. Accessed on 14 January 2022.

40. J. Venkatesan, 'Aadhaar infringes privacy', *The Hindu*, 23 September 2013, https://www.thehindu.com/news/national/aadhaar-infringes-privacy/article5160686.ece. Accessed on 29 September 2021.

41. Nandan Nilekani, 'Data to the People: India's Inclusive Internet', *Foreign Affairs*, September/October Issue, 2018, https://www.foreignaffairs.com/articles/asia/2018-08-13/data-people. Accessed on 14 January 2022.

42. Government of India, 'Annual Report 2012–2013', Ministry of Rural Development, Government of India, https://rural.nic.in/sites/default/files/MoRDEnglish_AR2012_13_0.pdf; 'The Mahatma Gandhi National Rural Employment Guarantee Act, 2005', Ministry of Rural Development, Government of India, https://nrega.nic.in/amendments_2005_2018.pdf. Accessed on 14 January 2022.

43. 'Report of the Comptroller and Auditor General of India on Performance Audit of Mahatma Gandhi National Rural Employment Guarantee Scheme', Ministry of Rural Development, Government of India, 2013, No. 6, https://cag.gov.in/cag_old/sites/default/files/audit_report_files/Union_Performance_Civil_Ministry_Rural_Development_6_2013.pdf. Accessed on 14 January 2022.

44. Ibid. 129–138.

45. PTI, 'Manmohan directs Planning Commission to address gaps in NREGA', *The Hindu*, 14 July 2002, https://www.thehindu.com/news/national/manmohan-directs-planning-commission-to-address-gaps-in-nrega/article3639426.ece. Accessed on 29 September 2021; Mihir Shah, ed., '"MGNREGA Sameeksha 2012": An anthology of research studies on the Mahatma Gandhi National Rural Employment Guarantee Act (2006-2012)—A report by the Ministry of Rural Development', Ministry of Rural Development, Government of India, 8 August 2012, https://www.indiawaterportal.org/articles/mgnrega-sameeksha-2012-anthology-research-studies-mahatma-gandhi-national-rural-employment. Accessed on 14 January 2022.

46. Government of India, 'Synopses of Agreements/Protocols/MOUs signed during visit of Chinese President Hu Jintao to India, (November 20–23, 2006)', Ministry of External Affairs, 21 November 2006, https://www.mea.gov.in/press-releases.htm?dtl/7426/Synopses+of+Agreements

+Protocols+MOUs+signed+during+; https://www.mea.gov.in/bilateral-documents.htm?dtl/6363/Joint+Declaration+by+the+Republic+of+India+an. Accessed on 14 January 2022.

47. ORF, 'An Assessment of President Hu's visit to India,' Observer Research Foundation, December 2006, https://www.orfonline.org/wp-content/uploads/2006/12/IssueBrief_7.pdf. Accessed on 14 January 2022.

48. Jabin T. Jacob, 'Manmohan Singh's Visit to China: New Challenges Ahead,' *Sage Publications: China Report*, 1 February 2008, Vol. 44, No. 1, pp. 63–70, https://doi.org/10.1177%2F000944550704400109. Accessed on 14 January 2022.

49. Jim Yardley and Somini Sengupta, 'Two Giants Try to Learn to Share Asia,' *The New York Times*, 13 January 2008, https://www.nytimes.com/2008/01/13/world/asia/13singh.html. Accessed on 14 January 2022.

50. Government of India, 'Speech by Prime Minister Dr Manmohan Singh at the Chinese Academy of Sciences, Beijing,' Ministry of External Affairs, 15 January 2008, https://mea.gov.in/outoging-visit-detail.htm?1445/Speech+by+Prime+Minister+Dr+Manmohan+Singh+at+the+Chinese+Academy+of+Social+Sciences+Beijing. Accessed on 14 January 2022.

51. Ibid.

52. 'Chinese PM Wen Jiabao begins bumper Indian trade trip,' BBC News, 15 December 2010, https://www.bbc.com/news/world-south-asia-11997221. Accessed on 14 January 2022.

53. PTI, 'China wants to deepen strategic cooperation with India: Hu Jintao,' *The Economic Times*, 30 March 2012, https://economictimes.indiatimes.com/news/politics-and-nation/china-wants-to-deepen-strategic-cooperation-with-india-hu-jintao/articleshow/12469429.cms. Accessed on 14 January 2022.

54. 'India Prime Minister Address,' C-Span, 19 July 2005, https://www.c-span.org/video/?187688-1/indian-prime-minister-address; 'There is much we can accomplish together,' *rediff.com*, 19 July 2005, https://www.rediff.com/news/2005/jul/19pmspeech.htm. Accessed on 14 January 2022.

55. 'Joint Statement Between President George W. Bush and Prime Minister Manmohan Singh,' The White House, 18 July 2005, https://georgewbush-whitehouse.archives.gov/news/releases/2005/07/20050718-6.html. Accessed on 29 September 2021. Accessed on 14 January 2022.

56. 'Interview: Indian Prime Minister Singh,' *The Washington Post*, 20 July 2005, http://www.washingtonpost.com/wp-dyn/content/article/2005/07/20/AR2005072001916.html. Accessed on 14 January 2022.

57. Ashley J. Tellis, 'Atoms for War?: U.S.–Indian Civilian Nuclear Cooperation and India's Nuclear Arsenal,' Carnegie Endowment for International Peace, 27 June 2006, http://carnegieendowment.org/files/atomsforwarfinal4.pdf. Accessed on 29 September 2021.

58. R. Nicholas Burns, 'Remarks as Prepared for the House International Relations

Committee Hearing, *The U.S. and India: An Emerging Entente?*, Washington, DC, 8 September 2005, quoted in Ashley J. Tellis, 'Atoms for War?: U.S.-Indian Civilian Nuclear Cooperation and India's Nuclear Arsenal', Carnegie Endowment for International Peace, 27 June 2006, http://carnegieendowment. org/files/atomsforwarfinal4.pdf. Accessed on 14 January 2022.

59. Ashley J. Tellis, 'Atoms for War?: U.S.-Indian Civilian Nuclear Cooperation and India's Nuclear Arsenal', Carnegie Endowment for International Peace, 27 June 2006, http://carnegieendowment.org/files/atomsforwarfinal4.pdf.

60. Sheela Bhatt, 'PM wants to quit over nuclear deal', *rediff.com*, 19 June 2008, http://www.rediff.com/news/2008/jun/19pm.htm. Accessed on 14 January 2022.

61. Somini Sengupta, 'Indian Government Survives Confidence Vote', *The New York Times*, 23 July 2008, https://www.nytimes.com/2008/07/23/world/asia/23india.html?_r=1&ref=world&oref=slogin. Accessed on 14 January 2022.

62. 'Frequently Asked Questions and Answers on Civil Liability for Nuclear Damage Act 2010 and related issues', Ministry of External Affairs, Government of India, 8 February 2015, https://www.mea.gov.in/press-releases.htm?dtl/24766/Frequently_Asked_Questions_and_Answers_on_Civil_Liability_for_Nuclear_Damage_Act_2010_and_related_issues; Rina Chandran, 'ANALYSIS-Land, liability bill keep India nuclear power in dark', Reuters, 1 April 2010, https://in.reuters.com/article/idINIndia-47381720100401; Government of India, 'The Civil Liability for Nuclear Damage Bill of 2010', PRS Legislative Research, 2010, https://prsindia.org/files/bills_acts/acts_parliament/2010/the-civil-liability-for-nuclear-damage-act,-2010.pdf. Accessed on 14 January 2022.

63. George Iype, 'The world needs India: Bush', *rediff.com*, 3 March 2006, https://www.rediff.com/money/2006/mar/03bush2.htm. Accessed on 29 September 2021.

64. Ashley J. Tellis, 'Manmohan Singh Visits Washington: Sustaining U.S.–Indian Cooperation Amid Differences', Carnegie Endowment for International Peace, November 2009, https://carnegieendowment.org/files/singh_visits_washington.pdf. Accessed on 29 September 2021.

65. Stephen P. Cohen and Sunil Dasgupta, 'Arms Sales for India: How Military Trade Could Energize U.S.–Indian Relations', *Foreign Affairs*, March–April 2011, https://web.archive.org/web/20110303220832/http://www.foreignaffairs.com:80/articles/67462/sunil-dasgupta-and-stephen-p-cohen/arms-sales-for-india. Accessed on 29 September 2021.

66. The White House, 'Remarks by the President to the Joint Session of the Indian Parliament in New Delhi, India', The White House, 8 November 2010, https://obamawhitehouse.archives.gov/the-press-office/2010/11/08/remarks-president-joint-session-indian-parliament-new-delhi-india. Accessed on 29 September 2021.

67. PTI, 'Say no to Bangalore, yes to Buffalo: Obama', *The Economic Times*,

5 May 2009, https://economictimes.indiatimes.com/tech/ites/say-no-to-bangalore-yes-to-buffalo-obama/articleshow/4484596.cms. Accessed on 14 January 2022.

68. Government of India, 'Joint Statement issued after the conclusion of U.S.–India Strategic Dialogue,' Ministry of External Affairs, 3 June 2010, https://mea.gov.in/bilateral-documents.htm?dtl/4119/Joint+Statement+issued+after+the+conclusion+of+US++India+Strategic+Dialogue. Accessed on 14 January 2022.

69. Government of India, 'India-Russia Relations,' Ministry of External Affairs, January 2014, http://www.mea.gov.in/Portal/CountryQuickLink/597_Russia_January_2014.pdf. Accessed on 14 January 2022.

70. Vladimir Radyuhin, 'Russia has stood by us: Manmohan,' *The Hindu*, 23 October 2013, https://www.thehindu.com/news/national/russia-has-stood-by-us-manmohan/article5261967.ece. Accessed on 29 September 2021.

71. Vladimir Putin, 'For Russia, deepening friendship with India is a top foreign policy priority,' *The Hindu*, 24 December 2012, https://www.thehindu.com/opinion/op-ed/for-russia-deepening-friendship-with-india-is-a-top-foreign-policy-priority/article4232857.ece. Accessed on 14 January 2022.

72. Ibid.

73. SATP, 'Joint Statement-Meeting between Prime Minister Dr Manmohan Singh and Pakistan President Mr Pervez Musharraf,' Institute for Conflict Management, 24 September 2004, http://www.satp.org/satporgtp/countries/india/document/papers/INDO-PAK_24Sep2004.htm. Accessed on 14 January 2022.

74. Michael Krepon, 'South Asia Confidence-Building Measures (CBM) Timeline,' Stimson, 14 April 2017, https://www.stimson.org/content/south-asia-confidence-building-measures-cbm-timeline. Accessed on 14 January 2022.

75. Stuart Croft, 'South Asia's Arms Control Process: Cricket Diplomacy and the Composite Dialogue,' *International Affairs*, Vol. 81, No. 5, October 2005, pp. 1039–1060, https://www.jstor.org/stable/3569074?seq=1#page_scan_tab_contents. Accessed on 14 January 2022.

76. Guardian Staff and agencies, 'Musharraf offers Kashmir "solution"', *The Guardian*, 5 December 2006, https://www.theguardian.com/world/2006/dec/05/pakistan.india. Accessed on 29 September 2021.

77. Fareed Zakaria, 'Terror in Mumbai' [video], YouTube (broadcast by CNN), 23 March 2013, https://www.youtube.com/watch?v=hmr9Zlh0YxE. Accessed on 14 January 2022.

78. BBC Sports, 'England to return home from India,' BBC, 27 November 2008, http://news.bbc.co.uk/sport2/hi/cricket/england/7751756.stm. Accessed on 29 September 2021.

79. Sebastian Rotella, 'In 2008 Mumbai Attack, Piles of Spy Data, But an Uncompleted Puzzle,' *ProPublica*, 21 December 2014, https://www.propublica.org/article/mumbai-attack-data-an-uncompleted-puzzle. Accessed on 14 January 2022.

80. TOI, 'There's No One Alive Here', *Sunday Times of India*, 30 November 2008, https://www.pressreader.com/india/the-times-of-india-new-delhi-edition/20081130/page/1. Accessed on 14 January 2022.

81. Husain Haqqani, *Pakistan: Between Mosque and Military*, Carnegie Endowment for International Peace, Washington, DC, 2005; Eric Schmitt and Somini Sengupta, 'Ex-U.S. Official Cites Pakistani Training for India Attackers', *The New York Times*, 3 December 2008, https://www.nytimes.com/2008/12/04/world/asia/04india.html?hp. Accessed on 14 January 2022.

82. SATP, 'Terrorists Attacks in Mumbai since 1993', Institute of Conflict Management, 2001, http://www.satp.org/satporgtp/countries/india/database/mumbai_blast.htm. Accessed on 14 January 2022; 'For the record: The 11/7 chargesheet', *rediff.com* 11 July 2007, http://specials.rediff.com/news/2007/jul/11slid1.htm. Accessed on 29 September 2021.

83. Eric Schmitt and Somini Sengupta, 'Ex-U.S. Official Cites Pakistani Training for Indian Attackers', *The New York Times*, 3 December 2008, https://www.nytimes.com/2008/12/04/world/asia/04india.html?hp. Accessed on 14 January 2022.

84. Angel Rabasa, et al., 'The Lessons of Mumbai', RAND Corporation, 2009, https://www.rand.org/content/dam/rand/pubs/occasional_papers/2009/RAND_OP249.pdf. Accessed on 14 January 2022.

85. Government of India, 'Dossier of evidence collected by investigating agencies of India', https://bit.ly/35VFFaP. Accessed on 14 January 2022.

86. Ibid.

87. Ibid.

88. Angel Rabasa, et al., 'The Lessons of Mumbai', RAND Corporation, 2009, https://www.rand.org/content/dam/rand/pubs/occasional_papers/2009/RAND_OP249.pdf. Accessed on 14 January 2022.

89. Outlook Web Desk, 'The Uneducable Indian', *Outlook*, 1 January 1970, https://www.outlookindia.com/website/story/the-uneducable-indian/239084. Accessed on 29 September 2021.

90. 'Interview: Indian Prime Minister Singh', *The Washington Post*, 20 July 2005, http://www.washingtonpost.com/wp-dyn/content/article/2005/07/20/AR2005072001916.html. Accessed on 14 January 2022.

91. James Glanz, Sebastian Rotella and David E. Sanger, 'In 2008 Mumbai Attacks, Piles of Spy Data, but an Uncompleted Puzzle', *The New York Times*, 21 December 2014, https://www.nytimes.com/2014/12/22/world/asia/in-2008-mumbai-attacks-piles-of-spy-data-but-an-uncompleted-puzzle.html. Accessed on 14 January 2022.

92. Ibid.

93. Ajai Sahni, 'Mumbai: The Uneducable Indian', *South Asia Intelligence Review*, Vol. 7, No. 21, 1 December 2008, https://www.satp.org/south-asia-intelligence-review-Volume-7-No-21. Accessed on 14 January 2022.

94. PTI, 'Headley's wife watched 26/11 "show", congratulated him: NIA', NDTV, 21 January 2012, https://www.ndtv.com/india-news/headleys-wife-watched-

26-11-show-congratulated-him-nia-568345. Accessed on 29 September 2021.

95. 'Backgrounder on Dirty Bombs', U.S.NRC, February 2020, https://www.nrc.gov/reading-rm/doc-collections/fact-sheets/fs-dirty-bombs.html. Accessed on 14 January 2022.

96. Ajai Sahni, 'Mumbai: The Uneducable Indian', *South Asia Intelligence Review*, Vol. 7, No. 21, 1 December 2008, https://www.satp.org/south-asia-intelligence-review-Volume-7-No-21. Accessed on 14 January 2022.

97. Richard A. Oppel Jr. and Salman Masood, 'Gunman in Mumbai Siege a Pakistani, Official Says', *The New York Times*, 7 January 2009, https://www.nytimes.com/2009/01/08/world/asia/08pstan.html. Accessed on 29 September 2021.

98. Ibid.

99. Cyril Almeida, 'For Nawaz, it's not over till it's over', *Dawn*, 12 May 2018, https://www.dawn.com/news/1407192. Accessed on 29 September 2021.

100. NIA, 'Vision & Mission', National Investigation Agency, Government of India, http://nia.gov.in/vision-mission.htm. Accessed on 29 September 2021.

101. ECI, 'General Elections 2009: Constituency Wise Detailed Result', Election Commission of India, https://eci.gov.in/files/file/2857-constituency-wise-detailed-result/. Accessed on 14 January 2022.

102. Himanshu Kaushik, 'A polling station for one voter', *The Times of India*, 3 March 2009, https://timesofindia.indiatimes.com/India/A-polling-station-for-one-voter-/rssarticleshow/4213160.cms. Accessed on 29 September 2021.

103. ENS, 'President rejects CEC advice, Navin Chawla stays', *The Indian Express*, 2 March 2009, http://archive.indianexpress.com/news/president-rejects-cec-advice-navin-chawla-stays/429613/; J. Balaji, 'Navin Chawla takes over as CEC', *The Hindu*, 22 April 2009, https://www.thehindu.com/todays-paper/Navin-Chawla-takes-over-as-CEC/article16621160.ece. Accessed on 14 January 2022.

104. INC, 'Lok Sabha Elections 2009: Manifesto Of the Indian National Congress', Indian National Congress, http://www.indiaenvironmentportal.org.in/files/Congress%20Manifesto.pdf. Accessed on 29 September 2021

105. Ibid.

106. BJP, 'Manifesto Lok Sabha Election 2009', BJP Central Library, http://library.bjp.org/jspui/bitstream/123456789/262/1/bjp_lection_manifesto_english_2009.pdf. Accessed on 5 February 2022.

107. Ibid.

108. Ibid.

109. Ibid.

110. Agencies, 'Cong got three out of every 10 votes polled in LS election', *The Indian Express*, 18 May 2009, https://indianexpress.com/article/india/politics/cong-got-three-out-of-every-10-votes-polled-in-ls-election/. Accessed on 14 January 2022.

111. Agencies, 'Manmohan Singh re-elected Cong Parliamentary Party leader', *The Indian Express*, 19 May 2009, http://archive.indianexpress.com/news/

manmohan-singh-reelected-cong-parliamentary-party-leader/462380/. Accessed on 14 January 2022.

112. PTI, '2G scam: SC judgement no indictment of UPA, BJP must apologise to nation for causing huge loss, says Kapil Sibal', *The Times of India*, 2 February 2012, https://timesofindia.indiatimes.com/india/2g-scam-sc-judgement-no-indictment-of-upa-bjp-must-apologise-to-nation-for-causing-huge-loss-says-kapil-sibal/articleshow/11726700.cms. Accessed on 14 January 2022.

113. PTI, '2G verdict: A Raja "virtually gifted away important national asset", says Supreme Court', *The Times of India*, 2 February 2012, https://timesofindia.indiatimes.com/india/2G-verdict-A-Raja-virtually-gifted-away-important-national-asset-says-Supreme-Court/articleshow/11728003.cms?referral=PM. Accessed on 29 September 2021.

114. Subhajti Sengupta and Suhas Munshi, '2G Scam Explained', News18, 2017, https://www.news18.com/news/immersive/2g-scam-explained.html. Accessed on 14 January 2022.

115. Nirnimesh Kumar, 'Bail to Kanimozhi, four others', *The Hindu*, 28 November 2011, https://www.thehindu.com/news/national/bail-for-kanimozhi-four-others/article2668196.ece. Accessed on 14 January 2022.

116. Aamir Khan and Abhinav Garg, '2G spectrum verdict: No proof of scam, says Court. A scam of lies, says Congress', *The Times of India*, 22 December 2017, https://timesofindia.indiatimes.com/india/2g-spectrum-verdict-no-proof-of-scam-says-court-a-scam-of-lies-says-congress/articleshow/62201212.cms. Accessed on 29 September 2021.

117. IANS, 'Waited seven years in vain for evidence: 2G Judge OP Saini', *The New Indian Express*, 21 December 2017, https://www.newindianexpress.com/nation/2017/dec/21/waited-seven-years-in-vain-for-evidence-2g-judge-op-saini-1733364.html. Accessed on 14 January 2022.

118. Dr Pooja Dasgupta and Tushar Kumrawat, 'Coal is Gold: The "Coalgate" Scam', *Global Journal of Commerce & Management Perspective*, March–April 2016, Vol. 5, No. 2, pp. 16–21, https://www.longdom.org/articles/coal-is-gold-the-coalgate-scam.pdf. Accessed on 14 January 2022.

119. Sanjay Dutta, 'CAG: Govt lost Rs 10.7 lakh crore by not auctioning coal blocks', *The Times of India*, 22 March 2012, https://timesofindia.indiatimes.com/india/CAG-Govt-lost-Rs-10-7-lakh-crore-by-not-auctioning-coal-blocks/articleshow/12360183.cms; Comptroller and Auditor General of India, 'Allocation of Coal Blocks and Augmentation of Coal production by Coal India Limited', Performance Audit, 2011–2012, https://timesofindia.indiatimes.com/realtime/Draft_CAG_report.pdf. Accessed on 14 January 2022.

120. Sanjay Dutta, 'CAG: Govt lost Rs 10.7 lakh crore by not auctioning coal blocks', *The Times of India*, 22 March 2012, https://timesofindia.indiatimes.com/india/CAG-Govt-lost-Rs-10-7-lakh-crore-by-not-auctioning-coal-blocks/articleshow/12360183.cms. Accessed on 5 February 2022.

121. PTI, 'Coal scam: Chronology of events', *The Hindu*, 25 August 2014, https://www.thehindu.com/news/national/coal-scam-chronology-of-events/

article6350481.ece. Accessed on 14 January 2022.

122. Dr Manmohan Singh, 'PM's statement in Parliament on the Performance Audit Report on Allocation of Coal Blocks and Augmentation of Coal Production', Former Prime Minister of India: Dr Manmohan Singh, 27 August 2012, https://archivepmo.nic.in/drmanmohansingh/speech-details.php?nodeid=1208. Accessed on 29 September 2021.

123. Sachin Parashar, 'Will quit if coalgate charges against me are proved: PM Manmohan Singh', *The Times of India*, 30 May 2012, https://timesofindia.indiatimes.com/india/Will-quit-if-coalgate-charges-against-me-are-proved-PM-Manmohan-Singh/articleshow/13651105.cms. Accessed on 14 January 2022.

124. Ibid.

125. Utkarsh Anand, 'SC questions govt on coal blocks allotment, strongly defends CAG', *The Indian Express*, 14 September 2012, http://archive.indianexpress.com/news/sc-questions-govt-on-coal-blocks-allotment-strongly-defends-cag/1002705/0. Accessed on 14 January 2022.

126. Sanjay Dutta and Mohua Chatterjee, 'All coal blocks awarded after 1993 illegal: Panel', *The Times of India*, 23 April 2013, https://timesofindia.indiatimes.com/business/india-business/All-coal-blocks-awarded-after-1993-illegal-Panel/articleshow/19686444.cms. Accessed on 14 January 2022.

127. Shuchi Srivastava and Rachita Prasad, 'Coalgate verdict: Worst fears of power companies come true', *The Economic Times*, 25 September 2014, https://economictimes.indiatimes.com/industry/energy/power/coalgate-verdict-worst-fears-for-power-companies-come-true/articleshow/43375725.cms. Accessed on 14 January 2022.

128. Sunil Yash Kalra, *Road to Commonwealth Games, 2010*, Penguin Group, New Delhi, 2010; DCWG, 'Delhi promised, Delhi delivered', Delhi XIX Commonwealth Games, 15 October 2010, http://d2010.thecgf.com/news/delhi_promised_delhi_delivered. Accessed on 14 January 2022.

129. BBC Sports, 'Australia say India should not host Commonwealth Games', BBC, 24 September 2010, http://news.bbc.co.uk/sport2/hi/commonwealth_games/delhi_2010/9029049.stm. Accessed on 29 September 2021.

130. Indo-Asian News Service, 'Who is Suresh Kalmadi?' NDTV, 24 December 2010, https://www.ndtv.com/india-news/who-is-suresh-kalmadi-442861. Accessed on 14 January 2022.

131. J. Balaji, 'Centre orders probe into CWG issues', *The Hindu*, 15 October 2010, https://www.thehindu.com/news/national/Centre-orders-probe-into-CWG-issues/article15781507.ece. Accessed on 14 January 2022.

132. Jason Burke, '"India has arrived": spectacular ceremony opens Commonwealth Games', *The Guardian*, 3 October 2010, https://www.theguardian.com/sport/2010/oct/03/commonwealth-games-opening-ceremony-delhi-india. Accessed on 14 January 2022.

133. 'Commonwealth Games Delhi 2010 Opening Ceremony Oct 3rd' [video], YouTube (broadcast by DoorDarshan), 23 November 2013, https://www.

youtube.com/watch?v=JuUR8lR50Yk&t=12146s. Accessed on 14 January 2022.

134. Agencies, 'CWG closing ceremony a big dampener', *The Indian Express*, 15 October 2010, http://archive.indianexpress.com/news/cwg-closing-ceremony-a-big-dampener/697743/. Accessed on 14 January 2022.

135. IOL, 'CWG: Spectacular closing ceremony', *Independent Online*, 14 October 2010, https://www.iol.co.za/sport/cwg-spectacular-closing-ceremony-686264. Accessed on 14 January 2022.

136. Boria Majumdar, 'Commonwealth Games 2010: The Index of a "New" India?', *Social Research: An International Quarterly*, 2011, Vol. 78, No. 1, pp. 231–254, https://www.jstor.org/stable/23347210. Accessed on 14 January 2022.

137. Government of India, 'GDP Growth Rate of India (Constant Prices) during 2001-02 to 2013-14', community.data.gov.in, 4 February 2015, https://community.data.gov.in/gdp-growth-rate-of-india-constant-prices-during-2001-02-to-2013-14/. Accessed on 14 January 2022.

138. Ibid.

139. WB, 'GDP per capita (current US$)', The World Bank, https://data.worldbank.org/indicator/NY.GDP.PCAP.CD?locations=IN. Accessed on 14 January 2022.

140. Ambar Narayan and Rinku Murgai, 'Looking Back on Two Decades of Poverty and Well-Being in India', World Bank Group, April 2016, https://openknowledge.worldbank.org/bitstream/handle/10986/24168/Looking0back0o00well0being0in0India.pdf;jsessionid=B4479ECAC620E3280DFFE65BA02CD09E?sequence=1; Kirthi Rao, 'India's poverty level falls to record 22%: Planning Commission', *Mint*, 29 July 2013, https://www.livemint.com/Politics/1QvbdGnGySHo7WRq1NBFNL/Poverty-rate-down-to-22-Plan-panel.html; PTI, 'Poverty rate fall steepest in UPA regime', *The Hindu Business Line*, 3 January 2014, https://www.thehindubusinessline.com/economy/poverty-rate-fall-steepest-in-upa-regime/article23118262.ece; Arvind Panagariya and Megha Mukim, 'A Comprehensive Analysis of Poverty in India', Policy Research Working Papers, 2013, No. 6714, http://hdl.handle.net/10986/16930. Accessed on 14 January 2022.

141. Keith Breene, '6 surprising facts about India's exploding middle class', *World Economic Forum*, 7 November 2016, https://www.weforum.org/agenda/2016/11/6-surprising-facts-about-india-s-exploding-middle-class. Accessed on 14 January 2022.

142. M. Bhadrakumar, 'Manmohan Singh's Foreign Policy Legacy', Strategic Culture Foundation, 30 January 2014, https://www.strategic-culture.org/news/2014/01/30/manmohan-singh-foreign-policy-legacy.html. Accessed on 14 January 2022.

143. George Mathew, 'A day in Manmohan Singh's village: Pakistan to make Gah a model village', *The Tribune*, 28 September 2004, https://www.tribuneindia.com/2004/20040928/edit.htm#6. Accessed on 14 January 2022.

144. Mark Tully, 'Manmohan Singh: Architect of the New India', *The Sikh Times*, 14 November 2005, http://www.sikhtimes.com/bios_111405a.html. Accessed

on 14 January 2022.

CHAPTER 14: SECULAR NEHRU TO DIGITAL MODI

1.   Sunil Prabhu, 'No Leader of the Opposition in the 16th Lok Sabha: Sources', NDTV, 9 June 2014, https://www.ndtv.com/india-news/no-leader-of-the-opposition-in-the-16th-lok-sabha-sources-576622. Accessed on 11 January 2022.

2.   ECI, 'Political Party wise seat won and valid votes polled in state', Election Commission of India, https://eci.gov.in/files/file/2823-political-party-wise-seat-won-and-valid-votes-polled-in-state/. Accessed on 11 January 2022.

3.   Justia, 'We Know A Thing Or Two Because We've Seen A Thing Or Two-Trademark Details', Justia, 13 February 2018, https://trademarks.justia.com/868/34/we-know-a-thing-or-two-because-we-ve-seen-a-thing-or-86834020.html; Also see *Cambridge Dictionary*, 'a thing or two', *Cambridge Dictionary* https://dictionary.cambridge.org/us/dictionary/english/a-thing-or-two. Accessed on 11 January 2022.

4.   C. Rajagopalachari, 'Why Swatantra?', *Mint*, 16 July 2016, https://www.livemint.com/Sundayapp/XlvTGlfJcdJu9mQGZcksTI/C-Rajagopalachari–Why-Swatantra.html. Accessed on 11 January 2022.

5.   Ashley J. Tellis, 'Narendra Modi and U.S.–India Relations', Carnegie Endowment for International Peace, 1 November 2018, https://carnegieendowment.org/2018/11/01/narendra-modi-and-u.s.-india-relations-pub-77861. Accessed on 11 January 2022.

6.   HT Correspondent, 'BJP names team for 2014, Modi at the helm', *Hindustan Times*, 22 July 2013, https://www.hindustantimes.com/delhi-news/bjp-names-team-for-2014-modi-at-the-helm/story-AfTPVV0qj5iPX8iljlpRMM.html. Accessed on 11 January 2022.

7.   EB, 'India's Economy Needs an Early Election', *Bloomberg*, 21 August 2013, https://www.bloomberg.com/opinion/articles/2013-08-20/india-s-economy-needs-an-early-election. Accessed on 11 January 2022.

8.   BJP, 'BJP Election Manifesto 2014', Bharatiya Janata Party Central Library, 2014, http://library.bjp.org/jspui/handle/123456789/252. Accessed on 11 January 2022.

9.   'Full text: BJP manifesto for 2014 Lok Sabha elections', News 18, 7 April 2014, https://www.news18.com/news/politics/full-text-bjp-manifesto-for-2014-lok-sabha-elections-679304.html. Accessed on 11 January 2022.

10. Ibid.

11. Shamni Pande, 'Case study: The strategy and tactics behind the creation of Brand Modi', Business Today, 8 June 2014, https://www.businesstoday.in/magazine/case-study/story/case-study-strategy-tactics-behind-creation-of-brand-narendra-modi-46222-2014-05-19; Fred Dews, 'Experts Discuss Historic BJP and Narendra Modi Victory in India's Elections', Brookings,

19 May 2014, https://www.brookings.edu/blog/brookings-now/2014/05/19/experts-discuss-historic-bjp-and-narendra-modi-victory-in-indias-elections/amp/. Accessed on 11 January 2022.

12. Shamni Pande, 'Case study: The strategy and tactics behind the creation of Brand Modi', Business Today, 8 June 2014, https://www.businesstoday.in/magazine/case-study/story/case-study-strategy-tactics-behind-creation-of-brand-narendra-modi-46222-2014-05-19. Accessed on 11 January 2022.

13. BJP, 'BJP Election Manifesto 2014', Bharatiya Janata Party Central Library, 2014, http://library.bjp.org/jspui/handle/123456789/252. Accessed on 11 January 2022.

14. Anirban Sen, 'IT sector exports to grow 13–15% in FY15, says Nasscom', Mint, 11 February 2014, https://www.livemint.com/Industry/BrMXBnGtlewsRoN99KqKCM/IT-sector-exports-to-grow-1315-in-FY15-Nasscom.html. Accessed on 11 January 2022.

15. Quoted in Shankkar Aiyar, Aadhaar: A Biometric History of India's 12-Digit Revolution, Westland Publications, New Delhi, 2017; Book Experts, 'Modi, Nilekani and Aadhaar', Swarajya, 24 July 2017, https://swarajyamag.com/economy/modi-nilekani-and-aadhar. Accessed on 11 January 2022.

16. Ibid.

17. Ibid.

18. 'The Aadhar of all things', The Hindu Business Line, 15 January 2018, https://www.thehindubusinessline.com/blink/cover/the-aadhaar-of-all-things/article9609603.ece. Accessed on 25 September 2021.

19. Suzanne Goldenberg, 'Boom time in India as the millennium bug bites', The Guardian, 30 December 1998, https://amp.theguardian.com/world/1998/dec/30/millennium.uk. Accessed on 11 January 2022.

20. Ruhi Tewari, 'Aadhaar, DBT get a lifeline, Modi to retain, push UPA schemes', The Indian Express, 7 July 2014, https://indianexpress.com/article/india/india-others/aadhaar-dbt-get-a-lifeline-modi-to-retain-push-upa-schemes/. Accessed on 11 January 2022.

21. Mint, 'Aadhaar bill passed in Lok Sabha', Mint, 11 March 2016, https://www.livemint.com/Politics/UgblAmPPHetk71sjQUqcvN/Aadhaar-bill-passed-in-Lok-Sabha-the-story-so-far.html. Accessed on 25 September 2021.

22. Promit Mukherjee, 'DBTL helps govt save Rs 10,000 crore as illegal LPG consumption falls', Mint, 3 July 2015, https://www.livemint.com/Industry/PGCreyRo9L9rCt3Vx3xyBO/DBTL-helps-govt-save-Rs10000-crore-as-illegal-LPG-consumpti.html. Accessed on 25 September 2021.

23. PTI, 'Aadhaar helped Modi government save $9 billion: Nandan Nilekani', The Economic Times, 13 October 2017, http://economictimes.indiatimes.com/articleshow/61064674.cms?utm_source=contentofinterest&utm_medium=text&utm_campaign=cppst. Accessed on 25 September 2021.

24. Tarini Puri, 'Soon, passport authorities to verify applicant identity with Aadhaar database', The Times of India, 1 May 2015, http://timesofindia.indiatimes.com/india/Soon-passport-authorities-to-verify-applicant-

identity-with-Aadhaar-database/articleshow/47115181.cms. Accessed on 25 September 2021.

25. PTI, 'Supreme Court Order on Aadhaar Puts Brakes on Election Commission's Project', NDTV, 14 August 2015, http://www.ndtv.com/india-news/supreme-court-order-on-aadhar-puts-brakes-on-election-commissions-project-1207330. Accessed on 25 September 2021.

26. Zia Haq, '40 million cows to get Aadhaar-like number at cost of Rs 50 crore in 1st phase', *Hindustan Times*, 3 February 2018, https://www.hindustantimes.com/india-news/40-million-cows-to-get-aadhaar-like-numb er-at-cost-of-rs-50-crore-in-1st-phase/story-9f50M1CkgBoCSym5SR1VzL.html. Accessed on 25 September 2021.

27. HT Correspondent, 'Full text of Supreme Court's judgment on Right to Privacy', *Hindustan Times*, 24 August 2017, https://www.hindustantimes.com/india-news/supreme-court-rules-privacy-is-fundamental-right-here-s-full-text-of-the-judgment/story-Wheiu7B8nbgbqtJYT1KzkO.html. Accessed on 25 September 2021.

28. K. Deepalakshmi, 'The long list of Aadhaar-linked schemes', *The Hindu*, 24 March 2017, https://www.thehindu.com/news/national/the-long-list-of-aadhaar-linked-schemes/article17641068.ece. Accessed on 25 September 2021.

29. Digital India, 'How Digital India will be realized: Pillars of Digital India', Digital India, 9 June 2019, http://digitalindia.gov.in/content/programme-pillars. Accessed on 31 January 2022.

30. Unique Identification Authority of India, 'Unique Identification Authority of India: Annual Report 2019–20', UIDAI, 2020, https://uidai.gov.in/images/AADHAR_AR_2019_20_ENG_approved.pdf. Accessed on 11 January 2022.

31. Arpita Chakrabarty, 'Almora temple makes Aadhaar cards mandatory for getting hitched', *The Times of India*, 10 October 2016, https://timesofindia.indiatimes.com/city/dehradun/Almora-temple-makes-Aadhaar-cards-mandatory-for-getting-hitched/articleshow/54768578.cms. Accessed on 25 September 2021.

32. PTI, 'Railways plans linking Aadhaar with concessional ticket booking', *The Economic Times*, 7 October 2016, http://economictimes.indiatimes.com/industry/transportation/railways/railways-plans-linking-aadhaar-with-concessional-ticket-booking/articleshow/54739933.cms. Accessed on 25 September 2021.

33. Roli Srivastava, 'Linking Aadhaar to better healthcare', *The Hindu*, 27 February 2016, http://www.thehindu.com/news/cities/mumbai/news/linking-aadhaar-to-better-healthcare/article8288043.ece. Accessed on 25 September 2021.

34. Anuj Srivas, 'Twenty Crore Bank Accounts Opened: Where Does Jan Dhan Yojana Go From Here? An Explainer', *The Wire*, 3 May 2016, http://thewire.in/33272/twenty-crore-bank-accounts-opened-where-does-jan-dhan-yojana-go-from-here-an-explainer/. Accessed on 25 September 2021.

35. Komal Gupta, Suranjana Roy and Apurva Vishwanath, 'Legal backing to

Aadhaar notified, NDA free to use it for government schemes', *Mint*, 14 September 2016, https://www.livemint.com/Politics/QziSIMW5zHveR0 G7IoLK2I/Legal-backing-to-Aadhaar-notified-NDA-free-to-use-it-for-go. html. Accessed on 25 September 2021.

36.   Unique Identification Authority of India, 'What are the possible criminal penalties envisaged against the fraud or unauthorized access to data?', Unique Identification Authority of India, Government of India, https://www.uidai.gov. in/289-faqs/your-aadhaar/protection-of-individual-information-in-uidai-system/1944-what-are-the-possible-criminal-penalties-envisaged-against-the-fraud-or-unauthorized-access-to-data.html. Accessed on 11 January 2022.

37.   Mint, 'EmTech India 2016: The digital future', *Mint*, 24 March 2016, http:// www.livemint.com/Industry/NszhXWnjGmYfYqyWIcI6jJ/EmTech-India-2016-The-digital-future.html. Accessed on 25 September 2021.

38.   Ibid.

39.   Narain D. Batra, 'India tries a Moonshot', *The Statesman*, 14 December 2016, https://www.thestatesman.com/opinion/india-tries-a-moonshot-1481754160.html. Accessed on 25 September 2021.

40.   Ibid.

41.   Ibid.

42.   Hannah Kuchler, 'Facebook, Google and the race to sign up India', *Financial Times*, 18 March 2016, https://www.ft.com/content/91539fc4-ebc5-11e5-888e-2eadd5fbc4a4. Accessed on 25 September 2021.

43.   Tata Trusts, 'Tata Trusts and Google join hands to launch Internet literacy campaign for women in rural India and their communities', Tata Trusts, 3 July 2015, http://www.tatatrusts.org/article/inside/Tata-Trusts-and-Google-join-hands-to-launch-Internet-literacy-campaign-for-women-in-rural-India-and-their-communities. Accessed on 11 January 2022; Ravi Agrawal, *India Connected*, Oxford University Press, New York, 2018.

44.   Anand Nayyar and Inderpal Singh, 'A Comprehensive Analysis of Goods and Services Tax (GST) in India', *Indian Journal of Finance*, February 2018, http://doi.org/10.17010/ijf/2018/v12i2/121377. Accessed on 11 January 2022.

45.   Bhanu Priya, 'Full Text Of PM Narendra Modi's Speech At GST Launch From Parliament, NDTV, 1 July 2017, https://www.ndtv.com/india-news/full-text-of-pm-narendra-modis-speech-at-goods-and-services-tax-launch-from-parliament-1719236. Accessed on 25 September 2021.

46.   GST Goods and Services Council, 'Vision & Mission', GST Goods and Services Council, https://bit.ly/3ux1RSS. Accessed on 11 January 2022.

47.   *India Today* Web Desk, 'GST: A 17-year-old dream, 17 phases towards creating history', *India Today*, 29 June 2017, https://www.indiatoday.in/india/story/gst-history-arun-jaitley-tax-reform-july-1-985482-2017-06-29. Accessed on 25 September 2021.

48.   Prabhash K. Dutta, 'GST: Meet the men behind India's biggest tax reform that's been in making for 17 years', *India Today*, 29 June 2017, https://www.

indiatoday.in/india/story/goods-and-services-gst-reformers-atal-bihari-asim-dasgupta-chidambaram-arun-jaitley-985352-2017-06-29. Accessed on 25 September 2021.

49. PMO, 'Excerpts from PM Modi's address to the nation: "Hoarded notes will become just worthless pieces of paper"', *The Indian Express*, 9 November 2016, https://indianexpress.com/article/business/banking-and-finance/narendra-modi-500-100-indian-rupee-notes-scrapped-4365069/. Accessed on 25 September 2021.

50. Ministry of Law and Justice, 'The Specified Bank Notes (Cessation of Liabilities) Ordinance, 2016', *The Gazette of India*, No. 10, https://dea.gov.in/sites/default/files/Ordinance%2010%20of%202016%2030.12.2016.pdf. Accessed on 11 January 2022.

51. Arun Enara and Mahesh R. Gowda, 'The enigma of demonetization and the unexplored consequences', *Indian Journal of Psychiatry*, 2018, Vol. 60, No. 1, pp. 6–9, https://doi.org/10.4103/psychiatry.indianjpsychiatry_196_17. Accessed on 11 January 2022.

52. BQ Desk, 'Demonetisation Was Not Designed Only To Fight Black Money, Says Finance Minister Jaitley', *Bloomberg|Quint*, 30 August 2017, https://www.bloombergquint.com/business/demonetisation-was-not-designed-only-to-fight-black-money-says-finance-minister-jaitley#gs.BQ0mi4A. Accessed on 25 September 2021.

53. Reserve Bank of India, 'Annual Report of the RBI 2017-18', Reserve Bank of India, rbi.org.in/Scripts/AnnualReportPublications.aspx?year=2021. Accessed 7 February 2022.

54. Vishnu Padmanabhan, 'From GDP growth to black money, costs outweigh benefits of demonetisation', *Mint*, 3 September 2018, https://www.livemint.com/Industry/G0nNMoXXS8eVmW1oqUa1TP/Demonetisation-has-impacted-GDP-growth-to-black-money.html. Accessed on 25 September 2021.

55. Ibid.

56. Ibid.

57. Manas Chakravarty, 'How much has demonetisation affected the stock market?' *Mint*, 3 January 2017, https://www.livemint.com/Money/hRb1noUQV17fmP0o1GNQEJ/How-much-has-demonetisation-affected-the-stock-market.html. Accessed on 25 September 2021.

58. Radhika Iyengar, 'Both sides of the coin: What top economists think about demonetisation', *The Indian Express*, 28 November 2016, https://indianexpress.com/article/india/india-news-india/both-sides-of-the-coin-what-top-economists-think-about-demonetisation/. Accessed on 25 September 2021.

59. Bhaskar Chakravorti, 'One Year After India Killed Off Cash, Here's What Other Countries Should Learn from It', *Harvard Business Review*, 2 November 2017, https://hbr.org/2017/11/one-year-after-india-killed-off-cash-heres-what-other-countries-should-learn-from-it; Amartya Lahiri, 'The Great Indian Demonetization', *Journal of Economic Perspectives*, Winter 2020, Vol.

34, No. 1, pp. 55–74, https://doi.org/10.1257/jep.34.1.55. Accessed on 11 January 2022.

60. Gabriel Chodorow-Reich, Gita Gopinath, Prachi Mishra, Abhinav Narayanan, 'Cash and the Economy: Evidence from India's Demonetization', *The Quarterly Journal of Economics*, 2019, Vol. 135, No. 1, https://scholar.harvard.edu/files/gopinath/files/crgmn_demonetization.pdf. Accessed on 19 October 2021.

61. 'Assembly Election 2017', Election Commission of India, https://eci.gov.in/assembly-election/assembly-election/. Accessed on 11 January 2022.

62. Rikhil R. Bhavnani and Mark Copelovitch, 'The Political Impact of Economic Shocks: Evidence from India's 2016 Demonetization', University of Wisconsin—Madison, January 2018, https://rbhavnani.github.io/files/BhavnaniCopelovitch.pdf; Abhijit Banerjee and Namrata Kala, 'The economic and political consequences of India's demonetisation', VoxDev, June 2017, https://voxdev.org/topic/institutions-political-economy/economic-and-political-consequences-india-s-demonetisation. Accessed on 8 October 2021.

63. Milan Vaishnav, Jayaram Ravi and Jamie Hintson, 'Is the BJP India's New Hegemon?', Carnegie Endowment for International Peace, 8 October 2018, https://carnegieendowment.org/2018/10/08/is-bjp-india-s-new-hegemon-pub-77406. Accessed on 11 January 2022.

64. Harish Damodaran, 'LPG, toilet, house: BJP built solid rural assets but income didn't rise', *The Indian Express*, 12 December 2018, https://indianexpress.com/article/explained/lpg-toilet-house-bjp-built-solid-rural-assets-but-income-didnt-rise-5489311/. Accessed on 11 January 2022.

65. Milan Vaishnav, 'India's Congress Party Rises from the Dead', *Foreign Policy*, 14 December 2018, https://foreignpolicy.com/2018/12/14/in-india-the-congress-party-isnt-dead-yet/amp/. Accessed on 25 September 2021.

66. Harish Damodaran, 'LPG, toilet, house: BJP built solid rural assets but income didn't rise', *The Indian Express*, 12 December 2018, https://indianexpress.com/article/explained/lpg-toilet-house-bjp-built-solid-rural-assets-but-income-didnt-rise-5489311/. Accessed on 11 January 2022.

67. Ashok Dalwai, Sarswati Bora and Pawanexh Kohli, 'More than 55% of Indians make a living from farming. Here's how we can double their income', World Economic Forum, 4 October 2017, https://www.weforum.org/agenda/2017/10/more-than-55-of-indians-make-a-living-from-farming-heres-how-we-can-double-their-income. Accessed on 25 September 2021.

68. ET Online, 'Why the farmers have stormed Delhi, what they want', *The Economic Times*, 30 November 2018, https://economictimes.indiatimes.com/news/et-explains/why-the-farmers-have-stormed-delhi-what-they-want/articleshow/66881527.cms. Accessed on 11 January 2022.

69. BBC, 'India farmers: Tens of thousands march against agrarian crisis', BBC *News*, 30 November 2018, https://www.bbc.com/news/world-asia-india-46396118. Accessed on 11 January 2022.

70. Prabhash K. Dutta, 'What is Swaminathan report that has kept farmers vs govt battle alive for 12 years?', *India Today*, 1 June 2018, https://www.indiatoday.

in/india/story/what-is-swaminathan-report-that-has-kept-farmers-vs-govt-battle-alive-for-12-years-1247810-2018-06-01. Accessed on 25 September 2021.

71. Quoted in Soutik Biswas, 'Why a problem of plenty is hurting India's farmers', BBC *News*, 8 June 2018, https://www.bbc.com/news/world-asia-india-40184788. Accessed on 25 September 2021.

72. Rajendra Jadhav and Mayank Bhardwaj, 'Insight: Collapse in India's onion prices could leave Modi smarting in election', Reuters, 28 December 2018, https://www.reuters.com/article/us-india-election-onions-insight/insight-collapse-in-indias-onion-prices-could-leave-modi-smarting-in-election-idUSKCN1OR045. Accessed on 25 September 2021.

73. PTI, 'Ram Mandir-Babri Masjid dispute: Mohan Bhagwat says time for patience over, calls for law for temple construction', *Firstpost*, 25 November 2018, https://www.firstpost.com/politics/ram-mandir-babri-masjid-dispute-mohan-bhagwat-says-time-for-patience-over-calls-for-law-for-temple-construction-5615191.html. Accessed on 25 September 2021.

74. Siddhant Mohan, 'Ram Mandir dispute: Saffron Posters dot roads to Ayodhya as Hindu groups gear up for showdown on 25 November', *Firstpost*, 22 November 2018, https://www.firstpost.com/india/ram-mandir-dispute-saffron-posters-dot-roads-to-ayodhya-as-hindu-groups-gear-up-for-showdown-on-25-november-5589871.html. Accessed on 25 September 2021.

75. GOI, 'Text of PM's Op-Ed in Wall Street Journal', PMINIDA, 26 September 2014, http://www.pmindia.gov.in/en/news_updates/text-of-pms-op-ed-in-wall-street-journal/. Accessed on 6 February 2022

76. Jason Burke and Ed Pilkington, 'Narendra Modi: US turns on charm as roadshow rolls into New York', *The Guardian*, 29 September 2014, https://www.theguardian.com/world/2014/sep/28/narendra-modi-india-new-york-prime-minister. Accessed on 11 January 2022.

77. David Hudson, 'President Obama Meets with Indian Prime Minister Narendra Modi', The White House, 30 September 2014, https://obamawhitehouse.archives.gov/blog/2014/09/30/president-obama-meets-indian-prime-minister-narendra-modi. Accessed on 25 September 2021.

78. Express News Service, 'PM Narendra Modi invites President Barack Obama to Republic Day parade', *The Indian Express*, 22 November 2014, https://indianexpress.com/article/india/politics/invited-obama-to-be-r-day-chief-guest-modi/. Accessed on 11 January 2022.

79. Anshu Lal, 'PM swearing-in: US media praises Modi for inviting all SAARC leaders', *Firstpost*, 27 May 2014, https://www.firstpost.com/world/pm-swearing-in-us-media-praises-modi-for-inviting-all-saarc-leaders-1543971.html. Accessed on 11 January 2022.

80. Ibid.

81. BBC, 'Pakistan PM Sharif to go to Modi inauguration in India', BBC *News*, 27 May 2014, https://www.bbc.com/news/world-asia-27554193. Accessed on 25 September 2021

82. V.S. Chandrasekar and Andrew MacAskill, 'Narendra Modi, Xi Jinping pledge to resolve India-China border dispute', *Mint*, 15 July 2014, https://www.livemint.com/Politics/7kuzKNe9PW3TND0AY13uYJ/Narendra-Modi-meets-Chinese-president-Xi-Jinping-ahead-of-Br.html. Accessed on 11 January 2022.

83. Niranjan Rajadyhaksha, 'Opinion | India's trade deficit with China has a geostrategic dimension', *Mint*, 17 April 2019, https://www.livemint.com/opinion/online-views/opinon-india-s-trade-deficit-with-china-has-a-geostrategic-dimension-1555442346843.html. Accessed on 11 January 2022.

84. GOI, 'Deputy Prime Minister of Russia meets Prime Minister', Ministry of External Affairs, Government of India, 19 June 2014, https://www.mea.gov.in/incoming-visit-detail.htm?23456/Deputy+Prime+Minister+of+Russia+meets+Prime+Minister. Accessed on 11 January 2022.

85. N. Ram, 'Modi's decision to buy 36 Rafales shot the price of each jet up by 41%', *The Hindu*, 18 January 2019, https://www.thehindu.com/news/national/modis-decision-to-buy-36-rafales-shot-the-price-of-each-jet-up-by-41/article26019165.ece. Accessed on 11 January 2022.

86. Rajesh Basrur, 'Modi's foreign policy fundamentals: a trajectory unchanged', *International Affairs*, 2017, Vol. 93, No. 1, pp. 7–26, https://doi.org/10.1093/ia/iiw006. Accessed on 11 January 2022.

87. Rajesh Basrur, 'Modi's foreign policy fundamentals: a trajectory unchanged', *International Affairs*, 2017, Vol. 93, No. 1, pp. 7–26, https://doi.org/10.1093/ia/iiw006. Accessed on 11 January 2022; Ravish Tiwari, 'BJP calls for a muscular foreign policy: Panchamrit to replace Panchsheel', *India Today*, 4 April 2015, http://indiatoday.intoday.in/story/bjp-foreign-policy-national-executive/1/428383.html. Accessed on 25 September 2021; Vidya Nadkarni, *Strategic Partnerships in Asia: Balancing without alliances*, Routledge, New York, 2010.

88. Serajul Quadir, 'India, Bangladesh sign historic land boundary agreement', Reuters, 6 June 2015, https://in.reuters.com/article/bangladesh-india-land-treaty-idINKBN0OM0IV20150606. Accessed on 11 January 2022.

89. Rupak Bhattacharjee, 'Delimitation of Indo-Bangladesh Maritime Boundary', Manohar Parrikar Institute of Defence Studies and Analyses, 19 August 2014, https://idsa.in/idsacomments/DelimitationofIndo-Bangladesh_rbhattacharjee_190814. Accessed on 11 January 2022.

90. Darshana M. Baruah, 'Maritime Security in the Bay of Bengal', Carnegie India, 1 March 2018, https://carnegieindia.org/2018/03/01/maritime-security-in-bay-of-bengal-pub-75754. Accessed on 11 January 2022.

91. PTI, 'India takes over operations of part of Chabahar Port in Iran', *The Economic Times*, 7 January 2019, https://economictimes.indiatimes.com/news/politics-and-nation/india-takes-over-operations-of-part-of-chabahar-port-in-iran/articleshow/67424219.cms?utm_source=contentofinterest&utm_medium=text&utm_campaign=cppst. Accessed on 11 January 2022.

92. Dipanjan Roy Chaudhury, 'India's 'global stature' and 'islamic component'

help it get OIC invite', *The Economic Times*, 25 February 2019, https://economictimes.indiatimes.com/news/politics-and-nation/indias-global-stature-and-islamic-component-help-it-get-oic-invite/articleshow/68145827.cms?from=mdr/. Accessed on 6 February 2022.

93. PTI, 'India invited as "Guest of Honour" to OIC meet, Sushma Swaraj to attend' *The Hindu Business Line*, 23 February 2019, https://www.thehindubusinessline.com/news/world/india-invited-as-guest-of-honour-to-oic-meet-sushma-swaraj-to-attend/article26349752.ece. Accessed on 11 January 2022.

94. World Bank Group and KNOMAD 'Migration And Remittances: Recent Developments and Outlook', KNOMAD: Migration and Development Brief 30, December 2018, https://www.knomad.org/sites/default/files/2018-12/Migration%20and%20Development%20Brief%2030.pdf. Accessed on 11 January 2022.

95. Indrani Bagchi, 'India, Israel elevate their ties to strategic partnership', *The Times of India*, 6 July 2017, https://timesofindia.indiatimes.com/india/india-israel-elevate-their-ties-to-strategic-partnership/articleshow/59461930.cms. Accessed on 11 January 2022.

96. Dipanjan Roy Chaudhury, 'PM Benjamin Netanyahu seeks alliances for peace & to fight radical Islam', *The Economic Times*, 17 January 2018, https://economictimes.indiatimes.com/news/politics-and-nation/pm-benjamin-netanyahu-seeks-alliances-for-peace-to-fight-radical-islam/articleshow/62533084.cms. Accessed on 11 January 2022.

97. MEA, 'India-Israel Joint Statement during visit of Prime Minister of Israel to India (January 15, 2018)', Ministry of External Affairs, Government of India, 15 January 2018, https://www.mea.gov.in/bilateral-documents.htm?dtl/29357/IndiaIsrael+Joint+ Statement+during+visit+of+Prime+Minister +of+Israel+to+India+January+15+2018. Accessed on 11 January 2022.

98. Alyssa Ayers, 'China's Mixed Message to India', Council on Foreign Relations, 17 September 2014, https://www.cfr.org/blog/chinas-mixed-messages-india. Accessed on 11 January 2022.

99. Ministry of External Affairs, 'Transcript of Media Briefing by Official Spokesperson in Hangzhou on Prime Minister's visit to China (September 04, 2016)', Ministry of External Affairs, Government of India, 5 September 2016, https://mea.gov.in/media-briefings.htm?dtl/27366. Accessed on 19 October 2021.

100. Shruti Godbole, 'Wuhan Summit: An important signal of intent by India and China', Brookings, 23 May 2018, https://www.brookings.edu/blog/up-front/2018/05/23/wuhan-summit-an-important-signal-of-intent-by-india-and-china/. Accessed on 11 January 2022.

101. David C. Mulford, 'Issue of Gujarat Chief Minister Narendra Modi's Visa Status', U.S. Department of State, 21 March 2005, https://2001-2009.state.gov/p/sca/rls/rm/2005/43701.htm. Accessed on 25 September 2021; BBC, 'Gujarat riot death toll revealed', BBC *News*, 11 May 2005, http://news.bbc.

co.uk/2/hi/south_asia/4536199.stm. Accessed on 25 September 2021.

102. Office of the Press Secretary, 'Readout of the President's Call with Prime Ministerial Candidate Narendra Modi of India', The White House, 16 May 2014, https://obamawhitehouse.archives.gov/the-press-office/2014/05/16/readout-president-s-call-prime-ministerial-candidate-narendra-modi-india. Accessed on 25 September 2021.

103. John Cassidy, 'What Does Modi's Victory Mean for the World?', *The New Yorker*, 16 May 2014, https://www.newyorker.com/news/john-cassidy/what-does-modis-victory-mean-for-the-world. Accessed on 11 January 2022.

104. Office of the Press Secretary, 'U.S.–India Joint Statement', The White House, 30 September 2014, https://obamawhitehouse.archives.gov/the-press-office/2014/09/30/us-india-joint-statement. Accessed on 11 January 2022.

105. Peter Baker and Gardiner Harris, 'U.S. and India Share Sense of Unease Over China', *The New York Times*, 26 January 2015, https://www.nytimes.com/2015/01/27/world/us-and-india-share-sense-of-unease-over-china.html. Accessed on 11 January 2022.

106. Lalit Mansingh quoted in Peter Baker and Gardiner Harris, 'U.S. and India Share Sense of Unease Over China', *The New York Times*, 26 January 2015, https://www.nytimes.com/2015/01/27/world/us-and-india-share-sense-of-unease-over-china.html. Accessed on 11 January 2022.

107. Vineeta Pandey, 'Together we can, and we must', The Pioneer, 30 June 2017, https://www.dailypioneer.com/2017/columnists/together-we-can-and-we-must.html. Accessed on 11 January 2022.

108. Ashley J. Tellis, 'Narendra Modi and US–India Relations', Carnegie Endowment for International Peace, 1 November 2018, https://carnegieendowment.org/2018/11/01/narendra-modi-and-u.s.-india-relations-pub-77861. Accessed on 11 January 2022.

109. Ministry of External Affairs, 'Brief on India–US Relations', Ministry of External Affairs, Government of India, June 2017, http://www.mea.gov.in/Portal/ForeignRelation/India_US_brief.pdf. Accessed on 11 January 2022.

110. Neha Mahajan, '"Zero defect, zero effect" to "Make in India": Modi's jugglery with words', *Hindustan Times*, 15 August 2014, https://www.hindustantimes.com/india/zero-defect-zero-effect-to-make-in-india-modi-s-jugglery-with-words/story-89z3Vdx20blLnQJxBoxbWN.html. Accessed on 11 January 2022.

111. PTI, 'India replaces China as top FDI destination in 2015: Report', *The Economic Times*, 21 April 2016, https://economictimes.indiatimes.com/news/economy/finance/india-replaces-china-as-top-fdi-destination-in-2015-report/articleshow/51932057.cms. Accessed on 11 January 2022.

112. 'Business Enabling Environment (BEE)', The World Bank, http://www.doingbusiness.org/en/data/exploreeconomies/india. Accessed on 11 January 2022.

113. Atmadip Ray and Saloni Shukla, 'Bank recapitalization: More money in the leaking boats?' *The Economic Times*, 1 November 2017, https://economictimes.indiatimes.com/industry/banking/finance/bank-recapitalisation-more-

money-in-leaking-boats/articleshow/61377232.cms. Accessed on 11 January 2022.

114. Parismita Goswami, 'Toilet-Ek Prem Katha success: Haryana Government directs village heads to watch Akshay Kumar's film', *International Business Times*, 17 August 2017, https://www.ibtimes.co.in/toilet-ek-prem-katha-success-haryana-government-makes-village-heads-watch-akshay-kumars-film-738702. Accessed on 11 January 2022.

115. 'Ayushman Bharat: National Health Protection Mission', india.gov.in, 22 October 2018, https://www.india.gov.in/spotlight/ayushman-bharat-national-health-protection-mission. Accessed on 26 September 2021; 'Ayushman Bharat Yojana', Reproductive Rights Initiative, https://reproductiverights.hrln.org/1918-2/. Accessed on 7 February 2022.

116. Government of India, 'Mudra', mudra.org, https://www.mudra.org.in/. Accessed on 11 January 2022.

117. Prajakta Hebbar, 'Cameron's Message To Modi's India: Acche Din Zaroor Aayega', *Huff Post*, 14 November 2015, https://www.huffingtonpost.in/2015/11/14/uk-pm-says-acche-din-aayega_n_8562120.html?_guc_consent_skip=1557410313. Accessed on 11 January 2022.

118. H. Plecher, 'India: Real gross domestic product (GDP) growth rate from 2014 to 2024', Statista, 6 November 2019, https://bit.ly/335BKHs. Accessed on 11 January 2022.

119. Ajay Chhibber, 'There are more questions than answers on back series GDP data', *The Economic Times*, 6 December 2018, https://economictimes.indiatimes.com/news/economy/policy/view-there-are-more-questions-than-answers-on-back-series-gdp-data/articleshow/66959795.cms. Accessed on 11 January 2022.

120. Arvind Subramanian, 'India's GDP Mis-estimation: Likelihood, Magnitudes, Mechanisms, and Implications', Working Papers: Centre for International Development at Harvard University, June 2019, No. 354, https://growthlab.cid.harvard.edu/files/growthlab/files/2019-06-cid-wp-354.pdf. Accessed on 11 January 2022.

121. Ibid.

122. Mahesh Vyas, '11 million jobs lost in 2018', Centre for Monitoring Indian Economy Pvt. Ltd., 8 January 2019, https://www.cmie.com/kommon/bin/sr.php?kall=warticle&dt=2019-01-08%2009:28:37&msec=666. Accessed on 11 January 2022; Corinne Abrams and Rosa de Acosta, 'Modi's World: See What India's Economy Has Done in Five Years', *The Wall Street Journal*, 22 April 2019, https://www.wsj.com/amp/articles/modis-world-see-what-indias-economy-has-done-in-five-years-11555925401. Accessed on 11 January 2022.

123. ILO, 'India Wage Report: Wage polices for decent work and inclusive growth', International Labour Organization, 2018, https://www.ilo.org/wcmsp5/groups/public/—asia/—ro-bangkok/—sro-new_delhi/documents/publication/wcms_638305.pdf. Accessed on 6 February 2022.

124. Ibid; Mahesh Vyas, 'Voters want jobs more than anything else', Centre for

Monitoring Indian Economy, 30 April 2019, https://www.cmie.com/kommon/bin/sr.php?kall=warticle&dt=2019-04-30%2011:46:41&msec=513. Accessed on 11 January 2022.

125. Surjit S. Bhalla, 'Like 2014, 2019 election is being contested around economy. Will the result be similar?', *The Indian Express*, 11 May 2019, https://indianexpress.com/article/opinion/columns/lok-sabha-elections-2019-narendra-modi-bjp-congressanother-black-swan-5722129/. Accessed on 11 January 2022.

126. ET Online, 'BJP manifesto highlights: The 75 promises for India', *The Economic Times*, 8 April 2019, https://economictimes.indiatimes.com/news/elections/lok-sabha/bjps-sankalp-patra-makes-75-resolutions-for-india/articleshow/68775256.cms. Accessed on 11 January 2022.

127. Ibid.

128. ET Online and Agencies, 'Congress releases manifesto for 2019 Lok Sabha elections, promises wealth and welfare', *The Economic Times*, 3 April 2019, https://economictimes.indiatimes.com/news/elections/lok-sabha/india/congress-releases-manifesto-for-2019-lok-sabha-polls-details-here/articleshow/68684073.cms. Accessed on 11 January 2022.

129. Ibid.

130. David Schultz and Manisha Madhava, 'How India holds an election with 900 million voters and 8,000 candidates', *The Washington Post*, 8 May 2019, https://www.washingtonpost.com/politics/2019/05/08/india-more-than-candidates-states-are-campaigning-parliament-seats/?utm_term=.9fee20d5f7a9. Accessed on 11 January 2022.

131. Yogendra Yadav, 'What 2019 polls mean for the idea of India', *Mint*, 26 May 2019, https://www.livemint.com/elections/lok-sabha-elections/what-2019-polls-mean-for-the-idea-of-india-1558876507713.html. Accessed on 11 January 2022.

132. TOI, 'Lok Sabha Election Results 2019', *The Times of India*, https://timesofindia.indiatimes.com/elections/results. Accessed on 11 January 2022.

133. Kat Devlin, 'A Sampling of Public Opinion in India', Pew Research Centre, 25 March 2019, https://www.pewresearch.org/global/2019/03/25/a-sampling-of-public-opinion-in-india/. Accessed on 11 January 2022.

134. Ibid.

135. NITI Aayog, 'Strategy for New India @75', NITI Aayog, November 2018, https://www.niti.gov.in/sites/default/files/2019-01/Strategy_for_New_India_0.pdf. Accessed on 27 September 2021.

136. Ibid.

137. Nitya Thirumalai, 'Lok Sabha Election Results: In Victory Speech, Narendra Modi Likens 2019 Polls to Mahabharata, Says Will Take Rivals Along Too', News 18, 23 May 2019, https://www.news18.com/news/politics/lok-sabha-election-results-in-victory-speech-narendra-modi-likens-2019-polls-to-mahabharata-says-will-take-rivals-along-too-2157207.html. Accessed on 11 January 2022.

138. Romila Thapar, 'They Peddle Myths and Call it History', *The New York Times*, 17 May 2019, https://www.nytimes.com/2019/05/17/opinion/india-elections-modi-history.html. Accessed on 11 January 2022.

CHAPTER 15: HOW INDIANS THINK

1. 'Constituent Assembly Of India Debates (Proceedings) - Volume XI', Constitution of India, 25 November 1949, https://www.constitutionofindia.net/constitution_assembly_debates/volume/11/1949-11-25#11.165.322. Accessed on 30 December 2021.

2. Francis Pritchett, 'Taraanah-i-Hindi', Columbia University, Department of South Asian Studies, 2004, http://www.columbia.edu/itc/mealac/pritchett/00urdu/taranahs/hindi_text.html. Accessed on 14 January 2022.

3. Shriaya Dutt, 'Amartya Sen says 'Jai Shri Ram' not linked to Bengali culture; BJP reacts', *The Tribune*, 6 July 2019, https://www.tribuneindia.com/news/archive/nation/amartya-sen-says-jai-shri-ram-not-linked-to-bengali-culture-bjp-reacts-798089. Accessed on 14 January 2022.

4. Sugata Bose, 'Rabindranath Tagore And Asian Universalism', Goldsmiths Research Online, p. 6, http://research.gold.ac.uk/20908/23/Rabindranath%20Tagore%20and%20Asian%20Universalism.pdf. Accessed on 14 January 2022.

5. Shuma Raha, 'Exploring the roots of Bengali exceptionalism', *The Asian Age*, 29 December 2017, https://www.asianage.com/books/291217/exploring-the-roots-of-bengali-exceptionalism.html. Accessed on 14 January 2022.

6. Sudeep Chakravarti, *The Bengalis: A Portrait of a Community*, Aleph Book Company, New Delhi, 2017, pp. 1–8.

7. Khushwant Singh, *The Sikhs*, Lustre Press, New Delhi, 1984; Patwant Singh, *The Sikhs*, Knopf, New York, 2000.

8. A.R. Venkatachalapathy, *Tamil Characters*, Pan Macmillan, New Delhi, 2019, pp. 1–8.

9. N.D. Batra, *Digital Freedom: How Much Can You Handle?*, Rowman & Littlefield, Lanham, 2008, p. 2.

10. A.K. Ramanujan, 'Is there an Indian way of thinking? An informal essay', *Contributions to Indian Sociology*, 1 January 1989, Vol. 23, No. 1, pp. 41–58, https://doi.org/10.1177/006996689023001004. Accessed on 14 January 2022.

11. Bobins Abraham, 'From Ganesha's Surgery To Internet In Mahabharat Times, Here Are Most Epic Quotes By Ministers', Indiatimes.com, 1 May 2018, https://www.indiatimes.com/news/india/from-ganesha-s-surgery-to-internet-in-mahabharat-times-here-are-most-epic-quotes-by-ministers-344534.html; The Washington Post, 'Narendra Modi wants to send Indians to space by 2022 but Hindu nationalists have bizarre ideas about science', *South China Morning Post*, 8 January 2019, https://www.scmp.com/news/asia/south-asia/article/2181082/hindu-nationalists-cite-legends-and-scriptures-evidence-

ancient. Accessed on 14 January 2022.

12. Quoted in V. Ravi Kumar, *Glimpses of Hindu Genius*, Suruchi Prakashan, New Delhi, 2009, p. 2.

13. K. H. Krishnamurthy, *Medicine and Surgery in Ancient India*, Samskrita Bharati, New Delhi, 2001, pp. 39–40; Valerie Debenedette, 'Sushruta, Ancient Indian Surgeon and Father of the Nose Job', *Mental Floss*, 31 July 2018, https://www.mentalfloss.com/article/502055/retrobituaries-sushruta-father-nose-job. Accessed on 14 January 2022.

14. Quoted in Stephen Knapp, *The Power of the Dharma: An Introduction to Hinduism and Vedic Culture*, iUniverse, Nebraska, 2006, p. 11.

15. Nicola Nymalm and Johannes Plagemann, 'Comparative Exceptionalism: Universality and Particularity in Foreign Policy Discourses', *International Studies Review*, Vol. 21, No. 1, 22 March 2019, pp. 12–37, https://doi.org/10.1093/isr/viy008. Accessed on 14 January 2022.

16. Francis Pritchett, 'Taraanah-i-Hindi', Columbia University, Department of South Asian Studies, 2004, http://www.columbia.edu/itc/mealac/pritchett/00urdu/taranahs/hindi_text.html. Accessed on 14 January 2022.

17. Nicola Nymalm and Johannes Plagemann, 'Comparative Exceptionalism: Universality and Particularity in Foreign Policy Discourses', *International Studies Review*, Vol. 21, No. 1, 22 March 2019, pp. 12–37, https://doi.org/10.1093/isr/viy008. Accessed on 14 January 2022.

18. Kate Sullivan, 'Exceptionalism in Indian Diplomacy: The Origins of India's Moral Leadership Aspirations', *Journal of South Asian Studies*, 1 September 2014, Vol. 37, No. 4, pp. 640–55, https://doi.org/10.1080/00856401.2014.939738. Accessed on 14 January 2022.

19. Ibid. 650.

20. Sunil Khilnani, et al., 'Nonalignment 2.0: A Foreign and Strategy Policy for India in the Twenty First Century', *Center For Policy Research*, https://www.cprindia.org/research/reports/nonalignment-20-foreign-and-strategic-policy-india-twenty-first-century. Accessed on 14 January 2022.

21. Ibid.

22. Patrick French, *India: A Portrait*, Knopf Doubleday Publishing Group, New York, 2011, pp. 323–358.

23. Yann Zopf, 'India's Biggest Challenge: Pursuing Reforms Needed to Sustain 8% Growth for Decades', *World Economic Forum*, 6 October 2016, https://www.weforum.org/press/2016/10/india-s-biggest-challenge-pursuing-reforms-needed-to-sustain-8-growth-for-decades/. Accessed on 14 January 2022.

24. 'Abrams V. United States: The Dissent That Shaped Free Speech', Constitutional Law Reporter, https://constitutionallawreporter.com/2015/09/24/abrams-v-united-states-the-dissent-that-shaped-free-speech/. Accessed on 14 January 2022.

INDEX